GALATIANS

THE NEW TESTAMENT LIBRARY
Current and Forthcoming Titles

Editorial Advisory Board

C. CLIFTON BLACK

M. EUGENE BORING

JOHN T. CARROLL

COMMENTARY SERIES

MATTHEW. BY R. ALAN CULPEPPER, MCAFEE SCHOOL OF THEOLOGY, MERCER UNIVERSITY

MARK. BY M. EUGENE BORING, BRITE DIVINITY SCHOOL, TEXAS CHRISTIAN UNIVERSITY

LUKE. BY JOHN T. CARROLL, UNION PRESBYTERIAN SEMINARY

JOHN. BY MARIANNE MEYE THOMPSON, FULLER THEOLOGICAL SEMINARY

ACTS. BY CARL R. HOLLADAY, CANDLER SCHOOL OF THEOLOGY, EMORY UNIVERSITY

ROMANS. BY BEVERLY ROBERTS GAVENTA, PRINCETON THEOLOGICAL SEMINARY

I CORINTHIANS. BY ALEXANDRA R. BROWN, WASHINGTON & LEE UNIVERSITY

II CORINTHIANS. BY FRANK J. MATERA, THE CATHOLIC UNIVERSITY OF AMERICA

GALATIANS. BY MARTINUS C. DE BOER, VU UNIVERSITY AMSTERDAM

EPHESIANS. BY STEPHEN E. FOWL, LOYOLA COLLEGE

PHILIPPIANS AND PHILEMON. BY CHARLES B. COUSAR, COLUMBIA THEOLOGICAL SEMINAR

COLOSSIANS. BY JERRY L. SUMNEY, LEXINGTON THEOLOGICAL SEMINARY

I & II THESSALONIANS. BY SUSAN EASTMAN, DUKE DIVINITY SCHOOL

I & II TIMOTHY AND TITUS. BY RAYMOND F. COLLINS, THE CATHOLIC UNIVERSITY OF AMERIC/

HEBREWS. BY LUKE TIMOTHY JOHNSON, CANDLER SCHOOL OF THEOLOGY, EMORY UNIVERSITY

JAMES. BY REINHARD FELDMEIER, UNIVERSITY OF GÖTTINGEN

I & II PETER AND JUDE. BY LEWIS R. DONELSON, AUSTIN PRESBYTERIAN THEOLOGICAL SEMINARY

I, II, & III JOHN. BY JUDITH M. LIEU, UNIVERSITY OF CAMBRIDGE

REVELATION. BY BRIAN K. BLOUNT, UNION PRESBYTERIAN SEMINARY

CLASSICS

HISTORY AND THEOLOGY IN THE FOURTH GOSPEL. BY J. LOUIS MARTYN,
UNION THEOLOGICAL SEMINARY, NEW YORK

IMAGES OF THE CHURCH IN THE NEW TESTAMENT. BY PAUL S. MINEAR,
YALE DIVINITY SCHOOL

PAUL AND THE ANATOMY OF APOSTOLIC AUTHORITY. BY JOHN HOWARD SCHÜTZ,
UNIVERSITY OF NORTH CAROLINA, CHAPEL HILL

THEOLOGY AND ETHICS IN PAUL. BY VICTOR PAUL FURNISH, PERKINS SCHOOL
OF THEOLOGY, SOUTHERN METHODIST UNIVERSITY

THE WORD IN THIS WORLD: ESSAYS IN NEW TESTAMENT EXEGESIS AND THEOLOG
BY PAUL W. MEYER, PRINCETON THEOLOGICAL SEMINARY

GENERAL STUDIES

THE LAW AND THE PROPHETS BEAR WITNESS: THE OLD TESTAMENT IN THE NE\
BY J. ROSS WAGNER, PRINCETON THEOLOGICAL SEMINARY

METHODS FOR NEW TESTAMENT STUDY. BY A. K. M. ADAM, UNIVERSITY OF GLASGO

NEW TESTAMENT BACKGROUNDS. BY CARL R. HOLLADAY, CANDLER SCHOOL OF
THEOLOGY, EMORY UNIVERSITY

Martinus C. de Boer

Galatians

A Commentary

© 2011 Martinus C. de Boer

2013 paperback edition
Originally published in hardback in the United States
by Westminster John Knox Press in 2011
Louisville, Kentucky

13 14 15 16 17 18 19 20 21 22—10 9 8 7 6 5 4 3 2 1

All rights reserved. No part of this book may be reproduced or transmitted in any form or by any means, electronic or mechanical, including photocopying, recording, or by any information storage or retrieval system, without permission in writing from the publisher. For information, address Westminster John Knox Press, 100 Witherspoon Street, Louisville, Kentucky 40202–1396. Or contact us online at www.wjkbooks.com.

Scripture quotations outside Galatians, unless otherwise identified, are from the New Revised Standard Version Bible. Copyright 1989, by the Division of Christian Education of the National Council of the Churches of Christ in the USA. Used by permission. All rights reserved. Except as otherwise specified, Galatians is cited from the author's translation; and AT signifies other author translations.

Scripture quotations marked RSV are from the Revised Standard Version of the Bible, copyright © 1946, 1952, 1971, and 1973 by the Division of Christian Education of the National Council of the Churches of Christ in the U.S.A., and are used by permission.

Book design by Jennifer K. Cox

Library of Congress Cataloging-in-Publication Data is on file at the Library of Congress, Washington, D.C.

ISBN 978-0-664-22123-2 (hardback)
ISBN 978-0-664-23982-4 (paperback)

∞ The paper used in this publication meets the minimum requirements of the American National Standard for Information Sciences—Permanence of Paper for Printed Library Materials, ANSI Z39.48-1992.

For

Marinus de Jonge
J. Louis Martyn
Paul W. Meyer
Christopher M. Tuckett

CONTENTS

Preface	xi
Acknowledgments	xiii
Abbreviations	xv
Bibliography	xix
Introduction	1
The Approach of This Commentary	1
A Note on the Translation	2
Addressees	3
Date	5
Structure	11
Overview	15

COMMENTARY

I. 1:1–10 The Letter Opening		**19**
1:1–5	Prescript	19
	Excursus 1: The Title "Apostle"	21
	Excursus 2: Galatians and Apocalyptic Eschatology	31
	Excursus 3: The Letter Opening	36
1:6–10	Rebuke and Imprecation	37
	Excursus 4: The New Preachers and Their Gospel	50
	Excursus 5: The Genre of Galatians and Paul's Use of Rhetorical Forms and Conventions	66

II. 1:11–2:21	**The Origin and the Truth of the Gospel**	**72**
1:11–17	The Origin of the Gospel 1: Paul's Conversion and Call	75
	Excursus 6: Paul's Language of Apocalyptic Revelation	79
1:18–24	The Origin of the Gospel 2: Paul's Visit with Cephas in Jerusalem	96
2:1–10	The Truth of the Gospel 1: The Apostolic Conference in Jerusalem	104
	Excursus 7: The Problem of Galatians 2:7b–8	119
2:11–14	The Truth of the Gospel 2: Conflict with Cephas in Antioch	128
2:15–21	The Truth of the Gospel for the Galatian Situation	139
	Excursus 8: Works of the Law	145
	Excursus 9: The Faith of Jesus Christ	148
III. 3:1–4:7	**The Spirit and the True Heirs of the Promise Made to Abraham**	**166**
3:1–5	The Reception of the Spirit in Galatia	168
	Excursus 10: The Greek Phrase *ex akoēs pisteōs*	174
3:6–14	The Blessing of Abraham and the Curse of the Law	184
	Excursus 11: Faith (*pistis*) in Galatians 3	192
3:15–22	The Promise to Abraham and the Law of Moses	216
3:23–29	The True Offspring of Abraham	237
	Excursus 12: The Baptismal Formula in Galatians 3:26–28	245
4:1–7	The True Heirs of the Promise	249
	Excursus 13: "The Elements of the World" in Galatians	252
	Summary of Section III	268
IV. 4:8–5:12	**The Grave Dangers Confronting the Galatians**	**269**
4:8–11	The Danger of Returning to Their Previous Religious Servitude	270
4:12–20	The Danger of Abandoning Paul and His Gospel	277

4:21–5:1	The Danger of Losing Their New Identity through Faulty Exegesis	285
	Excursus 14: Allegorical Interpretation	295
	Excursus 15: Why Isaiah 54:1?	303
5:2–6	The Danger of Becoming Separated from Christ and Grace	310
5:7–12	The Source of the Danger: The Leaven of the New Preachers	319
	Summary of Section IV	327
V. 5:13–6:10	**Life at the Juncture of the Ages**	**329**
5:13–24	Love and the Spirit's Strife against the Flesh	332
	Excursus 16: The Flesh as a Cosmic Power	335
	Excursus 17: The Fulfillment of the Law	343
5:25–6:10	Living by the Spirit and Fulfilling the Law of Christ	368
	Excursus 18: The Law of Christ	378
	Summary of Section V	392
VI. 6:11–18	**Epistolary Closing**	**393**
6:11–17	Recapitulation	394
	Excursus 19: The Israel of God	405
6:18	Final Benediction	410

Index of Ancient Sources   413

Index of Subjects and Authors   437

PREFACE

When I began work on this commentary, a visitor remarked, upon seeing the many earlier commentaries on Galatians arrayed on my bookshelf: "It has already been done!" Indeed. Commentators on Galatians, as on the many other major books of the New Testament, are not pioneers. They can only build on the work of many others who have preceded them. In this commentary I have benefited from the work of numerous previous commentators on Galatians. Deserving special mention are the commentaries of Ernest De Witt Burton, Hans Dieter Betz, Richard N. Longenecker, and J. Louis Martyn.

In writing a commentary on Galatians, one also quickly realizes that much more has been written about Galatians than can be read or, if read, acknowledged. For reasons of space I have omitted from the bibliography the many works that I also read and consulted but did not actually cite or refer to in the commentary. A commentary, after all, is not the best place to enter into intensive or extensive debate with one's fellow scholars. My procedure was as follows: I first produced my own provisional interpretation of the passage, working from the primary text. I then read widely in the secondary literature, including previous commentaries on Galatians. On this basis I adjusted my interpretation as needed while being careful to acknowledge my indebtedness for any new insights. Throughout the commentary, I have attempted to support my own interpretation with arguments based on a close reading of the Greek text in its literary and historical context. When called for, in my comment on a passage, I have sought to indicate where the difficulties lie, what the various interpretive options are, and what the major alternative interpretations in previous treatments of the passage in question have been. In matters that are particularly controversial or complicated (e.g., the faith of Christ in 2:16, the fulfillment of the law in 5:14, or the Israel of God in 6:16), I have supported my interpretation with an extended excursus in which the alternatives are reviewed and evaluated.

I was able to do serious work on the commentary during a research leave granted by the Faculty of Theology of my university in 2003–2004. A grant from the Netherlands Organisation for Scientific Research (NWO) enabled me to spend nearly three months at the University of Heidelberg, Germany, in the fall of 2003. I thank my hosts, Professors Gerd Theissen and Peter Lampe, for their hospitable reception. Dr. Beate Müller, Librarian at the Fakultätsbibliothek Theologie, provided generous assistance. I am also grateful for conversations I had during my time in Heidelberg with Robert Jewett and David Horrell. The latter gave me his thoughtful comments on draft material.

I want to express my gratitude to my students at VU University Amsterdam and to the members of the Amsterdam New Testament Colloquium, who have had to listen to several papers on Galatians during the last few years. I benefited greatly from their critical and appreciative comments. I am particularly grateful to my fellow New Testament scholars: Tjitze Baarda, Henk Couprie, Bert Jan Lietaert Peerbolte, Jan Krans, Peter-Ben Smit, Eduard Verhoef, and Arie Zwiep. My student assistants, Ben van Veen and Jan Mulder, made invaluable contributions to my research for the commentary.

I also benefited from the presentation of some of the material at the annual meetings of the Studiosorum Novi Testamenti Conventus (the society for Dutch-speaking New Testament scholars in the Netherlands and Flanders), the British New Testament Conference, the Society of Biblical Literature (both national and international), and Studiorum Novi Testamenti Societas (the international society for New Testament scholars).

My heartfelt thanks go also to the editors of New Testament Library, C. Clifton Black and John T. Carroll. The former skillfully guided the project to completion and made many helpful suggestions for improvement. It has also been a pleasure to work with the editors at Westminster John Knox: Dr. Jon Berquist, and his successor, Dr. Marianne Blickenstaff.

Special thanks go to my wife, Paula Pumplin, who cared for me above and beyond the call of duty when I suffered a severely broken ankle early in December 2009. The injury had a silver lining: The two months I was forced to spend at home, unable to walk, enabled me to put the finishing touches on the manuscript. Without Paula's completely selfless devotion and care, that would not have been possible.

Finally, I dedicate this commentary to four friends and colleagues without whom this commentary would never have been written. They will understand why.

Martin de Boer
March 1, 2010

ACKNOWLEDGMENTS

Citations of the Old Testament Pseudepigrapha are taken from *The Old Testament Pseudepigrapha*, edited by James H. Charlesworth (2 vols.; Garden City, N.Y.: Doubleday, 1983–85). Citations from the Dead Sea Scrolls are taken from *The Dead Sea Scrolls: Study Edition*, edited and translated by Florentino García Martínez and Eibert J. C. Tigchelaar (2 vols.; Leiden: Brill, 1997–98), and the columns of 1QH are keyed to this work. Citations from classical authors, Philo, Josephus, and the Apostolic Fathers are taken from the editions of the Loeb Classical Library (Cambridge, Mass.: Harvard University Press). Citations from the Mishnah are taken from *The Mishnah: Translated from the Hebrew with Introduction and Brief Explanatory Notes*, edited and translated by Herbert Danby (Oxford: Oxford University Press, 1933; repr., 1938).

The research for this commentary was made possible by a grant from the Netherlands Organisation for Scientific Research (NWO).

ABBREVIATIONS

AB	Anchor Bible
ABD	*Anchor Bible Dictionary*. Edited by D. N. Freedman. 6 vols. New York, 1992
AcT	Acta theologica: Supplementum
AGJU	Arbeiten zur Geschichte des antiken Judentums und des Urchristentums
alt.	altered
ANF	*Ante-Nicene Fathers*
ANTC	Abingdon New Testament Commentaries
AT	Author's Translation
BAG	Bauer, W., W. F. Arndt, and F. W. Gingrich. *Greek-English Lexicon of the New Testament and Other Early Christian Literature*. Chicago, 1957
BAGD	Bauer, W., W. F. Arndt, F. W. Gingrich, and F. W. Danker. *Greek-English Lexicon of the New Testament and Other Early Christian Literature*. 2nd ed. Chicago, 1979
BDAG	Bauer, W., F. W. Danker, W. F. Arndt, and F. W. Gingrich. *Greek-English Lexicon of the New Testament and Other Early Christian Literature*. 3rd ed. Chicago, 2000
BDB	Brown, F., S. R. Driver, and C. A. Briggs. *A Hebrew and English Lexicon of the Old Testament*. Oxford, 1907
BDF	Blass, F., A. Debrunner, and R. W. Funk. *A Greek Grammar of the New Testament and Other Early Christian Literature*. Chicago, 1961
BHT	Beiträge zur historischen Theologie
Bib	*Biblica*
BibInt	*Biblical Interpretation*
BJRL	*Bulletin of the John Rylands University Library of Manchester*
BNTC	Black's New Testament Commentaries
BZ	*Biblische Zeitschrift*
CBET	Contributions to Biblical Exegesis and Theology
CBQ	*Catholic Biblical Quarterly*

CNTC	Calvin's New Testament Commentaries
CTJ	*Calvin Theological Journal*
CurTM	*Currents in Theology and Mission*
FRLANT	Forschungen zur Religion und Literatur des Alten und Neuen Testaments
HNT	Handbuch zum Neuen Testament
IBS	*Irish Biblical Studies*
ICC	International Critical Commentary
Int	*Interpretation*
JBL	*Journal of Biblical Literature*
JHC	*Journal of Higher Criticism*
JSNT	*Journal for the Study of the New Testament*
JSNTSup	Journal for the Study of the New Testament: Supplement Series
JTS	*Journal of Theological Studies*
Jud	*Judaica*
KEK	Kritisch-exegetischer Kommentar über das Neue Testament (Meyer-Kommentar)
LCL	Loeb Classical Library
LEC	Library of Early Christianity
LSJ	Liddell, H. G., R. Scott, H. S. Jones, et al. *A Greek-English Lexicon.* 9th ed. with revised supplement. Oxford, 1996
MM	Moulton, J. H., and G. Milligan. *The Vocabulary of the Greek Testament.* London, 1930. Repr., Peabody, Mass., 1997
NA[27]	*Novum Testamentum Graece.* Edited by Eberhard and Erwin Nestle, Barbara and Kurt Aland, et al. 27th ed. Stuttgart, 1993. 9th, corrected printing, 2006
NIB	*The New Interpreter's Bible.* Edited by Leander Keck. Nashville, 1994–2004
NICNT	New International Commentary on the New Testament
NIGTC	New International Greek Testament Commentary
NovT	*Novum Testamentum*
NovTSup	Supplements to Novum Testamentum
NTD	Das Neue Testament Deutsch
NTL	New Testament Library
NTOA	Novum Testamentum et Orbis Antiquus
NTP	Novum Testamentum Patristicum
NTS	*New Testament Studies*
NTT	New Testament Theology
OTL	Old Testament Library
OTS	*Old Testament Studies*
PzB	*Protokolle zur Bibel*

RB	*Revue biblique*
SBLSBS	Society of Biblical Literature Sources for Biblical Study
SBLDS	Society of Biblical Literature Dissertation Series
SBLSymS	Society of Biblical Literature Symposium Series
SNTSMS	Society for New Testament Studies Monograph Series
SP	Sacra pagina
TB	Theologische Bücherei
TDNT	*Theological Dictionary of the New Testament*. Edited by G. Kittel and G. Friedrich. Translated by G. W. Bromiley. 10 vols. Grand Rapids, 1964–1976
THKNT	Theologischer Handkommentar zum Neuen Testament
ThT	*Theologisch tijdschrift*
WBC	Word Biblical Commentary
WUNT	Wissenschaftliche Untersuchungen zum Neuen Testament
ZNW	*Zeitschrift für die neutestamentliche Wissenschaft und die Kunde der älteren Kirche*

BIBLIOGRAPHY

Commentaries on Galatians Cited

References to commentaries in the main text and in the footnotes are by author and page number(s) only. Luther's two volumes may be distinguished by the part of Galatians in view.

Becker, Jürgen. "Der Brief an die Galater." Pages 7–103 in *Die Briefe an die Galater, Epheser und Kolosser*. By Jürgen Becker and Ulrich Luz. NTD 8.1. Göttingen: Vandenhoeck & Ruprecht, 1998.
Betz, Hans Dieter. *Galatians: A Commentary on Paul's Letter to the Churches in Galatia*. Hermeneia. Philadelphia: Fortress, 1979.
Bruce, F. F. [Frederick Fyvie]. *The Epistle to the Galatians: A Commentary on the Greek Text*. NIGTC. Grand Rapids: Eerdmans; Carlisle: Paternoster, 1982.
Burton, Ernest De Witt. *A Critical and Exegetical Commentary on the Epistle to the Galatians*. ICC. Edinburgh: T&T Clark, 1921. Repr., 1971.
Calvin, John. *The Epistles of Paul the Apostle to the Galatians, Ephesians, Philippians and Colossians*. CNTC. Grand Rapids: Eerdmans; Carlisle: Paternoster, 1996.
Dunn, James D. G. *The Epistle to the Galatians*. BNTC. London: A&C Black, 1993.
Fung, Ronald Y. K. *Galatians*. Grand Rapids: Eerdmans, 1988.
Hays, Richard B. "Galatians." Pages 181–348 in vol. 11 of *NIB*. Nashville: Abingdon, 2000.
Lightfoot, J. B. [Joseph Barber]. *Saint Paul's Epistle to the Galatians: A Revised Text with Introduction, Notes and Dissertations*. London and New York: Macmillan, 1887.
Longenecker, Richard N. *Galatians*. WBC. Dallas: Word, 1990.
Lührmann, Dieter. *Galatians*. A Continental Commentary. Minneapolis: Fortress, 1992.
Luther, Martin. *Lectures on Galatians 1535, Chapters 1–4*. In vol. 26 of *Luther's Works*. Edited by Jaroslav Pelikan and Walter A. Hansen. Saint

Louis: Concordia, 1963; and *Lectures on Galatians 1535, Chapters 5–6; Lectures on Galatians 1519, Chapters 1–6*. In vol. 27 of *Luther's Works*. Edited by Jaroslav Pelikan and Walter A. Hansen. Saint Louis: Concordia, 1964.

Martyn, J. Louis. *Galatians: A New Translation with Introduction and Commentary*. AB 33A. New York: Doubleday, 1997.

Matera, Frank J. *Galatians*. SP 9. Collegeville, Minn.: Glazier, 1992.

Metzger, Bruce Manning. *A Textual Commentary on the Greek New Testament*. 2nd ed. Stuttgart: German Bible Society, 1994.

Mussner, Franz. *Der Galaterbrief*. 5th ed. Freiburg: Herder & Herder, 1988.

Oepke, Albrecht. *Der Brief des Paulus an de Galater*. Revised by J. Rohde. 3rd ed. Berlin: Evangelische Verlagsanstalt, 1973.

Ridderbos, Herman N. *The Epistle of Paul to the Churches of Galatians*. NICNT. Grand Rapids: Eerdmans, 1953.

Rohde, Joachim. *Der Brief des Paulus an die Galater*. THKNT 9. Berlin: Evangelische Verlagsanstalt, 1989.

Schlier, Heinrich. *Der Brief an die Galater*. Repr. of 4th ed. KEK 7. Göttingen: Vandenhoeck & Ruprecht, 1961.

Vouga, François. *An die Galater*. HNT 10. Tübingen: Mohr Siebeck, 1998.

Williams, Sam K. *Galatians*. ANTC. Nashville: Abingdon, 1997.

Witherington, Ben, III. *Grace in Galatia: A Commentary on St. Paul's Letter to the Galatians*. Edinburgh: T&T Clark, 1998.

Ziesler, John. *The Epistle to the Galatians*. London: Epworth, 1992.

Other Literature

References to literature other than commentaries are by author, plus year of publication only when necessary to distinguish it from another work.

Abrams, M. H. [Meyer Howard]. 1988. *A Glossary of Literary Terms*. 5th ed. Fort Worth: Holt, Rinehart & Winston.

Anderson, Roger Dean, Jr. 1999. *Ancient Rhetorical Theory and Paul*. Rev. ed. CBET 18. Leuven: Peeters.

———. 2000. *Glossary of Greek Rhetorical Terms Connected to Methods of Argumentation, Figures and Tropes from Anaximenes to Quintilian*. Leuven: Peeters.

Arnold, Clinton E. 2005. "'I Am Astonished That You Are So Quickly Turning Away' (Gal 1.6): Paul and Anatolian Folk Belief." *NTS* 51:429–49.

Aune, David E. 1987. *The New Testament in Its Literary Environment*. LEC 8. Philadelphia: Westminster.

———, ed. 1988. *Greco-Roman Literature and the New Testament: Selected Forms and Genres*. SBLSBS 21. Atlanta: Scholars Press.

Aus, Roger D. 1979. "Three Pillars and Three Patriarchs: A Proposal concerning Gal 2:9." *ZNW* 70:252–61.
Baarda, Tjitze. 1992. "*Ti eti diōkomai* in Gal 5,11: Apodosis or Parenthesis?" *NovT* 34:250–56.
Bachmann, Michael. 1999. *Antijudaismus im Galaterbrief? Exegetische Studien zu einem polemischen Schreiben und zur Theologie des Apostels Paulus*. NTOA 40. Freiburg: Universitätsverlag; Göttingen: Vandenhoeck & Ruprecht. ET, *Anti-Judaism in Galatians? Exegetical Studies on a Polemical Letter and on Paul's Theology*. Translated by Robert L. Brawley. Grand Rapids: Eerdmans, 2008.
Barclay, John M. G. 1987. "Mirror-Reading a Polemical Letter: Galatians as a Test Case." *JSNT* 31:73–93.
———. 1988. *Obeying the Truth: A Study of Paul's Ethics in Galatians*. Studies of the New Testament and Its World. Edinburgh: T&T Clark.
———. 2002. "Paul's Story: Theology as Testimony." Pages 133–56 in *Narrative Dynamics in Paul: A Critical Assessment*. Edited by Bruce W. Longenecker. Louisville, Ky.: Westminster John Knox, 2002.
Barnikol, Ernst. 1998. "The Non-Pauline Origin of the Parallelism of the Apostles Peter and Paul: Galatians 2:7–8." *JHC* 5:285–300. Repr. of 1931 original.
Barrett, C. K. [Charles Kingsley]. 1982. "The Allegory of Abraham, Sarah, and Hagar in the Argument of Galatians." Pages 154–69 in *Essays on Paul*. Philadelphia: Westminster.
Bauckham, Richard J. 1979. "Barnabas in Galatians." *JSNT* 2:61–72.
Behm, Johannes. 1964. "ἀνατίθημι." *TDNT* 1:353–56.
Beker, J. Christiaan. 1980. *Paul the Apostle: The Triumph of God in Life and Thought*. Philadelphia: Fortress.
Bertram, Georg. 1967. "πατέω." *TDNT* 5:940–43.
———. 1971. "στρέφω." *TDNT* 7:714–29.
Betz, Hans Dieter. 1975. "The Literary Composition and Function of Paul's Letter to the Galatians." *NTS* 21:352–79.
———, 1992. "Apostle." *ABD* 1:309–311.
Betz, Otto. 1964. "στίγμα." *TDNT* 7:657–64.
Beuken, W. A. M. [Willem André Maria]. 1974. "Isaiah LIV: The Multiple Identity of the Person Addressed." *OTS* 19:29–70.
Blinzler, Josef. 1963. "Lexikalisches zu dem Terminus *Ta stoicheia tou kosmou* bei Paulus." Pages 429–43 in vol. 2 of *Studiorum Paulinorum Congressus Internationalis Catholicus 1961*. Rome: Pontifical Biblical Institute.
Borgen, Peder. 1995. "Some Hebrew and Pagan Features in Philo's and Paul's Interpretation of Hagar and Ishmael." Pages 151–64 in *The New Testament and Hellenistic Judaism*. Edited by Peder Borgen and Søren Giversen. Aarhus: Aarhus University Press.

Brawley, Robert L. 2002. "Contextuality, Intertextuality, and the Hendiadic Relationship of Promise and Law in Galatians." *ZNW* 93:99–119.
Breytenbach, Cilliers. 1993. "Versöhnung, Stellvertretung, und Sühne: Semantische und traditionsgeschichtliche Bemerkungen am Beispiel der paulinischen Briefe." *NTS* 39:59–97.
———. 1996. *Paulus und Barnabas in der Provinz Galatien: Studien zu Apostelgeschichte 13f.; 16,6; 18,23 und den Adressaten des Galaterbriefes.* AGJU 38. Leiden: Brill.
———. 2003. "'Christus starb für uns': Zur Tradition und paulinischen Rezeption der sogenannten 'Sterbeformeln.'" *NTS* 49:447–75.
Brondos, David A. 2001. "The Cross and the Curse: Galatians 3.13 and Paul's Doctrine of Redemption." *JSNT* 81:3–32.
Bruce, F. F. [Frederick Fyvie]. 1971. "Galatian Problems 3: The 'Other' Gospel." *BJRL* 53:253–71.
Büchsel, Frederick. 1964. "ἀλληγορέω." *TDNT* 1:260–63.
Bullinger, E.W., 1968 (reprint of 1898). *Figures of Speech Used in the Bible.* Grand Rapids: Baker.
Bultmann, Rudolf. 1951. *Theology of the New Testament.* Translated by Kendrick Grobel. Vol. 1. New York: Scribner.
———. 1968. "πείθω." *TDNT* 6:1–3.
Campbell, Douglas A. 1992. "The Meaning of *Pistis* and *Nomos* in Paul: A Linguistic and Structural Analysis." *JBL* 111:91–103.
———. 1994. "Romans 1:17—A Crux Interpretum for the *Pistis Christou* Debate." *JBL* 113:265–85.
Chester, Stephen. 2009. "It Is No Longer I Who Live: Justification by Faith and Participation in Christ in Martin Luther's Exegesis of Galatians." *NTS* 55:315–37.
Chibici-Revneanu, Nicole. 2008. "Leben im Gesetz: Die paulinische Interpretation von Lev 18:5 (Gal 3:12; Röm 10:5)." *NovT* 50:105–19.
Chilton, Bruce. 1987. *The Isaiah Targum: Introduction, Translation, Apparatus and Notes.* The Aramaic Bible 2. Wilmington, Del.: Michael Glazer.
———. 1992. "Amen." *ABD* 1:184–86.
Choi, Hung-Sik. 2005. "*Pistis* in Galatians 5:5–6: Neglected Evidence for the Faithfulness of Christ." *JBL* 124:467–90.
Collins, John J. 1984. *The Apocalyptic Imagination: An Introduction to the Jewish Matrix of Christianity.* New York: Crossroad.
———, ed. 1998. *The Origins of Apocalypticism in Judaism and Christianity.* Vol. 1 of *The Encyclopedia of Apocalypticism.* New York: Continuum.
Cosgrove, Charles H. 1988. "Arguing Like a Mere Human Being: Galatians 3.15–18 in Rhetorical Perspective." *NTS* 34:536–49.
Dahl, Nils A. 1950. "Der Name Israel." *Jud* 6:161–72.

Das, A. [Ajit] Andrew. 2000. "Another Look at ἐὰν μή, in Galatians 2:16." *JBL* 119:529–39.
Davies, W. D. [William David]. 1955. *Paul and Rabbinic Judaism*. Harper Torchbook. New York: Harper & Row. Original, 1948.
Davies, W. D. [William David], and Dale C. Allison. 1988. *The Gospel according to Saint Matthew*. Vol. 1. ICC. Edinburgh: T&T Clark.
Davis, Basil S. 1999. "The Meaning of προεγράφη in the Context of Galatians 3.1." *NTS* 45:194–212.
De Boer, Martinus C. 1988. *The Defeat of Death. Apocalyptic Eschatology in 1 Corinthians 15 and Romans 5*. JSNTSup 22. Sheffield: Sheffield Academic.
———. 1989. "Paul and Jewish Apocalyptic Eschatology." Pages 169–90 in *Apocalyptic and the New Testament: Essays in Honor of J. Louis Martyn*. Edited by Joel Marcus and Marion L. Soards. JSNTSup 24. Sheffield: Sheffield Academic.
———. 1998. "Paul and Apocalyptic Eschatology." Pages 345–83 in *The Origins of Apocalypticism in Judaism and Christianity*. Edited by John J. Collins. Vol. 1 of *The Encyclopedia of Apocalypticism*. New York: Continuum. Repr., pages 166–94 in *The Continuum History of Apocalypticism*. Edited by Bernard J. McGinn, John J. Collins, and Stephen J. Stein. New York: Continuum, 2003.
———. 2001. "The Appropriation of Jewish Apocalyptic Eschatology in the New Testament, Especially Paul." Pages 17–29 in *Hoffnung für die Zukunft: Modelle eschatologischen und apokalyptischen Denkens*. Edited by Ed Noort and Mladen Popovíc. Theologie zwischen Ost und West 2. Groningen: Groningen University Press.
———. 2002. "Paul, Theologian of God's Apocalypse." *Int* 56:21–33.
———. 2004. "Paul's Quotation of Isa 54.1 in Gal 4.27." *NTS* 50:370–89.
———. 2005. "Paul's Use and Interpretation of a Justification Tradition in Galatians 2.15–21." *JSNT* 28, no. 2:189–216.
———. 2007. "The Meaning of the Phrase *ta stoicheia tou kosmou* in Galatians." *NTS* 53:204–24.
———. 2008. "The New Preachers in Galatia: Their Identity, Message, Aims, and Impact." Pages 39–60 in *Jesus, Paul, and Early Christianity: Studies in Honour of Henk Jan de Jonge*. Edited by Rieuwerd Buitenwerf, Harm W. Hollander, and Johannes Tromp. NovTSup 130. Leiden: Brill.
———. 2010. "De Psalmen bij Paulus: LXX Psalm 142:2 in Galaten 2:16 and Romeinen 3:20." *Amsterdamse Cahiers voor Exegese van de Bijbel en zijn Tradities* 25:83–94.
Deissmann, Adolf. 1927. *Light from the Ancient East: The New Testament Illustrated by Recently Discovered Texts of the Graeco-Roman World*. 4th ed. London: Hodder & Stoughton.

Delling, Gerhard. 1967. "προλαμβάνω." *TDNT* 4:14–15.
De Vries, Carl E. 1975. "Paul's 'Cutting Remarks' about a Race: Galatians 5.1–12." Pages 115–20 in *Current Issues in Biblical and Patristic Interpretation*. Edited by Gerald F. Hawthorne. Grand Rapids: Eerdmans.
Dibelius, Martin. 1976. *James: A Commentary on the Epistle of James*. Translated by Michael A. Williams. Philadelphia: Fortress.
Di Mattei, Steven. 2006. "Paul's Allegory of the Two Covenants (Gal 4.21–31) in Light of First-Century Hellenistic Rhetoric and Jewish Hermeneutics." *NTS* 52:102–22.
Dodd, Brian J. 1996. "Christ's Slave, People Pleasers and Galatians 1.10." *NTS* 42:90–104.
Dodd, C. H. [Charles Harold]. 1968. "Έννομος Χριστοῦ." Pages 134–48 in *More New Testament Studies*. Manchester: University of Manchester Press.
Donaldson, Terence L. 1989. "Zealot and Convert: The Origin of Paul's Torah-Christ Antithesis." *CBQ* 51:655–82.
Downing, F. Gerald. 1996. "A Cynic Preparation for Paul's Gospel for Jew and Greek, Slave and Free, Male and Female." *NTS* 42:454–62.
Dunn, James D. G. 1990. *Jesus, Paul and the Law: Studies in Mark and Galatians*. London: SPCK.
———. 1993. *The Theology of Paul's Letter to the Galatians*. NTT. Cambridge: Cambridge University Press.
———, ed. 1996. *Paul and the Mosaic Law: The Third Durham-Tübingen Research Symposium on Earliest Christianity and Judaism (Durham, September 1994)*. WUNT 89. Tübingen: Mohr; Grand Rapids: Eerdmans.
———. 1997. "4QMMT and Galatians." *NTS* 43:147–53.
———. 1998. *The Theology of Paul the Apostle*. Edinburgh: T&T Clark.
———. 2002. "Once More, *Pistis Christou*." *JSNT* 85:75–96. Originally pages 730–44 in *Society of Biblical Literature 1991 Seminar Papers*. Edited by Eugene H. Lovering Jr. Atlanta: Scholars Press, 1991. Repr. as pages 61–81 in *Looking Back, Pressing On*. Edited by E. E. Johnson and D. M. Hay. Vol. 4 of *Pauline Theology*. SBLSymS 4. Atlanta: Scholars Press, 1997.
Du Toit, André. 1994. "Vilification as a Pragmatic Device in Early Christian Epistolography." *Bib* 75:403–12.
Eastman, Susan. 2001. "The Evil Eye and the Curse of the Law: Galatians 3.1 Revisited." *JSNT* 83:69–87.
———. 2006. "'Cast Out the Slave Woman and Her Son': The Dynamics of Exclusion and Inclusion in Galatians 4.30." *JSNT* 28, no. 3:309–36.
———. 2007. *Recovering Paul's Mother Tongue: Language and Theology in Galatians*. Grand Rapids: Eerdmans.
———. 2010. "Israel and the Mercy of God: Re-visiting Galatians 6.16 and Romans 9–11." *NTS* 56:356–95.
Elliott, John H. 1990. "Paul, Galatians, and the Evil Eye." *CurTM* 17:262–73.

Elliott, J. Keith. 1969. "The Use of ἕτερος in the New Testament." *ZNW* 60:140–41.
Elliott, Susan M. 2003. *Cutting Too Close for Comfort: Paul's Letter to the Galatians in Its Anatolian Context.* JSNTSup 248. London: T&T Clark International.
Esler, Philip F. 1994. "Sectarianism and the Conflict at Antioch." Pages 52–69 in *The First Christians in Their Social Worlds.* London and New York: Routledge.
———. 1995. "Making and Breaking an Agreement Mediterranean Style: A New Reading of Galatians 2:1–14." *BibInt* 3:285–314. Repr. as pages 261–81 in *The Galatians Debate: Contemporary Issues in Rhetorical and Historical Interpretation.* Edited by Mark D. Nanos. Peabody, Mass.: Hendrickson.
———. 1998. *Galatians.* New Testament Readings. London and New York: Routledge.
Fairchild, Mark R. 1999. "Paul's Pre-Christian Zealot Associations: A Reexamination of Gal 1.14 and Acts 22.3." *NTS* 45:514–32.
Fee, Gordon D. 1987. *The First Epistle to the Corinthians.* NICNT. Grand Rapids: Eerdmans.
———. 1994. *God's Empowering Presence: The Holy Spirit in the Letters of Paul.* Peabody, Mass.: Hendrickson.
Fitzmyer, Joseph A. 1978. "Crucifixion in Ancient Palestine, Qumran Literature, and the New Testament." *CBQ* 40:493–513.
———. 1987. *Paul and His Theology: A Brief Sketch.* Englewood Cliffs, N.J.: Prentice-Hall.
———. 1992. *Romans: A New Translation and Commentary.* AB 33. New York: Doubleday.
———. 1998. *The Acts of the Apostles: A New Translation and Commentary.* AB 31. New York: Doubleday.
Furnish, Victor Paul. 1968. *Theology and Ethics in Paul.* Nashville: Abingdon.
———. 1984. *II Corinthians.* AB 32A. Garden City, N.Y.: Doubleday.
García Martínez, Florentino, and Tigchelaar, Eibert J. C. 1997–98. *The Dead Sea Scrolls Study Edition.* 2 vols. Leiden: Brill.
Gaventa, Beverly Roberts. 1986. *From Darkness to Light: Aspects of Conversion in the New Testament.* Philadelphia: Fortress.
———. 1986a. "Galatians 1 and 2: Autobiography as Paradigm." *NTS* 28:309–26.
———. 1990. "The Maternity of Paul: An Exegetical Study of Gal 4:19." Pages 189–201 in *The Conversation Continues: Studies in Paul and John: In Honor of J. Louis Martyn.* Edited by Robert T. Fortna and Beverly Roberts Gaventa. Nashville: Abingdon.
———. 2007. *Our Mother Saint Paul.* Louisville, Ky.: Westminster John Knox.

Georgi, Dieter. 1992. *Remembering the Poor: The History of Paul's Collection for Jerusalem*. Nashville: Abingdon. German original, 1965.
Gordon, David T. 1989. "A Note on *Paidagōgos* in Galatians 3:24–25." *NTS* 35:150–54.
Grundmann, Walter. 1964. "ἄγγελος." *TDNT* 1:74–76.
———. 1964a. "ἐγκράτεια." *TDNT* 2:339–42.
Häfner, Gerd. 2001. "Zur Auslegung von προειρήκαμεν in Gal 1,9." *BZ* 45:101–4.
Hall, Robert G. 1987. "The Rhetorical Outline of Galatians: A Reconsideration." *JBL* 106:277–88.
———. 1996. "Arguing Like an Apocalypse: Galatians and an Ancient *Topos* outside the Greco-Roman Rhetorical Tradition." *NTS* 42:434–53.
Hanse, Hermann. 1935. "Δῆλον: Zu Gal. 3:11." *ZNW* 34:299–303.
Hansen, G. Walter. 1989. *Abraham in Galatians: Epistolary and Rhetorical Contexts*. JSNTSup 29. Sheffield: JSOT Press.
———. 1993. "A Paradigm of the Apocalypse: The Gospel in the Light of Epistolary Analysis." Pages 194–209 in *Gospel in Paul: Studies on Corinthians, Galatians and Romans for Richard N. Longenecker*. Edited by L. Ann Jervis and Peter Richardson. JSNTSup 108. Sheffield: Sheffield Academic Press.
Hardin, Justin K. 2008. *Galatians and the Imperial Cult: A Critical Analysis of the First-Century Social Context of Paul's Letter*. WUNT 2/237. Tübingen: Mohr Siebeck.
Harrill, J. Albert. 2002. "Coming of Age and Putting On Christ: The Toga Virilis Ceremony, Its Paraenesis, and Paul's Interpretation of Baptism in Galatians." *NovT* 44:252–77.
Hauck, Frederich, and Siegfried Schulz. 1968. "πραΰς, πραΰτης." *TDNT* 6:645–51.
Hays, Richard B. 1987. "Christology and Ethics in Galatians: The Law of Christ." *CBQ* 49:268–90.
———. 1989. *Echoes of Scripture in the Letters of Paul*. New Haven: Yale University Press.
———. 1989a. "'The Righteous One' as Eschatological Deliverer: A Case Study in Paul's Apocalyptic Hermeneutics." Pages 191–216 in *Apocalyptic and the New Testament: Essays in Honor of J. Louis Martyn*. Edited by Joel Marcus and Marion L. Soards. JSNTSup 24. Sheffield: Sheffield Academic.
———. 1992. "Justification." *ABD* 3:1129–32.
———. 2002. *The Faith of Jesus Christ: The Narrative Substructure of Galatians 3:1–4:11*. 2nd ed. Grand Rapids: Eerdmans; Dearborn: Dove Booksellers. Originally *The Faith of Jesus Christ: An Investigation of the Narrative Substructure of Galatians 3:1–4:11*. SBLDS 56. Chico, Calif.: Scholars Press, 1983.

———. 2002a. "Πίστις and Pauline Christology: What Is at Stake?" Pages 272–97 in *The Faith of Jesus Christ: The Narrative Substructure of Galatians 3:1–4:11*. 2nd ed. Grand Rapids: Eerdmans; Dearborn: Dove Booksellers. Originally pages 35–60 in *Looking Back, Pressing On*. Edited by E. E. Johnson and D. M. Hay. Vol. 4 of *Pauline Theology*. SBLSymS 4. Atlanta: Scholars Press, 1997.

Hengel, Martin. 1991. *The Pre-Christian Paul*. London: SCM; Philadelphia: Trinity Press International.

Holmberg, Bengt. 1998. "Jewish versus Christian Identity in the Early Church?" *RB* 105:397–425.

Hooker, Morna D. 1990. *From Adam to Christ: Essays on Paul*. Cambridge: Cambridge University.

Horrell, David G. 2000. "'No Longer Jew or Greek': Paul's Corporate Christology and the Construction of Christian Community." Pages 321–44 in *Christology, Controversy and Community: New Testament Essays in Honour of David R. Catchpole*. Edited by David G. Horrell and Christopher M. Tuckett. Leiden: Brill.

———. 2005. *Solidarity and Difference: A Contemporary Reading of Paul's Ethics*. London: T&T Clark International.

Horrell, David G., and Christopher M. Tuckett, eds. 2000. *Christology, Controversy and Community: New Testament Essays in Honour of David R. Catchpole*. Leiden: Brill.

Hultgren, Arland J. 1976. "Paul's Pre-Christian Persecutions of the Church: Their Purpose, Locale, and Nature." *JBL* 95:97–11.

Hunt, Arthur Surridge, and Campbell Cowen Edgar, eds. and trans. 1970. *Select Papyri*. Vol. 1. LCL 166. Cambridge, Mass.: Harvard University Press.

Jervis, L. Ann, and Peter Richardson, eds. 1993. *Gospel in Paul: Studies on Corinthians, Galatians and Romans for Richard N. Longenecker*. JSNTSup 108. Sheffield: Sheffield Academic Press.

Jewett, Robert. 1979. *Dating Paul's Life*. London: SCM.

———. 2002. "The Agitators and the Galatian Congregation." Pages 334–47 in *The Galatians Debate: Contemporary Issues in Rhetorical and Historical Interpretation*. Edited by Mark D. Nanos. Peabody, Mass.: Hendrickson. Original in *NTS* 17 (1970–71): 198–212.

Kahl, Brigitte. 2000. "No Longer Male: Masculinity Struggles behind Galatians 3:28?" *JSNT* 79:37–49.

Käsemann, Ernst. 1969. "On the Subject of Primitive Christian Apocalyptic." Pages 108–37 in *New Testament Questions of Today*. Philadelphia: Fortress. German original, 1962.

———. 1969a. "'The Righteousness of God' in Paul." Pages 168–82 in *New Testament Questions of Today*. Philadelphia: Fortress. German original, 1961.

———. 1971. "On Paul's Anthropology." Pages 1–31 in *Perspectives on Paul.* Philadelphia: Fortress.
Keck, Leander E. 1984. "Paul and Apocalyptic Theology." *Int* 38:229–41.
Keith, Chris. 2008. "'In My Own Hand': Grapho-Literacy and the Apostle Paul." *Bib* 89:39–58.
Kennedy, George A. 1963. *The Art of Persuasion in Greece.* London: Longman.
———. 1972. *The Art of Rhetoric in the Roman World.* Princeton: Princeton University Press.
———. 1984. *New Testament Interpretation through Rhetorical Criticism.* Chapel Hill: University of North Carolina Press.
Kern, Philip H. 1998. *Rhetoric and Galatians: Assessing an Approach to Paul's Epistle.* SNTSMS 101. Cambridge: Cambridge University Press.
Kim, Seyoon. 2002. *Paul and the New Perspective: Second Thoughts on the Origin of Paul's Gospel.* Grand Rapids: Eerdmans.
Knox, John. 1989. *Chapters in a Life of Paul.* Rev. ed. London: SCM.
Koch, Dietrich-Alex. 1986. *Die Schrift als Zeuge des Evangeliums: Untersuchungen zu Verwendung und zum Verständnis der Schrift bei Paulus.* BHT 69. Tübingen: Mohr.
———. 1999. "Barnabas, Paulus und die Adressaten des Galaterbrief." Pages 85–106 in *Das Urchristentum in seiner literarischen Geschichte: Festschrift für Jürgen Becker zum 65. Geburtstag.* Edited by U. Mell and U. B. Müller. Berlin and New York: de Gruyter.
Koet, Bart J. 1991. "Roeping of Bekering? Paulus volgens Handelingen vergeleken met de Paulus van Galaten." Pages 77–95 in *Eén auteur, twee boeken: Lucas en de Handelingen van de Apostelen.* Edited by Peter Schmidt. Leuven: Acco.
Kremendahl, Dieter. 2000. *Die Botschaft der Form: Zum Verhältnis von antiker Epistolographie und Rhetorik im Galaterbrief.* NTOA 46. Éditions universitaires Fribourg. Göttingen: Vandenhoeck & Ruprecht.
Kuck, David W. 1994. "'Each Will Bear His Own Burden': Paul's Creative Use of an Apocalyptic Motif." *NTS* 40:289–97.
Lambrecht, Jan. 1996. "Is Gal. 5:11b a Parenthesis? A Response to T. Baarda." *NovT* 38:237–41.
———. 1997. "Paul's Coherent Admonition in Galatians 6,1–6: Mutual Help and Individual Attentiveness." *Bib* 78:33–56.
Lategan, Bernard C. 1998. "Is Paul Defending His Apostleship in Galatians?" *NTS* 34:411–30.
Longenecker, Bruce W. 1998. *The Triumph of Abraham's God: The Transformation of Identity in Galatians.* Edinburgh: T&T Clark.
———. 1999. "'Until Christ Is Formed in You': Suprahuman Forces and Moral Character in Galatians." *CBQ* 61:92–108.

———, ed. 2002. *Narrative Dynamics in Paul: A Critical Assessment.* Louisville, Ky.: Westminster John Knox.
Lüdemann, Gerd. 1984. *Paul, Apostle to the Gentiles: Studies in Chronology.* Translated by F. Stanley Jones. Philadelphia: Fortress.
Lührmann, Dieter. 1980. "Tage, Monate, Jahreszeiten, Jahre (Gal 4,10)." Pages 428–45 in *Werden und Wirken des Alten Testaments.* Edited by R. Albertz et al. Göttingen: Vandenhoeck & Ruprecht.
Lull, David J. 1986. "The Law Was Our Pedagogue: A Study in Gal 3:19–25." *JBL* 105:481–98.
Lütgert, Wilhelm. 1919. *Gesetz und Geist: Eine Untersuchung zur Vorgeschichte des Galaterbriefes.* Gütersloh: Gütersloher Verlag.
Lyons, George. 1985. *Pauline Autobiography: Toward a New Understanding.* Atlanta: Scholars Press.
Malherbe, Abraham J. 1988. *Ancient Epistolary Theorists.* SBLSBS 19. Atlanta: Scholars Press.
Mann, Jacob. 1971. *The Palestinian Triennial Cycle: Genesis and Exodus.* Vol. 1 of *The Bible as Read and Preached in the Old Synagogue.* New York: Ktav.
Marcus, Joel. 1982. "The Evil Inclination in the Epistle of James." *CBQ* 44:606–21.
———. 1986. "The Evil Inclination in the Letters of Paul." *IBS* 8:8–21.
———. 2001. "'Under the Law': The Background of a Pauline Expression." *CBQ* 63:72–83.
Marcus, Joel, and Marion L. Soards, eds. 1989. *Apocalyptic and the New Testament: Essays in Honor of J. Louis Martyn.* JSNTSup 24. Sheffield: Sheffield Academic.
Martin, Dale. 1990. *Slavery as Salvation: The Metaphor of Slavery in Pauline Christianity.* New Haven: Yale University Press.
Martin, Troy W. 1995. "Apostasy to Paganism: The Rhetorical Stasis of the Galatian Controversy." *JBL* 114:437–61.
———. 1996. "Pagan and Judeo-Christian Time-Keeping Schemes in Gal. 4.10 and Col. 2.16." *NTS* 42:105–19.
———. 2003. "The Covenant of Circumcision (Gen 17:9–14) and the Situational Antitheses in Gal 3:28." *JBL* 122:111–25.
Martyn, J. Louis. 1991. "Events in Galatia: Modified Covenantal Nomism versus God's Invasion of the Cosmos in the Singular Gospel: A Response to J. D. G. Dunn and B. R. Gaventa." Pages 160–79 in *Thessalonians, Philippians, Galatians, Philemon.* Edited by Jouette M. Bassler. Vol. 1 of *Pauline Theology.* Minneapolis: Fortress.
———. 1997. *Theological Issues in the Letters of Paul.* Studies in the New Testament and Its World. Edinburgh: T&T Clark.

Mason, Steve. 2007. "Jews, Judaeans, Judaizing, Judaism: Problems of Categorization in Ancient History." *JSJ* 38:457–512.
Matlock, Barry. 2002. "'Even the Demons Believe': Paul and πίστις Χριστοῦ." *CBQ* 64:300–318.
Maurer, Christian. 1972. "μετατίθημι." *TDNT* 8:161–62.
———. 1972a. "προστίθημι." *TDNT* 8:167–68.
Meeks, Wayne A. 1974. "The Image of the Androgyne: Some Uses of a Symbol in Earliest Christianity." *History of Religions* 13:165–208.
Meiser, Martin. 2007. *Galater*. NTP 9. Göttingen: Vandenhoeck & Ruprecht.
Mell, Ulrich. 1989. *Neue Schöpfung: Eine traditionsgeschichtliche und exegetische Studie zu einem soteriologischen Grundsatz paulinischer Theologie.* BZNW 56. Berlin: De Gruyter.
Merk, Otto. 1969. "Der Beginn der Paränese im Galaterbrief." *ZNW* 60:83–104.
Meyer, Marvin W. 1987. *The Ancient Mysteries: A Sourcebook*. San Francisco: Harper & Row.
Meyer, Paul W. 2004. *The Word in This World: Essays in New Testament Exegesis and Theology*. NTL. Louisville, Ky.: Westminster John Knox.
Meyer, Rudolf. 1968. "περιτέμνω." *TDNT* 6:72–84.
Mitchell, Stephen. 1993. *The Rise of the Church*. Vol. 2 of *Anatolia: Land, Men, and Gods in Asia Minor*. Oxford: Clarendon.
Moore, George Foot. 1971. *Judaism in the First Centuries of the Christian Era*. 2 vols. New York: Schocken Books.
Morland, Kjell Arne. 1995. *The Rhetoric of Curse in Galatians: Paul Confronts Another Gospel*. Emory Studies in Early Christianity. Atlanta: Scholars Press.
Moule, C. F. D. [Charles Francis Digby]. 1959. *An Idiom Book of New Testament Greek*. 2nd ed. Cambridge: Cambridge University Press. Repr., 1982. 1st ed., 1953.
Mullins, Terence Y. 1972. "Formulas in New Testament Epistles." *JBL* 91:380–90.
Munck, Johannes. 1959. *Paul and the Salvation of Mankind*. Richmond: John Knox.
Murphy-O'Connor, Jerome. 1993. "Paul in Arabia." *CBQ* 55:732–37.
———. 1995. *Paul the Letter-Writer: His World, His Options, His Skills*. Good News Studies 41. Collegeville, Minn.: Michael Glazier.
———. 1997. *Paul, A Critical Life*. Pbk., Oxford: Oxford University Press. Original, 1996.
———. 1998. "Gal 4:13–14 and the Recipients of Galatians." *RB* 105: 202–7.
Nanos, Mark D., ed. 2002. *The Galatians Debate: Contemporary Issues in Rhetorical and Historical Interpretation*. Peabody, Mass.: Hendrickson.
———. 2002a. *The Irony of Galatians: Paul's Letter in First-Century Context*. Minneapolis: Fortress.
———. 2002b. "What Was at Stake in Peter's 'Eating with Gentiles' at Antioch?" Pages 282–318 in *The Galatians Debate: Contemporary Issues*

in Rhetorical and Historical Interpretation. Edited by Mark D. Nanos. Peabody, Mass.: Hendrickson.
Neyrey, Jerome H. 1988. "Bewitched in Galatia: Paul and Cultural Anthropology." *CBQ* 50:72–100.
Noort, Ed, and Mladen Popovíc. 2001. *Hoffnung für die Zukunft: Modelle eschatologischen und apokalyptischen Denkens.* Theologie zwischen Ost und West 2. Groningen: Groningen University Press.
Noth, Martin. 1957. "Die mit des Gesetzes Werken umgehen, die sind unter dem Fluch." Pages 155–71 in *Gesammelte Studien zum Alten Testament.* TB 6. Munich: Kaiser.
Oepke, Albrecht. 1965. "ἀποκαλύπτω, ἀποκάλυψις." *TDNT* 3:563–92.
Räisänen, Heikki. 1985. "Galatians 2:16 and Paul's Break with Judaism." *NTS* 31:543–53.
Rengstorf, Karl Heinrich. 1964. "ἀπόστολος." *TDNT* 1:407–45.
———. 1964a. "δοῦλος." *TDNT* 2:261–80.
Richards, Ernest Randolph. 1991. *The Secretary in the Letters of Paul.* WUNT 2. Tübingen: Mohr.
Richardson, Peter. 1969. *Israel in the Apostolic Church.* SNTSMS 10. Cambridge: Cambridge University Press.
Riches, John. 2007. *Galatians through the Centuries.* Blackwell Bible Commentaries. Oxford and Malden, Mass.: Blackwell.
Ropes, James Hardy. 1929. *The Singular Problem of the Epistle to the Galatians.* Cambridge, Mass.: Harvard University Press.
Rusam, Dietrich. 1992. "Neue Belege zu dem *Stoicheia tou kosmou* (Gal 4,3.9; Kol 2,8.20)." *ZNW* 83:119–25.
———. 2002. "Was versteht Paulus unter der Πίστις (Ἰησοῦ) Χριστοῦ (Röm 3,22.26; Gal 2,16.20; 3,22; Phil 3,9)?" *PzB* 11:47–70.
Russell, David Syme. 1964. *The Method and Message of Jewish Apocalyptic, 200 B.C.–A.D. 100.* OTL. London: SCM.
Sanders, E. P. [Ed Parish]. 1977. *Paul and Palestinian Judaism.* Philadelphia: Fortress.
———. 1983. *Paul, the Law, and the Jewish People.* Philadelphia: Fortress.
———. 1990. "Jewish Association with Gentiles and Galatians 2.1–14." Pages 170–88 in *The Conversation Continues: Studies in Paul and John in Honor of J. Louis Martyn.* Edited by Robert T. Fortna and Beverly Roberts Gaventa. Nashville: Abingdon.
———. 1991. *Paul.* Past Masters. Oxford and New York: Oxford University Press.
Sänger, Dieter. 1994. "'Verflucht ist jeder, der am Holze hängt' (Gal 3,13b): Zur Rezeption einer früher antichristlichen Polemik." *ZNW* 85:279–85.
———. 2002. "'Vergeblich bemüht' (Gal 4,11)? Zur paulinischen Argumentationsstrategie im Galaterbrief." *NTS* 48:377–99.

———. 2006. "'Das Gesetz is unser Παιδαγωγός geworden bis zu Christus' (Gal 3,24)." Pages 236–60 in *Das Gesetz im frühen Judentum und im Neuen Testament: Festschrift für Christoph Burchard zum 75. Geburtstag.* Edited by Dieter Sänger and Matthias Konradt. Göttingen: Vandenhoeck & Ruprecht; Fribourg: Academic Press.

Schewe, Susanne. 2005. *Die Galater zurückgewinnen: Paulinische Strategien in Galater 5 und 6.* FRLANT 208. Göttingen: Vandenhoeck & Ruprecht.

Schmidt, Andreas. 1992. "Das Missionsdekret in Galater 2.7–8 als Vereinbarung vom ersten Besuch Pauli in Jerusalem." *NTS* 38:149–52.

Schmidt, Peter, ed. 1991. *Eén auteur, twee boeken: Lucas en Handelingen van de Apostelen.* Leuven: Acco.

Schmithals, Walter. 1972. "The Heretics in Galatia." Pages 13–64 in *Paul and the Gnostics.* Translated by John E. Steely. Nashville: Abingdon.

Schrenk, Gottlob. 1949. "Was bedeutet 'Israel Gottes'?" *Jud* 5:81–94.

———. 1950. "Der Segenswunsch nach der Kampfepistel." *Jud* 6:170–90.

Schüssler Fiorenza, Elisabeth. 1983. *In Memory of Her: A Feminist Theological Reconstruction of Christian Origins.* New York: Crossroad.

Schweitzer, Albert. 1931. *The Mysticism of Paul the Apostle.* London: A&C Black. German original, 1930.

Schweizer, Eduard. 1988. "Slaves of the Elements and Worshipers of Angels: Gal 4:3, 9; Col 2:8, 18, 20." *JBL* 107:455–68.

Seesemann, Heinrich. 1967. "πατέω." *TDNT* 5:940–41, 943–45.

Silva, Moisés. 2001. *Interpreting Galatians: Explorations in Exegetical Method.* 2nd ed. Grand Rapids: Baker Academic.

Smit, Joop. 1989. "The Letter of Paul to the Galatians: A Deliberative Speech." *NTS* 35:1–26.

Smyth, Herbert Weir. 1956. *Greek Grammar.* Cambridge, Mass.: Harvard University Press.

Soards, M. L. 1988. "Seeking (*zētein*) and Sinning (*hamartolos* and *hamartia*) according to Galatians 2.17." Pages 237–54 in *Apocalyptic and the New Testament: Essays in Honor of J. Louis Martyn.* Edited by Joel Marcus and Marion L. Soards. JSNTSup 24. Sheffield: Sheffield Academic.

Stanley, Christopher D. 1990. "'Under a Curse': A Fresh Reading of Galatians 3.10–14." *NTS* 36:481–511.

———. 1992. *Paul and the Language of Scripture: Citation Technique in the Pauline Epistles and Contemporary Literature.* SNTSMS 74. Cambridge: Cambridge University Press.

———. 2004. *Arguing with Scripture: The Rhetoric of Quotations in the Letters of Paul.* New York and London: T&T Clark International.

Strelan, John G. 1975. "Burden-Bearing and the Law of Christ: A Re-Examination of Galatians 6.2." *JBL* 94:266–76.

Talbert, Charles H. 2001. "Paul, Judaism, and the Revisionists." *CBQ* 63:1–22.
Thurén, Lauri. 2000. *Derhetorizing Paul: A Dynamic Perspective on Pauline Theology and the Law*. WUNT 124. Tübingen: Mohr Siebeck.
Tolmie, D. François. 2005. *Persuading the Galatians: A Text-Centred Rhetorical Analysis of a Pauline Letter*. Tübingen: Mohr Siebeck.
———, ed. 2007. *Exploring New Rhetorical Approaches to Galatians*. AcT 9. Bloemfontein, S.A.: Publications Office of the University of the Free State.
Ukwuegbu, Bernard O. 2008. "Paraenesis, Identity-defining Norms, or Both? Galatians 5:13–6:10 in the Light of Social Identity Theory." *CBQ* 70:538–59.
Urbach, Ephraim E. 1987. *The Sages: Their Concepts and Beliefs*. Repr. of 2nd ed., 1979. Cambridge, Mass.: Harvard University Press.
Van Manen, Willem Christiaan. 1887. "Marcions brief van Paulus aan de Galatiërs." *ThT* 21:382–404, 451–533.
Verhoef, Eduard. 1979. *Er staat geschreven...: De Oud-testamentische citaten in de Brief aan de Galaten*. Meppel: Krips Repro.
Vos, Johan S. 2002. *Die Kunst der Argumentation bei Paulus*. WUNT 149. Tübingen: Mohr Siebeck.
Vouga, François. 1988. "Zur rhetorischen Gattung des Galaterbriefes." *ZNW* 79:291–92.
Walker, William O. 1997. "Translation and Interpretation of ἐὰν μή in Galatians 2:16." *JBL* 116:515–20.
———. 2003. "Does the 'We' in Gal 2.1–17 Include Paul's Opponents?" *NTS* 49:560–65.
———. 2003a. "Galatians 2:7b–8 as a Non-Pauline Interpolation." *CBQ* 65:568–87.
Wedderburn, Alexander J. M. 2002. "Paul's Collection: Chronology and History." *NTS* 48:95–100.
Weima, Jeffrey A. D. 1993. "Gal. 6:11–18: A Hermeneutical Key to the Galatian Letter." *CTJ* 28:90–107.
Westerholm, Stephen. 1988. *Israel's Law and the Church's Faith: Paul and His Recent Interpreters*. Grand Rapids: Eerdmans.
———. 2004. *Perspectives Old and New on Paul: The "Lutheran" Paul and His Critics*. Grand Rapids: Eerdmans.
White, John L. 1988. "Ancient Greek Letters." Pages 85–105 in *Greco-Roman Literature and the New Testament: Selected Forms and Genres*. Edited by David E. Aune. SBLSBS 21. Atlanta: Scholars Press.
Wilckens, Ulrich. 1971. "στῦλος." *TDNT* 7:732–36.
Williams, Sam K. 1987. "Again *Pistis Christou*." *CBQ* 49:431–47.
———. 1989. "The Hearing of Faith: Ἀκοὴ πίστεως in Galatians 3." *NTS* 35:82–93.
Willits, Joel. 2005. "Isa 54,1 in Gal 4,24b–27: Reading Genesis in Light of Isaiah." *ZNW* 96:188–210.

Wilson, Todd A. 2005. "'Under Law' in Galatians: A Pauline Theological Abbreviation." *JTS* 56:362–92.

———. 2007. *The Curse of the Law and the Crisis in Galatia: Reassessing the Purpose of Galatians*. Tübingen: Mohr Siebeck.

Winger, Michael W. 1986. "Unreal Conditions in the Letters of Paul." *JBL* 105:110–12.

———. 2000. "The Law of Christ." *NTS* 46:537–46.

Wischmeyer, Oda. 1986. "Das Gebot der Nächstenliebe bei Paulus: Eine traditionsgeschichtliche Untersuchung." *BZ* 30:161–87.

Witulski, Thomas. 2000. *Die Adressaten des Galaterbriefes: Untersuchungen zur Gemeinde von Antiochia und Pisidiam*. FRLANT 193. Göttingen: Vandenhoeck & Ruprecht.

Wright, N. T. [Nicholas Thomas]. 1991. *The Climax of the Covenant. Christ and Law in Pauline Theology*. Edinburgh: T&T Clark.

———. 1997. *What Saint Paul Really Said: Was Paul of Tarsus the Real Founder of Christianity?* Oxford: Lion.

———. 2005. *Paul: Fresh Perspectives*. London: SPCK.

Young, Norman H. 1987. "*Paidagōgos*: The Social Setting of a Pauline Metaphor." *NovT* 29:150–76.

INTRODUCTION

The Approach of This Commentary

Two recent books (Meiser; Riches)[1] have helpfully traced how Paul's Letter to the Galatians has been used and interpreted by Christian believers, theologians, historians, and commentators from the second century C.E. to our own time. By contrast, this commentary seeks to understand and to expound what the apostle was attempting to communicate to the very *first* users and interpreters of the letter, a group of believers in Christ living in Galatia in the middle of the first century C.E. The working assumption behind this quintessentially historical approach to understanding and expounding Paul's thought—his theology—in his Letter to the Galatians is twofold. First, we have a moral obligation to try to understand and to expound the Letter to the Galatians on Paul's own terms and not to attribute meanings to those terms that he (probably) did not intend.[2] Second, an understanding and an exposition of what Paul was seeking to communicate to his first, intended readers have some relevance for the manner in which the letter may be used and interpreted in current theological discussion and preaching.[3] A third assumption also plays a role: Ongoing developments in historical-critical research into Paul's Letter to the Galatians, and into earliest Christianity generally, require that the results of this research be critically harvested from time to time in the form of a commentary meant for a circle of readers wider than NT scholars alone.

The task of commenting on Paul's letter necessarily involves investigating how the first and intended readers of the letter, the believers resident in Galatia, may have heard what Paul was trying to communicate to them, given what

---

1. See the bibliography for complete information. In this volume, publications are cited by author (and year only when necessary to distinguish the work); commentaries are cited by author only.

2. Needless to say, many factors make this quest difficult and fraught (the historical distance between now and then, the linguistic and cultural barriers, the fact that every interpreter is not without presuppositions and expectations, etc.). That is not a reason for despair, but for humility with respect to one's own attempt to give an account of Paul's thought in this letter.

3. All texts, and perhaps especially theological texts, have a surplus of meaning, and are susceptible to a range of interpretations, but it would still be difficult, and morally dubious, to justify an appeal to Galatians that cannot be supported exegetically.

we know of their cultural-historical setting and of the occasion of the letter. Here too there is a working assumption: Paul cannot have intended what the Galatians were in no position to understand. A commentary on Paul's letter involves, therefore, taking into account the intended readers' likely reception of his words. A consequence of this approach is that considerable circumspection is required in using the other letters of Paul for the interpretation of Galatians. Those other letters were not available to the Galatians to help them make sense of Paul's words. This stricture counts especially for Romans, which has many thematic similarities with Galatians, particularly with respect to the matter of justification on the basis of faith rather than works of the law. Paul wrote Romans some years after he wrote Galatians, in completely different circumstances and for a completely different audience. What he wrote to the Romans about justification, faith, or the law may not, therefore, apply to what he was trying to convey about these matters to the Galatians.

The aim of this commentary, then, is to understand and to expound Paul's theology *as it unfolds* in this letter, and *as the Galatians* will probably understand it when they receive it.[4] For this reason, the commentary consistently uses the present tense with respect to Paul ("Paul probably means here to say that . . .") and the future tense with respect to the Galatians ("the Galatians will probably understand Paul to say that . . ."). The commentary thus asks its readers to imagine themselves as silent witnesses to Paul's dictation of the letter and to imagine how the letter will probably be received and understood in Galatia. This commentary does not pretend to be the last word on Galatians, and certainly not on Paul's theology in this letter. The ultimate purpose of this commentary is not to end the conversation about Galatians but to give it a new stimulus.

A Note on the Translation

The aim of the commentary requires a translation that seeks to be as faithful as possible to the Greek text that Paul wrote and the Galatians actually heard. The translation, therefore, seeks to stay as close as possible to Paul's Greek text, including on several occasions its garbled syntax, ambiguous formulations, and puzzling use of specific terms. Nevertheless, the translation also strives to be acceptable, idiomatic English.

The literalness of the translation means, inter alia, that it inevitably reflects the masculine bias of the original Greek, which was the common Greek of first century C.E. For example, on a number of occasions, Paul addresses the

---

4. By "Paul's theology in this letter" I mean not some thoroughly-worked-out system of thought, but merely his thinking about what he calls "the gospel" (1:11) as it comes to expression in this particular letter, which was written to a particular group of people living in a particular time and place.

Galatians as *adelphoi*, literally, "brothers." Because of its masculine bias, this term does not by modern definitions count as "inclusive language." The Greek term itself, however, has an inclusive meaning, being used by Paul to encompass both female and male believers in Galatia. To reflect this fact as well as the (for us, problematic) masculine bias of the term at the same time, the translation "brethren" has been chosen, meaning "sisters and brothers in Christ." The translation thus reflects Paul's text, warts and all.

The aim of providing a translation that is literal but also acceptable, idiomatic English recognizes that an overly literal translation can in some instances be misleading or incomprehensible. For example, for a portion of 2:6, the following translation has been adopted: "God shows no partiality" (following NRSV; cf. BDAG 584). An overly literal translation of the underlying Greek would yield: "God does not take the face of a person." Sometimes a definite article has been included where the Greek does not use one, or vice versa. This is normally a matter of style. For example, in the prescript where the Greek reads "God Father," the translation reads "God the Father." In 3:21, the Greek speaks literally of "the justification," but the translation has simply "justification." Such examples could be multiplied. The commentary tries to be transparent about such choices throughout so that readers can decide for themselves.

In short, the maxim, "As literal as possible, as idiomatic as required," has guided the translation process.

Addressees

Paul writes the letter to "the churches of Galatia" (1:2; cf. 1 Cor 16:1). The phrase is parallel to the expressions "the churches of Asia" in 1 Cor 16:19 and "the churches of Macedonia" in 2 Cor 8:1, where the geographical terms designate Roman provinces.[5] The same is probably true of the expression "the churches of Judea" in Gal 1:22, where "Judea" is evidently the Roman province encompassing the districts of Judea, Samaria, and Galilee (cf. 1 Thess 2:14).[6] The reference to "Galatia" in Gal 1:2, therefore, probably also designates the Roman province of that name. It is difficult, however, to determine where in

---

5. Paul tends to use Roman provincial names when referring to the areas where his churches are located, such as Macedonia (Rom 15:26; 1 Cor 16:5; 2 Cor 2:13; 7:5; 8:1; 11:9; Phil 4:15; 1 Thess 1:7–8; 4:10), Achaia (Rom 15:26; 1 Cor 16:15; 2 Cor 1:1; 9:2; 11:10; 1 Thess 1:7–8), Asia (Rom 16:5; 1 Cor 16:19; 2 Cor 1:8). Paul can even use the provincial names to refer to the believers living there, e.g., Achaia in Rom 15:26; 1 Cor 16:15; 2 Cor 9:2.

6. Elsewhere in Galatians, Paul uses regional designations, namely, "Arabia" (1:17; 4:25), which was a region not a Roman province, and the "districts [*klimata*] of Syria and Cilicia" (1:21), which were the regions after which the larger Roman province (Syria-Cilicia) was named (Betz 79 n. 222; Bruce 103; Longenecker 40; Vouga 37). Cf. 2 Cor 11:10 AT ("the districts of Achaia").

the Roman province of Galatia the churches addressed are located: in (or near) such northern cities as Ancyra (present-day Ankara), Pessinus, and Tavium (the North Galatia hypothesis)—or in such southern cities as Pisidian Antioch, Lystra, Iconium, and Derbe (the South Galatia hypothesis). The latter are specifically mentioned in Acts as the area of Paul's missionary activity during his first missionary journey for the church in Antioch in Syria (Acts 13:13–14:23); he passes through the first three cities a second time on his return to Antioch (14:21–27).[7]

Galatia was not only the Roman province of that name but also the region from which the much larger province (in the center of present-day Turkey) took its name.[8] Ancyra in the north lay at the center of this region, whereas the cities mentioned in Acts 13–14 lay in the regions of Pisidia and Lycaonia. The people living in the region of Galatia were ethnic Galatians.[9] The fact that Paul addresses his readers as "Galatians" in 3:1 would seem to decide the matter in favor of the region as the locale of the "churches in Galatia" (the "North Galatia" hypothesis), for it seems unlikely, if not exactly impossible, that Paul would refer to people who lived in Lycaonia and Pisidia as "Galatians," even if some of them may have been ethnic Galatians.[10] That Paul passed through the district of Galatia is also supported by Acts, which twice has Paul (the first time with Timothy and Silas/Silvanus) passing through "the Galatian region [*hē Galatikē chōra*]" (16:6; 18:23).[11] Acts clearly distinguishes this region from the regions of Pisidia and Lycaonia. It is true that Acts does not depict Paul as founding churches there on his first journey through the area; he simply passes through on his way to Macedonia. On the second journey, however, Paul goes "from place to place through the Galatian region and Phrygia, strengthening all the disciples" (Acts 18:23). Acts here assumes that Paul has founded a number of churches in Galatia (and Phrygia) the first time through.

Barnabas, who plays a prominent role alongside Paul in his initial travels in Acts 13–14, is not with Paul when he passes through "the Galatian region."

---

7. In Acts 16:1–5 Paul passes through Lystra, Iconium, and Derbe a third time.

8. In the same way, the Netherlands is commonly known as Holland, after the region in the west of the country (the current provinces of North and South Holland) where such well-known cities as Amsterdam, Rotterdam, and The Hague are located.

9. Ethnic Galatians were descendants of the Celts who originated in central Europe and settled in Britain, Gaul, northern Italy, Macedonia, and north-central Asia Minor. The Greek term *Galatai* appears to be a variant form of *Keltoi* or *Keltai* (Latin: Galli). See Bruce 3.

10. Breytenbach (1996: 152–67) shows that ethnic Galatians also lived in the south and thus concludes that Christians living there could also be addressed as "Galatians." But how likely is it that (virtually) all the members of the two or more (!) Galatian congregations in the south are also ethnic Galatians so that Paul can address them in this way?

11. More precisely, "the Phrygian and Galatian region" (16:6 AT); "the Galatian region and Phrygia" (18:23 AT). Koch (1999: 90) shows that "the Galatian region" is the northern region of the Roman province of Galatia, whose major cities were Pessinus, Ancyra, and Tavium.

Paul refers to Barnabas three times in the second chapter of Galatians (2:1, 9, 13) but does not mention him in the brief account of the apostle's initial contact with the Galatians in 4:12–15. If Barnabas had been with Paul at the founding of the Galatian churches, which is a necessary assumption of the "South Galatia" hypothesis (Acts 13–14), Barnabas would have been the senior partner (Acts 14:14: "the apostles Barnabas and Paul," in that order). Paul would then surely have mentioned him (Koch 1999: 93; Martyn 185; cf. Bauckham), despite the break with Barnabas caused by the incident in Antioch (2:11–14). Moreover, if Barnabas had been the founder of the Galatian churches alongside Paul, and the senior founder at that, Paul would scarcely have found it useful to his purposes to present the incident in Antioch as a suitable analogy for the problem in Galatia (see the commentary on this passage), since Barnabas is explicitly mentioned in this connection, being portrayed as standing on the same side as "the circumcision party" (2:12). The new preachers in Galatia (1:6–9; see Excursus 4), who were putting pressure on the Galatians to practice circumcision (6:12), would have exploited this fact against Paul, but Paul gives no indication that they had done so (Koch 1999: 96–97). The conclusion must then be that Barnabas was not present when Paul founded the churches in Galatia. That conclusion supports the "North Galatia" hypothesis.

According to Acts 13–14, Paul (accompanied by Barnabas) preaches in the local synagogues, bringing not only Gentiles but also many Jews to faith in Christ (Acts 13:43; 14:1). There is no corroboration of this picture in the Letter to the Galatians. Paul portrays himself in Galatians as the apostle to the Gentiles (1:15–16), and the Galatians to whom he writes are Gentile Christians (4:8–9). There is no indication that any of them are Jews by birth. This is consistent with the fact that there is no evidence for Jewish communities or synagogues in northern Galatia in the first century C.E. (Breytenbach 1996: 127–48; Mitchell 31–37). All things considered, it seems likely that the Galatians whom Paul addresses are ethnic Galatians living in the northern area of the Roman province of Galatia, not in the southern area as some of the evidence of Acts might suggest (see further comments on 1:2b and 3:1).

Date

Paul refers to the death or crucifixion of Christ in several places in Galatians (see esp. 3:1, 13). On the basis of the evidence provided by the Gospels and other sources, this event most probably took place in the year 30 C.E. Obviously the letter to the Galatians was written sometime after this event. But when exactly? In Gal 1:13–2:14, Paul gives a brief autobiographical narrative containing a number of temporal markers that provide the basis for constructing a relative chronology leading up to the writing of the letter:

1:13   For you have heard of my manner of life earlier [*pote*] in Judaism
1:15f. When [*hote*] God was pleased to apocalyptically reveal his Son in me
1:18   Then [*epeita*] after three years I went up to Jerusalem
1:21   Then [*epeita*] I went into the districts of Syria and Cilicia
2:1   Then [*epeita*] after fourteen years I again went up to Jerusalem
2:11   When [*hote*] Cephas came to Antioch

To transform this relative chronology into an absolute chronology, giving the calendar years in which the activities probably took place, it is necessary to bring information from outside Galatians to bear (see below, on 2 Cor 11:32–33 and Acts 18:12).[12]

1. *Paul as persecutor.* Paul calls the attention of the Galatians to his life before his conversion and call, when he was a persecutor: "For you have heard of my manner of life earlier in Judaism, that I persecuted the church of God beyond measure, and I sought to destroy it" (1:13; cf. Acts 8:1–3; 9:4–5, 21; 22:4, 7–8; 26:11, 14–15).[13] This activity probably took place in the early to mid-30s.

2. *Paul's conversion and call.*[14] Paul recounts his conversion (to Christ) and his simultaneous call (to apostleship) in or near Damascus: "[I received the gospel] through an apocalyptic revelation of Jesus Christ, . . . the One who set me apart from the womb of my mother and called me through his grace was pleased to apocalyptically reveal his Son in me, that I might preach him among the Gentiles . . ." (1:12, 15–16). After a sojourn in "Arabia," Paul "returned again to Damascus" (1:17), which implies that his conversion and call occurred in or near this city (cf. Acts 9:3–9; 22:6–11; 26:12–18). The event probably took place in 35 or 36 C.E., in light of the probable date of Paul's first visit to Jerusalem (see next point).

3. *Paul's first visit to Jerusalem "after three years."* "Then after three years I went up to Jerusalem to visit Cephas . . ." (1:18). Before his visit to Jerusalem, Paul was in Arabia and Damascus, though he does not indicate how much of

---

12. A chronology of Paul's travels, missionary labors, and letters must be based in the first instance on Paul's Letters. Acts, which was written several decades after Paul's death in the 60s, can be used only to corroborate or to elucidate the data from Paul's own letters. Where Paul and Acts disagree, Paul must be given priority since he was a participant in the events he describes, whereas the author of Acts almost certainly was not, the "we" passages in Acts (16:10–17; 20:5–15; 21:1–18; 27:1–28:16) notwithstanding (see Fitzmyer 1998: 98–103). It is not the purpose of this section to provide a full reconstruction of Paul's missionary career but to present the data necessary for establishing the probable date of Galatians.

13. Translations of passages from Galatians are fully explained and justified in the commentary below.

14. See comment on 1:12 for this terminology to describe what happened to Paul.

Date 7

the "three years" he spent in each location. The temporal notation "after [*meta*] three years" probably means "in the third calendar year after" a previous event (cf. Mark 8:31: "after three days" means "on the third of three days," Friday, Saturday, and Sunday). It covers a period of between one and three years by modern ways of measuring time.[15] The previous event from which Paul measures is probably his conversion and call (1:15–16), though it could also be his return to Damascus (1:17; cf. Acts 9:23). If Paul returned to Damascus in the same calendar year that his conversion and call took place (and we do not know whether that was or was not the case), the temporal phrase "after three years" could in fact cover both events. In 1:16–17, at any rate, Paul is at pains to point out that he did not "immediately" go up to Jerusalem after his conversion and call; 1:18 indicates that he waited "three years" to do so (Martyn 181–82).

Paul evidently went up to Jerusalem from Damascus (1:17). A passage from 2 Corinthians is relevant in this connection: "In Damascus," Paul writes here, "the governor under King Aretas guarded the city of Damascus in order to seize me, but I was let down in a basket through a window in the wall, and escaped from his hands" (2 Cor 11:32–33; cf. Acts 9:23–25 for a rather different version of this event). This turn of events was presumably the reason for Paul's decision to go up to Jerusalem to pay a visit to Cephas (see comment on 1:18). Extrabiblical sources indicate that Damascus was controlled by King Aretas IV of the Nabateans from 37–39 C.E. (Jewett 1979: 32–33; Murphy-O'Connor 1997: 4–7). Paul's departure from Damascus for Jerusalem must then have taken place within this time frame, thus around 38 C.E.

4. *Paul in Syria and Cilicia.* "Then I went into the districts of Syria and Cilicia" (1:21). After his two-week visit with Cephas in Jerusalem (1:18), Paul did not return to Damascus (it was evidently still too dangerous for him); he went instead "into the districts of Syria and Cilicia," adjoining territories in the northeast corner of the Mediterranean basin (see further comment on 1:21). The designation "Syria and Cilicia" was a fixed combination (cf. Acts 15:23, 41), which means that no conclusions can be drawn from it about the sequence of Paul's travels to the two regions. The leading city of Cilicia was Tarsus, which according to Acts was Paul's birthplace (Acts 9:11; 21:39; 22:3; 23:34). Antioch was the leading city of Syria, and Paul was closely associated with the church there (cf. Gal 2:11; Acts 11:25–15:35). According to Acts, Paul first went to Tarsus (traveling there by sea from Caesarea) and spent some time there (9:30), before being brought to Antioch by Barnabas (11:25–26). Some argue that Paul also went to Galatia (to the west and north of Cilicia) in this

---

15. By an ancient way of reckoning time, the interval between, e.g., December 1, 2009, and May 1, 2011, would be "three years," because three calendar years are involved—2009, 2010, and 2011—whereas by modern methods of calculation it would be only eighteen months.

period to found the churches to which he writes this letter (Dunn 80), or even further afield to Macedonia and Achaia (cf. Lüdemann 59–61; Knox 40–41). That is most unlikely. Paul uses the account of his activities in chapter 1 to show that he kept his distance, both literally and figuratively, from the church in Jerusalem during this period (see comments on 1:11–17 and 1:18–24). Missionary activity in Galatia and beyond, if it had occurred at this time, would have supported his case of "distance" from the Jerusalem church even more than the reference to Syria and Cilicia (Martyn 184).

This conclusion also excludes a particular interpretation of 2:5, where Paul writes that his refusal to submit to "the false brethren," who were seeking to compel the circumcision of Gentile believers in Antioch and/or Jerusalem, occurred "so that the truth of the gospel might abide [*diameinē*] for you [Galatians]."[16] The verb *diameinē*, "might abide" or "remain," could be taken to imply that the Galatian churches had already been founded at the time of the conference in Jerusalem described in 2:1–10 (Burton 86; Longenecker 53). Given 1:21, however, it is most unlikely that the churches of (north) Galatia had been founded before Paul's second visit to Jerusalem (see comment on 2:5).

5. *Paul's second visit to Jerusalem "after fourteen years."* "Then after [*dia*][17] fourteen years I again went up to Jerusalem with Barnabas, also taking Titus with me" (2:1). He and Barnabas went to the apostolic conference in Jerusalem (described in 2:6–10) as delegates of the church in Antioch to discuss the issue of the circumcision of Gentile believers (see comment on 2:1–3).[18] By modern ways of measuring time, the period in view is between twelve and fourteen years. Moreover, it is not absolutely clear from where Paul is measuring these "fourteen years": is it his conversion and call (1:15–16), or his first visit to Jerusalem (1:18)? Probably the first of these is in view (note "again," 2:1), which means that the period of time between his first and second visits to Jerusalem would be about ten or eleven years ("fourteen years" minus "three years," or 12–14 years minus 1–3 years by modern ways of reckoning). In short, Paul spent about a decade between his first and second

---

16. In the translations of Paul's Greek text, words in square brackets are explanatory comments or clarifying additions to the text.

17. Literally, "through," i.e., "after a lapse of" (cf. Mark 2:1; Acts 24:17).

18. Acts 15:1–29 is probably a variant account of the same event despite the fact that, according to Acts, Paul goes to Jerusalem for the third time in ch. 15 (it is perhaps even the fourth time, in view of the uncertain reading in 12:25). According to Acts, the second visit of Paul to Jerusalem occurs in 11:30, also with Barnabas. The meeting described in Gal 2:1–10, however, has more in common with the one described in Acts 15 than the one in Acts 11:30 (which was for famine relief). The central issue is the same, as are the key participants and the primary result: no circumcision for Gentile believers (cf. 15:1, 5, 28). See comment on 2:1–10.

visits to Jerusalem in Syria and Cilicia. The second visit to Jerusalem, and the apostolic conference that took place there, seem, therefore, to have taken place around 48 C.E.

6. *The incident at Antioch.* "When Cephas (Peter) came to Antioch" (2:11) after the conference in Jerusalem, Paul was evidently already there, as was Barnabas. While in Antioch, Cephas had for some time (Paul does not indicate how long) been eating with the Gentile believers in Christ before "certain people from James"[19] began to put pressure on him not to eat with uncircumcised Gentile believers. Cephas, one of the influential pillar apostles (2:9), succumbed to the pressure, "fearing those from the circumcision." He then made a practice of withdrawing and separating himself from the community's common meals: he no longer ate with Gentile believers (again, Paul does not indicate precisely how much time was involved). The remaining Jewish believers, "even Barnabas," followed his example. Paul was the only Jewish Christian in Antioch not to succumb to the pressure. Because of Cephas's position and influence, Paul reproached him before the entire Antioch church. This confrontation with Cephas apparently occurred a few months after the conclusion of the apostolic conference in Jerusalem (2:6–10). The confrontation could thus well have taken place in the same year as the apostolic conference.

7. *Paul founds the churches in Galatia.* Paul gives a brief account of this founding in 4:13–14: "You know that on account of an infirmity of the flesh I preached the gospel to you the earlier time, and your temptation in my flesh you did not despise or disdain, but you received me as an angel of God, as Christ Jesus." In view of the foregoing discussion, Paul must have founded the churches in Galatia after the incident with Peter in Antioch. Paul continued his missionary efforts but now without backing from the church in Antioch and without Barnabas as his missionary partner (see further the comment on 1:1). According to Acts, Paul was in Corinth "when Gallio was proconsul of Achaia" (Acts 18:12), which means in the summer of 51 C.E. (Murphy-O'Connor 1997: 21) or 52 C.E. (Fitzmyer 1987: 6–7). Taking into account Paul's other travels and missionary activities (in such places as Thessalonica, Philippi, Athens) before reaching Corinth, Paul probably founded the churches in (north) Galatia in 49 C.E. (cf. Acts 16:6).

8. *A second visit to the Galatian churches?* Did Paul visit the churches in Galatia a second time before writing the letter? That possibility is based on Paul's comment in 4:13 describing his founding visit to Galatia as "the earlier time," *to proteron*. Classically *to proteron* refers to the earlier of two occasions,

---

19. James, "the brother of the Lord" (1:19; cf. 2:9), is here in view. See comments on 1:19; 2:9, 12.

and that could then mean that Paul had been to Galatia a second time before writing the letter. The notion of two visits before the writing of the letter finds support in Acts, where Paul passes through the region of Galatia twice (Acts 16:6; 18:23).[20] In Hellenistic times, however, *proteron* had come to mean simply "earlier" (BDF #62) and *to proteron* "the first time" or "before" (BDAG 889; cf. John 6:62). Paul's use of this term, therefore, does not necessarily point to a second visit. Moreover, Paul probably does not have a second, intervening visit in view because it would have served his purpose in the context to mention such a visit if it had occurred (see comment on 4:13). That means that if Paul did indeed go through the Galatian region a second time, as Acts 18:23 reports, the letter was written before this second visit.

9. *New preachers come to the churches of Galatia*. Paul writes the Letter to the Galatians because it has come to his attention (he does not say how) that new preachers have come into the Galatian churches, and they are preaching "a different gospel" and insisting that Gentile believers must practice circumcision and observe the Mosaic law (1:6–9; 5:2–4; 6:12–13; Excursus 4). Christian Jews with similar views had sought to undermine Paul's proclamation of the gospel among the Gentiles in Antioch and Jerusalem ("the false brethren" mentioned in 2:4), and again in Antioch after the apostolic conference ("certain people from James" and "those from the circumcision" in 2:12–13). After the apostolic conference, James, Cephas, and "even Barnabas" had come to share, at least in part, their point of view (see comment on 2:11–14). The new preachers in Galatia probably saw themselves as authentic representatives of the Jerusalem church's view on Gentile converts' needing to practice the rite of circumcision, despite what Paul and the pillar apostles had agreed at the apostolic conference as recounted by Paul in 2:6–10. With this background, it seems likely that the new preachers came to Galatia not long after Paul had left: they dogged his steps in Galatia as "the false brethren," "the people from James," and "those from the circumcision" had done earlier (and as others would later, in Philippi and Corinth). The new preachers also rather quickly made an impact on the new converts in Galatia despite the fact that the latter "were running well" (5:7) when Paul departed. The arrival of the new preachers shortly after Paul's departure and their immediate impact upon the Galatians would explain why Paul reproaches the Galatians directly after the prescript (1:1–5) for "*so quickly* turning . . . to a different gospel" (1:6; see comment on this verse). The point of reference for this reproach is probably

---

20. Acts also supports two visits for those who adopt the "South Galatia" hypothesis (cf. Acts 13:1–14:20 with 14:21–24). If one then identifies Paul's second visit to Jerusalem in Gal 2:1–10 with the second visit to Jerusalem in Acts 11:30, one can date Galatians to before the Apostolic Council recounted in Acts 15, making Galatians the earliest known letter of Paul. But see notes 12 and 18.

Paul's founding of the churches and not the arrival of the new preachers, who are first explicitly mentioned in the next verse. Of course, it is not clear precisely how much time "so quickly" involves. It could be anywhere from a few weeks to a year or even two.[21]

10. *Paul writes the Letter to the Galatians.* Paul's reproach that the Galatians are even as he writes "so quickly turning" to a gospel different from the one he preached to them indicates not only that the new preachers arrived shortly after Paul founded the churches of Galatia, but also that the letter was in turn written shortly after these new preachers began to make an impact on the Galatians. Evidently one or more members of the Galatian churches rapidly informed Paul of the still-developing situation, either by letter or by emissary, or by both. As Paul writes the letter, he is convinced that he can yet turn the tide (cf. e.g., 3:1–2; 4:21; 5:2–4).[22] Where was Paul when he received this information and composed the letter in reply? We do not really know, but Corinth is a good candidate. According to Acts, Paul was in Corinth for a year and a half (18:11). Paul also wrote 1 Thessalonians from Corinth (cf. 1 Thess 3:1–2, 6 with Acts 18:1, 5), probably in 50 C.E. In that letter Paul does not use the language of justification, language that to a greater or a lesser extent reappears in all his remaining letters (except the very short Philemon); hence it is probable that Galatians was written somewhat later than 1 Thessalonians, as Paul's second surviving letter whose authenticity is undisputed. A likely date for the letter to the Galatians is thus 51 C.E.

Structure

A rule-of-thumb division of Galatians is the following:

Chapters 1–2: Autobiographical section
Chapters 3–4: Exegetical section
Chapters 5–6: Hortatory section

This division is a simplification and will only help us so far. For example, it hides the fact that the hortatory section probably begins not at 5:1 but at 5:13 (see below). Furthermore, Galatians is a letter with an epistolary opening and closing (see comment on 1:1–5 and Excursus 3). Taking this fact seriously leads initially to the following tripartite division:

---

21. It is difficult to think that if the lapse of time had been, say, four or five years, Paul could have convincingly written "so quickly" (see comment on 1:6).
22. This fact makes it unlikely that Paul, after a second visit to Galatia, wrote the letter while resident in Ephesus ca. 54 C.E., as thought by many who also adopt the North Galatia hypothesis, relying on Acts 18:23–24 as well as on a particular interpretation of Gal 4:13 to indicate two visits (see above).

1:1–5   Opening (Prescript: sender, recipients, grace greeting)
1:6–6:17 Body
6:18   Closing (Final grace benediction)

The place of 1:6–10 and 6:11–17 is, however, disputed, in part because these two passages do not conform to Paul's own use of epistolary conventions in his other letters. The first does not contain the characteristic elements of a thanksgiving prayer, and the second does not contain the greetings from or to third parties, nor a holy-kiss greeting, which are standard in Paul's other letters (White 97). In the above division, 1:6–10 is assumed to be the introduction to the letter body (it articulates the main theme or issue of the letter), whereas 6:11–17 functions as the conclusion to the letter body (it contains a personal authentication and appeal along with a recapitulation of the preceding discourse). One can also regard these verses as part of the opening and closing sections of the letter instead of as part of the epistolary body:

1:1–10   Opening
  1:1–5   Prescript (sender, recipients, grace greeting)
  1:6–10   Main theme/issue
1:11–6:10   Body
6:11–18   Closing
  6:11–17   Personal authentication, recapitulation, final appeal
  6:18   Final grace benediction

Thus 1:6–10 and 6:11–17 can be regarded as part of the body of the letter or as part of the opening and the closing respectively. The present commentary chooses the latter option (cf. Aune 1987: 184; White 97; see Excursus 3). Galatians 1:6–10 introduces the main theme of the letter, what Paul calls "the gospel of Christ" in 1:7. The problem here is that the Galatians are turning to "a different gospel," one preached by others (1:6–9). Instead of offering remarks of thanksgiving or blessing as Paul does in other undisputed letters in this part of the letter opening, he angrily rebukes the Galatians for turning to this different gospel and calls down an imprecation on the originators of it (see comment on 1:6–10). In turn, Gal 6:11–17 contains a recapitulation, first of Paul's rebuke of the new preachers active in Galatia and second of the gospel he preaches.

The letter body (1:11–6:10), in which Paul repreaches the gospel of Christ and refutes its counterfeit at the same time (see end of Excursus 5), can in turn be divided into four main sections: 1:11–2:21; 3:1–4:7; 4:8–5:12; 5:13–6:10. This division of the letter body needs some explanation.

While most everyone agrees that 3:1 begins a new section,[23] there is considerable diversity of opinion about where this section ends. To some extent

---

23. Bruce begins a new major section with 2:15 rather than with 3:1.

Structure

a decision depends upon where one thinks the so-called hortatory section of the letter begins. The first imperative in the second half of the letter actually occurs in 4:12, leading Longenecker to posit that the hortatory section begins there. Arguments can also be made based on 4:21, or even 4:30, verses where imperatives also occur (cf. Merk for a survey). The choice, however, usually comes down to 5:1 (e.g., Lightfoot; Burton; Bruce; Betz) and 5:13 (e.g., Matera; Martyn; Dunn; Becker; Williams; Vouga; Merk). For some, 5:1 cannot begin the hortatory section, because it forms, in their view, the conclusion to the previous passage (e.g., Schlier; Mussner; Fung; Longenecker; Martyn).[24] The present commentary also takes this view and regards 5:13 as the beginning of the hortatory section (see introduction to 5:13–6:10).

Where, then, does the section that begins at 3:1 end? With 5:12, or earlier? The opening verses of chapter 3 introduce a new theme into the letter, that of the Spirit: "This only I wish to learn from you: Did you receive the Spirit on the basis of works of the law or on the basis of what was heard of faith?" (3:2). The thrust of this rhetorical question is repeated in 3:5: Does God lavish the Spirit on the Galatians on the basis of works of the law or on the basis of what is heard of faith? The argument of the following verses is extremely difficult to follow at numerous points, but with 3:2, 5 as our guide, it seems that there is a unifying theme: the Spirit, or more fully, the reception of the promised Spirit (3:14; 4:6–7). The references to promise (3:14, 16, 18, 19, 22, 29), inheritance (3:18, 29; 4:1, 7), and divine sonship (3:26; 4:5–7) are different ways of articulating this overarching theme.

The Spirit as theme extends through 4:6–7. It again becomes a prominent theme in the hortatory section of the epistle (5:13–6:10). Though there are two references to the Spirit in the intervening verses (4:29; 5:5), the Spirit does not form the theme or focus of the material. The theme or focus of this material is the dangers confronting the Galatians if they adopt the message of the new preachers who are active in Galatia. The section functions as a series of *warnings* to the Galatians, but in terms of theological content, it signals various theological *dangers*. These various dangers are all variations on a single theme: the temptingly attractive, alternative gospel of the new preachers who have invaded the Galatian congregations. The point of the whole section is not to exhort the Galatians to live in a manner that accords with the gospel of Christ, which will be the purpose of the hortatory section (5:13–6:10), but to *prevent* them from being burdened by the putative gospel of the new preachers (5:1), a step Paul rather astonishingly equates with the Galatians' going back to their previous situation of religious servitude to "the elements [*ta stoicheia*]" (4:8–11). The present commentary thus regards 4:8–5:12, the material between 3:1–4:7 and 5:13–6:10, as a distinct major section within the letter body of Galatians.

---

24. Hays agrees but then takes 5:2 to be the start of the hortatory section.

With the opening and the closing, therefore, Galatians has six main sections, each with two or more subsections or definable paragraphs. Detailed justification for this division of the letter may be found in the introductions to each main section and in the comments on individual passages.

Section I: Letter Opening (1:1–10)
    1:1–5   Prescript
    1:6–10   Rebuke and Imprecation

Section II: The Origin and the Truth of the Gospel (1:11–2:21)
    1:11–17   The Origin of the Gospel 1: Paul's Conversion and Call
    1:18–24   The Origin of the Gospel 2: Paul's Visit with Cephas in Jerusalem
    2:1–10   The Truth of the Gospel 1: The Apostolic Conference in Jerusalem
    2:11–14   The Truth of the Gospel 2: Conflict with Cephas in Antioch
    2:15–21   The Truth of the Gospel for the Galatian Situation

Section III: The Spirit and the True Heirs of the Promise Made to Abraham (3:1–4:7)
    3:1–5   The Reception of the Spirit in Galatia
    3:6–14   The Blessing of Abraham and the Curse of the Law
    3:15–22   The Promise to Abraham and the Law of Moses
    3:23–29   The True Offspring of Abraham
    4:1–7   The True Heirs of the Promise

Section IV: The Grave Dangers Confronting the Galatians (4:8–5:12)
    4:8–11   The Danger of Returning to Their Previous Religious Servitude
    4:12–20   The Danger of Abandoning Paul and His Gospel
    4:21–5:1   The Danger of Losing Their New Identity through Faulty Exegesis
    5:2–6   The Danger of Becoming Separated from Christ and Grace
    5:7–12   The Source of the Danger: The Leaven of the New Preachers

Section V: Life at the Juncture of the Ages (5:13–6:10)
    5:13–24   Love and the Spirit's Strife against the Flesh
    5:25–6:10 Living by the Spirit and Fulfilling the Law of Christ

Section VI: Epistolary Closing (6:11–18)
    6:11–17   Recapitulation
    6:18   Final Benediction

The structure of the letter body (1:11–6:10) has been determined largely by attending to the theological themes addressed, as one can see from the titles given to the various sections and subsections. Each of the sections and

Overview 15

subsections also has a discernible rhetorical function, but the present commentary regards it as important to distinguish the thematic content from the rhetorical function of the material. This commentary focuses on Paul's message to the Galatians rather than on his rhetoric, even if the two cannot be separated (see further Excursus 5).

Overview

Commentary on each major section of the letter begins with an introduction giving an overview of the content, the literary structure, and its place in the letter as a whole. Each section is subdivided into two or more subsections, each consisting of a self-contained paragraph. Comment on each subsection (paragraph) begins with its place in Paul's developing argument, an overview of the important exegetical issues that the passage raises, and a division of the material into smaller "sense units." Each of the latter normally consists of several verses upon which detailed commentary is given. A concise overview of the letter as a whole is given here.

In Section I (The Letter Opening), Paul gives an indication of what the major accents or themes of his letter will be. In the first verse, he already makes clear what he will develop later in chapter 1: his apostleship has a divine origin, as does the gospel he preaches among the Gentiles (cf. 1:11–12, 15–16; 2:2). The salutation in 1:3 is an encapsulation of the gospel as Paul understands it: "Grace to you and peace from God the Father and our Lord Jesus Christ." This salutation is found in all his genuine letters (see comment on 1:3). Already in 1:4, Paul gives a contextually relevant application and summary of this gospel when he defines "the Lord Jesus Christ" in 1:4 as "the one who gave himself for our sins, that he might rescue us from the present evil age, according to the will of God and our Father."

Aside from indicating the sender and the recipients and greeting the latter, the prescript thus also functions to give the Galatians an immediate indication of Paul's own theological position, his own interpretation of the gospel, which revolves around God's grace and has an apocalyptic character (see comment on 1:4 and Excursus 2). In the next part of the Letter Opening (1:6–10), Paul states the primary theme of the letter, "the gospel of Christ" (1:7), and indicates the letter's occasion (new preachers have come to Galatia proclaiming "a different gospel"). The section contains a rebuke of the Galatians (1:6–7) and an imprecation upon the new preachers (1:8–9). The second part of the Letter Opening functions to indicate to the Galatians in no uncertain terms that the developments in Galatia are an extremely serious matter, demanding their immediate and utmost attention.

Section II (the first of the letter body), extending from 1:11 to 2:21, begins with a thesis statement: "For I make known to you, brethren, concerning the gospel that was preached by me, that it is not of human origin. For I neither received it from a human being nor was I taught [it], but [I received it] through an apocalyptic revelation of Jesus Christ" (1:11–12). This thesis statement provides a guideline for interpreting the first section of the letter body in particular. It concerns "the gospel," a term that occurs only in chapters 1 and 2 (1:6, 7, 11; 2:2, 5, 7, 14). In particular, two aspects of that gospel are emphasized: its origin in God and its divine truth. Both aspects are contained in the thesis statement of 1:11–12. Paul emphasizes the first aspect in 1:11–24 and the second in 2:1–21. A second contextualized summary of the gospel in the final paragraph (2:15–16) has a polemical thrust and lays the groundwork for Section III and its dense theological argument: "We Jews by birth and not sinners from the Gentiles, [16]because we know that someone is not justified on the basis of works of the law but through the faith of Jesus Christ, we too came to believe in Jesus Christ, so that we might be justified on the basis of the faith of Christ and not on the basis of works of the law, because on the basis of works of the law shall all flesh not be justified."[25]

In emphasizing the divine origin and truth of the gospel that Paul preached and still preaches to the Galatians, Section II also functions rhetorically to establish Paul's credibility as an authentic and reliable preacher of the gospel of Christ.

Section III argues that the gift or the promise of the Spirit depends not on observance of the law but upon "faith," meaning the faith of Christ, which is another way of speaking about his faithful, redemptive death (see Excursuses 9 and 11). Those who receive the Spirit from faith can consider themselves the legitimate offspring of Abraham, for they are heirs of the promise made by God to Abraham apart from any observance of the law. In fact, they have been liberated from the law and are not merely "sons [heirs] of Abraham" but also, and more important, "sons [heirs] of God." The Spirit of the faithful Christ, not the law, provides the basis for justification, which Paul understands to involve God's rectifying activity in the world. Section III is the theological heart of the epistle. In its climactic paragraph (4:1–7), Paul gives a third contextualized summary of the gospel (4:4–5): "When the fullness of time came, God sent forth his Son, having been born of a woman, having existed under the law so that he might redeem those under the law, so that we might receive adoption as sons."

Paul anticipates this summary with the concise declaration in 3:25: "Now that this faith [Christ] has come, we are no longer under a custodian [the law]" (cf. 3:23–24). Section III in particular can be read as a demonstration of this claim for the Galatian situation. Section III has a double rhetorical function,

---

25. The argument for regarding 2:15–16 as one long sentence may be found in the commentary below. Paul repeats the subject ("we," *hēmeis*) in v. 16 for emphasis.

to establish the plausibility of the gospel that Paul preaches, and to refute the "different gospel" being promoted by new preachers who have come into the Galatian churches (see on 1:6–9 and Excursus 4). One of Paul's key concerns in this section is to place some distance between God and the law in order in this way to undermine its status among his opponents as the divinely given solution for the human condition. The law is not the solution but part of the problem!

Section IV, which has been prompted and necessitated by the dire situation of the Galatian churches (cf. 1:6–9; 5:2–4; 6:12–13), articulates the (theological) dangers confronting the Galatians and serves as a transition from the doctrinal heart of the letter (the indicative) to the paraenesis (the imperative). If Section III is the theological heart of the letter, Section IV is its rhetorical heart. By means of the letter, Paul wants to keep the Galatians from following the demands of the new preachers who have come into the Galatian context and are wanting the Galatians to adopt the observance of the law, beginning with the rite of circumcision (see on 1:6–9 and Excursus 4). Nowhere does this rhetorical agenda become more visible than in Section IV. For this reason, 5:1 contains "the climactic exhortation of the letter" (Hays 187): "For freedom Christ has set us free! Stand fast, therefore, and do not be burdened again with a yoke of slavery!" The first half of this verse serves as a reminder of the second contextualized summary of the gospel in 4:4–5 (cf. 3:25). The immediate rhetorical point, however, is to be found in the negative exhortation in the second half of the verse: The Galatians are not to allow themselves to be burdened once again with the yoke of slavery that is the law (see comment on 5:1). In Section IV, Paul alerts the Galatians in no uncertain terms to the theological dangers of the message of the new preachers in their midst. Before attacking the source of the danger (the message of the new preachers) directly in the closing paragraph (5:7–12), Paul provides a fourth contextualized summary of the gospel in 5:5–6. Looking both backward and forward, this passage summarizes the message of the whole letter: "For we, through the Spirit from faith, are waiting for the hope of justification, for in Christ Jesus neither circumcision avails anything nor uncircumcision, but faith becoming effective through love."

Section V contains exhortation, or paraenesis, and also describes the believers' new life in the realm of the Spirit. Love is arguably the unifying theme (5:13–14, 22). Its central verse is probably 5:25: "If we live by the Spirit, let us also follow the Spirit." The section functions rhetorically to allay concerns that life without the law leads to moral chaos. A fifth contextualized summary of the gospel, also covering this section, occurs in the letter closing (6:15): "For neither circumcision is anything nor uncircumcision, but a new creation."

This summary corresponds to the summary given in the prescript (1:4 above): the "new creation" is the apocalyptic alternative for "the present evil age." The closing of Galatians has at least three functions: to authenticate the letter as from Paul (6:11), to rebuke the new preachers one last time (6:12–13), and to summarize the central message of the letter (6:14–15). Paul follows with a blessing of peace and mercy upon those who "follow this standard" (6:16) and a final appeal (6:17), before concluding with a grace benediction (6:18).

Paul's five linguistic summaries of the gospel are contextual, shaped by and for a particular context: the circumstances in Galatia. The fact that there are (at least) five different summaries suggests that no one linguistic formulation of the gospel is exhaustive. The five summaries are, then, mutually interpretive, representing different attempts by Paul to formulate the central message of the gospel for the Galatian situation at different points in his argument. The commentary seeks to shed some light on what Paul intends precisely to say with these contextualized summaries of the gospel, and on how the Galatians will probably hear what Paul says in and through them.

COMMENTARY

Section I: Galatians 1:1–10
The Letter Opening

Paul begins his letter to the Galatians with a prescript (1:1–5), followed by a short paragraph devoted to the letter's occasion and announcing its main theme, which is "the gospel of Christ" (1:6–10). Together these two paragraphs form the letter opening, the section that precedes the "body" of the typical Pauline letter (see Excursus 3, below). In the prescript Paul introduces two matters that provide nonnegotiable starting points for the argument that will follow in the remainder of the letter: (1) his calling to be an apostle comes directly from Christ and God, not from human beings; and (2) the gospel of Christ involves the rescue of human beings by God from "the present evil age" and thus from the malevolent powers that hold sway there (1:4).

1:1–5 Prescript

Ancient letters written in Greek commonly had a prescript consisting of three elements:

(a) the name of the author
(b) the name of the recipient
(c) a greeting from the author to the recipient

A simple example from the third century B.C.E. begins as follows:

(a) Dromon (b) to Zenon (c) greetings.[26]

Galatians, like all Paul's letters, follows this ancient epistolary convention, though with modifications:

---

26. Hunt and Edgar #91. An example from 41 C.E. (#107) reads: "Sarapion to our Heraclides greeting." For NT examples conforming to this pattern, see Jas 1:1; Acts 15:23; 23:26.

(a) "Paul . . . and all the brethren with me" (1:1–2a)
(b) "to the churches of Galatia" (1:2b)
(c) "Grace to you and peace . . ." (1:3a)

In this case, "Paul . . . and all the brethren with me" are the senders of the letter, though Paul is in fact its sole author ("with me"). As the naming of cosenders indicates, Paul expands or modifies the conventional three-part epistolary prescript in his own way. Some of the expansions and modifications found here recur in the prescripts to his other letters and are thus indicators of Paul's distinctive epistolary writing style (White 96–100). Others are unique to Galatians and provide important clues to this particular letter's occasion and to Paul's aims in the letter. The full text of the prescript reads as follows:

1:1 Paul, an apostle not from human beings nor through a human being, but through Jesus Christ and God the Father, the One who raised him from the dead, 2a and all the brethren with me,
2b to the churches of Galatia:
3 Grace to you and peace from God our Father and the Lord Jesus Christ,ᵃ 4 the one who gave himself forᵇ our sins, that he might rescue us from the present evil age, according to the will of God and our Father, 5 to whom be glory forever and ever. Amen.

a. There is very strong manuscript support (including $\mathfrak{P}^{46}$, B, D, H) for the reading "from God *the* Father and *our* Lord Jesus Christ" (assumed by the NRSV to be correct). Here NA²⁷ adopts the other reading, which also has good support (including ℵ, A, 33, 81), because it represents Paul's "stereotyped formula" (Metzger 520). On internal grounds, then, this reading (see above) is to be preferred.

b. There is good manuscript evidence for both *hyper* (on behalf of, for the sake of), adopted by NA²⁷, and *peri* (concerning). For the same variation, see 1 Thess 5:10. There is little difference in meaning or implication.

[1–2a] The "Paul" who is writing this letter is also the author of Romans, 1 and 2 Corinthians, Philippians, 1 Thessalonians, and Philemon. Whether this same Paul was also the author of Ephesians, Colossians, 2 Thessalonians, and the Pastoral Epistles (1 and 2 Timothy, Titus) is disputed. We really know about Paul only through the letters he actually wrote, though the disputed letters may preserve further valuable information even if they are pseudonymous. Some further information is found in the letter known as *1 Clement* (written from the church in Rome to the church in Corinth ca. 96 C.E.) and in the canonical Acts of the Apostles (probably written in the last decade of the first cent. C.E.). Particularly important is Acts, since it gives an account of Paul's missionary career from his conversion in the thirties of the first century to his journey to

The Letter Opening

Rome in the early sixties. The difficulty with Acts, however, is that its depiction of Paul is often at odds with what can be gleaned from Paul's own (undisputed) letters, written several decades earlier. A case in point is that Paul in Acts never writes any letters at all! The Paul of Galatians clearly writes letters, and he tells us much about himself, particularly in the first two chapters.

Paul does not write simply as a private person. He writes as an "apostle." The self-designation also occurs in the prescripts of Romans and 1 and 2 Corinthians (cf. Ephesians, Colossians, and the Pastoral Epistles).

Excursus 1: The Title "Apostle"

The English word, like the Latin *apostolus*, is a near transliteration of the Greek word *apostolos*. The latter, a passive verbal adjective used as a noun and closely related to the verb *apostellō* (to send), in the NT means "someone who has been sent (or commissioned)" by a third party (cf. John 13:16). An apostle is thus a delegate or an envoy who represents the one who has authorized or commissioned him or her. Paul assumes that this meaning is evident to his Gentile readers in Galatia even though the word rarely occurs with this meaning prior to and outside of the Christian literature that was produced in the first and second centuries C.E. (BDAG 122). Outside of Biblical Greek, it was used to mean various things in connection with naval expeditions and shipping (e.g., a fleet, a bill of lading, a certificate of clearance at a port), meanings of little discernible relevance here. Furthermore, the word is absent from the many works of the Alexandrian Jewish philosopher Philo, a contemporary of Paul, and there is only a single, sure instance of the term in the writings of the Jewish historian, Josephus (*Ant.* 17.300), writing in the later decades of the first century C.E. The word was thus not common among Greek-speaking Jews, and the explanation for the peculiar Christian usage of the term must be sought elsewhere. A plausible hypothesis is that the Greek term as used by the early Christians, including Paul, originates in a Hebrew and/or Aramaic equivalent. In the single instance of the term *apostolos* in the Septuagint, a variant reading of 3 Kingdoms (= 1 Kings) 14:6, it translates the Hebrew term *šālûaḥ*. Later rabbinic literature refers to the *šālûaḥ* (or *šālîaḥ*) as a commissioned, authorized envoy, which is also what an *apostolos* is (see BDAG 122; Rengstorf 1964; H. D. Betz 1992). The early Christians in Jerusalem and Palestine would have used the Aramaic counterpart (*šālîaḥā'*) for an apostle; this Aramaic term was then translated into Greek as *apostolos*, which became a technical term in Christian circles for a commissioned envoy or missionary (see comments on 1:17, 19 below).

The meaning of the title was not univocal among the early Christians, as we can see when Paul emphatically describes himself as "an apostle *not* from human beings nor through a human being, but through Jesus Christ and God the Father, the One who raised him from the dead." Here Paul claims that his apostolic commission did not result from human initiative: it did not originate "from" (*apo*) human beings (a group). Nor did any human being commission him: his apostleship was not "through" (*dia*) a human being (an individual).

Rather, he was sent forth by (*dia*) Jesus Christ and God the Father, here identified as the One who raised Jesus Christ from the dead. Jesus Christ and God the Father are portrayed as one unified and divine (= nonhuman) agency, with the preposition *dia* covering both as a unity. The preposition also does double duty, expressing both origin and agency (cf. Burton 4–5; cf. Gal 1:12, 15–16).[27]

Paul's words can be taken to mean that there were two types of apostles in his day, apostles commissioned by human beings on the one hand, and apostles commissioned by Jesus Christ and God on the other. There is good support for this interpretation of Paul's words. In 2 Cor 8:23, he himself refers to certain "apostles of the churches" (NRSV: "messengers of the churches"), evidently members of various Pauline churches charged with carrying funds collected for the church in Jerusalem (cf. Rom 15:25–27). In Phil 2:25, Paul calls Epaphroditus the "apostle" (NRSV: "messenger") of the church in Philippi. These "apostles of churches" have been commissioned by human beings (churches) with (it seems) a specific and thus temporary task in view (much like the rabbinic *šālûaḥ*). The "apostles of churches" are distinguished from "apostles of Jesus Christ" (1 Cor 1:1; 2 Cor 1:1; cf. Eph 1:1; Col 1:1; 1 Tim 1:1; 2 Tim 1:1; 1 Pet 1:1; 2 Pet 1:1). The latter are apostles who "have seen the [risen] Lord" (1 Cor 9:1; cf. 1 Cor 15:7–9) and thus have been commissioned *directly by him* for a specific task. In 1 Cor 15:8, Paul declares that he is the "last" of such apostles.

In this connection we observe that Acts maintains a similar distinction: there are "apostles" (1:26; cf. 2:37; 5:29) who are specially chosen "witnesses to his [Jesus'] resurrection" (1:22). According to Acts, these apostles "ate and drank with him after he rose from the dead" (10:41; cf. Luke 24:36–49). But there are also "apostles" who are sent out by churches as missionaries in the period after Jesus' ascension (described in Acts 1:9–11). This meaning of the term occurs only in 14:4, 14 where it is applied to *Paul* and Barnabas (cf. Gal 2:1, 9, 13). In Acts, then, Paul is called an apostle (along with Barnabas) only in the sense of having been commissioned for missionary activity (in connection with the so-called first missionary journey) by the church at Antioch (see 13:1–3), to which he appropriately returns and makes a report (14:26–28). In Acts, the apostles who are witnesses to the risen Jesus are limited to a circle of twelve (Judas being replaced in 1:15–26), and these twelve men not only "ate and drank with him after he rose from the dead" (Acts 10:41), but were also "witnesses to all that he did both in the country of the Jews and in Jerusalem" (10:39 RSV), "beginning from the baptism of John until the day when he was taken up from us" (1:22). These twelve apostles (cf. 1:26) were thus also companions of the pre-Easter Jesus (Luke 6:13; 9:10; 17:5). For the author of Acts, Paul cannot be an apostle in this double sense; he had not been a follower of Jesus before Easter, nor had

---

27. As Burton (6) writes: "It cannot be supposed that the apostle thinks of a more ultimate source than God of which God is the agent." See BDF #223.2.

The Letter Opening 23

he eaten and drunk with the risen Jesus before his ascension. (In Acts, it is the *ascended* Jesus who waylays Paul on the road to Damascus.) Though Paul is the leading figure of Acts and Christ's chosen "instrument" (Acts 9:15) for bringing the gospel to the Gentiles (cf. Acts 22:10, 14–15; 26:17–19), he could not be a member of the special circle of the twelve apostles (a notion found also in Rev 21:14). The Paul of Acts 14:4, 14 is an "apostle" only in a lesser sense, the sense that Paul himself specifically rejects in Gal 1:1 as a sufficient indication of his apostolic identity and call!

It is probable that Paul (like Barnabas) had in fact once been an apostle of the church in Antioch (cf. Gal 2:11 and see comment on 2:11–14). At some level Paul may see no contradiction between being an apostle of a church and being an apostle of the risen/ascended Christ.[28] Even in Acts, when Paul and Barnabas are set aside for their apostolic mission by the church at Antioch, "the Holy Spirit" plays the key role in the commissioning event (13:1–3). It is nevertheless clear that Paul in Gal 1:1 understands himself to be above all an apostle of the risen and ascended Christ. At the time he writes this letter, he is surely no longer an apostle of the church in Antioch, as he once was (see comment on 2:11–14). The point here is that no church commission *or the absence thereof* can alter his conviction that he has always been and will always remain an apostle of Christ, and thus of the God who raised him from the dead.

In view of the preceding discussion, it is unlikely that Paul's emphatic denial of human origin and agency is no more than a rhetorical device (Matera 41; Vos 89) whereby he can highlight the divine origin and agency of his apostolic commission and thus underline his special authority. Paul's sharply antithetical formulation ("not . . . nor . . . but") is to be taken as apologetic and polemical. But in what sense? Again, given the preceding discussion, it is unlikely that Paul is defending himself against the charge that he is merely a church apostle (cf. Acts 14:4, 14 above) and not an apostle of Christ as the apostles in Jerusalem are (cf. 1:17–19), though his words could at first glance easily be taken in this way. As he writes this letter, however, Paul is no longer an apostle of the church in Antioch, or of any other church. More likely, as indicated above, the complaint being lodged against Paul is that since he is no longer an apostle of the church at Antioch, which has a close working relationship with the mother church in Jerusalem (cf. Acts 11:19–15:35; Gal 2:12), he has no discernible mandate for his apostolic mission nor then for the gospel he preaches, a gospel that problematically deviates from that of the Jerusalem apostles (see comments on 1:6–10; 1:11–24; 2:8–9). In the opening verse of the letter, Paul seeks to undermine those who have made this charge, the new preachers who have come

---

28. The sharp distinction between the resurrection of Jesus and his ascension is Lukan; Paul does not appear to know it (cf. 1 Cor 15:1–11; Phil 2:9–11).

to Galatia with an alternate gospel (on the identity of these people, see comment on 1:6–7 and Excursus 4 below). He concedes that he has no apostolic mandate from a church, meaning the one in Antioch, or through the agency of some leading figure there or in Jerusalem ("not from human beings nor through a human being"), and claims that his apostolic mandate comes directly from Christ and the God who raised him from the dead (cf. 1:12, 15–16). He thus needs no other mandate.

The sharp contrast Paul here posits between human beings and God is theologically significant (Martyn 94–95, 137–44) and recurs elsewhere in the letter (see comment on 1:11–17). Moreover, Paul's placement of Jesus Christ on the divine side of that contrast is a remarkable move. This placement is perhaps not surprising to Christian readers today, familiar with the Nicene and Chalcedonian Creeds, or to those who read Galatians with the lens provided by the Gospel of John. Already in this letter, one of the earliest documents of Christianity, the identification of Jesus Christ as in some sense divine (the precise sense is a matter of endless debate) has been made.[29] The identification is made without elaboration or explicit justification. It is assumed as a matter of course: To be commissioned by Jesus Christ is to be commissioned not by a human being but by God.

Here Paul uses the term "Christ" as a second name for Jesus. The word in Greek simply means "anointed" and is a literal translation of the Hebrew or Aramaic counterpart ("messiah"; cf. John 1:41; 4:25). "Jesus Christ" means the same as "Jesus Anointed," or "Jesus, the Anointed One." On the basis of his earlier preaching, Paul's Galatian audience will presumably have a basic sense of its Jewish and OT origins, especially as applied to the king of Israel, and thus of its meaning: God's "anointed" bringer of salvation (cf. 1 Sam 2:10, 35; 12:3, 5; Ps 18:50; Lam 4:20; Hab 3:13; *Pss. Sol.* 17.32; see BDAG 1091; Burton 395–99). In 1:4, as elsewhere in this letter, Paul defines who this "Jesus Christ" is and the nature of the salvation he brings (see comment there).

Here God is defined specifically in relation to Jesus Christ rather than the reverse: "God the Father,[30] [namely,] the One who raised him from the dead." As Luther aptly observes: "He does not say: 'Through God, who has made heaven and earth, who is the Lord of angels, who sent Moses to Pharaoh, who brought Israel up out of Egypt'" (Luther 1535: 22). God, for Paul, is "the Father" who raised Christ from the dead. "God's identity is here given by his having raised Jesus from the dead, . . . making that act, indeed, the primal mark of his identity" (Martyn 85). Put otherwise, God's fatherhood of Jesus becomes

---

29. This does not mean that Paul denies, or would deny, that Jesus was a human being, only "that this term did not state the whole, or even the most important truth about him" (Burton 4).

30. The Greek has *patēr*, "Father," without the article. This is simply a matter of style. *Theos*, "God," also has no article for the same reason. See BDF #254.1, #257.3.

concretely visible for Paul in his act of raising Jesus from the dead.[31] The designation of God as "Father" anticipates the designation of Jesus as "his Son" in 1:16, and as "the Son of God" in 2:20 (cf. 4:4, 6). The father-son language for God and Jesus is not a Pauline invention; it is rooted in such classic "messianic" texts as 2 Sam 7:12–17; Ps 2:7–9 (cf. Acts 13:33); and Ps 89:26–29, as well as in Jesus' habit of addressing God as "Abba" (cf. Mark 14:36; Gal 4:6; Rom 8:15). The link between God as Father and God as the One who raised Jesus from the dead is perhaps an echo of the view (predating Paul) that Jesus either became or was revealed to be God's Son at his resurrection from the dead (cf. Rom 1:4; Acts 13:33).

The designation of God as the One who raised Jesus from the dead contains the only explicit reference to the resurrection of Jesus in Galatians, perhaps surprising in view of its greater prominence elsewhere in Paul's Epistles. This resurrection is the hidden reason why Paul can place Christ without explicit justification on the divine side of the human/divine contrast. The resurrection of Christ signifies for Paul (and other early Christians) not only that Jesus' body has not been left in the grave to rot (1 Cor 15:4–5) but also, and above all else, that God has "made him both Lord and Christ, this Jesus whom you crucified" (to use the language of Acts 2:36). Paul, like other early Christians, resorts to the metaphorical language of Ps 110:1 ("The LORD says to my lord, 'Sit at my right hand, until I make your enemies your footstool'") to give voice to this conviction (cf. 1 Cor 15:25; Rom 8:34; Col 3:1; Eph 1:20; Heb 1:3, 13; 8:1; 10:12–13; 12:2; 1 Pet 3:22; Matt 22:44; 26:64; Mark 12:36; 14:62; 16:19; Luke 20:42–43; 22:69; Acts 2:33–35; Rev 3:22). Implicit also in the reference to Christ's resurrection is an allusion to Paul's call to his specific apostolic task through the risen Christ (see comment on 1:12, 15–16).

Paul designates as cosenders of the letter "all the brethren with me" (1:2a). The "brethren" (*adelphoi*) here are other Christians, women as well as men; the Greek term, which is grammatically masculine, is semantically inclusive (see comment on 1:11). Paul does not, however, indicate who precisely these "brethren" are. He may be referring to a larger group of fellow Christians, perhaps the members of a local church, or to special coworkers, such as Timothy and Silvanus, who accompanied him on his travels (cf. 1 Thess 1:1; 1 Cor 1:1; 2 Cor 1:1; Phil 1:1; 4:3). Probably a combination of the two is in view. The intended rhetorical impact of these words is in any case evident. By referring to "all the brethren" with him as he writes his letter to the Galatians, Paul indicates for effect that he is not alone, that he is no isolated figure, that other Christian "brethren" lend their support to this epistolary communication and are silent witnesses to it.

---

31. Only in 1:3–4 does God's fatherhood of believers also come clearly into view. See comment there.

[2b] Paul writes this letter to "the churches of Galatia." Paul addresses his other letters to a single church, or a single group of Christians, located in a particular city (Thessalonica, Corinth, Rome, Philippi; also Philemon, though no city is named). In this case, he sends a letter to two or more "churches" (communities of Christians)[32] located in the Roman province of Galatia. That this is no mistake is shown by the reference to "the churches of Galatia" in 1 Cor 16:1. Where in the Roman province of Galatia are these churches located? As argued in the Introduction, the churches addressed are probably located in (or near) such northern cities as Ancyra (present-day Ankara), Pessinus, and Tavium (the North Galatia hypothesis) rather than in such southern cities as Pisidian Antioch, Lystra, Iconium, and Derbe (the South Galatia hypothesis). That conclusion is consistent with the fact that Paul will subsequently address his readers as "Galatians" in 3:1, which is most probably an ethnic designation for the inhabitants of northern Galatia (the region from which the much-larger Roman province took its name), and with the exclusively Gentile origin of the believers in Galatia (4:8–11).

Paul does not indicate how many churches are involved. "At least two" is all that can be concluded with confidence. These two or more churches are located in different cities; if they were in the same city, Paul would surely name it, as his letters to believers in Thessalonica, Corinth, Philippi, and Romans show. Galatians 4:13–14 indicates that the churches of Galatia are close geographically since this passage suggests that "Paul's illness had an impact on a relatively small number of people at the same time" (Murphy-O'Connor 1998: 205). This fact makes it unlikely that one church is located in Ancyra and another in Pessinus, lying some 160 kilometers (100 miles) to the southwest, and perhaps still another in Tavium, also 160 kilometers away but to the east (so, e.g., Martyn 15–17).[33] Perhaps we are to think of a church in one of these cities, such as Pessinus (Murphy-O'Connor 1997: 162; Esler 1998: 34; see comment on 4:3; 5:12), with other churches in nearby, dependent villages. We do not really know, though of course the Galatians do.

Paul does not here write "to the Galatians," as he could have done (3:1). He writes "to *the churches* of Galatia." This letter is no private communication, but a circular letter to churches from their founding apostle (cf. 4:13). Paul clearly takes the term to mean "communities of *believers in Christ*," and since he does not pause to explain or to justify his usage, he assumes that his intended Gentile readers in Galatia will also so understand the term. Just as the term *apostolos*, then, so also the word *ekklēsia* has come to have a particular, technical

---

32. Paul does not actually use the term "Christian" in Galatians (or his other letters), but see Acts 11:26, which indicates that the term originated in Antioch in the time of Paul. I use the term as a convenient synonym for "believer in Jesus Christ" (cf. 2:16; 3:22) or "someone who belongs to Christ" (cf. 3:29a; 5:24a).

33. The distances are given by Murphy-O'Connor 1998: 205; comparable distances are involved with respect to the cities in southern Galatia.

The Letter Opening

meaning distinctive to Christians, a meaning known even to the new Christians in Galatia. In the secular Greek spoken by the Galatians, the term simply means an "assembly," a "gathering," or a "meeting" (as in Acts 19:32, 39, 40–41), frequently of a political nature, and by extension "the people who are present at such an assembly, gathering, or meeting" (as in Acts 7:38; cf. BDAG; LSJ). These nuances of the term have hardly been lost in the instance of the term in Gal 1:2b, though here it also designates "the people who regularly gather or meet in a particular place" (as in Acts 15:41; Rev 1:4; and 1 Cor 16:1, where Paul also refers to "the churches of Galatia").[34] The churches of Galatia can be addressed even when they are not actually in assembly, though the letter will undoubtedly be read and thus heard in the meetings (for worship and fellowship) of the Galatian Christians (see on 1:3–5 below). The fact that Paul addresses them as "the churches" of Galatia is important in another respect: he addresses them in terms of their *identity* as congregations of Christ. Despite the terseness of the address (when compared with the fulsome way Paul addresses churches elsewhere, e.g., in Corinth or Rome), Paul reminds the Galatians from the start of their identity as communities of Christ. He has not yet given up on them.

[3–5] Characteristic of these last three verses of the prescript is their liturgical flavor, especially v. 5, which consists of a doxology with a concluding "Amen!" These verses are a clear indication that Paul expects the letter to be read aloud during a service of worship (Martyn 86, 91, 106; White 98), presumably once in each of the Galatian churches.

Instead of the normal greeting or salutation, Paul in v. 3 calls down God's blessing on the Galatian congregations, using a standard formula found in all his undisputed epistles: "Grace to you and peace from God our Father and the Lord Jesus Christ" (Rom 1:7; 1 Cor 1:3; 2 Cor 1:2; Phil 1:2; Phlm 3; 1 Thess 1:1).[35] For the customary *chairein*, "greetings" (cf. Jas 1:1; Acts 15:23; 23:26),[36] Paul has substituted the similar-sounding *charis*, "grace," and he has supplemented the latter with "peace" (*eirēnē*), the salutation customarily found in Jewish letters (*šālōm* in Hebrew, *shelam* in Aramaic).[37] That Paul's salutation is no

---

34. The Greek term does not yet mean a church building, as in later usage, or as the English term "church." See further the comments on "the church of God" in 1:13, and on "the churches of Judea that are in Christ" in 1:22.

35. In 1 Thess 1:1, however, Paul seems to have omitted "from God our Father and the Lord Jesus Christ."

36. Literally, "(I wish you) to rejoice," or more prosaically, "(I want you) to be happy." It is functionally equivalent to "Have a good day" or "All the best."

37. Cf. Ezra 4:17; 5:7; 2 Macc 1:1; *2 Bar.* 78.2–3. The Aramaic form occurs in Dan 4:1, translated by Theodotion (but not LXX) with *eirēnē*. Hellenistic letters frequently contained a wish for good health after the "greetings." For example: "Apollonios to Sarapion: . . . many greetings and continued good health" (cited by White 89). The wish for "peace" in Paul's salutation could also be construed as a substitute for this health wish.

ordinary, everyday greeting is demonstrated by the fact that grace and peace come "from God our Father and the Lord Jesus Christ." "Grace and peace" are thus the gospel that Paul preaches in a nutshell. In themselves the terms are rather vague. The remainder of the letter, including in the first instance the remainder of the prescript, may be read as Paul's unpacking of this encapsulation of the gospel for the Galatians in their particular time and situation. It may here, however, be said that "grace" is God's favor, referring (in Paul's usage) both to an activity and a sphere, by and in which believers are privileged to live (see comments on 1:6; 2:9, 21; 5:4; 6:18), whereas "peace" is that condition of eschatological well-being ("salvation") that only God can bring about (see comments on 5:22; 6:16).[38] "Grace" is shorthand for God's self-initiated saving action in Christ, "peace" for the result for believers (cf. Rom 5:1).

The preposition "from" (*apo*) here covers both God and Christ, just as the preposition "through" (*dia*) does in 1:1. Even though Paul can keep God and Christ distinct (see comment on 1:15–16 below), in matters of salvation he regards them as a single divine agent, which is another way of saying that Christ is assumed to be integral to the identity and the activity of God.[39] In this verse, God is called "our Father," making explicit what may already have been implicit in the opening verse with its reference to "God the Father": God is not only "the Father" of Christ; God is also "our Father," that is, of believers (cf. 3:26; 4:6–7).

For the second time in the prescript, Paul mentions Jesus Christ, this time designating him as "Lord," *kyrios*. This title occurs frequently in Paul's Letters (some 200 instances), with "Jesus (Christ) is Lord" a fundamental confession for Paul (1 Cor 12:3; Rom 10:9; 2 Cor 4:5; Phil 2:11). This title will probably be more meaningful to a Gentile audience than the title "Christ" (Messiah), for there were many "lords"—gods and goddesses, various deified rulers, and the Roman emperor—whose authority or power had to be acknowledged or reckoned with in the Greco-Roman world (Dunn 1998: 244–52). Paul's view of the matter is succinctly expressed in 1 Cor 8:5–6: "Even though there may be so-called gods in heaven or on earth—as in fact there are many 'gods' and many 'lords'—yet *for us* there is *one* God, the Father, from whom are all things and for whom we exist, and *one* Lord, Jesus Christ, through whom are all things and through whom we exist" (stress added). The title is not particularly crucial to the theology of Galatians (cf. 1:19; 5:10; 6:14, 18), but the lordship of Jesus

---

38. In Galatians Paul does not actually use the language of "salvation" (*sōzō, sōtēria*), though it is prominent elsewhere (e.g., Rom 1:16; 5:10; 10:10; 11:11; 2 Cor 6:2; Phil 1:19). The term is here used as convenient shorthand for what Paul is about to say in 1:4 (see comment there).

39. The fact that God and Christ are introduced in reverse order in 1:1 makes no difference in this regard. The order in 1:3 is customary for Paul in the salutation, whereas the order in 1:1 is determined by the subject matter, Paul's apostleship as originating directly in Jesus Christ and thus in the God who raised him from the dead.

The Letter Opening

Christ is a presupposition of everything Paul writes (see comment on 1:10). As Paul uses the title, it implies exclusivity.

In vv. 4–5 Paul expands his standard salutation (v. 3), with several clauses that have no parallel in his other letters and that represent a contextually relevant summary of the gospel as Paul understands it for the Galatian situation:

> . . . the Lord Jesus Christ,
> 4a the one who gave himself for our sins,
> 4b that he might rescue us from the present evil age
> 4c according to the will of God and our Father,
> 5 to whom be glory forever and ever. Amen.

In v. 4a, Paul identifies more precisely who the Lord Jesus Christ is for himself and, most importantly, for the churches of Galatia: ". . . the Lord Jesus Christ, [namely,] the one who gave himself for our sins."[40] Paul's formulation has similarities with confessional formulas found in 1 Tim 2:6 (the one "who gave himself a ransom for all") and Titus 2:14 ("who gave himself for us"), both using the aorist of the simple verb *didōmi*, as Paul does in 1:4a. Other texts use the compound *paradidōmi*, including Gal 2:20 (the "one who loved me and gave himself up for me"; cf. Eph 5:2, "Christ loved us and gave himself up for us"; 5:25, "Christ loved the church and gave himself up for her"). The wording of 1:4a ("for our sins") is most similar, however, to that of 1 Cor 15:3, where Paul quotes a known formula, one he had earlier passed on to the Christians in Corinth: "For I delivered to you . . . what I also received, namely, that 'Christ died *for our sins*'" (AT). It is thus probable that in 1:4a Paul is adapting this particular confession, with which the Galatians are also probably familiar, modifying it in two distinct ways: (1) He changes the finite verb construction (*Christos apethanen*, "Christ died") into a participial construction (*tou dontos heauton*, "the one who gave himself"), whereby he can join the confession to the name "the Lord Jesus Christ" at the end of v. 3. (2) He changes the notion of "dying for" to "giving himself for," whereby the active involvement and intentionality of Jesus Christ precisely as Lord comes to expression. He did not simply die: he gave himself. The point is repeated in different ways in 2:20; 3:13; and 6:14 (see comments there).

The formulation "for our sins" is ambiguous (cf. Breytenbach 2003). Its import cannot be determined simply by philological and grammatical analysis. These simple words not only assume more than is stated, they are also

---

40. One could translate with a simple relative clause: ". . . the Lord Jesus Christ, who gave himself for our sins" (so NRSV). But Paul does not here use the relative pronoun *hos* with an aorist indicative, as this translation would suggest, but rather a participial construction: *tou dontos*, best translated as "the one who gave" (more lit., "the one having given"). The latter does not merely further describe "the Lord Jesus Christ"; it *identifies* who he is.

shorthand for a profound and mysterious theological claim that resists rational analysis. The sense of the phrase in the tradition that Paul here adapts was probably "to deal with our sins," to forgive them so that they can no longer form an obstacle between "us" and God (cf. Rom 3:25; 5:8–9; Breytenbach 1993). What exactly these "sins" were (probably the collective transgressions of the law by God's people, Israel) and how exactly Jesus' death (or blood) could effect forgiveness of these sins are not indicated (cf. Matt 26:28; Eph 1:7).[41] In any case, Paul immediately interprets Christ's giving himself "for our sins" to effect not forgiveness but deliverance from an evil realm.[42] He could have written: Christ gave himself for our sins so that we might be forgiven, or "justified" (cf. 2:16 and comment there; Rom 3:25; 4:25; 2 Cor 5:19). Instead he writes that Christ gave himself for our sins "so that [*hopōs*] he might rescue [*exelētai*, from *exaireomai*] us from [lit., out of, *ek*] the present evil age [*tou aiōnos tou enestōtos ponērou*]" (v. 4b).[43] Paul thus shifts the import of the phrase "for our sins" from a forensic (judicial) frame of reference (the divine lawcourt) to a cosmological one (a cosmic conflict between God and malevolent powers for sovereignty over the human world): "The present evil age" is an all-encompassing sphere of evil that Paul frequently refers to elsewhere simply as "this age" (in Greek: Rom 12:2; 1 Cor 1:20; 2:6, 8; 3:18; 2 Cor 4:4) or, synonymously, as "this world" (1 Cor 3:19; 5:10; 7:31; cf. Eph 2:2). "This age" or "world" is in the hands of malevolent, enslaving powers (cf. 1 Cor 2:6; 15:24; 2 Cor 4:4). The notion is indebted to Jewish apocalyptic eschatology, in which the counterpart to "this age" (or "this world") is "the age" or "world to come" (cf. Matt 12:32; Mark 10:30; Luke 18:30; 20:35; Eph 1:21; 2:7; Heb 6:5; *1 En.* 71.15; *4 Ezra* [2 Esd] 6.9; 7.12–13, 50, 113; 8.1; *2 Bar.* 14.13; 15.8; 44.8–15; 83.4–9; *m. ʾAbot* 4:1; *m. Sanh.* 10:1; *b. Ber.* 9.5). The concept of the two ages is given classic expression in the apocalypse of *4 Ezra* [2 Esd] 7.50: "The Most High has made not one age [*saeculum*] but two" (cf. Eph 1:21; Matt 12:32; Luke 20:34–35). Paul himself does not explicitly refer to "the coming age" (*ho aiōn ho mellōn/erchomenos*), as do some NT texts (Matt 12:32; Mark 10:30; Luke 18:30; Eph 1:21), though there may

---

41. In the background probably lies the tradition, found in 2 and 4 Maccabees, of the righteous martyr whose death (blood) atones for the sins of the nation against God and his law. See, e.g., 2 Macc 7:32–38; 8:3; 4 Macc 6:27–29; 17:21–22.

42. The term *aphesis* (forgiveness) is notably absent from the undisputed Pauline Letters, though the idea is present in Rom 3:25; 4:6–8; 2 Cor 5:19.

43. The vocabulary is not characteristic of Paul: *hopōs* ("in order that, so that") occurs only here in Galatians (6 times elsewhere in the undisputed letters, 3 times in OT citations); he prefers *hina* (17 instances in Galatians alone). *Exaireomai* occurs only here in Paul's Letters (5 instances in Acts); he prefers *sōzō*, "save" (19 instances), and *rhyomai*, "rescue" (7 instances), elsewhere. The expression "the present evil age" occurs only here. Still, there is little reason to justify the view that Paul is here quoting from some formula since there is no parallel to the language and thought of Gal 1:4b elsewhere in the NT or other early Christian literature.

The Letter Opening

be an allusion to it in the reference to "the ends of the ages" (i.e., the end of the old age and the beginning of the new) in 1 Cor 10:11. The coming or new age is implied, however, when the present world-age is characterized as "*this* age/world" (Keck 234). Moreover, such expressions as "the kingdom of God" (Gal 5:21; cf. Rom 14:17; 1 Cor 4:20; 6:9, 10; 15:24, 50; 1 Thess 2:12; Eph 5:5; Col 4:11; 2 Thess 1:5; *As. Mos.* 10.1), "eternal life" (Gal 6:8; cf. Rom 2:7; 5:21; 6:22, 23; 1 Tim 1:16; 6:12; Titus 1:2; 3:7; Dan 12:2), and "new creation" (Gal 6:15; cf. 2 Cor 5:17; *1 En.* 72.1; *4 Ezra* [2 Esd] 7.75; *2 Bar.* 32.6) are surely other ways of speaking about the age or world to come, as indeed are "grace and peace" in 1:3. In the prescript, Paul points the Galatians to a cosmic conflict between two worlds, the world of God's "grace and peace" and that of "the present evil age."

Excursus 2: Galatians and Apocalyptic Eschatology

Galatians is often regarded as a letter from which apocalyptic eschatology (understood to involve a future expectation, the Parousia) is largely absent (Beker 37–58; contrast Martyn 97–105; 1997: 85–156, 176–182; Hansen 1993). Much depends on a proper definition (cf. de Boer 1988, 1989, 1998, 2001, 2002). As indicated in the comment on Gal 1:4b above, the notion of two world ages ("this age" and "the age to come") is fundamental to (Jewish or Christian) apocalyptic eschatology. Both ages are matters of revelation (cf. Rev 1:1):[44] the revelation of the new age simultaneously unmasks the present time as the old age that is doomed to pass away.

The dualism of the two ages exhibits two distinct patterns (or "tracks") in the available Jewish literature, one "cosmological," the other "forensic" (de Boer 1989, 1998). (1) According to the cosmological pattern, the created world has come under the dominion of evil, angelic powers in some primeval time, namely, in the time of Noah (for the idea of an angelic "fall," cf. Gen 6:1–6; *1 En.* 6–19; 64.1–2; 69.4–5; 86.1–6; 106.13–17; *Jub.* 4.15, 22; 5.1–8; 10.4–5; *T. Reu.* 5.6–7; *T. Naph.* 3.5; CD 2.17–3.1; *2 Bar.* 56.12–15; *L.A.B.* 34.1–5; Wis 2:23–24; Jude 6; 2 Pet 2:4). God's sovereign rights have been usurped, and the world, including God's own people, has been led astray into forms of idolatry. But there is a righteous remnant of people, chosen by God, who by their acknowledgement of and submission to the Creator, the God of Israel, bear witness to the fact that these evil cosmological powers are doomed to pass away. This remnant, the elect of God, awaits God's deliverance. God will invade the world, now under the dominion of the evil powers, and defeat them in a cosmic war. Only God has the power to defeat and to overthrow the demonic and diabolical powers that have subjugated and perverted the earth. God will establish his sovereignty very soon, delivering the righteous and bringing about a new age in which he will reign unopposed. God will have put right what has gone wrong in and with the world.

---

44. The use of the term "apocalyptic" for this type of eschatology is derived from the opening verse of the book of Revelation: "The revelation [*apokalypsis*] of Jesus Christ." For this reason, the book is also known as the Apocalypse (of John). See comments on 1:12 and 1:16 below.

This "cosmological" apocalyptic eschatology is to be found in perhaps its purest form in *1 Enoch* 1–36 but can best be illustrated here by *Assumption of Moses* 10:

> Then his [God's] kingdom (rule) will appear throughout his whole creation,
> Then the devil will have an end,
> Yes, sorrow will be led away with him.
> ....
> For the Heavenly One will arise from his royal throne,
> Yes, he will go forth from his holy habitation
> With indignation and wrath on behalf of his sons.
> And the earth will tremble . . .

This form of Jewish apocalyptic eschatology, in short, appears to involve "a cosmic drama in which divine and cosmic forces are at work" (Russell 269). This drama in turn suggests that the two ages are not only temporal epochs but also two spheres or zones in which certain powers hold sway or in which certain kinds of activity take place. The final judgment entails God's defeat and destruction of evil cosmic forces.

(2) The other pattern is a modified form of the first. In this pattern, the notion of evil, cosmological forces is absent, recedes into the background, or is even explicitly rejected (cf. *1 En.* 98.4–5; *Pss. Sol.* 9.4–5). Instead, the emphasis falls on free will and individual human decision. Sin is the willful rejection of the creator God (the breaking of the first commandment), and death is punishment for this fundamental sin. God, however, has provided the law as a remedy for this situation, and a person's posture toward this law determines their ultimate destiny. At the last judgment, conceptualized not as a cosmic war but as a courtroom in which all humanity appears before the bar of the Judge, God will reward with eternal life those who have acknowledged his claim and chosen the law and observed its commandments (the righteous), while he will punish with eternal death those who have not (the wicked). Whereas the wicked will be condemned, the righteous will be "justified" (declared right, vindicated).

This "forensic" (legal, judicial) form of apocalyptic eschatology is to be found in *4 Ezra* and *2 Baruch*, both of which emphasize the fall and the responsibility of Adam, the first and paradigmatic human transgressor (*4 Ezra* [2 Esd] 3.5–7, 20–21; 4.30–31; 7.118–119; *2 Bar.* 17.2–3; 23.4; 48.42–43; 54.14, 19; 56.6; cf. *1 En.* 69.6; *Jub.* 3.17–25; 4.29–30; *L.A.B.* 13.8–9; Sir 25:24; Wis 10:1). Evil angelic powers are absent from both works. According to *2 Baruch*, for example, "Adam sinned first and . . . brought death upon all; . . . each of us has become his [or her] own Adam" (54.14, 19). The destiny of each person is in one's own hands: "each of them who has been born from him [Adam] has prepared for himself [or herself] the coming torment; . . . each of them has chosen for himself [or herself] the coming glory" (54.15; cf. 51.16; 85.7). To choose the law is thus to choose the coming glory (cf. 17.4; 38.1–2; 48.22; 54.5). The present age is the time of *decision*. This form of apocalyptic eschatology, whose marks can still be traced in rabbinic literature, is marked by a legal piety in which personal responsibility and accountability are dominant.

Some works exhibit a blend of the two patterns, notably the Dead Sea Scrolls. In the latter, there is to be found both subjection to evil cosmological forces and human control of personal destiny, both predestination and exhortation to observe the law, both God's

The Letter Opening

eschatological war against Belial and his cohorts and God's judgment of human beings on the basis of their deeds or works (see 1QS 1–4; 1QM; CD). According to the Scrolls, the community as a whole as well as the individual members are under constant threat from evil cosmological powers (Belial, the Angel of Darkness, the Spirit of Falsehood or Deceit). To choose the law is thus to choose to stand in the protected sphere of God's own power (as represented by Michael, the Angel of Light, the Spirit of Truth). The law is God's powerful weapon whereby he enables the righteous believer to withstand the superhuman power of the demonic forces (cf. CD 16.1–3). Present existence is thus marked by a struggle between two contending groups of cosmological powers or spirits that seek to lay their claim on human beings. This struggle does not manifest itself only in the sociological separation of the righteous (the covenantal community) from the wicked (the world outside), but also in the choice that the individual, especially the member of the community, must make each day for God and his law. The struggle penetrates the heart of the individual (cf. esp. 1QS 3–4; Sanders 1977: 237–321, esp. 295). Much the same could be said for the book of *Jubilees* and the *Testaments of the Twelve Patriarchs* (Collins 1984: 111).

Paul's Letters also exhibit the characteristic concerns and ideas, or at least the language, of these two different patterns or "tracks" of Jewish apocalyptic eschatology. His use of the story of Adam in 1 Cor 15:21–22, 45–49 and Rom 5:12–21 (cf. 2 Cor 11:3; 1 Tim 2:13–14) betrays the influence of the tradition of interpretation of Adam and his disobedience found in *4 Ezra* and *2 Baruch*, while his not-infrequent references to Satan, always as the power hostile to God and the gospel of Christ (Rom 16:20; 1 Cor 5:5; 7:5; 2 Cor 2:11; 11:14; 12:7; 1 Thess 2:18; cf. 2 Cor 6:15; 1 Thess 3:5), suggest his deep indebtedness to the worldview of "cosmological" Jewish apocalyptic eschatology (cf. "the god of this age" in 2 Cor 4:4; "Beliar" in 2 Cor 6:15). The angelology of "cosmological" Jewish apocalyptic eschatology probably also lies behind the references to "the rulers of this age" in 1 Cor 2:6–8, the principalities and powers mentioned in Rom 8:38 and 1 Cor 15:24, and Paul's personification of Sin and Death as oppressive cosmic powers that rule over human beings (cf. Rom 5:12, 21; 1 Cor 15:26, 56). For this reason, Schweitzer concludes that Paul like Jesus "stood *closer* to the world of thought represented by the Book of Enoch," with its "cosmological" apocalyptic eschatology, than to that of "the Apocalypses of Baruch and Ezra," with their "forensic" apocalyptic eschatology (57, with added stress; so also Martyn 1997: 111–23; de Boer 1989: 182–85; 1998: 364–67). Galatians 1:4ab supports this conclusion (see comment above).[45]

In Jewish cosmological apocalyptic eschatology, the two ages are not simply, or even primarily, temporal categories, referring to two successive, discontinuous periods of world history ("ages"); they are also spatial categories, referring to two spheres or orbs of power, both of which claim sovereignty over the world. In "this age," alien, destructive powers have taken complete control of God's creation, including the cosmos of human beings, and perverted it. "This age" is, then, the realm of sin, death, and evil (what Paul in 1:4 refers to as "the present evil age"). Human beings are slaves of evil,

---

45. Unlike Paul, however, the new preachers in Galatia (see on 1:6–9 below and Excursus 4) stand closer to the world of thought represented in the *Psalms of Solomon*, *4 Ezra* (2 Esdras), and *2 Baruch*, i.e., to the *forensic* pattern of Jewish apocalyptic eschatology (see also comment on 2:15–16).

malevolent powers who have usurped God's rightful claim on the world. In "the age to come," which in Jewish apocalyptic eschatology is to be revealed in the future even as it already exists in heaven above, God will (once more) reign unopposed over the whole creation. For this reason, "the age to come" is the realm of righteousness, life, and peace. The powers of the new age (God and those whom he delegates, such as the Messiah) will thus at the end of time reveal themselves: from heaven above, they will invade the orb of the powers on earth below (the orb of Satan and his minions) and aggressively defeat them, thereby removing them from the creation and liberating human beings from their malevolent, destructive control. Within the framework of the apocalyptic dualism of the two world ages understood spatially as well as temporally, this end-time event (traditionally known as the "last judgment") is necessarily (1) cosmic in scope and implication (all peoples and all times are affected), (2) an act of God (God invades the human cosmos since human beings are in no position to liberate themselves from the evil powers), (3) rectifying (God puts right what has gone wrong in and with the world), and (4) eschatological (final, definitive, and irrevocable). In ancient Jewish apocalyptic eschatology, the turn of the ages, when "this age" is brought to an end and "the age to come" takes its place, will signify God's eschatological act of cosmic rectification.

In Paul's view, God has initiated this eschatological act of cosmic rectification in the person and the work of Jesus Christ. When God sent forth his Son into the world (4:4) to liberate human beings from enslaving powers (4:3–4), God began a unified apocalyptic drama of cosmic rectification that will reach its conclusion at Christ's Parousia (cf. 1 Thess 4:13–18; 1 Cor 15:20–28). Believers live neither in the old age nor in the new; they live at the juncture of the ages where the forces of the new age ("the kingdom of God") are in an ongoing struggle with the forces of the old age (esp. sin, death, and surprisingly, the Sinaitic law). Paul's christological adaptation of Jewish apocalyptic eschatology thus contains the well-known tension between an "already" (God has already acted apocalyptically to liberate human beings from enslaving powers) and a "still more" (God has not yet finished the job). With respect to Galatians, this tension is illustrated by 5:1 ("For freedom Christ has set us free! Stand fast, therefore, and do not be burdened again with a yoke of slavery") and 5:5 ("For we, through the Spirit from faith, are waiting for the hope of justification"). For Galatians as a whole, however, the emphasis falls decisively upon the "already" of God's apocalyptic action in sending forth his Son into the human world to liberate human beings from suprahuman, enslaving powers (cf. 3:13; 4:1–6).[46] This cosmological-apocalyptic perspective has implications for the meanings Paul attaches to the important terminology of justification (the verb *dikaioō* and the noun *dikaiosynē*) later in the letter. Paul first uses this terminology in 2:15–21 (cf. 3:6, 8, 11, 21, 24; 5:4–5). To anticipate the comment on that central passage: For the new preachers active in Galatia (1:6–9; Excursus 4), the terms *dikaioō* and *dikaiosynē* have the normal *forensic*-eschatological meanings: "justify" (declare right, vindicate, approve) and "justification" (God's declaration of vindication or approval and/or the resulting status of having been vindicated). For Paul, the terms *also* acquire a *cosmological*-eschatological nuance: "rectify" (make right,

---

46. See Martyn 1997: 121–22: "It is [in Galatians] the time after the apocalypse of the faith of Christ (3.23–25), the time of things being set right by that faith, the time of the presence of the Spirit, and thus the time of a new war of liberation commenced by the Spirit."

put straight) and "rectification" (God's act of putting things right and/or the resulting condition of having been rectified). In other words, God's justifying act is interpreted by Paul as God's act of cosmic rectification involving a "rescue from the present evil age" (1:4), liberation from the malevolent cosmic powers that hold sway there (3:13, 22–23; 4:3–5; 5:1, 16–24).

The notion of a present evil age assumes that the human condition for everyone (apart from God's deed in Christ) is a form of slavery or subjugation to evil powers:[47] "Then, when you did not know God," Paul will write the Galatians in 4:8, "you were slaves [*edouleusate*] of beings not gods by nature." For Paul, the problem that needs to be addressed, therefore, is not so much "sins," transgressions of divinely given commandments, as Sin, a malevolent enslaving and godlike power under which all human beings are held captive: "all things" have been "shut up . . . under Sin" (so 3:22; see comment there). Evidently in Paul's view, the "sins" of which the received tradition speaks (v. 4a) are not the actions of autonomous and free individuals who respond to God's law as they see fit, but the actions of slaves who do the will of their master, Sin, a power that Paul can also and more frequently in this letter refer to as "the Flesh" (see 5:13–24 and comment there). By giving himself "for our sins," Christ rescues "us" from "the present evil age," where Sin holds sway. That saving act, whereby human beings are liberated from the clutches of an otherwise closed world, is "according to the will of God and our Father" (1:4c).[48]

The verb *exaireō* ("rescue"), common in the LXX and used five times in Acts, means to rescue from an enemy, as illustrated by Acts 12:11: "Then Peter came to himself and said, "Now I am sure that the Lord has sent his angel and *rescued* me from the hands of Herod." The rescue from "the present evil age" is a recurring theme in Galatians, even though Paul does not repeat the verb "rescue." He uses synonyms such as "redeem" (*exagorazō*; 3:13; 4:5) and "set free" (*eleutheroō*; 5:1), the latter both in connection with the Mosaic law! It is one of the curious and challenging features of this letter that Paul speaks of all human beings before and apart from Christ as being "under the law" (3:23; 4:4–5, 21; 5:18), whereby the law is presented as an oppressive, enslaving power from which Christ "redeems" and "frees" human beings (Martyn 370–73). To be "under the law" is to be "under a curse" (3:10), "under a custodian" (3:25), "under guardians and household managers" (4:2), "under the elements of the world" (4:3, 9), and indeed "under Sin" (3:22). The crucial issue in this letter is not so much Sin (mentioned only twice in the remainder of the letter, in 2:17 and 3:22) as the law (some 30 instances).

---

47. Calvin (12) writes that "by this one word ["evil"], as by a thunderbolt, he [Paul] lays low human pride." We today might say that Paul here lays low human optimism.
48. The modifier "our" could also apply to God: "our God and [our] Father" (so NRSV).

The grammar of 1:4b, "that he might rescue [subj.] us from the present evil age," can be taken to refer to the future (a deliverance that will occur) as well as the present (a deliverance that has occurred). In a sense, Paul means "both now and in the future" (cf. 5:5), even if the accent falls on the present in the remainder of Galatians, especially in connection with the law (5:1). Until the Parousia, the deliverance achieved is in jeopardy, as the Galatian situation itself abundantly attests (see on 1:6–9 below), and is thus always dependent on Christ's continual rescuing activity as and through the Spirit (cf. 4:1–6). That ongoing rescuing activity, which has an apocalyptic character (see Excursus 2, above), can take the form of a letter from an apostle "not from human beings nor through a human being, but through Jesus Christ and God the Father, the One who raised him from the dead" (see Excursus 5, below).

By repeatedly using the first-person plural ("our Father," "our sins," "us"), Paul reminds the Galatians of their present status in Christ: they have been rescued, and shall continue to be rescued, "out of the present evil age" by Christ's having given himself for their sins. The appropriate response is to give "glory" (praise) to God "forever and ever," for as long as the new age lasts, which is forever.[49] With the final "Amen" (1:5), Paul invites the Galatians who shall be listening to his letter being read aloud to them to join him in a solemn affirmation of what God has accomplished in Christ for "us."[50]

Excursus 3: The Letter Opening

The comments on 1:1–5 have demonstrated that Galatians bears the marks of an ancient letter. The document begins in the way such letters normally do, with a three-part prescript consisting of sender, the addressees, and a greeting. As noted above, Paul modifies the conventional elements of the prescript in his own way. Some of his modifications recur in his other letters and are thus indicators of Paul's own epistolary style. Others are unique to Galatians and are determined by the particular situation in Galatia and Paul's response to this situation. Much the same can be said for the remainder of the letter: Paul makes use of conventional epistolary phrases and formulas, but he adapts them to his own epistolary style (as does any letter writer, ancient or modern, mostly subconsciously) on the one hand and to the particular occasion and his immediate aims on the other. As indicators of Paul's own distinctive epistolary style, the adaptations that recur in other letters provide important clues to the possible structure of the Letter to the Galatians, as we have already seen in connection with the prescript: Paul's modification of the normal greeting (*chairein*) found in Hellenistic letters into a "grace [*charis*] and

---

49. Literally, Paul writes "for the ages of the ages, " *eis tous aiōnas tōn aiōnōn* (Tob 14:15; 4 Macc 18:24; Phil 4:20; 1 Tim 1:17; 2 Tim 4:18; Heb 13:21; 1 Pet 4:11; numerous instances in Revelation), which is a more intense form of the common LXX idiom, "for the age of the age," *eis ton aiōna tou aionos*, which does not occur in the NT.

50. The wording of Gal 1:5 matches exactly the final words of 4 Maccabees (18:24). Paul is here indebted to Jewish liturgical language and formulas. See Chilton 1992.

The Letter Opening

peace" formula is found in all his (authentic) letters. This distinctive Pauline adaptation of the secular greeting formula introduces the third subsection of the prescript, which in Galatians is remarkably elaborate.

John L. White (97) has compared the various letters of Paul and constructed an abstracted outline of a Pauline letter, showing the features characteristic of his correspondence. In his view, Paul's letter opening characteristically consists of the prescript followed by a "thanksgiving prayer." This transitional section can be also be regarded as the opening section of the letter body instead of the second section of the letter opening (see Introduction: Structure). Unique to the Letters of Paul, Galatians has a rebuke and imprecation instead of a thanksgiving prayer (see below on 1:6–10). Still, like the thanksgiving prayer in the other letters of Paul, the rebuke and imprecation introduces the main theme of the letter, which is "the gospel of Christ" (1:7), and the issue that has occasioned the letter: the presence of new preachers in Galatia, those proclaiming "a different gospel" (1:6).

The letter opening of Galatians thus consists of the prescript plus the rebuke and imprecation, in 1:1–10 (so also, e.g., Rohde; Dunn; Matera; Anderson 1999: 144). In this analysis, the letter body proper begins at 1:11, not at 1:6 (as, e.g., Betz; Martyn).[51] That 1:11 begins a new section is indicated by the solemn introductory formula "I make known to you, brethren" (1 Cor 12:3; 15:1; 2 Cor 8:1; cf. 1 Thess 1:5; 1 Cor 1:11; 2 Cor 1:8; Rom 1:13; Phil 1:12). In this case, the formula introduces the issue that Paul will address in the first major section of the letter (1:11–2:21): the origin and (thus also) the truth of the gospel. This discussion will provide the basis for the remaining sections of the letter, in which Paul expounds the truth of the gospel for the Galatian situation.

1:6–10 Rebuke and Imprecation

This paragraph, which is part of the letter opening (Excursus 3), contains a rebuke followed by an imprecation. It also discloses the specific occasion of the letter: The churches of Galatia are currently hearing a gospel "different" from the one Paul initially proclaimed to them, and they are finding this different gospel rather attractive. Paul does not hesitate to express his alarm and displeasure at this turn of events in the process stating the main theme of the letter, what Paul calls "the gospel of Christ" in 1:7. The paragraph raises two potentially crucial issues for the interpretation of the letter: (1) the content of the "different gospel" together with the identity of those proclaiming it to the Galatians, and (2) the literary character or genre of the letter, particularly in connection with Paul's use of rhetorical forms and stratagems. We treat each issue in a separate excursus below, the first after the commentary on 1:6–9, the second after the commentary on 1:10.

The paragraph has three discernible subunits. In the first (1:6–7), Paul expresses his consternation at developments in Galatia. In the second (1:8–9), he anathematizes anyone who would preach a gospel contrary to the one he

---

51. Other commentators begin a major new section not at 1:11 but at 1:10 (Martyn) or 1:12 (Betz). The justification of the present division can be found in the comments on 1:10 and 1:11 below.

initially preached to the Galatians. He concludes (1:10) with a series of seemingly rhetorical questions about his aims and his use of rhetoric (the art of persuasive speaking and writing) to achieve them.

> **1:6** I am astonished that you are so quickly turning from the one who called you into the grace of Christ[a] to a different gospel, **7** which is not another, except that there are some who are unnerving you and wanting to turn the gospel of Christ into its opposite.
>
> **8** But even if we or an angel from heaven were preaching-a-gospel[b] to you[c] contrary to what we did preach to you, let that someone be an anathema. **9** As we have said before and I now say again: if someone is preaching-a-gospel contrary to what you received, let that someone be an anathema.
>
> **10** So am I now persuading human beings or God? Or am I seeking to please human beings? If I were still pleasing human beings, I would not be a slave of Christ.

a. Here NA[27] places *Christou*, "of Christ," in brackets since "the absence of any genitive qualifying *en chariti* ($\mathfrak{P}$46[vid], G, H[vid], it[g,ar], Marcion . . .) has the appearance of being the original reading, which copyists supplemented by adding *Christou* " (Metzger 520). The inclusion, however, has strong external support, including $\mathfrak{P}$51, ℵ, A, B, Ψ, 33, 81, 614, 1739, among others; furthermore D has *Iēsou Christou*, which is simply a variation of the simple *Christou* (other, lesser manuscripts have *theou*, "of God"). The addition of *Christou* (or of *Iēsou Christou*) seems at first sight easier to explain than its omission, but not if one takes into account the fact that Paul refers to "the grace of God" in 2:21 and to "his [God's] grace" in 1:15 in connection with his apostolic call, where the verb *kaleō*, used in 1:6, also occurs. For this reason, the addition of *Christou* is unlikely (one would expect *theou*, as in some manuscripts); it is easier to suppose that certain scribes found *Christou* incongruous and omitted it (others substituted *theou*). Galatians 6:18 ("the grace of our Lord Jesus Christ") shows that the expression "grace of Christ" is actually not un-Pauline (in 1:3, grace comes from both God and Christ). In any case, the immediate context makes it plain that the grace at issue pertains to Christ ("the gospel of Christ" in v. 7). As we shall indicate below, the genitive here is probably appositional or explanatory, "[God's] grace, which is Christ."

b. This is one word in the Greek, *euangelizētai*, which is a cognate of the word for gospel, *euangelion*.

c. The NA[27] also places *hymin*, "to you," in brackets, since some manuscripts place the word before the verb and others after it. Still other manuscripts omit the word altogether (see Metzger 521). It is probably original since it is easier to explain why scribes would delete the word than to insert it (the deletion generalizes the point, making it applicable to other settings).

[6–7] In his other letters, Paul normally follows the prescript with a paragraph that begins by giving thanks to God for the recipients (1 Thess 1:2–3; Phil

1:3; Rom 1:8; Phlm 4; 2 Cor 1:3 contains a blessing instead). This thanksgiving section is Paul's adaptation of the "worship formula" found in ancient letters, which "either follows or is blended with the formula for health" (Aune 1987: 163). Here is an example: "Antonius Longus to Nilous his mother, very many greetings. I pray always for your health; every day I make supplication for you before the Lord Serapis" (Hunt and Edgar #120). The Galatians may thus be expecting something similar at this point, perhaps something akin to the thanksgiving of 1 Corinthians with its mention of God's grace given in Christ to the church in Corinth: "I give thanks to God always for you because of the grace of God that has been given to you in Christ Jesus" (1 Cor 1:4–9).

In Galatians, however, the thanksgiving addressed to God is replaced by a rebuke (vv. 6–7) and an imprecation (vv. 8–9). The rebuke is addressed to the Galatians directly in vv. 6–7: "I am astonished [*thaumazō*] that you are so quickly turning from the one who called you into the grace of Christ to a different gospel, ⁷which is not another [gospel], except that there are some who are unnerving you and wanting to turn the gospel of Christ into its opposite."

The use of the verb *thaumazō* to express astonishment with an undertone of irritation or annoyance in letters is conventional; the verb functions to introduce a rebuke (Betz 46–47; Longenecker 11; Mullins 385–86; Hansen 1989: 33–42; Nanos 2002a: 39–42). Although the verb is conventional, an element of genuine astonishment on Paul's part is probably not to be excluded here (Longenecker 14). The verb expresses not simply Paul's surprise at the turn of events but also his deep consternation (cf. 4:20, "I am perplexed about you"). Paul directs a rebuke at the Galatians because they are in the process of deserting "the one who called them" and embracing a gospel "different" from the one Paul preached to them initially. Though sharp, the rebuke is nevertheless fraternal, as indicated by the fact that, beginning at 1:11 (the first verse of the letter body), Paul will address the Galatians nine times in the letter as "brethren" (*adelphoi*).

The verb "turn" (*metatithesthe*, present tense) was commonly used in connection with changing allegiances, such as turning from one school of thought to another or from one religion to another (e.g., 2 Macc 7:24; 11:24; see BDAG 642; Maurer 1972: 161–62; Betz 47 n. 41). Paul thus presents the Galatians' process of turning to that different gospel as a form of apostasy (cf. 5:4), undoubtedly to alert the Galatians to the seriousness of the situation in which they find themselves. The phrase "so quickly" (*houtōs tacheōs*) may simply be rhetorical, referring "to the ease with which the addressees were allegedly won over by the antagonists" (Thurén 65, following Rohde 38–39; cf. Lightfoot 75). Betz (47), who grants the rhetorical origin of the phrase, nevertheless observes that Paul's "words would make little sense . . . if a considerable length of time had passed since the founding of the churches." The point of reference is probably the founding of the churches by Paul and not the arrival of the new preachers mentioned in the next verse.

Paul could have rebuked the Galatians for "turning from my gospel to a different gospel." That the Galatians are doing precisely that is clear from what follows (1:8–9, 11: "the gospel that was preached by me"). In Paul's view, however, by turning to that different gospel, the Galatians are deserting and thus rejecting "the one who called" them "into the grace of Christ." The phrase "the one who called you" (*ho kalesas hymas*) is ambiguous, perhaps intentionally so. On the surface, it can be taken as a reference to Paul, who through the gospel he preached to the Galatians (1:8–9, 11) called them into the sphere of Christ's grace (see 1:1, 16). It is possible that the Galatians will so understand Paul's formulation, at least on a first hearing of the letter. Elsewhere, however, Paul uses this participial construction as a name for God (1 Thess 5:24; cf. 1 Cor 1:9; 1 Thess 2:12; Rom 4:17; 8:30; 9:12), and there are no instances of the verb elsewhere with him as the subject. In Paul's view, the caller is undoubtedly God (as in 5:8).[52] Yet Paul and the gospel he preaches are the means through which God calls. Paul's point, then, is that the Galatians, in turning their backs on him and his gospel, are actually turning their backs on God (cf. 4:9). In this way, Paul seeks to make it clear to the Galatians that the issue posed by that different gospel is not trivial; in his view, their true Christian identity and thus their salvation are at stake.

In this context the verb *kaleō*, "call," means more than a verbal invitation or summons since God's calling has effected a transfer "from the present evil age" (1:4) "into the grace of Christ," here regarded as a sphere into which the Galatians have been brought.[53] The genitive is probably descriptive, "the grace which is Christ," meaning "the grace of God which Christ represents" (Betz 48). As Gal 2:21 shows ("the grace of God"; cf. 1:3, 15; 2:9; 5:4; 6:18), "grace" is central to Paul's understanding of the gospel (see comment there), and he undoubtedly chooses the word here to form a contrast with the "different gospel," which by implication has nothing to do with grace as Paul understands it.

Like the terms "apostle" and "church," the term "gospel" (*euangelion*) quickly came to have a special, technical meaning among Christians, the good news about Christ (similarly the cognate verb *euangelizomai*, "to preach-the-gospel"). Of the seventy-six instances in the NT, sixty occur in the Letters of Paul. That it is not a distinctively Pauline word is indicated by the twelve occurrences in Matthew and Mark, and, conversely, by its surprising absence from Luke-Acts, given the important role of Paul in the second volume of that work. Paul assumes that the Galatians will understand what the word means and that

---

52. Traditionally, the one who called the Galatians has been thought to be Christ (Luther 1535; Calvin), but that seems unlikely, especially in view of the phrase "into the grace of Christ."

53. It is possible to understand the phrase "in [*en*] the grace of Christ" instrumentally, "by means of" (so Longenecker 15). But *en* with the verb *kaleō* often has the sense of "into," as in 1 Cor 7:15; 1 Thess 4:7; see also Rom 5:2 ("this grace in [*en*] which we stand").

The Letter Opening

the new missionaries in Galatia are also using the term for their proclamation (see further Excursus 4 below). The antecedents to the technical Christian usage have proved difficult to trace in both Jewish and non-Jewish sources. The LXX contains only a single instance of the noun and then in the plural form (2 Kgdms [2 Sam] 4:10), a form that also occurs a number of times in secular literature, especially in connection with the emperor cult (cf. Josephus, *J.W.* 4.168; 4.656). There are only a few known instances of the singular in non-Christian literature (e.g., Josephus, *J.W.* 2.420). The Christian usage is probably primarily rooted in such texts as LXX Isa 40:9; 52:7 (cited by Paul in Rom 10:15); Isa 60:6; 61:1–2 (cf. 11QMelch 2.15–24; LXX Joel 3:5), where the verb *euangelizomai* ("to preach-good-news") occurs in connection with the announcement of God's salvation (cf. Martyn 127–35; Dunn 1998: 164–69). The Galatians do not need to know this background to understand the meaning of the term, which in Greek simply means "good news." They will understand it as a technical term signifying the good news about Christ (1:7: "the gospel of Christ").

Paul does not indicate how he has come know that the Galatians are turning to "a different gospel," meaning a different version of the good news about Christ. Nor does he indicate the content of this gospel, only that it is "different" from his own. The Galatians certainly know how "different" it actually is; an interpreter and a reader today must rely on the data and hints given in the remainder of the letter to reconstruct at least its basic content. From those data and hints, it is evident that this gospel entails the observance of the law, beginning with circumcision, for the Gentile converts in Galatia (3:1–3; 4:21; 5:3–4; 6:12–13; see Excursus 4, below). In this verse, however, Paul's concern is only to alert the Galatians to the fact that the "different gospel" they are turning to entails deserting "the one who called" them "into the grace of Christ" (cf. 5:4).

In v. 7, which is tied syntactically to v. 6, Paul begins by denying that this "different [*heteron*] gospel" is in fact "another [*allo*]" gospel (1:7a). The two adjectives *heteros* and *allos* are frequently used interchangeably to mean "(an) other," also by Paul (Burton 420–22; J. K. Elliott; BDF #306; cf. 2 Cor 11:4; 1 Cor 12:9–10). Here, however, a case can be made for a distinction (Burton 24): The sense is that the "different gospel" cannot count as "another gospel" alongside the one Paul himself has preached and still preaches.[54] Anything other than "the gospel that was preached by me" (1:11) to the Galatians is not in fact "the gospel of Christ" (the good news of which Christ is the content). Paul's self-correction[55] is designed to rob that "different gospel" of the right to the label "gospel (of Christ)."

---

54. At first glance Gal 2:7–8 appears to countenance two distinct versions of the gospel, but that is not the case; see comment there.

55. Correction (*correctio*, *metabolē*) was a common rhetorical device to fasten the listener's attention on a particular point (Anderson 2000: 71).

Paul continues in what now becomes a run-on sentence by mentioning the source of that "different" so-called gospel. The "different gospel" is not actually "another" gospel "except that [*ei mē*] there are some [*tines*] who are unnerving you [*hoi tarassontes hymas*] and wanting [*thelontes*] to turn the gospel of Christ into its opposite." The conjunction *ei mē*, "except that," which unlike *alla* ("but") in v. 8 is a weak adversative (BDF #448.8), probably means "only the problem is that . . ." For Paul, then, that different gospel is not another gospel—only the problem is that there are "some" people now among the Galatians who are proclaiming what they mistakenly regard to be the gospel of Christ. Paul does not name the people he here rebukes, limiting himself to the vague "some" (cf. 4:17; 5:7, 10; 1 Cor 4:18; 15:12; 2 Cor 3:1; 10:2; Rom 3:8). The use of the vague "some" could be seen as a rhetorical device designed to minimize the importance and the number of these people in the eyes of the Galatians. Other plausible explanations include the following: Paul really does not know who these people are (he has never met them and has not been told who they are), and he does not really care (he wants to focus on the issues at stake). In any event Paul does not describe these people or their activities in a neutral way, as simply preaching a mistaken version of the gospel. He describes them rather in terms of their deleterious impact (1) on the Galatians themselves and (2) on "the gospel of Christ."

Impact 1. According to Paul, the unnamed people are first of all "unnerving" the Galatians, making them anxious. The verb is *tarassō* (v. 7; also used in 5:10, the only two instances in Paul's Letters), and a suitable English translation is not easy to find. Recognized possibilities include "disturb" (NAB; Betz; Dunn), "confuse" (NRSV, NIV), "trouble" (KJV, RSV), and "frighten (out of their wits)" (Martyn 112). The verb literally means to "stir up" or to "trouble," as water (John 5:7). In its metaphorical extension, the general meaning is "to cause inward turmoil" (Martyn 112: "mental anguish") and thus to "stir up, disturb, unsettle, throw into confusion" (BDAG 990; cf. John 11:33; 12:27; 13:21; 14:1, 27). In the Synoptics, the verb occurs only in the passive form, and the NRSV consistently translates it with "be terrified" or "frightened" (Matt 2:3; 14:26; Mark 6:50; Luke 1:12; 24:38). The translation "unnerve" seeks to encompass these various nuances (so also 5:10).

Paul does not, however, here explain why the Galatians are unnerved by the preachers of that "different gospel." He does not have to; the Galatians know the reason. Paul does not let on how he knows about the alarming impact of the new preachers and their "different gospel" on the Galatians. But the possibilities are limited: One or more members of the Galatian congregations loyal to Paul have sought him out, or have been asked to do so. A letter may also have been dispatched (cf. 1 Cor 7:1; 16:17). Paul here then only repeats what has come to his attention: the negative impact of the preachers of the "different gospel" on the Galatians themselves. They are being "unnerved." He repeats this fact in order to indicate his sympathy with the predicament of the churches he has founded in Galatia.

This interpretation of the verse means that Paul's comment about "those unnerving you" is not to be taken merely as rhetorical vilification of those preaching that "different gospel" (e.g., du Toit 409).[56] That Paul is not here indulging in rhetorical vilification receives confirmation in the interesting parallel in Acts 15:24, part of the official letter from the church in Jerusalem to the one in Antioch following the "Apostolic Council" (15:6–22): "We have heard that some persons [*tines*] from us have unnerved you [*etaraxan hymas*] you with words, unsettling your minds [*anaskeuazontes tas psychas hymōn*] . . ." (RSV, alt.).

This verse harks back to the beginning of Acts 15, which indicates the source of the mental distress in Antioch: "But some persons [*tines*] came down from Judea [to Antioch] and were teaching the brethren, 'Unless you are circumcised according to the custom of Moses, you cannot be saved'" (15:1 RSV).

The situation described in Gal 1:7 is analogous to the one in Acts 15: Some persons (*tines*) have come into the Galatian churches and are "unnerving" (*tarassō*) the Galatians with a message very similar to the one brought to the Gentile Christians in Antioch, according to Acts 15:1 (see Excursus 4, below). Without circumcision, they are excluded from salvation (cf. Gal 4:17).

Impact 2. Not only do the new preachers unnerve the Galatians; they also, according to Paul, "are wanting to turn [*metastrepsai*] the gospel of Christ into its opposite." The two actions of the new preachers probably go together, the second serving to explain the first: They are unnerving the Galatians precisely because they are wanting to turn the gospel of Christ into its opposite. Here again, however, a suitable, one-word translation of the highlighted verb (*metastrepsai*), not used by Paul elsewhere, has proved difficult. The most common translation is "pervert" (RVS, NRSV, KJV, NIV, NAB, NJB; Betz; Longenecker). Another alternative is "distort" (BDAG 641; Witherington). Both of these alternatives fail to do justice to the nuances of the verb in this context. Dunn renders with "to turn . . . [the gospel of Christ] into something else," which goes in the right direction since a possible meaning of the verb is to change something so that it turns into its opposite (Bertram 1971: 729; BDAG 641). Sirach, for example, warns its readers against a certain type of person capable of "turning [*metastrephōn*] good into evil" (11:31); and Acts 2:20 cites the prophecy of Joel 2:31 (LXX 3:4) warning that "the sun shall be turned [*metastraphēsetai*] into darkness." For this reason, Martyn renders the verb with "to change the gospel of Christ into its opposite," which is also the translation adopted here. Paul does not explain in what way the new preachers are wanting to turn the

---

56. It needs to be constantly remembered that Paul's comments about the new preachers, their intentions, and their activities can be verified by the addressees.

gospel of Christ into its opposite. Paul's rhetorical purpose here is limited to an attempt to alienate the Galatians from the preachers of that "different gospel" (which he has already declared to be a nongospel at the beginning of the verse) and to dissociate the latter from any legitimate connection with "the (true) gospel of Christ."

It could perhaps be argued that Paul, in order to achieve his purpose, is (once again) resorting to the common rhetorical stratagem of vilifying adversaries by questioning their motives. Paul's use of the participle *thelontes*, "wanting" (cf. 4:17; 6:12–13), encourages such an interpretation (cf. Martyn 112); so does the common translation of the infinitive *metastrepsai* as "to pervert." Yet there are two reasons why that reading of the verse may be dubious. First, the new preachers have come into the Galatian churches after their founding by Paul (4:13). Thus Paul's gospel was on the scene first. Since their arrival, the new preachers have undoubtedly been telling the Galatians that Paul's (version of the) gospel is inadequate, that without circumcision and a law-observant life their salvation ("justification") has not been and cannot be secured (see Excursus 4, below). The new preachers in Galatia are thus in fact "wanting" to substitute their (version of the) gospel (in which circumcision and law observance are fundamental also for Gentile believers) for Paul's gospel (in which circumcision and law observance play no role whatsoever). Paul actually could have written: "They are wanting to substitute their version of the gospel for mine." With that description of their activities, the new preachers would readily have agreed.

Second, much of the remainder of the letter (esp. from 2:15 onward) is Paul's attempt to demonstrate on substantive theological grounds why in his view the gospel of the new preachers turns the gospel of Christ into its very opposite (cf. esp. 2:15–21; 3:18; and comments there). It would be curious for Paul to do that if the closing clause of 1:7 were merely a rhetorical ploy and thus without real substance, as if he were only attacking unseen and unverifiable intentions. As the reference to "the grace of Christ" in 1:6 already suggests, and as the remainder of the letter attests, Paul's gospel is focused on God's grace in Christ, whereby the blessings of salvation are freely and *unconditionally* given (1:4, 6; 2:21; cf. 3:1–5; etc.); the gospel of the new preachers, however, is focused on circumcision and the law, whereby the blessings of salvation, especially "justification," are completely *conditional* on doing "works of the law" (2:16; 3:2, 5, 10; 5:4).[57] Paul's charge that the new preachers want "to turn the gospel of

---

57. The general expression "the blessings of salvation" is a convenient way of referring to, e.g., peace, the Spirit, being a "son" of God, love, eternal life, new creation, etc., mentioned elsewhere in the letter. As indicated in the comment on 1:3–5, Paul does not in Galatians actually use the language of "salvation" (*sōzō, sōtēria*), though it is prominent elsewhere (e.g. Rom 1:16; 5:10; 10:10; 11:11; 2 Cor 6:2; Phil 1:19). He does refer to "blessing," namely, "the blessing of Abraham," identified as the Spirit (3:14; cf. 3:8).

The Letter Opening 45

Christ into its opposite" in 1:7 is certainly uttered from his own perception and conviction about the meaning of the gospel, but the charge is also, and above all else, a theological evaluation of the new preachers and their program. For Paul, their "different gospel" turns the gospel of Christ on its head and is therefore a nongospel. He is going to show the Galatians (and the new preachers listening to the letter with them) why he believes that to be the case.

[8–9] Before Paul turns to substantive theological argument, however, he wants to undermine the authority of the new preachers in Galatia and to bolster his own. The latter occurs primarily in v. 10, the former in these two verses.[58] Paul here combats the evidently strong and tempting influence of these troublemakers by twice anathematizing those who would preach a gospel contrary to "the gospel preached by me" (1:11). Thus he writes in 1:8–9, "But even if we or an angel from heaven were preaching-a-gospel to you contrary to what we did preach to you, let that someone be an anathema [*estō anathema*]. ⁹As we have said before and I now say again: if someone is preaching-a-gospel contrary to what you received, let that someone be an anathema [*estō anathema*]."

"Here Paul is breathing fire" (Luther 1535: 55). An *anathema* (or in older Greek, *anathēma*, with a long *e*) literally means "something placed" or "set up" and thus "dedicated" to a deity, and in the LXX to the God of Israel (LSJ 104–5; BDAG 63; cf. Lev 27:28 LXX). It does not necessarily have a negative connotation, often (esp. in non-Biblical Greek, where the word is normally spelled *anathēma*) referring merely to a votive offering (cf. Plutarch, *Pel.* 29; Sophocles, *Ant.* 286; Jdt 16:19; 2 Macc 2:13; 9:16; Luke 21:5; Philo; Josephus). In the LXX as in the NT, however, it can mean "a curse" (Deut 13:16; 20:17; Acts 23:14), in the Semitism "to anathematize with an anathema," "to curse with a curse." In the LXX, where it most often translates the Hebrew *ḥērem* ("ban"), it often has the meaning "an object devoted to God in order that God can curse it"; something cursed by God is thus "an accursed thing" (e.g. LXX: Deut 7:26; 13:18 [17]; Josh 6:17–18; 7:11–13; Zech 14:11; cf. Behm 353–54). Paul uses it with this meaning in 1 Cor 12:3 ("No one who speaks by God's Spirit says 'Jesus is an anathema'" [AT]) and Rom 9:3 ("I could wish myself to be an anathema, away from Christ, for the sake of my brethren" [AT]). Paul's formulation in Gal 1:8–9 also occurs in 1 Cor 16:22: "If someone has no love for the Lord, let that someone be [*ētō*] an anathema" (AT). Paul is distinctive in using the term exclusively in connection with people (cf. Josh 7:12 for a precedent and Acts 23:14 for a parallel; see also Mark 14:71; Acts 23:12, 21, where the verb is used).

It is curious that Paul would use the word "anathema" since the meaning it has here (an object, or in this case a person, to be cursed by God) is found in the Septuagint, not in non-Biblical Greek (where the term, normally spelled *anathēma*,

---

58. This double agenda continues in the opening paragraphs of the letter's body (1:11–2:14).

was used to mean "a votive offering," as noted above).[59] Paul does not help his Gentile readers out by explaining or even translating the word, and for that reason a transliteration rather than a periphrastic rendering has been chosen. The context is probably enough to alert the Galatian readers (and readers today) to the intended sense, but the new preachers, who were well versed in the Jewish Scriptures (see Excursus 4), will be able to enlighten them (cf. Morland). The curse in v. 9 is clearly meant for them, rather than for the Galatians: "If someone is preaching-a-gospel contrary to what you received—and someone is in fact doing that—let that someone be an anathema."

The conditional clause in this verse presents a "real" or factual condition, in this case representing what is actually going on in the churches of Galatia.[60] Someone is preaching a gospel (*euangelizetai*, present indicative) contrary to what (*par' ho*) the Galatians received (*parelabete*). Paul here uses the generic singular *tis* ("anyone, someone") instead of the plural *tines* ("some people") to refer to the new preachers in Galatia (he means to say, "if someone, anyone of the new preachers"), though it is also possible that Paul has a (or the) leader of the group in mind (cf. the singulars in 3:1; 5:10 with the plurals in 1:7; 6:12). The word "gospel" (*euangelion*) does not actually occur here but is contained in the verb *euangelizetai*, "to preach-good-news." The prepositional phrase *par' ho*, which literally means "contrary to what," could also be taken to mean "alongside what," but that is unlikely here since Paul has just declared the "different gospel" not to be "another gospel" alongside the one he has preached (1:6–7). It is thus also clear that "the gospel of Christ" (1:7), equal to "the gospel preached by me" (1:11), is the unstated antecedent of the neuter relative pronoun *ho*. The Galatians have "received" this gospel from Paul (cf. the similar formulation in 1 Cor 15:1: "I make known to you . . . the gospel that I preached to you, which you also received" [AT]). Here he uses a verb that is a technical term for the reception of (human) tradition, the corresponding verb being *paradidōmi*, "to deliver, pass on" (cf. 1 Cor 15:3: "For I passed on to you . . . what I also received" [AT]). It is Paul's way of saying that "his" gospel was the first one on the scene in Galatia: The Galatians had received that gospel as an authentic message, and it had been enough (cf. 2:15–21; 3:1–5; 4:13–14; 5:7). The "different gospel" is now disrupting that initial reception; it is an interloper (cf. 5:2–4, 7).

In v. 9, as suggested above, Paul appears to be speaking over the heads of the Galatians to the new preachers, Christian Jews well versed in the Jewish

---

59. Only a single inscription from the first or second century A.D. (from Megara, between Corinth and Athens) attests the use of *anathema* in the sense used by Paul and the LXX (see BDAG 63; MM 33).

60. A formally "real" condition need not reflect reality, only the writer's presentation of reality. Here it does both.

The Letter Opening

Scriptures, who shall be listening to the letter with the Galatians. That may explain why Paul does not pause to explain the meaning of an anathema. They will know what he means. From the foregoing analysis, it is also evident that the third-person imperative, "Let that someone be an anathema," is tantamount to a prayer or a petition directed to God (see further the comment on "persuading God" in 1:10 below).

With respect to Paul's primary audience, the Galatians, his rhetorical purpose behind the solemn imprecation on the new preachers is reasonably clear, to undermine, even destroy, their influence on the Galatians and to alert the Galatians to the severe danger they are in. Not so clear, however, is why Paul is not satisfied with the curse in v. 9, but must lead up to it with the curse in v. 8, prefacing the former with a curious introduction as well ("As we have said before and I now say again"). He could have simply written the following: "There are some who are unnerving you and wanting to turn the gospel of Christ into its opposite, but . . . if someone is preaching-a-gospel contrary to the one you received, let that someone be an anathema." Paul does not keep it this simple and direct.

He begins v. 8 by positing two hypothetical possibilities: "But [*alla*] even if [*kai ean*] we or an angel from heaven were [now] preaching a gospel [*euangelizētai*, present subjunctive][61] to you contrary to the one we did preach [*euēngelisametha*, aorist indicative] to you, let that person be an anathema." In contrast to v. 9, the condition here is hypothetical not only because of the subjunctive mood in the conditional clause but also because of the conjunction *kai ean* ("even if"), which introduces a concession made purely for the sake of argument. In contrast to the conjunction *ean kai* ("although"), which concedes something to be in fact the case (BDF #374), the conjunction *kai ean* concedes, for the sake of argument only, an extremely remote possibility (Lightfoot 77; Burton 26; Mussner 60), indeed one that the writer regards as an absolute impossibility. That is surely the case here (rightly Calvin 15; otherwise Betz 53; Martyn 113–14; Dunn 45; Witherington 83). Paul regards it as impossible that either "we" (Paul himself)[62] or "an angel from heaven," meaning a messenger from God's side (cf. 4:14), would now be preaching a gospel "different" from the one "we" did in fact preach in Galatia. The concessive clause posits an entirely theoretical possibility for the sake of argument: Even if Paul or a heavenly angel were preaching another gospel, which neither

---

61. Some manuscripts, including the original hand of Sinaiticus, have the aorist subjunctive. The evidence for the present subjunctive is stronger ($\mathfrak{P}^{51vid}$, B, D, et al.). The present subjunctive posits an ongoing activity ("were now preaching"), whereas the aorist posits a potential activity ("were ever to preach").

62. The "we" is probably editorial, a substitute for "I" (cf. 4:13: "I preached-the-gospel to you," *euangelisamēn hymin*), though he may here be including coworkers (as perhaps in 1:9) and even "all the brethren" mentioned in 1:2a.

is actually doing, or could do, the gospel originally preached by Paul in Galatia remains unchanged and in force while Paul or that heavenly angel becomes an anathema in God's sight.

Paul could perhaps simply have referred only to himself here. Why then does he mention an angel from heaven as well? The introduction of this figure is important enough for Paul to allow the word "angel" to govern the verbs in both the conditional clause (*euangelizētai*) and the main clause (*estō*); both are third-person singular forms. Claims of revelations from or through an angel (a divine messenger) were not uncommon in antiquity (Betz 53 n. 84; Grundmann 1964). In 4:14 Paul remembers that the Galatians had received him "as an angel of God." The Galatians will thus readily understand what Paul is referring to in v. 9 and grasp the importance of such angelic revelations for authorizing a message, even more so if the new preachers in Galatia are appealing to angelic revelations to add weight and authority to their gospel (Betz 53; Martyn 113–14; cf. 3:19 and comment there). If Paul mentions the heavenly angel because the new missionaries in Galatia are making appeals to one or more angelic revelations for their gospel, he will then be sending the message that all such claims are false and deceptive. It is for Paul simply impossible for an angel from heaven ever to proclaim the "different gospel" of the other missionaries; Christ would then have died for no discernible purpose (cf. 2:21 and comment there). If the new preachers' appeal to an angel from heaven explains why Paul introduces this figure in v. 8, it is noteworthy that he himself does not make a positive appeal to an angelic revelation; in 1:11–12, 15–16 he goes over their heads and appeals directly to a revelation from God (see comments there).

Another possibility is that of Calvin (15), who surmises that Paul is trying to bolster the authority of his message over against that of the new preachers, who were appealing to the apostles James, Peter, and John in Jerusalem (2:7–9) as authorities for their gospel: "He saw that he and his teaching were attacked by the use of famous names. He replies that not even angels [never mind Jerusalem apostles] have the weight to overwhelm it."

The addition of the heavenly angel can perhaps best be explained as an intensification (an argument *a minori ad maius*, from the lesser to the greater). If it is excluded that Paul would ever have changed his tune, a fortiori it is even more unlikely (i.e., absolutely impossible) that an angel from heaven, speaking directly for God, would have done so. In view of 4:14 (cited above), the angel in this verse may contain a hidden reference to Paul: this reference to an angel from heaven could be simply another way of referring to himself in the eyes of the Galatians; he was for them (tantamount to) "an angel of God."

Whatever the reason for the mention of the angel, purely for the sake of argument Paul posits an event that he knows could never happen and in fact is

The Letter Opening

not happening, that he or an angel from heaven is preaching a gospel like the one being preached by the new missionaries in Galatia. If that were the case, a curse would have to be called down even on Paul himself or on that heavenly angel. The completely hypothetical curse of v. 8 thus adds tremendous rhetorical weight to the very real curse called down on the new preachers in v. 9. Paul's rhetorical aim is probably not only to alienate the Galatians from the new preachers, but also to bring the Galatians to ban them from their churches (Betz 54; Dunn 46–47; cf. 4:30 and comment there).

The preface to the conditional sentence anathematizing the new preachers in Galatia in v. 9 is curious, however: "As we have said to you before [*proeirēkamen*] and I now say again" (1:9a). There are two interrelated issues here: (1) Why does Paul say "we" and then "I"? (2) What is the import of "We have said to you before"? Paul's words seem to imply that he and his coworkers said something of the sort on a previous occasion, probably at the founding of the churches in Galatia (cf. 5:3, 21). Paul himself solemnly "now" says "again" what "we" have said "before." That would explain the first-person plural at the beginning and the subsequent switch to the first-person singular. At first sight it may seem implausible to think that Paul on his first (or second) visit to Galatia would take taken such extreme prophylactic measures, using a solemn cursing formula as well (so Häfner 103), but not if we assume that the Galatian churches were founded by Paul after his traumatic break (2:10–14) with the church at Antioch (Dunn 47; Bachmann). Paul evidently anticipated that the problem might occur, which explains his current consternation with the Galatians, who despite his precautionary steps are nevertheless in the process of succumbing to the "different gospel." The eventful break with Antioch (and Peter and Barnabas) would also explain the vehemence of his reaction to the presence of the new teachers in Galatia. This interpretation of the introduction of v. 9a further explains why the content and the wording of the imprecation in v. 9 do not precisely match those of v. 8; they match instead (more or less) the content and wording of Paul's previous teaching. That teaching is repeated in v. 9 for the situation in Galatia at the present moment.

In the given sequence the two imprecations of vv. 8 and 9 constitute an argument from the greater to the lesser (the reverse thus of the common *a minori ad maius* argument): If Paul or an angel from heaven would be an anathema if either one was now preaching a gospel contrary to the one Paul actually did preach (and neither he nor such an angel is now preaching such a gospel), how much more is someone else an anathema who at this very moment is preaching a gospel contrary to the one the Galatians did receive![63]

---

63. Cf. Luther (1535: 55), who observes that "clever debaters usually begin by criticizing themselves, in order that then they may be able to reprove others more freely and more severely."

Excursus 4: The New Preachers and Their Gospel

Galatians 1:6–9 indicates that Paul's Letter to the Galatians was not written in a historical vacuum[64] and that the identity of the new preachers active in Galatia, the content of their gospel, their aims in preaching this gospel, and their impact on the Galatians cannot be ignored in the interpretation of the letter: Paul's letter was written primarily to refute the gospel of the new preachers, to break their hold on the Galatian churches, and thus to bring the Galatians back to their (theological) senses (cf. 3:1–5). At this point it therefore will be useful to gather the pertinent information from the remainder of the letter in one place. Does it present a coherent and historically plausible picture of the new preachers, their gospel, their aims, and their impact on the Galatians?

In Gal 1:6–9, as we have seen in the commentary above, Paul expresses his astonishment that the churches of Galatia (1:2b) are in the process of turning to "a different gospel." This different gospel is attributed to certain people who, according to Paul, "are unnerving" the Galatians and "wanting to turn the gospel of Christ into its opposite." Paul then anathematizes someone who "is preaching a gospel contrary to" the one the Galatians "received," which is the gospel "we [Paul] did preach" to the Galatians (1:8–9). From this information and making allowances for Paul's rhetorically and polemically motivated formulations, we have drawn certain conclusions in the commentary above about the people he refers to:

1. They have come into the Galatian churches from outside. Paul clearly distinguishes those unnerving the Galatians ("some") from the Galatians themselves ("you"). This does not in itself mean that they are strangers to the cities or villages in which the Galatians themselves live (see further below). It does at least mean that they are not members of these churches.

2. Those supposedly unnerving the Galatians have come on the scene after Paul had founded the churches of Galatia: Paul here anathematizes someone (*tis*)[65] who "is [now] preaching a gospel" (*euangelizetai*, pres. ind., v. 9) contrary to the one the Galatians "received" (*parelabete*, aor. ind., v. 9), which is the one "we preached" (*euēngelisametha*, aor. ind., v. 8; cf. 1:11; 4:13).

3. As the previous point already indicates, the people supposedly unnerving the Galatians are preaching what they call "a gospel" (*euangelion*). Paul would hardly want to call their message "gospel" unless they themselves are designating it as such (Martyn 109; 1997: 13; *pace* Nanos 2002a: 142).

4. Furthermore, it is "a different gospel" (*heteron euangelion*), different in kind from the one Paul has preached to them. This gospel has to be considerably different from Paul's own; Paul's expressed consternation in this passage and the petition to let the new preachers be an anathema in God's eyes would otherwise be difficult to explain.

From these four points, we have concluded that the people Paul refers to in 1:6–9 are Christian preachers who have come into the Galatian churches founded by Paul with a version of "the gospel of Christ" different from Paul's own. We have accord-

---

64. See de Boer 2008 for an earlier version of this excursus. In addition to the standard commentaries, see also Martyn 1997: 7–24; Barclay 1987; 1988: 36–74; Sanders 1983: 17–29; Bruce 1971.

65. The singular is probably generic (representative), though Paul may have a leader of the group in view. See below on 3:1; 5:7, 10b.

The Letter Opening

ingly labeled them "the new preachers."[66] Two further conclusions have, however, been drawn from 1:6–9:

5. The new preachers are indeed "unnerving" the Galatians. Paul is not here simply vilifying the new preachers, or making false and slanderous accusations. His Galatian readers are in a position to corroborate this charge about the impact of the new preachers on the Galatians. Paul has undoubtedly learned of the deleterious impact of the new preachers on the Galatians from sources loyal to him in the churches of Galatia. There is something about the gospel of the new preachers that the Galatians find to be truly unnerving. It is causing them considerable mental distress.

6. The reason is that the new preachers are indeed wanting to substitute their version of the gospel for Paul's. Paul formulates their agenda in a polemical manner: they are "wanting to turn the gospel of Christ into its opposite." Paul's formulation entails a theological evaluation of their version of the gospel of Christ from the vantage point of his own understanding of that gospel. The gospel according to Paul is focused on "the grace of Christ" (cf. 1:15; 2:21), whereby the blessings of salvation are unconditionally given. By implication, the opposite of this gospel is one in which grace (as Paul understands it) plays no role and the blessings of salvation are made conditional. A conditional gospel is one that in Paul's view turns the gospel of Christ on its head so that it can no longer be called "gospel": it is no longer good news. The new preachers may well be arguing that it is actually Paul who has turned the gospel on its head and that they have come to set the gospel of Christ back on its feet. The new preachers probably then agree with Paul's implicit point: their gospel is the diametric opposite of his. However that may be, it is highly probable that the new preachers want to replace Paul's (version of the) gospel of Christ with their own (version).[67]

The six points above have been drawn exclusively from Gal 1:6–9 (in addition to the prescript, which explicitly names "the churches of Galatia") without reference to the remainder of the letter, to which we may now turn for further information. Much of the remainder (apart from 1:11–2:14 and 5:13–6:10) seeks to show on substantive theological grounds why the different gospel of the new preachers turns the gospel of Christ into its opposite and thus is not the (true and only) gospel of Christ. In the process, Paul directly and indirectly reveals much about the new preachers and their "different gospel." In this excursus, however, we confine ourselves to the verses in which Paul explicitly mentions the new preachers in order to provide a basic sketch of their identity, message, aims, and impact. We shall first briefly survey the relevant passages,

---

66. We could also call them "the new missionaries" or "the new evangelists," and sometimes will. "Evangelist" here means a preacher of the gospel (a message containing good news), not the author of a Gospel (a book narrating the ministry and passion of Jesus as good news, such as the four canonical Gospels).

67. It is thus possible to describe the new preachers from Paul's viewpoint as "the opponents" (e.g., Betz; Dunn), an epithet they could agree with since they do want to replace Paul's gospel with their own in Galatia, or from the Galatians' point of view as "the agitators" (Barclay 1988), or (following our translation of *hoi tarassontes* in 1:7) "the unnervers." We here describe them, following Martyn's lead (1997: 13), in terms of their primary activity: preachers who have recently come into the Galatian churches with a message they called "the gospel of Christ." Martyn himself prefers to call them "the Teachers."

interrogating them initially without reference to the contexts in which they occur and thus rather atomistically.[68] In a later step, we shall survey them again, this time with reference to the larger literary and argumentative contexts while also taking into account the other verses surveyed.

In providing a sketch we want to avoid two extremes: One extreme is to maintain that everything Paul says and writes about the new preachers is factual and unaffected by rhetorical or polemical aims. One of Paul's aims in this letter is to alienate the Galatians from the new preachers and their gospel. That Paul is not a neutral observer is obvious from Gal 1:6–9 (see above). The second extreme is to claim that everything Paul says about the new preachers in Galatia contains so much rhetorical and polemical distortion that no hard ("neutral") information about them can be gleaned from the text of Galatians. It is implausible, however, to maintain that Paul does not, at least along the way, pass on factual information about the new preachers (see the comments on 1:6–9 above). Paul is rhetorically constrained by the familiarity of his audience with the new preachers and their gospel. He cannot just make it all up as he goes. His words have to make contact with the experience and the knowledge of the Galatians if he is to accomplish his aims, if the letter is to serve as a vehicle of communication from him to the Galatians.

Beyond these two extremes, there is also a third option, to maintain that Paul has misunderstood the situation in Galatia or has been misinformed (cf. Schmithals). Hypotheses based on this option run the risk of claiming to understand the new preachers better than Paul or his informants, which is problematic since there is no other firsthand information about the situation in Galatia apart from Paul's own letter. Such hypotheses may also be irrelevant for the interpretation of the letter: In any event, Paul responds to the situation in Galatia as he perceives and presents that situation.[69] Resort to this option commends itself only if the information Paul provides in his letter lacks both internal coherence and historical plausibility.

Evidence in 3:1. "O unthinking Galatians! Who has bewitched you [*tis hymas ebaskanen*], before whose eyes Jesus Christ was portrayed as crucified?" The singular *tis* (here the interrogative pronoun "who?") is probably generic, as is the *tis* (the indefinite pronoun "someone") in 1:9, though Paul may perhaps have a leader of the new preachers in view. Paul characterizes the Galatians as "unthinking" because they have been "bewitched" by the new preachers. The language here is probably metaphorical and hyperbolic (see comment on 3:1). Paul perceives that the Galatians have, as even we might metaphorically say without thereby affirming a literalistic belief in magic or demons, "fallen under the spell" of the new preachers and their gospel. In his view, by turning from the one who has called them to a different gospel, they are no longer in their right minds. Paul thus ruefully acknowledges that the different gospel comes across as a plausible and attractive alternative to his own, perhaps also that its proponents are effective preachers of this gospel in that they have brought the Galatians to the point of adopting their views. Further to be noted is that Paul addresses his readers as "Galatians," which he could scarcely do in this context if the new preachers were also native

---

68. The exegetical justification for the translations and interpretations offered may be found in the various comments on the relevant passages later in the commentary.

69. It makes a difference for the reconstruction of the history of early Christianity, but that is not the concern of this commentary.

The Letter Opening

to the area (see comment on 1:2b). The new preachers are thus missionaries who come from outside the region of Galatia.

Evidence in 4:17. "They zealously court you but not in a good way; rather, they want to shut you out, so that you might zealously court them." Paul's comment on the new preachers, who remain unnamed and indeed unmentioned except as part of the verb *zēlousin* ("they court zealously"), is clearly designed to discredit them. If we "de-rhetorize" Paul's language (Thurén), two observations may be pertinent about the new preachers and their gospel: (1) The new preachers take a serious interest in the Galatians and in their salvation. They have a gospel to preach and want the Galatians to know its benefits. They would not have come to the Galatian churches if that were not so. (2) According to Paul, the new preachers in Galatia "want to shut" the Galatians "out" if they do not accept their version of the gospel. The new preachers present themselves (Paul claims) as gatekeepers, preventing entry into the realm of salvation and the benefits thereof unless their gospel is followed.

Evidence in 5:7. "You were running well. Who [*tis*] hindered you from being obedient to the truth?" This verse begins a discrete literary unit that ends at v. 12. Paul mentions the new preachers explicitly three times (in 5:7; 5:10b, 12).[70] If we leave Paul's own views and rhetoric aside, this verse confirms that the new preachers are interlopers. The Galatians started out with Paul's (version of the) gospel; once on their way, they were confronted with a different one.

Evidence in 5:10b. "He who is unnerving you will bear the judgment, whoever he may be." Paul uses the same verb (*tarassō*) that he used in 1:6: "those who are unnerving you." The singular (he) is probably generic, though once again he may be referring to the leader of the group (see above on 1:9; 3:1; 5:7).

Evidence in 5:12. "Would that those who are upsetting you also practice castration!"[71] Important for our purposes here is the characterization of the new preachers as "those who are upsetting you" (*hoi anastatountes hymas*). The verb used is a virtual synonym of the one used in 1:6 and 5:10b and thus adds nothing new. The repeated attention paid to the negative impact of the new preachers on the Galatians (1:6; 5:10b, 12) is noteworthy, however.

Evidence in 6:12–13. "Those who are wanting to make a good showing in the flesh, these are putting pressure on you to practice circumcision, only in order that they not be persecuted for the cross of Christ. For not even those who practice circumcision themselves keep the law, but they are wanting you to practice circumcision in order that they may boast in your flesh." Taking into account Paul's rhetorically and polemically motivated formulations, we may discern four items of hard information about the new preachers; all four concern the practice of circumcision:

1. The new preachers (and the community/ies from which they come) are identified as "those who practice circumcision," meaning "the circumcisers" (*hoi peritemnomenoi*).[72]

---

70. On the use of the singular *tis*, see above on 3:1.
71. For this translation and its implications, see the comment on 5:12.
72. The present tense gives the correct reading, not the perfect (*hoi peritetēmenoi*); see comment on 6:13. For the translation of *peritemnesthai* as "to practice circumcision" (present middle) instead of as "to be circumcised" or "to receive circumcision" (present passive), see the comments on 5:2–3 and 6:12–13.

The new preachers (and the community/ies from which they originate) themselves practice circumcision. They are thus Jews as well as Christians, since circumcision was the crucial identifying mark of Jews in the Greco-Roman world (cf. Tacitus, *Hist.* 5.5.2: "They adopted circumcision to distinguish themselves from other peoples by this difference"; Josephus, *Ant.* 1.192).[73]

2. The circumcisers are concerned about "keeping [*phylassousin*] the law." (Paul insinuates that they do not practice what they preach). The law in question is the law given to Moses on Mount Sinai (cf. 3:17, 19; 4:25) and preserved in the Pentateuch, where the command to practice circumcision originates (Gen 17:9–14). Circumcision is thus part of something greater, the Mosaic law.

3. The circumcisers "are wanting you to practice circumcision" (*thelousin hymas peritemnesthai*). They want the Galatians to practice circumcision despite the fact that they (the Galatians) are already believers in Christ.

4. "These [people] are putting pressure on you to practice circumcision" (*houtoi anankazousin hymas peritemnesthai*).[74] The new preachers are not satisfied merely with expressing what they desire the Galatians to do, leaving it up to them to follow their instructions as they see fit. They are also putting pressure on them to proceed to the practice of circumcision.[75]

Paul divulges this information in the closing passage of the epistle, a paragraph he has added in his own hand (6:11). It is the clearest indication of the identity of the new preachers and of their gospel. This gospel involves the practice of circumcision as an essential element; the practice of circumcision is in turn linked to "keeping the law."[76]

With the information gleaned from 6:12–13, the other passages in which the new preachers are mentioned fall into place, and a relatively coherent picture of their identity, message, aims, and impact emerges. We survey the passages again, this time in reverse order and with attention also to the larger literary and argumentative context.

Context for 5:12. Paul's wish that the new preachers unsettling the Galatians "practice castration" thinly disguises a reference to their desire that the Galatians now begin practicing circumcision. (He recommends that they take the knife used for circumcision and go a step further.) Indeed, Paul explicitly mentions circumcision in the previ-

---

73. "Those who practice circumcision" could in theory refer to Gentile Christians in Galatia who had adopted the practice, but that is unlikely given the syntax of 6:13, which demands that "those who practice circumcision" are also those who "are wanting you [the Gentile Galatians] to practice circumcision."

74. For this reason, the new preachers have traditionally been labeled "Judaizers," though that is a misnomer, since the Greek verb "to Judaize," *ioudaïzein* (used by Paul in Gal 2:14), means "to live in a Jewish manner," not "to put pressure on others to live in Jewish manner." Gentile Galatians adopting circumcision could hence accurately be labeled Judaizers; see comment on 2:14.

75. The nature of this pressure is not explained, but see on 4:17 above.

76. Difficult to evaluate are Paul's seemingly hyperbolic accusations in 6:12–13 that the new preachers want to make a good showing in the flesh, that they avoid persecution for the cross of Christ, that they themselves do not keep the law, and that their real goal is to boast in the Galatians' (circumcised) flesh. The accusations are clearly designed to put the new preachers in a bad light. On the possibility that these accusations nevertheless provide clues to the deeper motivations of the new preachers for their activities in Galatia, see Jewett 2002 and the comment on 6:12–13.

ous verse. The new preachers have evidently told the Galatians that Paul himself "still proclaims circumcision" (*peritomēn eti kēryssō*, v. 11), a charge he indignantly denies.

Context for 5:10b. This half verse precedes Paul's reference to proclaiming circumcision in 5:11. The new preachers are "unnerving" the Galatians probably because they are telling them that they must practice circumcision (and thus that Paul's gospel is to be abandoned).

Context for 5:7. The new preachers have placed an obstacle in the race that the Galatians were running. That obstacle is circumcision. Here we cannot ignore that 5:7 comes on the heels of a passage in which Paul urgently points to the danger to which the new preachers have exposed the Galatians: "Look, I, Paul, say to you that if you were to practice circumcision [*peritemnēsthe*, pres. mid. subj.], Christ will avail you nothing. I again testify to everyone practicing circumcision [*panti anthrōpō peritemnomenō*, pres. mid. ptc.] that he [or she][77] is someone obligated to do the whole law (*holon ton nomon poiēsai*). You have become separated from Christ, you who are seeking to be justified [*dikaiousthe*] in the law; you have fallen from grace" (5:2–4).

It is clear that the crucial issue is "practicing circumcision." Will the Galatians practice circumcision as the new preachers want them to? The information about the new preachers and their intentions divulged in 6:12–13 is here being presupposed. In 5:2–4, as in 6:13, Paul indirectly indicates that the new preachers presume a link between the practice of circumcision and the observance of "the (whole) law" ("doing the law" in 5:3 means essentially the same thing as "keeping the law" in 6:13). The practice of circumcision, they are telling the Galatians, obligates the practitioner also "to do" (*poiēsai*) the (remainder of the) law.[78] For this reason, presumably, Paul in 4:21 characterizes the Galatians who are contemplating practicing circumcision as "those who are wanting to be under the law." By embracing the gospel of the new preachers, the Galatians are "seeking to be justified in (the sphere of) the law." This descriptive comment is shared

---

77. It may seem ridiculous to add "or she" here, since the circumcision in view involves the penis. But the issue is "practicing circumcision," and that is a community matter, one in which the women members would also have a say as mothers of infant (and older) sons who need to be presented for circumcision (see Exod 4:25 where Zipporah, Moses' wife, circumcises their son). As soon as the boys and the men in the Galatian churches allow themselves to be circumcised, the practice will become both a family and a community concern: Henceforth parents will together present their infant sons on the eighth day (Gen 17:12) for the rite. Both parents, the mother as well as the father, will thereby acknowledge the importance of the rite for belonging to the Jewish community with its commitment to doing the law. In that sense, they will all be "practicing circumcision."

78. At first sight Gal 5:3 seems to indicate that Paul is newly informing the Galatians about the link between the practice of circumcision and the observance of the whole (Mosaic) law. In 6:13, however, Paul charges that "those who practice circumcision [the new preachers] do not themselves keep the law," which seems to imply that the new preachers believe that circumcision and law observance go hand in hand (in Paul's view, they fail to live up to what they believe). In 5:3, Paul emphasizes the "*whole*" law, to underscore the far-reaching consequences of beginning with circumcision. The new preachers undoubtedly believe that the practice of circumcision obligates the practitioners to do "the [undivided] law" (just like the Christian Jews in Acts 15:5), but they do not present this obligation as a terrible burden as Paul now does (a "yoke of slavery," according to 5:1). See comment on 5:3.

ground between Paul and the Galatians: in other words, the Galatians agree with this statement. The striving of the Galatians for justification almost certainly reflects the influence of the new preachers. For the new preachers, to begin practicing circumcision is to make a commitment "to do" the Mosaic law, with the aim of "being justified [by God] in the law" (5:4).

Context for 4:17. Paul's comment comes after he has described his founding of the Galatian churches and the good relationship he had with them. The new preachers have disturbed this situation profoundly and threatened that relationship. According to Paul, they "want to shut [the Galatians] out." From this charge it can reasonably be concluded that the new preachers are putting considerable pressure on the Galatians to embrace their gospel, an inference confirmed by 6:12–13 (see above). On a theological level, they are probably exerting such pressure by telling the Galatians that apart from law observance, they are excluded from membership in God's people, the descendants of Abraham (cf. 3:7, 29). Without the law, they are saying, the Galatians fall under the curse of Deut 27:26 (3:10; cf. Martyn 30), whereby they are effectively excluded from "the blessing of Abraham" (cf. 3:14). On a social level, the new preachers may be exerting such pressure by literally excluding the Galatians from their table fellowship, including the Lord's Supper (cf. Barclay 1988: 59). The combination of theological and social exclusion would help to explain why the Galatians have become "unnerved" by the new preachers (1:7).[79]

Context for 3:1. The Galatians have fallen under the spell of the new preachers, even though Paul had proclaimed Christ crucified to them (3:1), which for him sums up "the gospel of Christ" (1:7). Paul poses a pertinent question to the unthinking Galatians in the following verse: "This only I wish to learn from you: Did you receive the Spirit on the basis of works of the law or on the basis of what was heard of faith?" (3:2). The answer is as plain to the Galatians as it is to Paul: "works of the law," doing (the commandments of) the law, had nothing to do with their reception of the Spirit (cf. 3:5). Circumcision is undoubtedly covered by the broader expression "works of the law" (cf. 2:16; 3:5, 10), since the next verse contains a probable allusion to this fleshly rite: "Are you so unthinking, having begun with the Spirit, are you now ending up with the flesh?" (3:3; cf. the use of the term "flesh" in 6:12–13 above).[80] It is evident from the context that the new preachers are telling the Gentile Christians in Galatia that the reception of the Spirit is conditional upon doing the law, beginning with circumcision (cf. Sanders 1983: 19).[81]

---

79. The theological exclusion of the Galatians would reinforce the social exclusion, and vice versa.

80. For Paul, the term "flesh" here may also be a reference to the fearsome cosmic power he calls "the Flesh" in 5:13–26, where that power stands opposed to the Spirit. Paul would then be implying that the Galatians, by taking up fleshly circumcision, will leave the realm of the Spirit and end up in that of the Flesh. See comment on 3:3.

81. Given the rhetorical question in 3:3, it is for some interpreters conceivable "that Paul's missionary efforts were taken as merely the first step, and that the opponents claimed to provide the necessary and final measures to bring salvation to completion and perfection" (Betz 136). This line of interpretation takes the verb *epiteleisthe* in 3:3 to mean not "ending up with" but "a perfecting or completing of what was already there" (Jewett 2002: 342). There are two significant problems

The Letter Opening

It is but a short step back from 3:1–5, with its twofold mention of "works of the law," to 2:15–16, where Paul claims that "we Jews by birth, . . . we too came to believe in Jesus Christ, so that we might be justified on the basis of the faith of Christ and not on the basis of works of the law." The new preachers, themselves Jews by birth, have surely come to believe in Christ Jesus, just as Paul, but they do not share Paul's view that a believer is justified (2:16), or receives the gift of the Spirit (3:2, 5), apart from "works of the law." The practice of the rite of circumcision is thus part of a wider issue in Galatia, whether believing in Christ can and ought to be supplemented by the observance of the law. The new preachers are convinced that believing in Christ can be, in fact must be, combined with doing the law.

To support their case, the new preachers are undoubtedly appealing to the Scripture of the Jews, in particular to Gen 17:9–14, where God requires Abraham and his descendants to keep his covenant with them by practicing male circumcision. From v. 10 the passage is directed to the descendants of Abraham, among whom the new preachers surely count themselves. The second-person pronoun "you" changes almost imperceptibly from singular to plural forms in that verse (the plural forms have been italicized):[82]

> And God said to Abraam, "You shall keep my covenant, you and your seed after you for their generations. ¹⁰And this is the covenant that you shall keep between me and *you*, and between your seed after you for their generations; every male of *you* shall be circumcised. ¹¹And *you* shall be circumcised in the flesh of *your* foreskin, and it shall be for a sign of a covenant between me and *you*. ¹²And a child of eight days shall be circumcised by *you*. Every male throughout *your* generations. . . . ¹³shall surely be circumcised, . . . and my covenant shall be on *your* flesh for an everlasting covenant. ¹⁴And an uncircumcised male who will not be circumcised in the flesh of his foreskin on the eighth day, that person shall be utterly destroyed from his nation, for he has rejected my covenant."(Gen 17:9–14 LXX)

That the new preachers appeal to Gen 17:9–14 and the covenant of circumcision with Abraham can be deduced from the fact that in a long section of the letter (3:6–29), Paul addresses a crucial question: Who are the true offspring of Abraham? The answer of the

---

with this line of interpretation: (1) It presupposes that the new preachers see no necessary link between the gift or reception of the Spirit and the observance of the law (their position would then be that the Galatians already have the Spirit; they now also need the law). The rhetorical question in 3:2 presupposes, however, that the new preachers see the former to be entirely dependent on the latter. (2) It implies that Paul acknowledges circumcision to produce or lead to the perfection promised by the new preachers. One way to avoid this implication is to regard the question as ironic, even sarcastic (Martyn 289, among others). This is possible, but the other rendering of the verb in question ("ending up with," as the complement to "beginning with"; cf. Phil 1:6; 2 Cor 8:6) is more plausible, since the question is then straightforward and makes good sense: The Galatians started off on the right road; they now are in danger of ending up at the wrong destination. See also Barclay 1988: 39, 49.

82. The new preachers are probably quoting the LXX to the Greek-speaking Galatians (as Paul does in the letter). Hence the following translation is based on the LXX text.

new preachers was undoubtedly: those who practice circumcision, thereby obligating themselves to do "the (remaining) works of the law" (3:2, 5, 10).[83]

Is the information gleaned from text of Galatians about the new preachers and the importance they attach to circumcision historically plausible? The search for an answer to that question demands that we survey texts that seem to provide parallels to this information.

A partial parallel to the Galatian situation (Barclay 1988: 55–56) is provided by the story of Izates, king of Adiabene, told by the Jewish historian Josephus, whose life and career overlapped with those of Paul. Izates contemplates being circumcised and becoming a Jew but hesitates to take this step. He is even told by a Jew named Ananias that he could worship the God of Israel without being circumcised. But he was subsequently challenged by another Jew named Eleazar to do what the law commanded:

> For when he [Eleazar] came to him [Izates] to pay him his respects and found him reading the Law of Moses, he said: "In your ignorance, O king, you are guilty of the greatest offence against the Law and thereby against God. For you ought not merely to read the Law but also, and even more, to do [*poiein*] what is commanded in it. How long will you continue to be uncircumcised? If you have not yet read the Law concerning this matter [presumably Gen 17:9–14 is in view], read it now, so that you may know what an impiety it is you commit." (*Ant.* 20.44–45)

Izates subsequently agrees to take the required step.

More pertinent perhaps, if somewhat later, is the Justin Martyr's *Dialogue with Trypho* (Talbert 5). When Justin, a Gentile, has told Trypho, a Jew, of his conversion to Christ, Trypho tells him that this means nothing unless he becomes circumcised and then commits himself to observing the law: "If, then, you are willing to listen to me, . . . first be circumcised, then observe what ordinances have been enacted with respect to the Sabbath, and the feasts, and the new moons of God; and, in a word, do all things which have been written in the law: and then perhaps you shall obtain mercy from God" (*Dial.* 8; trans. in *ANF* 1:198–99).[84]

The dialogue partner of Justin is a Jew, not a Christian Jew, however. Is there evidence outside of Galatians for Christian Jews with an approach to Gentiles similar to that of the new preachers in Galatia? Acts, whose account often contradicts or deviates from that found in Paul's own letters, confirms the plausibility of the picture drawn in Galatians. According to Acts 15:1 (cited above in the comment on 1:6–7), "Some people came down from Judea [to Antioch] and were teaching the brethren, 'Unless you are circumcised according to the custom of Moses, you cannot be saved'" (RSV). This turn of events eventually leads to the so-called apostolic council (15:6–22) in Jerusalem, at which

---

83. See Barclay (1988: 54–56) for other texts, many closer to the time of Paul, as unambiguous as Gen 17:9–14 itself is. "Armed with such unambiguous texts," Barclay writes (53), "the agitators could readily demonstrate that, to share in the Abrahamic covenant and the Abrahamic blessing (Gen 12:3; 18:18; etc.), the Galatians needed to be circumcised; indeed such was the command of God in their Scriptures."

84. Cf. Jas 2:10; 4 Macc 5:20–21; 1QS 1.13–18; *m. ʾAbot* 2:1; 4:2 (more texts in Longenecker 227).

Paul and Barnabas also take part. At the conclusion of this meeting, "the apostles and the elders" in Jerusalem write an official letter to the church in Antioch, and in that letter they report that "some persons from us have unnerved you (*etaraxan hymas*) with words, unsettling your minds" (15:24 RSV, alt.). As noted above, the verb used here is *tarassō*, "unnerve," the verb that Paul uses in Gal 1:7 and 5:10b. The situation presupposed in Acts 15 is analogous to the one presupposed in Gal 1:7 and 5:10b: Some persons (*tines*) have come into the church in Antioch from elsewhere (Jerusalem) and "have unnerved" (*tarassō*) the Gentile members with the message that they must practice circumcision in order to be saved. Accepting Jesus as Messiah is not enough. Furthermore, before the meeting actually gets underway, certain believers (described as coming from the Pharisaic party) make their position plain to both the delegation from Antioch and the leaders of the Jerusalem church: "It is necessary [1] to circumcise them [Gentile believers], *and* [2] to charge them to keep the law of Moses" (15:5 RSV; cf. Gal 5:3; 6:13).

Other passages in Acts also indicate that a mission to Gentiles without requiring circumcision and law observance caused resistance among Christian Jews in Judea (10:1–11:18, esp. 10:28, 45–47; 11:2–3, 18), particularly in connection with the work of Paul (21:20–22). Noteworthy are two passages: (1) Acts 10:44–45 recounts the amazement of circumcised believers that Gentiles receive the gift of the Spirit simply by "hearing the word," the message about Christ (as in Gal 3:2, 5); circumcision and law observance do not enter into the equation, much to their surprise (Acts 11:17–18). (2) Acts 21:20–21 refers to Christian Jews who are "all zealous for the law" and who have heard that Paul has been teaching "all the Jews who are among the Gentiles to forsake Moses, telling them not to circumcise their children or observe the customs" (RSV). The author of Acts himself wants to allay this charge and, as the Letter to the Galatians shows, Paul was telling Jews no such thing; rather, he was telling *Gentiles* that they did not need to circumcise or observe the law. In any event, Acts preserves a tradition about some Christian Jews who were zealous for the law and also extremely suspicious of Paul, of his views on the law in connection with his missionary activities among the Gentiles. Paul himself in the Letter to the Galatians points to the resistance of certain Christian Jews in Jerusalem (he labels them "false brethren") to his circumcision-free gospel and his missionary efforts among Gentiles (Gal 2:4).[85]

In the case of the Galatian churches, to be sure, we are dealing with what appears to be an active mission to Gentiles by Christian Jews with a gospel different from Paul's, a mission beyond the bounds of Judea (see Martyn 1997: 7–24), something of which Acts seems to know little or nothing (cf. Acts 8:1–40; 11:19–26). In Acts, the opponents of Paul in the cities of the Greco-Roman world are Jews, not Christian Jews. In this striking difference, we must give priority to the information contained in Paul's Letters since these letters represent the primary evidence for the course of events in the 50s of the first century.[86] Paul's Letter to the Philippians and his Second to the Corinthians

---

85. The later *Pseudo-Clementine* literature (containing *The Ascents of James* and *The Preachings of Peter*) preserves a fierce polemic against Paul by Christian Jews. For the relevant texts, see Betz 331–33; for discussion and application, see Martyn 117–26; 1997: 9–24.

86. Where the information of Acts diverges from that found in the Letters of Paul, the latter must always be given priority. Acts can thus be used only to confirm information derived from Paul's Letters, not to disconfirm such information. See Knox 19.

also indicate that there were Christian-Jewish missionaries who resisted Paul's efforts among the Gentiles in other places, although it is not certain that the Christian Jewish missionaries in Galatia, Philippi, and Corinth all had the same views about the relation between the observance of the law (or circumcision) and believing in Christ.[87] Paul's picture of the new preachers contains some distinctive features, but the picture nevertheless remains historically plausible.

The foregoing survey and analysis of the primary evidence (passages in Galatians in which Paul explicitly mentions the new preachers, and parallel texts) indicate that the information Paul divulges about the new preachers is internally coherent and historically plausible. That information enables us to give the following brief sketch of the new preachers, their identity, message, aims, and impact.

1. *Their identity.* The new preachers are Christian Jews who preach the gospel to Gentiles.[88] They are missionaries who have come from elsewhere. Where are they from? That is difficult to say with any certainty, though Gal 1:11–2:14 indicates that they probably have some relation to the church in Jerusalem and believe themselves to represent its views concerning a mission to the Gentiles (see comments on 1:11–2:14; 4:21–5:1).[89]

2. *Their gospel.* For the Gentile Christians in Galatia, the gospel of the new preachers amounts to the following: "You believe in Christ—fine; but you must now also observe the law, beginning with the rite of circumcision."[90] In normal circumstances, in their own mission to Gentiles who have not (in their view) been misled by Paul, the new preachers probably reverse the order of Christ and the law: "First observe the law, beginning with the rite of circumcision, and you may then also believe in Jesus." The assumption behind both summaries of their gospel is that a Gentile must first be

---

87. On this matter, 2 Cor 11:4 does bear some striking similarities to Gal 1:6–9; 3:1–5: "For if some one comes and preaches another Jesus [*allon Iēsoun*] than the one we preached, or if you receive a different spirit from the one you received, or if you accept a different gospel [*euangelion heteron*] from the one you accepted, you submit to it readily enough" (RSV). See also 2 Cor 11:22–23: "Are they Hebrews? So am I. Are they Israelites? So am I. Are they descendants of Abraham [cf. Gal 3:6–9, 29]? So am I. Are they servants of Christ? I am a better one" (RSV). See Phil 3:2, with its wordplay allusion to circumcision (*peritomē*) and those (Christian Jews) who promote the practice: "Beware of the dogs, beware of the evil workers, beware of those who mutilate [*katatomē*] the flesh."

88. They are Christian Jews, not Jewish Christians (for the distinction, see Martyn 1997: 9–24). Christian Jews and Jewish Christians have in common that they were both born into the Jewish community and its religion. For Christian Jews, however, circumcision remains of central importance (Gal 5:2–3; 6:12–13); for Jewish Christians, such as Paul, it has become a matter of indifference (see Gal 5:6; 6:15).

89. There is no good reason to think that those unnerving the Galatians were gnostics (Schmithals), a group of Paul's own Gentile converts (Munck), or local synagogue Jews (Nanos 2002a; Walker 2003a), or that there was a double front in Galatians (Lütgert; Ropes). For these theories, see especially the surveys provided by Bruce 1971 and Barclay 1988.

90. This conclusion has a long history. Already in the second century, the Marcionite Prologue to the Letter to the Galatians (preserved in Latin translations of the original Greek) gives a similar assessment: "The Galatians are Greeks. They at first received the word of truth from the apostle, but after his departure they were tempted by false apostles to turn to the law and circumcision" (quoted from Bruce 1971: 254).

The Letter Opening   61

incorporated into the covenant people of Israel in order to receive the benefits of salvation made available through Christ. For this reason, the new preachers are not content with merely completing Paul's gospel: they are determined to replace it (see comment on 1:6–9). In their view, the Galatians cannot obtain the benefits of faith in Christ apart from the observance of the law. Christ is here subordinate to the law, rather than (as for Paul) the other way around.[91] The benefits of salvation for the new preachers can be summed up by the word "justification," a cornerstone of their gospel (2:16, 21; 3:6, 8; 5:4). What does justification mean and entail for the new preachers? I shall propose an answer in the comment on 2:16.[92]

3. *Their aims.* The new preachers in Galatia want the Galatians to begin practicing circumcision and then to observe the Mosaic law, thereby becoming members of the people of Israel. That aim also involves another, to substitute their (version of the) gospel for Paul's. To accomplish the latter, they also seek to discredit Paul and his apostleship (see the comment on 1:1).

4. *Their impact.* The new preachers are effective missionaries, since the Galatians are in the process of embracing their gospel (1:6; 3:1; 4:10, 21). The Galatians have evidently fallen under their spell (3:1), which may explain why they would even consider undertaking the practice of circumcision, no small step for an adult man especially in antiquity (no anesthesia, the high risk of infection, social derision).[93] The new preachers are telling the Galatians that unless they begin practicing circumcision, they cannot partake of Christ's benefits, cannot receive justification.[94] In their gospel, justification is thus entirely conditional on doing the law. By putting considerable pressure on the Galatians to begin the practice of circumcision and to observe the (remaining commandments of the) law, the new preachers have succeeded in deeply "unnerving" (1:6; 5:10b) and "upsetting" (5:12) the Galatians.

[10] In the last verse of the letter opening, Paul begins by posing two interrelated rhetorical questions: "So am I now persuading human beings or God? Or am I seeking to please human beings?" The conjunction "so" (*gar*) indicates that this verse belongs with v. 9 and thus with the letter opening, rather than with the letter body (so Martyn; Vouga), which begins in 1:11. This conjunction commonly expresses cause or reason ("for") and sometimes introduces

---

91. Martyn appropriately writes that "the Law is itself both the foundation and the essence of their good news" (1997: 13), and that the new preachers (as we call them) "view God's Christ in the light of God's Law, rather than the Law in the light of Christ," while avoiding "every suggestion that God's Law and God's Christ could be even partially in conflict with one another." Jesus is thus "the Messiah of the Law, deriving his identity from the fact that he confirms—and perhaps even normatively interprets—the law" (17). See further the comments on 2:15–21; 3:6–22.

92. Missing from the parallel texts cited above in support of the plausibility of the picture that Paul presupposes of the new preachers and their gospel is the theme of justification/righteousness. See, however, the comment on 2:16.

93. See Barclay (1988: 46–47) on the disdain that the practice elicited among Greco-Roman writers, though S. Elliott thinks the attitude was different in the region of Galatia.

94. Barclay (1988: 52–72) gives a thoughtful discussion of the theological and social factors that could have played a role in the new preachers' attempts to make the Galatians conform.

a clarification (cf. BDAG 189–90; BDF #452). Here it probably signals an inference (cf. Burton 31; Longenecker 18): the question in v. 10a constitutes an inference prompted by the anathema that Paul has just called down on his opponents in v. 9: Is Paul thereby in some manner trying to "persuade human beings or God"? The temporal adverb "now" (*arti*), which is the emphatic first word of v. 10 in the Greek, picks up the "now" (also *arti*) at the beginning of v. 9 and so refers back to the anathema in that verse: "So am I *now* (with the anathema just uttered) persuading human beings or God?"

Though Paul formally poses the two rhetorical questions in v. 10 to himself about his own actions and intentions, he evidently expects the Galatians to know the answers as well as he does. The answer to the second question ("Am I seeking to please human beings"?) is clearly "No," given the sentence that follows: "If I were still pleasing human beings, I would not be a slave of Christ" (v. 10c). In this contrary-to-fact conditional sentence, Paul in effect claims that he is indeed a slave of Christ and *therefore* does not spend his time "pleasing" human beings, as he once evidently did. Pleasing human beings (or trying to) is incompatible with being a slave of Christ. The verb "please" (*areskō*) has a clearly negative import in this context: it means to "flatter" or "curry favor with" (BDAG 129), to tell people what they want to hear. The answer to the first question ("Am I now persuading human beings or God?") is less than self-evident, however: Is it "neither human beings nor God" (Betz; Dunn); "human beings, not God" (Bruce; T. Martin 1995: 447; Bultmann 1968: 2); "God, not human beings" (Luther 1535; Martyn; Matera; Lyons 136–46); or even "both human beings and God"? A choice among these possibilities depends in part on the meaning of the verb "persuade" (*peithō*) in this context. Does it have a positive connotation ("appeal to, win over, seek the approval of") or a negative one ("cajole, mislead, seduce, corrupt") in this context (cf. BDAG 791; Bultmann 1968: 1), as does the verb "to please" in v. 10c?

"To persuade human beings" (*anthrōpous peithein*) is a definition of rhetoric going back to Plato (*Prot.* 352E: *peithein tous anthrōpous*; cf. *Gorg.* 452E: "to persuade the multitude," *peithein ta plēthē*), who already recognized the dubious uses to which public oratory could be put (Betz 54–55). Paul's use of the phrase "to please human beings" (*anthrōpois areskein*) reflects this negative evaluation of rhetoric, at least as frequently practiced: Users of rhetoric were commonly suspected of being people pleasers, telling their audience what it wanted to hear, often for personal gain, by using flattery, deception, and specious argumentation (cf. 1 Thess 2:4–5). Rhetoric in the form of sophistry was derided by the Platonic-Aristotelian philosophical tradition (cf. Vos 1–24), where teaching was the preferred alternative. If "pleasing human beings" has this negative connotation in v. 10bc, it seems that "persuading human beings" in v. 10a has the same negative connotation. Both mean "to curry favor" or "to tell people what they want to hear," and the like. Thus, if Paul is not "seeking to

The Letter Opening 63

please human beings" (v. 10bc), he also cannot be seeking to "persuade" them (v. 10a). Both expressions mean the same thing and have the same connotation in this context. If Paul is not seeking to "persuade human beings," he must be seeking to "persuade" God instead, or (which means the same thing) "pleasing" him, as in 1 Thess 2:4–5 where Paul contrasts pleasing God (allowed) with pleasing human beings (not allowed). The first question can be split into two: "For am I now persuading human beings? [No!] Or [am I not rather persuading] God? [Yes!]" This interpretation of v. 10a makes good sense in the larger context, being consistent with the sharp contrast between human beings and God (Martyn 139; Vouga 25) discernible in 1:1 and 1:11–12 (see comments there), and is thus to be preferred.

Since the verb "to persuade" with the term "human beings" as its direct object evidently has a decidedly negative connotation, Paul's use of this verb with God as the object is not without a strong element of paradox and irony (cf. Ridderbos 55), just as his use of the verb "to please" in 1 Thess 2:4–5 and by implication in Gal 1:10b, where the full implied answer may be "No, I do not please human beings, but God." The same element of irony and paradox counts for Paul's description of himself as "a slave of Christ" in a letter whose primary theme is freedom from slavery (5:1; cf. 1:4; 2:4; 3:13; 4:5).[95]

The question that remains is in what sense the anathema called down on the new preachers in 1:9 can count as an instance of "persuading God." The use of the same expression by the Jewish historian Josephus may provide an answer. In his account of the sack of Jerusalem by the Egyptian king Shishak (2 Chr 12), Josephus adds to the biblical account the report that "although Roboamos [Rehoboam] and the multitude, who were shut up in the city, ... entreated God to grant them victory and deliverance, they did not prevail upon God [did not persuade God, *epeisan ton theon*] to side with them" (*Ant.* 8.255). Particularly of interest is Josephus's retelling of the story of Balaam and Balak (Num 22–24): Balaam wants to erect altars and offer sacrifices so that "if possible I may be able to persuade God [*peisai ton theon*] to allow me to bind these people (the Israelites) with curses [*arais*]" (*Ant.* 4.123; cf. Num 23:13). In these two texts, the idea of "persuading God" is tantamount to a prayer or a petition; it is not a matter of rational persuasion. In v. 10a, then, it becomes clear that the imperative of 1:9, "If someone is preaching-a-gospel contrary to what you received, let that someone be an anathema" is a petition directed to God.

It nevertheless remains difficult to determine why Paul has included v. 10 in this Letter to the Galatians, especially since v. 11 actually follows rather well on v. 9. The rhetorical *function* of the verse is certainly evident: Before turning to a defense of the gospel that he preached to the Galatians (1:11–12), Paul

---

95. Paul in Gal 5:13 makes the paradox explicit ("You were called into freedom, ... but through love be slaves of one another"). See comment there.

will have established that he is to be trusted, claiming that his "persuasion" is employed to "please" not human beings, but God. What has prompted him to make such a character (*ēthos*) argument (cf. Aristotle, *Rhet.* 1.2.1356a) at this point in his letter? It could be construed as Paul's intentional employment of a standard rhetorical stratagem: It was evidently common practice for orators who do not spare their audiences for the sake of the truth (cf. Paul in 1:8–9) to distinguish themselves from those who merely flatter and please their audiences (Vos 96–98). Paul makes use of this rhetorical *topos* (standard topic) to establish his credibility as a preacher of the (true) gospel, preparing the way for the argument to follow in 1:11–12.

While this reading of the verse is clearly possible, there are solid indications that Paul is responding to a particular charge from the new preachers in Galatia, that he is a sophistic people pleaser with his circumcision-free version of the gospel (Burton 30–34; and many others).[96] That hypothesis finds support in the close connection between v. 10 and the preceding verses, where Paul rebukes the new preachers in Galatia and calls down God's curse upon them in v. 9. Furthermore, in v. 10c, Paul claims that he would not be a slave of Christ if he were "still" a people pleaser. Paul is evidently rebutting a charge that he is a people pleaser because he, though a circumcised Jew himself (Phil 3:5) who sees nothing wrong with circumcision for Jewish believers in Christ (cf. Gal 5:6; 6:15), has omitted circumcision from his preaching to the Gentiles in Galatia, thereby making the gospel easy for them to accept ("cheap grace"). With the little adverb "still," Paul concedes that he had indeed been a people pleaser *before* he became a slave of Christ. He thereby alludes to his pre-Christian life as a zealous Pharisaic Jew (1:13–14; cf. Phil 3:5) when he, as Gal 5:11 indicates, was "still [*eti*] proclaiming circumcision" (see comment there). For polemical reasons and with the benefit of hindsight, Paul now regards "proclaiming [i.e., advocating] circumcision" as a form of people pleasing. Paul has here neatly turned the tables on the new preachers in Galatia: If he were to advocate circumcision in Galatia as the new preachers are doing, he would be telling them what *they* want to hear! As the anathema of v. 9 amply illustrates (Burton 31; Mussner 63; Vos 97), much to the certain discomfort of the new preachers who will be listening to the letter with the Galatians, Paul does not curry favor with

---

96. Cf. 1 Thess 2:4–6; 1 Cor 1:17; 2:1–2; 2 Cor 4:2. Esler (1998: 67) writes that "a significant strand of ancient Graeco-Roman rhetoric . . . advised that speakers should incorporate into their speeches references to the case they thought was being made against them." He quotes a passage from the pre-Christian and anonymous *Rhetoric to Alexander* in support of this observation: "If then one is under suspicion of wrongdoing in the past, one must employ anticipation in addressing one's audience and say: 'I am well aware that a prejudice exists against me, but I will prove that it is groundless.' You must then make a brief defense in your proem [and Gal 1:6–10 is arguably the proem or introduction to Paul's letter], if you have anything to say on your own behalf, or raise objections to the judgments which have been passed on to you" (1436b–1437a).

The Letter Opening

human beings, whether they be Galatians or new preachers: "So am I *now* [with the anathema] trying to seek the approval of human beings—or of God?" The answers will be as clear to the Galatians as to the new preachers themselves.

The second question (v. 10b) now also comes into sharper focus: "Or am I seeking to please human beings, pandering to them with my circumcision-free gospel, as the new preachers allege?" If Paul were a people pleaser in the manner the new preachers allege, he would not be a slave of Christ, the Lord for whom he suffers and whose scars he bears (5:11; 6:12, 17).[97] As the apostolic slave of Christ (cf. Rom 1:1), Paul no longer spends his time "pleasing (other) human beings," telling them what they want to hear about "the gospel of Christ" (1:7), and flattering them with rhetorical display or manipulating them with lies (cf. 1 Cor 4:1–5).[98] Like any other slave in similar circumstances, he has no choice except to please his Lord (Gal 1:3) and thus to serve what he calls "the truth of the gospel" (2:5, 14; cf. 1 Cor 9:16 RSV: "For necessity is laid upon me. Woe to me if I do not preach the gospel!"). Paul's character argument emerges from an accusation that he was a sophistic people pleaser; his response to the gospel of the new preachers—the anathema of 1:9—demonstrates the contrary to be the case.

To sum up: In the second paragraph of the letter opening, Paul rebukes the Galatians for being in the process of turning from God, the one who has actually called them, to a different version of "the gospel of Christ," propounded by new preachers (evangelists and missionaries) who have come into the Galatian churches from elsewhere. These new preachers are unnerving the Galatians and wanting to turn the gospel of Christ into its opposite. The result is that it can no longer, in Paul's view, be called "gospel." He therefore rebukes the new preachers even more sharply than he rebukes the Galatians themselves; Paul underlines his rebuke with an imprecation, asking God to anathematize them for preaching a gospel contrary to the gospel he himself preached to the Galatians initially, which the Galatians had also received. In the final verse, Paul digresses momentarily from his focus on the gospel of Christ to combat an accusation against his character, a charge that his version of the gospel is no more than a form of people pleasing that omits crucial elements from the gospel message: circumcision and the consequent obligation to observe the law. Such people pleasing, he claims, would be inconsistent with his identity as a slave of Christ, whose work must reflect the will of his Master. His only loyalty is to the gospel of Christ as originally preached in Galatia, the gospel of God's grace in Christ,

---

97. Cf. B. Dodd; Lightfoot 79. To be a slave of an important person brought status to such a slave (cf. D. Martin). Since Christ was also important to the Galatians, Paul could also be claiming leadership status by claiming to be Christ's special slave.

98. As Martyn (136–37) writes, "His identity as apostle and slave of Christ is given him by God, not by a crowd that is pleased with his preaching."

which would remain true and in force even if he or an angel from heaven were now also preaching that conditional, counterfeit gospel of the new preachers. The (true) gospel cannot be altered.

Excursus 5: The Genre of Galatians and Paul's Use of Rhetorical Forms and Conventions

As the comments on 1:1–10 have demonstrated, Galatians is clearly a letter. In this opening section of the letter, and particularly in 1:1–5, Paul uses and adapts for his own purposes the conventions of letter writing used in the ancient world.[99] But what sort of letter is it? Adolf Deissmann made a famous distinction between a "letter," an ephemeral, nonliterary, normally quite brief document meant for a particular, real addressee in a particular time and place—and an "epistle," a longer, conscious work of literature cast in the form of a letter but addressed to a wide audience and meant for publication. The distinction does not really work for the Letters of Paul, which fall somewhere between the two categories.[100] Paul's authentic letters are real letters, addressed to particular audiences about particular issues in particular times and places, as the comments on 1:1–10 have indicated for Galatians, yet they are not ephemeral communications written in the frequently vulgar style of the ancient letters to which Deissmann appeals. Paul writes not as a private individual to friends or family but as an apostle of Christ to churches of Christ (not even Philemon is an exception). The letters were read out loud to the members when they assembled for worship and fellowship (cf. 1 Thess 5:27; Col 4:16); they were undoubtedly copied (cf. 2 Pet 3:16), as their survival alone attests.[101] Their literary artistry and rhetorical aspects (see above on 1:10 and further below) also set them apart from the usually brief private communications found by Deissmann in the garbage dumps of Egypt. The high average length of Paul's Letters distinguishes them not only from the short private letters used by Deissmann but also from the letters of Cicero, Seneca, or Pliny the Younger, which were also on average considerably shorter than Paul's (Anderson 1999: 112, citing the work of Richards).

The fact that Paul's Letters, including Galatians, were meant to be read out loud and thus heard implies that they were experienced by their intended audiences, including the churches of Galatia, as a type of speech. (We do not know who brought Paul's letter to the churches of Galatia, nor do we know who read it out loud to them.) Paul presumably wrote his letters taking this fact—the oral and aural nature of the initial communication—into account (even if he also reckoned with the possibility, perhaps probability, that the letter would be read and heard more than once). In such a situation, rhetoric, in the positive sense of effective (persuasive) public speaking or oratory (cf. Plato, *Gorg.*

---

99. For readable overviews and critiques, see Murphy-O'Connor 1995 and Anderson 1999; further Longenecker c–cxix; Esler 1998: 14–20, 58–75; Sänger 2002 (with massive bibliography).

100. Anderson (1999: 109–17) shows that the distinction does not hold for other ancient letters either.

101. Cf. Anderson (1999: 113–14), who writes that "it was normal practice in Roman society to copy private letters received, in order to share them around (especially from well-known or important persons)."

The Letter Opening

452E; Aristotle, *Rhet.* 1.2.1355b),[102] would be a significant factor (cf. Gal 4:20: "I could wish to be with you now and to change my tone"). Certainly "Paul could not expect to be persuasive unless there was some overlap between the content and form of what he said and the expectations of his audience" (Kennedy 1984: 10; cf. Esler 1998: 19).

Rhetoric as just defined originated in the Greek city-state and, despite abuses (see above on 1:10),[103] was a highly prized skill in the ancient Greco-Roman world, especially for those in positions of influence and power. Ancient education focused on developing this skill (Kennedy 1963, 1972, 1984), as the evidently large number of treatises and handbooks on the subject attest (Kennedy 1984: 10; Anderson 1999: 36–107).[104] "As a result," writes Esler (1998: 15), "anyone who wished to persuade an audience to a particular view or action would inevitably have been impelled by this aspect of the culture to utilise rhetoric." Beginning with Aristotle, ancient writers on rhetorical theory commonly distinguished three categories, or "species," of rhetoric: (1) forensic (also known as judicial or apologetic) rhetoric, used in a court of law to defend a client (or negatively, to accuse a defendant) before a jury or a panel of judges; (2) deliberative (hortatory, advisory) rhetoric, used in public assemblies to persuade the audience to undertake (or not to undertake) a particular course of action under consideration, and (3) epideictic (demonstrative, encomiastic, laudatory) rhetoric, used at festivals, celebrations of victory, commemorations, and the like to praise (or negatively, to blame and denigrate). By its nature, forensic rhetoric focuses on an assessment of *past* actions (who did what and why), whereas deliberative rhetoric focuses on a consideration of possible *future* actions (what the audience must do, or not do); epideictic rhetoric in turn focuses on the *present* situation (who is to be praised, or blamed, for the current state of affairs).

In a preliminary study from 1975 and then in his magisterial commentary of 1979 (14–25), Hans Dieter Betz has proposed that Galatians is to be regarded as "an apologetic letter," whose body (1:6–6:10, according to Betz) is arranged in accordance with the conventions of *forensic* rhetoric as described and attested in ancient treatises and handbooks. "The apologetic letter, such as Galatians, presupposes," according to Betz (24), "the real or fictitious situation of the court of law, with jury, accuser, and defendant. In the case of Galatians, the addressees are identical with the jury, with Paul being the defendant, and his opponents the accusers. This situation makes Paul's Galatian letter a self-apology, delivered not in person but in a written form." Betz argues that aside from the epistolary frame (1:1–5 and 6:11–18), Galatians is arranged or structured as such a speech ought to be according to ancient theorists writing on the subject:

---

102. This definition is to be distinguished from Quintilian's definition of rhetoric (*Inst.* 2.15.38) as *scientia bene dicendi*, the knowledge of how to speak well (Kennedy 1984: 13) and from the modern, popular understanding of rhetoric as empty, pompous speechmaking.

103. Acceptable public oratory would seek to persuade through careful, rational argument, whereas the unacceptable form (sophistry) would make use of flattery, deception, and other "rhetorical" tricks (see Vos).

104. Important surviving examples include Aristotle, *Rhetoric* (4th cent. B.C.E.); the anonymous *Rhetoric to Herennius* (beginning of the first cent. B.C.E.); Cicero, *On Invention* and *Partitions of Oratory* (first cent. B.C.E.); and Quintilian, *On the Education of an Orator* = *Institutio oratoria* (end of the first cent. C.E.).

1:6–11   *Exordium*, or introduction, stating the central issues at stake and establishing the character of the speaker
1:12–2:14 *Narratio*, or narration, outlining the facts of the case
2:15–21   *Propositio*, or proposition, stating the central issues to be proved
3:1–4:31   *Probatio*, or confirmation, developing the key arguments
5:1–6:10   *Exhortatio*, or exhortation (paraenesis), to action

In addition, according to Betz, the epistolary postscript contains a further element of a typical forensic speech: the *peroratio*, or *conclusio*, which recapitulates or summarizes the case being made (6:11–17).

Since Betz launched his thesis and supported it in his commentary, Galatians has been a storm center of scholarship around the issue of Paul's use of rhetorical forms and conventions. Betz's thesis has come in for some fierce criticism on several grounds. (1) Betz was unable to provide an example of an apologetic letter from the ancient world with which Galatians could be compared; furthermore, epistolary theorists also do not mention this category as a possibility (Anderson 1999: 116).[105] (2) As Betz himself realized, exhortation (5:1–6:10) is not normally part of a forensic speech. The *exhortatio* is the weakest part of Betz's proposal. (3) In favor of Betz's thesis, to be sure, is the *narratio* (1:12–2:14), but Kennedy (1984: 145) has shown that such a narrative element was not absent from deliberative or epideictic speeches. Kennedy observes further that Galatians 1:12–2:14 also does not attempt to do what a *narratio* in a judicial speech normally does, provide a statement of the facts directly at issue: "It is supporting evidence for Paul's claim in 1:11 that the gospel he preached was not from man, but from God" (145). (5) Finally, Kennedy (1984: 151) points out that Paul's overall aim is not to persuade the Galatians to change their opinion of him, as Betz's thesis holds, but instead, as shown by the closing paragraph of the letter, to persuade them not to begin practicing circumcision.

After Betz's work, numerous scholars have followed Kennedy in regarding Galatians as an example of deliberative rhetoric (cf., e.g., Hall 1987; Vouga 1988; Smit 1989; the commentators Matera and Witherington). Hansen (1989) and Longenecker propose a mediating position: Galatians is primarily forensic until 4:11 (the rebuke section), primarily deliberative thereafter (the request section).[106] The scholars show little agreement, however, on the formal "arrangement" (*dispositio*) of Galatians as a specimen of deliberative rhetoric (see the surveys provided by Murphy-O'Connor 1995: 78; Kern 91). Furthermore, the problem of the exhortation remains. A section of exhortation may seem more appropriate to deliberative than to forensic rhetoric (Kennedy 1984: 145; Hall 1987: 281; Witherington 28), but Anderson (1999: 131) observes that rhetorical theorists "never discuss general *exhortatio* at all, whether the genre is deliberative or not." Smit recognizes the problem, but then argues that Gal 5:13–6:10 must be a later

---

105. For the epistolary theorists, see Malherbe. There were two handbooks devoted entirely to the subject, Pseudo-Demetrius, *Typoi epistolikoi*, who discusses 21 types of letters; and Libanius (or Proclus), *Epistolimaioi characteres*, who enumerates 42 types of letters! An apologetic letter is not one of them.

106. Kremendahl in turn argues that Galatians is patterned on a forensic speech until 5:6; from 5:7, Paul uses epistolary paraenesis.

The Letter Opening

interpolation! Still other scholars have argued that Galatians exhibits the marks of epideictic rhetoric (e.g., Nanos 2002a: 329–31).[107]

The efforts to classify and to outline Galatians as if it were a speech (whether forensic or deliberative, or a combination of the two) with an epistolary wrapper are probably misguided, as two recent monographs have sought to show (Kern 258 and passim; Anderson 1999: 117–27). Galatians after all is not a speech written down, but a genuine letter, consciously written as such, even if it was also meant to be read out loud and thus heard. Ancient rhetorical theorists paid no attention to letter writing before the fourth century C.E. (Julius Victor), whereas epistolary theorists paid little or no systematic attention to rhetoric (Malherbe 3–4).[108] "For what," asked Cicero (*Fam.* 9.21.1) rhetorically in the first century B.C.E., "does a letter have in common with a speech in court or an assembly?" (*quid enim simile habet epistula aut iudicio aut contioni?*).[109] Anderson concludes that Galatians cannot "reasonably be divided into the various *partes* of a speech" (1999: 144) and that "it is vain to attempt to strictly apply a scheme of classification designed for speeches to letters" (117; cf. Kern 166).[110] In addition, Kern surveys early Christian writers on their views of Paul's style and discovers, as classical and patristic scholars before him have done, that for the church fathers Paul was "no rhetorician or high-born orator but a humble author of weighty letters" (203).

Anderson (1999: 126), however, also points out that while Paul's Letters (like other ancient letters) "cannot simply be forced into the threefold structural categorization of ancient rhetoric," they may still "have been influenced by rhetorical methods of style and argumentation more generally." A similar point is made by Esler (1998: 61), who argues that though the structure of Galatians is not patterned on that of a formal deliberative speech, the letter nevertheless *functions* deliberatively: it seeks to persuade or dissuade. Similar arguments have been made by those who discern elements of epideictic rhetoric in Galatians. Kennedy (1984: 19) thinks that "all discourse," oral or written, can be classified in terms of the three species of rhetoric, even though there are also mixed forms. This claim means that Paul's discourse in Galatians must conform to one or more of these species of rhetoric at all points. That the matter may not be so simple is indicated by Quintilian, a near contemporary of Paul, who makes a plea for other species of rhetoric (*Inst.* 3.4.3; cf. Murphy-O'Connor 1995: 68): "On what kind of oratory are we to consider ourselves to be employed when we complain, console, pacify, excite, terrify, encourage, instruct, explain obscurities, narrate, plead for mercy, thank, congratulate,

---

107. Nanos (2002: xvi n. 5) gives an extensive list of scholars supporting each classification.

108. Malherbe observes that "while the discussions of letter writing in these manuals [those of Pseudo-Demetrius and Pseudo-Libanius] are systematic, there is no evidence to indicate that they were part of a rhetorical system" (3–4).

109. On this issue, see further Sänger 2002: 380–86.

110. Quintilian also makes the following interesting observation in connection with the handbooks and their rules (*Inst.* 2.13.7; cf. Murphy-O'Connor 1995: 86): "The rules of rhetoric have not the formal authority of laws or decrees of the plebs, but are, with all they contain, the children of expediency. I will not deny that it is generally expedient to conform to such rules, otherwise I would not be writing now. But if our friend expediency suggests some other course to us, why, we shall disregard the authority of the professors and follow her." Theoretical handbooks and treatises are one thing; actual practice and reality another.

reproach, abuse, describe, command, retract, express our desires and opinions, to mention no other of the many possibilities?"

The variety of rhetorical styles noted by Quintilian is reminiscent of the variety of epistles listed in the two epistolary handbooks known from antiquity (Sänger 2002: 385). To reduce genres of rhetoric to three may thus be an oversimplification.

Summary. Some parts of Paul's Letter to the Galatians may usefully be characterized as specimens of forensic, deliberative, or epideictic rhetoric, but to classify the letter as a whole under one of these headings probably distorts its character, particularly when accompanied by an attempt to make Galatians fit the structure of a forensic, deliberative, or epideictic speech as prescribed by the handbooks.[111] A letter is a flexible medium of communication; its form and content are determined not by theoretical considerations and fixed rules, but by the concrete situation it seeks to address (Sänger 2002: 385–86). Conventions provide guidelines, not a straitjacket. Paul undoubtedly used certain rhetorical devices or stratagems (we have pointed out a number of them already in the commentary on 1:6–10). The "three modes of artistic proof" (Kennedy 1984: 15) outlined by Aristotle (*Rhet.* 1.2.1356a) deserve special mention here: (1) the *ēthos*, or character argument, whereby an author seeks to establish his credibility or trustworthiness with the audience in view (see above on 1:10 and below on 1:11–2:14); (2) the *pathos*, or emotion argument, referring to an author's attempt to appeal to the audience's feelings as a technique of persuasion; and (3) the *logos*, or logical argument, found in the discourse itself; this proof can be either inductive (proceeding from examples to a general conclusion) or deductive (a claim supported by a reason; Kennedy 1984: 15–16). In the course of the commentary, we shall note various instances of these and other rhetorical devices or strategies used by Paul (cf. Tolmie 2005, 2007). Paul's use and application of such rhetorical devices may often be more subconscious than conscious, not only because rhetoric was a pervasive element of ancient culture, but also because many common rhetorical devices may well characterize all human discourse in whatever time or place (Kennedy 1984: 10).

But more must be said. Kennedy also observes that "there is a distinctive rhetoric of religion, . . . at the heart of [which] lies authoritative proclamation, not rational persuasion" (1984: 6). Paul, he notes in critique of Betz , did not choose to defend himself; instead, "he preached the gospel of Christ" (1984: 143) And Anderson (1999: 119) makes the interesting comment that "Paul's letters were substitutes not for a conversation," as letters normally were,[112] "but for a sermon/speech." Martyn (21) has made a strong argument for regarding Galatians as "a substitute" for "an argumentative sermon

---

111. If push comes to shove, it must be said that Galatians as a whole has the most affinities with deliberative rhetoric, particularly in view of Section IV (4:8–5:12), but then in a negative sense: Paul wants to keep the Galatians from adopting the views of the new preachers active in Galatia with respect to circumcision and the law. See Excursus 4 and Introduction: Structure.

112. See the definitions of a letter according to ancient writers in Malherbe 12: "A letter is one half of a dialogue (Dem. 233) or a surrogate for an actual dialogue (Cic. *Ad Fam.* 12, 30, 1). In it one speaks to an absent friend as though he were present (Cic. *Ad Fam.* 2, 4, 1; Sen. *Ep.* 75, 1; Ps. Lib. 2, 58; Jul. Vic.). The letter is, in fact, speech [the spoken word] in the written medium (Cic. *Ad Att.* 8, 14, 1; 9, 10, 1; 12, 53; Sen. *Ep.* 75, 1). A letter reflects the personality of the writer (Cic. *Ad Fam.* 16, 16, 2; Sen. *Ep.* 40, 1; Dem. 227; Philostr.)."

The Letter Opening

preached in the context of a service of worship—and thus in the acknowledged presence of God." A "sermon" here is understood to be a theological speech proclaiming the gospel within the context of a worship service. This thesis takes seriously not only the primary theme of the letter as announced in 1:6–10 ("the gospel of Christ") and the theological content of the letter as a whole, but also the liturgical features of Paul's utterances at the beginning (see comment on 1:3–5 above) and at the end (see comment on 6:18 in particular).[113] Martyn concedes that the letter contains elements that could support both the forensic and deliberative analyses of the letter (cf. Longenecker), but nevertheless maintains that "the body of the letter as a whole is a rhetorical genre without true analogy in the ancient rhetorical handbooks of Quintilian and others" (23).

According to Martyn, then, the primary concern of Paul's sermon in letter form is "to *repreach* the gospel in place of its counterfeit" (23, stress added). In his repreaching of the gospel, Paul begins not from a common rhetorical and thus human point of departure but from "the divine and thus nonrhetorical point of departure" of Christ's death and resurrection (148), an event that marks God's apocalyptic invasion into the world to liberate human beings from enslavement to cosmic powers (23; see comment on 1:4 above). In Paul's "evangelistic argument," rhetoric may have its place, but "the gospel itself is not fundamentally a matter of rhetorical persuasion (1:10–12)" (23). Paul is not trying to persuade the Galatians that faith is to be preferred to the law; rather, he is "constructing an announcement designed to wake the Galatians up to the real cosmos, made what it is by the fact that faith has now *arrived* with the advent of Christ" (Gal 3:23–25)." Paul's rhetoric is thus not so much "hortatory and persuasive" (though it is that too) as "revelatory and performative," since it "presupposes God's action through Paul's words."[114] The Galatians "need to be taught by God . . . so that they *see* the cosmos that God is bringing into existence as his new creation. Their need of real vision is what basically determines the nature of Paul's rhetoric" (23, stress original).

Though Martyn himself does not use this designation, it may be appropriate to label Galatians as not only "a highly situational sermon," as Martyn does here, but also as an intensely *apocalyptic* sermon (cf. Hall 1996). It is a sermon whereby God invades and shatters the world of the new preachers, the world predicated on the law and its observance or nonobservance (see comment above on 1:4b and below on 1:11–12, 15–16; 5:6; 6:15), and enables the Galatians to see and to know once again God's utterly new creation. As Paul writes the letter, he is expecting it to be experienced by the Galatians as such an apocalyptic sermon.

---

113. See White 98: "When Paul addressed his congregations, he imagined them at worship and himself as officiating at the service. It is for this reason that he combines epistolary conventions with the language of thanksgiving, blessing, and prayer, and why salutation is enjoined as a religious act (e.g., the holy kiss)."

114. Cf. Martyn 1991: 161: "Paul wrote Galatians in the confidence that *God* intended to cause a certain event *to occur* in the Galatian congregations when Paul's messenger read the letter aloud to them. . . . The author we see in the course of reading Galatians is a man who *does* theology by writing in such a way as *to anticipate* a theological *event*" (with original stress).

Section II: Galatians 1:11–2:21
The Origin and the Truth of the Gospel

In 1:6–10, the primary theme of the letter has been introduced: it is "the gospel of Christ" (1:7). Christ, whom God raised from the dead (1:1), is for Paul "the one who gave himself for our sins, that he might rescue us from the present evil age, according to the will of God and our Father" (1:4). In this section of the letter, Paul identifies the gospel of Christ as "the gospel that was [initially] preached by me [to you Galatians] [*to euangelion to euangelisthen hyp' emou*]" (1:11) and as "the gospel that I [still now] proclaim [*kēryssō*] among the Gentiles" (2:2). Through this gospel, God has called the Galatians "into the grace of Christ" (1:6).

The unifying theme of this section is this (Pauline) gospel, but the focus is not so much on its content as on its divine origin (1:11–24) and its truth (2:1–21). After the opening paragraph (1:11–12), Paul refers several more times to "the gospel" in this section (2:2, 5, 7, 14), twice in the pregnant phrase "the truth of the gospel" (2:5, 14). The cognate verb "to preach the gospel" (*euangelizomai*), also first used in the letter opening (1:8–9), occurs again in 1:16 and 23, as well as in 1:11. There is, somewhat surprisingly, no further instance of the noun in the letter and only two further instances of the verb, in 3:8 (in the compound form "to preach the gospel in advance," *proeuangelizomai*) and 4:13. The content of the gospel preached by Paul is not made explicit before the closing paragraph of the section (2:15–21) and then largely by way of the negation of the counterfeit gospel proclaimed by the new preachers: "Justification" does *not* occur "on the basis of works of the law," as they claim, but rather "on the basis of the faith of Christ" (*ek pisteōs Christou*). This articulation of the gospel forms the basis for the argument in the remainder of the letter.

The opening and closing paragraphs of the section enclose a brief autobiographical narrative (1:13–2:14), in which Paul gives an account of his contacts with the church in Jerusalem, particularly with the leading apostles there: James (1:19; 2:9, 12), Cephas/Peter (1:18; 2:7, 8, 9, 11, 14) and John (2:9). The account covers nearly twenty years, stretching from his pre-Christian life as a (Pharisaic) Jew and persecutor of the church of God (1:13–14) to his conflict with Peter in the

The Origin and the Truth of the Gospel 73

church of Antioch (2:11–14; cf. Acts 15:22–35). It includes his call to become an apostle of Christ to the Gentiles (1:15–17), his first visit to the church in Jerusalem after three years (1:18–20), his time in the regions of Syria and Cilicia (1:21–24), and his second visit to the church in Jerusalem after fourteen years (2:1–10). The conflict in Antioch, instigated by "emissaries from James" in Jerusalem and abetted by "the circumcision party" there (2:12; cf. Acts 10:45; 11:2), led to a traumatic parting of the ways between Paul and his coworker Barnabas (2:13) as well as Peter (2:14), the church in Antioch (2:11, 14), and thus also the church in Jerusalem, which was under the leadership of James (2:12). Paul writes Galatians after this decisive parting of the ways, an event that colors his autobiographical narrative from beginning to end. Paul's agenda in this narrative is to show that the gospel he has preached (1:11–24) and still preaches (2:1–21) has *not* been received or learned from these (human) apostles and thus does not depend on them for its truth, yet *also* that they gave it their unreserved seal of approval on his second visit to Jerusalem, having perceived God's effective presence in his proclamation and activity (2:1–10). The fundamental issue at stake is what Paul calls "the truth of the gospel" (2:5, 14), a truth that is predicated on its divine origin (1:11–24). The following outline of the section emerges:

1:11–17   The Origin of the Gospel 1: Paul's Conversion and Call
1:18–24   The Origin of the Gospel 2: Paul's Visit with Cephas in Jerusalem
2:1–10   The Truth of the Gospel 1: The Apostolic Conference in Jerusalem
2:11–14   The Truth of the Gospel 2: Paul's Conflict with Cephas in Antioch
2:15–21   The Truth of the Gospel for the Galatian Situation

The autobiographical narrative proper (1:13–2:14) is characterized by the repeated use of temporal markers. The important ones are the following:

1:13   "For you have heard of my manner of life earlier [*pote*] in Judaism . . ."
1:15   "When [*hote*] God was pleased . . ."
1:18   "Then [*epeita*] after three years . . ."
1:21   "Then [*epeita*] I went . . ."
2:1   "Then [*epeita*] after fourteen years . . ."
2:11   "When [*hote*] Cephas came to Antioch . . ."

The section can credibly be read as Paul's response to certain charges coming from the new preachers in Galatia, claiming that since he is no longer connected with the church in Antioch, his mission to the Gentiles lacks any legitimate basis. The new preachers are suggesting to the Galatians that Paul is a freebooter, without authority and authorization to continue his missionary activity among the Gentiles (see comment on 1:1). As a freebooter, moreover, Paul has come up with a (version of the) gospel that is theologically the opposite of the (version of the) gospel that the new missionaries are preaching to the Galatians (see comment on 1:7). Paul, they charge, has invented this gospel himself (see comment on 1:10), distorting what he had received or been taught on his visits to Jerusalem and in the church at Antioch (cf. Martyn 169, 178). Their own version, they are undoubtedly telling the Galatians, stands in continuity with the gospel being proclaimed by the founding apostles of the mother church in Jerusalem (cf. 4:26), a claim that Paul tries to qualify in this letter (see comments on 2:7–8, 15–21). For the new preachers, too, the key issue is less Paul's apostolic credentials and legitimacy than the gospel that he preaches (see on 1:6; Lategan), even if the two issues are inextricably connected for both sides. Furthermore, the claim of the new preachers that their gospel stands in continuity with the gospel as preached in Jerusalem implies that they themselves are active in Galatia with the blessing of James and the church in Jerusalem (see comments on 2:11–14 and 4:25–27); they may therefore be "apostles" (not of the risen Christ, as Paul is, but) of the church in Jerusalem (see on 1:1). The new preachers probably understand it as part of their task in Galatia to undermine or to "correct" the work of Paul among the Gentiles (see Excursus 4, above).

Paul's response is to say that since the gospel preached by him came directly from God, the apostles in Jerusalem had nothing to do with determining its content; his gospel cannot be dismissed as a distorted version of theirs. On his second visit to Jerusalem, however, the Jerusalem apostles did recognize its divine origin and thus its truth, and they gave to him (and Barnabas) "the right hand of partnership" (2:9). The appeal of the new preachers to the apostles in Jerusalem in order to undermine the gospel preached by Paul is thus actually without substance. Paul also wants to show that his break with Antioch was not his fault, as the new preachers may be claiming, but that of Barnabas, Peter, and James—who failed, in Paul's view, to understand and to carry through the full implications of their insight at the meeting in Jerusalem into the origin and the truth of the gospel being preached by Paul to the Gentiles. Paul needs to provide this account of his dealings with Jerusalem in order to reestablish his credibility in the churches of Galatia, credibility undermined by the new preachers and their gospel (Burton 35). Only when he has reestablished his credibility, his trustworthiness, can he respond on theological and exegetical grounds, as he begins to do in the closing paragraph of the section.

This section of the letter is one of the major sources for the historical reconstruction of Paul's life and career, and indeed of early Christianity. The material can be read for this purpose, and frequently has been, often at the expense

The Origin and the Truth of the Gospel 75

of recognizing that Paul's autobiographical narrative is as much his "witness to God's activity" (Martyn 161) as it is to his own (cf. Gaventa 1986a). In this commentary we shall read and interpret the section as an integral part of Paul's epistolary communication to the churches of Galatia: What does Paul want to say here to the Galatians—and through them to the new preachers who will be listening to the letter with them?

1:11–17 The Origin of the Gospel 1: Paul's Conversion and Call

This paragraph has three discernible parts or sense units (vv. 11–12, 13–14, and 15–17) with a common theme: Paul's insistence that the gospel he preached to the Galatians when he first came to them (4:13) does *not* have a human origin. Each part seeks in its own way to undergird this claim. The alternative, that this gospel came to Paul directly from God through an apocalyptic revelation of Christ, receives (unfortunately, from our point of view) considerably less emphasis here and no elaboration. The word "not" occurs three times in the first part, then twice more in the third. And the second part is meant to support the claim that he had *not* received the gospel from, or been taught it by, a human being. It came into his life unexpectedly and its source was God.

> 1:11 For[a] I make known to you, brethren, concerning the gospel that was preached by me, that it is not of human origin. 12 For I neither received it from a human being nor was I taught [it], but [I received it] through an apocalyptic revelation of Jesus Christ.
>
> 13 For you have heard of my manner of life earlier in Judaism, that I persecuted the church of God beyond measure, and I sought to destroy it, 14 and I advanced in Judaism beyond many of my own age among my people, being to a greater degree a zealot for my patriarchal traditions.
>
> 15 And when [God],[b] the One who set me apart from the womb of my mother and called me through his grace, was pleased 16 to apocalyptically reveal his Son in me, that I might preach him among the Gentiles, I did not immediately confer with flesh and blood, 17 nor did I go away[c] to Jerusalem to those who were apostles before me, but I went away into Arabia and again I returned to Damascus.

a. The manuscript evidence is evenly divided between *de* (a weak conjunction meaning "and, but"), which is often better left untranslated, and *gar* ("for"). Supporting the former are $\mathfrak{P}^{46}$, ℵ*, A, and others; supporting the latter are B, D*, and others. Internal considerations can also support either reading: Paul uses *de* in the parallels in 1 Cor 15:1 and 2 Cor 8:1, but he uses *gar* in Gal 1:10, 12, and 13. Scribal assimilation can thus explain both readings.

b. The manuscripts are divided on the presence or absence of the word "God," but even if not original, it is clear that "God" is meant in any case. It is also easier to explain its inclusion if the original text did not contain it than its omission if it was originally part of the text (see Metzger 521–22). It is not found in 𝔓⁴⁶ and B.

c. Following the reading of 𝔓⁵¹, B, D, F, G, *pc* (*apēlthon*). 𝔓⁴⁶ has simply "went" (*ēlthon*), whereas ℵ, A, Ψ, and others have "went up" (*anēlthon*); cf. 1:18; 2:1.

[11–12] That 1:11 begins a new section is here indicated by the vocative "brethren" (*adelphoi*) combined with the epistolary formula "I make known to you" (cf. 1 Cor 15:1; 2 Cor 8:1). By addressing the Galatians as *adelphoi*, "brethren" (the masculine plural is inclusive for Paul in that both women and men are intended), Paul adopts a familial or fraternal tone, indicating that he has not given up on the Galatians, despite the rebuke of the previous paragraph. They remain brothers and sisters in Christ.[115] With his solemn introduction, "I make known to you," Paul begins the letter body (see Excursus 3) and states the primary thesis of this section (and in a way of the whole letter), that the gospel he has preached to the Galatians *ouk estin kata anthrōpon*, "is *not* of human origin" (so also NRSV; Dunn). The phrase *kata anthrōpon* (lit., "according to a human being"), which is classical (cf. BDAG 81), is difficult to render into suitable English.[116] The following clause (1:12a) discloses its basic import in this context: Paul denies that the gospel he has preached (and still preaches) comes "from a human being [*para anthrōpou*]." His gospel thus does not have a human origin and is not a human production or invention.

If the conjunction "for" (*gar*) is original, it would seem to signal a clarification of 1:9, and not of 1:10, which we have argued above is a digression or an aside. If the *gar* is not original, Paul has used *de* instead because of the intervening 1:10. The thought of 1:11 in any case picks up the thread of Paul's argument from 1:9: "If someone is preaching a gospel [*euangelizetai*] contrary to what you received [from me], let that someone be an anathema. . . . For I make known to you, brethren, concerning the gospel [*to euangelion*] that was preached [*euangelisthen*] by me, that it is not of human origin."

Paul can call down an anathema on the "different gospel" because the gospel preached by him, he knows without the shadow of a doubt, was then and still "is" (*estin*) no mere human construction. It is God's own gospel. Paul here designates "the gospel" as "the gospel that was preached by me" to distinguish it from that "different gospel" (1:6)—which is not the gospel of Christ (1:7)—being preached by the new missionaries in Galatia. The first part of 1:12 provides a clarification of this assertion: (a) "for [*gar*] I [*egō*] neither

---

115. The use of this term for fellow believers was not distinctive to Paul or to Christians; cf. BDAG 18; MM 9; Burton 36.

116. Other possibilities include: "after man" (KJV); "in a human way, from a human standpoint" (BDAG); "man's gospel" (RSV); "something that man made up" (NIV); "human in nature" (Betz); "from a human point of view, according to human will or thought" (Burton); "simply human" (Longenecker); and the like.

The Origin and the Truth of the Gospel   77

[*oude*] received [*parelabon*] it from a human being [*para anthrōpou*]," (b) "nor [*oude*][117] was I taught [it by a human being]."

The use of the emphatic *egō* ("I") implies a contrast, probably with the new preachers: *He*, unlike the new preachers,[118] did not receive the gospel that he preached in the form of an already-existing tradition passed on to him, nor had he learned it as a student receiving catechetical instruction from a teacher.[119] In short, the gospel that Paul preached in Galatia did not, so he claims, come to him by human traditioning or learning processes. If not a human tradition or construction, passed on or taught in the normal human manner, this gospel must of necessity be of divine origin. That is the implication of 1:12c, even though Paul does not here write: "but from God [*para theou*]." Instead, he makes the same point by writing that the gospel came to him "through an apocalyptic revelation of Jesus Christ [*di' apokalypseōs Iēsou Christou*]" (cf. 1:1).

Verse 12c nevertheless remains terse and unforthcoming, perhaps because Paul's emphasis falls on where the gospel he preached does *not* come from rather than on where it does. He postpones any elaboration until 1:15–16, where he interprets the reference to the "apocalyptic revelation of Jesus Christ" in 1:12c to mean that "God was pleased . . . to apocalyptically reveal [*apokalypsai*] his Son in me." That elaboration indicates that 1:12c may be paraphrased as follows: "through God's apocalyptic revelation of his Son, Jesus Christ, in me." Jesus Christ is here presented as the content rather than as the origin or agent of the apocalyptic revelation in Paul's life (an objective rather than a subjective genitive). The content of the gospel is thus "Jesus Christ" or simply "Christ" (1:7). The intervening verses (1:13–14) concern Paul's pre-Christian life as a Pharisaic zealot who persecuted the church of God; that means that "the apocalyptic revelation of Jesus Christ" of 1:12c must be a reference to Paul's conversion by God (from what he calls his "manner of life earlier in Judaism" to another manner of life "in Christ"), an event he also regards as his call to apostleship. For Paul, if not for anyone else, conversion to Christ and call to apostleship coincide (see comment on 1:15–17 below).[120]

---

117. Other manuscripts read *oute* instead, with no difference in meaning.

118. Less likely is a comparison with the Twelve: "I, too, just like the Twelve, did not receive it from a human being" (so Burton 39).

119. The new preachers presumably would claim that their gospel tradition has its ultimate source and origin in God or Christ, much as Paul does in 1 Cor 11:23 ("from the Lord")! Cf. *m. ʾAbot* 1:1: "Moses received the law from Sinai and committed it to Joshua, and Joshua to the elders, and the elders to the Prophets; and the Prophets committed it to the men of the Great Synagogue." Cf. also 1 Cor 15:1–5.

120. Whether "conversion" is the right word here is partly a matter of definition (see Gaventa 1986). The word can be understood actively or passively. In the former case, "conversion" means a person's considered, autonomous change from one religion to another. This understanding of conversion does not apply to Paul since he did not (a) voluntarily (b) change from one religion (Judaism) to another (Christianity). In Paul's case, "conversion" is to be understood passively (cf.

The translation of the noun *apokalypsis* in 1:12c and of the cognate verb, *apokalypsai* (aor. inf.), in v. 15 is of crucial importance. The noun is normally translated simply as "revelation" (cf. NRSV, NIV, NJB, NAB, KJV). The word literally means "unveiling," a lifting of the veil, as also the Latin *revelatio*, from which our word "revelation" is obviously derived (cf. BDAG 112). The basic sense here then is that of a visible disclosure (cf. the much more detailed and embellished accounts in Acts 9:3–9; 22:6–11; 26:12–18), in this case of "Jesus Christ." Such an interpretation is consistent with Paul's claim to have "seen the Lord" (1 Cor 9:1) and with his report that the risen Christ "appeared to me" (15:8), using a form of the verb *horaō*, "to see," in both cases. The other translation of the Greek term, "apocalypse," which is a near transliteration, occurs commonly today as a designation for a particular genre of literature, such as the apocalypses of Daniel and *4 Ezra* (2 Esdras), the Synoptic apocalypse found in Mark 13, and the book of Revelation, which is also known as the Apocalypse of John. The latter begins with exactly the same expression that Paul uses in 1:12c, "an *apokalypsis* of Jesus Christ" (Rev 1:1a),[121] which may indicate the genre of the book and/or (more likely) its contents (objective genitive). The opening line of the Apocalypse of John is the source of the term "apocalyptic" to designate a particular understanding of the world and of God's relation to it in both early Judaism and early Christianity, even when such a worldview is found in other forms of literature as well, such as the Letters of Paul (see comment on 1:4b and Excursus 2 above). It is clear that Paul does not here use the term as a genre designation, as if he had received the gospel by reading and studying an apocalypse such as the book of Revelation (which in any case was written several decades after Paul wrote this letter). Paul nevertheless uses the noun *apokalypsis* in 1:12c (and the verb *apokalypsai* in 1:16) with the "apocalyptic" overtones and implications associated with the book of Revelation and other such literature, warranting the translation "apocalyptic revelation" for *apokalypsis* in 1:12c (and the translation "apocalyptically reveal" for the cognate verb in 1:16; Martyn 144, 157).[122] This translation serves to reflect what the immediate context clearly indicates, that the "*apokalypsis* of Jesus Christ" was experienced and

---

4:9: to be known by God rather than the other way around): it describes the advent of Christ into his life, an advent that meant the death of his manner of life in the religion of Judaism and the creation of a new manner of life in Christ (cf. 2:19–20). Christ here is no religion (not even "Christianity") but the end of all religion (cf. Martyn 163–64), whether that be the religion of the law or that of "the elements of the world" (4:3, 8–10). See further Gaventa 1986: 22–28; and the comments on 1:15–16; 2:15–21; 4:1–7, 8–10.

121. The Greek expression in Rev 1:1 (*Apokalypsis Iēsou Christou*) is often translated "*The revelation of Jesus Christ*" (NRSV), even though it is formally indefinite.

122. Strictly speaking, "apocalyptic revelation" (like "apocalyptically reveal") is redundant. But the English word "revelation" no longer has the "apocalyptic" connotations of the Greek original in some contexts. See Excursus 6, below.

The Origin and the Truth of the Gospel

interpreted by Paul as an "apocalyptic" event whereby God not only disclosed to him the true identity of Jesus Christ (he is God's Son) but also put an end to his old way of life in order to give him a new one in its stead (cf. Lührmann 17–18; Martyn 144). With respect to his own life, Paul "underlines the sharp *discontinuity* between the old age of sincere Law observance and the new age of apostolic vocation" (Martyn 157, with emphasis original).

Excursus 6: Paul's Language of Apocalyptic Revelation

Paul uses the term *apokalypsis* in different ways, and the context is often a significant factor in determining both its reference and its sense (de Boer 2002).[123] The noun and its cognate verb *apokalyptō* are rather rare in secular sources and do not have the theological weight they carry for Christian writers (Oepke 1965: 570–71). The noun occurs in the LXX only four times, with the meaning "disclosure" or "revelation" (1 Kgdms [1 Sam] 20:30; Sir 11:27; 22:22; and *Odes Sol.* 13.32 [in some editions of LXX]). Of the numerous instances of the verb in the LXX, where it commonly means "to uncover" or "to disclose," the instances of Isa 53:1 and 52:10, both referring to God's saving "arm," are particularly noteworthy: "O Lord, who has believed our report? And to whom has the arm of the Lord been revealed [*apekalyphthē*]?" (53:1 LXX). "And the Lord shall reveal [*apokalypsei*] his holy arm in the sight of all the nations (*panta ta ethnē*); and all the ends of the earth shall see the salvation [*sōtēria*] that comes from our God" (52:10 LXX).

Paul makes notable use of Second Isaiah in Gal 1:16 (Isa 49:1, 6) and elsewhere in Galatians (4:27 quotes Isa 54:1). He was therefore probably familiar with Isa 53:1 and 52:10 (53:1 is partially quoted in Rom 10:16), where the "revelation" of God's arm is no mere disclosure of previously hidden information or of a heavenly mystery, but the visible coming of God to effect salvation in the world. Paul uses the term in three distinct ways but in each case the term carries an "apocalyptic" nuance similar to that found in the two passages from Isaiah:

1. Apokalypsis as the Parousia. In 1 Cor 1:7, Paul describes the Corinthians Christians as waiting for "the *apokalypsis* of our Lord Jesus Christ," which refers to the Parousia (cf. 1:8; 15:23–28). Paul does not describe the Corinthians as waiting for the direct communication of heavenly mysteries, of divine information, in a dream, mystical trance, or a moment of spiritual ecstasy, but for the visible reappearance on the world scene of Jesus himself. This usage of the term conforms to what many scholars and probably most Christians today take the word "apocalyptic" to signify: Jesus' Parousia as a future, cosmic event (cf. Excursus 2 above). The revelation—apocalypse—of Jesus Christ concerns his visible eschatological appearance at his Parousia, and this is clearly an apocalyptic *event* whereby this evil age is finally and irrevocably destroyed "so that God may be all in all" (1 Cor 15:23–28; cf. 1 Thess 4:13–18). Second Thessalonians 1:7 speaks similarly and more clearly of "the revelation [*apokalypsis*] of the Lord Jesus from heaven with his angels of power" (AT; cf. also 2 Thess 2:3, 6, 8). The "revelation" here referred to is no mere disclosure of previously hidden heavenly secrets, nor is it simply information about future

123. Presupposed is the discussion found in Excursus 2 on Galatians and apocalyptic eschatology.

events: instead, it is actual eschatological activity and movement, an invasion of the world below from heaven above, which is also in a sense an invasion of the present by the future.

Given 1 Cor 1:7, then, "the *apokalypsis* of Jesus Christ" in Gal 1:12 could be regarded as an anticipation of the future, objective revelation of the Lord at his Parousia, a sort of personal Parousia for Paul himself. For Gal 1, the difficulty with this interpretation is that Paul wants to say something about the origin of the gospel that he now, in the present, proclaims among the Gentiles (1:16; 2:2). This present gospel does not have its origin in the future apocalypse of the Lord at his Parousia, but in an apocalypse that Paul can refer to as a past event. Nonetheless, 1 Cor 1:7 does show that for Paul the term *apokalypsis* can have a definite (future) "apocalyptic" meaning (cf. further, Rom 2:5; 8:18–19; 1 Cor 3:13).

2. *Apokalypsis as disclosure of divine mysteries through the Spirit.* Elsewhere in 1 Corinthians, Paul does appear to use the term *apokalypsis* in connection with the communication of heavenly or divine mysteries in the present, to those who are already believers. "When you come together," the apostle writes in 1 Cor 14:26, "each one has a hymn, a lesson, *a revelation [apokalypsis]*, a tongue, or an interpretation" (cf. 1 Cor 14:6; Eph 1:17). These instances of Paul's use of the noun *apokalypsis*, and of its cognate verb, *apokalyptō* (1 Cor 2:10; 14:30; Phil 3:15), concern the disclosure of heavenly secrets or information to an individual believer (who mediates what has been seen and heard to others). In 1 Corinthians 14, Paul makes a close connection between revelation and prophetic speech; visionary experiences as such play no discernible role and are not mentioned (cf. 14:6, 29–31; 2:10; also Phil 3:15). These prophetic revelations during the gatherings of the community in Corinth are, however, caused by the Holy Spirit, and this Spirit represents for Paul the apocalyptic-eschatological presence and activity of Jesus Christ and thus of God in the life of believers (see Fee 1994; comments below on Gal 3:1–5; 4:6). Even here, then, the term *apokalypsis* receives from Paul a distinctive apocalyptic-eschatological nuance: Christian existence in the world always entails for Paul participation in the apocalyptic rescuing activity of God in Christ (see comments on 1:4b and 2:19–20).

The "*apokalypsis* of Jesus Christ" in Gal 1:12c is somewhat different from the revelations of 1 Corinthians 14, however. The law-observant zealot and persecutor of the church of God was not waiting for a revelation during a worship service of Christians in Corinth or elsewhere. He did not ask for the revelation referred to in 1:12c or seek it out. Furthermore, this revelation was not simply a disclosure of information, the unveiling of something previously hidden, but a cataclysmic, life-changing event. The revelations of 1 Corinthians 14 enable Christians "to stay in"; the revelation of 1:12c enabled the persecutor of God's church "to get in."

Much the same can be said about 2 Cor 12:1–4, to which interpreters also appeal in an effort to explain Paul's usage in 1:12c. In 2 Cor 12:1, Paul mentions "visions [*optasiai*] and revelations [*apokalypseis*] of the Lord [*kyriou*]," where the phrasing seems to provide a near parallel to "a revelation of Jesus Christ," *apokalypsis Iēsou Christou*. The terms "visions" and "revelations" seem to be roughly synonymous (cf. 12:7, where the latter term, again plural, recurs as a summary). Together they point to the visionary and auditory disclosure of heavenly secrets to an individual, in this case Paul himself evidently. But this passage is the exception that proves the rule, partly because Paul

The Origin and the Truth of the Gospel

seeks here utterly to relativize the importance of such visionary, revelatory experiences (cf. 12:5–7), much as he does glossolalia in 1 Corinthians 14 or the revelation from an angel in Gal 1:8. He uses the word "revelation" in 2 Cor 12:1 in a sense not typical of him elsewhere. Apart from 2 Cor 12:1–4, a revelation is not for Paul a private matter; it has communal implications and is placed in a communal context, as 1 Corinthians 14 shows. Furthermore, the "visions and revelations" of 2 Cor 12:1–4 are rather different from the *one* revelation of Jesus Christ in Gal 1:12c, which gave Paul the content of his gospel and dramatically changed his life from persecutor to apostle.

3. Apokalypsis as a reference to God's cataclysmic invasion of the world in Christ. Aside from Gal 1:12c, Paul also uses the term and its cognate verb elsewhere in connection with the gospel that he preaches in the present. This gospel is fundamentally oriented to and surely based upon an event in the past, the death and resurrection of Jesus, and thus not on an event in the future, the Parousia. The question is whether Paul's use of these terms in connection with the gospel that he preaches in the present, and with an eye on the current situation of Christians in the world, has to do with the visible, eschatological action and movement of God—with the invasion of "the present evil age" by God Himself.

There are expressions by the apostle that suggest an affirmative answer to this question. In Rom 1:16–17, Paul claims that in the gospel "the righteousness of God *is being revealed* [*apokalyptetai*] from faith for faith" (alt.).This gospel is "the power of God [*dynamis theou*] for salvation." Paul here relates the verb *apokalyptō* directly to the notion of "the power of God." The gospel here evidently involves an apocalyptic-eschatological event in the present: The righteousness of God becomes visible and powerful, or powerfully visible, in the gospel itself, and for that reason within the sphere of faith that it creates and brings into being. Faith is elicited or created by the gospel of God's powerful righteousness. Faith (*pistis*; "believing," *pisteuō*) in this passage of Romans is evidently for Paul a form of sharing in God's eschatological revelation, in God's eschatological activity and movement. Through the gospel a believer is taken up into this eschatological activity in order to participate in it, to become a part of it. Faith thus means for Paul that a believer can truly see and perceive this action, this movement, of God *into* (and then *in*) the world. The movement and presence of God are to be seen in the crucified Christ, whom God raised from the dead (Rom 1:1–4). Further, that this activity and movement of God involves judgement upon "this world" is evident in Rom 1:18–32: The revelation of God's righteousness "through faith for faith" also means that "the wrath of God," normally associated with the Parousia (cf. Rom 2:5; 5:9; 1 Thess 1:10), "is [now also] being [powerfully] revealed [*apokalyptetai*] from heaven against all ungodliness and wickedness of those who by their wickedness suppress the truth" (Rom 1:16–18, alt.). The creation of something eschatologically new in the world, faith, also entails God's judgment of a world marked by its absence before and apart from Christ.

Particularly relevant here is Gal 3:23, since it provides the only other instance of the verb in Galatians. Paul here characterizes faith itself as something which is "revealed," using the passive form of the verb *apokalyptō*: "Now before faith came [*elthein*], we were being held in custody under the law, being confined until faith should be revealed [*apokalyphthēnai*]." Here the verb *apokalyptō*, "to reveal," is being used as a synonym for the verb *erchomai*, "to come [on the world scene]":

Faith came (*elthein*).
Faith was revealed (*apokalyphthēnai*).

"Faith" was "revealed" and thus "came" (3:23, 25) onto the world stage, just as Christ himself did, as is clear from 3:19: "the law ... was added ... until the offspring [= Christ, 3:16] should come [*elthē*]." Christ entered—came into—a world in subjection to inimical enslaving powers (4:3, 8), in this case the law (3:25), in order to liberate human beings from their subjugation (cf. 5:1). To anticipate the comment on this passage later, the context indicates that Paul here understands "faith" to be a metonym for Christ himself (see also the comment on 1:23 below): "the law was our custodian until Christ [came on the scene], so that we might be justified on the basis of faith [i.e., by Christ]. Now that this faith [Christ] has come [*elthousēs*] [on the world scene], we are no longer under a custodian" (3:24–25). In this passage, then, the verb *apokalyptō* (3:23) means "apocalyptically reveal." On the basis of the usage in 3:23 as well as contextual considerations, that is also the probable meaning of the verb in 1:16: God apocalyptically revealed his Son in Paul's former life, thereby ending that life and creating a new one. Mutatus mutandis, the noun in 1:12c must mean "apocalyptic revelation," since it refers, as noted above, to the same event. It is a concise way of saying what 1:16 also says: God invaded Paul's life with Jesus Christ, his Son. On the other side of this apocalyptic event, and as an extension of it, Paul began to preach the gospel that he has preached to the Galatians (1:11) and still proclaims among the Gentiles (2:2). In the latter passage, Paul uses the noun *apokalypsis* for the second and last time in Galatians; the term also has the meaning "apocalyptic revelation" there (see comment on 2:2).

Galatians 1:12c is elliptical, containing no verb. In view of v. 12a, Paul probably intends that his Galatian readers and hearers complete the thought as follows:

1. For neither did I receive it [*parelabon auto*] from a human being,
2. nor was I taught [it],
3. but [I received it, *parelabon auto*] through an apocalyptic revelation of Jesus Christ.

The verb "received" (*parelabon*) here means the same as "was given"; in his reception of the gospel "through an apocalyptic revelation of Jesus Christ," Paul was no more than a recipient, as indeed he would have been if he had received it from a human being as a tradition (or had been taught it by a teacher). Paul has already used this verb (1:9) in connection with the Galatians who "received" (*parelabete*) the gospel that he preached to them, and he will use the uncompounded form in connection with the Galatians having "received" (*elabete*) the Spirit (3:2; also 3:14). It is thus evident that Paul is comfortable with the verb "receive" (*paralambanō*) in connection with "the gospel" (cf. 1 Cor 11:23; 15:1–3; Phil 4:9; 1 Thess 2:13; 4:1). For this reason, the contrast in 1:12 is not between "receiving from a human being" and "an apocalypse of Jesus Christ," but between two modes of receiving: "[receiving the gospel] from a human being" and "[receiving the gospel] through an apocalyptic revelation of Jesus Christ." Paul received it "through" (by means of) the latter.[124]

What Paul claims about this reception of the gospel he preached to the Galatians seems, however, to contradict what he will write in 1 Cor 15:1–5, where the wording is strikingly similar to that found in Gal 1:11–12:[125]

Gal 1:11–12	1 Cor 15:1–5 [AT]
I make known to you [*gnorizō de hymin*], brethren [*adelphoi*], concerning the gospel that was preached [*to euangelion to euangelisthen*] by me [which you received, *parelabete*; 1:9],	I make known to you [*gnorizō de hymin*], brethren [*adelphoi*], the gospel that I preached [*to euangelion ho euēngelisamēn*] to you, which you also received [*parelabete*] . . .
that it is not of human origin. For I neither received [*oude parelabon*] it from a human being nor was I taught [it], but [I received it] through an apocalyptic revelation of Jesus Christ.	for I passed on to you . . . what I also received [*parelabon*]: that "Christ died for our sins according to the Scriptures" . . .

In 1 Cor 15:1–5, what Paul "received" (was given by human beings) and "passed on" (transmitted to other human beings) as "the gospel" consisted of an already-fixed verbal tradition, whereas in Gal 1:12 what he received "through an apocalyptic revelation of Jesus Christ" (and by implication passed on to the Galatians, who "received" it) was no such thing. The fact that Paul in 1:4a has seemingly cited and adapted a key element of the gospel tradition found in 1 Cor 15:3–5, that "Christ died for our sins" (see comment on 1:4a above), suggests, however, that there is less of a contradiction than appears at first sight.

The issues at stake in the two texts are different. In 1 Cor 15:1–11, the issue is the resurrection of Christ, and Paul seeks to let the Corinthians know that his preaching of Christ's resurrection was common apostolic preaching from the beginning: "Whether then it was I or they, so we [all] preach and so you believed" (1 Cor 15:11 RSV). The content of "the gospel" transmitted in the existing tradition concerns primarily the death and resurrection of Christ "according

---

124. An alternative if less likely possibility would be to assume the verb *edidachthēn*, "I was taught [the gospel]," in v. 12c—following v. 12b, where Paul claims that he "was not taught [it by a human being]," and similar to 1 Thess 4:9, where Paul describes the Thessalonian Christians as *theodidaktoi*, "those taught by God." Verse 12b could then be rendered: "But [I was taught the gospel by God] through an apocalyptic revelation of Jesus Christ." Again, the issue is not teaching as such, but the source of the gospel.

125. The Galatians themselves may be completely unaware of this problem, unless they are familiar with the tradition of 1 Cor 15:1–5, a portion of which Paul cites in 1:4 (see comment there).

to the Scriptures" (1 Cor 15:3–5). In Galatians, the issue is whether Gentile believers in Christ need to be compelled to do the law, beginning with circumcision. As the account of his second visit to Jerusalem makes plain (2:1–10), Paul's preaching of a circumcision-free and law-free gospel for the Gentiles is *not* based on common apostolic tradition, going back to the beginning (cf. Acts 10:34–11:18, esp. 10:45; 11:1–2, 18). Paul locates the origin of the gospel he has preached to the Galatians and still proclaims among the Gentiles (Gal 2:2) in the event of God's apocalyptic revelation of his Son in his life at a particular moment in his life (cf. Eph 3:3, 6; Acts 9:15; 22:21; 26:17). Its content is evidently God's unconditional grace for Gentile believers, indeed (as Paul will insist) for all who believe, whether Gentile or Jew: justification takes place as a result of "the faith of Christ" and not as a result of "works of the law" (Gal 2:16; see comment there). "The (one) gospel" can thus be authentically expressed in different verbal formulations, some of them rooted in tradition received and passed on (as in 1 Cor 15:1–5), others not (as in Galatians).

For Paul, moreover, the criterion of the gospel's truth in both 1 Corinthians and Galatians is the crucified Christ, whom God raised from the dead (Gal 1:1; 1 Cor 15:12–18):

Gal 3:1	1 Cor 2:2 (cf. 1:18, 23)
"[When I came to Galatia,] Jesus Christ was portrayed as crucified before your eyes"	"[When I came to Corinth,] I decided to know nothing among you except Jesus Christ, and him crucified"

The diverse formulations of "the gospel" in particular situations or in ongoing traditions must all be subject to this criterion, whatever their supposed origin. The "different gospel" of the new preachers is rejected and attacked by Paul because it does not, in his estimation, meet this fundamental criterion (see on 1:6–9). What must also be added here is that "the apocalyptic revelation of Jesus Christ" to which Paul refers is probably the source of this criterion of discernment and evaluation in the first place (see further below on 1:15–16). He has given this criterion, which is itself the gospel (cf. 3:1), a contextual application and elaboration for the Gentiles in Galatia (cf. comment on 2:15–21).

[13–14] The mention of the apocalyptic revelation of Jesus Christ now causes Paul to remind the Galatians ("for you have [already] heard"[126]) of the context in which that apocalyptic revelation took place: his "manner of life [*anastrophē*] earlier [*pote*] in Judaism [*Ioudaïsmos*]." *Anastrophē* can also mean "conduct" or

---

126. Paul does not say how. Cf. 1:23, with its reference to Paul's notoriety as a persecutor of Christians in the past.

The Origin and the Truth of the Gospel

"behavior" (BDAG 73; cf. Eph 4:22; 1 Tim 4:2; Heb 13:7; Jas 3:13; 1 Pet 1:15, 18; 2:12; 3:1, 2, 16; 2 Pet 2:7; 3:11), and that is where Paul's focus lies in these verses (cf. 2 Macc 6:23). The "Judaism" referred to is the Pharisaic variety, since in his letter to the Philippians (3:5 AT), Paul says that he had once been "according to the law a Pharisee,"[127] though the Galatians may not be aware of such distinctions or care about them. In his "manner of life in [Pharisaic] Judaism," Paul kept himself busy with three interrelated activities, all of them far removed from a willingness to receive the gospel or to learn it from another human being (parallels with the account in Acts are given in the footnotes):

1. I persecuted [ediōkon][128] the church of God[129] beyond measure [kath' hyperbolēn],[130] and
2. I sought to destroy [eporthoun] it,[131] and
3. I advanced [proekopton] in Judaism beyond many of my own age [synēlikiōtas] among my people [en tō genei mou], being to a greater degree a zealot [zēlōtēs][132] for my patriarchal traditions [tōn patrikōn mou paradoseōn].[133]

---

127. Cf. Acts 23:6; 26:5: "I have belonged to the strictest sect of our religion and lived as a Pharisee."

128. Cf. Acts 26:11 RSV: "In raging fury, ... I persecuted [ediōkon] them even to foreign cities [Damascus in 9:2]"; 22:4 RSV: "I persecuted [aor.] this Way to the death, binding and delivering to prison both men and women"; further 9:4-5; 22:7-8; 26:14-15.

129. Cf. Acts 8:1-3: "And Saul [Paul] was consenting to his [Stephen's] death. And on that day a great persecution arose against the church in Jerusalem. ... But Saul was ravaging the church, and entering house after house, he dragged off men and women and committed them to prison" (RSV, alt.).

130. Cf. Acts 26:9-12. Paul's phrase, which is classical, is fairly common in his letters (Rom 7:13; 1 Cor 12:31; 2 Cor 1:8; 4:17), occurring nowhere else in the NT. It does not necessarily mean "violently" (NRSV), though there are good indications at the end of v. 13 (destroying the church) and in v. 14 (zeal) that Paul's persecuting activity did entail violence (see below).

131. The verb Paul uses is a conative imperfect (BDF #326). Cf. Acts 9:21: "And all who heard him [Paul] were amazed, and said, 'Is not this the man who made havoc [porthēsas; lit., 'who destroyed'] in Jerusalem of those who called on this name?'" (RSV).

132. This word is a noun (BAGD 427; LSJ 755), though it is often translated as if it were an adjective: "zealous" (NRSV, NIV, KJV; Burton; Betz; and other commentators).

133. Cf. Acts 22:3:"[I was] brought up in this city at the feet of Gamaliel, educated according to the strict manner [kata akribeian] of the law of our fathers [tou patrōou nomou], being a zealot [zēlōtēs] for God as you all are this day" (NRSV, alt.); Josephus, Vita 191: "The sect of the Pharisees ... have the reputation of being better than others in exactness [akribeia] concerning the rules of their fathers [peri ta patria nomima]"; Ant. 13.297: "The Pharisees had passed on to the people certain regulations [nomima] handed down by former generations [ek paterōn diadochēs] and not recorded in the laws of Moses, ... those which were from the tradition of the fathers [ta d' ek paradoseōs tōn paterōn]"; Philo, Spec. 2.253: "There are thousands who have their eyes upon him [God], zealots for the laws [zēlōtai nomōn], strictest guardians of the ancestral institutions [phylakes tōn patriōn akribestatoi], merciless to those who do anything to subvert them." Cf. Mark 7:3-5.

The three main Greek verbs are all imperfect, indicating repeated or continuous action ("I was persecuting," etc.) over a period of time, the time of his pre-Christian and preapostolic "manner of life in Judaism." That Paul is here not merely exaggerating for rhetorical effect (so Koet 80) is indicated by Acts where close parallels to Paul's formulations occur (see also Josephus and Philo).[134]

Paul is one of only two authors in the first century C.E. to use the term "Judaism," the other being the author of 4 Maccabees (4:26).[135] This author is in turn dependent on 2 Maccabees, written in the first century B.C.E. about events the century before, in which the author employs the term three times (2:21; 8:1; 14:38) to designate the religion of the Jews (or Judeans), here as the alternative to the "Hellenism [*Hellēnismos*]" (4:13) that Antiochus IV Epiphanes wanted to impose upon the inhabitants of Judea. The term "Judaism" is not found again in extant literature before the letters of Ignatius (*Magn.* 10.3; *Phld.* 6.1), this time as the alternative to "Christianity [*Christianismos*]." Paul's use of the term in Galatians seems to stand midway between its use in 2 Maccabees and Ignatius. To the Galatians, Paul's "Judaism" will be understood as the religion of the Jews (Judeans), who in the Diaspora distinguish themselves from their Gentile neighbors by observing the Mosaic Law, particularly in keeping the commandments pertaining to the circumcision of sons, the observance of the Sabbath, and the eating and preparation of food. Paul, however, presents his own manner of life in this Judaism as a thing of the past (cf. Phil 3:4–9), now that he has become a slave and an apostle of Christ (1:1, 10). Indeed, his agenda in the Letter to the Galatians is to repreach the gospel of Christ in such a way as to make the religion of the law (Judaism) unnecessary, superfluous, and even dangerous (5:2–4) for the Gentiles in Galatia, thereby countering the "different gospel" of the new missionaries, who are attempting to impose the law on them. Paul is already here functioning as a paradigm, as he does more clearly in what follows (cf. Lyons; Gaventa 1986a; Hansen 1993).

Paul's account of his manner of life in Judaism is brief, but the focus falls on his persecuting (*ediōkon*) "the church of God" and his attempt to destroy (*eporthoun*) it (1:13), as it does in two other passages where Paul mentions his pre-Christian, preapostolic past: "For I am the least of the apostles, unfit to be called an apostle, because I persecuted [*ediōxa*] the church of God [*tēn ekklēsian tou theou*]" (1 Cor 15:9). "According to the law, [I was] a Pharisee; according to zeal [*zēlos*] [for the law], [I was] a persecutor [*diōkōn*] of the

---

134. See the previous seven footnotes.
135. The Judaism here referred to is not of course "rabbinic Judaism," which first emerged in the late first century C.E. and of which modern Judaism is the heir. The term could perhaps best be rendered "early Judaism," or "pre-Judaism." Mason argues that in Paul's time the term "did not yet mean 'Judaism' as a comprehensive system and way of life" (471) but that it meant "Judaizing," in Paul's case, "a violent harassment of Jesus' followers (Gal 1:13) out of zeal, as he puts it, for the ancestral traditions (1:14)" (469).

The Origin and the Truth of the Gospel

church [*tēn ekklēsian*]; according to the righteousness that is in the law, [I was] blameless" (Phil 3:5-6 AT).

The latter passage indicates that Gal 1:14, where Paul refers to himself as a zealot (*zēlōtēs*) for his ancestral traditions (those pertaining to the law),[136] also probably has his persecution of the church in view. In Jewish thought in Paul's time, "zeal" was often associated with an ardent, even murderous defense of the law, which functioned as a boundary marker, distinguishing Jews from the surrounding Hellenistic culture. First Maccabees recounts how "a Jew came forward in the sight of all to offer sacrifice on the altar in Modein, according to the king's [Antiochus Epiphanes'] command." The account then continues: "When Mattathias saw it, he burned with zeal [*ezēlōsen*] and his heart was stirred. He gave vent to righteous anger; he ran and killed him on the altar. At the same time, he killed the king's officer who was forcing them to sacrifice, and he tore down the altar. Thus he burned with zeal [*ezēlōsen*] for the law, just as Phinehas did against Zimri son of Salu" (2:23-28).

According to Num 25:6-15, Phinehas slew Zimri son of Salu, an Israelite, and his Midianite wife, because he regarded intermarriage with foreigners as objectionable. Phinehas is praised for this act because "he was zealous [*ezēlōsen*] for his God" (25:13 LXX). In Sir 45:23-24, Phinehas is feted "for being zealous [*zēlōsai*] in the fear of the Lord." Presumably Paul's zeal was like that of Phinehas (cf. 4 Macc 18:12; Philo, *Spec.* 1.56) and Mattathias (cf. Josephus, *Ant.* 12.271), and it led him to persecute "the church of God" beyond measure and even to seek to destroy it.[137] The verb *portheō*, "destroy," has violent overtones, being used by Josephus for the destruction of towns and villages (*J.W.* 4.405, 534) and the devastation of Jerusalem (*Ant.* 10.135; cf. Hengel 71). Acts also portrays the pre-Christian Paul (Saul) as a violent persecutor (8:3; 9:1; 22:4; 26:10). Verse 14 (Paul's intense zeal for his ancestral traditions concerning the law) is thus an explanation for 1:13 (his persecution of "the church of God" and his attempt to destroy it).

When Paul refers to "the church of God" (*tēn ekklēsian tou theou*) in v. 13, as in 1 Cor 15:9, in connection with his persecuting activity, he is probably referring not to "the Christian community at large" (Burton) but to the Jerusalem church in particular. According to Acts 8:1-3, Paul's efforts were initially directed against "the church in Jerusalem" (cf. 9:13, 21; 26:10), and there probably were no other churches to speak of at the time. Its members

---

136. In Paul's mind, the "patriarchal traditions" may have to do with the oral law of the Pharisees (Lightfoot 82; cf. Mark 7:1-5), but the law as such may be in view (Calvin 19; Martyn 155). In the phrase, the Galatians will probably hear simply a reference to "Judaism" and the observance of the law among Jews of whatever party.

137. There have been attempts to suggest that Paul the zealot for his ancestral traditions was actually a Zealot, like "Simon the Zealot" (Acts 1:13): e.g., Lightfoot 81-92; Fairchild. Most commentators disagree (also Donaldson 673).

were all Christian Jews. The use of the word *ekklēsia* for the Christian assembly is probably rooted in the Hebrew *qāhāl* (and its Aramaic equivalent); the Greek term is used more than a hundred times in the LXX as a translation of this Hebrew term. In Neh 13:1, the Hebrew *qāhāl hāʾĕlōhîm*, "the assembly [congregation] of God," is translated in the LXX as *ekklēsia theou*, "assembly of God" (cf. Deut 23:1–4, where *qāhāl yhwh*, "the assembly of Yahweh," is translated by the LXX as *ekklēsia kyriou*, "the assembly of the Lord"; also 1 Chr 28:8). A near equivalent occurs in 1QM 4.10: *qāhāl ʾēl*, "the assembly of God." It is thus quite possible that the earliest Christians in Jerusalem regarded themselves as "the assembly (church) of God" in the last days and that this self-designation was translated into Greek accordingly, to be subsequently applied to other communities of Christians in Judea (1 Thess 2:14) and elsewhere (1 Cor 1:2; 10:32; 11:16, 22; Acts 20:28; 1 Tim 3:5, 15). That "the church of God" in v. 13 probably refers, at least primarily, to the community of Christian Jews located in Jerusalem[138] does not necessarily mean that Paul was not active elsewhere in the immediate vicinity, especially as time went on (cf. "the churches of Judea" in Gal 1:22–23; see comment there). In the account of Acts, Paul was also active in Damascus, where there were also "disciples" (9:19); according to his own account in Galatians, Paul "returned again" to that city (1:17) not long after his apostolic call (1:16), which means not only that this event occurred in or near Damascus but also that he must have been active as a persecutor there. The genitive "of God" in any event clearly shows whose side God was on in Paul's retrospective look at his "way of life earlier in Judaism." He now knows that he persecuted the church that had been gathered by God.

Paul does not indicate here (or indeed elsewhere) exactly *why* he persecuted the church of God.[139] For Paul it is important to mention to the Galatians only *that* he had done so and that his action followed from his zealous devotion to the law. What Paul found objectionable in the acceptance of Jesus as the Messiah by fellow Jews, he does not say. In vv. 13–14, Paul has a limited and specific agenda. "The whole of this narrative," writes Calvin (18), "was put in as an argument," whereby Paul "relates that in all his life he had such an abhorrence" of the gospel "that he was its mortal enemy and a destroyer" of the church. "From this," continues Calvin, "we infer that his conversion was divine," brought about by God. Paul turns to his pre-Christian, preapostolic "manner of life in Judaism" not only to show that he had not received or learned the gospel from any human source, but also to place the event of God's apocalyptic revelation of Jesus Christ (1:12c) in the context of his former life in Judaism, when he was a persecutor of God's own church and sought to destroy it out of intense

---

138. Paul gives no indication that his persecuting activity was aimed at only a part of this church, e.g., the Hellenists in Acts 6–8 (so Dunn 59).

139. Acts is also silent on the matter. On this issue, see Hultgren; Martyn 161–62.

The Origin and the Truth of the Gospel 89

(Pharisaic) zeal for his "patriarchal traditions," for the law.[140] The gospel he preached to the Galatians, and which he still preaches, was thus "hardly the message that a zealot and former persecutor would devise" (Matera 62).

[15–17] One of the remarkable features about these three verses, which are one long sentence, is that a subordinate temporal clause rather than the main clause contains Paul's elaboration of his conversion and call,[141] to which he alluded at the end of 1:12: "And [*de*] when [God,] the One who set me apart from the womb of my mother and called me through his grace, was pleased to apocalyptically reveal his Son in me, that I might preach him among the Gentiles . . ." (vv. 15–16b).

The main clause, containing the primary message of the passage for the Galatians, concerns his (minimal or nonexistent) contacts with other human beings, especially the Jerusalem apostles, in the first two to three years (1:18) after his conversion and call: "I did not immediately confer with flesh and blood, nor did I go away to Jerusalem to those who were apostles before me, but I went away into Arabia and again I returned to Damascus" (vv. 16c–17).

The issue here is the origin of Paul's gospel (1:11–12)—it is "*not* of human origin"—and he is trying to show in vv. 16c–17 that he could not possibly have received it from other human beings, least of all from the apostles in Jerusalem. Paul's agenda is thus not to give a full account of his conversion and call, but to present them together as a divine act in which human beings played no role whatsoever (cf. 1:1, 11–12).

The subordinate clause (vv. 15–16b) with which Paul begins thus looks forward (to vv. 16c–17) rather than backward (to vv. 13–14). Nevertheless, a connection to what precedes is established by *hote de*, "And when," which assumes that Paul's "manner of life earlier [*pote*] in Judaism" (v. 13) is the context within which God's apocalyptic revelation of his Son occurred. The activities reported in vv. 16c–17 occurred after this cataclysmic event that Paul in 2:19–20 will characterize as a crucifixion with Christ.

The key claim in the subordinate temporal clause is that "God[142] was pleased [*eudokēsen*] . . . to apocalyptically reveal [*apokalypsai*] his Son in me [*en emoi*]" (vv. 15a, 16a). That claim refers specifically to Paul's conversion[143]

---

140. Paul's formulations (advancement in Judaism beyond his contemporaries, even more a zealot for his ancestral traditions than they) suggest that Paul's understanding of Pharisaism was probably not wholly shared by other Pharisees.

141. Paul's apostolic call was at the same time his conversion; see comment on 1:12 above. On the meaning and the appropriateness of the latter term in Paul's case, see note 120 above.

142. Whether *theos*, "God," belongs to the original text is not certain, but there is no doubt that God is meant.

143. See note 120 above on the use of this term. It is to be understood passively (Paul was converted by God from his manner of life in Judaism to Christ), not actively (as though Paul on his own initiative changed religions).

(from his previous manner of life in Judaism to Christ, a change effected by God), and it is complemented by language that pertains specifically to his apostolic call: "the One who set me apart [*aphorisas*; cf. Rom 1:1] from the womb of my mother and called me through his grace [cf. 1 Cor 15:10] ... that I might preach him among the Gentiles" (vv. 15bc, 16b). We discuss each in turn, first the call and then the conversion, even though the two events actually coincide in Paul's case, at least in his presentation to the Galatians. The accounts of Paul's "Damascus road experience" in Acts (9:3–9; 22:6–11; 26:12–18) support this presentation, even though Acts refrains from calling Paul an apostle of Christ.

For many interpreters, v. 15bc ("the One who set me apart from the womb of my mother [*ek koilias mētros mou*] and called [*kalesas*] me through his grace") and v. 16b ("that I might preach [*euangelizōmai*] him [God's Son] among the Gentiles [*en tois ethnesin*]") contain an allusion to the call of the prophet Jeremiah in Jer 1:5 (LXX): "And the word of the Lord came to me, saying, 'Before I formed you in the womb [*en koilia*] I knew you, and before you came forth from [your] mother [*ek mētras*], I consecrated you; I appointed you a prophet to the Gentiles [*eis ethnē*]." Jeremiah's mission to the Gentiles is not salvific, however, in contrast to Paul's, which is (Koet 83 n. 5; cf. Jer 1:10, 15–16). A more pertinent parallel may be found in the second Servant Song of Second Isaiah, 49:1–6 (LXX), especially vv. 1 and 6 (Koet 82–83; and many commentators): "Listen to me, islands; pay attention, Gentiles [*ethnē*]: ... From the womb of my mother [*ek koilias mētros mou*][144] he [God] called [*ekalesen*] my name. ... And he said to me: '... I have appointed you ... to be a light for the Gentiles [*eis phōs ethnōn*] for salvation until the end of the earth.'"

The motif of the Servant as a light to the Gentiles (*ethnē*) already occurs in the first Servant Song (42:6). As a light to the Gentiles, the Servant (*pais*), identified as Jacob in LXX 42:1 (cf. 41:8–9), will "open the eyes of the blind, lead out from their bonds those who have been bound and from the prison house also those who sit in darkness" (42:7 LXX); therefore in the name of this Servant "shall the Gentiles hope" (42:4 LXX). In Isa 49:1, the Gentiles are singled out and invited to listen to the Servant. Moreover, the Servant, who is to be a light to the Gentiles for salvation unto the end of the earth (49:6), describes God as "the one who formed me from the womb [*ek koilias*] to be his own slave [*doulos*]" (49:5). In an analogous manner, Paul, a "slave of Christ" (Gal 1:10) called to preach him as God's Son among the Gentiles (v. 16b), describes God as "the one who set me apart from the womb of my mother [*ek koilias mētros mou*] and called me through his grace." God's setting Paul apart thus occurred "before birth, before human nurturing, before cultural socialisation, and before Paul himself became a human agent" (Barclay 2002:139). It is perhaps no mere coincidence that the Paul of Acts quotes Isa 49:6 to describe his missionary task

---

144. These words are exactly the same as Paul's in v. 15b.

The Origin and the Truth of the Gospel

in Acts 13:47 (cf. Acts 1:8); Acts may here preserve an authentic reminiscence of the importance of the passage for Paul's own understanding of his apostolic vocation. In the three accounts of Paul's call in Acts, his mission "among the Gentiles" also plays an increasingly prominent role (9:15; 22:21; 26:17–18).[145]

Paul's use of ideas and words from Isa 49:1–6 is clearly limited and selective. The Servant's task as God's own slave is also to "gather Jacob . . . and Israel" to God (49:5). Paul does not see such a gathering to be part of his apostolic vocation (Gal 2:7–8; contrast Acts 9:15). His focus remains on preaching the gospel to the Gentiles: "God was pleased to apocalyptically reveal his Son in me, that [*hina*] I might preach him among the Gentiles."

Perhaps the key phrase in 1:15bc, 16b is the characterization of God as "the One who . . . called me through his grace," *ho . . . kalesas dia tēs charitos autou*, in 1:15b, which applies not only to Paul's apostolic call but also to his conversion to Christ, recounted in the following clause (1:16a). In 1:6, God is described as "the One who called [*ho kalesas*] you [the Galatians] into the grace [*en chariti*] of Christ" (see comment there). As noted in the comment on 1:3, God's "grace," a synonym for God's free and unconditional liberating love (cf. 2:20), is both a sphere (as in 1:6) and a power (as in v. 15c) in and by which human beings can live as God's "new creation" (6:15). As far as his conversion is concerned, Paul presents himself as a paradigm of someone who has been called by God through grace into grace (see below on 2:9 and 2:19–21).

In 1:15a and 16a (God "was pleased to apocalyptically reveal his Son in me"), which specifically concern Paul's conversion rather than his call, he refers to a past event and emphasizes the divine initiative: "God was pleased" [*eudokēsen*, aor. ind.], which means "God himself decided." Paul had nothing to do with it, a point emphasized by the characterization of God as the One who set him apart from birth and called him (in or near Damascus) by his grace. This God, who acts in sovereign freedom, decided "to apocalyptically reveal his Son in me." The verb is *apokalypsai* (inf.), which is cognate to the noun *apokalypsis*, used in 1:12c: "an apocalyptic revelation" (see Excursus 6, above, on the translation of these terms). It is important to observe that in 1:16 Paul does not use the verb "to see," *horaō*, with himself as the subject (as in 1 Cor 9:1), but the verb *apokalyptō*, of which God is the subject. What *Paul* saw is not here at issue, but what *God* was pleased to reveal. Paul wants to give full attention not to his own human experience, his vision of the risen Lord, but to the "apocalyptic" activity and movement of God into and in his life. Paul's narrative is not so much autobiography as testimony (Martyn; Barclay 2002: 139).

---

145. The phrase "among [*en*] the Gentiles" also occurs in 2:2; see the comment on 2:8 for the possible implications ("to the Gentiles" or "in Gentile lands"?).

In this connection, the meaning of the prepositional phrase *en emoi* ("in me") in 1:16 needs to be properly understood: "God was pleased to apocalyptically reveal his Son *in me*." Commentators give three rather different interpretations to this phrase:

View 1. The phrase *en emoi* has the same meaning as the simple dative *emoi*, "to me" (e.g., Martyn; cf. BDF #220.1). This interpretation fits well with the idea of an (experienced) objective revelation to Paul, which is what seems to be involved in the appearances of the risen Christ recounted in 1 Cor 15:5–9. The problem with this interpretation, however, is that Paul could very easily and clearly have used a dative, as he does elsewhere when using the same verb (Phil 3:15; 1 Cor 2:10; 14:30; cf. Matt 16:17).

View 2. The phrase *en emoi* means "through me" (e.g., Lightfoot; Dunn; Hays). According to this interpretation, the first part of 1:16 ("apocalyptically reveal his Son in/through me") looks forward to the following subordinate clause ("in order that I might preach him among the Gentiles"). This interpretation means that God reveals his Son among the Gentiles through the preaching work of Paul. Romans 1:17 could support this interpretation: the righteousness of God is revealed "in" (*en*), and thus through, the gospel that Paul preaches. But the syntax of Gal 1:15–16 can scarcely support this interpretation. The revelation of God's Son "in" Paul took place in the past (God *was pleased* to reveal). The present preaching activity (*euangelizōmai*, pres.) of Paul among the Gentiles was the purpose and thus the *consequence* (*hina*) of the revelation of God's Son "in" Paul, not a part of that revelation.

View 3. The phrase *en emoi* is to be taken literally, meaning "within me" (e.g., Burton). In this case, we would be dealing with an inner, subjective revelation and experience (cf. 4:6; 2 Cor 4:6). This interpretation seems to be the most natural. The context, however, lays no emphasis on a subjective (mystical or inner) experience by Paul. In Paul's very concise report about "the apocalyptic revelation of Jesus Christ," there is no trace of a journey to heaven during a dream, a vision, or a trance whereby he received his gospel or came into contact with the risen Christ. The subjective explanation can only appeal to the phrase *en emoi* itself. That might be sufficient, except that there is another, more convincing possibility:

View 4. The phrase *en emoi* means "in my former manner of life" (de Boer 2002: 31). The phrase refers to Paul's earlier manner of life in what he calls "Judaism" (1:13–14; see comment above). The apocalyptic revelation of God's Son "in" Paul stands in direct relation to his previous manner of life (*anastrophē*) "in" (Pharisaic) Judaism (1:13–14) when, according to his own report, he persecuted "the church of God" (cf. Phil 3:6) and "advanced in Judaism" beyond many of his contemporaries, "being to a greater degree a zealot" for his ancestral traditions. As noted previously, "the apocalyptic revelation of Jesus Christ" about which Paul writes in v. 12c took place in

The Origin and the Truth of the Gospel

the past and resulted in Paul's becoming a preacher of the gospel among the Gentiles, a result intended by God. The context suggests then that the phrase "in me" must mean "in the midst of my former career as a Pharisaic zealot who persecuted the church of God." The action of God brought this career to an end. We can paraphrase 1:15–16b as follows: "God invaded my life as a Pharisaic zealot and persecutor of the church with his Son, thereby bringing this life to an end, so that I could subsequently preach God's Son among the Gentiles, as I now do."

The context thus confirms that Paul wants the Galatians to understand that "the *apokalypsis* of Jesus Christ" (1:12c), whereby "God was pleased to reveal [*apokalypsai*] his Son in me" (1:16a), means that God entered into the life of Paul, the persecutor of God's church and an extremely zealous, law-observant Pharisee, in order to bring that manner of life to a complete and irrevocable end. That is, Paul wants them to understand this event "apocalyptically": in his own life, Paul personifies the radical discontinuity between the two ages (this one and the one to come) characteristic of all apocalyptic eschatology, whether Jewish or Christian (see Excursus 2). Through the gracious act of God, a radical discontinuity came into being between Paul the persecutor of God's church and Paul the apostle to the Gentiles. This action of God in his own life is thus interpreted and presented by Paul as an apocalyptic-eschatological event, or to put it somewhat more carefully, as his *participation* in an apocalyptic-eschatological (thus cosmic) event, that of "Jesus Christ," God's "Son" (see below on 2:19–20, where Paul uses the language of crucifixion with Christ to express this participation). For Paul, furthermore, the discontinuity between "then" and "now" does not primarily involve a subjective and inner experience, but an objective and visible reality. One manner of life had been utterly destroyed, and a new one had taken its place. The apocalyptic revelation of God's Son "in" Paul was no private, merely personal event but a public one as well. The public life of Paul was completely changed, as everyone—friend or foe, believer or opponent in Galatia—could see and confirm (cf. 1:23!).

Paul in 1:12c has referred to the apocalyptic revelation of "Jesus Christ"; in v. 16a he refers to God's having apocalyptically revealed "his Son" in his former manner of life. Since he refers to "the Son of God, Jesus Christ" in 2 Cor 1:19, the switch from "Jesus Christ" to "his Son" could be simply a stylistic variation. That the reference to Jesus as God's Son in v. 16a may not be such a stylistic variation, nor merely arbitrary, is suggested by the first account of Paul's call in Acts, where his first words as a believer in Christ are "He is the Son of God!" (9:20). The importance that the designation will come to have for Paul is indicated by the opening verses of Romans, where Paul will refer to "the gospel of God . . . concerning his Son" and to "the gospel of his Son" (Rom 1:1, 3, 9). The claim, or insight, that Jesus is God's "Son" is not unique to Paul in the NT (cf. esp. Mark 1:1; 14:61; John 20:31) and is probably rooted in the fact that the Davidic king on whom Jewish messianic expectations were based is called God's (adopted) son in 2 Sam 7:12–14 (cf. Heb 1:5; 4Q174 1.10–13); Ps 2:7 (cf. Heb 1:5; 5:5; Acts 13:33); and Ps 89:26–27 (88:27–28 LXX).[146] Jesus' habit of referring to God as "Abba," Father (Mark 14:36; cf. Gal 4:6; Rom 8:15), may also have played a role in its prominence among early believers in Jesus as the Messiah. For Paul, as for other NT writers, the designation points to Jesus' special, unique relationship with God, which is distinguished from that of believers, who are "sons" of God only by adoption (Gal 4:6–7; cf. Rom 8:23). As God's Son sent into the world (Gal 4:4–5; Rom 8:3, 32), Jesus acts completely in accordance with the will or intention of God, his Father (Gal 1:1–4; cf. Rom 5:10; 1 Cor 1:9; 15:28; 2 Cor 1:19; 1 Thess 1:10), and for that reason he stands wholly in God's favor (Gal 1:1; Rom 1:1–4).

When God invaded Paul's life as a zealous Pharisee and persecutor of the church, he did so with his Son, Jesus Christ. In this event, Paul came to understand that the crucified Jesus, whose followers he had been persecuting, had been raised and thus vindicated by God as his Son (Gal 1:1; cf. Rom 1:3–4). Paul in effect realized for the first time that the crucified Christ was also the risen Christ, approved by God. In his preaching of the gospel, however, Paul astonishingly preached precisely the reverse, that the risen Christ was also the crucified Christ. When Paul first went to Galatia, he did not speak about his personal vision of the risen Christ. On the contrary, according to 3:1, he placarded the crucified Christ before the eyes of the Galatians, the Christ who on the stage of human history died on a cross. This Christ is "the Son of God, the one who loved me and gave himself up for me" (2:20; see comments on 2:19–21 and 3:1).

We now turn to the main clause of 1:15–17. It consists of four coordinate clauses, two negative ones followed by two positive ones:

> [16c]I did not immediately [thereafter][147] confer with flesh and blood,
> [17a]nor did I [at that time] go away to Jerusalem to those who were apostles before me,
> [17b]but I [immediately][148] went away into Arabia
> [17c]and [after that] again I returned to Damascus [where I stayed put].

---

146. In the Dead Sea Scrolls, divine sonship sometimes seems to be an attribute of the Messiah, at least by implication: 4Q246; 4Q174; 1QSa 2.11–12; see also *4 Ezra* (2 Esd) 7.28–29; 13.32, 37, 52; 14.9.

147. Following Longenecker 33, who discusses other ways of understanding *eutheōs*, "immediately": Some prefer to take the adverb, not with the negative formulation in 1:16c, but with the first affirmative clause in 1:17b, e.g., NIV: "I did not consult any man, nor did I go up to Jerusalem.... but I went *immediately* into Arabia" (also Lightfoot; Burton). The adverb probably goes, given the word order, with the negative clause in 1:16c, but there is in fact no discernible difference in meaning: What Paul did not immediately do is the opposite of what he did (immediately) do: go away into Arabia.

148. See previous note.

The Origin and the Truth of the Gospel

As far as the thought goes, 1:16c and 1:17b go together (Paul did not immediately go and confer with flesh-and-blood human beings following his apostolic call; rather, he went off immediately into Arabia), as do 1:17a and 1:17c (Paul did not in this initial period of time as apostle visit with the apostles before him in Jerusalem; rather, after his stay in Arabia, he returned to Damascus, where he stayed put).

The issue here is the origin of Paul's gospel (1:11–12)—it is *"not* of human origin"—and he is trying to show in 1:16c–17 that he could not possibly have received it from other human beings. Thus he first informs the Galatians about what he did *not* do when God called him: he did not "confer [*prosanethemēn*] with flesh and blood." The phrase "flesh and blood" is an idiom that functions as a metonym for human beings as distinct from God (cf. 1:1, 11–12), emphasizing in this context their insignificance (cf. 1 Cor 15:50; Matt 16:17; Eph 6:12; Sir 14:18; 17:31). Does the verb exclude all other contacts with human beings, even other Christians? That is unlikely (cf. Acts 9:10–19; 22:12–16), and the verb implies only that he did not consult (talk formally) with anyone about the gospel so as to receive an authoritative interpretation of it (cf. Dunn 67; MM 546; LSJ 1501), certainly not—and this is probably the key point—the apostles in Jerusalem. For Paul did *not* go away to (the church in) Jerusalem, to those who were apostles before him. He does not specify who precisely these apostles were, but he is certainly not referring to apostles of churches (2 Cor 8:23; Phil 2:25; Acts 14:4, 14), but to apostles of the risen Christ like himself (1 Cor 9:1; see comment on 1:1 above). For Paul, such apostles are a group wider than the Twelve (contrast Acts 1:26; Rev 21:14), if only because he includes himself in it (Gal 1:18, "before me"). The apostles of Christ whom Paul here has in view are probably not only Cephas (Peter) and John (1:18–19; 2:8–9) but also James (1:19; 2:9) and Barnabas (2:1, 9; 1 Cor 9:1, 5–6; cf. Acts 14:4, 14). According to 1 Cor 15:5–8, the risen Christ appeared not only "to Peter and the Twelve," but also "to James and then to all the apostles." Just as Peter is actually one of "the Twelve" though here formally distinguished from them, so also James is actually one of "the apostles" though formally distinguished from them. The expression "all the apostles" here seems to mean "all the other apostles." Despite this reference to "all the apostles," Paul still goes on to refer to himself separately: "Last of all . . . he appeared also to me. For I am the least of the apostles . . . because I persecuted the church of God" (1 Cor 15:8–9). In 1 Cor 9:5, Paul mentions "the other apostles and the brothers of the Lord and Cephas." This formulation would appear to distinguish "apostles" from "brothers of the Lord," yet Cephas (Peter) is clearly an apostle for Paul (Gal 1:18–19; 2:8), and the brothers of the Lord probably also are in his view, as is Barnabas, whom he mentions in the next verse (1 Cor 9:6; cf. 9:1).

Instead of going to Jerusalem, the first thing Paul did after his conversion and call was to go away to "Arabia." The term comes from a Hebrew word meaning "dry area" or "desert." Arabia here refers to the kingdom of the Nabateans, ruled by King Aretas IV, that extended from near Damascus down the east side of the Jordan all the way to the Gulf of Aqaba (Murphy-O'Connor 1993; BDAG 127; Josephus, *J.W.* 5.159; *Ant.* 18.112; Diod. Sic. 19.94.1; cf. 2 Cor 11:32–33, where Paul mentions Aretas). Paul thus went to Gentile territory. He does not say what he did there, but as Luther rhetorically asks: "What else was he to do but preach Christ?" (Luther 1535: 74). He subsequently (but we do not know precisely when) "returned again" to Damascus, which lay on the boundary between Arabia and Syria. The adverb "again" implies that his conversion and call took place in or near Damascus (cf. Acts 9:3; 22:6; 26:12, 20). He does not tell how long he stayed in Damascus or what he did there. By informing his Galatian readers that he returned again to Damascus, he makes the point that he did not go to Jerusalem during this initial period of his life as a Christian and as an apostle. He had no contact with the apostles in Jerusalem and thus could not have received or learned the gospel that he preached to the Galatians from them (with the implication that "his" gospel could then be construed as a distortion or a misunderstanding of what they had taught him). They had nothing to do with it. The gospel he preached to the Galatians originated in God's apocalyptic disclosure of his Son in his life.

Summary. In the first part (1:11–12) of this passage, Paul asserts that the gospel he preached in Galatia does not have a human origin. He therefore did not receive it in the form of a tradition that had been passed on to him by human beings (such as the apostles in Jerusalem), nor had he learned it from them. His gospel originates in God via an apocalyptic revelation of Jesus Christ, not in human traditioning or learning processes. The second and third parts substantiate the claim that he did not receive it from (other) human beings. Before his call, Paul was a zealous (Pharisaic) Jew and persecutor of the church of God, thus not in any way receptive to the message of the gospel (1:13–14). And when God did apocalyptically reveal his Son in his life, so that he might preach him among the Gentiles, Paul did not right away confer with mere human beings about it, not even with the apostles in Jerusalem. Instead, he immediately went off to Arabia before returning to Damascus, where he stayed put (1:15–17). His contacts with the (human) apostles of the church in Jerusalem in this early period were thus nonexistent. The gospel he preached in Galatia and still preaches everywhere can therefore not be a distorted version of something he had learned from them.

1:18–24 The Origin of the Gospel 2: Paul's Visit with Cephas in Jerusalem

This paragraph has two distinguishable parts or sense units, vv. 18–20 and vv. 21–24. In the first part, Paul describes in broad strokes his first trip to Jerusalem

The Origin and the Truth of the Gospel

after three years of working on his own as the apostle of Christ to the Gentiles. He went there merely to visit Cephas (Peter) and saw no other apostle except James. The visit with Peter, he wants the Galatians to know, was brief, a mere two weeks and thus much less than the roughly three years he had been working on his own. In the second part, Paul relates that after this initial visit to Jerusalem, he went off to the Gentile districts of Syria and Cilicia, and thus far from Jerusalem and the church located there. He had nothing to do with the churches of Judea, including the mother church in Jerusalem, for more than a decade. On the historical level, the point is that for this long period of time, he was unknown by sight, if not by reputation, to the churches of Judea, notwithstanding his visit to Jerusalem. They could not have commissioned him nor given him the gospel that he was supposed to preach to the Galatians. On a theological level, these churches nevertheless acknowledged that God was present in his apostolic ministry among the Gentiles from the start.

> 1:18 Then after three years I went up to Jerusalem to visit Cephas, and I remained with him fifteen days. 19 I did not see another of the apostles except James, the brother of the Lord. 20 With respect to what I am writing to you, I assure you in the presence of God that I am not lying.
>
> 21 Then I went into the districts of Syria and Cilicia. 22 I was unknown by sight to the churches of Judea that are in Christ. 23 Only, they kept hearing, "The one persecuting us earlier is now preaching the faith that he was earlier seeking to destroy." 24 And they were glorifying God in me.

[18–20] Paul here grudgingly admits that he did go up to Jerusalem "after three years" in order "to visit" (*historēsai*) Cephas and that he stayed with him for "fifteen days," which by modern ways of reckoning amounts to fourteen days, or two weeks. "After [*meta*] three years" probably means "in the third calendar year after" a previous event and covers a period from between one and three years by modern ways of measuring time (see Introduction: Date). Paul is probably measuring from the year of his conversion and call (1:15–16), rather than from the year of his return to Damascus (1:17; cf. Acts 9:23), though these two events could actually have taken place in the same year. As already indicated above, Cephas (*Kēphas*) is the apostle commonly known as Peter (*Petros*; cf. John 1:42), though that is difficult to prove on the basis of Galatians alone (see comment on 2:7–9).[149] Paul prefers the former name (four times in both Galatians and 1 Corinthians), using the latter only in 2:7–8 (twice). *Kēphas* is derived from the Aramaic word for rock, *kepha*, whereas *Petros* comes from

---

149. The fact that some, mostly Western, manuscripts read "Peter" (*Petros*) in 1:18 indicates that in the early church, it was assumed that Cephas and Peter were the same person. "Cephas" is supported by the best manuscripts.

the Greek word for rock, *petra* (see Matt 16:18). Both are nicknames ("Rock"); neither is attested as a proper name prior to the NT. Paul does not indicate here whether this nickname has some special theological or missionary significance for him or for Christian Jews. When Paul reports that he "stayed with him" (*epemeina pros auton*), he presumably means that he lodged in Cephas's home (cf. Acts 18:3, Codex D, *pros autous*; *Did.* 12.2, *pros hymas*); Cephas was his host. Paul does not bother to tell the Galatians that Cephas/Peter was then (and still is at the time of writing) the leading apostle among the Twelve (cf. 1 Cor 15:5), nor that at the time of Paul's first visit Peter was probably the leader of the church in Jerusalem (cf. Acts 3:1–12:19; 15:7). This can only mean that the Galatians have already been informed about Cephas, most likely by the new preachers in Galatia.

The most discussed issue in this verse is the sense of the verb translated "visit," *historēsai*. Paul uses it in connection with his purpose in going to Jerusalem, "to visit Cephas." (He only "saw" James in passing.) The verb can mean "to visit a person for the purpose of inquiry" (LSJ 842) and thus in this case "to obtain information from" Peter (TEV), presumably about Jesus (Dunn 1990: 110–13). But the verb can also mean simply "to visit," "to make the acquaintance of," or "to get to know" (NRSV, NIV, NEB, REB; Burton; Betz; Longenecker; Martyn), and that is normally the case when it has a personal object, as here (e.g., Josephus, *J.W.* 6.81; cf. BDAG 483). The first meaning does not serve Paul's purpose at all, whereas the second does: His purpose in this section is to minimize the importance of his contacts with Jerusalem (1:17) *as far as the gospel* he preached to the Galatians (1:11) is concerned. He expresses this purpose by pointing out that he did not go to Jerusalem until "three years" after his conversion and call (perhaps not until three years after his return to Damascus, which could involve an even longer period of time between conversion/call and the first visit to Jerusalem), and by emphasizing that he had received the gospel that he preached to the Galatians (1:11) directly through an apocalyptic revelation of Jesus Christ (1:12). Paul's point in 1:18 cannot then be that he received instruction at the feet of Peter about "the gospel," and the verb *historēsai* thus cannot here mean, or be taken by the Galatians to mean, "to receive the gospel from" or "to be taught the gospel by" Peter (cf. 1:12). If the verb does still carry the nuance of "to get information from" (Dunn), it means in this context that Paul went to get information from Peter about Peter himself, not about "the gospel." Peter and Paul undoubtedly did talk about more than the weather (C.H. Dodd, cited by Dunn 1990: 127), but the content of the gospel that Paul preached to the Galatians was already essentially fixed (see further on 2:7–10). He merely went to Jerusalem to get to know (about) Peter, probably because Peter was (according to the tradition known to Paul) the first of the Twelve to whom the risen Christ appeared (1 Cor 15:5) and because he had been "entrusted with the gospel to the circumcision [Jews]," just as Paul

The Origin and the Truth of the Gospel

had been "entrusted with the gospel to the uncircumcision [Gentiles]" (2:7; see comment there).

As for the other apostles, Paul "saw" [*eidon*] none of them "except [*ei mē*] James, the brother of the Lord." Paul's language can be read to mean that he saw no other apostles aside from Cephas, but that he did also see James, who was not an apostle but "the brother of the Lord" (e.g., Lührmann). That is not the most natural way to understand Paul's syntax, however (Lightfoot; Burton; Bruce; Longenecker). Paul probably assumes here that James is also an apostle (cf. 1 Cor 9:5; 15:7; and comment on 1:17a above). James (Jacob) was a common name among Jews, and the initial specification of James as "the brother of the Lord" (no longer necessary when he is mentioned again in 2:9, 12) probably distinguishes him from other apostles called James, particularly James the son of Zebedee (Acts 1:13; 12:2; etc.) and James the son of Alphaeus (Matt 10:3; Mark 3:18; Luke 6:15), both members of the Twelve. It is perhaps obvious why the James the brother of the Lord (cf. Mark 6:3) would be distinguished by his relationship to Jesus, rather than by his relationship to his father ("the son of Joseph"). Paul assumes that the Galatians will recognize the importance and authority of this James in the church of Jerusalem; by the time Paul writes this James had become the leading figure in Jerusalem (cf. 2:9, 12; Acts 12:17; 15:13; 21:18; see comment on 2:7–10). If Paul "got to know" Peter, he only "saw" James, implying that the contact was minimal and without real significance.

Paul follows the mention of his seeing James with an asseveration: "With respect to what I am writing to you [here about the nature and limits of my contacts with the apostles in Jerusalem], I assure you[150] in the presence of God that I am not lying" (cf. Rom 9:1; 2 Cor 11:31). This solemn oath is another indication that the letter will be read aloud in the context of a worship service, and thus in the presumed presence of God. With the oath, Paul seeks to establish the trustworthiness of his account in the eyes of the Galatians, and it implies that they may doubt his account. The new preachers in Galatia have probably given the Galatians another account, claiming that Paul had learned the correct version of the gospel from the apostles in Jerusalem, but that he had adulterated it or deviated from it in an unacceptable way, mainly by not saying anything about circumcision and the observance of the law. The gospel he eventually preached in Galatia, they have told the Galatians, was not the gospel he had learned originally from the apostles. Paul responds by pointing out that he had gone up to Jerusalem three years after his conversion and call and then only to make Peter's acquaintance, staying a mere two weeks. He had in fact seen none of the other apostles, except James, the brother of the Lord.

---

150. The phrase "I assure you" is a periphrastic rendering of the exclamatory particle *idou*, which means "Look!" or "Notice!" (cf. BDAG 468).

On the essential point, namely, that Paul had not learned the gospel that he preaches to the Gentiles from the apostles in Jerusalem, the account of Paul's first visit to Jerusalem in Acts 9:26–31 agrees with Paul's own: When Paul went to Jerusalem for the first time after being forced to leave Damascus (9:23–25; cf. 2 Cor 11:32–33), he was brought by Barnabas "to the apostles." For Acts, "the apostles" were the Twelve (cf. Acts 1:26), a group that did not include James (12:17; 15:13; 21:18) or Paul (see comment on 1:1). Their leader and spokesman was Peter (1:13, 15; 2:14, 37–38; etc.). To "the apostles," including Peter, Paul recounted "how on the road he had seen the Lord, who had spoken to him, and how in Damascus he had spoken boldly in the name of Jesus" (9:27). The apostles, including Peter, said nothing to him and thus did not give him the content of his proclamation. After this initial meeting with Peter and the apostles, Paul "was with them, going into and out of Jerusalem, speaking boldly in the name of the Lord" (9:28 AT). He did and proclaimed in Jerusalem what he had already been doing and proclaiming in Damascus. There is not a hint that Paul received instruction about Jesus or the gospel from any of "the apostles," not even Peter. James does not even enter into the picture. Paul's solemn asseveration in Gal 1:18 thus finds corroboration in Acts.

[21–24] Paul "then" (*epeita*) went to the Gentile "districts" (*klimata*; Rom 15:23; 2 Cor 11:10) of Syria and Cilicia, thus far from the Jerusalem church and the apostles there. The two adjoining territories lay in the northeast corner of the Mediterranean basin, forming in Paul's time one Roman province, Syria-Cilicia (Bruce 103). The leading city of Syria, and the capital of the Roman province, was Antioch, at the time one of the largest and most important cities of the Roman Empire. Galatians 2:11 indicates that the church in Antioch was Paul's primary base of missionary operations for much of the "fourteen years" (2:1) between the first and second visits to Jerusalem, and for a brief period of time thereafter (cf. Acts 11:25–15:35). The leading city of Cilicia was Tarsus (Acts 21:39), which according to Acts was Paul's birthplace (9:11; 21:39; 22:3; 23:34). Acts also reports that Paul went directly (traveling by sea from Caesarea) to Tarsus, thus Cilicia, after his first visit to the church in Jerusalem and spent some time there (9:30), before being brought to Antioch, thus Syria, by Barnabas (11:25–26). Paul gives no hint about the sequence, the designation "Syria and Cilicia" being a fixed combination (cf. Acts 15:23, 41). It is unlikely that Paul also went to Galatia in this period to found the churches to which he writes this letter (Dunn 80), or even further afield to Macedonia and Achaia (cf. Lüdemann 59–61; Knox 40–41); he would certainly have mentioned such missionary activity, especially in Galatia, if he had undertaken it, for that would have supported his case of independence from the Jerusalem church even more than the reference to Syria and Cilicia (Martyn 184).

As a result, Paul "was unknown by sight [lit., by the face] to the churches of Judea that are in Christ" (1:22). Here, as in 1:23, Paul uses a periphrastic

The Origin and the Truth of the Gospel

imperfect tense, implying some duration (BDF #353): *ēmēn agnooumenos*, literally, "was being unknown." The interpretation of 1:22 is often posed in terms of the following two alternatives: (1) Paul was unknown by sight to the churches of Judea only after his call when he had become an apostle, but not before that event, when he was the persecutor (Hultgren). *Or* (2) Paul was unknown by sight to the churches of Judea both before and after his call, thus both as persecutor and as apostle (e.g., Martyn; Vouga). Galatians 1:21 indicates, however, that the issue is whether Paul was unknown to the churches of Judea *in the years following his first visit to Jerusalem*, after which he went to the districts of Syria and Cilicia. In short, Paul appears to have in view only the more than ten years between his first visit to Jerusalem (1:18) and his second visit (2:1–10).[151] The expression "the churches of Judea" is parallel to the expressions "the churches of Galatia" (1:2), "the churches of Macedonia" (2 Cor 8:1), and "the churches of Asia" (1 Cor 16:19), where the geographical terms designate Roman provinces (see comment on 1:2b above). Probably, then, the Roman province of Judea is meant here, encompassing not only the original region of Judea near Jerusalem but also the regions of Samaria and Galilee (Bruce 103; Longenecker 41; cf. Acts 9:31). After passing through the province of Judea on his way to Syria and Cilicia after his first visit to Jerusalem,[152] Paul was *from then on* and *for more than a decade* personally unknown to the Jewish Christian churches in Judea, including the one in Jerusalem. He could not therefore have been an apostle of these churches, charged with preaching a version of the gospel approved by the Jerusalem apostles, one that he allegedly distorted when he went to Gentile territory. He has always been the apostle of Christ to the Gentiles, preaching the gospel that he also preached to the Galatians, from the moment of his conversion and call.

Paul's claim about being unknown by sight (if not by reputation) is thus not absolute, manifestly focusing on the time between his first and second visits to Jerusalem and not on the time before the first visit, including his career as a persecutor prior to his conversion and call. Only the time period between the first and second visits to Jerusalem is really relevant to Paul's concern in this subsection (1:21–24), to let the Galatians know that his contact with the Jerusalem apostles after his visit with Peter was nonexistent, just as it was in the three years between his conversion/call and his first journey to Jerusalem (1:16c–17). He has just reported that he spent two weeks in Jerusalem, and the journey to and from Jerusalem must have involved travel through Judea. Before ending

---

151. Paul in Gal 2:1 says "fourteen years," which means twelve to fourteen years by modern ways of measuring time (see Introduction: Date). If these years are being measured from Paul's conversion and call, as is probably the case, then the time between his first and second visits to Jerusalem would be about ten to twelve years ("fourteen years" minus "three years").

152. Paul does not indicate the route he took, but he definitely had to go through parts of Judea. As indicated above, Acts has him go from Jerusalem to Caesarea on the coast and then by boat to Cilicia (9:30).

up in Syria and Cilicia, therefore, Paul had been seen in Judea, especially if "Judea" here includes Jerusalem as of course it can. (He emphasizes in 1:18–19 that of the *apostles* he had contact only with Peter and James, not that he saw no other believers in Christ on this journey).[153] Paul's seemingly superfluous characterization of the churches of Judea as being "in Christ" (cf. 1 Thess 2:14) probably represents abiding respect for the efforts of Peter as the apostle to the Jews of Judea in the many years prior to Paul's second visit (cf. Gal 2:7–8; Acts 9:32–11:18), despite what happened in Antioch afterward (Gal 2:11–14).[154] These churches too are "in Christ" (cf. 2:4, 17; 3:14, 26, 28; 5:6), even if they do remain law observant (see comment on 1:23 and 2:16 below). Nowhere in Galatians does Paul see his mission to the Gentiles as the substitute for, or as the successor to, Peter's original mission to the Jews. The latter has its place in God's saving activity through Christ, as has his circumcision-free mission to the Gentiles (cf. 2:7–8). For the Galatians, and the new preachers listening to the letter with them, a key point of 1:22 may be that Paul stayed out of Peter's mission field to the Jews (Judea/Palestine), implying that the new missionaries ought to stay out of his mission field among the Gentiles (cf. 2:7–8).

Paul was thus unknown by sight to the churches of Judea for many years. "Only" (*monon*) the members of these churches "kept hearing" (lit., "were hearing," *akouontes ēsan*) a rumor about Paul during these years, a rumor that Paul now cites for the benefit of the Galatians: "The one persecuting [*diōkōn*] us earlier [*pote*] is now preaching the faith that he was earlier [*pote*] seeking to destroy [*eporthei*]" (1:23). The Greek words highlighted recall Paul's account of his persecuting activity in 1:13: "you have heard of my manner of life earlier [*pote*] in Judaism, that I persecuted [*ediōkon*] the church of God beyond measure, and I sought to destroy [*eporthoun*] it." Paul has thus probably formulated the content of the rumor in his own words for the most part. It is not a verbatim citation[155] of what the Christians in Judea were actually saying (they, presumably, would have spoken Aramaic anyway).

---

153. It cannot be excluded that apart from the church in Jerusalem (see comment on 1:13 above and 1:23 below), Paul was known by sight to the churches of Judea *before* his first visit to Jerusalem, even though there is no explicit indication in either his own letters or in Acts that he was active there (i.e., outside Jerusalem) as either persecutor or apostle (see comment on 1:13). Many such churches, however, were founded in the years after his conversion and call (cf. Acts 9:32–11:18), though probably not all (cf. Acts 8:1–40; 9:31), when he was occupied elsewhere (first in Arabia and Damascus, and then in Syria and Cilicia).

154. Paul and Peter may have come to a preliminary understanding during Paul's first visit to Jerusalem on the parallel missions indicated in 2:7–9, since those verses seem to hint at a previously-agreed-upon arrangement between the two (Martyn 172). See Excursus 7.

155. Against Betz 81. The *hoti* may be recitative (BDF #470), as Betz notes, but statements can be given the appearance of being literal quotations when they give only the basic sense of what was actually said, using the author's own words. That is the case here.

The Origin and the Truth of the Gospel

Seemingly unusual for Paul is the expression "preaching the faith" (*euangelizetai tēn pistin*), where "the faith" appears to be a virtual synonym for "the gospel" (cf. 1:11: "the gospel preached by me," *to euangelion to euangelisthen hyp' emou*). "The faith" would here then refer not to the act of believing (*fides qua creditur*), but to what is believed (*fides quae creditur*). This is not Paul's normal usage, as Burton (64) points out, who thus thinks "faith in Christ" is Paul's intended meaning. In 1:16, however, Paul has posited the person of Christ as the object of the verb *euangelizomai*: "that I might preach [*euangelizōmai*] him [*auton*, God's Son] among the Gentiles." The parallelism is striking:

1:16 preaching God's Son
1:23 preaching the faith

The parallel indicates that "the faith" in 1:23 may refer to "the faith of the Son of God" (2:20) or "of [Jesus] Christ" (2:16), which would mean that Paul is using the word "faith" in 1:23 as a metonym for the Son of God or Christ, as he does in 3:23–26 (see end of Excursus 6; and comments on 2:16; 3:23–26).[156] To preach "the faith" is to preach "God's Son" or "Christ." Whatever the precise nuance or origin of "preaching the faith" here, it is in any case noteworthy that Paul attributes to the law-observant members of the churches of Judea the notion that faith (thus not the law!) is definitive for Christian identity even for those who are Jews by birth (cf. 2:15–16; 3:28).

The verbal connections and parallels pointed out above between 1:23 and 1:13 indicate that the "us" in the rumor about Paul probably corresponds to "the church of God," which is the mother church in Jerusalem (see comment on 1:13–14). The members of the churches of Judea outside Jerusalem ("they"), founded after Paul's call and as a result of Peter's mission, have thus heard from their mother church in Jerusalem ("us") that the former persecutor of the church of God (the church in Jerusalem) was now, lo and behold, "preaching the faith" that he was earlier seeking to destroy (also Witherington 125).[157]

As a result, the churches of Judea, including the one in Jerusalem, "were glorifying [impf.] God in me [*en emoi*]" (1:24). The phrase *en emoi* can be construed as causal, "because of me" (NRSV, NIV). Paul has used the same phrase in 1:16a (God was pleased to apocalyptically reveal his Son "in me") and it there means "in my manner of life earlier in Judaism" (cf. 1:13 and the comment on 1:16a). Here the phrase may have an analogous meaning: Paul's *new* manner of life as the apostle of Christ to the Gentiles. The churches of Judea recognized

---

156. On the phrase *pistis (Iēsou) Christou / huios tou theou*, "the faith of (Jesus) Christ / the Son of God," in 2:16 and 2:20, see comment on 2:16 and Excursus 9.

157. Though Paul does not distinguish Jerusalem from Judea in 1:22, he does do that in 1:23 (cf. e.g., Matt 3:5).

the work of God in Paul's new manner of life, "preaching the faith" to Gentiles apart from having been instructed by the apostles of their mother church in Jerusalem. During this early period, there was thus no opposition to Paul and his mission from the churches of Judea.

Verse 24 leads up to the next passage, in which Paul will show that the Jerusalem church and its apostles unconditionally affirmed his circumcision-free mission to the Gentiles. It also stresses once again that Paul's gospel, just like his apostleship (1:1), does not have a human origin (1:11–12). Paul attempts to substantiate this claim in 1:13–24 through an autobiographical narrative of his contacts with Jerusalem from before his conversion and call to his initial visit with Peter in Jerusalem, where he also saw James. The gospel that Paul preached to the Galatians (1:11) was not received by Paul from other human beings, nor was he taught it (1:12). Those are "the historical facts of the case" he presents to the Galatians. Paul does not try to demonstrate where the gospel he preached does come from, from God acting through an apocalyptic revelation of his Son, Jesus Christ, in Paul's life (1:12, 15–16). God's role in Paul's conversion and call, and subsequently in his activity as apostle, is not a matter of historical demonstration nor of rational proof but, as 1:24 and 1:15–16 both indicate, of testimony, confession, and the insight granted by faith. The churches of Judea shared his own insight and claim that God was indeed at work in his preaching of the gospel to the Gentiles.

2:1–10 The Truth of the Gospel 1:
The Apostolic Conference in Jerusalem

This passage is the third paragraph of the first major section of the letter body (1:11–2:21). In the previous two paragraphs (1:11–17 and 1:18–24), the overarching theme was the claim that "the gospel that was preached [to you Galatians] by me . . . is not of human origin" (1:11), but comes from God (1:12, 15–16). Except for a brief getting-acquainted visit with Peter, Paul's contact with the human authorities in Jerusalem was nonexistent (1:17–24). He therefore did not get "his" gospel, which is actually *the* gospel, from them in any way, shape, or form. In this unit and the next one (2:11–21), the overarching theme is "the truth of the gospel" (2:5, 14), the truth of "the gospel that I proclaim among the Gentiles" (2:2). The truth of this gospel was acknowledged by the "pillars" James, Cephas, and John in Jerusalem, but was subsequently undermined in Antioch by Cephas and others, including Barnabas. The truth of the gospel—"our freedom [from the imposition of the law], which we have in Christ Jesus" (2:4)—is not elaborated until the closing paragraph of the section (2:15–21), where Paul begins to turn his attention once more directly to the situation in Galatia: justification occurs not by "works of the law" but by "the faith of Christ." Between 1:11–24 and 2:1–21 are the following noteworthy parallels and contrasts:

Gal 1:11–24	Gal 2:1–21
"the gospel that was preached by me" to the Galatians in particular	"the gospel that I proclaim among the Gentiles" generally
this gospel "is not of human origin"	"the truth of the gospel"
Paul received it "through an apocalyptic revelation of Jesus Christ"	This was made known to the "pillars" in Jerusalem "in accordance with an apocalyptic revelation"
Positive story involving primarily Cephas but also James	Negative story involving primarily Cephas but also James
Paul now preaches "the faith" that he was earlier trying to destroy	Paul preaches "the faith of Christ"

In the present passage, Paul wants the Galatians to know (1) that the apostolic leaders in Jerusalem—James, Cephas, and John—acknowledged "the truth of the gospel" (esp. re the freedom of Gentiles not to practice circumcision) that he was and is still proclaiming among the Gentiles, and (2) that their acknowledgement too was the work of God. The passage has three subunits: 2:1–3; 2:4–5; and 2:6–10. The first is a summary of his second visit to Jerusalem. In it he discloses the success of this visit, using the concrete example of Titus to make the point: Titus, though a Gentile, was not compelled to be circumcised! The second subunit informs the Galatians that Paul had met with considerable resistance from a specific group in Jerusalem, whom he labels "the false brethren." Paul (and Barnabas and Titus) did not submit to them for a moment, with the result that "the truth of the gospel" could abide (remain in force) for the Galatians. In the third subunit, which in Greek is one long, convoluted sentence, Paul informs the Galatians that the three acknowledged leaders in Jerusalem, James, Cephas, and John, had recognized God's presence in his proclamation of the gospel to the Gentiles and had affirmed it with "the right hand of partnership." They laid no demands on him at all; only he and Barnabas were politely asked to remember the poor in Jerusalem, which Paul was indeed eager to do.

2:1 Then after fourteen years I again went up to Jerusalem with Barnabas, also taking Titus with me. 2 I went up in accordance with an apocalyptic revelation, and I shared with them the gospel that I proclaim among the Gentiles, but privately with the acknowledged leaders, lest somehow I was running or had run for nothing. 3 But not even Titus, who was with me, though he was a Greek, was compelled to be circumcised.

4 But on account of the secretly-brought-in false brethren, who came in to spy out our freedom, which we have in Christ Jesus, in order that

they might enslave us, **5** to whom we did not yield in submission for a moment, so that the truth of the gospel might abide for you.

6 From those acknowledged to be something—what sort of people they were earlier matters nothing to me: God shows no partiality—for the acknowledged leaders added nothing to me, **7** but to the contrary, when they came to see that I had been entrusted with the gospel to the uncircumcision, just as Peter to the circumcision, **8** (for the One who worked in Peter for the apostleship to the circumcision also worked in me for the Gentiles), **9** and when they came to recognize the grace that had been given to me, James and Cephas[a] and John, those acknowledged to be pillars, gave to me and Barnabas the right hand of partnership, that we go to the Gentiles and they to the circumcision, **10** only that we remember the poor, which very thing I was indeed eager to do.

a. Some manuscripts read "Peter" (*Petros*), including $\mathfrak{P}^{46}$ (also some old Latin manuscripts, D, F, G, Marcion, and others). The same variation is found in lesser manuscripts for 1:18. In 2:9, the manuscripts that read "Peter" also place Peter before James, with the exception of $\mathfrak{P}^{46}$ and it[r] (Metzger 522–23). These readings are clearly secondary.

[1–3] These first three verses serve as a summary of Paul's second visit to Jerusalem. The remaining verses (2:4–10) give additional details, added by Paul to highlight the significance of what happened, or rather what did not happen: Titus, Paul's Greek coworker, was *not* compelled to be circumcised (2:3). Some interpreters place 2:3 with 2:4–5 (e.g., Longenecker; Martyn), arguing that 2:3–5 forms a discrete literary unit breaking the flow of the account in 2:1–2, 6–10. But 2:3 mentions Titus as does 2:1, and the conjunction "but" (*alla*) joins 2:3 directly to 2:2 (Paul was not running and had not run for nothing!). It gives the major result of the meeting in Jerusalem, one that the Galatians will need to know while facing the agenda of the new preachers in Galatia, which is to compel the Galatians to practice circumcision (5:2–4; 6:12–13; Excursus 4). Galatians 2:3 already implies that Paul's circumcision-free gospel was recognized as God's work by the church in Jerusalem, in particular by "the acknowledged leaders," *hoi dokountes* (lit., "those seeming [to be something])." Paul uses the latter expression four times in this passage:

2:2   "the acknowledged leaders [*hoi dokountes*]"
2:6a "those acknowledged to be something [*hoi dokountes einai ti*]"
2:6b "the acknowledged leaders [*hoi dokountes*]"
2:9   "those acknowledged to be pillars [*hoi dokountes styloi einai*]"

In 2:9, "those acknowledged to be pillars" are identified as James, Cephas, and John (see on 2:9 below). The expression *hoi dokountes*, which is classical (BDAG 255; LSJ 442), does not necessarily have an ironic or derogatory connotation. Used absolutely, it can mean "the influential men" (BDAG 255), "those who were of repute" (2:2, 6 RSV), "the acknowledged leaders" (NRSV) or something similar. In Paul's repeated use of the term, it does seem to have an ironic flavor (cf. Plato, *Apol.* 21B, 41E; *Gorg.* 472A), especially discernible in 2:6, where he relativizes the importance and the stature of the men involved, at least in the eyes of the new preachers (see comment below). Presumably the new preachers in Galatia have introduced the expression into the Galatian setting, seeking to impress upon the Galatians the authority of these men of repute.

As the time notation in 2:1 indicates ("after fourteen years"), Paul spent more than a decade between his first and second visits to Jerusalem in Syria and Cilicia, thus a considerable length of time away from the church of Jerusalem and its sphere of influence.[158] The first time he went to Jerusalem, he apparently went alone (1:18). The second time he went up to Jerusalem "with Barnabas, also taking Titus with me." Barnabas is mentioned again in 2:9 as Paul's close associate (cf. 1 Cor 9:6), which he would remain until the incident in Antioch (2:13; see comment there). In Acts, Barnabas, a Jewish Christian from Cyprus, is depicted as Paul's mentor, introducing him to "the apostles" in Jerusalem (9:27). The Jerusalem church eventually sends Barnabas to Antioch (11:22), where he seems to have become the leading figure (13:1), forging a close working relationship with Paul, after bringing him to Antioch from Tarsus (11:25-26, 30; 12:25; chs. 13–14). In Acts 15:2, "Paul and Barnabas" and some others are appointed to go to Jerusalem to discuss the issue of the circumcision of Gentile believers (15:1–2, 6) with "the apostles and the elders" (15:2).[159] In Gal 2:11–13, Paul and Barnabas are (back) in Antioch after the conference with the apostles in Jerusalem recounted in 2:1–10 (cf. Acts 15:35). It therefore seems likely that in verse 1 of the present passage,

---

158. The time indication "more than a decade" covers different possible interpretations of the phrase "after [*dia*] fourteen years." (For *dia* meaning "after a lapse of," cf. Mark 2:1; Acts 24:17). See Introduction: Date. By modern ways of measuring time, the period of time in view could be between 12 and 14 years. It is not certain where Paul is measuring these "fourteen years" from. It could be his conversion and call (1:15–16) or his first visit to Jerusalem (1:18). Probably the first of these is in view (note "again"), which means that the period of time between his first and second visits to Jerusalem would be about 10 years. This issue is more important for establishing a scientific chronology of Paul's life and career, and the date of the writing of Galatians, than for the interpretation of the passage at hand.

159. According to Acts, Paul goes to Jerusalem for the third time in chapter 15 (it is perhaps even the fourth time, in view of the uncertain reading in 12:25). The second visit of Paul to Jerusalem occurs in 11:30, also with Barnabas. The meeting described in Gal 2:1–10, however, has much more in common with the meeting described in Acts 15:1–29 than the one in Acts 11:30 (which was for famine relief). The central issue is the same, as are the key participants and the primary result: no circumcision for Gentile believers (cf. 15:1, 5, 28). See Lightfoot 123–28; Silva 132–36.

Paul and Barnabas went as delegates of the church in Antioch and that the gospel Paul was proclaiming among the Gentiles was indeed also at that time the gospel being proclaimed by Barnabas and the church in Antioch (cf. 2:9, where Barnabas is also given "the right hand of partnership"). Paul does not mention Antioch in 2:1–3 probably because he is no longer associated with the church there (cf. 2:11–14). Barnabas's role too is diminished in light of the parting of their ways indicated in 2:13 (cf. Acts 15:37–39). Furthermore, only Paul's proclamation is relevant for the Galatians, since Barnabas was probably not involved in the founding of the Galatians churches (see Introduction: Addressees).[160] That the circumcision of Gentile believers was indeed the make-or-break issue as in the account of Acts is only obliquely indicated by Paul, in his reference to the fact that Titus was not compelled to be circumcised even though he was a Greek. Titus, who (strangely) is nowhere mentioned in Acts, was undoubtedly an important figure in Paul's mission. In 2 Corinthians he plays a crucial role in Paul's relationship with the Corinthian church and in the collection for Jerusalem (2:13; 7:6, 13, 14; 8:6, 16, 23; 12:18; cf. further 2 Tim 4:10; Titus 1:4). Paul refers to him there as "my brother [in Christ]" (2 Cor 2:13) and as "my partner and co-worker in your service" (2 Cor 8:23). The added phrase "also taking Titus with me" in 2:1 intimates that Paul took Titus, an uncircumcised Greek (2:3), for a specific purpose, to display the fruit of his gospel.

In 2:2a, Paul claims that he "went up [i.e., to Jerusalem] in accordance with an apocalyptic revelation [*kata apokalypsin*]." Whether the preposition *kata*, "in accordance with," here implies "as a result of" or "for [the purpose of]" (cf. 2 Cor 11:21; John 2:6; Josephus, *Ant.* 3.268) is difficult to decide (cf. BDAG 512–13). The former is the usual interpretation, leading to the translation "by revelation" (KJV, RSV) or "in response to a revelation" (NRSV, NIV), both meaning "because God revealed to me that I should go" (Martyn).[161] But "for [the purpose of] an (apocalyptic) revelation" may also be possible particularly in view of the fact that 2:2a is but the first and introductory part of one long sentence:

1. I went up [to Jerusalem] in accordance with an apocalyptic revelation

---

160. On the basis of 2:1, it is difficult to judge whether the Galatians have already heard about Barnabas and his association with Paul. If so, they have been informed by the new preachers, who have presented Paul's former close associate as their ally in the struggle for the hearts and minds of the Galatians (cf. 2:13).

161. Paul says nothing about the circumstances (a worship service? a dream?) and content of this revelation (a prophecy? a vision?); one can (dubiously) use Acts to fill in some of the details (cf. 11:28–30; 13:1–3; 16:9–10). Paul's reserve in this matter is to be respected (see on 1:15–16 above).

The Origin and the Truth of the Gospel

2. and [*kai*] I shared with them [the members of the church in Jerusalem] the gospel that I proclaim[162] among the Gentiles, but privately with the acknowledged leaders [the pillars James, Cephas, and John],
3. lest somehow I was running[163] or had run for nothing.

Verse 2:2a thus points forward to what happened in Jerusalem, and the verb *anebēn*, "I went up," can be deemed a complexive aorist, whereby a series of actions are retrospectively regarded as a whole (cf. BDF #332). The following paraphrase is the result: "My whole journey to Jerusalem, including what happened during my stay there, was a matter of God's revelatory activity and intention."

Just as in 1:12, so also here, Paul conjoins a reference to "the gospel" with a reference to an *apokalypsis* (cf. 1:15–16). In 1:12, this term means "apocalyptic revelation," describing God's redemptive intrusion into Paul's previous manner of life as a zealous law-observant persecutor of God's church in order to give him a new manner of life as the apostle of Christ to the Gentiles (see comments on 1:12, 15–16; and Excursus 6 above). Analogously, through Paul's second visit to Jerusalem, God effected what Paul calls "an apocalyptic revelation" in the lives of the pillar apostles in Jerusalem, who "came to see" (*idontes*) that his proclamation of the gospel to the uncircumcised had been entrusted to him by God (2:7), and who "came to recognize" (*gnontes*) the grace granted to him by God (2:9). Everything here turns on the action of God in the life and work of Paul, including his visit to Jerusalem. This visit as a whole, not just the initial decision to go, was "in accordance with an apocalyptic revelation," thus in line with God's apocalyptic-eschatological redemptive activity in Christ (see Excursuses 2 and 6 above). In Paul's account, then, his second visit to the church in Jerusalem functioned as an apocalyptic revelation for the pillar apostles, as the means whereby God invaded their world to disclose to them—concretely in the persons of Paul, Barnabas, and Titus—the truth of the gospel (cf. Martyn 188, 190, 200–203). Their world would never be the same,

---

162. Paul here uses the verb *kēryssō* (cf. 5:11; Rom 10:8; 1 Cor 1:23; 15:11; etc.) as a virtual synonym of *euangelizomai*, used in 1:8, 9, 11, 16, 23; 4:13. In contrast to the English present tense used here ("I proclaim"), the present tense of the Greek can be construed (cf. Smyth #1888) as referring to action contemporaneous with an event in the past ("I shared . . . the gospel that I was [then] proclaiming") or as referring to action at the time of writing ("I shared . . . the gospel that I am [still] proclaiming"). Both are probably in view.

163. Or: "lest somehow I should [from then on] run for nothing," understanding *trechō* to be a present subjunctive rather than present indicative. If the latter, the action is contemporaneous not with the time of writing but with that of the main verb "shared with," hence the translation "was [at that time] running." The present indicative is probably intended given the following aorist indicative, *edramon*, "had run" (against Burton 73; Betz 87; Longenecker 49; BDAG 901; with NRSV; Martyn).

in spite of the fact that Cephas, and probably James too, later sought to turn the clock back (cf. 2:11–14).

On either interpretation of 2:2a, the rhetorical function of the appeal to divine revelation is clear. Paul indicates that he had not gone up to Jerusalem (1) because the apostles who resided there had summoned him or called him on the carpet, or (2) because he had felt a personal need to have their official stamp of approval (or that of the church there) for his gospel and his apostleship to the Gentiles. In 1:1, 11–24, Paul has already asserted that his gospel and apostleship have God's approval and backing; they need no other approval. Yet 2:2a also indicates that Paul does not regard the acknowledgement of his mission by the pillars in Jerusalem to be an indifferent matter, either theologically or practically (see on 2:2c and 2:7–9 below).

In 2:2b, Barnabas falls out of the picture until 2:9, perhaps because as Paul writes the letter, he and Barnabas have parted company; Barnabas no longer preaches the gospel Paul preaches (cf. 2:13; Acts 15:37–39). For the Galatians, at any rate, the issue is the gospel that Paul, their founding apostle, was proclaiming and is still proclaiming. The verb translated "shared with" (*anethemēn*, the aorist of *anatithēmi*) is difficult (just like the verb "visit with," *historēsai*, in 1:18). In the middle voice (as here), the verb can mean "to lay something before someone for consideration," or "to communicate, refer, declare," with the connotation of a "request for a person's opinion" (BDAG 74, referring to Polybius 21.46.11, and other texts). If that is the meaning here, it cannot be taken to imply that Paul submitted his gospel to the Jerusalem church and the pillars for their approval, as if Paul by going to Jerusalem acknowledged their superior authority in such matters (cf. Dunn 1990: 113–16). The context alone forbids such a conclusion (see on 1:11–24 above). The verb here probably has the simple meaning "communicate to" or "share with," as in 2 Macc 3:9 and Acts 25:14. Paul shared his gospel first with the church ("them"; cf. Acts 15:4–5) and then privately with the pillars (cf. 15:6), so that they would come to see that God had entrusted him with the gospel to the Gentiles and would come to recognize God's grace in his present manner of life (Gal 2:7, 9).

How then are we to interpret 2:2c, where Paul expresses the fear that he was (at that time) running or (in the years before the visit) had run for nothing? The verb "to run" (*trechō*) here is a metaphor meaning "to exert oneself" for a goal (cf. 5:7; 1 Cor 9:24–26; Phil 2:16). In the context, Paul's surprising expression of uncertainty cannot mean that he had any doubt in his own mind about the validity of his gospel, its origin in God, and its truth, but only that the Jerusalem apostles were in a position to hinder and even to thwart his mission among the Gentiles. The fear that Paul expresses is for the communities he (with Barnabas) had already founded as daughter churches of the one in Antioch, where he was based at the time (cf. Acts 15:21, 36, 41). If the Jerusalem apostles had rejected Paul's gospel, which at that time was also Antioch's gospel, the continuing

The Origin and the Truth of the Gospel 111

existence of Gentile congregations in Syria and Cilicia, called into being by the circumcision-free gospel, would have been jeopardized. In the end, Paul's fear proved to be groundless: "but [*alla*] not even Titus, who was with me [right there in Jerusalem], though he was a Greek [thus a Gentile, not a Jew], was compelled [*ēnankasthē*] to be circumcised" (2:3). At the conference in Jerusalem, Titus represented the fruit of Paul's mission to the Gentiles generally. The verb here translated "compelled" in the present tense means "to put pressure on," in the aorist "compelled," implying that the pressure applied has achieved its goal. Titus, despite being put under severe pressure by "the false brethren" or their allies in Jerusalem (2:4–5), was *not* successfully "compelled" (by them) to be circumcised (by, or with the consent of, Paul).[164] Thus Burton (75) writes: "So far were they from carrying through their demand that not even Titus, who was there on the ground at the time, and to whom the demand would first of all apply, was circumcised." The failure of their pressure on Titus to achieve their desired goal already signals to the Galatians that Paul's gospel was acknowledged by the pillars, as he will say with so many words in 2:7–9, and thus that the new preachers who "are putting pressure [*anankazousin*]" on the Galatians "to practice circumcision" (6:12), just as the false brethren did on Titus, cannot appeal to the apostles in Jerusalem as support for their "different gospel" (1:6).

[4–5] Paul could have stopped there, with 2:3, and left the Galatians with an account of his second visit to Jerusalem to match the brevity of the account of his first visit in 1:18–20. The key point has been made: the circumcision of Gentile converts was not demanded or insisted upon by the leaders in Jerusalem, and Paul's circumcision-free gospel had won the day. But already in 2:3 Paul has intimated that this result had not been easy to achieve. There had been another group, not to be identified with the pillars, who had offered considerable resistance to Paul's gospel, putting severe pressure on Titus to be circumcised—by (or with the consent of) Paul, who was Titus's mentor (cf. Acts 16:1–3). The pressure on Titus was also effectively pressure on Paul (and

---

164. Paul's words are sometimes read in another way: Titus was not compelled to be circumcised: he voluntarily allowed himself to be, with Paul's approval (cf. Timothy in Acts 16:1–3). The assumption here is that Paul objected to compulsion; for the rest he was indifferent with respect to circumcision (5:6; 6:15). Thus as long as Titus was not compelled, Paul would have had no objection. (This interpretation also appeals to variant readings in 2:5; see note below). However, three considerations speak against this interpretation: (1) In 2:4–5, Paul indicates that he did not yield for one moment to the "false brothers" from whom the pressure that Titus be circumcised surely came. (2) In 6:12, he will charge the new preachers in Galatia with putting pressure (*anankazousin*) on the Galatians to begin practicing circumcision; his purpose behind this charge can hardly be that the Galatians are to begin this practice voluntarily. (3) He is trying to prevent the Galatians from undertaking the practice of circumcision, going so far as to declare that if they do, Christ will be of no benefit to them, they will have been severed from Christ, and they will have fallen away from grace (5:2–4). It therefore can hardly suit his purpose in this letter to suggest in any way that Titus was indeed circumcised, especially with Paul's approval.

Barnabas) to yield to the demand of this group that the practice of circumcision be required of Gentile believers. Willy-nilly, Titus became a test case for the proponents of circumcision for Gentile Christians. Paul now gives a brief account of his evidently traumatic clash with these people whom he labels "the false brethren," meaning believers in Christ not true to the gospel (cf. 2 Cor 11:26). The memory of the encounter causes his grammar to break down, for these two verses do not contain a complete sentence but a prepositional phrase at the beginning, which is followed by four subordinate clauses, piled up one on top of the other:

4aBut [*de*] on account of the secretly-brought-in false brethren,
4bwho came in to spy out our freedom, which we have in Christ Jesus,
4cin order that [*hina*] they might enslave us,
5ato whom[165] we did not yield in submission for a moment,
5bso that [*hina*] the truth of the gospel might abide for you.

The initial prepositional phrase (2:4a) probably can be paraphrased as follows: "but the pressure to circumcise Titus came from the secretly-brought-in false brethren, who..." When Paul refers to "the secretly-brought-in false brethren [*tous pareisaktous pseudadelphous*], who came in to spy out our freedom," he seems to presuppose activity that took place in a church where such freedom (from the requirement of circumcision) was the norm. The church in Antioch is the most likely candidate, given the evidence of Gal 2:11–12, where Paul, Cephas, and Barnabas are all in Antioch following the Jerusalem conference. The account in Acts 15:1–2 supports this inference: "Some people [*tines*]" came down from Jerusalem to Antioch (cf. Gal 2:12) and "were teaching the brethren, 'Unless you are circumcised according to the custom of Moses, you cannot be saved'" (RSV, alt.). Paul and Barnabas engage in "no small dissension and debate" with these new teachers, and the result is that Paul and Barnabas and

---

165. There is ancient evidence of attempts to improve the difficult grammar of these verses, thereby also changing the sense: (1) the omission "to whom" (*hois*) by Marcion, syr^p, and others, leading to the following sentence: "But on account of [*dia*] the ... false brethren, ... we did not yield for a moment," i.e., to the pillar apostles. Some modern interpreters effect a similar change in the plain meaning by arguing that *hois* = *dia hous*, "on account of whom" (Vouga 46), to correspond to the *dia* in 2:4a. (2) The omission not only of "to whom" but also of the negative "not" (*oude*), mainly by Western manuscripts including D (see Burton 85): "On account of the ... false brethren, ... we did yield for a moment [to the pillar apostles]." Paul was thus not uncompromising but accommodating (cf. 1 Cor 9:22–23), at least for a moment and for a good cause. In this attempt to improve the grammar and the sense, perhaps inspired by the account of Paul's circumcising Timothy in Acts 16:1–3, Paul agreed to the circumcision of Titus to prevent a break with the church in Jerusalem (see previous note), so that the truth of the gospel could be preserved for the Galatians. The inclusion of both *hois* and *oude* is however widely supported by the Greek manuscript tradition, with the exception of the first hand of D, as well as by versional and patristic witnesses (Metzger 522–23; Bruce 113–15).

"some of the others" are appointed to go to Jerusalem "to the apostles and elders about this question" (RSV). Some such scenario seems to be assumed here by Paul. Paul characterizes those who had come into the Antioch church as "the secretly-brought-in [*pareisaktous*] false brethren" (cf. BDAG 774), though it is not really clear if the verbal adjective *pareisaktous* (only here in the NT) has the passive meaning the form would suggest (so Burton 78, who adds that "the idea of surreptitiousness," or "secrecy," is not "at all clearly emphasised" either). The ancient lexicographer Hesychius (5th cent. C.E.) defined it with the term *allotrios*, "alien," "strange," or "hostile" (cf. BDAG 774; Burton 78). Paul could simply mean that the false brethren were present as an alien and hostile element at the meetings of the Antioch church, a conclusion supported by the following clause: "they [the false brethren] came in [*pareisēlthon*] to spy out our freedom." The verb *pareiserchomai* literally means "to come in alongside," as in Rom 5:20, where "the law came in alongside" a situation already fully determined by the twin powers of Sin and Death (Rom 5:12, 20–21). In Gal 2:4, the false brethren "came in alongside" a situation already fully determined by the freedom of the Antioch church ("our freedom") not to impose circumcision on its Gentile members. The verb often implies an element of stealth (Burton 83; BDAG 774), a nuance reinforced by the presence of the verb "to spy out," *kataskopēsai*.

Paul assumes here that "freedom" (*eleutheria*), however defined, is by definition a good and desirable thing, and the Galatians will undoubtedly share that assumption (cf. 3:28; 5:1). The "freedom" referred to here, however, is specifically freedom from the imposition of circumcision and, by implication, of (the remainder of) the law (cf. Acts 15:5). This is the freedom "which we [believers] have [*echomen*] in Christ Jesus" (see comment on 5:1). It is noteworthy that Paul here says "we," not "[you] Gentiles," and also uses a present tense, thereby being able to include his Galatian readers.[166] "In Christ Jesus" here means both "through Christ Jesus," meaning through his redemptive dying "for us" (cf. 1:4; 3:13; 4:4–5), and "in the sphere of his lordship," in the same way that "grace" for Paul is both a redemptive power and a sphere in which believers can live (see comments on 1:3, 6, 15; 2:9, 19–21; 5:4).

When Paul and Barnabas went up to Jerusalem, "the false brethren" probably went back there as well. But even if they did not, there were surely other representatives of "the circumcision party" (2:12) in Jerusalem (cf. Acts 10:45; 11:2). According to Acts 15:4–5, believers described as belonging to

---

166. The present tense of the Greek *echomen* in this subordinate clause can properly be construed as signifying continuous action contemporaneous either with the action of the main verb ("They came in to spy out our freedom, which we [Antiochene Christians] had [at the time in question] in Christ Jesus") or with the time of writing ("They came in to spy out our freedom, which we [believers everywhere now] have in Christ Jesus"). The ambiguity, which an English translation must resolve in favor of one of the alternatives, allows Paul to include the Galatians—and allows the Galatians, when they hear the letter, to include themselves.

the Pharisaic party in Jerusalem "rose up" (RSV), presumably at the meeting of Paul and Barnabas with "the church and the apostles and the elders," and said, "It is necessary to circumcise them, and to charge them to keep the law of Moses" (RSV), a requirement that evidently had not occurred to the leadership of the Jerusalem church previously. A similar situation seems to be presupposed by Paul's account. In 2:2, Paul mentions but does not emphasize a meeting with the church in Jerusalem, referring to its members simply as "them." "The false brethren" who had earlier traveled to Antioch (or their allies in Jerusalem) were surely present. Their vociferous opposition to Paul's circumcision-free gospel probably lies behind the private meeting that he and Barnabas arranged with the pillar apostles (2:2).[167]

The primary purpose of the false brethren in going to Antioch "to spy out [undermine or subvert] our freedom" was undoubtedly to compel (2:3) the circumcision of Gentile believers, or as Paul polemically phrases it, "in order that [*hina*] they might enslave us [*hēmas katadoulōsousin*] [to the law]." Paul's account is colored not only by his desire to discredit the proponents of circumcision for Gentile believers but also by his own theological presuppositions. For the first time in the letter, it here becomes clear that circumcision and thus also the law represent for Paul a form of slavery (cf. 4:21–31), from which Christ "has freed us" (5:1; cf. 3:13; 4:4–5; 5:13). Again he says "[all of] us," whether Jewish or Gentile by birth, and not "you [Gentiles]." Paul can call the Christian Jews promoting circumcision "false brethren" (cf. 2 Cor 11:26) precisely for this reason, that they threatened to enslave "us" to the law. By their actions in Antioch and Jerusalem, they placed themselves over against the freedom that Christ has effected by his death (cf. 1:4; 3:13; 4:4–5; 5:1). Their "gospel," like that of the new preachers now active in Galatia, was "a different gospel," one that turned "the [true] gospel of Christ" into its very opposite (1:6–7).

Paul and Barnabas ("we"), however, "did not yield [*eixamen*]" to the false brethren "in submission [*tē hypotagē*, lit., in the submission] for a moment [*pros hōran*, lit., for an hour]."[168] Not in Antioch, not in Jerusalem. It had evidently been a considerable struggle. Paul now states the purpose of his fierce resistance, which at the same time is its result: "so that [*hina*] the truth of the gospel [*hē alētheia tou euangeliou*] might abide [*diameinē*] for you [Galatians]." The verb *diameinē*, "might abide," could be taken to imply that the Galatian churches had already been founded at the time of the conference in Jerusalem (Burton 86; Longenecker 53). The phrase *pros hymas* would then have to be understood to mean "with you" (as in 1:18), instead of "for you."

---

167. Cf. Martyn 196. It is implausible, and not necessary, to assume, as Dunn (97) and Witherington (136) do, that the false brethren had "infiltrated" this private, by-invitation-only meeting in Jerusalem.

168. This is an idiom favored by Paul (cf. 2 Cor 7:8; 1 Thess 2:17; Phlm 15).

It is unlikely, however, that the churches of Galatia had been founded before Paul's second visit to Jerusalem (2:1; see comment on 1:21). An alternative would be to take *pros hymas* to mean "with you Gentiles in general," hence without the implication that the Galatian churches had already been founded (Dunn 101). However, "for you Galatians" is also a possible interpretation of *pros hymas*, whereby the clause as a whole can be taken to mean the following: "so that the truth of the gospel would still be around later, for you Galatians." The result of Paul's refusal to yield to the demand for subjection to the views of the false brethren and their allies is then that "the truth of the gospel" was preserved for the Galatians. The expression "the truth of the gospel" probably means "the truth contained in, and so belonging to, the gospel" (Burton 86), or "the gospel's truth" (possessive genitive). The context suggests that this truth is to be identified as "our freedom [from the imposition of the law], which we have in Christ Jesus." The gospel is a matter of God's grace and thus imposes no prior conditions (cf. 1:6; 2:21).

In 6:12, using the same verb that he has used in 2:2, Paul will charge the new preachers in Galatia with "putting pressure" (*anankazousin*) on the Galatians to practice circumcision, just as the false brethren had put pressure on Titus to be circumcised, though without success. The Galatians must not yield, not even for a moment, to the new preachers, just as Paul and Barnabas did not yield, not even for one moment, to the false brethren in Antioch and Jerusalem. The truth of the gospel is unequivocal and nonnegotiable.

[6–10] In Paul's account of the conference in Jerusalem, "the false brethren" had applied considerable pressure on Paul to effect the circumcision of Titus, but "the acknowledged leaders" evidently had not (against Lightfoot 105–6; Burton 77, 84; Dunn 96). The account of the conference in Acts 15:6–29, which despite some notable differences probably refers to the same event, also gives no reason to think that the leadership of the Jerusalem church put any pressure on Paul (or Barnabas) to be accommodating on the issue of circumcision; in that account, as in Paul's report here, the leaders in Jerusalem were themselves under pressure from a discrete group in the church to impose circumcision on Gentile believers (Acts 15:4–5), but they did not succumb (15:6–11, 13–21).[169] It is in any case the burden of Gal 2:6–10 to underscore the unequivocal support

---

169. The issue of the circumcision of Gentile believers became urgent only after nearly twenty years of mission and growth. Until the conference (ca. 48 C.E.), the Jerusalem apostles had evidently accepted the circumcision-free church of Antioch and its mission among the Gentiles without reservation, as their approval of Paul and Barnabas at the conference further indicates, and as Paul's argument in 2:15–16 will demonstrate on theological grounds (see comment). For the circumcision party in Jerusalem (2:13; Acts 10:45; 11:2), the presence of uncircumcised Gentile believers was evidently an anomaly that needed to be addressed and rectified. The issue probably came to a head because of the success of the circumcision-free mission led by Paul and Barnabas as missionaries ("apostles"; Acts 14:4, 14) of the church in Antioch (cf. Acts 13:1–3; 14:24–28).

that "the acknowledged leaders" of the Jerusalem church (2:2, 6d), the so-called "pillars" (2:9b), gave Paul on this score, as the main sentence (in italics below) of the passage indicates:

> ⁶ᵃFrom those acknowledged to be something— ⁶ᵇwhat sort of people they were earlier matters nothing to me: ⁶ᶜGod shows no partiality— ⁶ᵈ*for the acknowledged leaders added nothing to me,* ⁷ᵃ*but, to the contrary,* when they came to see that I had been entrusted with the gospel to the uncircumcision, ⁷ᵇjust as Peter to the circumcision—⁸for the One who worked in Peter for the apostleship to the circumcision also worked in me for the Gentiles—⁹ᵃand when they came to recognize the grace that had been given to me, ⁹ᵇ*James and Cephas and John, those acknowledged to be pillars, gave to me and Barnabas the right hand of partnership,* ⁹ᶜ[agreeing] that we go to the Gentiles and they to the circumcision, ¹⁰only that we remember the poor, which very thing I was indeed eager to do.

The italicized words give the main thought of the passage. The rest is commentary.

The syntax in 2:6 is garbled, as was also the case in 2:4–5, but the main thought is clear, and it comes at the end of the verse: "for the acknowledged leaders added nothing to me [*emoi ouden prosanethento*],"[170] meaning that they did not add the requirement of circumcision for Gentile believers (cf. 2:3) to the gospel that "I proclaim among the Gentiles" (2:2).[171] "On the contrary," Paul will continue in 2:7a, "James and Cephas and John, those acknowledged

---

170. Paul here uses the aorist middle of the verb *prosanatithēmi* ("added"). He also uses the aorist middle of this verb in 1:16, where it means "confer," which is the more commonly attested meaning (cf. BDAG 876; LSJ 1501): "I did not confer [*prosanethemēn*] with flesh and blood" (see comment on 1:16). Just as the English verb "confer" can mean "consult [with someone]" and "bestow [something on someone]," so also the Greek verb *prosanatithēmi* in the middle voice, besides meaning "to offer or dedicate beside," can mean "to confer [with someone]," as in 1:16, and "to add [something to someone]," as in 2:6d. See Burton 89–91. One is tempted to translate the phrase in 2:6d as "They conferred nothing on me," thereby honoring the recollection of 1:16; see next note.

171. According to Witherington (136), "Paul is saying that the Jerusalem authorities added nothing to (and subtracted nothing from) his own status or honor rating. This came to him from God's grace. He was not beholden to them for the fact that he was a Christian and a Christian apostle." One could then indeed translate the relevant phrase in 2:6d as "They conferred nothing on me," i.e., no status (see previous note). In favor of this interpretation is the indirect object "to me" (*emoi*), instead of "to my gospel" or something similar, and the reference to "face" in 2:6c (see below). The *emoi* is also placed at the head of the clause, thus in an emphatic position. Both interpretations make good sense (see on 2:9 below), though the first interpretation (they added nothing to Paul's gospel) is to be preferred since the key issue is the gospel that Paul preaches, not Paul's apostolic status, which in the following verses is not particularly emphasized.

The Origin and the Truth of the Gospel

to be pillars, gave to me and Barnabas the right hand of partnership" (2:9b). In driving this point home, Paul runs the risk of granting the pillar apostles too much authority, as if his gospel and his apostleship depended on them and their approval. His difficulty becomes apparent in 2:6, where he twice refers to the acknowledged leaders, *hoi dokountes*, in Jerusalem (see already in 2:2). In 2:6a, they are described as "those acknowledged to be something [*hoi dokountes einai ti*]," in other words, "those who are looked up to as authorities" (Lightfoot 107). At this point Paul's syntax once again breaks down,[172] probably because he is about to appeal to the pillar apostles in Jerusalem as support for his gospel, thereby seeming to grant to them authority in such matters, which would concede too much to the new preachers in Galatia. For Paul, the truth of the gospel does not really depend on the pillars' approval (even though their failure to provide it might have been disastrous for his mission and for the unity of God's church). He thus interrupts himself to relativize the position of the pillar apostles in the eyes of the new preachers and thus also in the eyes of the Galatians: "⁶ᵇwhat sort of people they were earlier matters nothing to me: ⁶ᶜGod shows no partiality."

Paul's use of tenses in 2:6a–c is noteworthy. The pillar apostles are referred to in the present tense: "those acknowledged [*hoi dokountes*] to be something" at the time of writing. The new preachers in Galatia undoubtedly look up to the pillar apostles as authorities. Paul here acknowledges that fact. In 2:6b, however, Paul uses a past tense: "what sort of people [*hopoioi*] they *were* [*ēsan*] earlier [*pote*] . . ." Paul presumably is here looking back to the status of the pillar apostles at the time of the conference. Their status then was probably based on a combination of factors: (1) their personal knowledge of, and relationship with, the earthly Jesus (Cephas and John had been disciples of Jesus before Easter, and James was "the brother of the Lord"); (2) their identity as apostles of Christ, who had seen the risen Lord (cf. 1 Cor 9:1–5; 15:3–8; see comments on 1:1, 17, 19); and (3) their leading roles in the church of Jerusalem ("pillars") for nearly two decades (see on 2:9b below). What sort of status they had earlier (*pote*), Paul writes, "matters nothing to me [*ouden moi diapherei*]." This statement can be interpreted in one of two ways: their status "*still* matters nothing to me, anymore than it did then" (Martyn), or their status "matters nothing to me *now*, although it did once" (Dunn). If the former, Paul is seeking once again to underline his independence from the Jerusalem apostles, even if their approval of his mission was a crucial and welcome event. If the latter, then the change in attitude is probably due to the conflict with Cephas and the emissaries from James in Antioch (2:11–14); Paul writes Galatians after this traumatic event has taken place, and though he does not seem to have given up on the church

---

172. He perhaps was intending to write, "From those acknowledged to be something, I received nothing" (cf. Burton 87).

in Jerusalem and its leaders (2:10; cf. 1 Cor 9:1–6; 15:1–9; Rom 15:25–28), he regards them differently now.[173] In either case, the point is that the status of the pillars cannot be brought to bear on the present argument (Betz 95), for as Paul now explains, "God shows no partiality" (also NRSV; BDAG 584), which is a translation of *prosōpon [ho] theos anthrōpou ou lambanei*, literally, "God does not take the face of a person" (cf. Luke 20:21), meaning that God is not impressed by considerations of external status. The "face" here is the social role of a person, the "mask" one has on in social affairs (Lightfoot 108; cf. e.g., Luke 20:21; LXX: Lev 19:15; Deut 1:17; 10:17; 16:19). If God is not impressed by considerations of external status, treating everyone the same, the Galatians (Paul implies) should also not be impressed: "The status of the acknowledged leaders at the time of the conference thus cannot be used as an argument for—or against—my gospel, as the new preachers would have you think."

In any case, those acknowledged leaders "added nothing" to Paul, added nothing to his circumcision-free gospel, "but to the contrary" (Gal 2:7a), they in fact recognized God's presence in his mission and affirmed it with a handshake. The main thought, "James and Cephas and John . . . gave to me and Barnabas the right hand of partnership" (2:9b), is preceded by two parallel participial clauses (2:7a, 9a), giving the reasons for the positive reaction of the acknowledged leaders in Jerusalem. These two clauses are interrupted by a theologically loaded parenthesis (2:8). The syntax, though not as garbled as in 2:6a, is still rather complex and characterized by ellipses (rectified by the words supplied in brackets):

> [7a]when they came to see [*idontes*] that I had been entrusted[174] [by God] with the gospel to the uncircumcision, [7b]just as Peter [had been entrusted by God with the gospel] to the circumcision
> [8](for the One who worked in Peter for the apostleship to the circumcision also worked in me for [the apostleship to] the Gentiles),
> [9a]and when they came to recognize [*gnontes*][175] the grace which had been given to me [by God] . . .

---

173. It seems that Paul's relationship with Peter and Barnabas eventually improved, if the evidence of 1 Corinthians is any indication: Peter/Cephas is mentioned four times (1:12; 3:22; 9:5; 15:5) and Barnabas once (9:6), without evident rancor. James is another story (see on 2:12 and 4:25–27).

174. The verb is the perfect *pepisteumai*, lit., "I have been entrusted," and could also be so translated here. This perfect can be construed as signifying completed action relative to the main verb in the text, which here is actually *edōkan*, "they gave," in 2:9b—or as signifying completed action relative to the time of the writing of the letter. In the former case, English demands a pluperfect construction ("had been entrusted"), in the latter a perfect construction ("have been entrusted"). The ambiguity of the Greek allows Paul to mean both: "I had been and have been entrusted."

175. The participles in 2:7a and 9a are both ingressive, or inceptive, aorists.

The Origin and the Truth of the Gospel

Paul's use of the terms "circumcision" (*peritomē*) and "uncircumcision" (*akrobystia*, lit., "foreskin") in these verses is another indication that the circumcision of Gentile believers was the crucial point at issue at the conference, just as it is now in Galatia. The terms are here being used metonymically to designate groups of peoples: respectively, the people who practice circumcision, Jews (cf. 2:9c; Rom 3:30; 4:9), and the people who do not, Gentiles (cf. Gal 2:8, 9c; Rom 2:26; 3:30; 4:9). Paul had (and still has)[176] been entrusted with "the gospel to the uncircumcision" (*to euangelion tēs akrobystias*, lit., "the gospel of the circumcision"), whereas Peter had (and presumably still has) been entrusted with "[the gospel] to the circumcision" ([*to euangelion] tēs peritomēs*, lit., "[the gospel] of the circumcision"). The genitive here is one of direction (BDF #163; Burton 93; Martyn 202), given the metonymical uses of the terms "circumcision" and "uncircumcision," as well as the phrases "to [*eis*] the Gentiles" and "to [*eis*] the circumcision" in 2:8 and 9c. Paul's words can be taken to mean that there are two (different) gospels (Betz 96; Longenecker 55), one for the Jews ("a circumcision gospel") and another for the Gentiles ("an uncircumcision gospel"), yet they can also be taken to mean that the *one* gospel is to be proclaimed to the two different groups (Martyn 202; Witherington 140). The latter interpretation is to be preferred, since it is consistent with what Paul has written earlier, in 1:6–9, 11–12 (see comments above), and will write in 2:15–16 (see comment below). In 2:7, there is but *one* gospel in view, even if this gospel can receive different formulations in different contexts (see comment on 1:11–12). That *one* gospel, whose hallmark is "grace" (1:6, 15; 2:9a, 21), had (and has) been entrusted to Paul for proclamation to the Gentiles and to Peter for proclamation to the Jews.

Excursus 7: The Problem of Galatians 2:7b–8

Galatians 2:7b–8 ("just as Peter to the circumcision, for the One who worked in Peter for the apostleship to the circumcision also worked in me for the Gentiles") presents several difficulties. Among these are the following:

1. The presence of 2:7b–8 makes the syntax of 2:7–9a rather complex and blurs the parallelism of the participial phrase in 2:9a ("when they came to recognize . . .") to the one in 2:7a ("when they came to see . . ."). The passage reads much more smoothly and clearly without 2:7b–8: "[7a]when they came to see [*idontes*] that I had been entrusted with the gospel to the uncircumcision, . . . [9a]and when they came to recognize [*gnontes*] the grace that had been given to me, [9b]James and Cephas and John . . . gave to me and Barnabas the right hand of partnership."

2. In 2:7b–8, Paul twice refers to Cephas as Peter (see comment on 1:18 above). He does so nowhere else. Four times elsewhere in Galatians he uses Peter's Aramaic

---

176. See note 174 above.

nickname "Cephas" instead (1:18; 2:9, 11, 14),[177] and he uses it another four times in 1 Corinthians (1:12; 3:22; 9:5; 15:5). (There are no other instances of "Cephas" in the Pauline Letters or indeed in the NT, apart from John 1:42, where "Cephas" is said to mean "Peter.") An unsuspecting reader could get the impression that Peter and Cephas, mentioned for the second time in 2:9 (after 1:18), are two different people, Peter being the missionary to the Jews and Cephas being one of the three pillars of the Jerusalem church. Paul does not explicitly indicate that they are one and the same.

3. In 2:7b–8, only Paul and Peter are mentioned in terms of the two parallel missions to Gentiles and Jews. According to 2:9b–c, which contains the main sentence of the subunit 2:6–10, Paul *and Barnabas* ("we"), representing the church in Antioch, are to preach the gospel to the Gentiles, whereas Cephas (assuming him to be Peter) together with *James* and *John* ("they"), representing the church in Jerusalem, are to preach the gospel to the Jews. Galatians 2:7b–8 thus does not seem to fit very well in the context.

Taken together, such observations[178] have led to two major proposals: First, Gal 2:7b–8 is an early (second-cent.) interpolation, perhaps directed against Marcionites, for whom Paul was the only true apostle (see van Manen; Barnikol; Walker 2003a). The purpose behind the interpolation was to put Peter on an equal level with Paul, consistent with the views of the Roman church and its allies elsewhere. Already in *1 Clement*, written from the church in Rome to the one in Corinth around 96 C.E., Peter and Paul are the two leading apostles, being called "the greatest and most righteous pillars" (5.2). The interpolation hypothesis could also explain why the variant reading "Cephas" for "Peter" does not occur in any known manuscript containing 2:7b–8, whereas the variant reading "Peter" for "Cephas" does occur in manuscripts (particularly "Western" ones, including in all cases Codex D) containing 1:18; 2:9, 11, 14. The variant "Peter" for "Cephas" in these four verses can be readily explained as having occurred under the influence of the use of "Peter" in 2:7b–8, once the latter passage had been inserted. Against this hypothesis, however, is the fact that this variant does not occur in the other four passages where Paul refers to "Cephas," all of them, as it happens, in 1 Corinthians (1:12; 3:22; 9:5; 15:5). The hypothesis assumes that "Cephas" was no longer understood at a later time and had to be replaced by "Peter," whose status as the apostolic equal of Paul had to be emphasized; then why not also in 1 Corinthians, a letter already known to the writer of *1 Clement* (47.1)? Furthermore, in 2:7b–8, Peter is entrusted with "the gospel to the circumcision," and it is hard to see how Peter's "apostolate to the circumcision" could have been relevant to the issues of the second century. Already in Acts (10:1–11:18; 15:7–11), he is being portrayed as the one with whom a mission to Gentiles began (cf. 1 Peter). Thus Galatians 2:7b–8, though syntactically awkward, seems to be original.

---

177. According to the best manuscript evidence (lesser, mostly Western or Byzantine manuscripts for each verse read "Peter"). Curiously, the variant reading "Cephas" (replacing "Peter") is unattested for 2:7b–8.

178. Others include the claim that certain expressions here are un-Pauline: "the gospel of circumcision," "[the gospel] of uncircumcision," and "the apostolate of the circumcision" (Betz 96–97, using his translations); also the verb *energeō* ("work") followed by a simple dative instead of a prepositional phrase beginning with *en*, as in 3:5; Rom 7:5; 1 Cor 12:6; 2 Cor 1:6; 4:12; Phil 2:13; 1 Thess 2:13 (Walker 2003a: 579).

The Origin and the Truth of the Gospel

According to the second major proposal, Paul is quoting, or using key words derived from, an official document, a "protocol," agreed to at the Jerusalem conference (cf. Betz 97; Bruce 120–21; Longenecker 55–56; Vouga 47). The problems with this hypothesis are numerous: (1) Paul does not indicate that he is citing such a protocol; (2) there is no further evidence that such a protocol existed; (3) the use of "Peter" rather than "Cephas" for a document originating in Aramaic-speaking Jerusalem remains difficult to explain, given the fact that Paul uses the Aramaic "Cephas" elsewhere (one would expect "Cephas" in 2:7b–8 and "Peter" in 1:18; 2:9, 11, 14); (4) the evident tension with the report of what was agreed to at the Jerusalem conference in 2:9b–c remains and indeed becomes more acute.

A hypothesis that overcomes some of these difficulties is that of A. Schmidt, who is followed by Martyn (204, 212). In this view, these verses "contain the kernel of an earlier agreement reached by Peter and Paul on the occasion of Paul's first visit to Jerusalem (1:18)," while 2:9b–c "reports that at the time of the meeting that earlier agreement was also adopted (and adapted) by James and John, representing the Jerusalem church with Peter, and by Barnabas as one of the Antioch representatives" (Martyn 212). Peter and Paul had thus reached a rudimentary and informal understanding of the parallel missions to Jews and Gentiles, one that would be formally confirmed at the Jerusalem conference by the representatives of the two churches.

Even with this hypothesis, two questions remain unanswered: (1) Why does Paul write "Peter" instead of "Cephas" in 2:7b–8? A possible reason is that he wants to bring out the symbolic meaning of the name for his Galatian readers (Lührmann 39–40; Becker 35; Vouga 47–48): Peter was "the rock" of the law-observant church in Jerusalem (cf. Matt 16:18). Paul assumes that the Galatians will understand that "Peter" is a nickname meaning "Rock," and that it is the Greek translation of "Cephas." The first mention of Cephas in 1:18 already suggests that the Galatians were familiar with the name; at least Paul assumes such familiarity on their part. (2) Why does Paul refer only to himself and Peter in 2:7b–8? Because at the time of the Jerusalem conference, Paul was the leading missionary of the Antioch church to the Gentiles, whereas Peter was the leading missionary of the Jerusalem church to the Jews. Paul and Barnabas formed a missionary team, to be sure, as did Cephas and John, but Paul and Cephas were the recognized leaders of, respectively, the mission to the Gentiles and the mission to the Jews (see comments on 2:7b–8 and 9b above).

In Gal 2:7b–8, Paul seems to assume (1) that the Galatians will understand that Peter and Cephas, who is mentioned for the second time in 2:9 (cf. 1:18; 2:11, 14), are one and the same person (see Excursus 7, above); and (2) that Peter was the leading missionary of the Jerusalem church, working together with John to bring the gospel to the Jews (a picture implied by 2:9b and confirmed by Acts 1–5), just as Paul at the time of the conference was the leading missionary of the Antioch church, working closely with Barnabas to bring the gospel to the Gentiles (a picture presupposed by 2:1 and confirmed by Acts 13–15). For this reason, presumably, Paul can refer here simply to Peter and himself, rather than to "Peter and John" and "me and Barnabas." Their particular leadership roles in the two missions may already be implied by Gal 1:18, where Paul (without mentioning Barnabas) goes up to visit Cephas (without mentioning John), with James getting only a passing nod (1:19).

The passive form of the verb "had been entrusted" (*pepisteumai*) in 2:7a is a circumlocution for the divine activity (a "divine passive"), as is the passive participle "was given" (*dotheisan*) in 2:9a. That surmise is supported by 2:8, where Paul refers to God as "the One who worked," "was effective" (*ho energēsas*), in both him and Peter. This verse, formally an aside, seems to express Paul's own theological position, one also shared, he implies, by the pillar apostles in Jerusalem; the aside is here for the benefit of the Galatians and the new preachers who shall be listening to the letter with them. Paul refers here to Peter's "apostleship to the circumcision." He applies the word "apostleship" twice elsewhere to himself (Rom 1:5; 1 Cor 9:2). Romans 1:5 recalls the vocabulary used here: "We have received *grace* and *apostleship* to bring about the obedience of faith among all the *Gentiles*." In 2:8 the omission of the word "apostleship" in connection with Paul is thus probably stylistic, a matter of ellipsis, and of no further significance, any more than is the omission of the word "gospel" in connection with Peter in 2:7b; thus Paul writes in 2:8: "For the One who worked in Peter for the apostleship to the circumcision [*eis apostolēn tēs peritomēs*] also worked in me for [the apostleship to] the Gentiles [*eis ta ethnē = eis apostolēn tōn ethnōn*]."[179]

Verses 2:7a and 9a together recall Paul's conversion and call to apostleship in 1:15–16: "*The One who* . . . called me through his *grace* was pleased to apocalyptically reveal his Son in me, that I might preach him among *the Gentiles*." With "grace," Paul could be alluding not simply to his conversion and call, but also, and perhaps chiefly, to the gospel (cf. 1:6; 2:21; 5:4); in that case, 2:7a and 9a contain an instance of synonymous parallelism, the latter repeating the thought of the former in different words: The pillar apostles extended the right hand of partnership to Paul and Barnabas once they saw (*idontes*) that Paul "had been entrusted" by God "with the gospel" to the Gentiles (7a), that is to say, once they recognized (*gnontes*) "the grace that had been given" to him by God (9a). The pillar apostles acted as they did when they were able to perceive God's grace-full presence and activity in the calling and the work of Paul "among the Gentiles." Paul places their new perception under the rubric "apocalyptic revelation" (2:2a; see comment there): God caused them to perceive that he was present in Paul's proclamation of the gospel, meaning the gospel of God's grace in Christ, to the Gentiles, just as he was in Peter's proclamation of the gospel, meaning the gospel of God's grace in Christ, to the Jews. The pillars' new perception and recognition, effected by God, enabled them to give to Paul

---

179. Burton (94) rightly adds: "That *apostolēn* is omitted because of an unwillingness on Paul's part to claim apostleship for himself is excluded alike by the whole thought of the sentence and by 1:1."

The Origin and the Truth of the Gospel

(and Barnabas) "the right hand of partnership" in the proclamation of the one gospel (cf. Martyn 200–210).

James is probably "James, the brother of the Lord" (1:19), rather than James the son of Zebedee, who was killed some years before by King Herod Agrippa I (Acts 12:1–2). The fact that James is mentioned first (contrast 1:18–19) suggests that by the time of the conference he was the leading figure in the Jerusalem church, an inference further supported by the account of the conference in Acts 15 (15:13; cf. 12:17; 21:18). Another reason for mentioning him first could be to highlight the fact that "even the leader known to be a strict adherent of the law came to see that God was at work in Paul's circumcision-free mission to Gentiles" (Martyn 204; cf. Hegesippus, *apud* Eusebius, *Hist. eccl.* 2.23.4–18). By the time Paul writes Galatians, furthermore, James has probably become the leading authority for the new preachers and for the circumcision party in Jerusalem; Paul wants to emphasize that at this crucial conference, James himself acknowledged Paul and his circumcision-free gospel to Gentiles, even if he does so no longer (cf. comments on 2:12 and 4:25–27). Cephas, or Peter (2:7–8), was the leader among the Twelve (cf. 1 Cor 15:5; cf. Gal 1:18 and comment there) and probably also the leading missionary of the Jerusalem church (see on 2:7–8 and Excursus 7 above). John is probably John the son of Zebedee, who is mentioned a number of times in Acts as Peter's close associate and missionary partner (3:1, 3–4, 11; 4:13, 19; 8:14). Cephas and John seemed to have formed a missionary partnership, much like Paul and Barnabas (see comments on 2:9c below and on 2:7–8 above). John was plainly the junior partner. The sense of 2:9b can perhaps be rendered as follows: "James, as well as Cephas and John, the missionary partners of the Jerusalem church, . . . gave to me and Barnabas, the missionary partners of the Antioch church, the right hand of partnership."

All three (James, Cephas, John) were probably regarded as apostles by Paul (see comments on 1:17, 19 above), and thus probably by the Jerusalem church as well. Paul indicates that these three apostles were known as "pillars" in the church of Jerusalem. He refers to them as "those acknowledged [*hoi dokountes*] to be pillars" (for *hoi dokountes*, see comment on 2:1–3 and 2:6a–c, above). The image is that of a building whose roof is held up by pillars. The term is obviously being used metaphorically to designate "those upon whom responsibility rests" (Burton 96). This metaphorical use of the term occurs in classical and Jewish as well as Christian writings (Burton 96; Longenecker 57; BDAG 949); the Galatians will thus have had little trouble in grasping its basic significance here, whatever its precise origin and import may have been.[180]

---

180. The origin and import of the metaphor as applied to James, Cephas, and John can only remain a matter of speculation, since Paul does not explain the image nor is it found in other NT texts. Among the possibilities are the following: (1) There is evidence that "the church of God"

The three "pillars" shook hands with Paul and Barnabas, meaning that they accepted the circumcision-free mission to the Gentiles as sponsored by the church in Antioch. The "giving of the right hand" was a custom "as a pledge of friendship or agreement" (Burton 95; cf. e.g., 1 Macc 6:58 LXX; Josephus, *Ant.* 18.328–329). The pillars in Paul's account, however, each offered to Paul and Barnabas not so much the right hand of friendship or agreement as that "of partnership." The Greek word *koinōnia*, often here translated "fellowship" (KJV, NRSV, NIV), means "sharing" or "participation" (BDAG 552–53; cf. Acts 2:42; Rom 15:26; 1 Cor 1:9; 10:16; 2 Cor 6:14; 8:4; 9:13; 13:13; Phil 1:5; 2:1; 3:10; Phlm 6; Heb 13:16; 1 John 1:3, 6–7). Here the sharing involves "partnership" (NJB, NAB; cf. Phil 1:5): joint and equal participation in the work of God (2:7–8). The nature of that partnership is spelled out in the two parallel subordinate *hina*-clauses in 2:9c–10:

> ⁹ᶜthat [*hina*] we go to the Gentiles [*eis ta ethnē*] and they to the circumcision [*eis tēn peritomēn*],
> ¹⁰only that [*hina*] we remember the poor, which very thing I was eager to do.

The elliptical *hina* clause in 2:9c is probably not an adverbial purpose clause ("they gave us the right hand of partnership *in order that* we go to the Gentiles and they to the circumcision"), but a noun clause explicating the partnership in view: "They gave us the right hand of partnership, [agreeing] that we [of the church in Antioch, on the one hand, go] to the Gentiles and they [of the church in Jerusalem, on the other hand, go] to the circumcision [the Jews]." The "we" undoubtedly refers to Paul and Barnabas as the missionary team of the Antioch church, whereas the "they" refers specifically to Cephas and John (see above on 2:7b–8 and 9b) as the missionary team of the Jerusalem church.[181] The mission of Paul and Barnabas to the Gentiles on behalf of the church in Antioch was not a rival of, nor a deviation from, the mission of Cephas and John to the Jews on behalf of the church in Jerusalem; the former shared in God's work just as much as the latter. Paul's basic point here is that the three recognized men of importance in Jerusalem, to whom the new preachers in Galatia are appealing to cast doubt on the legitimacy of the circumcision-free gospel Paul had

---

(1:13) was regarded as the eschatological temple of the new age inaugurated by Christ (cf. 1 Cor 3:10–17; Eph 2:21; Rev 3:12; Wilckens). The three apostles thus functioned as "pillars" in God's new temple, "the church of God" in Jerusalem (see comment on 1:13). (2) In rabbinic traditions, the three patriarchs Abraham, Isaac, and Jacob, were regarded as the pillars of Israel and indeed the world (Aus). Perhaps the three apostles were regarded by the church in Jerusalem as pillars of the new Israel and indeed of the new world inaugurated by Christ. The Galatians will not have to know any of these things to understand the metaphor, which was widespread in the ancient world.

181. The "we" and "they" can thus also be taken to mean simply "the church of Antioch" and "the church of Jerusalem," respectively (Georgi 32).

The Origin and the Truth of the Gospel

preached to the Galatians (1:11), had actually affirmed the circumcision-free gospel that he and Barnabas were then proclaiming (2:2) on behalf of the church in Antioch. Paul shared his gospel with the pillar apostles in a private meeting (2:2), and they responded not with negotiations and demands but solely with their approval: "When the apostles had heard Paul's Gospel, they . . . simply and unhesitatingly embraced his doctrine" (Calvin 30).[182]

In 2:9c, as in 2:8, Paul posits two parallel missions, one to the Gentiles and one to the Jews. It is difficult to determine with certainty whether the envisioned division of labor was to be ethnic or territorial. If the former, Paul and Barnabas were to proclaim the gospel solely to Gentiles wherever they lived, and Peter and John solely to Jews wherever they lived. If the latter, Peter and John would be confined to Jewish territory, meaning Palestine, whereas Paul and Barnabas would be confined to Gentile territory, the Mediterranean basin beyond Antioch. Paul and Barnabas could then also preach the gospel to Jews resident in their territory, just as Peter and John could preach the gospel to any Gentiles resident in Palestine. Among the considerations in favor of the first ("ethnic") option are the following:

1. Paul's terminology ("the circumcision" and "the uncircumcision" = "the Gentiles") seems to presuppose an ethnic division.
2. The Galatians themselves are all Gentiles (4:8–10).
3. Paul's other letters indicate that he preached the gospel to Gentiles, not to Jews (contrary to the impression created by Acts).
4. In Rom 11:13, he specifically characterizes himself as "the apostle of [= to] the Gentiles" (cf. Rom 1:5; 15:16, 18).

In favor of the second ("territorial") option are the following considerations:

1. Paul twice uses the phrase *eis ta ethnē*, literally, "in the direction of the Gentiles" (2:8, 9c; cf. 2 Cor 10:16), not the dative *tois ethnesin*, "to the Gentiles," as one might expect (Burton 98).
2. He has already twice, in 1:16 and 2:2, referred to proclaiming the gospel *en tois ethnesin*, "among the Gentiles," again instead of *tois ethnesin*, "to the Gentiles."
3. In 1:17–23, Paul emphasizes that he kept his *geographical* distance from Jerusalem and Judea, thus from Jewish territory (see comments there), where the pillar apostles were the authorities and the Jerusalem church sponsored a mission to Jews.

---

182. The picture presented by Acts 15 is somewhat different; there something is added to Paul's gospel of grace, namely, the so-called apostolic decree mandating that Gentiles "abstain from what has been sacrificed to idols and from blood and from what is strangled and from fornication" (15:29 NRSV).

4. Two short passages in Paul's Letters suggest that Paul also preached to Jews, as does Acts, where Paul routinely goes to the synagogue first upon entering a new city (cf. 17:1–2: "as was his custom"): in 1 Cor 9:20, Paul claims that "to the Jews I became as a Jew," and in 2 Cor 11:24 he reports that he five times received the synagogue punishment of thirty-nine lashes.[183]

The formulations in 2:6–10 are probably too vague to come to a certain conclusion here (Vouga 49). In any case, it is possible that Paul (or the church in Antioch) and Peter (or the church in Jerusalem) may themselves have had conflicting or even unclear views about the matter. For the Galatians, the distinction will probably be of no concern or consequence; either way, Paul's rhetorical point is the same: the Gentile Galatians "fall under Paul's sphere of influence" (Matera 83), not that of Jerusalem.

Verse 2:10 indicates a second dimension to the partnership between Antioch and Jerusalem: "Only [they asked] that [*hina*] we [of the church in Antioch] remember the poor [of the church in Jerusalem], which very thing I [Paul] was indeed eager to do." The first part of this verse (2:10a) emphasizes "the poor," since it literally reads: "only the poor, that we remember [them]." The verb "remember" is present tense in the Greek (*mnēmoneuōmen*), denoting continuous or ongoing action; in this case, it is not certain whether Paul means "continue to remember" the poor, or "make a practice of remembering" the poor (Burton 99). With the adverb "only," here replacing an expected *kai* ("and"), Paul indicates to the Galatians that the request for the Antioch church and its representatives to "remember the poor" was a matter of secondary importance compared to the division of labor agreed to in 2:9c. Nevertheless, the remembrance of "the poor" was for Paul a sign of partnership between the two churches, for "the poor" here are not the poor in general but specifically the poor of the church in Jerusalem, as indicated by the context:

Gal 2:9c	Gal 2:10a
"we [of the church in Antioch]"	"we [of the church in Antioch] remember"
"they [of the church in Jerusalem]"	"the poor"

In 2:10a, as in 2:9c, Paul is explicating the nature of the partnership between the two churches of Antioch and Jerusalem. The "we" contained in the verb

---

183. Martyn (213–16) argues, however, that in 1 Cor 9:20 Paul has only the Jerusalem conference described in Gal 2:1–10 in view, whereas in 2 Cor 11:24 he is referring to punishment received by Jews for preaching the gospel to *Gentiles* (cf. 1 Thess 2:16, where Jewish hostility to Paul's preaching the gospel to Gentiles is indicated). If so, the value of Acts diminishes on this point, since it can hardly be used against Paul's own testimony.

mnēmoneuōmen, "we remember," of 2:10a thus corresponds to the pronoun "we" (*hēmeis*) of 2:9c: both signify the Antioch congregation. In the same way, the term "the poor" (*tōn ptōchōn*) corresponds to the "they" (*autoi*) of 2:9c. It is even possible that "the poor" was an honorific title for (the members of) the Jerusalem church as such, signifying its humility and dependence on God (cf. "the poor in spirit" in Matt 5:3; 1QM 14.7) as well as its eschatological self-consciousness and dignity as the community of the last days (Georgi 33–35). To "remember" these poor (the Jerusalem church as a whole) could then mean no more than to "to keep them in mind," perhaps in the sense of "to recognize their significance" (cf. Heb 13:7; Georgi 38; Longenecker 60) or "to pray for them" (cf. 1 Thess 1:3; 1 Macc 12:11).

That "the poor" in Jerusalem may designate people who really were materially impoverished is suggested by Rom 15:26, where Paul refers to "the poor among the saints in Jerusalem," doing so in connection with a collection of money from (some of) his churches for these poor (Rom 15:25–27; cf. 1 Cor 16:1–4; 2 Cor 8–9). In 1 Cor 16:1–3, Paul also mentions "the collection for the saints" that is to be taken to Jerusalem, giving the Corinthian church the same instructions that he gave "to the churches of Galatia" (16:1): "On the first day of every week, each of you is to put aside and save whatever extra you earn, so that collections need not be taken when I come." In Rom 15:26, then, "the poor" are a group within the Jerusalem church, and the poverty is not spiritual but material. To "remember the poor" in 2:10 would thus seem to imply not merely praying for them but also collecting funds on their behalf. Thus when Paul refers to "the poor" in 2:10a, he probably has in view, at least primarily, the materially poor members of the Jerusalem congregation; it is in any event likely that the Galatians will so understand the term.

The collection to which Paul refers in 2:10a, however, is probably *not* to be identified with the collection for "the poor among the saints in Jerusalem" about which Paul writes in his later correspondence (1 and 2 Corinthians; Romans). In 2:10a, Paul refers to (1) ongoing collection efforts (2) organized by the Antioch church (cf. Acts 11:27–30),[184] whereas in Romans and the Corinthian correspondence (including 1 Cor 16:1, where he mentions the role of the Galatian

---

184. In Acts 11:27–30, the church in Antioch provided famine relief for the church in Jerusalem during the reign of the emperor Claudius (41–56 C.E.), with Barnabas and Paul bringing the collected funds to Jerusalem (cf. Josephus, *Ant.* 20.50–51 for the famine in Palestine in 45–47 C.E.). In the scheme of Acts, this visit of Paul to Jerusalem (with Barnabas) occurred prior to the conference in Jerusalem recounted in Acts 15 (= Gal 2:1–10), but this is extremely unlikely since Paul's own chronology in Gal 1–2 does not allow a visit to Jerusalem (with or without Barnabas, for famine relief or some other purpose) between his first visit to Jerusalem to make Peter's acquaintance (1:18) and his second for the conference (2:1). See Burton 67–68. If the report in Acts 11:27–30 is historical, the visit recounted there must have taken place after the conference (Georgi 44–45) and been the result of what was agreed between the two churches as indicated in Gal 2:10a.

churches) he refers to (1) a onetime collection effort (2) organized by himself (Martyn 225; Wedderburn 96).

That Paul is no longer involved in the former collection is probably indicated by 2:10b, where Paul changes to the first-person singular and a past tense: "which very thing [remembering the poor] *I was* indeed eager [or hastened] to do [*espoudasa*]." At least at the time of the conference and thus in the (brief) interval between the conference and the incident at Antioch (2:11–14), Paul made a conscientious, diligent effort (BDAG 939) to "remember the poor" of the church in Jerusalem. He did so as a member and a missionary of the church in Antioch (cf. Acts 11:27–30).[185] After his break with Barnabas and Antioch (Gal 2:11–14), he initiated his own collection, one in which the Galatians would also be invited to participate (1 Cor 16:1; Martyn 222–28; Georgi). Thus in his own way, Paul would honor the commitment made under different circumstances at the conference in Jerusalem. At this conference, the request to remember the poor in Jerusalem was, Paul implies, a recognition of the full partnership of the Antioch church in the missionary efforts of the Jerusalem church and its pillar apostles. The two churches were of one mind, specifically in the recognition of the legitimacy of the circumcision-free mission of Antioch to the Gentiles, as carried out by Paul and Barnabas. The "acknowledged leaders" (2:2, 6, 9) thus at that time recognized "the truth of the gospel" (2:5), even if two of them (Cephas and James) later betrayed it (2:11–14 below).

2:11–14 The Truth of the Gospel 2: Conflict with Cephas in Antioch

This passage constitutes the fourth paragraph of the first major section of the letter body (1:11–2:21). In the first two paragraphs (1:11–17 and 1:18–24), the focal theme was the origin of the gospel that Paul preached to the Galatians. In the preceding paragraph (2:1–10) and this last one, the focal theme is "the truth of the gospel" (2:5, 14). If in the preceding paragraph, the pillar apostles in Jerusalem acknowledged the truth of the gospel that Paul was proclaiming among the Gentiles (the freedom of Gentile Christians not to practice circumcision and the remainder of the law), in this paragraph two of the pillars, Cephas and James, have (in Paul's view) turned their backs on it. Cephas (Peter) came to Antioch, and at the behest of emissaries from James in Jerusalem withdrew from table fellowship with Gentile believers in Antioch. Cephas's action caused Paul to confront him and once more to stand firm for the truth of the gospel. Paul gives a theological justification and elaboration of the truth of the gospel in 2:15–21, thereby turning his attention once more directly to the situation in

---

185. The aorist tense, *espoudasa,* could perhaps be taken to refer to the famine relief visit recounted in Acts 11:27–30 ("which very thing I had indeed hastened to do," i.e., prior to the conference in the famine relief visit), but this is unlikely since Paul's chronology of his visits to Jerusalem does not allow for such a visit; see previous note.

The Origin and the Truth of the Gospel

Galatia. It is difficult to know where Paul's account of the incident in Antioch stops and where his application of the truth of the gospel to the situation in Galatia begins. In 2:14, Paul quotes what he said to Cephas in Antioch some years before, but it is unclear where the quotation stops. Beginning with 2:15–16, words he addressed to Cephas in Antioch merge with words he now directs primarily to the new preachers in Galatia, who, like Cephas and Paul himself, were Jews by birth.

This passage can readily be divided into three sense units: the first is a summary of Paul's confrontation with Cephas in Antioch (2:11), the second recounts what Cephas did in Antioch and why (2:12–13), and the third gives Paul's reaction to Cephas's behavior: he rebuked him before a plenary assembly of the Antioch church (2:14). That rebuke provides a point of connection with the situation in Galatia and thus also constitutes a transition to the next passage, where Paul will rebuke the new preachers in Galatia. The encounter with Cephas in Antioch is thus presented as an analogy to the situation in Galatia.

2:11 But when Cephas[a] came to Antioch, I opposed him to his face, because he stood condemned.

12 For before certain people came from James, he was eating with the Gentiles, but when they came, he drew back and separated himself,[b] fearing those from the circumcision; 13 and the remaining Jews [also][c] played the hypocrite with him, so that even Barnabas was led away with their hypocrisy.

14 But when I saw that they were not behaving correctly with respect to the truth of the gospel, I said to Cephas in the presence of all: "If you, being a Jew, are living in a Gentile manner and not in a Jewish manner, how can you be putting pressure on the Gentiles to practice Judaism?"[d]

    a. Byzantine and Western manuscripts (including D) read "Peter." See the comments on 2:7–9 and Excursus 7 above.

    b. $\mathfrak{P}^{46}$ reads: "For before *someone* came from James, *they were eating* with the Gentiles, but when *he* [Cephas] came, he drew back and separated himself." The first two readings have little further support, but the third ("but when *he* came," *hote de ēlthen*) is also supported by ℵ, B, and D*, and probably arose under the influence of 2:11a, which also begins "but when he came" (*hote de ēlthen*), referring to Cephas.

    c. Some good witnesses read *kai* here (ℵ, A, C, D, et al.), but other good witnesses omit the word ($\mathfrak{P}^{46}$, B, et al.).

    d. "To practice Judaism" is a translation of the present infinitive *ioudaïzein*, which means "to be living in the Jewish manner," "to adopt Jewish customs," and the like; see comment on 2:14 below.

This passage assumes a certain sequence of actions that are here summarized and taken to be historical:

1. Cephas came to Antioch sometime after the conference recounted in 2:1–10.[186]
2. Cephas then ate with "the Gentiles," meaning Gentile believers in Christ (cf. Rom 15:16, 27), and did so over a period of time (*synēsthien*, impf.).
3. Emissaries from James in Jerusalem arrived on the scene and objected to Cephas eating with Gentile believers.
4. Cephas then made a practice of withdrawing (*hypestellen*, impf.) and separating himself (*aphōrizen*, impf.) from the community's meals: he no longer ate with Gentile believers of the church in Antioch.
5. Following Cephas's example, the "remaining Jews," meaning the Jewish believers in Christ, did the same, including Barnabas. The church of Antioch was thereby split into two groups, one Jewish, the other Gentile, no longer sharing the same table at mealtimes.
6. By their exclusion from table fellowship with Jewish believers, Gentile believers in Antioch were either intentionally or effectively being put under pressure "to practice Judaism." Only so could the two groups once again share the same table.
7. Paul reacted to this situation in a plenary assembly of the Antioch church, rebuking Cephas with a pointed question for not behaving in line with "the truth of the gospel," which holds that God's grace in Christ is unconditional for all who believe (1:6, 15; 2:9a, 16, 21) and means concretely that Gentile Christians are exempt (free) from the observance and thus also from the imposition of the Mosaic law.

[11] The Antioch that Paul refers to is Antioch on the Orontes (modern Antakya in Turkey), in the northeast corner of the Mediterranean basin. It was the capital of the Roman province of Syria and the third most populous city of the Roman Empire, after Rome and Alexandria. According to Acts, the church in Antioch was the first to attract Gentile believers (11:19–30). This church subsequently sponsored a circumcision-free mission to Gentiles, with Paul and Barnabas as its missionary team (Acts 13:1–14:28), and initiated the conference with the Jerusalem church in response to the demand of a particular faction in the Jerusalem church that Gentile believers also practice circumcision and observe the law (Acts 15:1–35; see comment on Gal 2:1–10 and Excursus 4).

---

186. It has sometimes been asserted that the incident in Antioch preceded the conference and may even have provided the occasion for it. But that is not the most natural way to read the passage. It is difficult to think that Paul could have gone to Jerusalem as a delegate of the Antioch church with Barnabas after the incident in Antioch. Nothing indicates that Paul's views prevailed. On the contrary, he seems to have lost the debate.

Paul does not explain why Cephas (Peter) came to Antioch, and it is idle to speculate since there are no other sources reporting such a visit (Peter disappears from the narrative of Acts after he gives a speech at the conference in 15:7–10). More important for Paul is what he did in Antioch once he arrived, as described in Gal 2:12–13.

The remainder of v. 11 constitutes a summary of Paul's confrontation with Cephas before the Antioch church: "I opposed him [*antestēn*] to his face [*kata prosōpon*], because he stood condemned." Paul thereby highlights what for him is the important point, his necessary opposition to Cephas to defend "the truth of the gospel." What Paul's opposition consisted of and why Cephas "stood condemned" are recounted in v. 14: Paul sternly reprimanded Cephas "in the presence of all" because he was "putting pressure on" Gentile believers "to practice Judaism." He was thus not "behaving correctly with respect to the truth of the gospel," the very truth he had earlier seen and recognized at the conference in Jerusalem (2:1–10).

Difficult is the phrase "stood condemned [*kategnōsmenos ēn*]." The Greek has the form of a periphrastic pluperfect (perfect participle with an imperfect of the verb *eimi*), which would normally be translated "he had been condemned": Paul, looking back at an event that occurred some years before, reports that when he confronted Cephas at the assembly of the Antiochene Christians, he "had [already] been condemned" (by the Gentile Christians of Antioch? by Paul? by God?). The participle can also be construed as a predicate adjective: hence the translation "stood condemned" (RSV), meaning "existed in a state of condemnation" (lit., "was having been condemned"). Paul's thought is probably that Peter's action, described in the following verses as hypocritical, condemned him (Lightfoot 103; Burton 103; Bruce 129; cf. 1 John 3:20–21), and thus that he "stood self-condemned" (NRSV). It is likely that Paul also believes that Cephas stood condemned before (or by) God (e.g., Longenecker 72; Martyn 232; cf. 1:8–9 above; *Ps.-Clem. Hom.* 17.19; Josephus, *J.W.* 1.635; 7.154), though it is less certain that the Galatians will catch this nuance. Paul's basic point is that Peter did something that deserved condemnation. He now goes on to explain why.

[12–13] These verses explain how it came about that Cephas was putting pressure on Gentile believers in Antioch "to practice Judaism" (v. 14) so that "he stood condemned": "¹²ᵃFor [*gar*] before certain people came from James,[187] he was eating with the Gentiles, ¹²ᵇbut when they came, he drew back and separated himself, fearing those from the circumcision; ¹³and the remaining Jews [also] played the hypocrite with him, so that even Barnabas was led away with their hypocrisy."

---

187. Or, following the word order of the Greek: "certain people from James came." There seems to be little difference in meaning or implication.

In 2:12a, Paul reports that over a period of time after his arrival in Antioch, Cephas "was eating" (*synēsthien*, impf.) with "the Gentiles," meaning Gentile believers of the church in Antioch (cf. Acts 10:9–11:18).[188] But then "certain people [*tinas*] from [*apo*] James," the leader of the church in Jerusalem, came on the scene (see on 2:9 above). These unnamed people were probably James's emissaries, people who acted on his instructions; it is otherwise difficult to explain why Paul does not simply refer to them as coming "from Jerusalem."[189] By referring to these emissaries merely as "certain people," Paul tries to minimize their importance and their number in the eyes of the Galatians. Their impact on the life of the Antioch church upon arrival indicates that they carried considerable authority, that of James himself. Paul does not say why they were sent to Antioch by James; he says only that their arrival marked the end of Peter's eating with the Gentile believers in Antioch. When they arrived, Peter "drew back" (*hypestellen*, impf.) and "separated" (*aphōrizen*, impf.) himself for the remainder of his stay in Antioch. Paul does not say how long Cephas stayed in Antioch.[190]

Peter's withdrawal had a powerful impact on the other Jewish believers in Antioch (2:13). They "played the hypocrite with [*synypekrithēsan*] him, so that even Barnabas was led away with their hypocrisy [*hypokrisei*]." Paul's charge of hypocrisy is clearly polemical. He implies that their actions were not consistent with what they knew to be true (cf. 2:15–16 below: "we Jews by birth . . . *know* that someone is not justified on the basis of works of the law"). Paul's disappointment in Barnabas, his mentor and missionary partner, is evident (for Barnabas, see comments on 2:1, 9). Barnabas's decision to follow Cephas's example left Paul in a weak and lonely position (cf. Col 4:11). Of the Jewish believers, he alone refused to give in to the demands of the emissaries from James. The fact that the other Jewish believers in Antioch followed Cephas's example suggests that the emissaries from James objected not only to Cephas's eating with Gentile believers but also to other Jewish believers' doing so. James's emissaries focused their efforts on Cephas because of his stature as a pillar apostle and his leading role in the mission "to the circumcision" (2:7–9), perhaps assuming that if he buckled, the others would too.

According to Paul, Cephas withdrew and separated himself not from conviction but from fear: he was afraid (*phoboumenos*, "fearing," a causal participle) of

---

188. Such meals probably included the eucharistic meal (Lord's Supper) of the community in Antioch, which would have been combined with a normal supper (cf. 1 Cor 11:17–34).

189. The prepositional phrase "from James" makes it unlikely that Paul is referring to people who appeal to James as their authority without his approval or knowledge, as is sometimes proposed (under the influence of Acts 15:24).

190. Burton (107), followed by Longenecker (75), suggests that the imperfect tenses imply that Cephas "gradually" withdrew and separated himself. The imperfects could equally well indicate that he did so immediately and then made a practice of withdrawing and separating himself.

The Origin and the Truth of the Gospel   133

"those from the circumcision" (*hoi ek peritomēs*), or "the circumcision party." With this designation, Paul could simply be referring to Jews, whether Christian or non-Christian (cf. Rom 4:12; Col 4:11). The same phrase appears in Acts 11:2–3, in a setting analogous to the one in Gal 2:11–14: After Peter returns to Jerusalem from Caesarea, where the Gentile yet God-fearing Cornelius and his household have become believers (Acts 10:1–48), "those from the circumcision" (AT) ask him to explain his behavior: "Why did you go to uncircumcised men [Gentiles] and eat with them?" "Those from the circumcision" seem to be Christian Jews in Jerusalem (as 11:18 bears out), and that is probably also the case in Gal 2:12b (against Jewett 2002 and Longenecker 73–75, who argue that "zealot-minded Jews" antagonistic to Christian Jews' fraternizing with Gentiles are in view). If so, they could represent either the Jerusalem church as a whole or, more probably, a particular faction within that church, "the circumcision party" (cf. Acts 15:1, 5 KJV) comprising Christian Jews who were "zealots for the law" (Acts 21:20 AT; see comment on 1:13–14 above). In the account of Acts, Peter stands his ground against the criticism of these Christian Jews (11:4–17), silencing their criticism and leading them to glorify God and to say: "Then to the Gentiles also God has granted repentance unto life!" (11:18 RSV). Acts 10:45 prepares the way for this outcome, reporting that certain "believers from the circumcision [*hoi ek peritomēs pistoi*]" (AT), meaning believers of Jewish birth, had accompanied Peter to Caesarea and were amazed that "the gift of the Holy Spirit had been poured out even on the Gentiles!"

In Paul's account of the situation in Antioch, the roles are reversed: the circumcision party stood firm and Cephas gave way. The emissaries from James represented the interests and the viewpoints of the circumcision party in Jerusalem, and that fact indicates that James too had come to share their views (as he evidently also does in Acts 21:18–20). For all intents and purposes, James and his emissaries to Antioch were also (in Paul's perception at any rate) members of the circumcision party based in Jerusalem; that party had come to dominate the Jerusalem church after the conference recounted in Gal 2:1–10, mainly by bringing James around to their point of view (cf. 4:26–27 and comment there; Acts 21:17–26).[191] Only such a turn of events can explain why Paul reports that Cephas feared them enough to change his own practice.

---

191. Paul does not say that James agrees with him, which he would have done had that been the case. Yet Paul refrains from attacking James directly in the present passage (also 4:25–27), perhaps for two reasons: (1) James was the leader of the church in Jerusalem, who had recognized the truth of the gospel at the conference there some time before (2:9); and (2) Paul hopes to win him (and, more important, the church in Jerusalem) back, in part with his own collection for the poor there (cf. Rom 15:25–27; 1 Cor 16:1–4; 2 Cor 8–9). (Acts does not mention this collection, though there may be an allusion to it in 24:17.) The author of Acts, it is true, portrays James as a mediating, moderating figure (15:13–29; 21:24–25). In Acts 21, when Paul returns to Jerusalem for the last time, he meets with James and "all the elders." James functions here as the chairman of the

Paul does not indicate precisely what Cephas had to fear from the circumcision party, nor does he explicitly indicate why James and his emissaries, acting at the behest of the circumcision party, objected to Cephas and other Jewish believers' eating with Gentile believers. There are three main possibilities:

1. They objected to Cephas and other Jewish believers' having an indifferent attitude toward the observance of the food laws when dining with Gentile Christians who did not observe such food laws. Jews, and thus also Christian Jews who wished to remain scrupulous about observing the law, did not eat certain foods, pork being the best-known example (Lev 11:1–23; Deut 14:3–21; 1 Macc 1:47; 2 Macc 6:18–21; 7:1; Tob 1:10–11; Josephus, *Ant.* 3.259–260; 4.137). The importance of keeping such food laws for conscientious Jews is indicated by 1 Macc 1:62–63: "But many in Israel stood firm and were resolved in their hearts not to eat unclean food. They chose to die rather than to be defiled by food or to profane the holy covenant; and they did die." Jews would also normally insist that permitted food be properly prepared (Lev 17:10–15; cf. Acts 15:20, 29; 21:25) and not contaminated by idolatry (Lev 17:8–9; 2 Macc 6:7; Josephus, *Life* 14; cf. Acts 15:20, 29; 1 Cor 8:1–6; 10:23–30). In Greco-Roman culture, meat and wine were commonly dedicated to the local gods and could then not be consumed by conscientious Jews (cf. Dan 1:8; Jdt 12:1–4; Add Esth 14:17; cf. Sanders 1990: 178; Esler 1994: 67; 1998: 104–8).[192] It was thus difficult for Jews to eat with Gentiles; the Roman historian Tacitus (*Hist.* 5.5.2) observed that "they eat separately" (*separati epulis*). Yet Paul does not explicitly mention food laws anywhere in the passage.

2. A variation on this first interpretation is that the emissaries from James were concerned only about Cephas's own observance of the food laws, thus not about the observance of the food laws by the other Jewish believers. Peter,

---

board of elders. James and these elders run interference for Paul against the suspicions of Christian Jews who are "zealots for the law" (21:20 AT) and who have heard (misleading and untrue) rumors about Paul's view of the law, namely, that he is "teaching all the Jews who are among the Gentiles apostasy from Moses, by telling them not to circumcise their children or observe the customs" (21:21 AT). James and the elders recommend that Paul demonstrate to these zealots that he is an observer of the law (21:24), which he does (21:26). That the historical James may well have shared the views of these Christian Jews more than Acts lets on is suggested by his later reputation among Christians Jews as a strict observer of the law (Hegesippus, in Eusebius, *Hist. eccl.* 2.23.4–18). Even in Acts 21, James and the elders function as spokesmen of the Christian Jews to Paul: Their first reaction to him is to articulate the concerns and the viewpoints of these zealous Jewish believers and their opposition to his work. James and the elders could not very well ignore them, since, as they themselves tell Paul, there were "many thousands" of such Christian Jews in Jerusalem, and "all" of them "zealots for the law."

192. Esler argues that the problem of Christian Jews "eating with" Christian Gentiles in Antioch would only have emerged in connection with the Lord's Supper, where there would be a sharing of food, wine, and vessels (cf. 1 Cor 10:16–17); at other meals, Jewish believers could and would have brought and eaten their own food, with Gentile believers doing the same (1998: 101–2). But there is no indication in the text for such a distinction.

being the apostle to the Jews (2:7–9), ought to observe these laws, since he would otherwise jeopardize his missionary efforts among Jews (cf. Martyn 242, Sanders 1990: 186; Dunn 126). In this interpretation, the demand that Cephas observe the food laws was a direct consequence of what was agreed at the Jerusalem conference: "The separation of the mission to the Jews from that to the Gentiles would imply that Peter would retain his Jewish way of life, and that included first of all dietary and purity laws. As a result, cultic separation would have to be observed also during table fellowship with Gentile Christians. This was especially important in the Diaspora, where defilement was most likely to occur" (Betz 108; cf. Burton 106). This interpretation does not, however, explain why Barnabas, Paul's missionary partner to the Gentiles who was also present at the Jerusalem conference and party to what was agreed to there, ended up going along with Cephas. Nor why the other Jewish believers also did so.

3. The emissaries from James and the circumcision party objected to Cephas and Christian Jews eating with uncircumcised Gentiles under any circumstances. The underlying assumption of this view is that Gentiles were by definition sinners (cf. e.g., Isa 14:5; 1 Macc 1:34; 2:48; *Pss. Sol.* 1.1–8), a view Paul himself momentarily adopts for the sake of argument when he contrasts "we Jews by birth" with "sinners from the Gentiles" in 2:15 (see comment on this verse below). In *Jubilees* 22.16, Abraham tells Jacob: "Separate yourself from the gentiles, and do not eat with them. . . . Because their deeds are defiled, and all their ways are contaminated, and despicable, and abominable." What Peter (in Acts 10:28) initially tells the Gentile-though-God-fearing Cornelius and the Gentiles assembled with him in his house is consistent with this seemingly extreme view of the matter: "You yourselves know that it is illicit [*athemiton*][193] for a Jewish man to associate intimately with [*kollasthai*] or to visit [*proserchesthai*] a foreigner [*allophylos*, someone of another tribe, a Gentile]" (AT). The implication is that Jews did not normally visit Gentile homes or share meals with them. Peter continues by saying that "God [however] has [now] shown me to call *no one* profane [*koinon*] or unclean [*akatharton*]" (AT). The implication of this saying is that Gentiles were regarded by (certain?) Jews as "profane" and "unclean."[194] For this reason, "the circumcision party" (also mentioned in Gal 2:12) asks Peter upon his return to Jerusalem: "Why did you go to uncircumcised men [lit., men of the foreskin] and eat with them?" (11:2–3). There is no suggestion here that the problem is the failure of these Gentiles to observe the food laws; the problem

---

193. According to BDAG 24, this word "refers prim[arily] not to what is forbidden by ordinance but to violation of tradition or common recognition of what is seemly or proper." The translation "illicit" is taken from Esler 1998: 95; BDAG suggests "forbidden."

194. Whether the words ascribed to Peter in Acts are representative of what Jews generally thought about such matters is a question pursued further and sharply debated by Dunn 117–23 (cf. 1990); Sanders 1990; Esler 1998: 94–116 (cf. 1994; 1995); Holmberg; and Nanos 2002b; particularly in connection with table fellowship and eating customs.

is the fact that they are uncircumcised (as in Acts 15:1, 5) and thus by definition "profane" and "unclean." The observance of food laws by Gentiles, perhaps out of consideration for Jewish sensibilities, would in this view be totally insufficient and largely irrelevant, important as the observance of these food laws was for Jews themselves. The emissaries from James, representing the views of the circumcision party in Jerusalem, would similarly have regarded attempts by the Gentile Christians in Antioch to observe the food laws as insufficient and largely irrelevant. The food laws were for Jews, not for Gentiles. What Cephas effected with his behavior, the separation of Jewish and Gentile believers in Antioch into two commensality groups, would thus have been intended by James and his emissaries (Holmberg 410–11). Paul's response to Cephas in v. 14 below suggests, however, that James and his emissaries saw the separation as a step to another goal: to convince the Gentile believers that they too had to become fully law observant. In this interpretation, Jewish believers could eat with Gentile believers only if they became Jews, if they practiced circumcision and the remainder of the law (cf. Gal 5:3; Acts 15:1, 5). The views of the circumcision party thus matched those of "the false brethren" at the Jerusalem conference (Gal 2:4–5); they also match those of the new preachers now active in Galatia (see Excursus 4, above). As indicated, the next verse gives reason to think that this third explanation for Cephas's withdrawal from the common table in Antioch is to be preferred to the other two.

[14] Paul's attention remains fixed on Cephas, rather than on Barnabas or on the emissaries from James. Cephas was for him the key. If Cephas had stood his ground and remained consistent, all would have been well. Paul sprang into action against Cephas when he saw (*eidon*) that "they" (the Jewish believers) were not "behaving correctly [*orthopodousin*] with respect to [*pros*] the truth of the gospel,"[195] that truth being God's unconditional grace in Christ for all who believe (1:6, 15; 2:9a, 16, 21) and thus, concretely, the freedom of Gentile believers in Antioch from the imposition of the law (2:4–5). Paul took Cephas to task before the whole congregation: "If you, being a Jew [i.e., a Jewish believer], are living in a Gentile manner and not in a Jewish manner, how can you be putting pressure on the Gentiles [i.e., Gentile believers] to practice Judaism?"

Cephas was addressed by Paul as "a Jew" (*Ioudaios*), meaning a Jewish believer (cf. 2:13), rather than merely as a "Jew by birth" (cf. 2:15).[196] As such, he was "not living in a Jewish manner." Here "to live in a Jewish manner" (*zēn Ioudaïkōs*, lit., "to live Jewishly") clearly means "to observe the law" (*poiēsai ton nomon*, 5:3), whereas "to live in a Gentile manner" (*zēn ethnikōs*, lit., "to live Gentilely") by contrast means "not to observe the law," with the

---

195. Other possible ways to translate the Greek include "he was not straightforward about the truth of the gospel" and "he was not progressing toward the truth of the gospel" (cf. BDAG 722).

196. Against Lightfoot 114; Vouga 57.

The Origin and the Truth of the Gospel 137

added implication of unhindered social intercourse with Gentiles.[197] The two expressions "not to live in a Jewish manner" and "to live in a Gentile manner" are thus virtually synonymous in this context,[198] and they serve to emphasize the point that Cephas was not law observant when Paul confronted him. To be sure, Cephas was at that point no longer eating with Gentile believers, but Paul evidently preferred to take Cephas's withdrawal as an unfortunate and temporary aberration from his normal practice, in any event as inconsistent with his inner convictions (cf. 2:15–16: "We Jews by birth ... know that ..."). Perhaps apart from the food laws, Cephas was still living "in a Gentile manner" (e.g., with respect to the observance of festivals). The rebuke was meant to bring Cephas back to his senses, to help him (and the other Jewish believers) rediscover his (and their) true Christian identity (Holmberg 1998). If Cephas was not law observant, it was inconsistent for him "to be putting pressure [*anankazeis*]" on the Gentile believers in Antioch "to practice Judaism." It is not clear whether Paul means that Cephas himself intentionally and explicitly put such pressure on the Gentile believers, or whether he effectively did so through his action of withdrawing and separating himself from them. As indicated above, it seems likely, or at least plausible, that exerting such pressure was among the aims of James's emissaries and the circumcision party. The verb "to practice Judaism," from the present infinitive *ioudaïzein*, must here mean "to be law observant" (cf. BDAG 478: "live as one bound by Mosaic ordinances or traditions"). There are good reasons to think, however, that more is involved in Paul's question to Cephas, and in Paul's use of this verb, than simply that Gentile believers are being put under duress to observe the Jewish food laws.

The key lies in Paul's use of the verb "to put pressure on," *anankazō*, which in the aorist (past) tense means "compelled" (referring to pressure successfully applied). Paul's use of this verb here can be no accident, given the fact that the new preachers in Galatia are charged with "putting pressure" on the Galatians "to be practicing circumcision" (6:12):

2:14 Peter was "putting pressure" (*anankazeis*) on the Gentile believers of Antioch "to practice Judaism" (*ioudaïzein*).

6:12 The new preachers are "putting pressure" (*anankazousin*) on the Gentile believers of Galatia "to practice circumcision" (*peritemnesthai*).[199]

---

197. For the emissaries from James and the circumcision party "to live in a Gentile manner" would mean "to live sinfully"; cf. the last paragraph of comment on vv. 12–13 above and the contrast between "Jews by birth" and "sinners from the Gentiles" in 2:15. See also comment on 2:17 below.

198. For this reason, perhaps, 𝔓[46] omits the phrase "and not in a Jewish manner."

199. For the translation of the present (or imperfect) middle of *peritemnō* as "to practice circumcision," see comments on 5:2–3 and 6:12 (also Excursus 4).

By using the verb *anankazō* in his question to Cephas in Antioch, Paul posits an analogy between what Peter was doing in Antioch on the one hand and what the new preachers are now doing in Galatia on the other. (He thereby puts Cephas in the same camp with the new preachers, the emissaries from James, and the circumcision party.) Something similar had also happened at the conference in Jerusalem, where "the false brethren" had, without success, put pressure on Titus to be circumcised: "But Titus, a Gentile believer, was not compelled [*ēnankasthē*] to be circumcised" (2:3).

The practice of circumcision by Gentile believers is the specific issue in Galatia (5:2–4; 6:12–13; cf. 3:3); it was the specific issue at the conference in Jerusalem (2:3); given the parallels between 2:3, 6:12, and 2:14, it was probably also the specific issue in Antioch. It is true that the verb "to practice Judaism" (*ioudaïzein*) does not necessarily involve circumcision (cf. Plutarch, *Cic.* 7.6; Josephus, *J.W.* 2.463; Ign. *Magn.* 10.3), though it does not necessarily exclude it either. In Josephus, *J.W.* 2.454, the commander of the Roman garrison, Metillus, saves his own life by promising "to practice Judaism even as far as circumcision" (*kai mechri peritomēs ioudaïzein*). In Esth 8:17 LXX, "Many of the Gentiles were practicing circumcision [*perietemonto*] and [were practicing] Judaism [*ioudaïzon*] for fear of the Jews." In both passages, the verb "to practice Judaism" implies becoming a Jew by adopting the practice of circumcision as the initial step.

The pressure that Cephas was putting on the Gentile believers in Antioch "to practice Judaism" (*ioudaïzein*) thus probably involved not simply food laws, which Paul nowhere explicitly mentions, but observing "the whole law," beginning with circumcision (5:3; Betz 112; Longenecker 78; Esler 1998: 137; Holmberg 411; Nanos 2002b: 304). Only under those conditions were Cephas, the emissaries from James, the circumcision party, and the other Jewish believers in Antioch, even Barnabas, prepared "to eat with" Gentile believers in Antioch. Before the Gentile believers had met those conditions, they were to be excluded from the common table (cf. 4:17).

For the Galatians, Paul wants to highlight the fact that Cephas, one of the pillar apostles who had acknowledged the truth of the gospel at the conference in Jerusalem, had not behaved correctly as far as the truth of the gospel was concerned. It is not in Paul's interest here to suggest in any way that Cephas had actually and finally repudiated or betrayed that truth. Perhaps for that reason, he does not report what Cephas had said in reply. The answer he thinks Cephas should have given is in any event contained in the question: "You are right, Paul; I should know better. I should continue to act in accordance with what I know to be the truth of the gospel, as I have done in the past, and not put pressure on Gentile believers to become Jews." In 2:15–21, Paul will show the new preachers in Galatia on theological grounds why that should have been Cephas's answer.

2:15–21 The Truth of the Gospel for the Galatian Situation

In the previous passage, Paul was giving an account of his confrontation with Cephas (Peter) in Antioch and rebuking him for not behaving correctly with respect to the truth of the gospel. His short but telling rebuke of Cephas (in 2:14) turns into a rebuttal of the new preachers in Galatia (in 2:15–16). The present passage supports the assumption that the new preachers in Galatia were Jews "by birth" (2:15), like Cephas and like Paul himself. Paul here makes a startling claim, one clearly (still) unacceptable to these new preachers in Galatia (and presumably also to Cephas, Barnabas, the emissaries from James in Jerusalem, and Christian Jews in Antioch): Works of the law are completely *irrelevant* for justification. The only thing that matters is "the faith of Christ." This is the truth of the gospel that Paul now proclaims to the new preachers in Galatia, hoping that they will see and acknowledge it as James and John and Cephas had earlier done in Jerusalem (2:9). The new preachers are Christian Jews, accepting Jesus as the Messiah but still taking their theological bearings from the law (see Excursus 4, above); on the other hand, Paul has become a Jewish Christian, no longer taking his theological bearings from the law but from Christ, in particular his death on the cross (2:19–21).

In this paragraph, which concludes the first major section of Galatians, Paul gives his second contextually relevant summary of the gospel (the first occurs in 1:4). Paul's theological convictions are here given sharp, antithetical formulation, especially in 2:16, where he asserts with great emphasis that "someone is justified" (*dikaioutai*) not "on the basis of works of the law" (*ex ergōn nomou*),[200] but only "on the basis of the faith of Christ" (*ek pisteōs Christou*).[201] This fundamental theological principle, formulated on the run, informs the theology of the remainder of the letter, even though the specific language of justification is largely left behind by the end of chapter 3, recurring only in 5:4–5. An interpretive crux here is the phrase *pistis (Iēsou) Christou*, literally, "(the) faith of (Jesus) Christ" (vv. 16a, c), which can be understood to refer to "(a human being's) faith in Christ" (an objective genitive) or to "Christ's own faith(fulness)" (a subjective genitive).[202] A decision on this point is of major importance for understanding Paul's theology in this letter (and probably in the others as well) and thus also for the particular message he wants to give to his Galatian readers. The verb "to justify" (*dikaioō*) and the expression "works

---

200. Literally, "from works of law." The absence of the article with the word *nomos* in prepositional phrases is common in Paul and appears to be primarily a matter of style (cf. BDF #258.2; Moule 113).

201. Literally, "from faith of Christ." Here too the absence of the definite article with the word *pistis* is a matter of style. See previous note.

202. It can also be understood as a genitive of authorship (the faith that comes from Christ, is created by him) or as a genitive of quality (Christ-faith). See Excursus 9, below.

of the law" (what are these works, and what is the problem with them?) also require careful exegetical attention.

The passage can be divided into three discrete sense units: (1) vv. 15–16, (2) vv. 17–18, and (3) vv. 19–21. The first contains a thesis, that a person is not justified as a result of works of the law but only as a result of "the faith of Christ." The third unit picks up the argument begun in the first (the word "law" provides the link). The second is a digression in which Paul responds to charges directed to him personally. He continues with the first-person mode of discourse in the third section because he recognizes that he (still) stands theologically alone among Christians who are also Jews "by birth." His own views are not (yet) shared by the new preachers in Galatia, who, like the emissaries from James, represent the views of the circumcision party in Jerusalem (see above on 2:12–13). Paul presents himself here as a paradigm for how Christ's death by crucifixion puts an end to the world determined by (works of) the law. The passage concludes with an argument for the absolute incompatibility of the law and the death of Christ in the matter of "justification" (*dikaiosynē*). On that argument, which is Paul's elaboration of the thesis found in 2:16, hangs Paul's entire theology in this letter.

> **2:15** We Jews by birth and not sinners from the Gentiles, **16** because[a] we know that someone is not justified on the basis of works of the law but through the faith of Jesus Christ,[b] we too came to believe in Jesus Christ,[b] so that we might be justified on the basis of the faith of Christ and not on the basis of works of the law, because on the basis of works of the law shall all flesh not be justified.
>
> **17** (But if by seeking to be justified in Christ, we ourselves were found also to be sinners, is Christ then[c] a servant of Sin? Of course not! **18** For if I am building up again these things that I tore down, I am establishing myself a transgressor.)
>
> **19** For I through the law died to the law, that I might live to God.[d] I have been crucified with Christ. **20** I no longer live, but Christ lives in me. The life I now live in the flesh, I live in faith, that of the Son of God,[e] the one who loved me and gave himself up for me. **21** I do not nullify the grace of God, for if justification is through the law, Christ died for nothing.

a. There are other ways to punctuate the Greek. Verse 15 may be regarded as an independent sentence ("We ourselves [are] Jews by birth and not Gentile sinners. Because we know . . ."). In support of this division is the conjunction *de* (left untranslated) at the beginning of v. 16 in some important manuscripts (ℵ, B, C, D*, among others), though there are also very good manuscripts that omit this word (including $\mathfrak{P}^{46}$, A, Ψ, 33, 1739, 1881), for which reason the word has been placed between brackets by NA^{27}. The given translation assumes that the conjunction is not original and that vv. 15–16 form one sentence.

The Origin and the Truth of the Gospel 141

b. Manuscripts are divided on the order. Some read "Christ Jesus," other "Jesus Christ." There is little discernible difference in meaning or implication, since in what follows, Paul abbreviates to "Christ."

c. The Greek term here is *ara*. With a circumflex accent it functions as an interrogative particle; with an acute accent it is simply an inferential particle. The manuscripts differ in the accenting, or lack an accent altogether ($\mathfrak{P}^{46}$, ℵ, A, B*, C, D). The sentence can thus be construed either as a question or as a statement. If the sentence is construed as a statement, the meaning would change considerably: "If seeking to be justified in Christ, we ourselves were found also to be sinners, then Christ is a servant of Sin." Paul's follow-up exclamation "Of course not" (*mē genoito*, lit., "May it not be so") really makes sense only if the preceding sentence is a question, as is regularly the case when Paul uses the exclamation "Of course not!" elsewhere (cf. 3:21; 1 Cor 6:15; 10 instances in Romans).

d. In the KJV, NIV, and RSV, the numbering is slightly different: v. 19 ends here instead of after the next short sentence ("I have been crucified with Christ").

e. Strong witnesses ($\mathfrak{P}^{46}$, B, D*) read "of God and Christ," but there are also good witnesses for the most commonly adopted reading (ℵ, A, C, Ψ, 33, 1739, and others). It is easier to explain a change from "Son of God" to "God and Christ" than the reverse; for this reason, "Son of God" is probably the original reading (Metzger 524).

[15–16] These two verses consist of one long sentence that is crucial to the interpretation of the whole letter. The sentence contains three subordinate clauses (vv. 16a, c, d), all of which contain a reference to, and a firm rejection of, justification on the basis of works of the law. The main sentence, which has a positive thrust, is to be found in vv. 15 and 16b, italicized below:

¹⁵*We Jews by birth*²⁰³ *and not sinners from the Gentiles,*
¹⁶ᵃbecause we know that someone is not justified
on the basis of works of the law
but through the faith of Jesus Christ,
¹⁶ᵇ*we too came to believe in Jesus Christ,*
¹⁶ᶜso that we might be justified
on the basis of the faith of Christ
and not on the basis of works of the law,
¹⁶ᵈbecause on the basis of works of the law shall all flesh not be justified.

Paul has to repeat the "we" (*hēmeis*) in v. 16b because of the long intervening subordinate clause (v. 16a). The main sentence, a *captatio benevolentiae* (an expression of goodwill or friendship, in this case toward fellow Jewish believers in Christ), represents the starting point in Paul's theological rebuttal of the new preachers and their attempt to impose circumcision and other works of the law on Paul's Galatian converts. Paul may have said something similar to

---

203. Literally, "by nature," *physei*.

Cephas in Antioch, but now he directs these words primarily to the new preachers in Galatia. Paul thus begins by pointing out what he and the new preachers have in common: He and the new preachers (all of them "Jews by birth" like Cephas) also (*kai*)—meaning just like the Gentiles in Galatia (or Antioch)—"came to believe [*episteusamen*][204] in Jesus Christ." In the main sentence, Paul is completely silent on the matter of the law and its observance; the only relevant point is that he and Jews "came to believe in Jesus Christ."

Paul uses the verb *pisteuō* ("believe") with the meaning "believe" only three times in the letter (2:16; 3:6, 22);[205] only here does he use the construction with the preposition *eis*, "believe in" (cf. Rom 10:14a; Phil 1:29). In 3:6, a quotation from Gen 15:6, the construction is *pisteuein* plus the dative, which normally means "believe something to be true, give credence to," whereas in 3:22 the verb is used absolutely, with no object, "those who believe," though "in [*eis*] Christ" is probably to be mentally supplied (see comments on these two verses). The nuance of the construction "believe in" is trust or reliance upon (BDAG 817). One could thus translate: "We too have placed our trust in, come to rely upon, Jesus Christ."

As part of his *captatio benevolentiae*, Paul contrasts "we Jews by birth" and "sinners from the Gentiles" at the beginning of the sentence (v. 15). He could simply have said: "We Jews by birth, . . . we too have come to believe in Jesus Christ." In Antioch, however, Cephas, Barnabas, and the other Jewish believers who had fallen under the influence of the emissaries from James and the circumcision party in Jerusalem had been telling Gentile believers that Gentiles, being without the law, are by definition sinners according to that standard. In Galatia, the new preachers, spiritual relatives of the circumcision party in Jerusalem, are now telling the Gentile Galatians (cf. 4:8–9) the same thing: Gentiles who had come to believe in Christ without also becoming law-observant Jews nevertheless remain (Gentile) sinners. Paul momentarily adopts this perspective of the new preachers in order to point out to them that "we Jews by birth," and thus *not* Gentile "sinners," *still* came to believe in Christ, whereby "we" implicitly conceded that "works of the law" were inadequate for "justification," a point driven home in the latter part of v. 16. In v. 21, Paul will point out that if justification were indeed possible through the law, Christ would have died for no evident reason (see comment below).

The three subordinate clauses in v. 16 make Paul's agenda with respect to "works of the law" explicit. They are closely related to one another in terms of wording and content. Whereas the main sentence has a positive thrust ("We too came to believe in Jesus Christ"), the subordinate clauses all contain

---

204. An ingressive, or inceptive, aorist.
205. He also uses this verb in 2:7 with the meaning "to entrust [someone with something]"; see comment there.

The Origin and the Truth of the Gospel

a single, sharp negation: *Works of the law are irrelevant for justification.* That the emphasis falls on this negation is further indicated by the structure of these clauses in relation to one another. The first clause begins with the negation of works of the law as the source of justification, and the third clause ends emphatically with that negation. The second clause has been structured to provide a transition to the last clause. It is also the case, however, that over against the threefold rejection of justification on the basis of works of the law, Paul twice places justification through (*dia*) or on the basis of (*ek*) "the faith of (Jesus) Christ."

In the first subordinate clause, Paul gives the reason why "we Jews by birth" came to believe in Jesus Christ (v. 16b): "because we know that someone [*anthrōpos*] is *not* justified on the basis of [*ek*]²⁰⁶ works of the law but [*ean mē*] through [*dia*] the faith of Jesus Christ" (v. 16a). He appeals here to knowledge shared by believers who, like himself and Peter, are Jews by birth ("because we know that . . ."). Is Paul, then, making use of already-existing views and formulations in this clause? Is everything after the phrase "because we know that" (lit., "knowing that," *eidotes hoti*) in v. 16a a quotation from a formula? There are no certain answers to these questions (see Dunn 1990: 188–96; Martyn 263–75). Nevertheless, it seems that Paul is citing (from) known material in v. 16a and—this is the crucial point—that three key terms in v. 16 have not been coined by Paul himself nor introduced by him into the Galatian setting: "works of the law" (*erga nomou*), "the faith of Jesus Christ" (*pistis Iēsou Christou*), and "to be justified" (*dikaiousthai*). Some important building blocks of his theology in this letter (and subsequently in Romans) have evidently been given to him by those opposing his work in Galatia.

At least five considerations speak in favor of regarding v. 16a as a quotation whose content was known to, and perhaps even given its specific formulation by, the new preachers in Galatia: (1) As already indicated, the introductory words "because we know that" (*eidotes hoti*) suggest that what follows may be a quotation, in whole or in part. (2) The preposition "through" (*dia*) in the phrase "through the faith of Jesus Christ" is remarkable, given the fact that in v. 16c, where Paul clearly and unmistakably stakes out his own position, he uses the preposition *ek* ("from, on the basis of") instead of *dia*: "from [*ek*] the faith of Christ" in antithetical contrast to "from [*ek*] works of the law."²⁰⁷ (3) Paul does not pause to explain or to define the meaning of the verb *dikaioō*, "justify." That the verb was being used in the proclamation of the new preachers and thus known to the Galatians is indicated by its occurrence in 5:4, where Paul

---

206. Without substantially altering the meaning, one can also translate the preposition "as a result of" or "by means of."

207. The preposition *dia* itself is not un-Pauline (cf. 3:14, 26; Phil 3:9), but in combination with the other considerations, its presence here indicates that it may be part of the quoted formula.

warns the Galatians: "you who are seeking to be justified [*dikaiousthe*][208] in the law" (5:4a), as the new preachers want (cf. 5:8–12), have been "separated from Christ" and "have fallen from grace" (5:4b). It occurs further only in v. 17 and in 3:8, 11, and 24, where Paul seeks to undermine the theology of the new preachers. (4) Without introduction or elaboration, Paul employs two crucial expressions in v. 16a: "works of the law" (*erga nomou*) and "the faith of Jesus Christ" (*pistis Iēsou Christou*). At issue in v. 16 are not the basic referential meanings of these terms (the realities to which they refer)[209] but rather the substantive *relationship* between them in connection with the matter of "justification."

Finally (5), the conjunction *ean mē*, translated as "but" above, literally and normally means "if not" and thus "except" or "unless" (BDAG 267; Burton 121; Dunn 1990: 195–96, 208). It has only this latter meaning elsewhere in Paul (Rom 10:15; 11:23; 1 Cor 8:8; 9:16; 13:1; 14:6–7, 9, 11, 28; 15:36; cf. Das 530–31). With this meaning the conjunction could be taken to imply that someone is not justified as a result of works of the law *unless* by way of "the faith of Jesus Christ." In other words, "the faith of Jesus Christ" is compatible with, or complements, works of the law in the matter of justification. Given v. 16c, where works of the law and the faith of Christ are regarded as mutually exclusive in the matter of justification, *ean mē* must mean "but" for Paul himself, despite the pattern of his usage elsewhere (so most interpreters).[210] But Paul's interpretation of v. 16a in v. 16c also indicates that if he had been composing freely, he would have avoided the ambiguous *ean mē* in favor of the unambiguous adversative *alla* ("but"), of which there are twenty-three instances in Galatians alone (1:1, 8, 12, 17; 2:3, 7, 14; 3:12, 16, 22; 4:2, 7, 8, 14, 17, 23, 29, 30, 31; 5:6, 13; 6:13, 15). In v. 16a, then, Paul is apparently appealing to a formula stemming from Christian Jews in which "works of the law" and "the faith of Jesus Christ" were regarded as compatible and complementary. Christian Jews, including the new preachers in Galatia, would have understood the ambiguous *ean mē* as exceptive (Das 537–39). Under

---

208. Paul here uses a conative present tense, indicating an attempt. He does not mean that the Galatians "are being justified in the law," but that they are trying to be (BDF #319).

209. The referential meanings of terms are to be kept distinct from the theological ones: what are the deeper theological implications of the realities to which the terms refer? The former are matters of description; the latter, which have to do with the "sense" or the "significance" of concepts, are matters of theological evaluation and insight. Two parties can agree on the former, yet disagree sharply about the latter.

210. See Räisänen 547. For other interpretations of *ean mē* as exceptive also for Paul, yet consistent with the meaning "but," see Lightfoot 115; Burton 121; Fung 115; Longenecker 83–84; Walker 1997. This solution interprets the exceptive clause in one of two complementary ways: (1) as limiting only the principal clause ("Someone is not justified . . . except through the faith of Jesus Christ") or (2) as being elliptical ("Someone is not justified as a result of works of the law; [someone is not justified] except through the faith of Jesus Christ").

The Origin and the Truth of the Gospel 145

the tutelage of the new preachers in Galatia, the churches there will also so understand it. Paul is out to correct this reading of the shared formula in the latter half of v. 16.

In sum, it appears that everything in v. 16a after the introductory phrase "because we know that" is a direct citation of a formula.[211] Paul and his dialogue partners in this passage, the new preachers in Galatia (like other Jewish believers), thus agree on the referential meanings of the two key expressions in v. 16a: "works of the law" (*erga nomou*) and "the faith of Jesus Christ," which Paul abbreviates in v. 16c to "the faith of Christ" (*pistis Christou*). Each expression has been the focus of sharp scholarly debate, and for this reason a separate excursus is devoted to each expression below. As explained in Excursus 8, the "works of the law," for both Paul and the new preachers in Galatia, refer simply to the actions or deeds demanded by the Mosaic law without distinction (between, e.g., cultic and moral laws) and without regard to the manner in which these deeds are performed ("legalism"); the phrase can be rendered "the observance (the doing) of the law."

Excursus 8: Works of the Law

This expression occurs for the first time in Galatians in 2:16, where Paul uses it three times. It also occurs in 3:2, 5, 10 (as in Rom 3:20, 28). In v. 16a, Paul gives, as we have seen above, the distinct impression that he is citing a Jewish Christian formula and that the expression "works of the law" was an integral part of that formula. He appears to assume that the meaning of the expression is evident to other Christians who were Jewish by birth as well as to the Gentile Christians in Galatia, who have undoubtedly been instructed in this matter by the new preachers who have come there (1:6–9; Excursus 4).

The expression is curiously absent from the remainder of the NT as well as from the LXX. The Hebrew OT also contains no precise equivalent. The only exact parallel is to be found in a document from the Dead Sea Scrolls known as 4QMMT, which is part of a letter. In one fragment of this document (4Q398 frg. 14–17 2.2–4), the author writes: "We have written to you some of *the works of the law* [*ma'ăśê ha-Torah*] that we think are good for you and for your people, for we saw that you have intellect and knowledge of the law" (alt.). Here the expression seems to mean "the precepts [or commandments]

---

211. Martyn brings some weighty arguments against this conclusion (264 n. 158): In comparable justification formulas used by Paul (in Rom 3:25; 4:24; 1 Cor 6:11), there is, according to Martyn, "no hint of a polemical antinomy that would place opposite one another Christ's faithful deed in our behalf and our observance of the Law" (268). Martyn thus attributes all the negatives in 2:16 to Paul's hand (with the third borrowed from Ps 142:2 LXX [143:2 MT]). In his view (270), Paul has also coined the expression "the faith of Jesus Christ." Since Paul does not, however, pause to explain the three key terms he uses, it seems plausible to conclude that they are also part of the formula on which he here relies. Furthermore, in the interpretation of the new preachers in Galatia, or in that of other Christians of Jewish birth, v. 16a does not contain the antinomy that Paul perceives in it.

of the law." Bachmann (33–56) has argued that the expression *erga nomou* also refers to this in Paul's Letters: The "works of the law" are the commandments of the (Mosaic) law preserved in the Pentateuch (cf. 3:10–21), irrespective of whether these commandments are actually done.

There are other texts among the Dead Sea Scrolls, however, where the term *ma'ăśîm* ("works") must refer to the actual observance or doing of the precepts of the law: "And when someone enters the covenant to behave in compliance with all these decrees, enrolling in the assembly of holiness, they shall examine their spirits in the community, one another, in respect of his insight and *his deeds in the law* [*ma'ăśêw ba-Torah*]" (1QS 5.20–21; alt.; the same formulation occurs in 1QS 6.18).

In the following lines, the expression "his deeds in the law" becomes simply "his deeds" or "their deeds" (1QS 5.23–24; cf. 1QS 4.25; 6.17). Further, the section of 4QMMT quoted above (4Q398 2.7) ends with the statement: "And it shall be reckoned to you as justification when you *do* [*'āsâ*] what is upright and good before him, for your good and that of Israel" (alt.). The verb *'āsâ*, "do," is from the same root as the noun *ma'ăśîm*. The *ma'ăśê ha-Torah*, then, clearly are precepts to be done, so that the expression can also be taken to mean "the works/deeds required by the law."

In the Hebrew OT, furthermore, the term *ma'ăśeh* (pl., *ma'ăśîm*) means "deed(s)" or "work(s)" (BDB 795; cf., e.g., Gen 20:9; 44:15; Exod 23:12). In Exod 18:20, Moses must teach the people "the statutes and instructions and make known to them the way they are to go and *the work that they shall work*" (alt.). The last phrase means the same as "the deed that they shall do." Here we find the noun *ma'ăśeh* with the verb *'āsâ* ("do") in a context pertaining to law observance, as in 4QMMT and 1QS above. The LXX changes the singular to a plural, using *erga*: "You [Moses] shall testify to them the ordinances of God and his law, and you shall show them the ways in which they shall walk in them and the works [*erga*] that they shall do [*poiēsousin*]."

In Gal 3:10–12, where the topic is those who live by "works of the law" (*erga nomou*, 3:10), Paul twice quotes passages from the LXX in which the verb "do" (*poieō*) occurs, as it does in Exod 18:20 above: The point of all the things written in the book of the law is "to *do* them" (Deut 27:26), for "the one who *does* them shall live in them" (Lev 18:5).[212] In Rom 3:20, 28, Paul refers to "works of the law"; in Rom 3:27; 4:2, 6 he simply refers to "works" (*erga*), without the qualification "of the law," similar to 1QS above. The context and the subject matter, which is justification on the basis of "works," indicate that "works" here are primarily, though perhaps not exclusively, "works of the law," especially circumcision (Rom 4:10–12). Further, given what Paul writes in Rom 4:4, the "works" referred to must be "deeds" performed by human beings: "Now to one who works [*ergazomai*], wages are not reckoned as a gift but as something due." For Paul, then, as for the formula he cites in v. 16a, "the works of the law" are the actions performed or carried out in obedience to the many commandments of the Mosaic law as preserved in the Pentateuch. The phrase "works of the law" thus refers to the actual "observance (doing) of the law."

In the interpretation of Paul, two questions have commonly been posed in connection with his rejection of "works of the law" as the source of justification: (1) Is Paul's

---

212. The corresponding Hebrew passages use the verb *'āsâ*.

The Origin and the Truth of the Gospel   *147*

rejection of "works of the law" actually a rejection of "legalism"? (2) Do "works of the law" refer to all the commandments that are to be done or only some selection of them? These questions can now also be posed to the formula Paul takes over in 2:16.

1. *Legalism rejected?* The claim that Paul does not reject the law as such but only "legalism" arises in part from the positive things he says about the law in Romans (cf. 7:12: "The law is holy, and the commandment is holy and just and good"). "Legalism" can be understood in at least three different ways, though it always implies a wrong attitude toward the law and thus a sinful misuse of it (cf. Westerholm 1988: 105-35): (a) The law is observed in order to achieve or to earn salvation ("works-righteousness"); the works done can then be construed as an attempt to "bribe" God. (b) The law is observed in such a way as to lead to self-righteousness or boasting in one's achievements and good works, either before God or before others. (c) The law is observed in a purely formal, external way, according to the letter and not according to its spirit. There is not a shred of evidence that legalism in any of these forms is at issue in Galatians.[213] For both Paul and the cited formula, works of the law refer simply to the observance of the law, whether that observance be "legalistic" or not.

2. *Select laws rejected?* The view that Paul has only a particular selection of works of the law in view arises in part from his seeming embrace of a portion of the law later in Galatians (the commandment to love one's neighbor as oneself from Lev 19:18 in Gal 5:14; 6:2)[214] and again in Romans (13:9). There are two primary variations on this approach: (a) Paul rejects the cultic, ceremonial sections of the law (e.g., circumcision, food laws), but not the moral law (cf. Rom 13:8-10, where some of the Ten Commandments in addition to the love commandment are quoted with approval). (b) Paul rejects the portions of the law that set Jews apart from Gentiles, such as circumcision, food laws, and special feast days, especially the Sabbath (Dunn 1990: 191, 196; also Hays 239). "Works of the law" are these "badges" of Jewish identity (Dunn 1990: 194), "Paul's way of describing in particular the identity and boundary markers" in which "the typical Jew placed his confidence," whereby he "documented his membership of the covenant" and distinguished himself and his people from the Gentiles (Dunn 1990: 220, 221, 224). In favor of this interpretation is the contrast between "we Jews by birth" and "sinners from the Gentiles" in 2:15 and the fact that Paul in Galatians specifically mentions circumcision (2:3, 7-9, 12; 5:2-3, 6, 11; 6:12-13, 15), alludes to food laws (2:11-14), and names feast days (4:10).[215] That "works of the law" cannot be limited to these three, however, becomes clear when Paul in 5:3 warns the Galatians that everyone who practices circumcision is "obligated to do the whole law" (see comment there). As

---

213. Whether this conclusion also counts for Romans must be left aside here.

214. See Excursus 17, however, for another interpretation of Paul's citation of Lev 19:18 in Gal 5:14.

215. In Dunn's view, such covenantal identity markers also led to a wrong "attitude to the law as such.... The law as fixing a particular social identity, as encouraging a sense of national superiority and presumption of divine favour by virtue of membership of a particular people—that is what Paul is attacking" (1990: 224). But such an attitude is one thing; the definition of "works of the law" as badges of identity is another. Dunn would presumably stick by his limited definition of "works of the law" apart from the presence or absence of the attitude of covenantal, nationalistic pride, which is a form of "legalism" (see previous point). Cf. Dunn 1998: 354-59.

Westerholm (1988: 118) writes, Paul places "the particular issue [of circumcision] in the broader context of a discussion of the origin, nature, and function of the Mosaic law as a whole." The warning found in 5:3 explains why Paul can use the term "law" as a synonym for "works of the law" in 2:21, as in 3:11 and 5:4, where justification "in the law" is rejected, just as justification "on the basis of works of the law" is rejected in 2:16 (cf. the juxtaposition of "works of the law" and "law" in Rom 3:20). In 4:5 Paul claims that those to whom Christ was sent to redeem were "under the law," not then under some portion of it.[216] These considerations also apply to the view that Paul draws a distinction between the ritual law and the moral law. The "works of the law" apply to any and all deeds required by the law.

Summary. For Paul, as for the formula he cites, "works of the law"(*erga nomou*) are the actions or deeds demanded by the law without distinction and without regard to the manner in which these deeds are performed.

In turn, the expression *pistis Iēsou Christou* in v. 16a, for both Paul and his dialogue partners in Galatia, refers not to "[our] faith in Jesus Christ," but to "Jesus Christ's [own] faith" or "faithfulness," as manifested in his atoning death. This interpretation of the phrase is justified in the following excursus.

Excursus 9: The Faith of Jesus Christ

The expression "the faith of Jesus Christ" (*pistis Iēsou Christou*) in v. 16a seems to have been part of a formula Paul cites (see above). The same or similar expressions occur in v. 16c ("the faith of Christ"), v. 20 ("the faith of the Son of God"); 3:22 ("the faith of Jesus Christ"); Rom 3:22 ("the faith of Jesus Christ"), 26 ("the faith of Jesus"); and Phil 3:9 ("the faith of Christ"). Does Paul mean "[a human being's] faith in Jesus Christ" (objective genitive) or "Jesus Christ's [own] faith[fulness]" (subjective genitive)? A mediating position would be to render "faith effected by Christ" (genitive of authorship) or "Christ-faith" (genitive of quality), though these two options are like the first in that the faith of believers is primarily in view. This issue of interpretation continues to be a matter of sharp debate.[217]

Faith of believers? Among the arguments in favor of the first interpretation (faith in Jesus Christ), which is common and traditional (NRSV, RSV, NIV, NJB, NAB), are the

---

216. In his commentary on Galatians, Dunn appears to take a more nuanced view of the issue: "'Works of the law' would mean in principle all that the faithful Israelite had to do as a member of the chosen people, that is, as distinct from 'Gentile sinners.' But in practice there were a number of test cases, several specific laws, . . . boundary markers where the distinctiveness of Jew from Gentile was most at stake" (136); see also Dunn 1997; 1998: 358.

217. For an overview of the debate, with extensive bibliographies, see the essays of Hays 2002a; Dunn 2002; Rusam 2002; Matlock. Hays argues for the subjective genitive (as do, e.g., Martyn; Matera; Longenecker), Dunn for the objective (so also, e.g., Burton; Betz; Matlock), and Rusam for a genitive of authorship. Williams (70) argues it is both Christ's faith and the "answering faith" of human beings, what he also calls "Christ-faith" (1987: 446), i.e., a Christian's faith is like that of Christ. Aside from being the creator of the believer's faith, Christ also, according to Williams, functions as its "exemplar."

The Origin and the Truth of the Gospel

following: (1) The expression *pistis Iēsou Christou* is parallel to the phrase "we came to believe [have faith] in [*episteusamen eis*] Christ Jesus" in v. 16b; it must then mean "faith in Jesus Christ." (2) A similar parallelism occurs in 3:6–7, where Paul glosses the citation of Gen 15:6, Abraham "believed [*episteusen*] God, and it was reckoned to him as justification," with the words, "Know therefore that those who are from faith [*hoi ek pisteōs*], these people are the sons of Abraham." The parallelism indicates that "faith" here means "believing," so that "those from faith" are "those who believe [in Christ]." (3) If "works of the law" refers to a human activity, *pistis Iēsou Christou* does as well; faith is the human response to God's act of grace. (4) Christ never appears in Paul as the subject of the cognate verb "to believe, trust, have faith in," *pisteuein*, as one might expect if Christ's own faith(fulness) were meant.

Faith of Christ? In favor of the second interpretation (Jesus Christ's own faith or faithfulness) are the following arguments:

1. In 3:22, Paul refers once again to "the faith of Jesus Christ," as he does in 2:16a; in the verses that immediately follow (3:23–25), Paul speaks of "Faith" (*pistis*) in a personified way, as a virtual synonym for Christ (3:24): Faith "came" onto the world stage at a certain juncture in time (3:23, 25), as Christ himself did (3:19). As a result "we are no longer under a custodian" (3:25), meaning not "under the law" (3:23), which was "our custodian until [*eis*] Christ" (3:24), that is, "until [*eis*] Faith should be revealed" (3:23). Faith is not here an intrinsic human possibility nor even a human activity. In these verses, as perhaps already in 1:23 (see comment there), "Faith" functions as a metonym for Christ (see comment on 3:23–25, and the end of Excursus 6). "Faith" here is thus something that belongs to or defines Christ himself.

2. Galatians 3:22 shows that the phrase *pistis Iēsou Christou* is probably to be construed as a subjective genitive: "that the promise [of the Spirit] be given on the basis of the faith of Jesus Christ [*pistis Iēsou Christou*] to those who have faith [in him] [*hoi pisteuontes {eis auton}*]." To translate the phrase here as an objective genitive would produce a meaningless tautology: "that the promise [of the Spirit] be given on the basis of [their] faith in Jesus Christ to those who have faith [in him]."

3. If Paul had wanted to say "faith in [Jesus] Christ," he would have used an expression such as *pistis eis Christon* (found in Col 2:5), corresponding to the verbal construction *pisteuein eis*, "believe in," in Gal 2:16b.[218]

4. The formulation *pistis Iēsou Christou* has an exact parallel in *pistis Abraam* in Rom 4:16; the latter undoubtedly means "the faith of Abraham," not "faith in Abraham" (also 4:12, "the faith of our father Abraham").[219]

---

218. Put otherwise, the case for construing *pistis Iēsou Christou* as an objective genitive ("faith in Jesus Christ") would carry more weight if the corresponding verb, *pisteuō*, had the meaning "have faith *in*, believe *in*, rely *upon*" in its transitive usage (i.e., when taking an accusative direct object). In its transitive usage, however, the verb (with a double accusative) means "to entrust (someone with something)," as in Gal 2:7. The connotations "to believe *in*, have faith *in*, rely *upon*" can only apply to the construction *pisteuō eis*, used in Gal 2:16b (or to the construction *pisteuō* with the dative, as in Gal 3:6), i.e., when the verb is intransitive. See P. Meyer 115 n. 82; cf. BDF #163.

219. Cf. Rom 3:3: "the *pistis* of God," where the genitive is also subjective. There are no parallels to the objective genitive interpretation of *pistis Christou* in Paul's own letters, and there is

5. In Gal 1:1, Paul posits an antinomy between human activity and God's action in Christ ("Paul, an apostle not from human beings nor through a human being, but through Jesus Christ and God the Father"), as he does in 1:11–12 (his gospel is "not of human origin" but came "through an apocalyptic revelation of Jesus Christ"); he probably does the same here, setting over against each other (a) a human activity, the observance of the law; and (b) God's own gracious, justifying act, "the faith of Jesus Christ" (cf. 2:21: "the grace of God").

6. In Rom 1:5, Paul describes faith as obedience, in the phrase "the obedience of faith" (= the obedience that is faith); in Rom 5:19, he refers to "the obedience" of Christ, which can then also be described as his *pistis*, as perhaps in Rom 1:17 ("from [Christ's] faith to [our] faith"; cf. Jesus as "faithful," *pistos*, in his death in Heb 2:17; 3:2; Rev 1:5; 3:14; 19:11).

7. The parallel with Gal 2:21 indicates that *pistis Iēsou Christou* must refer to Christ's death (his "obedience" in Rom 5:19):

Gal 2:16a	**Gal 2:21**
justification	justification
from works of the law	through the law
versus	*versus*
justification from	justification from
pistis Iēsou Christou	Christ died

The arguments for the second interpretation seem stronger than the arguments for the first; hence, the second interpretation is to be preferred both here and in Gal 3:22. In the formula from which Paul cites, and for Paul himself, *pistis Iēsou Christou* refers in the first instance to Christ's faithfulness to God, and thus also his trust in or reliance upon God, as this faithfulness came to concrete, visible expression in his death.[220] Christ's *pistis* does not, then, refer so much to a subjective attitude on the part of Christ as to an objective event: his atoning death on a cross. In 1:4, Paul has cited and modified a formula concerning this atoning death, the formula preserved in 1 Cor 15:3: "Christ died for our sins" (cf. Rom 3:21–26; 4:25). This formula was probably also known to the Galatians and to the new preachers who have taken up residence among them (see comment on 1:4). Paul adapts this formula again in 2:20, referring there to "the faith of the Son of God," who is defined specifically as "the one who loved me and gave himself up for me" (see comment below).

Summary. It seems highly probable that for Paul and for other believers who are Jews by birth, "*pistis* (*Iēsou*) *Christou* is a summary description of Christ's faithful death" (Hays 2002a: 287). It is "Christ's faithfulness as embodied in his death on the cross" (Hays 240). Such is the referential meaning of the phrase for both Paul and the new preachers in Galatia. (See further Excursus 11 on the meaning of *pistis* in the remainder of Galatians.)

---

only one relatively clear instance of an objective genitive after *pistis* in the whole NT (Mark 11:22: "Have faith in God," *echete pistin theou*).

220. For the implications for the interpretation of similar constructions in 3:7 and 3:22, see comments on those verses.

The Origin and the Truth of the Gospel

The particular point at issue between Paul and the new preachers in v. 16 is the meaning of "justification"[221] in the quoted formula found in v. 16a, which can now be paraphrased as follows: We know that "someone is not justified on the basis of the observance of the law except through [by means of] the faithful death of Jesus Christ."

The present tense of the verb "is justified" (*dikaioutai*) in the cited formula of v. 16a is timeless and thus indicates that a basic principle is involved. The passive voice is probably to be construed as a circumlocution for God's activity (a divine passive): It is God who "justifies" (cf. 3:8, "God justifies"). For this reason, it is misleading to speak of "justification *by* works (of the law)" or even of "justification *by* faith." In both cases, the question at issue is justification *by God* (P. Meyer 115 n. 82). For the same reason, it is also misleading to regard justification as a matter of being able to identify who belongs to the people of God, "how you tell who belongs to the community" or "to the covenant family" (Wright 1997: 119, 122; cf. Wright 2005: 112). This interpretation obscures the fact that for Paul, as indeed for the new preachers in Galatia, justification is a divine activity, not a human one. As a divine act, justification, whether it occurs in the present or the future, is *always* "a matter of promise and expectation" (Käsemann 1969a: 170). On these matters, Paul and the new preachers are in complete agreement.

But they do disagree on an important point: the reference of the word "someone" (*anthrōpos*). The new preachers in Galatia, to whom Paul specifically directs this passage, understand the word in this formula as follows: We know that "someone, meaning a Jew or an Israelite, is not justified on the basis of the observance of the law except through [by means of] the faithful death of Jesus Christ."

The shared formula as understood by the new preachers was probably originally used in missionary activity by Christian Jews (led by Cephas) among their fellow Jews. The framework is and remains "covenantal nomism" (Sanders 1977: 75, 180, 236): God's gracious covenant with the people of Israel, entailing observance of the law as the people's response and responsibility within that covenant relationship. Christian Jews were convinced, however, that the observance of the law does not bring justification apart from the faithful, atoning death of Jesus Christ for the sins of the nation (cf. 1:4 and comment there). That was the burden of their message to their fellow Jews. The formula would apply to Gentiles only to the extent that they also became part of Israel, which is what the new preachers in Galatia have been telling the Gentile Christians there (5:2–4; 6:12–13). Hence, for the new preachers, the word "someone" in the formula must refer to a Jew or an Israelite.

---

221. For instructive yet diverse discussions of justification, see Bultmann 1951: 270–85; Westerholm 1988: 141–50; Sanders 1991: 44–76; Hays 1992; Wright 1997: 95–133; Dunn 1998: 334–89; Westerholm 2004: 352–407.

As the remainder of v. 16 indicates, Paul reads the formula in v. 16a in the following way: We know that "someone, meaning *a Gentile as well as a Jew*, is not justified on the basis of the observance of the law, but [someone is justified only] through [by means of] the faithful death of Jesus Christ."[222]

Paul here takes over the key terms of the formula, retaining their referential meanings with the exception of "someone" (*anthrōpos*): Justification is not just for Jewish believers but also for Gentile believers (cf. Rom 3:28). In Paul's interpretation, moreover, the observance of the law and the faithful death of Jesus Christ are *mutually exclusive* rather than complementary when it comes to justification. That Paul reads the formula in this way becomes polemically clear in v. 16c: "[We Jews by birth too came to believe in Christ Jesus, just like the Gentiles] so that [*hina*] we [too] might be justified on the basis of the faith of Christ and *not* on the basis of works of the law."

The point is driven home by v. 16d: "because [*hoti*] on the basis of works of the law, all flesh shall *not* be justified [*ou dikaiōthēsetai*]," and that means that *no one* shall be so justified (BDF #302.1). The language is largely borrowed from Ps 143:2 (142:2 LXX, "because everyone living shall not be justified before you," meaning that no living being shall be justified before God). Paul weaves into the words of the psalm the phrase "on the basis of works of the law," as he also does in Rom 3:20 ("therefore, on the basis of works of the law all flesh shall not be justified before him" [AT]). In both places, he (or his LXX text?) also substitutes the words "all flesh" (a Hebraism) for "everyone living" (cf., e.g., LXX: Pss 64:3 [65:2E]; 135:25 [136:25E]; 144:21 [145:21E]), probably to emphasize the collective vulnerability and weakness of human beings and to distinguish them from God (see comment on v. 20).[223] Paul does not indicate in any way that he is relying upon or quoting from the (OT) Scripture, as he does later in Gal 3–4. The words from Scripture are simply incorporated into what amounts to a declaration.[224]

The cited formula assumes that *before and apart from Christ*, "someone [a Jew or an Israelite] is justified [*dikaioutai*]" by God purely "on the basis of

---

222. If the conjunction *ean mē* is still to be regarded as exceptive (see n. 210 above), then Paul understands it to modify the verb *dikaioutai*, not the whole of the preceding clause, as do the new preachers: "Someone is not justified . . . except through the faith of Jesus Christ." The same result is achieved if the exceptive clause is regarded as an ellipsis: "Someone is not justified on the basis of law observance, [someone is not justified] except through the faith of Jesus Christ."

223. There may also be an allusion to circumcision, which Paul explicitly characterizes as a fleshly act in 6:12–13 (cf. already 3:3).

224. Paul perhaps does not let on that he is quoting because he knows that the new preachers (1) could point out that the words "on the basis of works of the law" do not occur in Ps 142:2 LXX (143:2E), and (2) could interpret the passage to mean that "No one shall be justified before God *apart from* works of the law"! At issue for Paul, however, is not the right interpretation of a particular scriptural text but "the truth of the gospel." He borrows scriptural language to declare that truth. See de Boer 2010.

observing the law." The imagery behind the verb is that of a lawcourt in which God functions as a judge, as in Ps 142:2 LXX (143:2E), whose language Paul borrows in v. 16c, as we saw in the previous paragraph (cf. LXX: Mic 7:9; Isa 43:9; 43:26; 50:8; 53:11). The term "justify" is thus here forensic, or judicial: The person who observes the law is justified, or approved, by God—declared to be righteous, to be in the right.[225] In this scheme, God declares righteous those who by observing the law "are" righteous and thus also in terms of their relation to God (cf. Ps 119:1-8). They have in effect proved themselves to be righteous and deserving of their vindication (cf. Deut 25:1): Well done, good and faithful servants! In the apocalyptic Judaism of Paul's time, justification had come to have a distinctly eschatological dimension; Paul articulates this view when he writes in Romans that "the doers of the law shall be justified (declared right, vindicated)" (Rom 2:13 RSV alt.), meaning by God at the last judgment, when "sinners" or "the wicked" will be condemned (cf. Rom 2:5-8; Matt 12:36-37; *Pss. Sol.* 2.34-35; 13.11-12; 14.1-3, 9-10; 15.12-13; *4 Ezra* [2 Esd] 7; *2 Bar.* 14.12; 38.1-2; 46.6; 48.22; 51.3, 7; 54.5; 57.2). This understanding of justification is at home in one particular strand of Jewish apocalyptic eschatology in Paul's time; the forensic pattern in which personal accountability and the obligation to choose the law are paramount considerations (see Excursus 2, above).

This understanding of justification is essentially also that of the new preachers now active in Galatia. The latter are telling the Gentile Christians there that even as believers in Christ they need "to do" the law (3:10, 12; 5:3), beginning with circumcision (5:2-3; 6:12), if they want to be justified (5:4) when Christ returns for judgment. Only so do they have "the hope of justification [*dikaiosynē*]" (5:5), that is, of divine approval and vindication. By turning to the "different gospel" (1:6) of the new preachers, the Galatians are wanting "to practice Judaism" (2:14) and as a result are also "seeking to be justified [*dikaiousthe*] in the law" (5:4). In the view of the new preachers, then, justification is something that will occur for the law-observant believer in the future. They understand Christ's faithful death not as a justifying act, an act of vindication and approval, but as an atonement for the past sins of the nation against God and his law (see 1:4 and comment there; 1 Cor 15:3). This faithful death did not put an end to law observance for Jewish believers, but it obligates those so forgiven now to obey it all the more, to reach a level of law-based righteousness (*dikaiosynē*) surpassing that of other (nonbelieving, non-Christian) Jews (cf. Matt 5:17-20). Applied to the Gentile Christians in Galatia, the traditional missionary formula that Paul cites in v. 16a is being interpreted by the new preachers in Galatia to indicate that Gentile believers in Christ also have to

---

225. The verb (like its cognate noun *dikaiosynē*) has a range of meanings (cf. LSJ 429; BDAG 247-49). Paul's use of language from Ps 142:2 LXX (143:2E) provides a clue to the meaning it has in this context.

become part of the law-observant covenantal people of Israel in order "to be justified" in the future, at Christ's return (see Excursus 4).

Especially in v. 16c ("so that we might be justified on the basis of the faith of Christ and *not* on the basis of works of the law"), Paul rhetorically dissociates justification from law observance and associates it exclusively with the faithful death of Christ.[226] Both steps are equally important and have far-reaching theological consequences. The subordinating conjunction *hina* ("so that") probably does not point to Paul's own purpose or to that of other Christian Jews in coming to believe in Christ; the purpose is probably God's: "so that, as God wills [cf. 1:4], we might be justified . . ." It is unclear, however, whether the temporal reference of v. 16c (*dikaiōthōmen*, aor. subj.) is future ("so that we might be justified by God in the future") or present ("so that we might be justified by God, as we now are").[227] If the latter, the clause of v. 16c is then best understood as signifying (God's intended) result: justification is coordinate with the coming to believe in Christ (*pisteuō eis Christon*), which is thereby joined to, or made dependent on, Christ's faithful death (*pistis Christou*), just as justification itself is. In the next clause (v. 16d), however, Paul uses a future tense ("shall be justified," *dikaiōthēsetai*, from Ps 142:2 LXX [143:2E]), and in 5:5 he will speak of "the hope of justification." Paul still refers to justification as a future expectation in line with the formula he cites and the views of the new preachers in Galatia (also 2:17; see comment below).

It is difficult not to read Galatians through the lens of Romans, where Paul explicitly and unambiguously identifies Christ's faithful death as God's act of eschatological justification, whereby "having faith" and "being justified" are coordinate events in the present for the believer (cf. Rom 3:21–26; 4:1–8; 5:1–10; 8:30; 1 Cor 6:11). That move also makes it possible for Paul to include the notion of forgiveness in the meaning of justification (Rom 3:25; 4:6–8; 5:8–9).[228] In the Jewish-Christian formula from which Paul cites in Gal 2:16a, "to justify" means "to declare righteous those who by observing the law are righteous," or "to declare observers of the law to be in the right." Justification here is not God's forgiveness for having transgressed the law, but God's approval for having observed it, to a greater or a lesser extent.[229] By claiming

---

226. Wright's claim (1997: 119; 2005: 112) that, for Paul, justification is an issue of membership in God's covenantal people thus applies not to Paul (as Wright thinks) but to the new preachers in Galatia. Paul dissociates justification from law observance and thus from the covenantal identity based on that law. See comment on v. 19 below.

227. The remaining uses of the verb "to justify" in 3:8, 11, 24; and 5:4 are just as ambiguous on this score, at least syntactically (see comments on these verses).

228. For a link between forgiveness and justification, see 1QS 11.11–15; LXX: Mic 7:8; Isa 43:25–26.

229. In *4 Ezra* and the Dead Sea Scrolls, the demand is that the law be kept "perfectly" (*4 Ezra* [2 Esd] 7:89; 1QS 3.1–11; 4.22; 8.1). For a more moderate view, see the *Psalms of Solomon*,

in Galatians that justification occurs as a result of the faithful death of Christ and not as a result of law observance, Paul intimates, but does not yet say in so many words, that justification occurs *now* for those who "have come to believe in Christ Jesus," not (just) in the future (cf. 1:4 and comment there). Once justification is made exclusively dependent on Christ's faithful, atoning death, justification also comes to entail and thus also to mean forgiveness, as it clearly does in the passages in Romans.[230] Justification can no longer be, therefore, a matter of approving the righteous (those who do right by observing the law) but of accepting sinners ("the ungodly" of Rom 4:5; 5:6), despite their sinfulness (cf. Rom 3:25; 4:6–8; 5:8).[231] Paul goes even a step further, however, since for him justification cannot mean only "to accept" sinners but also "to rectify" them, to make them righteous, by freeing them from the powers of Sin and Death, as Rom 5:12–6:23 bears out (see Käsemann 1969a; de Boer 1988: 152).[232] Paul takes the first steps toward this "cosmological" redefinition of the forensic-eschatological understanding of justification among his fellow Jewish believers in the present passage, especially in Gal 2:20–21 (see comment below; cf. earlier comments on 1:4 with Excursus 2, and on 1:12, 15–16 with Excursus 6). In vv. 15–16, however, these steps to Paul's striking redefinition of justification as involving God's powerful, apocalyptic rectifying action in the present remain inchoate.

For Paul's argument in v. 16, the precise definition of "justification" (present or future? forensic or cosmological?) is not at issue. For the moment, he leaves intact the meaning attributed to it by his adversaries in Galatia, even if he also sets the stage for a new understanding of justification later in the passage. He contents himself with rhetorically separating "justification" (however defined) from law observance and binding it instead and exclusively to Christ's faithful

---

which repeatedly contrast "the sinners" and "the righteous," who are described as "those who live [*tois poreuomenois*] in the righteousness [*dikaiosynē*] of his commandments, in the law" (*Pss. Sol.* 14.2). The righteous also sin, but God "will forgive . . . those [righteous ones] who have sinned" (9.7) and "will wipe away their mistakes with discipline," whereas "sinners shall be taken away to destruction" (13.10–11; cf. 3.3–12; 15.12–13). Hence, "the discipline of the righteous (for things done) in ignorance is not the same as the destruction of the sinners" (13.7).

230. Martyn (1997: 141–56) discerns this meaning already in pre-Pauline tradition (1 Cor 6:11; Rom 3:25–26a; 4:25), as does de Boer (1988: 235 n. 35). It seems, however, that the equation of forgiveness through the atoning death of Christ with present justification is Paul's doing. See Bultmann 1951: 276; Sanders 1977: 471.

231. Paul's new use of the verb "to justify" has led to considerable confusion. The Greek verb in the LXX normally means "to declare someone righteous who is righteous from observing the law," whereas Paul makes it mean "to declare the sinner righteous even though one is a sinner," providing the exegetical foundation for the notion of justification as the imputation of (a fictional) righteousness (cf. Luther 1535: 123, 132–33).

232. In this way Paul avoids the implication that the justification of the sinner is merely a legal fiction, as Luther's interpretation suggests (see previous note). That Luther's views were ultimately more nuanced on this matter is shown by Chester.

death. For someone who has come to believe in Christ, the law has become completely irrelevant for "justification" (however defined).

[17–18] These two verses seem to constitute a parenthesis. Paul here defends himself against a particular charge that was probably made against him and Peter (and other Jewish Christians) already in Antioch (note the past tense in v. 17: "we were found"). He anticipates that the same charge will again be made in Galatia. These verses, therefore, have the character of a preemptive strike. The charge against Paul in Antioch came down to this: By "seeking to be justified in Christ" alone, apart from the observance of the law, Paul and Peter ("we") proved themselves to be "sinners," just like the Gentiles, who do not have the law (v. 15); Christ had thus effectively been brought into the service of fostering rather than of preventing sinful behavior! Paul indignantly denies this to be the case in a question to which he himself provides the answer: "But if by seeking to be justified in Christ we ourselves were found also to be sinners, is Christ then [*ara*] a servant of Sin? Of course not!"[233]

The opening phrase, "by seeking to be justified" (*zētountes dikaiōthēnai*), seems inappropriate at first glance, since justification for Paul is not something to be sought (a human achievement) but to be received (a matter of God's grace).[234] The phrase "to seek to be justified" is traditional and probably reflects a formulation of Paul's detractors in Antioch and (potentially) in Galatia. According to Paul in Rom 10:3, Jews who do not accept Christ are "ignorant of the justification [*dikaiosynē*] that comes from God and are seeking [*zētountes*] to establish their own" (AT). Such Jews would perhaps retort that in observing the law, they were seeking *God's* justification, meaning God's justifying verdict of approval at the last judgment (see on v. 21, below). In Rom 10:20, a quotation from Isa 65:1, God "has been found by those who did not seek" him, by the Gentiles (alt.). The verb "to seek" thus marks the religious quest for what is still missing or hidden from life on earth: human beings "seek God" (Acts 17:27) or "glory and honor and immortality" (Rom 2:7). Greeks "seek wisdom" (1 Cor 1:22 RSV). Followers of Jesus are to "seek first the kingdom of God and its righteousness" (Matt 6:33 AT), and believers are to "seek the things that are above, where Christ is" (Col 3:1). By using the phrase "seeking to be justified in Christ" in v. 17, Paul adopts this perspective, with the distinct implication that justification is to occur in the future (see above on vv. 15–16). But the *time* of justification is less important for the present argument than the

---

233. The Greek is *mē genoito*, lit., "may it not be so!" (cf. 3:21; 1 Cor 6:15; 10 instances in Romans).

234. Soards tries to get around the problem by translating and punctuating as follows: "But if we were found seeking to be justified in Christ [by observing the law], indeed we ourselves are sinners. Is Christ then an agent of sin? Certainly not." Soards takes the participle "seeking" to be supplementary (instead of circumstantial), completing the thought of the main verb "we were found." The word order in Greek does not easily support this possible reading.

basis on which it occurs (v. 16), or in v. 17, the *area* within which it is sought. Paul's formulation "seeking to be justified *in* Christ" forms the counterpart to "seeking to be justified *in* the law" in 5:4 (cf. 3:11: "no one is justified *in* the law"). In 5:4, Paul tells the Galatians: "You who are seeking to be justified [*hoitines dikaiousthe*]²³⁵ in the law" "have become separated from Christ" and "have fallen from grace." Those "who are seeking to be justified in the law" can be characterized as those "who [are trying to] live [*tois pereuomenois*] in the righteousness [*dikaiosynē*] of his [God's] commandments, in the law," as *Pss. Sol.* 14.2 puts it. The phrase "in the law" is not instrumental (a law-observer seeks to be justified not by the law but by God); neither is the phrase "in Christ" in v. 17 (Burton 124). Both phrases are locative, indicating the place, or the sphere, within which justification is being sought. Under the prodding of the new preachers, the Galatians are attempting to be justified "in the sphere of the law," whereas Paul, Peter, and other Jewish Christians in Antioch were "seeking to be justified in the sphere of Christ," in the territory where Christ is Lord (1:3). That territory is the community of people, both Jew and Gentile, who have "come to believe in Jesus Christ, so that" they "might be justified on the basis of Christ's faith and *not* on the basis of works of the law" (v. 16bc).

In so seeking to be justified, Paul and Cephas "were found [by the followers of the circumcision party in Antioch] to be sinners," just like the Gentiles (v. 15), who do not have the law. The verb "were found" (*heurethēmen*) here has the sense of "proved to be" (BDAG 412). Paul and Cephas had thereby, so the charge ran, effectively made Christ "a servant of Sin," the power that rules over Gentile sinners, beyond the bounds of nomistic Israel. Sin (*hamartia*) appears to be personified (hence the capital *S*) as a power, as in 3:22 (cf. Rom 3:9; 5:12–21). This understanding of Sin is probably Paul's and represents his own formulation of the charge being made against him. In Gal 3:22, as in Rom 3:9, Paul will obliterate the distinction between Jew and Gentile with respect to the hegemony of Sin: Apart from Christ, "all things," not just the Gentile world, are "under Sin," and that also means that all people, not just Gentiles, are "sinners" (cf. Rom 3:23). In this verse, however, Paul is content simply to dismiss the conclusion that Christ is Sin's servant (*diakonos*) as absurd: "Of course not!"

In v. 18, Paul tries to substantiate this dismissal of the charge with an argument, keeping at least one eye focused on the Galatian situation: "For if I am building up again [in Galatia, as Peter did earlier in Antioch] these things which I tore down [in Antioch], I am [now] establishing myself a transgressor." This sentence (in the Greek as in its translation) has the form of a real condition, but the sense is probably no different from that of a contrary-to-fact condition: "If I were building up again [which I am not] these things which I tore down, I would

---

235. As indicated earlier, the Greek verb *dikaiousthe* in this text is a conative present tense, signifying an attempt and thus warranting the translation "You are *seeking* to be justified."

be [but I am not] establishing myself a transgressor." Paul uses the form of a real condition for the sake of a logical argument: if such and such is the case, such and such must follow. Paul now refers exclusively to himself, for he knows that Peter and the other Jewish Christians in Antioch have deserted him, having capitulated to the demands of the circumcision party (see on 2:12–13). A transgressor (*parabatēs*) here must be what Paul elsewhere calls "a transgressor *of the law*" (Rom 2:25, 27; cf. Jas 2:9, 11). As he points out in Rom 4:15, "Where there is no law there is no transgression" (RSV) and thus also no transgressor.[236] That helps then to explain the imagery of building up and tearing down "these things" with which the verse begins. "These things" are the works of the law (v. 16), and they are like a wall (cf. Eph 2:14) dividing Jewish believer from Gentile believer in their relationship to Christ. Thus, if Paul is now rebuilding (reinstituting) the things (the works of the law) he earlier tore down (abrogated), he is indeed what the followers of the circumcision party in Antioch claimed he was: a transgressor of the law, for he would then once again be placing himself under the law's authority. But since Paul is *not* building the law up again, he cannot be a transgressor of it. If the law is now irrelevant for justification (v. 16), so also are transgressions of that law, for "where there is no law there is no transgression" of it either. A believer in Christ has been decisively separated from the law, as v. 19 now makes plain.

[19–21] Verse 18 presupposed what Paul in v. 16 three times asserted with insistent clarity: no one is or will be justified on the basis of observing the law. After the digression in vv. 17–18, Paul gives the reasons for this startling claim in vv. 19–21 and does so in abbreviated, staccato fashion:

[19a]For I through the law died to the law, that I might live to God.
[19b]I have been crucified with Christ.
[20a]I no longer live, but Christ lives in me.
[20b]The life I now live in the flesh, I live in faith,[237]
[20c]that of the Son of God, the one who loved me and gave himself up for me.
[21a]I do not nullify the grace of God,
[21b]for if justification is through the law, Christ died for nothing.

---

236. The terms "sinners" and "transgressors [of the law]" are not always or necessarily synonyms, as often supposed (e.g., Longenecker 91), especially when, as here, "sinners" are synonymous with Gentiles: From a Jewish standpoint, Gentile "sinners" live without the law (and thus contrary to God's will and intention) and so cannot be (intentional) transgressors of it; "transgressors" of the law refer to members of the covenant people, Jews by birth, who were given the law to live by and who for one reason or another "transgress" its statutes or its overall intent.

237. Both vv. 20a and 20b begin with the postpositive particle *de*, which often functions merely as a particle of continuation (BDAG 213) and is then best left untranslated, as here. In v. 20a, a second instance of *de* is probably adversative, however: "but [*de*] Christ lives in me."

Paul continues the first-person mode of discourse he began in v. 18 and now presents himself not as an example (as in v. 18) but as a paradigm of the born Jew who has come to believe in Christ (v. 16b): His life is no longer determined by the law but by Christ. For this reason, he can also function as a paradigm for the Gentile Christians in Galatia who "want to be under the law" (4:21).

Verses 19–21, which are the theological high point of the first two chapters and crucial to the interpretation of the remainder of the letter, constitute Paul's (further) interpretation of his conversion and call as recounted in vv. 13–16 (see comment there). The following parallels are particularly noteworthy:

Gal 1:13–16	Gal 2:19–21
in me (*en emoi*)	in me (*en emoi*)
patriarchal traditions	the law
his Son	the Son of God
his grace	the grace of God

As we saw in the comment on 1:16, the "apocalyptic revelation of Jesus Christ" (1:12c), whereby God "was pleased to apocalyptically reveal his Son in me" (1:16a), means for Paul that God entered into the life of the persecutor of God's church and of the law-observant Pharisaic zealot in order to bring that manner of life to a complete and irrevocable end. Paul understands this event, and wants the Galatians to understand this event, "apocalyptically," as God's sovereign redemptive act whereby he effected a radical discontinuity between Paul the law-observant persecutor of God's church and Paul the apostle of Christ to the Gentiles, between who Paul was then and who he is now.

The apocalyptic discontinuity between "then" and "now," discernible in 1:13–16, is emphasized anew in v. 19a with the claim that "I through the law died to the law, that I might live to God."[238] "To die to something" is metaphorical and means to become separated from it (cf. Rom 6:2, 10, 11; 7:6): Paul became separated from the law (*nomos*). The "law" from which Paul has been separated here refers to "the sum of specific divine requirements given to Israel through Moses" (Westerholm 1988: 108), the Sinaitic legislation (Gal 3:17, 19–20; 4:25) preserved in the Pentateuch (cf. 4:21); "the law" is thus shorthand for "works of the law" (2:16; 3:2, 5), the deeds or actions that the Mosaic law requires. With respect to this law, Paul's "I" (*egō*) has ceased to exist; it is thus his nomistic "I"—the "I" that finds its identity and its hope of justification (5:5) in (the observance of) the law—that has died.

---

238. The Greek word for "law" (*nomos*), used twice, does not have the article in v. 19a, yet *the* (Mosaic) law must be in view. The omission of the article is here a matter of style. See note 200 above.

The most difficult part of this verse is Paul's claim that he died to the law "through the law [*dia nomou*]."[239] A reader familiar with the Letter to the Romans would expect Paul to say that he died to the law *through Christ*: "You were made dead to the law through the body of Christ, that you might belong to another, to him who was raised from the dead" (Rom 7:4, alt.). And indeed, Paul seems to be saying as much in Gal 2:19b: "I have been crucified with Christ." Paul's point here appears to be that his nomistically determined "I" died to the law through being (metaphorically yet truly) "crucified with Christ." Paul's death to the law was no self-chosen path; it occurred in his being "crucified with Christ," an event that took place on the Damascus road (see comment on 1:13–16). The implication of Paul's assertion that he died to the law by being "crucified with Christ" is that (the observance of) the law played a role in bringing about the death of God's Son on the cross: he was crucified "through the law." Paul, however, says that he himself died to the law "through the law." The explanation is probably to be found in 1:13–16, on which the present passage elaborates and with which the Galatians are also familiar:[240] Paul himself died to the law "through the law" because his zealous devotion to the law and its "works" led him to persecute the very church of God (Ziesler 22), effecting a collision between the law and Christ, the final result of which was his death to that law (1:13–14).

The other side of dying to the law is living "[in relation] to God" (RSV, NRSV) or, with little difference in meaning, "for God" (NIV, NAB). That was the purpose of his dying to the law, that (*hina*) he could "live to [or for] God." Paul here posits what the new preachers in Galatia (as yet) regard as a startling and unacceptable contrast between the law and God, or more precisely, between observing the law and living to or for God. This contrast was already implied in his account of his conversion and call in 1:13–16 (see comment above) and is a necessary correlate of the theological principle given expression in v. 16: justification does not occur on the basis of law observance but only on the basis of Christ's faithful death, which is God's apocalyptically redemptive act. Paul himself now "lives to/for God" in his work as an apostle of Christ (1:1, 16).

Paul's claim to "have been crucified with Christ" (v. 19b) cannot be taken literally. His language is metaphorical and hyperbolic, yet also realistic and serious (cf. 5:24; 6:14); it is not just a figure of speech, but a vivid interpretation of a truly painful and real experience. As already indicated above, Paul means that his nomistically determined "I" was destroyed in the crucifixion

---

239. It is astonishing that there are no variant readings for this phrase.
240. The verse is often interpreted by making complicated theological appeals to other passages in Galatians (e.g., 3:13, 19–23) or Romans (esp. ch. 7). Presumably, however, Paul is here saying something that the Galatians will be able understand on the basis of what he has already written.

The Origin and the Truth of the Gospel

of Christ (cf. 3:1 and comment there). Christ's crucifixion was an event on the stage of human history that Paul regards as the central moment in God's apocalyptic-eschatological act of cosmic rectification through the person and work of Christ, his Son (see Excursus 2, above). In Paul's understanding of the gospel, everyone who "has come to believe in Christ Jesus" (v. 16a) participates in, is joined to or taken up into, this all-embracing cosmic, apocalyptic event that spells the end of the old age, where malevolent powers hold sway over God's creation; it thus also signifies the beginning of God's reign ("the kingdom of God"), through which human beings are delivered "from the present evil age" (1:4), after which they can truly "live to God." The extreme language of crucifixion with Christ gives expression to one key element of such participation, the end or the permanent loss of a previous manner of life (cf. 5:24; Rom 6:6), in this case one determined by the law. Crucifixion with Christ represents for the individual believer the destruction of one's participation in the old age, where the law functions as an oppressive, enslaving power (see comments on 3:19–23; 4:4–5 below). When Paul says he has been "crucified with Christ," he also means that he has been rescued from the present evil age (1:4; see comment there).[241]

Verse 20a makes the same point, using other words: "I [egō] no longer live, but [de] Christ lives in me." The "I" that no longer lives is the nomistically determined "I," the "I" that was a zealot for the ancestral traditions and persecuted God's church (1:13–14). It is Christ, meaning his Spirit (3:2, 5, 14; 4:6), who now lives "in me" (en emoi), giving Paul a new identity, a new self. The death of Paul's nomistic "I" had left him, as it were, an empty container, which Christ subsequently filled, creating a new "I" (cf. Barclay 2002: 142–43: the self has been "reconstituted"). Paul uses the same expression (en emoi) that he has already used in 1:16: God "apocalyptically reveal[ed] his Son *in me*." In 1:16 the phrase "in me" probably means "in my former manner of life as a zealous Pharisee who persecuted the church of God" (see comment on 1:16a). Through the apocalyptic revelation of his Son, God brought this manner of life to a definitive end. In the present verse, the phrase most probably means "in my current manner of life as an apostle who preaches God's Son among the Gentiles." Thus in his current life, which is public and social (Williams 75), Christ "lives in" Paul; he lives in Paul's preaching activity as Christ's apostle

---

241. Paul's "participationist" language is not here sacramental (as for many commentators who read Rom 6:1–10 into Gal 2:19), but informed and shaped by the categories and motifs native to Jewish cosmological apocalyptic eschatology (see Excursus 2). The interpretation of this passage has been much hampered by the tendency to read it through the lens provided by Romans and thus to make it seem more complicated than it already is (see, e.g., Betz 123–24). "Mysticism" (Longenecker 93) is also an inappropriate description of Paul's language, unless one means what Schweitzer (3) called "eschatological mysticism": being taken up into a cosmic event.

among the Gentiles.[242] The difference between "in me" in 1:16a and "in me" in v. 20a is the difference between the zealot for the law and persecutor of God's church that Paul was, and the apostle of Christ that he now is. In the crucifixion of his old self with Christ, a new self has been given to Paul, created by Christ.

The fact that Christ now lives in him, determining his identity and his activity, does not mean a removal from recognizably historical and thus human life on earth: "The life I now live in the flesh, I live in faith"[243] (v. 20b). "Flesh" denotes the substance that covers a human being's bones (BDAG 914), the material substratum of all human existence at the present time. Human beings in their totality can, therefore, be characterized as "flesh and blood" (1:16) or as "all flesh" (2:16), in part to distinguish them from God. The "flesh" in 2:20b is the sphere of what is mortal (susceptible to death) and weak (vulnerable to disease).[244] The flesh also lies behind the human propensity to sinful behavior (5:19–21) and human vulnerability to malevolent cosmic powers such as Sin (2:17; 3:22).[245] To live "in the flesh" (*en sarki*) is to live in a sphere or an area characterized by these realities (Burton 138). The life Paul "now" lives in this sphere—as a believer in Christ, as an apostle, and after his death to the law—he lives "in faith." This faith is not his own but "that of the Son of God" (v. 20c). The construction here (*pistis . . . tou huiou tou theou*) is a variation on *pistis (Iēsou) Christou*, "the faith of (Jesus) Christ" in v. 16. As in v. 16, "the faith of the Son of God" (v. 20c) refers to the Son's own faith, in particular his faithful, atoning death on the cross (see Excursus 9). Paul perhaps switches here to the Son-of-God title for two reasons: (1) because he has used this title in 1:16 and (2) because he wants to indicate that "the faith of Christ" is God's own saving act. In v. 20d, Paul immediately defines "the Son of God" as "the one who loved me [*tou agapēsantos me*] and gave himself up for me [*kai paradontos heauton hyper emou*]" (cf. Rom 4:25: "who was given up on account of our trespasses" [AT]). Paul in Gal 2:20 alludes back to 1:4a and his definition of Jesus Christ there ("the one who gave himself for our sins," *tou dontos heauton hyper tōn*

---

242. This interpretation does not exclude the notion of Christ's dwelling inside Paul (or the believer) in some sense, as in 4:6: "God sent forth the Spirit of his Son into [*eis*] our hearts." The *focus* of Paul's autobiographical narrative in 1:13–2:21, however, is the history of the gospel in human affairs, i.e., in *interpersonal* relationships (against, e.g., Betz 124). The human "I" is not for Paul abstracted from the interconnections that such interpersonal relationships create (culture, language, history, etc.).

243. Literally, "What [*ho*] I now live in [the] flesh, I live in [the] faith . . ." On this peculiar use of the neuter relative pronoun *ho* at the beginning of a clause and meaning "as to what," see Smyth #2494. The clause beginning with this pronoun may stand in apposition to the main clause, and that appears to be the case here.

244. Cf. 4:13–14, where Paul refers to "an infirmity of the flesh" and "my flesh."

245. See comment on 5:13–24 and de Boer 1988: 131–32: "Human creatureliness, weakness, and need for dependency on God also imply human susceptibility to the sway of evil cosmological powers" (on 1 Cor 15:26, 54–56).

hamartiōn hēmōn). The preposition *hyper* in v. 20b (as in 1:4a) means "for the sake" or "benefit of," not "instead of" (cf. Eph 5:2: "Christ loved us and gave himself up for us"; 5:25: "Christ loved the church and gave himself up for her"). The second participle, *paradontos* ("gave up"), is probably explanatory of the first, *agapēsantos* ("loved"): "the one who loved me, that is, gave himself up for me." The Son of God's love was thus not a disposition but a concrete act of self-sacrifice; put otherwise, the Son of God's self-sacrifice was an act of love "for me." Paul refers to himself, but he expects the new preachers and the Galatians also to say it after him and to apply it to themselves. The present situation of every believer is that the believer both lives "in the flesh" and "in the faith of God's Son." Living "in the flesh" is the universal human condition; living "in the faith of God's Son" is the privilege of believers. Paul's point is that the believer's life in the sphere of the flesh is now being determined by life in the sphere of Christ's faithful death, giving life in the flesh a completely different character, one marked by the experience and the knowledge of God's grace (v. 21a).

Verse 21 is the climax of the first two chapters: "I do not nullify the grace of God [as the new preachers do with their "different gospel"], for if justification is [in fact] through [works of] the law [as the new preachers claim], then [let us be clear about this:] Christ died for nothing." In v. 21a, Paul refers back to his testimony in 1:15 that God "called [him] through his grace" (cf. 2:9). God's act of grace in Christ to him is however paradigmatic for all believers (cf. 1:3, 6). The verb "to nullify," also used in 3:15 in connection with a testament, is a judicial (forensic) term meaning "to declare invalid" (BDAG 24). Verse 21a could be read to indicate that the new preachers are accusing Paul of nullifying God's grace, perhaps as expressed in the giving of the law (cf. Burton 140; Martyn 259; cf., e.g., *2 Bar.* 44.14). But the accusation probably runs in the other direction, since the reference to God's grace is probably meant to recall the references to God's grace in 1:15 and 2:9. By saying that he does not nullify God's grace in Christ, Paul implies that the new preachers with their law-based gospel are doing precisely that (just as Cephas and other Jewish believers did earlier in Antioch).

In v. 21b, the issue is once again explicitly "justification" (*dikaiosynē*), as it was in v. 16 (*dikaiousthai*). "Justification through the law" seems to be simply another way of saying "to be justified on the basis of works of the law" (cf. 5:4–5). The noun then means either "God's justifying pronouncement" ("justification") or "the status of having been justified by God" (the "righteousness" that comes from God); both can be in view at the same time (cf. Mic 7:9 LXX), and both are forensic-eschatological (see comment on v. 16 above). For the new preachers in Galatia, who have adopted and adapted the categories and perspectives of Jewish forensic apocalyptic eschatology (see Excursus 2), those who shall be justified (declared righteous) by God are in fact now "righteous," thus "living as God's people" (Ziesler 30) and rightly related to God, by virtue of their observance of the law (cf. *Pss. Sol.*14.2).[246] The eschatological verdict of divine justification will confirm their status and also eternalize it: the life of God's people in the new age beyond the judgment will be characterized by the same righteousness (cf. 3:21 and comment there). For the new preachers, it is therefore a matter of urgency that the Galatians observe the law, beginning with the practice of circumcision. In a substantive argument, Paul tries to undermine this position, believing that the "different gospel" of the new preachers turns "the gospel of Christ into its opposite" (1:7; see comment there): It effectively nullifies God's grace. To paraphrase v. 21b only slightly: If justification is indeed attainable through observing the law, as the new preachers claim,[247] then (*ara*) it must follow that Christ died for nothing: needlessly (*dōrean*, lit., "gratuitously"). But Christ did die, and did so "for our sins" (1:4). This fact cannot be wished away or reduced in importance. The corollary to v. 21b is thus that if justification occurs on the basis of Christ's faithful death, as Paul believes to be the case (v. 16), works of the law must be entirely superfluous and irrelevant. To rely on them is to "[seek to] nullify" God's grace in Christ (cf. 1:6). Paul here drives a wedge between the law and justification—indeed, between the law and God (see below on 3:19–22).[248]

The theme of justification that reemerges in v. 21 is to be read through the lens provided by vv. 19–20. By referring explicitly to Christ's death ("Christ died," *Christos apethanen*) and setting that death over against justification through the law, Paul alludes back to vv. 19–20 and the theme of dying to the law ("I *died* [*apethanon*] to the law") and being crucified with Christ ("I have been crucified *with Christ* [*Christō*]"). Paul thereby implies that the new preachers' understanding of *dikaiosynē* in v. 21 as purely forensic-eschatological is inadequate. *Dikaiosynē* for Paul cannot merely be God's forensic-eschatological acquittal of the righteous in the future; even more it is God's putting right (rectifying) what is wrong in the human world (Martyn), in the present as well as in the future.[249] God not only justifies (declares right) in the future, but also rectifies (makes right) in the present; God does so concretely by joining believers to the death of Christ, thereby separating them from the powers that enslave: Sin (v. 17; cf. 3:22) and the law (cf. 2:4; 4:1–5). Back in

---

246. Wright's interpretation of 2:21 (2005: 113), that *dikaiosynē* here means "covenant status" or "covenant membership," certainly applies to the new preachers.

247. Paul uses the form of real condition here, though the sense is actually unreal (contrary to fact), as in v. 18 (see comment there): If righteousness were through the law (which it is not), then Christ died for nothing (which he certainly did not). Cf. BDF #360; Winger 1986.

248. He thus also drives a wedge between the Sinaitic covenant and justification (contrast Wright 1997; 2005). See the comments on 3:15–18 and 4:21–5:1 below.

249. On "the righteousness of God" in Paul as God's saving action and power, see Käsemann 1969a.

The Origin and the Truth of the Gospel 165

1:4, Paul has defined the "Jesus Christ" in whom "we [Jewish believers] too came to believe" (2:16b) as "the one who gave himself for our sins, that he might rescue us from the present evil age, according to the will of God and our Father." Paul has interpreted the atoning death of Jesus apocalyptically, as God's act of deliverance from an evil realm (see comment there). For the sake of argument, Paul adopts the language of justification, but the context in which he places it forces it to take on a different meaning, that of God's rectifying power (Martyn 272–73).

In the remainder of the letter, the language of justification (*dikaiousthai, dikaiosynē*) in Galatians is almost exclusively confined to chapter 3 (the verb appears in 3:8, 11, 24; the noun in 3:6, 21), where Paul attempts to refute the so-called gospel of the new preachers exegetically.[250] Justification language disappears from the letter after 3:24, reappearing only briefly in 5:4–5, where Paul makes a last-ditch attempt to keep the Galatians from practicing circumcision and "seeking to be justified in the law," as the new preachers want. The justification language is thus that of the new preachers, not that of Paul. (It is entirely absent from his earliest letter, 1 Thessalonians, which shows that he could preach the gospel to the Gentiles without it.) He does not resort to this language in his third contextualized summary of the gospel (4:1–7), where he concludes his refutation of the "different gospel" (1:6) of the new preachers (3:1–4:7). The Paul of Galatians prefers the language of deliverance (1:4), crucifixion with Christ (2:19; 6:14), redemption (3:13; 4:5), liberation (5:1), and walking by the Spirit (5:16). This language is much more important to his own theological understanding of Christ's death and resurrection than is the language of justification.[251] In this passage (2:15–21), he focuses on justification because of its importance to the new preachers in Galatia, so that he can show them, as well as the Galatians who have fallen under their influence, that works of the law are completely *irrelevant* for justification. The only thing that matters is "the faith of Christ." This is the truth of the gospel that Paul has now disclosed to the new preachers in Galatia and thereby also to the Galatians themselves.

---

250. Furthermore, the two expressions introduced alongside the language of justification in 2:16—"works of the law" and "the faith of (Jesus) Christ"—occur for the last time in 3:10 and 3:22 respectively.

251. This judgment applies only to Galatians and makes no claims about Romans or about Paul's theology as a whole.

Section III: Galatians 3:1–4:7
The Spirit and the True Heirs of the Promise Made to Abraham

This section is the theological heart of the epistle. As indicated in the Introduction, it argues that the gift or the promise of the Spirit depends not on observance of the law but upon "faith," meaning the faith of Christ, which is another way of speaking about his faithful, redemptive death (see Excursuses 9 and 11). Those who receive the Spirit from faith can consider themselves the legitimate offspring of Abraham, for they are heirs of the promise that God made to Abraham apart from any observance of the law. In fact, they have been liberated from the law and are not merely "sons [heirs] of Abraham" but also, and more important, "sons [heirs] of God."

The section functions (and this may also be Paul's conscious purpose) primarily to refute the "different gospel" being promoted by the new preachers who are active in the churches of Galatia, yet at the same time it functions to establish the plausibility of the gospel that Paul preaches. The antinomy between "works of the law" (= observance of the law) and "the faith of Christ" (= Christ's faithful death), introduced in 2:16, is here carried forward and appears to underlie the whole section. If justification (3:6, 8, 11, 21, 24) depends on Christ's faithful death, so does the reception of the Spirit. The burden of the section is to demonstrate *why* the observance of the law is in fact irrelevant for receiving the Spirit and for that very reason also irrelevant for participating in God's "justification" (*dikaiousthai, dikaiosynē*) of the world in and through Christ. As the comments on 2:16 and 2:21 have indicated, "justification" for Paul does not only mean, as it does for the new preachers, eschatological vindication (being declared righteous in the future, at the Parousia)—but also, and primarily, "rectification" (being made right, and in the present as well as in the future). The term "justification" has been retained to indicate that the meaning Paul attaches to the term is not inherent in the term itself but is a consequence of the argumentative and theological contexts in which he places and uses it. The Spirit of the faithful Christ, not the law, is the power by which God from now on rectifies what has gone wrong in and with the world.

Paul does not, however, stop at demonstrating the irrelevance of the law since the coming of Christ, even though his argument can at times be read

The Spirit and the True Heirs of the Promise Made to Abraham 167

in that way (e.g., 3:25). In this section he also tries to place some distance between God and the law in order in this way to undermine its status among his opponents as the divinely given solution for the human condition. The law is severed from promise, blessing, justification, Christ, life, perhaps even God (see on 3:19–20), and depicted exclusively as the source of a curse (3:10–15) and as an imprisoning and enslaving power (3:23–25; 4:3) whose time has come to an end through the redemptive work of Christ (3:13, 25; 4:4–5). This depiction of the law is undoubtedly the most controversial part of the passage, indeed of the whole letter.

The argument of the section is extremely difficult to follow at numerous points, but there is a discernible unifying theme: the Spirit (or more fully, the reception of the promised Spirit). This theme is signaled by the opening paragraph (3:1–5), where Paul wants to learn from the Galatians whether they received, and still receive, the Spirit "on the basis of works of the law"—or "on the basis of what was, and is, heard of faith." Each of the remaining four subsections ends, as does the first paragraph, with a climactic reference to the Spirit:

3:6–14 The Blessing of Abraham and the Curse of the Law: "Christ redeemed us from the curse of the law, . . . in order that we might receive the promise of the Spirit [the promised Spirit] through faith" (3:14).

3:15–22 The Promise to Abraham and the Law of Moses: "The Scripture shut all things up under Sin in order that the promise [the promise of the Spirit] might be given to those who believe on the basis of the faith of Jesus Christ" (3:22).

3:23–29 The True Offspring of Abraham: "If you are Christ's, then you are the offspring of Abraham, heirs according to a promise [God's promise of the Spirit]" (3:29).

4:1–7 The True Heirs of the Promise: "Because you are sons [of God], God sent forth the Spirit of his Son into our hearts crying 'Abba, Father!' So you are no longer a slave but a son; if a son, also an heir [heir of the promised Spirit], through God" (4:6–7).

The references to promise (3:14, 16, 18, 19, 22, 29), inheritance (3:18, 29; 4:1, 7), and divine sonship (3:26; 4:5–7) are different ways of articulating the overarching theme of the section, which is the Spirit. The primary issue addressed in the section is this: Who are the heirs of the promise made to Abraham, that promise being the Spirit that the Galatians have already received and still receive? Paul's answer is that the heirs are those who are "from faith [*ek pisteōs*]" (3:8), meaning the faith of Christ (see Excursus 11), and not, as the new preachers are claiming, those who are "from works of the law [*ex ergōn nomou*]" (3:10). Section III is Paul's commentary on this central thesis.

Finally, Paul's argumentation in this section resists systematization. The precise relationship between the reception of the Spirit, believing, justification, and baptism into Christ remains largely inchoate and unarticulated, as does the precise relationship between promise, inheritance, descent from Abraham, and divine sonship. The interpreter must frequently struggle to determine how Paul sees the relationship of the one to the other. Paul's form of argumentation here is not systematic, but associative. A word in the last verse of each subsection becomes a catchword, triggering the need for further treatment, though always in relationship to the overarching theme, which is the Spirit:

3:1–5   The last word of the passage is "faith," and "faith" becomes the object of further reflection in the unit that follows (3:7, 8, 9, 11, 12, 14).

3:6–14 In the last verse, Paul refers to "the promise of the Spirit," thereby using the term "promise" for the first time in the letter. "Promise" thereupon becomes the leitmotif of the next passage (3:16, 17, 18 [2x], 19, 21, 22).

3:15–22 In the last verse, Paul mentions "the faith of Jesus Christ" (using this full expression for the first time since 2:16) and this faith becomes the object of further reflection vis-à-vis the law in the passage that follows (3:23, 24, 25, 26).

3:23–29 Paul calls believers in Christ "heirs according to a promise" in v. 29 and goes on to develop the notion of "an heir" in the concluding passage of Section III (4:1, 7).

Paul's basic concern in all these subsections is to let the Galatians know that the reception of the Spirit—which is positively related to believing, justification, promise, inheritance, and being sons or offspring of Abraham and sons of God— is in no way dependent on, or related to, the observance of the law. Throughout the section, Paul goes out of his way to put the law in a very bad light.

3:1–5 The Reception of the Spirit in Galatia

Paul's letter takes a new turn in 3:1. He addresses his readers in Galatia directly for the first time since 1:11. (They were last mentioned in 2:5.) Paul also here introduces references to the Spirit. By doing so, he not only establishes a connection between the reception of the Spirit and justification; he also makes a direct appeal to the experience of the Galatians. Was and is the experience of the Spirit among the new Christians in Galatia in any way dependent on their observance of the law? The answer is as clear to the Galatians (or should be) as

The Spirit and the True Heirs of the Promise Made to Abraham 169

it is to Paul. The answer also has far-reaching implications for the law and its place in God's justifying (3:6, 8, 11, 21, 24) and redeeming (3:13; 4:5) activity in Christ, and Paul goes on to make these explicit in the paragraphs that follow. This passage contains a series of questions, divided over two subunits (vv. 1–2 and vv. 3–5). The two subunits both begin with Paul's referring to the Galatians as "unthinking" and both end with a rhetorical question pertaining to the Spirit and contrasting "works of the law" with "what is heard of faith."

3:1 O unthinking Galatians, who has bewitched you,[a] before whose eyes Jesus Christ was portrayed as crucified?[b] 2 This only I wish to learn from you: Did you receive the Spirit on the basis of works of the law or on the basis of what was heard of faith?
3 Are you so unthinking, having begun with the Spirit, are you now ending up with the flesh?[c] 4 Have you experienced so many things in vain, if indeed they were also in vain?[d] 5 Therefore, the One who lavishes the Spirit on you and works deeds of power among you—on the basis of works of the law or on the basis of what is heard of faith?

    a. The variant reading *te aletheia mē peithesthai* ("so as not to be persuaded by the truth"), inserted at this point (cf. KJV), is not original, having been taken from 5:7 (Metzger 534). The best manuscripts do not include the phrase (ℵ, A, B, D*, 33*, 81, 1739).
    b. Some manuscripts, including D, have the words *en hymin* ("among you") after the verb. The best manuscripts do not support this reading (Metzger 524–25).
    c. This verse could also be understood as two questions: "Are you so unthinking? Having begun with the Spirit, are you now ending up with the flesh?"
    d. One may punctuate differently: "Have you experienced so many things in vain?— if indeed they were also in vain!"

The question in v. 1 and the two in vv. 3–4 are genuine questions, expressing concern about the spiritual (or mental) health of the Galatians. Paul's consternation is also evident in these questions. The parallel questions in vv. 2 and 5 are rhetorical questions to which Paul already knows the answer and to which he expects the Galatians, if they are not as "unthinking" as he characterizes them in vv. 1 and 3, also to know the answers.

[1–2] The interjection "O unthinking Galatians!" with which the paragraph begins expresses Paul's deep perplexity and concern about the intended readers (or listeners) of this letter in Galatia. Back in 1:11, they are affectionately called *adelphoi* (brethren, i.e., sisters and brothers in Christ). Here the tone is once again reproachful (as in 1:6–7). The term "Galatians" probably designates the inhabitants of the region known as Galatia (ethnic Galatians) rather than the inhabitants of the Roman province of Galatia, which included other regions and ethnic groups (see Introduction: Addressees). Whatever the case may be, the recipients of the letter will probably not appreciate being addressed as "unthinking." Is Paul himself not being "unthinking" (thoughtless) here? Does he not risk losing his audience at this juncture by resorting to such language?[252] The answer to these questions depends in part on the meaning of the word "unthinking" in Greek (*anoētoi*), here translated literally and meaning "lacking in the power of perception" (Burton 143). The word refers to people who are not in their right minds or lack insight. In Rom 1:14, Paul uses the word as the antonym of "wise," which lies behind the common translation of the word as "foolish." The issue is not a natural deficiency (low intelligence) but a failure of "spiritual discernment" (Longenecker 99; cf. Betz 130). Paul is asking the Galatians to step back and look at themselves. The rhetorical questions that follow in vv. 2 and 5, to which the Galatians already know the answers, are intended to shake them out of their mental stupor so that they can see that the bewitching message of the new preachers in Galatia is false and in fact irrelevant to their own experience.

By asking "Who has bewitched you?" Paul suggests that the Galatians have fallen under the hypnotic spell of the new preachers in Galatia. Paul here uses the singular *tis* ("who?"), with which the verb (*ebaskanen*) agrees. This singular is either generic (generalizing) or refers indirectly to a leading figure among the new preachers in Galatia (see comments on 1:9 and 5:10b). The Greek verb (*baskainō*) implies exerting evil influence through "the evil eye" (BDAG 170; see Deut 28:54 LXX; MM 106). Paul is probably speaking figuratively, as many ancients and not only moderns were quite capable of doing.[253] "It would be overpressing the facts," observes Burton (144), "to infer from Paul's use of this word that he necessarily believed in the reality of magic powers, and still more so to assume that he supposed the state of mind of the Galatians to be the result of such arts." Betz (131) points out that the figurative use of the term was common from the time of Plato in connection with rhetorical manipulation (also Vouga 66–67) and that the variant reading *tē alētheia mē peithesthai* ("so as not to be persuaded by the truth"), taken from 5:7 (see note above), further supports the figurative interpretation of the verb *baskainō*. With figurative seriousness, Paul refers to the malignant effect of the new preachers' message on the minds and the perceptions of his Galatian audience. Their minds have been affected and for the worse. They are "in thrall" to the message of the new preachers and in the process of turning away from the gospel that Paul initially preached

---

252. Martyn (281) calls Paul's language "acerbic." Witherington (201) thinks Paul is trying "to persuade" the Galatians "and if need be shame them." Betz (130) argues that Paul's "biting and aggressive" language is an "insult," but also notes that this sort of language was "commonplace among the diatribe preachers of Paul's day." For examples, see Luke 24:25; Philo, *Somn.* 2.181.

253. Other views may be found in J. H. Elliott; Neyrey; Longenecker 1998: 26, 153–55; 1999; Eastman 2001; Nanos 2002a: 279–80.

to them (cf. 1:6–7; 5:2–7).[254] That is the point, and we may paraphrase it as follows: Have you Galatians lost your (Christian) minds through the new preachers who have come to Galatia?

The following clause indicates that Paul would not expect this to happen to those who had heard the gospel of Christ—or as Paul puts it, to those "before whose eyes Jesus Christ was portrayed as crucified." The Greek verb translated "portrayed" is *prographō*, which literally means "to write before," where "before" can have a spatial import ("in front of") or a temporal one ("in advance, earlier"). If one adopts the temporal meaning, Paul could be referring either to his initial preaching of the gospel to the Galatians (cf. 4:13), to what he has just written about Jesus' death in the immediately preceding verses (2:19b–21; cf. Eph 3:3), or even to the OT Scriptures as testimony to Christ (cf. Rom 15:4; 1 Cor 15:3–4). The first of these is to be preferred.[255] The mention of the eyes of the Galatians makes a reference to the immediately preceding verses and a possible allusion to unspecified OT passages equally improbable. The spatial import can be expressed in one of two ways: "to proclaim publicly" or "to placard publicly" (cf. BDAG 867), the latter in the sense of "to set forth as a public notice" (LSJ 1473; cf. Burton 143: "a public proclamation on a bulletin-board").[256]

These two meanings are not necessarily mutually exclusive, though given the peculiar circumstances under which Paul came to preach the gospel to the Galatians (see 4:12–20), it is difficult to think that his proclamation took place in a large public area (the agora or central city square, for example). Furthermore, in contrast to the general picture created by Acts, the Letters of Paul himself give the overall impression that Paul began his evangelizing activity not in the agora, nor in the local synagogue, but in the workshop and the home (cf. 1 Thess 2:9; Acts 18:2–3). His "public" in these settings was rather modest. The meaning "to placard publicly" may thus be the most appropriate since this meaning, when taken metaphorically, implies a vivid, verbal portrait of the event of Jesus' crucifixion before an audience, however small or large (Martyn 283; Betz 131). This interpretation is further supported by the reference to the eyes of the Galatians. The temporal and spatial elements can be combined: Jesus Christ was vividly portrayed as crucified before the Galatians when Paul

---

254. Martyn (282–83) observes: "Given the Gentile aversion to circumcision [cf. Josephus, *Ant.* 20.139; *J.W.* 2.454], the Teachers must indeed have been virtual magicians to have made the Galatians long to come under the law." It would of course be wrong to conclude on the basis of this statement that Martyn believes in the actual efficacy of magic any more than Paul.

255. The ancient copyists who inserted "among you" (*en hymin*) after the verb evidently so understood it as well.

256. Burton (144) maintains that the verb is unattested with the meaning "paint" and that even for the uncompounded form of the verb, *graphō*, the meaning "paint" is rare and attested only much earlier than the NT (also Lightfoot 134). See further Davis.

first came to Galatia (cf. 1 Cor 2:1–2, where Paul reports that when he first came to Corinth he also proclaimed "Christ crucified").

The term "crucified," here as in 1 Cor 1:23 and 2:2, is a perfect passive participle in the Greek, literally meaning "having been crucified." The normal meaning of the Greek verb is "to nail to a cross" (BDAG 941) and by extension "to kill or execute by crucifixion." The sense of the perfect tense here is thus "having been put to death on the cross" and not "having been affixed to the cross and [still] hanging there" (Burton 144). With his use of the perfect tense, Paul refers to a past event with continuing importance for the present identity of Jesus Christ and for the salvation he bestows (cf. 2:19b: "I have been crucified with Christ"). The resurrection does not mean that the crucifixion can be relegated to the past and forgotten. As Paul's reference to his crucifixion with Christ in 2:19 indicates (see comment there), the appeal to Christ's crucifixion in this verse instead of merely to his death (as in 2:20c–21) calls attention to the manner of Jesus' death as an apocalyptic event, as an event that announces and effects the end of the world (cf. 1 Cor 1:18–19), in this case the world of law observance (cf. 2:16, 19; 3:25; 4:4–5; 6:14–15). In Christ's crucifixion a world has been destroyed, and that is what Paul wishes to emphasize in this context by characterizing Jesus Christ as "having been crucified" (see comments on 1:4; 2:19–20; 5:11; 5:24; 6:14). For the Galatians to take up law observance as part of their new Christian identity would thus be tantamount to returning to that world from which Christ has delivered them (see 4:8–11 and comment there). The implications for the Mosaic law are radical and disturbing (see esp. 3:15–22; 4:4–5 and comments there).

In verbally portraying Christ crucified before the Galatians, Paul also probably referred to Christ's "dying for our sins" (1:4; cf. 1 Cor 15:3) or to Christ's love "for us" as disclosed in his death (2:20; cf. Rom 5:8). If Paul had not done so, the crucifixion of Jesus could only have been perceived and experienced by the Gentile Galatians as utter "foolishness" (1 Cor 1:23) instead of as God's paradoxical saving power (cf. 1 Cor 1:18, 24; Gal 3:13; 4:5). Christ died precisely to deliver the Galatians (and all other human beings) from the present evil age (1:4), and thus to transfer them into a new world (the new creation) characterized above all else by the utterly self-sacrificing love made visible in Christ's gruesome death (2:20; 5:14, 22; 6:2, 15). The end of one world (the present evil age) and the beginning of the other (new creation) occur in that single event. For the Galatians themselves, the destruction of the old world and the advent of the new one effectively occurred when Paul vividly portrayed Jesus Christ as the crucified one, thereby causing them to believe in Christ (2:16) and (at precisely the same moment) bringing the Spirit into their lives (see on 3:2 below). How then could the Galatians possibly have allowed themselves to be bewitched by new preachers' insisting on law observance as a necessary condition for the reception of the Spirit and for membership in God's people? The "different

The Spirit and the True Heirs of the Promise Made to Abraham   173

gospel" of the new preachers has, in Paul's view, been disproved in advance of their arrival by events in Galatia itself.

In v. 2, Paul poses a rhetorical question: "This only I wish to learn from you: Did you receive the Spirit on the basis of works of the law or on the basis of what was heard of faith?" Paul is confident that the Galatians know the answer, as the introductory statement clearly shows. The word "only" points to "a decisive argument" (Burton 147); Paul knows that he has here "a knock-down proof for his case" (Barclay 1988: 83). The Galatians have indeed received the Spirit, and they know as well as Paul that this event occurred not because they began to observe the law but because they had heard his proclamation of the crucified Christ, thereby coming to believe.

Since the notion of "receiving" the Spirit is found elsewhere in the NT (Acts 2:38; John 20:22), Paul is probably not introducing a new idea here. Both he and the new preachers, as well as the Galatians, spoke of "receiving" the Spirit (from God). This means that all sides also spoke of "the Spirit." At issue between Paul and the new preachers in Galatia in this verse is not the nature of the Spirit or its divine origin (see the comment on 3:5; cf. 3:14; 4:6; 5:16), but the circumstances under which it was originally received: Was it received as a result of works of the law, or as a result of what was heard of faith?

"Works of the law" are mentioned here for the second time in the letter (cf. 2:16). These "works" are the actions performed or carried out in obedience to the many commandments preserved in the Pentateuch (see comment on 2:16 and Excursus 8). Especially but not only circumcision is in view (2:3; 5:2–3, 11; 6:12–13). The Galatians did not receive the Spirit as a consequence of such actions. Observance of the law had nothing to do with the bestowal or the reception of the Spirit in Galatia. Since Paul largely repeats the point in v. 5, it may well be that the new preachers in Galatia believe that the reception of the Spirit was predicated upon, or in some way linked to, observing the law (see comment on v. 5). If so, Paul is reminding the Galatians that their own experience proves such a link between law observance and the reception of the Spirit to be utterly false and irrelevant.

For Paul as for the Galatians, the Spirit was bestowed not "on the basis of works of the law" but "on the basis of what was heard of faith." The Greek behind this expression (*ex akoēs pisteōs*) has proved difficult to interpret, as can be seen from the various translations that have been proposed. For example:

"by hearing with faith" (Bruce; Dunn; RSV)
"by believing what you heard" (Longenecker; NRSV, NIV, REB, NJB)
"by [the] proclamation of [the] faith" (Betz)
"through the proclamation of the gospel" (Hays 2002: 196)
"by the proclamation that has the power to elicit faith" (Martyn; Hays)

The uncertainty in this context arises from the fact that *akoē* is taken to mean either "hearing" or "proclamation," whereas *pistis* is understood to mean either "the faith that believes," meaning "[the human act of] believing"—or "the faith that is believed," meaning "the gospel [message]." Hays may well be right when he observes, "Perhaps the truth of the matter is that Paul's compressed language will not answer all the questions we would like to put to it and that he did not intend a clear distinction" (2002: 131). The choice in favor of "what was heard of faith," therefore, can make no claim to certainty.

Excursus 10: The Greek Phrase *ex akoēs pisteōs*

This excursus briefly outlines the grammatical problems and options that confront the interpreter with the phrase *ex akoēs pisteōs*. The preposition *ex* (from *ek*) can be translated in different ways, with little difference in meaning: "on the basis of," "through," "by," or "as a result of." The noun *akoē* can have four distinguishable meanings: the ear, the faculty of hearing, the act of hearing, and a message that is proclaimed and/or heard (BDAG 31; cf. Hays 2002 124–32). In this context, only the latter two are possible:

a. the act of hearing, or
b. a proclamation, message, or report either as proclaimed (active) or as heard (passive)

The matter is complicated further by the precise meaning of the word "faith" (*pistis*) in this context. The options are normally two:

c. (the human act of) believing (*fides qua creditur*), or
d. that which is believed, meaning the gospel message (*fides quae creditur*)

These possibilities thus allow at least four different renderings of the phrase in which the genitive relationship between *akoē* and *pistis* can be interpreted in various ways:

1. With a + c: by hearing with faith, that is, by a faithful hearing (genitive of quality; BDF #165). Other possibilities here are by a hearing that comes of faith (so Lightfoot 135: "a subjective genitive"), or by a hearing that is believing (a genitive of apposition or of content; BDF #167).[257]
2. With a + d: by a hearing of the faith / the gospel (objective genitive; cf. BDF #163; Calvin 48).
3. With b + c: through the proclamation that creates or elicits faith/believing (genitive of goal or purpose; cf. BDF #166).[258]

---

257. Cf. Moule 175: "hearing and believing"; Burton 147: "of a hearing of faith," "a believing-hearing"; Williams 1989: 90: "the hearing of faith."
258. Cf. BDAG 36: "as the result of a message (proclamation) which elicited (only) faith," similar to Martyn's "by the proclamation that has the power to elicit faith" (284; cf. 289: "to elicit, to ignite, to kindle faith"). Martyn appeals to John 5:29 where "a resurrection of life" (*anastasis zōēs*) clearly means "a resurrection *to* life" (288 n. 21; cited in BDF #166).

The Spirit and the True Heirs of the Promise Made to Abraham 175

4. With b + d: through the proclamation of the faith / the gospel (objective genitive), or through the proclamation of which the faith / the gospel is the content (genitive of apposition).

An understanding of the phrase similar to the third option presumably lies behind the rendering of Longenecker (101–3): "on the basis of believing what you heard." This rendering is also found in NRSV, NIV, REB, and NJB. This solution would attain some plausibility if the word order of the Greek were the reverse: *ek pisteōs akoēs*, "from an act of believing the gospel message" (cf. Hays 2002: 125 n. 18). A further problem with this understanding of the phrase is that it could be taken to imply that believing (faith) is an existing human possibility outside of or prior to the message, whereas the rendering "through the proclamation that creates or elicits faith" assumes that the human response of faith is created by the gospel message and that both are something new in the world (see on 3:23–25, where the latter finds support).

That Paul probably intends *akoē* to refer to the message (proclamation) as heard by the Galatians, rather than "hearing," finds support in his use of this word in 1 Thess 2:13 and Rom 10:16–17.[259] A rather literal translation of the former would be: "When you received a word of what was heard [*logos akoēs*] from us of God, you accepted it not as a word of human beings but as . . . a word of God." The word here means "a message heard" and not "hearing." The "word of God" is a message that the Thessalonians heard coming from Paul's mouth. The same is true in Rom 10:16–17: "But they have not all obeyed the gospel; for Isaiah says, "Lord, who has believed what he has heard [*akoē*] from us?" [from Isa 53:1 LXX]. So faith [*pistis*] comes from what is heard [*ex akoēs*], and what is heard [*akoē*] comes by the preaching [*rhēma*] of Christ" (RSV). Paul thus uses the term in a passive sense, to refer to a proclamation as heard: the point of reference is the hearer who hears a message rather than the speaker who utters it. Hence the translation "what was heard" for the instance in v. 2.

With respect to *pistis*, neither "believing" (*fides qua creditur*) nor "the gospel [message]" (*fides quae creditur*) is probably a correct translation, given the use of the term in the immediately preceding paragraph (2:15–21). The term occurs three times in 2:15–21. In 2:16 Paul has twice referred to "the faith of [Jesus] Christ," and in 2:20 to "the faith of the Son of the God." This phrase could mean "human faith in [Jesus] Christ / the Son of God" (the traditional rendering), but it more probably refers to Christ's (the Son of God's) own faith (or faithfulness), and in particular to his faithful death on the cross (see Excursus 9 and comment on 2:15–16). Thus, in the three instances of the noun prior to 3:2, it has referred to Christ's own faith(fulness) as disclosed in his death on the cross, a death explicitly mentioned four times in the four verses

---

259. The only other instance in Paul's recognized letters occurs in 1 Cor 12:17, where it means "ear" or "faculty of hearing" (see BDAG, 36).

immediately preceding 3:2 (2:19, 20, 21; 3:1). If that is a correct interpretation of the instances of the term *pistis Christou / huiou theou* ("the faith of Christ / the Son of God") in 2:16 and 20, it follows that *pistis* in 3:2 (and mutatis mutandis, in 3:5) most probably has the same referential meaning it had in 2:15–21: the faith of Christ, the Son of God himself. That is, if *pistis* in 2:16 and 2:20 does indeed refer to Christ's own faith or faithfulness—if that is what Paul intended and what the Galatians will have heard—then it is probable that *pistis* in 3:2 (and 3:5) is intended by Paul to have the same referential meaning and will be heard by Galatians to have this referential meaning as well. The noteworthy parallelism between 3:2 and 2:16 supports this line of interpretation:

3:2 the reception of the Spirit "on the basis of [*ek*] works of the law" *or* "on the basis of [*ek*] what was heard of faith"

2:16 justification "on the basis of [*ek*] works of the law" *or* "on the basis of [*ek*] the faith of Christ."

Therefore, "faith" in 3:2 seems to have the same reference as "faith" in 2:16. In short, if 2:16; 2:19–21; and 3:1 are any guide, the phrase *ex akoēs pisteōs* in 3:2 may be paraphrased as follows: "on the basis of what was heard of the faith of Christ,"[260] that is, "of Christ's faithful death on the cross."

Three brief comments on this paraphrase are in order. (1) In a sense "Christ's faithful death on the cross" is indeed "the gospel [message]" that is believed, but the specific reference of the term *pistis* remains Christ's own faith or faithfulness rather than what human beings believe about it. (2) It actually makes little or no difference if the Galatians will take *akoē* to mean "hearing" instead of "what was heard." The word can be taken to mean "hearing" or "what was heard" without affecting the basic sense.[261] (3) With respect to the referential meaning of *pistis*, the offered paraphrase represents not only the probable intention of Paul, who has just dictated 2:15–3:1, but also the probable reception of his words by the Galatians, who will just then have heard the same passage read aloud to them.

In this line of interpretation, Paul is not contrasting two human acts—observing the law and believing in Christ (Dunn 154)—but a human act (observing the law) and God's act in Christ (Martyn 286–89). Here the specific concern of Paul is not the faith (the believing activity or response) of the Galatians (what they did), but the manner in which they received the Spirit (what happened to them). They received the Spirit when they heard the message of Christ crucified (3:1).

---

260. This rendering understands the phrase *akoē pisteōs* to involve an objective genitive.

261. Witherington (212), following Lightfoot (135), argues that Paul contrasts observing the law and "another human activity of the Galatians, namely, 'hearing.'" But hearing (as opposed to listening) is for Paul not a human activity, but a human "passivity." Sounds fall on the ear and one hears them. Hearing involves no effort or decision whatsoever.

The Spirit and the True Heirs of the Promise Made to Abraham 177

No doubt what the Galatians heard from the mouth of Paul elicited their faith or trust (and this implication can hardly be excluded here, given the announcement in 2:16 that "we came to believe in Christ," and the claim in 3:22 that "the promise [of the Spirit] on the basis of the faith of Jesus Christ is given to those who believe"), but that is not what the words *ex akoēs pisteōs* refer to. The words refer to the proclamation of Christ's faithful death as heard by the Galatians and what happened to them when they heard it: They received the Spirit not as a result of anything they did (works of the law), but as a result of the proclamation of the crucified Christ falling on their ears (what was heard of his faith).

To sum up, Paul's rhetorical question may be paraphrased as follows: Did you receive the Spirit as a result of observing the commandments of the Mosaic law, or as a result of what you heard from me of Christ's faithful death on the cross? The Galatians know the answer as well as Paul does.

[3–5] After the rhetorical question of v. 2, Paul now poses a genuine question: "Are you so unthinking, having begun with the Spirit, are you now ending up with the flesh?" He once again refers to the Galatian Christians as unthinking, sincerely questioning the extent of their spiritual health. The repetition drives the wake-up call home.[262] True, they had begun with the Spirit, but they are now in danger of "ending up with the flesh." The two verbs "begin" and "end" form a natural contrasting pair (cf. Phil 1:6; 2 Cor 8:6), as do "Spirit" (or "spirit") and "flesh" (cf. Gal 5:13–6:10; Rom 1:3–4; 2:28–29; 1 Cor 5:5; 2 Cor 7:1; Phil 3:3–4; Col 2:5; 1 Tim 3:16). In view of Gal 6:12–13, "flesh" here is most probably a pointed reference to circumcision,[263] the act whereby the fleshly foreskin of the penis is removed: "For those who are wanting to make a good showing in the *flesh*, these are putting pressure on you to practice circumcision; . . . they are wanting you to practice circumcision in order that they may boast in your *flesh*."

In Gen 17, which the new preachers in Galatia are undoubtedly calling to the attention of the Galatian Christians (see Excursus 4; cf. 4:21–30), God says to Abraham: "Every male of you shall be circumcised. And you shall be circumcised in the *flesh* of your foreskin, and it shall be a sign of a covenant between me and you, . . . and my covenant shall be upon your *flesh* for an everlasting covenant" (Gen 17:10–11, 13 LXX). The allusion to circumcision in 3:3 will surely not escape the Galatians, and even less so the new preachers among them.

---

262. Paul could have asked: "Having begun with faith [Christ crucified], are you now ending up with works of the law?" But his rhetorical question in v. 2 concerned the reception of the Spirit, and to that topic he returns here.

263. The link to circumcision is further supported by the use of the verb *epiteleō* in 3:3 "in connexion with the performance of religious duties" (MM 247). Betz (132) points to the "cultic overtones" of both verbs (begin, end) in certain contexts (e.g., mystery religions).

Three other interpretations of this seemingly simple verse are possible, however. They are not necessarily incompatible with the one above.

View 1. The Galatians (and the new preachers among them) will understand the term "flesh" as an allusion to what Paul in 5:16 characterizes as "the [evil] desire of the flesh" (*epithymia sarkos*; Martyn 289–94). This stock expression (cf. Rom 13:14; 1 John 2:16) probably represents the Hebrew *yetser basar* (= *yēṣer bāśār*), "the impulse [or inclination] of the flesh" (see comment on 5:16). The rabbinic literature of a later time refers to this impulse of the flesh as "the evil impulse," *yetser harah* (= *yēṣer hāraʿ*; see Davies 20–31). According to the *Community Rule* from Qumran (1QS), a member of the community is not to "walk in the stubbornness of his heart in order to go astray following his heart and his eyes and the musings of his inclination [*yēṣer*]. Instead he should *circumcise* in the Community *the foreskin of his tendency* [*yēṣer*]" (1QS 5.4–5).[264] The language of circumcision is here being used metaphorically, and the import of this metaphorical use is clear: the literal circumcision of the foreskin (which signifies a male's incorporation into God's covenant people) also involves, or should involve, the cutting away of the fleshly impulse to wrongdoing. It is entirely conceivable that the new preachers were propounding a similar teaching: incorporation into the people of the covenant and the law through the rite of circumcision is also an antidote for the fleshly impulse to sinful behavior (see on 5:16). When the Galatians, after being instructed about the impulse of the flesh by the new preachers, hear Paul's question in 3:3 for the first time, they may readily understand it to imply that ending up with fleshly circumcision is tantamount to ending up with the fleshly impulse, which turns the teaching of the new preachers on its head. Paul's formulation of the question is thus part of his campaign against the views of the new preachers.

View 2. For Paul himself, "the desire [or impulse] of the flesh" is a sign of something much more powerful in human life, a fearsome, cosmic power called "the Flesh," which stands opposed to the Spirit (see comments on 5:13–6:10). By taking up fleshly circumcision, Paul implies, the Galatian Christians will leave the realm of the Spirit and end up in that of the Flesh. It is difficult to know, however, whether the Galatians (and the new preachers listening to Paul's letter with them) will catch this possible allusion to the Flesh as a cosmic power in the initial reading (or hearing) of the letter. They may well make the connection on a rereading, or a rehearing, just as later interpreters have done.

View 3. The latter part of the question that Paul poses can be rendered in another way: "Are you now being *perfected* by means of the flesh?" (taking the verb *epiteleisthe* as a passive instead of a middle).[265] This rendering implies that

---

264. On "flesh" as the locus of sinful impulses and needing purification by God's spirit, see 1QS 3.9; 4.20–21; 11.9.

265. Lightfoot (135) points out that the middle voice is not attested elsewhere in the LXX or NT.

the new preachers had linked the rite of circumcision and subsequent adherence to the law to a notion of perfection. There is good evidence for this notion in Jewish thought of the time. In the book of *Jubilees*, a retelling of Genesis and Exodus, God asks Abraham to be "perfect" (15.3). According to 23.10, Abraham was indeed "perfect in all of his actions with the LORD." According to the later Mishnah (*Ned.* 3:11), "Great is circumcision, for in spite of all the virtues that Abraham our father fulfilled, he was not called 'perfect' until he was circumcised, as it is written, 'Walk before me, and be thou perfect [*tāmîm*]' [Gen 17:1]."[266] The *Community Rule* (1QS) emphasizes from beginning to end the importance of "walking perfectly" (*tāmîm*) on paths laid out or revealed by God (cf., e.g., 1QS 1.8; 2.2; 3.3–4, 9; 5.24; 9.2, 5–6, 8–9, 19; 11.17). A passage in another document (CD 2.14–16) makes an explicit connection between walking in perfection and resistance to the evil impulse: "And now, my sons, listen to me and I shall open your eyes so that you can see and understand the deeds of God, so that you can choose what he is pleased with and repudiate what he hates, so that you can *walk perfectly* on all his paths and not allow yourselves to be attracted by the thoughts of a guilty inclination (*yēṣer*) and lascivious eyes." Similar views can also be found in Jewish Christian texts. According to *Didache* 6.2, "If you can bear the entire yoke of the Lord [i.e., the whole law], you will be perfect [*teleios*]." Most interesting in this regard is Jas 2:21–23: "Was not Abraham our father justified by works [*ex ergōn*], when he offered his son Isaac upon the altar? You see that faith was active along with his works, and faith was completed [*eteleiōthē*] by works [*ex ergōn*]" (RSV).

The new preachers in Galatia could thus conceivably have said to Paul's Galatian converts: by undertaking the rite of circumcision, you will not only enter the covenant community; you will also be enabled to achieve a form of perfection, in your living (walking) according to the law of God, which is God's remedy for the fleshly impulse. The first step on the road to perfection is circumcision, as it was for Abraham (cf. Gen 17:1 above). Works of the law, beginning with circumcision, produce perfection, complementing faith. In this line of interpretation, it is possible "that Paul's missionary efforts were taken as merely the first step, and that the opponents claimed to provide the necessary and final measures to bring salvation to completion and perfection" (Betz 136). Paul's question in v. 3 would then be alluding to fleshly circumcision as a step on the way to perfection: having begun with the Spirit, are you now being perfected (on the way to perfection) by undertaking fleshly circumcision?

As already indicated in Excursus 4, there are three significant problems with this line of interpretation: (1) It presupposes that the new preachers see no necessary link between the gift or reception of the Spirit and the observance of the law. Their position would then be as follows: Thanks to Paul, the Galatians

---

266. The Mishnah in its final form dates from ca. 200 C.E. but contains earlier traditions.

already have the Spirit; they now also need the law, and we are here to give it to them. The rhetorical question back in v. 2 presupposes, however, that the new preachers see the Spirit to be entirely dependent on the law. (2) It implies that the new preachers have a positive attitude toward what Paul has already accomplished in Galatia. That is unlikely (see 1:6–9 and comment there). (3) It implies that Paul acknowledges circumcision to produce or lead to the perfection promised by the new preachers. One way to avoid this implication is to regard the question as ironic, even sarcastic (Martyn 1997: 289, among others). This is possible, but the other rendering of the verb in question ("ending up with," as the complement to "beginning with"; cf. Phil 1:6; 2 Cor 8:6) is more plausible, since the question is then straightforward and makes very good sense: Though the Galatians started off on the right road, they are now in danger of ending up at the wrong destination. Paul is deeply concerned, as the next question bears out.

In v. 4 Paul poses another genuine question: "Have you experienced so many things in vain, if indeed they were also in vain?" The verb "experienced" (*epathete*) is the past tense (aorist) of a verb (*paschō*) which elsewhere in Paul's genuine letters (1 Cor 12:26; 2 Cor 1:6; Phil 1:29; 1 Thess 2:14), the remainder of the NT, and the LXX always means "suffer" or "endure" in an unfavorable sense (BDAG 785). That meaning is difficult to sustain here, though not impossible. The Gentile Christians in Galatia could have suffered persecution at the hands of their Gentile neighbors (4:29; 6:12; cf. 1 Thess 2:14; 1 Pet 4:12–14; 5:9). In literature outside of the Bible, however, "experience" is a common meaning of the verb; the adverbs "favorably" (*eu*) and "unfavorably" (*kakōs*) frequently accompany the verb to indicate whether the experience was pleasant or unpleasant (see BDAG 785; LSJ 1347). If "experienced" is the intended meaning of the verb, Paul is presumably referring especially to the work of the Spirit among the Galatians, which is mentioned in the immediately preceding and following verses. It also seems likely that the Gentile Galatians will so understand the verb, given the context in which it is being used.

The last clause of v. 4 expresses the hope that what the Galatian Christians have experienced of the Spirit may not actually have been for nothing. Paul is deeply concerned about the situation, but he would not be writing the letter if he thought it was hopeless. By adding the clause, he causes the Galatians to share his hope and his concern. These considerations would also apply if suffering and persecution are in view.

Paul concludes the argument in this paragraph with another rhetorical question: "Therefore, the One who lavishes the Spirit on you and works deeds of power among you—[does He do so] on the basis of works of the law or on the basis of what is heard of faith?" (v. 5). The verse is elliptical; the words "does He do so" have no counterpart in the Greek. To this rhetorical question about the Spirit, as to the very similar one in v. 2, Paul knows the answer, and he expects the Galatians also to know the answer if they will stop being unthinking and stop listening to the so-called gospel of the new preachers. There are, however, two key differences from the question in v. 2. Attention shifts from the past ("you received" in v. 2, presumably referring to the time that the Galatians first heard the message of faith) to the present ("he who lavishes," a present participle, *ho epichorēgōn*, in v. 5). There is also a change of subject, from "you" in v. 2 to God in v. 5, for He is the one who lavishes the Spirit even now, not on the basis of "works of the law" but on the basis of "what is heard of faith," as God had done when the Galatians first heard the gospel (see comment on v. 2). The Greek verb translated to "lavish" means "generously provide" or "supply" what is needed (BDAG 387), and that nuance is probably present here (cf. Rom 5:5). The overall point is that observing the law is totally irrelevant to God's activity of providing the Spirit to the Galatians. God lavishes the Spirit on the Galatians through what is heard of faith—the faith of Christ—not through the observance of the law. God is no more tied to the law than the Galatians ought to be!

As in v. 2, Paul's point is probably directed against the new preachers in Galatia and their insistence on a connection between the works of the law and the Spirit. In *Jubilees* 1.23–24, where God makes an eschatological promise to Moses on behalf of his people Israel, the observance of the law (the doing of the commandments) seems to be a consequence of the gift of a holy spirit at the eschaton (cf. Ezek 11:19–20): "And I shall cut off the foreskin of their heart and the foreskin of the heart of their descendants. And I shall create for them a holy spirit, and I shall purify them so that they will not turn away from following me from that day and forever. And their souls will cleave to me and to all my commandments. And they will do my commandments."

In a similar way, the new preachers in Galatia are probably saying to the Galatians that the initial reception of the Spirit will lead to what amounts to an ongoing perfect observance of the law (see on v. 3) in the new age inaugurated by Christ (cf. Matt 5:17–20). According to them, the continuing gift of the Spirit enables believers to observe the law completely, once the practice of circumcision has been adopted as the first step. As in v. 2, Paul reminds the Galatians in v. 5 that their own experience of the Spirit proves such a link between law observance and the ongoing work of the Spirit to be utterly false and irrelevant.[267] The Spirit depends on "what is heard of faith," what is heard of Christ's faithful death (2:16; 3:1).

---

267. Martyn (284) surmises that in the worship services of the Galatian churches, the new preachers (whom he calls "the Teachers") "are showing the Galatians that Law-observant exegesis of the Scriptures is the means by which one can be assured of a steady supply of the Spirit and its wonder-working power." These worship services, therefore, "are focused not only on the observance of the Law but also and concretely on exegesis of the Law as the faithful activity to which God responds by continuing to give the Spirit" (Martyn 286, following Georgi 258–64).

In v. 5 God is described not only in terms of generously supplying the Spirit but also in terms of working "deeds of power" among (or in) the Galatians. Indeed, in the Greek the two descriptions of God are coordinate, with the Greek definite article *ho* covering both participles: "the One who lavishes the Spirit on you *and* works [*energōn*] deeds of power among [or in] you." This means that God's giving of the Spirit also involves his working powerful deeds, and vice versa. The two go together. But what exactly are these deeds of power (*dynameis*)? That is an extremely difficult question to answer. The word does not occur elsewhere in Galatians, and Paul does not bother to explain what he means. Presumably the Galatians will know what he is referring to. There seem to be three possibilities, all based upon information provided in Paul's two Letters to the Corinthians:

View 1. The Galatians themselves were enabled by the Spirit to work deeds of power, here understood to be miracles. The word *dynamis* was commonly used for power, might, force, and the like, including the power to work miracles or wonders, and hence also for a deed of power or a miracle (cf. BDAG, 262–63). In 1 Cor 12:4–11, Paul asserts that "there are varieties of gifts [*charismata*], but the same Spirit" (v. 4 RSV; cf. v. 11), and he goes on to list a number of them: "to one is given through the Spirit a word of wisdom [v. 8 AT], . . . to another gifts of healing [v. 9], . . . to another workings [*energēmata*] of *deeds of power* [*dynameis*; v. 10 AT]," and so on. These gifts, or the exercise of them, are labeled "the manifestation of the Spirit" (v. 7). Twice more in this chapter, Paul refers to the working of deeds of power: "God has appointed in the church first apostles, second prophets, third teachers, then [workers of] *deeds of power*. . . . Are all apostles? Are all prophets? Are all teachers? Are all [workers of] *deeds of power*?" (1 Cor 12:28–29, alt.). However, what these "deeds of power" are remains uncertain. Fee (595) surmises that the term here "covers a broad range of supernatural events that ordinary parlance would call miraculous," including healings and exorcisms. The phrase "works deeds of power among you" in Gal 3:5 could also then, and perhaps more plausibly, be rendered "works powers in [and thus through] you," on the model of Matt 14:2 (Lightfoot 136), where it is said of John the Baptist that healing "powers are at work in him [*hai dynameis energousin en autō*]."

View 2. The deeds of power are the miracles that Paul himself performed among the Galatians ("among you") as an apostle of Christ. In 2 Cor 12:12, Paul writes: "The signs of a true apostle were performed among you in all patience, with signs and wonders and *deeds of power*" (RSV, alt.). Presumably, Paul is here referring to the sorts of miracles attributed to him in Acts 14:8–10; 16:16–18; 19:11–12; 20:7–12; 28:1–9 (cf. Acts 2:22; 15:12; Rom 15:19). In his comment on 2 Cor 12:12, Furnish (1984: 556) claims that Paul is probably referring to "some kind of miraculous occurrences, perhaps healings, which took place (despite the silence of Acts 18) when he was preaching the gospel" to the Corinthians. The same could thus apply to Paul's initial preaching of the gospel to the Galatians (cf. 4:13–14).

View 3. The "deeds of power" concern the initial coming to faith of the Galatians and the diverse manifestations of the Spirit that followed. In 1 Cor 2:1–5, Paul writes of first coming to the Corinthians and proclaiming to them "Jesus Christ and him crucified" (2:2). He continues: "And I was with you in weakness and in much fear and trembling; and my speech and my message were not in plausible words of wisdom, but in demonstration of the Spirit and of power [*dynamis*],[268] that your faith [*pistis*] might not rest in the wisdom of men but in the power [*dynamis*] of God" (1 Cor 2:3–5 RSV). Paul here links a number of items that are also linked in Gal 3:1–5: the proclamation of Christ crucified, the Spirit, and power (specified further as "the power of God"). Fee (95) maintains that, in view of Paul's references to his "weakness" (1 Cor 2:3), the powerful demonstration of the Spirit in 1 Cor 2:1–5 probably does not refer to deeds of power (miracles) of the sort mentioned in 2 Cor 12:12, but to the "actual conversion" of the Corinthians themselves, "with the concomitant gift of the Spirit, which was probably evidenced by spiritual gifts" (such as those mentioned in 1 Cor 12). One such manifestation of the Spirit could be the "deeds of power" (usually understood to be miracles) in 1 Cor 12:10, 28–29, but other manifestations of the Spirit may also be in view.

Galatians 3:5 could be interpreted in a similar way. According to 3:2, the Galatians first received the Spirit as a result of "what was heard of faith," as a result of what they heard of Christ and his faithful death on the cross. They undoubtedly came to believe in Christ, or to place their trust in him, at the same time (cf. 2:16). According to 3:5, God *continues* to supply the Galatians with the Spirit and *continues* to work deeds of power in or among the Galatian Christians on the same basis. The deeds of power referred to may thus not be limited to miracles of healing and the like but may also include the moment the Galatians first came to believe in Christ and a diverse array of charismatic or spiritual gifts of the sort enumerated in 1 Cor 12. Believing in Christ is itself for Paul a work of God, a "miracle." As noted above, God's giving of the Spirit and his working of such powerful deeds are coordinate activities; the one activity entails the other. Paul's understanding of the Spirit comes here into partial view: the Spirit is God's eschatologically new, apocalyptically powerful presence in the world (see further comments on 4:6; 5:16).

How then is God, the supplier of the Spirit and the worker of deeds of power, present among Galatians? Surely the answer cannot be doubted. The experience of the Galatians itself is the proof that God is active and present among

---

268. Fee (95) comments: "The combination here is probably very close to a hendiadys (the use of two words to express the same reality: 'the Spirit, that is, Power')." For this reason, to "speak of the Spirit is automatically to speak of power (cf. Rom 15:13, 19)."

them not as a result of their observance of the law, but as the result of what they continue to hear of Christ and his faithful death. In sum, in 3:1–5, Paul has begun to establish the plausibility of the gospel preached by him and to refute the different gospel of the new preachers by appealing to the Galatians' own experience of the Spirit: it had, and has, nothing to do with observance of the law and everything to do with what they have heard, and continue to hear, of Christ's faithful death.

3:6–14 The Blessing of Abraham and the Curse of the Law

Paul has just reminded the Galatians of something they already know from their own experience: the Spirit that they had received when they came to believe in Christ was given to them, not as a result of their observance of the law, but as a result of the proclamation they heard of Christ's own faith: his faithful death on the cross on their behalf. God continues to lavish the Spirit on them on the very same basis, as they also know from firsthand experience. The reception of the Spirit was and is not in any way dependent upon the Galatians' observing the law. The present passage now argues that the reception of the Spirit "through faith" (v. 14), meaning the faith of Christ (see Excursus 11, below), has made Gentile believers, no less than Jewish believers, the (metaphorical and theological) "sons [*huioi*] of Abraham," thus *heirs* of the promise that God made to the patriarch (vv. 7, 14).[269] That promise concerned the gift of the Spirit, which for this reason is called "the blessing of Abraham" (v. 14). The Spirit attests to the present reality of justification, which for Paul entails God's apocalyptic rectification of the human cosmos (vv. 8, 11; cf. 2:16, 21; 3:24–26; 5:5). The metaphorical and theological "sons of Abraham"—a group that includes Gentile as well as Jewish believers, and female believers as well as male (cf. 3:28)—are thus "those who are from faith" (*hoi ek pisteōs*), those who derive their identity from faith (v. 9). By contrast, "those who are from works of the law" (*hosoi ex ergōn nomou eisin*), those who derive their identity from works of the law, do not receive this blessing but stand "under a curse" (v. 10). Paul thereby implies that for the Galatians to begin observing the law is to go under a curse and to leave behind the blessing of the Spirit. Curse and blessing are mutually exclusive, as in Deut 27–30, from which Paul quotes in

---

269. Paul's picture of sons and heirs is determined (a) by ancient patriarchal society in which sons inherited from their fathers (cf. Gal 4:1–2) and (b) by the particular instance of Abraham, whose heir was his son, Isaac (cf. 4:28). For this reason, the translation "children" for the Greek *huioi* ("sons") would be misleading, distorting Paul's point: the issue is not simply the offspring (descendants) of Abraham but his *heirs*. Paul continually modulates and subverts this patriarchal picture, however, in the remainder of the letter, most notably in 3:28 ("in Christ there is no male and female") and 4:21–5:1 (the allegorical interpretation of the story of Sarah and Hagar). See comments on these passages and on 4:1–7.

v. 10 (Deut 27:26). Paul instructs the Galatians that Christ, through his faithful death, has "redeemed [all of] us" precisely from "the curse of the law," so that "the blessing of Abraham" might come "to the Gentiles" who believe as well as to the Jews who believe, so that "we [believers] might [all] receive the promise of the Spirit through the faith [of Christ]" (vv. 13–14).

Three related assumptions appear to lie behind Paul's argument in this passage: (1) The God of Jesus is also the God of Abraham. (2) The gift of the Spirit that God has bestowed and still bestows (3:1–5) on those who "have come to believe in Christ" (2:16b) is the fulfillment of a promise that God made to Abraham. (3) This gift is given to the "sons of Abraham" (v. 7), to his "offspring" (*sperma*) and "heirs" (*klēronomoi*, 3:29). Paul does not pause to justify these three assumptions since they evidently represent common ground between him and the new preachers in Galatia. The point of contention is whether God's promise to Abraham finds its fulfillment in "those who are from faith" (v. 7) or in "those who are from works of the law" (v. 10). Who are truly the "sons [offspring and heirs] of Abraham": the former or the latter? Paul has been forced to address this issue because the new preachers have been telling the Galatians that by practicing circumcision, a rite that for Jews began with Abraham (Gen 17:9–14), and then observing the remainder of the Law (5:2–4; 6:12), they will become "sons" or "offspring" of Abraham (3:7, 29), and so members of the covenant people of Israel. Only as such can they also be "heirs" (3:29) of "the promise of the Spirit" (3:14). Paul here addresses the issue of the identity of Abraham's progeny because the new preachers have raised this issue, and he does so by interpreting "the Scripture" (v. 8)—to which they themselves appeal—in a new way, one determined by his own understanding of "the gospel of Christ" (1:7). He will disclose to the Galatians that "the Scripture" (the Jewish writings that Christians came to know as the OT) supports the identification of "the sons of Abraham" with "those who are from faith," and thus that the promised Spirit was meant for them exclusively, not (also) for "those who are from works of the law." The issue of the true progeny of Abraham runs through the remainder of chapter 3, reaching its culmination in the last verse, where Paul asserts that those who belong to Christ are "the [real] offspring of Abraham" because they are "heirs according to a promise" (3:29), a promise in which the law and its observance play no role whatsoever. Every positive statement about "faith" in this chapter implies a negative one about "works of the law," in accordance with the antinomy postulated in 2:16, 21.

This passage has three sense units. In the first (vv. 6–9), Paul identifies "those who are from faith" as the exclusive "sons" of Abraham. In the second (vv. 10–12), Paul seeks to show that "those who are from works of the law" are under a curse and that the law is therefore utterly incompatible with faith since the latter bestows a blessing. In the third (vv. 13–14), Paul proclaims that

Christ has redeemed "[all of] us" from the law's curse, whereby "we [all]" could "receive the promise of the Spirit through faith."

3:6 Just as Abraham: "He believed God, and it was reckoned to him as justification."[a] **7** Know therefore that those who are from faith, these people are the sons of Abraham. **8** The Scripture, having foreseen that God justifies the Gentiles on the basis of faith, preached the gospel in advance[b] to Abraham: "In you shall all the Gentiles be blessed." **9** So then, those who are from faith are blessed with the faithful Abraham.

10 For those who are from works of the law are under a curse. For it stands written: "Accursed is everyone who does not remain in all the things written in the book of the law so as to do them." **11** And because no one is justified before God in the law, it is evident that "the just one from faith shall live." **12** The law, however, is not "from faith," but "the one having done them shall live in them."

13 Christ redeemed us from the curse of the law, having become a curse for us, because it stands written: "Accursed is everyone who hangs on a tree," **14** so that the blessing of Abraham might come to the Gentiles in Christ Jesus,[d] so that we might receive the promise[c] of the Spirit through faith.

a. All Greek words from the stem *dikai-* (*dikaiosynē, dikaioō, dikaios*) in this passage (as in 2:15–21) have been translated using words from the stem "just-" (justification, justify, just), in order to preserve as much as possible the visual, aural, and semantic relationships among them, evident in the Greek. Other possible translations (rectification/righteousness; rectify, make righteous, or declare righteous; and the like) obscure these relationships to a greater degree. The primarily forensic nuances of the Greek terms thereby also remain discernible; these form the shared starting point for Paul and the new preachers in Galatia. Yet in the process of articulating his own theology, Paul gives them new, nonforensic meanings (see comment on 2:15–16 and further below).

b. The words "preached the gospel in advance" render a single Greek word, *proeuēngelisato*.

c. Influenced by the use of the term earlier in the verse, some manuscripts, including 𝔓46 and D, here have *eulogian* ("blessing"). Supporting the chosen reading are ℵ, A, B, C, Ψ, 33, and 1739, among others.

d. Some manuscripts read "in Jesus Christ," instead of "in Christ Jesus." There is probably no difference in meaning. See on 2:16 for the same variation there.

[6–9] In v. 6 Paul introduces the figure of Abraham. Why? One probable reason is that the Galatians have been hearing much about Abraham from the new preachers in Galatia, who claim that by practicing circumcision as Abraham did and thereby committing themselves to doing the law the Galatians will become

The Spirit and the True Heirs of the Promise Made to Abraham 187

"sons of Abraham," thus heirs of "the promises" (3:16, 21) God made to Abraham. Genesis 17:9–14 almost certainly plays a central role in their preaching:

> ⁹And God said to Abraam, "You shall keep my covenant, you and your seed after you for their generations. ¹⁰And this is the covenant that you shall keep between me and *you*, and between your seed after you for their generations; every male of *you* shall be circumcised. ¹¹And *you* shall be circumcised in the flesh of *your* foreskin, and it shall be for a sign of a covenant between me and *you*. ¹²And a child of eight days shall be circumcised by *you*. Every male throughout *your* generations . . . ¹³shall surely be circumcised, . . . and my covenant shall be on *your* flesh for an everlasting covenant. ¹⁴And an uncircumcised male who will not be circumcised in the flesh of his foreskin on the eighth day, that person shall be utterly destroyed from his nation, for he has rejected my covenant.

This translation is based on the LXX, since that is the Bible being used by both the new preachers and Paul. Where the second-person pronoun "you" represents a plural form in the Greek, it has been italicized. These plurals indicate that the passage was composed with later generations in view.

Moreover, in Jewish tradition contemporary with Paul, Abraham is regarded as the first proselyte who abandoned idolatry in exchange for the worship of the one true God (cf. e.g., Philo, *Abr.* 60–88). He subsequently became the founding patriarch of Israel by taking up the practice of circumcision, as God commanded according to Gen 17:9–14, and by keeping the law even before it was given to Moses on Mount Sinai:

Genesis 26:5 LXX: Your father Abraham obeyed my voice and kept my charges and my commandments and my statutes and my laws.
Sirach 44:19–20 LXX: Abraham was the great father of a multitude of nations, and no one has been found like him in glory. He kept the law of the Most High, and entered into a covenant with him; he certified the covenant in his flesh.
Jubilees 23.10: For Abraham was perfect in all his actions with the LORD and was pleasing through righteousness all of the days of his life.
Jubilees 24.11: Your father [Abraham] obeyed me and observed my restrictions and my commandments and my laws and my ordinances and my covenant.

Paul ignores these and other texts to which the new preachers may be appealing for their gospel, citing instead a biblical text (Gen 15:6 LXX) that links Abraham, believing, and justification without mentioning a single commandment: "Just as Abraham: 'He believed [*episteusen*] God, and it was reckoned to him as justification [*dikaiosynēn*]'" (v. 6). From this text, Paul will in the next verse draw the conclusion that only "those who are from faith" are truly the "sons" (heirs) of Abraham. Paul will allude to this text again in v. 8a and in v. 9 (see comments below).

It is impossible to know whether Paul has chosen this text on his own initiative or is responding to an interpretation of it by the new preachers in Galatia. Allusions to and partial quotations of this text can be found in contemporary Jewish literature, indicating that it was the object of reflection. The author of 1 Macc 2:52, for example, echoes Gen 15:6 when he asks: "Was not Abraham found faithful in testing [cf. Gen 22:1–19], and it was reckoned to him as justification?" (RSV). The reckoning of justification to Abraham follows from his obedience to God in connection with the requested sacrifice of his son Isaac (cf. Sir 44:20; *Jub.* 17.15–16). Abraham further functions here as the model of zeal for the law, for the cited verse is preceded by the following: "Now children, be zealous for the law, and give your lives for the covenant of our fathers. And remember the works [*erga*] of the fathers, which they did [*epoiēsan*] in their generations; and receive great honor and an eternal name" (1 Macc 2:50–51 LXX, AT; see Excursus 8). In Ps 106:31–32 (105:31–32 LXX), the Phinehas who slew Zimri son of Salu and his Midianite consort (Num 25:6–15) is presented as a model zealot (as he is in 1 Macc 2:23–28) whose violent deed "is reckoned to him as justification." This echo of Gen 15:6 suggests that Phinehas's deed is implicitly "Abrahamic." The Qumran document devoted to "works of the law," *ma'ăśê ha-Torah* (4QMMT = 4Q398), seems to echo Gen 15:6 when it promises: "It shall be reckoned to you [pl.] as justification when you do [*'āsâ*] what is upright and good before him, for your good and that of Israel" (alt.; see Excursus 8). Here the reckoning of justification is made contingent on doing the law. The Jewish Christian author of James interprets Gen 15:6 to mean that "someone is justified on the basis of [*ek*] works and not on the basis of [*ek*] faith alone" (2:23–24 AT), though the author is probably here responding to Paul and his putatively one-sided interpretation of the Genesis passage, whereby works are expressly excluded. Genesis 15:6, part of the core Scripture of the Jews (the Torah), was thus interpreted in a way consistent with the portrait of the fully law-observant and obedient Abraham, seen in the passages cited from Sirach and *Jubilees* above (cf. Longenecker 110–12). Paul gives Gen 15:6 a new and daring interpretation, one consistent with and even determined by the antinomy between "works of the law" and "the faith of Christ" posited in 2:16 (and 2:21). The key for Paul is that the passage makes no mention of the law or of a commandment at all in connection with justification. Abraham receives justification simply on the basis of his belief in God.

Paul's introduction to the citation is abrupt, leading some interpreters to suggest that "just as" (*kathōs*) is an abbreviation for "just as it stands written" (*kathōs gegraptai*; cf., e.g., Rom 1:17; 1 Cor 1:31), which would mean that the word "Abraham" belongs to the text being cited from Gen 15:6 rather than to the introductory formula (so Betz 140; Vouga 71; Dunn 160): "Just as it stands written: 'Abraham believed God, and it was reckoned to him as justification.'" The citation then seems to match the text of the LXX exactly, except that in the LXX the verb ("believed") actually stands before the subject (*episteusen Abram* instead of *Abraam episteusen*, as Paul has in v. 6). Paul follows the inverse word order of the LXX text when he cites Gen 15:6 in Rom 4:2, which indicates that his failure to do so here, in v. 6, is probably intentional. It thus seems likely that "Abraham" belongs to the citation's introductory formula: "Just as Abraham: 'He believed God . . .'" (so RSV, NRSV, NIV, NAB). The introductory formula means "and so it was with Abraham" (Lightfoot), "take Abraham as the example" (Longenecker), or "things were the same with Abraham" (Martyn). Paul's way of introducing the citation remains peculiar and without parallel, however, and it is thus unclear whether Paul actually intends to mark the words from Gen 15:6 as a quotation, as he does in Rom 4:2 (introducing the quotation with "What does the Scripture say?" cf. Gal 3:8, 10, 13), or simply weaves them into his own text, as the NRSV assumes: "Just as Abraham 'believed God, and it was reckoned to him as righteousness,' so, you see, those who believe are the descendants of Abraham." The NRSV with its quotation marks (omitted by KJV, NJB) knows that Paul is quoting from Gen 15:6, and Paul surely knows he is quoting from Gen 15:6, but will the Gentile Galatians know this, at least on a first reading? Ancient Greek manuscripts of the NT unfortunately contain little or no punctuation, and we do not know what Paul intends nor whether the person who shall read the letter aloud to the Galatians will pause or wink knowingly, nor then how the Galatians will hear these words. In favor of a marked quotation are (1) v. 7, which draws a conclusion (*ara*, "therefore") from the words about Abraham in v. 6, and (2) v. 8a, which restates this conclusion as something foreseen by "the Scripture" (see comment below). The new preachers in Galatia will surely recognize Paul's words as a quotation. Still, the fact that Paul does not unambiguously mark the words cited from Gen 15:6 as a quotation may indicate that what the person of Abraham did is more important to him than the fact that the report of it is found in "the Scripture." As the peculiar introduction indicates ("Just as Abraham . . . ," v. 6), Abraham *himself* is being summoned as an authority here, not the Scripture as such.

Verse 6 assumes what is made plain in v. 8, that Abraham "believed" a promise that God made to him, that promise (according to Paul) being, "In you [Abraham] shall all the Gentiles be blessed" (a quotation from Gen 12:3 with elements from 18:18; see comment below). This promise presupposes and includes another promise: Abraham would be blessed with a son and thus an heir (cf. v. 7). This promise is found in Gen 15:2–5, immediately preceding the report of Abraham's believing response in 15:6, and anticipated by Gen 12:2 ("I will make you into a great nation" [RSV]). "To be blessed" thus presupposes and includes "to have many descendants and heirs." The verb *pisteuein*, "believe," when followed by a dative as here (*tō theō*, lit., "to God," v. 6),[270] normally means "give credence to someone about something" or "to believe something to be true" (cf. BDAG 816–17) and not "place one's trust in" (which is the meaning of the verb in Gal 2:16, where it is followed by a prepositional phrase beginning with *eis*: "We came to believe [place our trust] *in* Christ Jesus," *episteusamen eis Christon Iēsoun*). Abraham thus "believed God," that is, he believed God's promise to be true and reliable (cf. 4:28). This conviction (cf. Rom 4:21) was "reckoned to him as justification [*dikaiosynē*]," meaning that Abraham was recognized as "just" (*dikaios*, "righteous") by God because by believing God's promise he proved himself also to have acted justly and thus to be just. Since God's promise preceded Abraham's believing, the latter was not a self-generated decision on the part of Abraham; it was called into being by God's promise itself, which fell on the ears of Abraham, just as the proclamation of the faithful death of Christ on the cross fell, and continues to fall, on the ears of the Galatians, bringing the gift of the Spirit with it (see comment on 3:2, 5). Abraham believed, as it were, on the basis of what was heard of God's promise.

Specifically, Abraham provides an analogy ("just as") for those who "have come to believe in Christ Jesus" so that they "might be justified on the basis of the faith of Christ and not on the basis of works of the law" (2:16). However, we must stress that Abraham provides *only* an analogy, and a rough one at that, for believers in Christ. It cannot be pressed too far, for obvious reasons: The "believing" of Christians involves (1) placing trust in (2) Christ (*pisteuein + eis*), whereas the "believing" of Abraham involves (1) giving credence to (2) God (*pisteuein* + dative). The "believing" of Christians is thus not only different in kind from that of Abraham; it is also directed to Christ, not to God.[271] Furthermore, their justification, unlike Abraham's, is already contained in God's prior act in Christ: his faithful death on the cross. Their believing in Christ, as their reception of the Spirit demonstrates (3:1–5), signifies their participation in this cosmic event for which "justification" in the sense of "declare just/righteous" provides an inadequate description; God rectifies

---

270. Paul uses this construction also in Rom 4:3 (again quoting Gen 15:6); Rom 4:17; and 10:16 (quoting Isa 53:1) (cf. BDF #294.2).

271. This observation provides the basis for the view that Abraham's faith is the model for Christ's own faith since the latter was also directed to God, as was Abraham's (Hays 2002: 173). While God's raising Jesus may have been understood by Paul as tantamount to the justification (vindication) of the faithful Jesus, Paul speaks in v. 8 of God's "justifying the Gentiles," not of Christ's doing so. Paul has not yet thought through all the possible ramifications of his contextually generated appeal to Abraham.

(makes just/righteous) those who believe in Christ by delivering them from enslaving powers, one of these being "the curse of the law" (3:13). Abraham, therefore, is not here for Paul the model for believers in Christ; he is not the first Christian. Paul's appeal to Gen 15:6 serves a specific and limited purpose, to show the Galatians (and the new preachers who shall be listening to the letter with them) that the exclusive relationship between "believing" (*pisteuein*) and "justification" (*dikaiosynē, dikaiousthai*) posited in 2:16, 21 has its precedent, and thus its anticipation, in (the story of) the first patriarch himself.[272] Paul will now go on to exploit that precedent and that anticipation throughout the remainder of chapter 3.

In v. 7, Paul asks the Galatians to embrace the exegetical conclusion he draws from the scripturally recorded example of Abraham: "Know [*ginōskete*][273] therefore that those who are from faith, *these* people [*houtoi*] are the sons of Abraham." The formulation appears to be polemically motivated, to counter the message of the new preachers in Galatia: It is because of the latter that "Paul (a) places his exegetical emphasis on an expression not found in the text": "the sons of Abraham"; and "(b) answers a question not posed in that text": Who are truly the sons of Abraham? (Martyn 299–300). Paul's answer to this question is that the people of faith—and by implication *not* the people practicing fleshly circumcision and observing the law—are truly "sons of Abraham." Paul here completely redefines the descendants of Abraham, on the basis of the Spirit rather than on the basis of the fleshly descent (cf. 3:3; 4:21–5:1).

The phrase "those who are from faith" is a rendering of the Greek *hoi ek pisteōs*, literally, "those from faith." The sense is "those who derive their identity from faith" (cf. Martyn 299) and thus "live on the basis of faith." Whose faith is here being referred to, however? The faith of believers (the traditional view), Christ's faith, or perhaps some combination of the two (e.g., Martyn 299)? If Paul had wanted to refer straightforwardly to the faith of believers, he could have written *hoi pisteuontes*, "the believing ones," as he does in 3:22. The phrase he does use, *ek pisteōs* ("from faith"), is an abbreviation of *ek pisteōs Christou* ("from the faith of Christ"), used in 2:16. In view of such considerations, it is probable that Paul is referring, at least primarily (Matera 118), to Christ's own faith (see

---

272. Paul's "methodology," which was commonly used in his time, "is to find passages in the Scriptures which had the same terminology one was using in the argument" (Betz 138), even if the precise meanings of those terms in the cited texts are different to a greater or a lesser extent from the meanings for the author making the citations. Paul reads the OT as testimony to Christ (cf. Koch 1986); put otherwise, the starting point for his exegesis of the OT is the new situation brought about by Christ's death and resurrection. The same is probably true of the new preachers in Galatia, even though they draw different conclusions (see below).

273. The verb can also be construed as an indicative (e.g., Martyn; Longenecker), in which case Paul would be disclosing something to the Galatians instead of exhorting them to share his insight. Even the imperative carries the sense of disclosure, however.

Excursus 11, below): "Those who are from faith" derive that identity from "the faith of Christ," from the event of Christ's faithful death (2:16, 21; 3:1, 13).

Since "those who are from faith" have in fact "come to believe [*episteusamen*] in Christ" (2:16b), the phrase *hoi ek pisteōs* can rightly be understood to include or to signify such humans' believing in Christ (*pisteuein eis Christon*) at a secondary level. In Romans, as in other letters, Paul can even unambiguously call such believing in Christ *pistis*, "faith" (e.g., Rom 1:5). In Galatians, however, Paul appears to use the term *pistis* consistently as shorthand for *pistis Christou*.[274] The primary *referential meaning* of *pistis* in Galatians, therefore, is (apart from 5:22) always the faith of Christ himself: his faithful death on the cross, not human faith in Christ, which is but a secondary, subordinate implication of the phrase. In Galatians, Paul uses the verb, not the noun, for human believing/faith, and then sparingly (only 2:16; 3:6, 22). Human beings who have come to believe in Christ are justified not on the basis of their own believing response but "on the basis of [*ek*] the faith of Christ," the Christ who "gave himself for us" (1:4), "who loved me and gave himself up for me" (2:20), who did not "die for nothing" (2:21), and who "was portrayed as crucified before your eyes" (3:1). Those who have come to believe in Christ can therefore be called "those who are from faith," meaning those who derive their identity from Christ's faithful death and henceforth live on that basis.

Excursus 11: Faith (*pistis*) in Galatians 3

There are fourteen instances of the term in chapter 3 (vv. 2, 5, 7, 8, 9, 11, 12, 14, 22, 23 [2x], 24, 25, 26). In 3:22, as in 2:16, Paul employs the prepositional phrase *ek pisteōs* (*Iēsou*) *Christou*, "from [on the basis of] the faith of [Jesus] Christ." Between these two verses, he *five* times employs the phrase found in 3:7, *ek pisteōs*, "from [on the basis of] faith" (cf. 3:24; 5:5; Rom 1:17; 3:26, 30; 4:16; 5:1; 9:30, 32; 10:6; 14:23)[275]:

2:16	*ek pisteōs Christou*, "from the faith of Christ"
3:7, 8, 9, 11, 12	*ek pisteōs*, "from faith"[276]
3:22	*ek pisteōs Iēsou Christou*, "from the faith of Jesus Christ"

The shorter phrase appears, therefore, to be for Paul an abbreviated version of the longer. Further support for this hypothesis can be found in 3:24, where the *hina* clause is parallel to the one in 2:16b:

---

274. The instance in Gal 5:22 is the exception that proves the rule: *pistis*, which here means "trustworthiness, reliability," occurs seventh (!) in a list of the fruit of the Spirit. It does not here mean "faith" or "trust" in Christ (see comment there).

275. The occurrences are confined to Galatians and Romans (21 instances). See next note.

276. In v. 11, the phrase occurs in the quotation from Hab 2:4, also cited in Rom 1:17. Did Paul derive the phrase from this text? So Campbell 1992; 1994. The Galatians would not know this, however, before hearing Gal 3:11, but even then Paul does not indicate that he is quoting from Hab 2:4 (see comment on Gal 3:11).

3:24 "so that [*hina*] we might be justified [*dikaiōthōmen*] on the basis of faith [*ek pisteōs*]"

2:16 "so that [*hina*] we might be justified [*dikaiōthōmen*] on the basis of the faith *of Christ* [*ek pisteōs Christou*]"

Here then the phrase *ek pisteōs* is the equivalent of *ek pisteōs Christou*. There is also the phrase *dia tēs pisteōs*, "through the faith," in 3:14 (also 3:26), which can be understood as an abbreviated form of the phrase "through the faith of Jesus Christ," *dia pisteōs Iēsou Christou* in 2:16a[277] (cf. Rom 3:22, 25, 30, 31).[278]

The hypothesis that the prepositional phrase *ek pisteōs* is an abbreviation of the phrase *ek pisteōs (Iēsou) Christou* holds firm, whether the genitive construction in the latter is objective ("faith in Christ") or subjective ("faith of Christ"). Indeed, the hypothesis is generally assumed to be true without argument by those who maintain that the genitive is objective: for them "faith" (*pistis*) in Galatians is almost always "faith in Christ."[279] In Excursus 9, however, it was argued that the genitive is probably subjective and that the expression *pistis (Iēsou) Christou* (or the functional equivalent in 2:20, "the faith of the Son of God") is probably to be interpreted as "a summary description of Christ's faithful death" (Hays 2002a: 287). Decisive in this matter is the occurrence of *pistis* in Gal 3:23-25, where Paul uses the term in a personified way: Faith "came" onto the world stage at a certain juncture in time (3:23, 25), as Christ himself did (3:19). As a result "we are no longer under a custodian" (3:25), "under the law" (3:23), which was "our custodian until [*eis*] Christ" (3:24), meaning "until [*eis*] Faith should be revealed" (3:23). *Pistis* seems here to be not the faith of the believer in Christ, but Christ's own *pistis*. Paul uses the word "Faith" as a metonym for Christ himself (see Excursus 9 and comments on 1:23; 3:23-25). In 3:24, "to be justified on the basis of faith" then means "to be justified on the basis of Christ's faith" (cf. 2:16b). That conclusion must then also apply to 2:16.

The two remaining instances of *pistis* in Gal 3 occur in the phrase *ex akoēs pisteōs* (3:2, 5). Here too the *pistis* in view is probably that of Christ. The phrase means "on the basis of what was/is heard of the faith of Christ," that is, "of his faithful death on the cross" (see comment on 3:1-5).[280] In sum, *pistis*, "faith," in Galatians 3 always has the referential meaning *pistis Christou*, "the faith *of* Christ" (2:16, 20; 3:22).

In Gal 3:8, Paul makes the assumed connection between Abraham's believing God (Gen 15:6) and God's prior promise to him (Gen 12:3) explicit: "[8a]The Scripture, having foreseen [in Gen 15:6] that God justifies the Gentiles on the basis of faith, [8b]preached the gospel in advance to Abraham: [8c]'In you shall all

---

277. Also Gal 3:26 in 𝔓[46].

278. The prepositions *ek* and *dia* seem to be interchangeable for Paul, though he seems to favor the latter in this matter. See comment on 2:15–16 above.

279. The one unambiguous exception is the instance in 5:22.

280. There are three further instances of the noun in Galatians, apart from the previously noted 5:22. The two instances in 5:5 ("we, through the Spirit from faith, wait for the hope of justification") and 5:6 ("faith becoming effective through love") as well as the one in 6:10 ("the household of faith") can also be interpreted as referring to Christ's faith (see comments). See also 1:23.

the Gentiles be blessed' [Gen 12:3]." Paul's personification of "the Scripture" (*hē graphē*, i.e., the OT), attributing to it foresight (of God's justification of the Gentiles on the basis of faith) and intentionality (preaching the gospel in advance to Abraham), is probably rhetorically motivated. The new preachers attach great importance to the Scripture: it is undoubtedly *the* authority for them. Paul now solemnly summons this witness for his own theology, against the new preachers and their "different gospel" (1:7). The personification is thus not to be unduly pressed; it is probably a mere figure of speech (Burton 160; Longenecker 115), serving a rhetorical purpose, to undermine the theology of the new preachers in Galatia on their own terms. For Paul himself, the gospel is the final and in fact sole authority, as the previous two chapters of the letter have repeatedly emphasized.[281] In v. 8a, Paul means to say that God's justification of the Gentiles on the basis of faith, rather than on the basis of the law, is actually attested in "the Scripture": "it stands written" (*gegraptai*) there (cf. vv. 10, 13), as his quotation and interpretation of Gen 15:6 in vv. 6–7 have just demonstrated and as his allusion to the same passage in v. 9 ("faithful Abraham") will further underline. The verb *dikaioi*, "justifies," is probably a timeless present, corresponding to the passive *dikaioutai*, "is justified," also a timeless present, in 3:11a and 2:16a. As a matter of principle, and as foreseen by the Scripture, God justifies the Gentiles (Gentile believers, as in 2:12) on the basis of faith, the faith of Christ (see Excursus 11, above). The verb itself, therefore, does not indicate when exactly justification takes place, whether now or in the future; the *time* of justification is not at issue in Paul's claim. For the new preachers, however, it can be said that justification (involving forensic-eschatological vindication) is a future expectation, whereas for Paul justification—God's powerful, invasive rectification of the human world—is now already taking place (see comments on 2:16–17, 21; 5:5; Excursuses 2 and 4).

Genesis 12:3, cited in v. 8c ("In you shall all the Gentiles be blessed"), is the promise that God made to Abraham, resulting in Abraham's believing God. As indicated above, the presupposition of this promise appears to be God's closely related promise that he would make of Abraham "a great nation" by providing him with a son and thus an heir (Gen 12:2; cf. 13:16; 15:2–5). In this promise, Abraham himself is to be blessed by God: "I will make you a great nation and I will bless you and magnify your name and you will be blessed" (12:2 LXX). Paul introduces a modification into his quotation from Gen 12:3, which in the

---

281. Before this passage, Paul makes no explicit appeal to passages from the Scripture (cf. comment on 2:16d). As 1 Thessalonians shows, Paul can preach the gospel to Gentiles without quoting the OT. It is thus improbable that, as Tolmie (2005: 111) says, Paul's "appeal to Scripture was based on the belief that it has the last word on any issue, since it transcends all human discussion and argumentation" (similarly, Stanley 2004: 173). This comment attributes to Paul what is probably true of his opponents, the new preachers in Galatia. For Paul, the gospel is the standard (cf. 6:15) of all truth, including that of "the Scripture."

LXX reads, "In you shall all the *tribes* of the earth be blessed." He has changed "all the tribes of the earth" to "all the Gentiles [*panta ta ethnē*]." That change has been derived from LXX Gen 18:18 (cf. 22:28; 26:4), where the promise is repeated ("in him [Abraham] shall all the Gentiles [*panta ta ethnē*] of the earth be blessed"). The adaptation of Gen 12:3 to 18:18 serves Paul's immediate purpose, to underline the justification of "the Gentiles" and *their* reception of the Spirit.[282] Paul refers later in this passage to "the blessing of Abraham" (v. 14), identifying the latter with the promised Spirit. Paul thus understands Gen 12:3 to promise the gift of Christ's Spirit (cf. 4:6) to the Gentiles. Since the Spirit was given "as a result of what was heard of [Christ's] faith" (3:2; see comment there), Paul can introduce the quotation of Gen 12:3 with the words: "the Scripture ... preached the gospel in advance [*proeuēngelisato*] to Abraham" (v. 8b).

As indicated above, Paul assumes in his argument (1) that the God of Jesus is also the God of Abraham, (2) that the gift of the Spirit, which God has bestowed and still bestows (3:1–5) on those who "have come to believe in Christ" (2:16b), is the fulfillment of a promise God made to Abraham, and (3) that this gift is given to the "sons of Abraham" (v. 8), to his "descendants" (*sperma*) and "heirs" (*klēronomoi*) (3:29). The new preachers in Galatia, who are Christian Jews, probably share these assumptions, none of which can be derived from Genesis itself (cf. Burton 156–59). Both Paul and the new preachers, therefore, do exegesis of the OT backward, as it were. They start from the present situation, from the present experience of the Spirit, and assume that the gift of the Spirit stands in continuity with God's dealings with the founding patriarch of Israel. They both identify the Spirit as "the blessing of Abraham." For the new preachers, however, that Spirit, like the blessing of Abraham, is closely linked to law observance (see comment on 3:1–5 above) and thus provides the basis

---

282. Paul has used the term *ethnē* seven times in Gal 1–2 to refer to Gentiles in distinction from Jews (1:16; 2:2, 8, 9, 12, 14, 15). In the Genesis texts the term probably means "nations," however, thus including Israel: According to Gen 18:18 LXX, "Abraham will become a great and populous nation [*ethnos*], and in him shall all the nations [*ethnē*] of the earth be blessed," presumably including the nation of Israel. This understanding of the term could actually serve Paul's purpose in the present context, since he has asserted in 2:15–16 that everyone, Jew as well as Gentile, who has come to believe in Christ is justified on the same basis, the faith of Christ and not observance of the law. Verse 8 could thus be rendered: "The Scripture, having foreseen that God justifies the nations [those of the Gentiles as well as that of the Jews] on the basis of faith, preached the gospel in advance to Abraham: 'In you shall *all* the nations [those of the Gentiles as well as that of the Jews] be blessed.'" In v. 14, "the blessing of Abraham" is identified as "the promise of the Spirit" (see comment below), and it is something "we" all (both Gentile and Jewish believer) receive. Against the rendering "nations" in v. 8, however, is the usage in the previous two chapters, noted above, where *ethnē* always means "Gentiles" (as differentiated from "Jews" or "the circumcision"). That is also clearly the meaning in v. 14 (see comment). Furthermore, if Paul had wanted to say "all peoples" he could presumably have quoted Gen 12:3 LXX exactly, leaving in the phrase "all the tribes of the earth."

for justification in the future. For Paul, the Spirit is linked to Christ's faithful death, which is God's rectifying power already at work in the world.

In v. 9 Paul draws a conclusion from the way in which he has conjoined Gen 15:6 and Gen 12:3: "So then, those who are from faith [*hoi ek pisteōs*] are blessed with the faithful [*pistos*] Abraham." The formulation is polemical. The latter part of the verse ("are blessed with the faithful Abraham") is an allusion to the story of the near sacrifice of Isaac (Gen 22:1–19) and its interpretation in contemporary Jewish tradition. The promises that God makes to Abraham in Gen 12:2–3 LXX ("I will make you a great nation, and I will bless you and magnify your name, and you will be blessed, . . . and in you shall all the tribes of the earth be blessed") are reiterated in Gen 22:17–18 LXX, where they are linked to Abraham's obedience: "I will indeed bless you [with multitudinous descendants], . . . and in your offspring shall all the Gentiles [*panta ta ethnē*] of the earth be blessed, *because you have obeyed my voice*." Here "all the Gentiles" (or nations) are blessed along with Abraham because of his obedience to God in connection with the near sacrifice of Isaac. In Sir 44:19–23, as in 1 Macc 2:52 (quoted above), Abraham is called "faithful" (*pistos*) precisely for having obeyed God's instructions in connection with Isaac (cf. *Jub.* 17.15–16); his faithful obedience provides the basis for the blessing of his offspring:

> Abraham was the great father of a multitude of nations [*ethnē*; cf. Gen 17:5; Rom 4:17], . . . and when he was tested [Gen 22:1–19], he proved faithful [*pistos*]. Therefore the Lord assured him with an oath that the nations would be blessed [*eneulogēthēnai ethnē*] through his offspring [*en spermati autou*; cf. Gen 22:18; 28:14]; that he would make him as numerous as the dust of the earth, and exalt his offspring like the stars, and give them an inheritance from sea to sea and from the Euphrates to the ends of the earth [cf. Gen 12:1–2, 7; 13:14–18; 15:5–6, 18; 17:4–8, 16–21; 18:18; 22:17; 28:14]. To Isaac also he gave the same assurance for the sake of his father Abraham [cf. Gen 22:17–18; *Jub.* 24.11]. The blessing [*eulogia*] of all people and the covenant he made to rest on the head of Jacob; he acknowledged him with his blessings [*eulogiai*], and gave him his inheritance [*klēronomia*].

Such passages indicate that for the new preachers the phrase "in you [Abraham]" in Gen 12:3 probably means "in your offspring [*sperma*]," in Abraham's fleshly, law-observant descendants down the generations, beginning with the patriarch Isaac and followed by Jacob (cf. Gen 28:14 LXX: "in you [Jacob] and in your offspring shall all the tribes of the earth be blessed"). In their interpretation of these passages, the new preachers in Galatia are probably telling the Galatians that "inasmuch as it is in Abraham that all the nations are to be blessed, the Gentiles to be blessed must be in Abraham, i.e., incorporated into his descendants by circumcision" (Burton 159).

In short, for the new preachers, "those *who are from works of the law* are blessed with the faithful Abraham." The polemical nature of Paul's formulation

The Spirit and the True Heirs of the Promise Made to Abraham

thereby becomes evident: "So then, *those who are from faith* are blessed with the faithful Abraham."

The people who live on the basis of (Christ's) faith(ful death) are the true offspring of Abraham, being heirs of the promise that God made to Abraham. They are blessed with the promised Spirit (v. 14), whose bestowal rests on faith, just as justification does, as the precedent provided by the patriarch himself demonstrates.[283] The adjective *pistos* for Paul means "believing God and his promise," alluding back to v. 6 and its quotation from Gen 15:6, not "obeying God and his law," as in the Jewish tradition from which the new preachers take their bearings. Paul thereby dissociates "the faithful [*pistos*] Abraham" from law observance and associates him with "the faith of Christ." In the next passage (3:15–22), Paul will identify Abraham's "offspring" as Christ himself (and, by implication, those who belong to him), thus not as the people of the law who stand in genealogical and historical continuity with the biological descendants of Abraham, beginning with Isaac (cf. 4:21–5:1; see comment there).

To summarize: For the new preachers, law-observant believers are blessed along with the faithful (law-observant) Abraham; for Paul, believers defined by Christ's faith(ful death) are blessed along with the faithful (God-believing) Abraham. That blessing is the Spirit (v. 14), attesting the reality and the promise of "justification," which for Paul is God's rectifying action. The continuity between God's dealings with Abraham and his rectifying action in Christ rests solely on God's making good on his promise to Abraham, not on Gentile believers' attaching themselves to the historical, fleshly descendants of Abraham through circumcision and law observance.[284]

[10–12] The thought in these three verses and in the two that follow is particularly difficult to follow, though perhaps less so if one keeps Paul's focus in mind: the problem he discerns in the (observance of the) law. This short unit is not about faith, but about the law:

v. 10: "Those who are from works of the law are under a curse."
v. 11: "No one is justified before God in the law."
v. 12: "The law is not 'from faith.'"

The positive things Paul has to say about faith here function merely as a foil for the negative things he says about the (observance of the) law. In these verses

---

283. Paul ignores the promises made to Abraham concerning a multitude of physical descendants who would inherit the land. There is for him a single relevant promise, which he identifies as the gift of the Spirit, whereby many spiritual descendants of Abraham come into being. See comments on 3:14 and 3:15–18 below.

284. Here Paul is polemicizing not against Jews and Judaism, but against Christian Jewish missionaries who want to convince or even compel Gentile believers in Christ to become Jews as a precondition for obtaining salvation (justification).

his primary purpose is to refute the law-based gospel of the new preachers and thus to undermine their influence on the Galatians (see Excursus 4).

The unit begins with an astonishing assertion in v. 10a: "For those who are from works of the law are under a curse." The expression "works of the law" (2:16; 3:2, 5) means "the observance—the doing [*poieō*]—of the law," as the present passage with its double use of the verb *poieō* ("to do") demonstrates (see Excursus 8 and further below). "Those who are from works of the law" (*hosoi ex ergōn nomou eisin*) are those who derive their identity from observance of the law and thus live on the basis of such observance.[285] Paul evidently begins with the conjunction "for" (*gar*) because he had "those who are from works of the law" in mind when he formulated the polemically motivated preceding verse. The sense can be captured with the following paraphrase: "Those who live from faith, *not* those who live from law observance, are blessed with the faithful Abraham, *for* those who live from law observance are in fact under a curse" (see comment on v. 9 above). The conjunction here probably introduces a clarification: "for you see . . ." (cf. BDAG 189; Longenecker 116).

In v. 13, Paul will refer to the curse of v. 10a as "the curse of the law" (see comment there). A curse is the opposite of a blessing (cf. Gen 12:3; Deut 27–30): the two are mutually exclusive. For Paul, they constitute an apocalyptic antinomy that came into being with Christ, whereby the Spirit also for the first time came on the human scene. To be under a curse is thus to be deprived of a blessing, in this case, the blessing of the promised Spirit (3:14). In Paul's view, then, those "under a curse" (*hypo kataran*) are still stuck "in the present evil age" (1:4), where malevolent powers hold all human beings "under" their control, one of these cosmic powers evidently being the law itself (3:23; 4:4–5, 21). To be under a curse, here the curse of the law, is to be outside the realm of salvation (see comments on 1:4; 3:23–26; Excursus 2). The remainder of this subunit constitutes Paul's attempt to substantiate this astonishing and, for the new preachers, offensive claim, that those who live from the law are in fact "under a curse":

> [10b]For it stands written: "Accursed[286] is everyone who does not remain in all the things written in the book of the law so as to do [*poiēsai*] them" [Deut 27:26 LXX]. [11]And because no one is justified before God in the law, it is evident that "the just one from faith shall live" [Hab 2:4 LXX]. [12]The law, however, is not "from faith," but "the one having done [*poiēsas*] them shall live in them" [Lev 18:5 LXX].

---

285. The verb "to live" here has an ethical import, meaning simply "to have one's existence in the flesh [cf. 2:20] ordered or determined by" (cf. 5:25) or "to walk by" (cf. 5:16). See comment on vv. 11–12 below.

286. The Greek word is an adjective *epikataratos* ("accursed"), not a past participle as the English translation "cursed" (NRSV) might suggest.

Particularly noteworthy is Paul's use of quotations from the OT to make his case. As in 3:6–9, Paul's exegetical efforts seek to meet the new preachers on their own turf, that of "the Scripture" (3:8) that they hold dear and to which, unlike Paul, they grant absolute authority (see Excursus 4). Paul finds that the Scripture itself supports his view of the law, particularly in v. 10, where v. 10a represents Paul's surprising interpretation of Deut 27:26, cited in v. 10b. In the LXX, the latter passage reads: "Accursed is every human being [*anthrōpos*] who does not remain in all[287] the words of this law so as to do them."

Paul, who introduces the quotation with a solemn introductory formula ("for it stands written"), changes the latter part of the verse: "Accursed [= under a curse] is everyone who does not remain in[288] all the things written in the book of the law so as to do them." Paul has thus changed the phrase "all the words [*logois*] of this law" into "all the things written in the book of the law." The alteration reflects the wording found in other passages with a similar message in later chapters of Deuteronomy (LXX), especially 28:58 ("all the things written in this book"), but also 29:19 ("all the curses [*arai*] of this covenant that are written in the book of this law") and 30:10 ("all his commandments, ordinances, and judgments that are written in the book of this law"). In these passages from Deuteronomy, "this law" is probably the legislation contained in the book of Deuteronomy itself, whereas "*the* law" in Paul's citation refers to the Sinaitic legislation as a whole, which is the meaning the term *nomos* has elsewhere in Gal 2:15–4:7. The "book of the law" is then, for Paul, probably the Pentateuch (see comment on 4:21).

Apart from the change from "*this* law" to "*the* law," the modifications that Paul introduces to the citation from Deut 27:26 do not appear to be significant and may not even originate with Paul. The real difficulty lies with Paul's interpretation of Deut 27:26: observers of the law are accursed! Yet Deut 27:26 seems to assert precisely the opposite: *non*observers of the law are accursed! This passage (also in the form in which Paul quotes it) seems on its face to fit the theology of the new preachers in Galatia better than that of Paul. How, then, can Paul hope to convince his Galatian readers or the new preachers who shall be listening to the letter with them? Has Paul misinterpreted the text or even committed an exegetical blunder? The manuscript history of Galatians does not promote this drastic conclusion, however, for no scribe has seen fit to correct or to improve v. 10 so as to remove the supposed contradiction between Deut

---

287. Here the underlying Hebrew text (MT) has no word corresponding to "all." Both Paul and the LXX do contain this word, a solid indication, among others, that Paul's citation follows the LXX text, not that of the MT.

288. According to manuscripts $\mathfrak{P}^{45}$, ℵ*, B, and others, Paul omits the Greek preposition *en*, found in LXX, but it is also not necessary since the compound Greek verb *emmenei* (= *en* + *menei*) contains it. The inclusion of the preposition by other scribes (A, C, D, and others) serves to conform Paul's citation to the LXX text.

27:26 and Paul's interpretation of it in v. 10a.[289] A common, traditional solution to the problem is to attribute to Paul the assumption that no one in fact does or is even able to do "*all* the things written in the book of the law" (cf. 6:13). For this reason, according to Paul's supposed reasoning, those who derive their identity from law observance must inevitably fall under the curse of Deut 27:26 (Calvin 53; Burton 164–65; Mussner 224–26; Longenecker 118; Dunn 171; Anderson 1999: 158), or at least under the constant *threat* of this curse (Stanley 1990; Williams 89–90; Witherington 233). One problem with this interpretation is that it implicitly attributes to Paul the (theoretical) notion that perfect or complete observance of the law brings a blessing rather than a curse, which seems to contradict the assertion of v. 10a and the thrust of the argument from 2:15–16 onward. Furthermore, in 2:16 and 21, Paul does not contrast "the faith of Christ" with imperfect or incomplete observance of the law but simply with observance of the law as such (see end of Excursus 8; Martyn 310). Nor does he write "under the threat of a curse" in v. 10a, but "under a curse" (also v. 13). Imperfect or incomplete observance of the law does not seem to be the issue for Paul; the problem is the law itself (cf. 3:19–22 and comment there).

Another solution is to attribute to Paul the assumption that Israel now (as he writes the letter) experiences being accursed by being "in exile" (Wright 1991: 144–47; followed by Hays 258–59), as was the case when the book of Deuteronomy itself was published (Noth). Thus Paul would be telling the Galatians that by adopting observance of the law, they would be placing themselves under a curse alongside Israel. Paul himself, however, shows no awareness elsewhere that Israel felt itself to be accursed in this manner (Dunn 172; Kim 136–40; Tolmie 2005: 116). Furthermore, in v. 11 he speaks in an individualizing way about no one's being justified before God in the sphere of the law (see comment below).

A more attractive solution works from the assumption that Paul is citing a favorite text of the new preachers for his own purposes. It is certainly easy to imagine them appealing to Deut 27:26 to impress upon the Galatians the importance of keeping the law: "Unless you begin practicing circumcision and then observe the [remainder of the] law, you will be deprived of the blessing of Abraham, which is the promised Spirit, and the curse of Deut 27:26 will fall on you instead." In this reading, the new preachers—not Paul himself—use Deut 27:26 as a threat or a warning (Martyn 311; Wilson 2007). They do so, not because the Galatians are imperfectly observing the law, but because they have not put themselves under it in the first place.[290] A presupposition of the appeal

---

289. The only variant NA[27] discusses is the inclusion or the omission of the preposition *en* ("in") in the citation from Deut 27:26; see previous note.

290. The new preachers may have found Deut 27:26 useful as a threat because it is the only passage in the OT that explicitly links the terms "law" and "curse" (Sanders 1983: 21). The new preachers' use of this text may be one reason for the Galatians becoming "unnerved" (1:7; 5:10; cf. Martyn 309) and then "bewitched" (3:1). Cursing was not taken lightly in the ancient world (see comment on 1:8–9).

to Deut 27:26 appears to be that the law has universal applicability: at the last judgment all human beings are to be judged by that standard, both those who observe and those who do not observe the law, thus both Jew and Gentile (cf. Rom 2:12–15; *4 Ezra* [2 Esd] 7.37; *2 Bar.* 15.5; 48.40). In this way, everyone, the Gentile as well as the Jew, falls "under the law," not in Paul's sense of enslavement under a malevolent power (cf. 3:23 and comment there), but in the sense of accountability to the law and its standard (cf. Marcus 2001). Paul cites Deut 27:26, cleverly using this assumption of the universal applicability of the law held by the new preachers in Galatia, to substantiate the claim that it is the people of the law—specifically the new preachers themselves and any Gentile Christians in Galatia tempted by their gospel—who fall under its curse, no less than the nonobservers of whom Deut 27:26 speaks! Paul has prepared the way for this daring interpretation in the previous nine verses, where he has emphasized that the blessing of the promised Spirit and justification come only to those who live from faith, not to those who live from observing the law. For this reason those who live from law observance, no less than those who do not, are of necessity under a curse—that of the law, whose stipulations they seek to do! The curse falls on the observer as well as the nonobserver (or imperfect observer) of the law (cf. Martyn 311; Lührmann 61), thus on everyone who is not "in Christ Jesus" (v. 14a).[291]

In the following two verses, Paul seeks to show that this reading of Deut 27:26 makes sense, largely repeating points made earlier: Since there is no justification in the law (v. 11), the law has nothing to do with (Christ's) faith (v. 12), which, as Paul has already repeatedly emphasized, is the sole basis for justification (cf. 2:16, 21; 3:6–9; Excursus 11). The key difference here is that Paul now uses formulations derived from Scripture (the LXX) to support these claims anew, even though the two quotations from Scripture found here are not marked in contrast to those in v. 10 and v. 13 (see below). The basic point of the two verses is a negative one about the law, namely, that it is "not from faith" (v. 12a), thereby placing those who (seek to) find their identity in law observance under its curse, as Paul has stated in v. 10a. That the issue here is still the curse mentioned in v. 10 is shown by the fact that in v.13 Paul refers again to this curse, labeling it "the curse of the law," from which Christ has redeemed "us." The overarching theme of vv. 10–12 is thus the curse of the law. The unstated premise of the argument of these two verses has been made explicit in v. 9—*those who live from faith* are blessed with the faithful Abraham—and will be again in v. 14: it is "through faith," not by doing the law, that believers have received and

---

291. For Paul, then, the expression "those who are from works of the law" (v. 10a) is finally objective, describing the universal human situation apart from Christ, not subjective, as the translation "those who *rely* or *depend* on works of the law" (NRSV, NIV, NJB, NAB) might imply. By "wanting to be under the law" (4:21), the Galatians are returning to the condition of slavery, from which they have been liberated (cf. comments on 4:8–10, 21; 5:1, 4).

continue to receive "the blessing of Abraham": the promised Spirit, attesting the new basis for justification, which is the faith of Christ (cf. 3:1–5). For this reason, then, those who live from law observance are under a curse (v. 10a), which for Paul is the only alternative to the blessing, which is the Spirit. This either/or has been created by coming of Christ and his Spirit (see on 3:23–25; 4:4–7).

Verses 11 and 12 present a number of much-debated exegetical difficulties that require careful unpacking. The two verses go together, the second building directly on the first, while also harking back to v. 10:

> [11a]And because [*hoti de*] no one is justified before God in the law, [11b]it is evident that [*dēlon hoti*] "the just one from faith shall live" [Hab 2:4 LXX]. [12a]The law, however, is not "from faith," [12b]but "the one having done them shall live in them" [Lev 18:5 LXX].

The translation of v. 11 given above requires some explanation since it is normally translated as follows (e.g., Burton; Betz; Longenecker; Dunn; Martyn; Williams; Vouga; cf. Hanse):

> [11a]And that [*hoti de*] no one is justified before God in the law is evident [*dēlon*], [11b]because [*hoti*] "the just one from faith shall live."[292]

In this translation v. 11a constitutes Paul's interpretation of Hab 2:4, cited in v. 11b. The translation assumes that the second *hoti* clause (v. 11b) is causal, rather than the first (v. 11a). It is a translation encouraged by the editors of the critical Greek text (NA[27]), who have placed a comma between *dēlon* ("it is evident") and *hoti* ("because/that"). In the translation preferred here, the first *hoti* clause is regarded as causal instead of the second one (also Witherington 348; Hays 259; Wright 1991: 149 n. 42; Kim 129):

> [11a]And because [*hoti de*] no one is justified before God in the law, [11b]it is evident that [*dēlon hoti*] "the just one from [*ek*] faith shall live."

In this translation the language from Hab 2:4 is used to state a conclusion. There are two reasons why this translation is to be preferred: (1) The expression *dēlon hoti* ("it is evident that") is probably a unified expression (cf. BDAG 222; Ign. *Eph* 6.1) that Paul himself also uses in 1 Cor 15:27 ("it is plain that . . ."). There is thus good reason to place a comma before *dēlon* rather than after it. (2) Paul's train of thought makes good sense with the proposed translation.[293]

---

292. Cf. NRSV: "Now it is evident that no one is justified before God by the law; for 'The one who is righteous will live by faith'"; similarly other versions and commentators.

293. If one adopts the other translation, the conclusion of Williams (90) lies close to hand: "Verse 11a stands independent of what precedes, neither supporting nor further developing the thought of verse 10."

The expression "No one is justified before God in the law" recalls the similar expression in 2:16a: "No one is justified on the basis of works of the law." Paul is thus repeating a principle formulated earlier. He now says "in [*en*] the law," instead of "on the basis [*ek*] of works of the law," under the influence of the citation from Deut 27:26 in the previous verse: "remain *in* [*emmenei*] all the things written *in* [*en*] the book of the law" (cf. 5:4). He thereby also anticipates the citation from Lev 18:5 in v. 12: "The one having done them shall live *in* [*en*] them" (in all the things written in the book of the law).[294] The law and its commandments here constitute a realm or a sphere determining a person's existence, the manner in which one "shall live." Precisely *because* no one is justified before God in the law (v. 11a), a claim Paul has found corroborated by Deut 27:26, it becomes evident that "the just one from [Christ's] faith shall live" (cf. 2:16; 5:4).[295] The only alternative to law observance for Paul is "faith," an alternative that he has not thought up or chosen himself but has come into the world with Christ (3:23–25). It is in fact the given from which he argues, even if his argument runs formally in the other direction, from the perceived problem (the inability of the law to provide justification) to the solution (Christ's "faith" as the sole source of justification).[296]

Paul's citation of Hab 2:4 in v. 11b does not match the LXX text exactly. The LXX manuscripts of Hab 2:4 have two solidly attested readings, both containing the possessive "my" (Verhoef 72). The translations given here follow exactly the word order of the Greek text, where the prepositional phrase "from faith" stands between the subject and the verb, as it does in Paul's citation:

"The just one from *my* faith shall live." (א, B, W*)
"*My* just one from faith shall live." (A, et al.; cf. Heb 10:38)

Both readings diverge from the underlying Hebrew text (MT), which reads: "The just one in *his* faith [*beʾĕmûnātô*] shall live." The second reading from the LXX could be construed accordingly: "My just one from *his* faith shall live," the absence of the possessive being merely stylistic. In the first LXX reading, which has stronger support than the second, the "faith" being referred to must be

---

294. To translate the preposition *en* with "by" in vv. 11 and 12, as is often done (e.g., NRSV), obscures these connections and also hides its spatial connotations.

295. Otherwise Burton (166), who considers but then quickly dismisses this possibility. According to Burton, that the first *hoti* clause is the subject of *dēlon* "is proved by the fact that the following clause is a quotation from O.T., and therefore, valuable proof of the apostle's assertion while not itself requiring to be proved." But Paul does not mark Hab 2:4 as a quotation; the words from this passage are woven into his own argument. Furthermore, Paul has modified the meaning of the language of Hab 2:4 significantly to fit that argument; see just below.

296. Paul's mode of argumentation is dialectical: since Christ's coming has shown law observance to place its adherents under a curse, that curse can be used to demonstrate that no one is justified in the law and thus that (Christ's) faith alone justifies.

that of God. In the MT and in both LXX readings, but especially the first, "faith" (*pistis*, *'ĕmûnâ*) clearly means "faithfulness," whether that of God or that of a human being. For the MT and the second LXX reading, the faithfulness in view has to do with faithful law observance on the part of a just person (who is just precisely because of observing the law faithfully). In 1QpHab 8.1–3 we find Hab 2:4 interpreted in this way: "Its interpretation concerns all observing the Law in the House of Judah, whom God will free from the house of judgment on account of their toil and their loyalty to the Teacher of Righteousness." Faith here has to do with law observance. Paul, however, uses the text to *undermine* law observance. For him, as opposed to the new preachers in Galatia, faith and law observance are mutually exclusive.

Paul omits the possessive "my" with the word "faith" (see the first and better-attested reading from the LXX). He does not write "my faith." Given the fact that Paul's citation of Hab 2:4 in Rom 1:17 also lacks this possessive, it is possible that Paul's LXX text did not contain it (see the second and more weakly attested LXX reading). In any case Paul does not indicate to the Galatians that he is citing from Hab 2:4. He does not introduce the quotation with words such as "it stands written," as he does when he quotes Hab 2:4 again in Rom 1:17 and as he does to introduce the quotation from Deut 27:26 in v. 10. The words from Hab 2:4 are woven into his own argument, and the Galatians will hear his words as follows:

> And because no one is justified before God in the law, it is evident that the just one from faith [*ek pisteōs*] shall live.

The inclusion of the possessive "my" would thus be misleading and confusing. Furthermore, Paul has already used the prepositional phrase *ek pisteōs* ("on the basis of/from faith"), without a possessive, three times in the previous paragraph (3:7, 8, 9), and he will use it again in the following verse (12) and in 3:24 (also 5:5). In Paul's mouth, and in the ears of the Galatians, the phrase is an abbreviation of the phrase *ek pisteōs (Iēsou) Christou* ("on the basis of the faith[fulness] of [Jesus] Christ"), found in 2:16 and 3:22 (see Excursuses 9 and 11, above). Thus the language that Paul cites from Hab 2:4 will be understood by the Galatians as follows: "The just one on the basis of Christ's faith shall live." The faith explicitly and primarily being referred to, therefore, is not the believer's (as in the MT and the second LXX reading), nor God's (as in the first LXX reading), but *Christ's*.[297]

The formulation taken over from Hab 2:4 contains three further ambiguities that have been matters of discussion and debate:

---

297. In a sense, Christ's faith(fulness) can be regarded as God's own faithfulness for Paul (cf. Rom 3:3). In this way, Paul's interpretation stays close to the first and better attested LXX reading discussed above.

Issue 1. Who exactly is "the just one"? In view of v. 11a ("No one is justified before God in the Law"), "the just one" of Hab 2:4 is for Paul probably "the justified one" (cf. Burton 166).[298] Verse 11 indicates neither *what* "justification" consists of nor *when* it occurs (neither is at issue here), though there are indications (a) that for Paul justification is actually to be understood as God's apocalyptic rectifying activity in Christ, and (b) that God has begun that rectifying activity in Christ's faithful death (see comment on 2:15–21). Verse 11b can thus be paraphrased as follows: "The one being rectified [= the believer in Christ] on the basis of Christ's faithful death shall live."

Issue 2. Does the prepositional phrase *ek pisteōs* ("from/on the basis of [Christ's] faith") modify the subject *ho dikaios* ("the just one"), the verb *zēsetai* ("shall live"), or perhaps both (Martyn)?[299] Put otherwise, does Paul mean to say "The one justified on the basis of Christ's faith shall live," or "The one justified shall live on the basis of Christ's faith"? This issue is closely related to a third:

Issue 3. Does the verb "shall live" in v. 11b refer to eschatological life or simply to a manner of conduct or existence, as in 2:14 ("You [Cephas] . . . are living in a Gentile manner and not in a Jewish manner") or 2:20 ("The life I now live in the flesh, I live in faith, that of the Son of God")? In the latter case, the verb "to live" is apparently akin to the verb "to walk" (Gr. *peripatō*; Heb. *hālak*) when used metaphorically to characterize conduct or a manner of living (cf. 5:16, 25).

To take the prepositional phrase *ek pisteōs* with the subject *ho dikaios* is consistent with 2:16 ("Someone is not justified on the basis of works of the law but . . . on the basis of the faith of Christ"); the whole of v. 11 can then be read as a restatement of that verse, using slightly different words: "Because no one is justified . . . in the law, it is evident that the one justified on the basis of [Christ's] faith shall live." The new element is the promise of life ("shall live"), taken from Hab 2:4, which then seems to have an eschatological meaning (new life in Christ, whether before or after the Parousia). If Paul had wanted to say this clearly, however, he could have placed the prepositional phrase between the article and the noun (*ho ek pisteōs dikaios*; cf. 3:8: *ek pisteōs dikaioi*). To take the phrase *ek pisteōs* as modifying the verb is consistent with Hab 2:4 (both in LXX and the underlying MT), where the phrase also clearly modifies the verb, not the subject (Fitzmyer 1992: 264–65). Verse 11b then provides a suitable contrast to the citation from Lev 18:5 in v. 12b: "The one having done them [the things that the law requires] shall live [*zēsetai*] in them." The verb "shall

---

298. Hays (2002: 134–38) has argued that "the just one" is Christ rather than the believer, but that does not seem likely since it makes the relationship between the two halves of the verse (more) difficult.

299. This issue has also been much debated in connection with Rom 1:17; see Fitzmyer 1992: 264–65.

live" here does not have an eschatological meaning (see on v. 12 below), nor then does the same verb in v. 11b, except perhaps as a secondary implication. (If asked, Paul would certainly say that "to live from faith" is to live in the new age inaugurated by Christ, but that is not at issue here.) The prepositional phrase thus probably modifies the verb. Even in this case, however, it can be presupposed that "the just one" is someone who is justified "on the basis of faith," so that a full paraphrase would read as follows: "Someone who is being justified [rectified] on the basis of Christ's faith shall henceforth also live on the basis of Christ's faith."

In v. 12a, Paul quotes the prepositional phrase *ek pisteōs* from v. 11b (Hab 2:4) in order to contrast it with the law: "The law, however [*de*], is not 'from faith.' . . ." Here "the law" is shorthand for "the works of the law" (3:10; cf. 2:19, 21), an expression that means "the observance of the law." Paul thus declares in v. 12a that the "doing" (3:10, 12) of the law is not "from faith," meaning it has nothing in common with the latter (see on 3:19–22). He supports this assertion with an abbreviated citation of Lev 18:5 in v. 12b (Stanley 1992: 244–45): "But [as the new preachers know] 'the one having done [*ho poiēsas*] them [*auta*] shall live [*zētesai*] in them [*en autois*]'" (v. 12b). The doer of the commandments "shall live *in them*," not then "on the basis of faith" (v. 11b).

Leviticus 18:5 is no arbitrary choice. The full text of Lev 18:5 LXX (mss. א, A) reads: "And you shall keep all my ordinances and all my judgments, and you shall do [*poiēsete*] them [*auta*], which having done [*ha poiēsas*] someone shall live [*zēsetai*] in them." The first half of this passage is similar in content to the latter part of Deut 27:26, as Paul has quoted it in v. 10 ("All the things written in the book of the law so as to do them [*poiēsai auta*]"). He thus does not need to cite the whole of Lev 18:5; he can confine himself to the last half, which also contains the verb "to do" (*poieō*). In quoting this part of Lev 18:5, Paul conforms the wording ("having done them," *poiēsas* [*auta*]) to that of Deut 27:26 as quoted by him in v. 10 ("to do them," *poiēsai auta*) In both cases, then, he uses an aorist form of the verb *poieō* and the direct object *auta*, "them," referring to "all the things written in the book of the law," meaning the body of commandments and stipulations it contains (cf. Rom 10:5). The final "in them" (*en autois*) in the citation from Lev 18:5 is also a reference to these commandments and stipulations. In his citation of these OT passages, Paul uses a common exegetical technique, the interpretation of passages in Scripture on the basis of shared key words: Lev 18:5 uses a verb also found in Deut 27:26 ("to do," *poieō*) and another also found in Hab 2:4 ("to live," *zaō*). With respect the latter verb, the future form *zēsetai* ("shall live") is used in both texts, strengthening the connection. The pregnant use of the preposition "in" (*en*) in both Deut 27:26 and Lev 18:5 also strengthens the link between these two texts, as does the use of *auta* ("them"). The relationship of the citation in

v. 12 to the ones in the two prior verses can be displayed as follows (the shared words have been italicized):

Deuteronomy 27:26 in Gal 3:10: "Accursed is everyone who does not remain *in* [*en*] all the things written *in* [*en*] the book of the law so as *to do them* [*poiēsai auta*]."
Habakkuk 2:4 in Gal 3:11: "*The* [*ho*] just one from faith *shall live* [*zēsetai*]."
Leviticus 18:5 in Gal 3:12: "*The* [*ho*] *one having done them* [*poiēsas auta*] *shall live* [*zēsetai*] *in* [*en*] *them* [*autois*]."

Every word in the citation of Lev 18:5 thus corresponds to a word in the citations found in vv. 10 and 11. Paul thereby can present Lev 18:5 as the (positive) summary of the latter part of Deut 27:26 and as the contrary of Hab 2:4. Thus to "live in them" (v. 12) means the same as to "remain in all the things written in the book of the law" (v. 10); "to live in them" then also means that an adherent of the law is "to do them." "To live *in them*," however—and this is Paul's concrete point—has nothing to do with "living *from faith*" (v. 11). They represent two distinct modes of "living." In this context, the verb "to live" is being used to mean "to conduct one's life in a certain way" (cf. 2:14: "living in a Gentile manner"), "to have one's existence ordered or determined by" (cf. 5:16: "to live by the Spirit") or "to exist in a certain sphere" (cf. 2:20: "to live in the flesh"; Rom 6:2: "to live in sin"). The import is thus ethical rather than soteriological or eschatological. At issue is not simply behavior but also identity, for to live in the law's commandments is to derive one's identity from law observance (v. 10a). For Paul, those who "live" from the works of the law "live" under a curse, that of the law itself (v. 13).

To live "in" the observance of the law (v. 12) and to live "from faith" (v. 11) are, then, presented as two mutually exclusive modes of being (cf. Chibici-Revneanu). As already indicated above, the verb "to live" probably does not have an eschatological or soteriological import in either v. 11b or v. 12b (cf. Deut 30:16), as often argued. It refers simply to conduct or existence qualified or determined by one thing (law observance) or another (faith). As Lührmann (61) points out, "the juxtaposition of Hab 2:4 and Lev 18:5 . . . can have the power of proof only if *live* in the two texts is understood without any emphasis and not taken in the sense of the full promise of life." The future tense is not so much promissory as determinative: The just one shall from now on "live" on the basis of faith (v. 11b; cf. 2:20), just as someone who is committed to doing the law's commandments shall henceforth "live" in them (v. 12b; cf. 2:14: "living in a Jewish manner"). The meaning of "shall live" is the same as the one found in *Pss. Sol.* 14.1–3, which itself echoes the language of Lev 18:5: "The Lord is faithful . . . to those who walk in [*en*] the righteousness [*dikaiosynē*] of his ordinances, in [*en*] the law, which he commanded us for our life [*zōē*]; the devout of the Lord shall [as they have to this moment] live [*zēsontai*] in [*en*] it forever."[300]

When the verb "to live" is interpreted in this noneschatological way, Paul's concern in vv. 11 and 12 cannot be either to solve or to underscore a seeming contradiction in Scripture—between Hab 2:4 (promising eschatological life on the basis of faith) and Lev 18:5 (*falsely* promising eschatological life in the realm of the law).[301] In neither case does Paul even explicitly indicate that he is quoting. The only such indication in v. 12 is that the quoted material stands in syntactical tension with what precedes (Stanley 1992: 37). Whether that would have mattered to the Galatians is a moot question. Paul borrows words from the Scripture, to which the new preachers probably attach primary importance, but the meaning of those words is more important to him than the source from which they come. Paul's concern in vv. 11–12, when taken together with v. 10, is to show that "living in" (the works of) the law, which is a matter of "doing" the law's commandments and seeking to be justified (in the future) on this basis (cf. 5:4), is utterly incompatible with "living on the basis of Christ's faith," which is a matter of God's grace and receiving the Spirit, which attests God's rectifying activity in the world (2:21). Paul's focus in 3:10–12 is on the problem that he discerns with observing the law: those who live from law observance "live" under its curse. For this reason, the (observance of the) law "is not from faith" (*ouk estin ek pisteōs*), since "faith" conveys a blessing, not a curse. In sum, vv. 11–12 may be paraphrased as follows:

> Since no one is justified before God in the sphere of law observance, it is plain that someone who is justified on the basis of Christ's faith shall henceforth live (exist) only on the basis of that faith. Observance of the law, however, has nothing in common with faith, since those who have committed themselves to doing what the law requires shall henceforth live (exist) in that realm, and that means living under its curse.

[13–14] The previous verses could give the impression that observance of the law (leading, in Paul's view, inevitably to a curse) and (Christ's) faith (conveying a blessing on those who believe in him) are matters of choice: The

---

300. The eschatological interpretation of Lev 18:5 is attested in the targums, which are from a later period: "And you shall keep my statutes and my judgments, which if a man do he shall live by them an everlasting life" (*Targum Onqelos*); "And you shall keep my statutes, and the order of my judgments, which if a man do he shall live in them, in the life of eternity, and his position shall be with the just" (*Targum Pseudo-Jonathan*; quoted from Longenecker 120). If asked, the new preachers in Galatia would undoubtedly confirm that justification on the basis of law observance contains the promise of eschatological life beyond the final judgment, but that does not seem to be the point at issue in Paul's citation of Lev 18:5 in v. 12.

301. Martyn (328–34) gives an extensive discussion of this issue, with bibliography.

The Spirit and the True Heirs of the Promise Made to Abraham

Galatians are being called upon to choose between his gospel and that of the new preachers (see comment on 1:6–9 and Excursus 4). That Paul is not calling upon the Galatians to make a decision between two modes of being Christian is indicated by these final two verses, in which Paul repreaches the gospel of the crucified Christ that he had preached to them initially (3:1), now formulating what they initially heard (*akoē*; 3:2, 5) in a manner designed to address the issue at hand, the law and the curse under which it places all human beings:

> [13a]Christ redeemed us from the curse of the law, [13b]having become a curse for us, [13c]because it stands written: "Accursed is everyone who hangs on a tree" [Deut 21:23], [14a]so that the blessing of Abraham might come to the Gentiles in Christ Jesus, [14b]so that we might receive the promise of the Spirit through faith.

Verse 13a (the main clause) and v. 14b (a subordinate clause dependent on v. 13a) are bound to each other by Paul's use of the first-person plural pronoun ("us," "we") in both clauses:

> [13a]Christ redeemed [all of] *us* from the curse of the law, . . .
> [14b]so that *we* [who believe, including Gentiles] might [all] receive the promise of the Spirit through faith.

The particular difficulties of vv. 13bc and 14a should not be allowed to obscure the primary, plain message of vv. 13a and 14b, which carry the main thought of this sense unit: Christ redeemed "us" from the curse of the law, so that "we" might receive the promise of the Spirit [as "we" indeed have] through faith (cf. 3:1–5). The first-person plural in v. 14b shows that the same pronoun in v. 13a cannot be restricted to Jewish believers, as sometimes argued (Burton 169; Betz 148 n. 101; Witherington 236–38; Hays 262) and as was the case in 2:15–16. For Paul, Gentiles as well as Jews fall under the law's curse (see comment on v. 10 above), and Gentile believers as well as Jewish ones received and continue to receive the Spirit (cf. 3:2: "You Galatians received the Spirit"); they all received, and continue to receive, it "through [Christ's] faith," thus not through law observance (see on v. 14 below). Paul's use of the first-person plural pronoun is rhetorically effective: it obliterates the distinction between Jew and Gentile (cf. 3:28) that lies at the heart of the theology of the new preachers in Galatia (cf. comment on 2:15–16; Rom 3:22).

In both v. 13a and v. 14b, furthermore, as in v. 13b ("having become a curse for us"), Paul uses probably traditional formulations: the claim that "Christ" (*Christos*) did something "for us" (*hyper hēmōn*) through his death (1:4; 2:20; cf. 1 Cor 15:3); the notion of "receiving" (*lambanō*) the Spirit (3:2; Acts 2:38; John 20:22); the expression "the promise of the Spirit" (*hē epangelia tou pneumatos*), also found in Acts 2:33 (cf. Luke 24:49; Acts 1:4–5; Eph 1:13; Heb

9:15); and the prepositional phrase "through faith," *dia tēs pisteōs* (2:16; 3:26; cf. Rom 3:25). The use of the first-person plural is probably also an indicator of traditional material. Paul thus plants his repreaching of the crucified Christ in the soil of received, common tradition (cf. 1:4; 1 Cor 15:3–5). He deploys the already-traditional formulations in a contextually relevant way, namely, by introducing the notion of liberation from the law's curse.

In v. 13a, the verb *exagorazō* ("redeem") is a commercial term sometimes used in connection with buying back slaves (BDAG 343; Diodorus Siculus 15.7.1; 36.2.2) and means "to ransom" (BDAG 525). Paul thus conceptualizes the human predicament apart from Christ as a form of slavery (cf. 2:4–5; 4:1–3): Apart from Christ, human beings (Gentiles as well as Jews) are enslaved "*under* [*hypo*] a curse" (v. 10a), that of the law (13a). As noted in the comment on v. 10a, those "under a curse" are, in Paul's view, still stuck "in the present evil age" (1:4) where malevolent powers hold all human beings "under" their control. One of these cosmic powers evidently is the law itself, as the parallel passage in 4:4–5 shows: "God sent forth his Son . . . so that he might redeem (*exagorasē*) those *under* the law." To be "under the law" (*hypo nomon*, 3:23; 4:4–5, 21) is thus to be "under a curse," *hypo kataran* (v. 10a), that of the law itself (see comments on 1:4; 3:23–26; Wilson 2005). Since to be *hypo nomon* is to be *hypo kataran*, the expression "the curse of the law" probably means that the law itself is a curse (the curse, which is the law), not simply that it effects or pronounces such a curse (cf. comments on 3:19–25).[302] The tense of the verb is aorist: Christ "redeemed" (*exēgorasen*, v. 13) those who believe in him from the curse of the law, in order to give them "the blessing of Abraham," the promised Spirit (v. 14). For the people of faith, *the* redemptive event has occurred, the end of the old age (that of the law and its curse) has come. The import of the verb "redeem" is not to be pressed unduly, as if Christ's death were the price he had to pay, giving something to someone (e.g., Satan). To redeem a slave is to set that person free. The verb used here is virtually synonymous with the one used in 1:4 (*exaireō*, "rescue") and means "to liberate (from)" (BDAG 343; cf. 5:1).

In v. 13b Paul indicates how this redemption was achieved, by Christ's "having become [*genomenos*] a curse [*katara*] for [*hyper*] us."[303] The ambiguity of the participle (*genomenos*, aor.) allows diverse interpretations of this passage. It could in principle be construed as temporal ("after/when Christ had become a

---

302. Paul is much more nuanced in his Letter to the Romans, never referring to the law as, or in connection with, a curse. Still, he can characterize the human condition before and apart from Christ as existence "under the law," contrasting that condition with that of being "under grace" (6:14–15).

303. For a brief overview of the many interpretations that this passage has elicited, see Betz 150–51; Brondos 3–10. Much effort has been expended on seeking to understand what Paul does *not* say or explicate: how Christ's "becoming a curse for us" actually effects or contributes to "our" redemption from the curse of the law (see the comment on 1:4a). The comment below will assume that the verse is intelligible on the basis of what Paul says here and elsewhere in Galatians.

curse for us") or causal ("because he had become a curse for us"). The participle is probably best understood to express means ("*by* having become a curse for us"; Burton 172), though Paul does not elaborate or specify. It is furthermore difficult to determine whether Christ's becoming a curse "for us" constitutes his redeeming work or is to be distinguished from it, if not separated from it. If the former, Christ's redemptive work is accomplished by his becoming a curse on the cross. If the latter, his becoming a curse precedes his redemptive work, which is then to be identified with his resurrection (cf. Rom 4:25: "Christ was raised for our justification"). The resurrection of Christ is surely presupposed, as 1:1 shows (God "raised him from the dead"). According to 1 Cor 15:17, Christ's death has no saving effects without the resurrection: "If Christ has not been raised, . . . you are still in your sins," the sins "for" which "Christ died," according to 1 Cor 15:3. The death and resurrection of Christ are two sides of the same saving event, that saving event in v. 13 being "our" liberation from the curse of the law.

The solemnly introduced citation from Deut 21:23 in v. 13c—"because it stands written, 'Accursed [*epikataratos*][304] is everyone who hangs on a tree'"—indicates that the noun "curse" in v. 13b is being used figuratively to mean "accursed" (= "being under a curse"): "Christ became a curse, i.e., accursed, for us" (Burton 171; Vouga 76; Mussner 233; Williams 93; cf. LXX: Jer 24:9; 33:6 [26:6E]; 51:8 [44:8E]). Paul has probably used the noun "curse" (*katara*) to provide a verbal link to the mention of "the curse [*katara*] of the law" in v. 13a (cf. v. 10a: "under a curse").[305] The phrase "for us" recalls the similar phrase in 2:20: The Son of God who "loved me and gave himself up *for* [*hyper*] me," for my sake (cf. 1:4: "the one who gave himself *for* [*hyper*] our sins," as in 1 Cor 15:3). The sense of v. 13ab, therefore, is not "Christ redeemed us from the law's curse by having allowed himself to become accursed in our place" (so, e.g., Bultmann 1951: 296–97), but rather "Christ redeemed us from the law's curse by having allowed himself to become accursed for our benefit." The substitutionary meaning ("in our place" or "in our stead") would imply that Christ took upon himself a penalty that ought to be imposed on human beings. For Paul, however, human beings apart from Christ are already under a curse (v. 10a); the issue is redemption from this already-existing situation. The phrase "having become a curse [i.e., accursed] for us" is evidently meant to call attention to the depth of Christ's love (2:20): He went so far as to share "our" predicament of

---

304. The Greek word is an adjective (hence "accursed"), not a past participle, as the English translation "cursed" (e.g., NRSV) might suggest.

305. The theory that Paul here uses the noun "curse" under the influence of the Hebrew text of Deut 21:23 (*Kî-qillat ʾĕlōhîm*, "a curse of God") is thus unnecessary. Consistent with the Hebrew text, later translators of the OT into Greek (Aquila and Theodotion) have *katara theou*, "a curse of God." Paul, however, says not that Christ redeemed us from the curse of God, but rather from the curse of *the law*; see below.

being under the law and its curse.[306] Christ's "having become [*genomenos*] a curse for us" means the same as Christ's "having become [*genomenos*] under the law" (4:4), just as "to redeem [*agorazō*] us from the curse of the law" means the same as "to redeem [*agorazō*] those under the law" (4:5). The idea is not that Christ became the curse from which "we" are then granted an exemption, but that Christ shared "our" predicament in order to liberate "us" from that predicament, along with himself (cf. Rom 6:9; 1 Cor 15:21).[307]

In what sense Christ became "accursed" is indicated through the citation from Deut 21:23: someone who is hung on a "tree" (*xylon*) is accursed, as (by implication) Christ was when he was nailed to a cross.[308] Deuteronomy 21:23 originally had nothing to do with execution by crucifixion, but with the display of an already-executed criminal on a tree:

> If there be sin in anyone [with respect to] a judgment of death and he dies and you hang him on a tree, his body shall not remain all night upon the tree, but you shall by all means bury it on that day; for *cursed by God is everyone hanging on a tree*; and you shall by no means defile the land that the Lord your God gives you for an inheritance. (Deut 21:22–23 LXX)

The part that Paul quotes from this passage was also interpreted as a reference to crucifixion by the writers of the Dead Sea Scrolls (4QpNah; 11QTemple 64.6–13), whereby "tree" was understood to mean "cross" (cf. Acts 5:30; 10:39; 1 Pet 2:24; Fitzmyer 1978). In this respect, Paul's citation of Deut 21:23 does not mark a new interpretive move on his part. Paul's citation does not, however, exactly match the LXX text in some important ways (cf. Verhoef 81–86; Stanley 1992: 245–48):

> Paul: "Accursed [*epikataratos*] is everyone who hangs [*pas ho kremamenos*] on a tree."
> LXX: "Cursed [*kekatēramenos*][309] by God [*hypo theou*] is everyone hanging [*pas kremamenos*] on a tree."

Some of these differences can be readily explained as due to the influence of Deut 27:26, as cited in v. 10:

---

306. Verse 13a–b is probably Paul's contextually determined interpretation of traditional formulations of Christ's dying "for us" or "for our sins" (see comment above; Dunn 177); Paul himself has introduced the language of liberation from the law's curse (contra Betz 150; Longenecker 121–23).

307. Cf. Phil 2:7–8: "He emptied himself, taking the form of a slave, having become [*genomenos*] in the likeness of a human being [cf. Gal 4:4: 'having come [*genomenos*] from a woman'], ... he humbled himself, having become [*genomenos*] obedient unto death, even death on a cross" (AT).

308. Burton (173) correctly observes: "The quotation ... is introduced to support the statement that Christ became a curse, not that he thereby 'delivered us from the curse of the law,' or that it was 'for us.'"

309. A perfect passive participle, lit., "having been cursed [by God]."

The Spirit and the True Heirs of the Promise Made to Abraham 213

Deuteronomy 27:26 in Gal 3:10: "Accursed [*epikataratos*] is everyone who [*pas hos*] does not remain . . ."

Deuteronomy 21:23 in Gal 3:13: "Accursed [*epikataratos*] is everyone who [*pas ho*] hangs on a tree."

By far the most important change, however, is Paul's omission of the prepositional phrase "by God" (*hypo theou*) from the citation of Deut 21:23.[310] One can explain the omission of the phrase to be the inevitable consequence of the change from a perfect passive participle (*kekatēramenos*, "cursed") to a passive adjective (*epikataratos*, "accursed"), whereby the prepositional phrase has become grammatically awkward (there being no parallel for such a construction in the LXX or the NT). Paul's omission of the phrase, one can then argue, is of no substantial significance; he still means that Christ became "cursed by God" because "the curse of the law" is "the curse of God" (Calvin 55; Longenecker 122; Dunn 177; Stanley 1992: 247; Tolmie 2005: 122). The conformation of the text of Deut 21:23 to that of Deut 27:26 proves to be significant, however, in demonstrating this interpretation to be utterly wrong. Paul's omission of the prepositional phrase "by God" is not a stylistic matter but a substantive, theological one, since v. 10 concerns a curse pronounced *by the law*, not a curse pronounced *by God*. That v. 10 is to be read in this way is indicated by vv. 8 and 11, where Paul places the law and God on opposite sides of a great divide: "God justifies the Gentiles on the basis of faith" and for that reason "no one is justified before God in the law." God bestows a blessing (the Spirit); the law places those who observe it under its curse (v. 10). According to v. 13bc, then, Christ became a curse (accursed), not because he was cursed by God, but because he was cursed by the law (Burton 168–72; Rohde 144; Martyn 321, 326). The conformation of the citation from Deut 21:23 to Deut 27:26 in v. 10b also suggests that Christ, in being cursed by the law, shares the predicament of humanity, which is cursed by the same law; he "became under the law" (4:4–5), thus also under its curse, together with those whom he redeemed (cf. Hooker). While the two curses of Deut 27:26 and 21:23 may in fact be different curses in Deuteronomy itself, Paul has brought them close together through the changes he has introduced into his citation from Deut 21:23.

Verse 13, then, can be paraphrased as follows: "Christ liberated all of us from the law's curse [Deut 27:26] by allowing himself to become accursed by the law for our benefit, for as someone who was crucified, he stood accursed in the eyes of the law [Deut 21:23], just as we did." As indicated above, unstated but presupposed in v. 13 is the conviction that God raised the crucified Christ

---

310. The LXX resolves the ambiguity of the Hebrew "a curse of God," reproduced by the literal translations of Aquila and Theodotion, which can mean either "cursed by God" (subjective genitive) or "cursed [an offense] to God" (objective genitive). See Lightfoot 152.

from the dead (1:1), thereby delivering him from the curse under which he had voluntarily placed himself (cf. 1:4; 2:20). Those who have come to believe in him (2:16b) now share in his victory over the curse of the law, being given the blessing of the promised Spirit in its stead (Hooker; see on v. 14, below). Paul cites Deut 21:23 to show the Galatians and the new preachers who shall be listening to the letter with them that in "the Scripture" to which they appeal, "it stands written" that even Christ himself (!) stands accursed, just as "it stands written" that those who live from law observance are accursed. The law is a cursing force, not one that mediates the blessing promised to Abraham. It is possible (Hultgren 102–4; cf. Sänger 1994) that before his conversion and call, Paul used this text to call into question the claim of Christian Jews that Jesus was the expected Messiah of Israel; if so, he now uses it to show that where Christ and the law collide, it is the law, not Christ, that must give way. They do not complement each other as in the gospel of the new preachers; to the contrary Christ has triumphed over the law's curse, putting an end to its malevolent effects on human life.

Verse 14 consists of two *hina* clauses, which express a combination of purpose and result ("so that"). Both clauses are dependent on the main clause, found in v. 13a ("Christ redeemed us from the curse of the law"). As noted above, the second *hina* clause uses a first-person plural, as does v. 13a, which means that the first *hina* clause is transitional, providing a bridge from the theme of curse and blessing (a theme for which Paul is indebted to the new preachers in Galatia) to that of the Spirit, which is thereby identified as "the blessing of Abraham" (an expression used in Gen 28:4 LXX): the blessing that God promised to Abraham and his descendants (Gen 28:3–4; see comment on vv. 8–9 above):

> Christ redeemed us from the curse of the law . . .
> so that the blessing of Abraham [the promised Spirit] might in Christ Jesus come [as it has] to the Gentiles,
> [i.e.,] so that we [who believe, including Gentiles] might receive [as we all have] the promise of the Spirit through [Christ's] faith.

In v. 14a, the phrase "to the Gentiles" stands emphatically at the beginning of the clause in the Greek: literally, "so that *to the Gentiles* the blessing of Abraham might come. . . ." The share of the Gentiles in the benefits of Christ's faithful death has been the theme throughout the passage. The purpose of Christ's death (and resurrection) was thus that the blessing of Abraham might also come to the Gentiles, without their having to observe the law. The prepositional phrase "in Christ Jesus" in v. 14a is the opposite of the phrase "in the law" in v. 11a (cf. "remain in all the things written in the book of the law" in v. 10b, and "shall live in them" in v. 12b), and the counterpart to "in you

[Abraham]" in the citation from Gen 12:3 in v. 8. For Paul, to be "in Christ" is to be "in Abraham," and not to be "in the law." In the sphere of Christ's lordship, a sphere created by his redemptive death on the cross, the Spirit is given to all who believe, Gentiles included; the law does not enter into the picture. At the same time, the phrase "in Christ Jesus" can also be understood instrumentally— "through Christ Jesus"—in which case the parallelism with the phrase "through [Christ's] faith" (v. 14b) becomes evident (see Excursus 11; Matera 120–21).[311] The expression "through faith" (*dia tēs pisteōs*) harks back to the expression "through the faith of Jesus Christ" in 2:16a, which Paul has taken over from existing Jewish Christian tradition (cf. 3:26 and comment there; Rom 3:25). The article with "faith" in the Greek is being used anaphorically, to refer back to a previous instance: "through the faith already referred to."

The particular focus on "the Gentiles" throughout this passage gives way to the unity of believers, whether Jewish or Gentile, in the shared reception (cf. Acts 2:38; John 20:22) of the promised Spirit in v. 14b, harking back to 3:1–5 ("You received the Spirit"). Here for the first time in the letter, Paul introduces the word *epangelia*, "promise," which does not occur in the LXX text of Genesis. Paul uses it in the probably traditional phrase "the promise of the Spirit" (Acts 2:33; cf. Luke 24:49; Acts 1:4–5), which means "the promise that is the Spirit" (a genitive of apposition). The term "promise" is thus being used passively to designate "what was promised," warranting the translation "the promised Spirit." That promised Spirit is the blessing of Abraham (cf. Isa 44:3 LXX: "I will pour out my spirit on your offspring and my blessing on your children").[312] Those who receive the Spirit are Abraham's true heirs, not those who live from law observance. At the end of v. 14, therefore, Paul grounds his argument—and the experience of his audience—not in "the Scripture," but in the tradition shared by all believers, whether Jewish or Gentile, concerning the reception of the promised Spirit through the faithful death of Christ.

To sum up: The reception of the Spirit through faith, meaning the faith of Christ, has made Gentile believers, no less than Jewish believers, the (metaphorical and theological) "sons of Abraham," thus the rightful heirs of the promise that God made to the faithful patriarch. That promise concerned the gift of the Spirit, which is "the blessing of Abraham." Those believers who insist on deriving their identity from works of the law instead of from Christ's faith do not receive this blessing but stand under a curse, that of the law itself. The Galatians will not want to take this step, for as Paul reminds them, Christ

---

311. Cf. 3:22, where Paul refers to the promise (the Spirit) that is given to those who believe "on the basis of (*ek*) the faith of Jesus Christ."

312. Some would prefer to identify the blessing of Abraham with justification (Burton 175; Fung 141; Williams 94; Witherington 228). The parallelism of the purpose clauses indicates, however, that the Spirit is specifically meant. The Spirit provides the basis for justification, which, at least in Galatians, is always a matter of expectation and promise (see on 2:16, 21; 5:5).

has redeemed "us" all from the curse of the law by his faithful death, precisely so that the blessing of the faithful Abraham might come to the Gentiles who believe as well as to the Jews who believe, so that "we" might all receive the promised Spirit through the faith of Christ.

3:15–22 The Promise to Abraham and the Law of Moses

At the close of the previous paragraph, Paul has referred to "the promise of the Spirit" (3:14), using what was probably a more widely known expression (Acts 2:33; cf. Luke 24:49; Acts 1:4–5; see comment on 3:14). Thereby he has for the first time introduced into his argument against the proclamation of the new preachers in Galatia the term "promise" (*epangelia*). Though the noun and its cognate verb are not actually found in the LXX text of Genesis, the term accurately describes the nature of what God declares to Abraham in Gen 12:2–3; 15:2–5; 17:1–8; and 18:18 (see comment on Gal 3:8). Having introduced the reference to "the promise of the Spirit" in 3:14, God's promise to Abraham now becomes the primary theme of the present passage: the noun "promise" occurs six times (3:16, 17, 18 [2x], 21, 22) in this connection and the verb once (3:19). The noun is found only one more time in Gal 3, in v. 29, where Paul summarizes his argument to that point by telling the Galatians that they are "the offspring of Abraham, heirs according to a promise." There are two further instances in 4:21–5:1, where Paul once again returns to the figure of Abraham and the question of his offspring "according to the Spirit" (4:29); the latter are identified as "children of promise in the pattern of Isaac" (4:28), Isaac himself having been "begotten through a promise" (4:23).

For Paul, as for the new preachers now active in Galatia, God's promise to Abraham that in him all the Gentiles (or nations) would be blessed (3:8) found its fulfillment in the eschatological gift of the Spirit, which is thus called "the blessing of Abraham" (3:14). Whenever Paul here refers to "promise" in the present passage, therefore, he also has in view the fulfillment of that promise in the gift and the reception of the Spirit, whereby new "sons" of Abraham" (3:7) are being produced, specifically among the Gentiles (see introduction to Section III: 3:1–4:7, above). For Paul, furthermore, the recipients of that eschatological blessing are believers "whose identity derives [exclusively] from faith" (3:7; see comment there), *not* believers "whose identity derives [primarily] from works of the law" (3:10). In Paul's view, the latter remain under a curse, that of the law itself (3:10, 13).

This passage carries forward the argument of the previous passage. In the latter, Paul has sought to associate the figure of Abraham exclusively with the justification of believers on the basis of Christ's faithful death and to dissociate his blessing (the promised Spirit's producing offspring for Abraham) from the observance of the law. In the current passage, he seeks to associate the

The Spirit and the True Heirs of the Promise Made to Abraham 217

"promise" (3:16, 17, 18 [2x], 21, 22)[313] that God made to Abraham exclusively with Christ (3:16), and thus to dissociate it from "the law" (3:17, 18, 19, 21 [3x]) of which Moses was "the mediator" (3:19–20) on Mount Sinai (cf. 4:25). Both passages end with similar *hina* clauses, demonstrating that the basic issue throughout is the gift and the reception of the Spirit "through" (*dia*) or "from" (*ek*) Christ's faith:

3:14 "that we [who believe] might receive the promise of the Spirit through [Christ's] faith"
3:22 "that the promise [of the Spirit] from the faith of Jesus Christ be given to those who believe"

The passage falls readily into two discrete units. In the first, Paul maintains that the promise to Abraham constituted "a covenant" validated by God that the coming of the law at a later time could not nullify or change. He thereby makes explicit what he has already assumed to be the case in the previous passage (3:6–14): the promise that God made to Abraham has nothing to do with the law or its observance. In the second unit, Paul addresses the question that will be on the minds of the Galatians and the new preachers who shall be listening to the letter with them: "Why then the law?" Paul's difficult answer, in which he separates the law from God, leads inevitably to a second question: "Is the law then against the promises of God?" The second unit of this passage is probably the most opaque of the whole letter. The two units are closely bound to each other by the single issue of the relationship between the Abrahamic promise and the Mosaic law—or rather, the lack of any relationship between them.

3:15 Brethren, I am speaking in a human way: no one annuls or appends a codicil to a validated will even of a human being. **16** The promises, however, were spoken to Abraham and to his offspring. It does not say "and to the offsprings," as referring to many, but as referring to one, "and to your offspring," which is Christ. **17** I mean this: the law, having come after four hundred thirty years, does not invalidate a covenant previously validated by God[a] so as to void the promise. **18** For if the inheritance were on the basis of a law, it would no longer be on the basis of a promise. But God has graciously given it to Abraham through a promise.

19 Why then the law?[b] It was added for the sake of the transgressions, until the offspring for whom it had been promised should come, having been arranged through angels by the hand of a mediator. **20** A mediator is not of one; God, however, is one. **21** Is the law then against the promises of God?[c] Not at all. For if a law had been given that is able to make alive,

---

313. See below on why the term is plural in 3:16, 21.

justification would indeed be on the basis of the law.ᵈ **22** But the Scripture shut all things up under Sin, so that the promise from the faith of Jesus Christ be given to those who believe.

    a. The Textus Receptus adds here the words *eis Christon*, "until/unto Christ" ("with Christ in view"), which seem to have been inspired by v. 16 and 3:24.
    b. Here 𝔓46 and some other, primarily Western manuscripts read, "Why then the law of practices [*praxeōn*]?" This reading is secondary, representing an attempt to specify what sort of law Paul here has in view.
    c. Some good manuscripts omit *tou theou,* "of God" (𝔓46, B), whereas other good manuscripts include these words (א, A, C, D, and the vast majority). The NA²⁷ places them in brackets.
    d. Instead of *ek nomou* ("from, on the basis of the law"), B and 𝔓46 read *en nomō* ("in the law"), as in 3:11 and 5:4. Both are Pauline (for *ek nomou*, see 3:18) and they amount to the same thing: to seek justification in the sphere of the law is to seek it on that basis.

[15–18] Here Paul addresses the Galatians as *adelphoi*, "brethren," for the first time since 1:11 (see comment there). The term, grammatically masculine in Greek, is semantically inclusive of both women and men. In 1:11 Paul has told the "brethren" that the gospel preached by him is not "a human matter," *kata anthrōpon*; he here tells the "brethren" that he now wants to speak to them "in a human way," also *kata anthrōpon*. Paul thereby seems to alert his readers in advance that the following analogy between a human being's last will and testament and God's promissory covenant with Abraham has its limits, something every interpreter of the passage needs to remember. Paul's primary aim is to undergird his attempt to dissociate the promise that God made to Abraham (and thus also the fulfillment of that promise through the gift of the Spirit) from the law (and thus also from the observance of that law). He does so by likening the "covenant" (v. 17) that God made with Abraham—the covenant of promise (Gen 15:18; 17:1–8), not that of circumcision (17:9–14)—to a human will or testament (v. 15):

> ¹⁵No one annuls or appends a codicil[314] to a validated will [*diathēkē*] even of a[nother] human being [let alone one of God]. . . . ¹⁷I mean this: the law, having come after four hundred thirty years, does not invalidate a covenant [*diathēkē*] previously validated by God so as to void the promise.

A very literal translation of v. 15 would yield: "I speak in a human way: *even of a human being a validated will no one annuls.*" The adverb "even" (*homōs*)

---

    314. The verb *epidiatassomai* ("to add a codicil") is not attested prior to the instance in this verse (BDAG 370). Josephus uses the noun *epidiathēkē* in connection with a codicil to a will in *Ant.* 17.226 (cf. Bruce 171).

indicates that God's "covenant" with Abraham, the subject of v. 17, is being illuminated by the analogy of a human "will" in v. 15, rather than the reverse (cf. Burton 178–79; Longenecker 127). When accented with an acute accent on the first syllable, the word *homōs* can mean "nevertheless" or "yet," implying a contrast ("I speak in a human way; nevertheless . . ."), but when accented with a circumflex on the second syllable, the word can mean "likewise," implying a comparison (cf. LSJ 1230; BDF 450.2; BDAG 710; NRSV, NIV). That difference has led to somewhat different translations and interpretations of the verse. The analogy in question arguably has elements of both contrast and comparison; the translation "even" (also NJB, RSV; Ridderbos; Dunn) can cover both, whatever the proper accenting may be.

The analogy between a human will and God's covenant with Abraham is facilitated by the fact that in Greek the word for both is the same, *diathēkē*. The word commonly means "will" or "testament" in Hellenistic Greek and "covenant" in the LXX. In the analogy that Paul posits between them, v. 16 can best be understood as a (rather awkward) parenthesis, giving Paul's peculiar interpretation of Gen 17:8, whereby he makes plain that the promises to Abraham have to do with Christ, and Christ alone (see comment on v. 16 below). The analogy should not be pressed by adding or speculating about elements that are not there (e.g., the fact that a human testator dies, whereas God does not; the dogmatic presupposition that whereas human beings can and do change their minds, God does not). The argument is implicitly *a minori ad maius*: what counts for a merely human *diathēkē* (it cannot be nullified or changed by a third party) counts even more for God's *diathēkē* with Abraham (it cannot be nullified or changed by the law, here implicitly regarded as a third party). Like a human testator, God may dispose of his goods (the inheritance) according to the terms of the *diathēkē* validated by him. The testator sets the terms of his will unilaterally; God likewise sets the terms of his covenant with Abraham unilaterally. "Validated" (*kekyrōmenēn* in v. 15; *prokekyrōmenēn* in v. 17) here means "ratified" in some official, public way and thus "legally binding" (BDAG 579, 872) for all concerned.

It is clear from the context that "no one" in v. 15 means "no one except the testator himself should he be so inclined" (*contra* Matera 130; Vouga 79). The exception is consistent with contemporary Greek and Roman law.[315] The point is that someone *else*, a third party or an outsider, cannot tamper with the testator's legally validated will. By the same token, "no one" can annul or append a

---

315. For discussion of the background, see Longenecker 128–30. If one argues that the term *diathēkē* in v. 15 refers to a covenant (treaty or agreement) between two equal human parties (so Burton 179, 502), which is a meaning attested in the LXX (cf., e.g., Gen 21:27, 32; 26:28; 31:44), then one would have to paraphrase "no one, except by mutual consent between the two parties to the said covenant" (cf. Josh 9:15–20). But the analogy concerns third-party tampering.

codicil to God's promissory covenant with Abraham except God himself—but for Paul, God has certainly not modified the promise to Abraham, as the coming of Christ and his Spirit attest. Moreover, the covenant validated by God is not an agreement between two parties, any more than a human will is, but an arrangement initiated and adhered to by God alone, as is the case in Gen 17:1–8 LXX:[316]

> [17:1]And Abram was ninety-nine years old, and the Lord appeared to Abram and said to him, I am your God, be well-pleasing before me, and be blameless. [2]And I will establish *my covenant* between me and you, and I will multiply you exceedingly. [3]And Abram fell upon his face, and God spoke to him, saying, [4]. . . "*My covenant* is with you, and you shall be a father of a multitude of nations. [5]And your name shall no more be called Abram, but your name shall be Abraham, for I have made you a father of many nations. [6]And I will increase you very exceedingly, and I will make nations of you, and kings shall come out of you. [7]And I will establish *my covenant* between you and thy seed after you, to their generations, for *an everlasting covenant*, to be your God, and of your seed after you. [8]And I will give to you and to your seed after you the land in which you sojourn, even all the land of Canaan for an everlasting possession,[317] and I will be God to them."

Three times God refers to "*my* covenant," which is "an everlasting covenant." This covenant consists solely of God's promises, given in Gen 17:2–8. The only thing Abraham does is to fall on his face and listen; he does not say a word, and he is not asked to do anything. The covenant in view in Gal 3:17 is thus, for Paul, identical with God's promises to Abraham, especially that he would become the father of a multitude of nations (cf. Rom 4:17 and comment on v. 16 below), *not* the covenant that requires Abraham to do his part by keeping the commandment of circumcision (Gen 17:9–14).

Two crucial and (doubtless in the eyes of the new preachers in Galatia) controversial assumptions appear to lie behind Paul's reasoning. The first is that the "coming" (rather than the "giving") of the law is *not* to be understood as God's act whereby he (as the sovereign testator) intended either to annul (*athetei*) his own covenant (*diathēkē*) with Abraham or, as the new preachers in Galatia may have been claiming (Martyn 337), to append a specifying codicil to it (*epidiatassetai*). For the new preachers, the law was added to the promise by God and represents a further specification of the covenant with Abraham, spelling out the obligations of the people of Israel to the God of Abraham ("covenantal nomism"). Paul's use of the verb "annul" reflects his

---

316. For this reason the word *diathēkē* in v. 15 cannot mean "covenant" (see previous note) in the sense of an agreement or treaty between two human parties. The analogy only works if the *diathēkē* in v. 15 is as one-sided as the *diathēkē* in v. 17.

317. Cf. Gen 15:18 LXX: "In that day the Lord made a covenant with Abram, saying, 'To your offspring I will give this land, from the river of Egypt to the great river Euphrates.'"

The Spirit and the True Heirs of the Promise Made to Abraham 221

own view that the law and the covenant of promise are incompatible: the law, if added by God, would in Paul's view represent a nullification of God's promissory covenant with Abraham, whereby God invalidates (*akyroi*) it so as to void (*katargēsai*) the promise he made to Abraham (Gal 3:17). God certainly did not do that (cf. Cosgrove). Paul thus likens the coming of the law after the covenant of promise validated by God to a third party tampering with a validated (legally ratified) human will (*diathēkē*). Consistent with this, Paul will maintain in vv. 19–20 that the law "was added" (*prosetethē*) to the promise, "having been arranged [*diatageis*] through [the intervention of] angels"; Moses, the mediator of the law to Israel, did not serve as a mediator for God but for these angels (see comment below).

In this connection one may ask how Paul could ignore Gen 17:9–14 (cf. Rom 4:10–12) and the commandment to circumcise sons given there: "And God said to Abraham, 'You also shall fully keep my covenant [*diathēkē*], you and your offspring after you for their generations. And this is the covenant that you shall fully keep between me and you, and between your offspring after you for their generations: every male of you shall be circumcised'" (Gen 17:9–10 LXX). A possible answer is that Paul works from the assumption that God's promise to Abraham concerning offspring (Gen 15:1–6; 17:1–8), to which the term "covenant" is applied before and apart from any mention of circumcision in Gen 17:2, 4, 7 (cf. already in Gen 15:18), preceded the commandment to circumcise (17:9–14), just as the fulfillment of the promise in the birth of Isaac (21:1–3) preceded the latter's circumcision (21:4). The promise and the fulfillment of that promise thus had nothing whatsoever to do with Abraham's obeying the commandment to circumcise his sons. Paul furthermore includes the circumcision commandment under the notion of "the law," perhaps on the basis of Lev 12:3, which mandates the circumcision of a male child on the eighth day but makes no allusion to Abraham. By saying that the law (including, then, the commandment to circumcise) came 430 years after the promise, he in effect emphasizes that the former did not come on the heels of the latter;[318] in driving this temporal wedge between the promise and the law (including, it seems, the circumcision commandment), Paul prepares the way for the conceptual wedge he will drive between them in v. 18: the two are in principle mutually exclusive.

Paul's second assumption in vv. 15, 17–18 appears to be that the promise that God made to Abraham concerns Christ himself and thus, by implication, the Spirit ("the inheritance" of v. 18) that believers in Christ receive. The parenthetical v. 16 functions to make this assumption explicit (cf. 3:8): "The

---

318. According to the Hebrew text of Exod 12:40, Israel spent 430 years in Egypt (400 years according to Gen 15:13; Acts 7:6; Josephus, *J.W.* 5.382; *Ant.* 2.204), but according to Exod 12:40 LXX, Israel spent 430 years "in Egypt *and Canaan*" (also Josephus, *Ant.* 2.318), thus apparently measuring from the time of Abraham, as Paul does (see Lührmann 70; Longenecker 133; Vouga 80–81).

promises [*hai epangeliai*], however [*de*], were spoken [by God] to Abraham and to his offspring [*sperma*]. It [the text] does not say 'and to the offsprings,' as referring to many, but as referring to one, 'and to your offspring,' which [offspring] is Christ." The conjunction "however" (*de*) indicates that v. 16 serves to prepare the way for v. 17: the promissory covenant validated by God in the latter verse has ultimately to do with Christ. For Paul, the promises made to Abraham, which constitute the content of the covenant made with Abraham in Gen 17:1–8, were also made to Christ, who is identified as Abraham's sole offspring and thus heir (cf. Matt 1:1). The text from which Paul here quotes is probably Gen 17:8 LXX: "And I will give to you *and to your offspring* after you the land in which you sojourn, even all the land of Canaan for an everlasting possession."[319] God speaks this promise only to Abraham, but he makes it clear that it also applies to his offspring. The promise made to Abraham is also made to his (yet unborn) offspring in the sense that it will find its fulfillment in the birth of offspring. Yet Paul's interpretation of Gen 17:8 is peculiar for at least two reasons:

Peculiarity 1. Paul identifies "the offspring" (*to sperma*) of Abraham as Christ himself (cf. v. 19), rather than as believers in Christ, which would seem to make better sense given 3:7 (the people of faith are "sons of Abraham") and especially 3:29 ("You [Galatians] are [collectively] the offspring of Abraham"). Paul bases his identification on the fact that the word *sperma* (lit., "seed") in Gen 17:8 is singular. The Greek word *sperma* can have a collective meaning, however, just like the English word "seed" or "offspring," referring to many descendants rather than to just one. That is the most natural way to understand the term *sperma* in Gen 17:8, as Paul seems to recognize in specifically rejecting what was probably the interpretation of the word by the new preachers in Galatia: they understand the phrase "and to your offspring" to mean "and to your descendants." Paul denies that the phrase is to be interpreted "and to the offsprings (*spermata*)," thus "as referring to many."[320] Paul himself, however, uses the singular *sperma* with a collective meaning in 3:29, where, as indicated above, he designates those who belong to Christ collectively as the "offspring of Abraham" (*tou Abraam sperma*).

Paul's interpretation of *sperma* in Gen 17:8 as referring to one descendant is not impossible, given the ambiguity inherent in the word itself. In Gen

---

319. Cf. Gen 13:15: "for all the land that you see I will give to you *and to your offspring* forever" (cf. 24:7, which refers back to 13:15 and/or 17:8). Paul is probably citing from Gen 17:8, however, since the word "covenant" occurs in the immediate context (17:2, 4, 7), whereas that is not the case with respect to Gen 13:15 (or 24:7). On the other hand, Gen 15:18 (note 317 above) refers to a "covenant" with Abraham but not to his "offspring."

320. The plural form *spermata*, which is unusual with the meaning "descendants" (Lightfoot 142; cf. Dan 11:31, Theod.; 4 Macc 18:1), is probably from Paul himself having been coined to highlight the key point, that the term *sperma* is technically singular, not plural.

22:16–17; 24:7, the term appears to apply to Isaac, at least primarily. Relevant in this connection is 2 Sam 7:12–14, where David's "offspring" is his son Solomon. In 4QFlor (4Q174) 1.10–11, furthermore, this text is given a messianic interpretation, whereby "offspring" is taken to refer to the Messiah:

> [And] YHWH [de]clares to you that "he will build you a house. I will raise up your seed (offspring) after you and establish the throne of his kingdom [for ev]er. I will be a father to him and he will be a son to me." This (refers to the) "branch of David," who will arise ... in the [l]ast days, as it is written: "I will raise up the hut of David which has fallen" [Amos 9:11].

Paul's interpretation of the singular "seed" in Gen 17:8 is similar, as indeed is his approach to "the Scripture," which he also interprets as referring to the Messiah. For Paul, the Messiah has already come in the person of Jesus Christ, all the more reason for him to read "the Scripture" messianically, through a christological lens. The fact, however, that Paul can also use the term *sperma* collectively to refer to those who belong to Christ (3:29) indicates that his primary concern in focusing on the singularity of the term *sperma* in v. 16 is to facilitate the christological interpretation of Gen 17:8, not to limit Abraham's offspring to a single individual (cf. Gal 4:27–28). In 3:22b and more explicitly in 3:23–29, Paul will indicate that "Christ" is a corporate figure, including those who belong to him solely on the basis of his faith. For this reason both Christ and those who belong to him on the basis of his faith can be called "the [promised] offspring" of Abraham (see comment on 3:29). As Lightfoot (142) comments: "The question therefore is no longer one of grammatical accuracy, but of theological interpretation." Paul's christological interpretation enables him to exclude the interpretation of Gen 17:8 probably being advocated by the new preachers in Galatia, who identify Abraham's offspring as the law-observant people of Israel through history, a people now being restored and renewed by the Messiah, Jesus (Betz 157; Martyn 343–47). For Paul, the promise of Gen 17:8 refers not to the law-observant people of Israel through history, culminating in the law-observant church, but to Christ himself. Between the promise and Christ, therefore, there were no offspring of Abraham, no heirs of the promise that God made to Abraham. The inheritance, the Spirit, became available only with the coming of Christ (see comment on 3:23–29).

Peculiarity 2. Genesis 17:8 mentions only one promise (that of the land), whereas Paul refers here, as in v. 21, to "the [pl.] promises" of God to Abraham (cf. Heb 11:17). Apart from these two instances, Paul uses the singular "promise" (8 times), identifying that singular promise with the Spirit (3:14). It is curious that he would here use the plural, especially since he wants to emphasize the fact that the word *sperma* in Gen 17:8 is singular! By using the plural "promises," Paul acknowledges either (1) that the one promise was made numerous times or (2) that God made a number of promises to Abraham: namely, the promise of land (Gen 17:8; also 12:7; 13:14–17; 15:7, 18–20; 24:7), that of a son and heir (17:15–22; also 15:2–4; 18:9–15), and that of many descendants (Gen 17:1–7; also 12:2 [which Paul quotes in Gal 3:8]; Gen 15:5 [which Paul quotes in Gal 3:6]; Gen 18:18; 22:17). The promise of land in Gen 17:8 plays no role in Paul's argument whatsoever. For Paul, the Spirit has taken the place of the land (see on 3:6–9, above, and on 3:18, below).[321] This one fundamental promise presupposes and includes the other two, however: Abraham will have a son and heir, and he will through that son and heir become the father of many descendants (Gen 15:4–5; 17:4–7, 15–22; cf. 28:14). For Paul, the latter two promises find their fulfillment only in Christ and in those who belong to him (see on Gal 3:29; cf. 4:27; Rom 4:16–18). Paul thus speaks of "promises" because the promise of the Spirit encompasses the other two, which are also interpreted christologically. The promises spoken to Abraham apply also to his offspring and find their fulfillment in his offspring. That offspring is Christ and those who belong to him (3:29; see comment there), not, therefore, the ethnic, law-observant people of Israel, to which the Gentile believers in Galatia are being asked to attach themselves even as believers in Christ. Christ creates a new people, actually a new humanity for both Jews and Gentiles (see comment on 3:28).

In v. 18a, Paul returns to the analogy of a will when he refers to "the inheritance" (*klēronomia*) in connection with the promise to Abraham. Not surprisingly, the verb "to inherit" (*klēronomeō*) occurs in association with the promises to Abraham concerning a son (and thus an heir) and the land (LXX: Gen 15:3–4, 7–8; 21:10; 22:17; 28:4).[322] For Paul, however, the inheritance referred to in v. 18 is specifically the Spirit, as it will be for the Galatians and the new preachers hearing the letter with them.[323] Paul formulates a principle in v. 18a, equal in importance to the one in 2:21(see comment there): "For if the inheritance [of the Spirit] were on the basis of a law [= the law of Moses] it would no longer be on the basis of a promise [= the promise to Abraham]." From the context it is evident that Paul here has, respectively, the Mosaic law and the promise to Abraham in view, even if his formulation is generalizing: a promise (any promise) is different in character from a law (any law). The principle enunciated here anticipates Paul's in Rom 11:6: "But if it is by [God's] grace [*charis*], it is no longer on the basis of works [of the law]; otherwise grace would no longer be grace."

---

321. The same is probably true of the new preachers; see comment on 3:6–8.

322. Genesis 31:14 contains the only instance of the noun *klēronomia*, "inheritance," in the LXX text of Genesis.

323. For the spiritualization of the notion of inheritance to denote an eschatological gift or reality (e.g., "eternal life"), see *Pss. Sol.* 14.5, 9–10; 15.10–11; 17.23; Mark 10:17; Matt 5:5; 19:29; 25:34; Luke 10:25; 18:18; Acts 20:32; Heb 1:14; 1 Pet 1:4; 3:9; Rev 21:7; etc. In Gal 5:21, Paul refers to inheriting "the kingdom of God" (also 1 Cor 6:9–10; 15:50; cf. Eph 5:5; Matt 25:34; Jas 2:5); see comment at Gal 5:21. Cf. also Rom 4:13–14; 8:17; Col 3:24; Eph 1:14, 18; 5:5; Titus 3:7.

In conclusion, in v. 18b, Paul points to what God has already done, using a verb (*charizō*) that is a cognate of the noun *charis*, "grace" (cf. 1:3, 6, 15; 2:9, 21). The verb is in the perfect tense, indicating a past event with ongoing effects in the present: "But God has graciously given [*kecharistai*] it [the inheritance of the Spirit] to [the sons of] Abraham through a promise [= the promise of the Spirit]." The perfect tense of the verb indicates that Abraham is being presented as a collective personality (cf. "in you" in 3:8), as is Christ in v. 16 (see comment above). His name now evidently stands for the metaphorical and theological "sons of Abraham" (3:8), who have inherited what God had promised in his *diathēkē* with Abraham. If Abraham stands for the sons of Abraham, the word "promise" in v. 18b also acquires a passive sense, "what was promised": the Spirit (cf. 3:14). What was promised is identical with the inheritance obtained, the Spirit that attests the rectifying presence of God in the world through the faith of Christ. "Graciously given" means "freely and unconditionally given" and implies a contrast with the law: the obtaining of the inheritance (the Spirit) is not at all conditional upon human beings' observance of the law (see comments on 1:6–9 and 3:1–5). In the Greek the last word in the sentence is "God" (v. 18): Paul emphasizes God as the ultimate source and bestower of the inheritance. To capture this emphasis, the word has been placed at the beginning in English translation: "But *God* has graciously given . . ." The fulfillment of the promise was and is in no way dependent upon human beings observing the law. The fulfillment of the promise made to Abraham has been and remains entirely *God's* doing.

To sum up: Paul has argued in 3:15–18 that the promise that God made to Abraham concerns Christ and does not have, and never did have, anything to do with the law or its observance. That is so for two reasons: First, the law came on the scene centuries after the promise. There is a yawning and unbridgeable temporal chasm between the promise and the law. Second, promise (the promise to Abraham) and law (the law of Moses) are conceptually incompatible. They exclude each other. God, acting freely, granted the inheritance (the Spirit) to Abraham's heirs purely on the basis of promise (the promise to Abraham), which means that law (the law of Moses) was and is and always will be totally irrelevant to its reception.

[19–22] Verses 19–22 are closely related to the preceding verses, forming with them a discrete unit (see introductory comments to 3:15–22).[324] In v. 19 Christ is referred to, without further explanation, as "the offspring," clearly an allusion back to v. 16, where he is identified as Abraham's "offspring" (*sperma*, "seed"). The verbs "added" in v. 19b and "arranged" in v. 19d stay with the image of a will or testament introduced in v. 15–18 (see below). The issue in

---

324. Other commentators see 3:19–22 as forming a unit with 3:25–29 instead of with 3:15–18 (Betz; Longenecker; Martyn).

vv. 15–18 is the relationship between "the promise(s)" and "the law," and that remains the issue in vv. 19–22.

In v. 19a, Paul asks the question that will also be on his listeners' minds by this point: "Why then the law?" (v. 19a).[325] The question has undoubtedly been directly prompted by the observation in v. 17 that the law came 430 years after the promise. The form of the question implies that the purpose and origin of the law is at stake. Paul does not ask: "Why then did *God give* the law?"[326] In v. 17, he has implied that the God who had everything to do with the promise to Abraham had nothing to do with the law; it simply "came" or "happened" (*gegonōs*, the perfect participle of *ginomai*), and then as an illegitimate attempt to change God's promissory covenant (*diathēkē*) with Abraham. Paul will continue to imply, if not explicitly say, that God had nothing to do with the law, particularly in v. 21, which contains a contrary-to-fact sentence: "For if a law had been *given* [by God] that could make alive"—Paul implies that God has never given such a life-giving law—"justification would indeed be on the basis of the law [*ek nomou*]" (see further comment below). Since God did not give such "a law," justification does not occur on the basis of (the observance of) "the law." The question "Why then the law?" thus already presupposes that God did *not* give the law, certainly not as a life-giving instrument of justification. This claim follows almost inevitably from the preceding argument, beginning at 2:15, in which Paul has built up a set of antinomies:

faith of Christ	works of the law
death of Christ	the law
what was heard of faith	works of the law
the blessing of Abraham	the curse of the law
God's promise to Abraham	the much-later-arriving law

The Spirit that God bestows (3:1–5, 14) as well as the justifying (rectifying) action of God to which it attests (2:16; 3:6, 7, 11) are associated exclusively with the items in the left column and expressly dissociated from those in the right column, all of which have to do with the law. Only through "faith" (i.e., the faith of Christ) do believers in Christ obtain "the inheritance" (3:18), thereby becoming "sons (= heirs) of Abraham" (3:7; cf. 3:29). In vv. 19–22 of the present passage, Paul continues this process of rhetorical and theological association

---

325. Another possible translation is "*What* then is the law?" (so Lightfoot 144; Betz 161; cf. 1 Cor 3:5). Paul's answer presupposes, however, that "why" is intended, as Betz's later paraphrase "What then is the meaning of the Torah?" indicates (163; cf. Burton 187).

326. Cf. John 1:17: "The law indeed was given [by God] through Moses"; Exod 31:18 RSV: "He [God] gave to Moses . . . the two tables of the testimony"; Lev 26:46 LXX: "These are the judgments and the ordinances and the law, which the Lord gave between him and the sons of Israel on Mount Sinai by the hand of Moses"; Neh 10:29 AT: "the law of God, which was given by the hand of Moses."

and dissociation between the promise and the law. Paul's answer to the question posed in v. 19a, "Why then the law?" thus seeks only to distance God from the law even further. Verses 21–22 drive the point home: as in 2:15–3:18, God and justification are associated exclusively with the promise and intentionally dissociated—indeed, distanced—from the law (cf. 3:6, 8, 11, 17, 18):

> ¹⁹ᵇIt [the law] was added [*prosetethē*; to the promise that God made to Abraham some 430 years earlier] for the sake of the transgressions, ¹⁹ᶜ[but then only] until the offspring [Christ, 3:17] for whom it [the inheritance, 3:18] had been promised should come [whereby the added law was retroactively shown to be illegitimate tampering with God's promissory covenant with Abraham], ¹⁹ᵈhaving been arranged [*diatageis*] through [the intervention of] angels by the hand of a mediator³²⁷ [Moses]. ²⁰A mediator³²⁸ is not [a mediator] of one [party, but of more than one; in the case of Moses, then, of the angels]; God, however, is one [party, thus needing no mediator; Moses could not then have mediated the law for God].

There are three key issues to be resolved in this passage: (1) the meaning of the prepositional phrase "for the sake of the transgressions" in v. 19b, (2) the meanings of the verbs "added" (*prosetethē*) in v. 19b and "arranged" (*diatageis*) in v. 19d, and (3) the import of the remarkably opaque v. 20.³²⁹ It will be useful to discuss them in reverse order, since the interpretation of v. 20 affects the interpretation of the two verbs mentioned, and the interpretation of the latter is in turn important for interpreting the phrase "for the sake of the transgressions."

Issue 3. The assumption underlying the argument of v. 20 appears to be that a mediator is needed only when the party initiating a particular transaction consists of a plurality. (Whether the other party to the transaction is also a plurality

---

327. "By the hand [*en cheiri*] of a mediator" echoes the stereotypical LXX phrase "by the hand [*en cheiri*] of Moses" (e.g., Lev 26:46 LXX, quoted above: "These are the judgments and the ordinances and the law, which the Lord gave between him and the sons of Israel on Mount Sinai by the hand of Moses"; there are 9 instances in Numbers, and a further 10 in the remainder of the OT). The Galatians, having been tutored by the new preachers among them, will certainly catch the allusion to Moses in his role as mediator. Moses is called "mediator" in Philo, *Somn.* 1.143; *Mos.* 2.166; cf. *As. Mos.* 1.14.

328. The Greek of v. 20 actually reads "*the* mediator," but given the present tense of the verb "is" (*estin*), the article here is probably generic (otherwise Bruce 179), best rendered into English as "a mediator." The Galatians are to apply what Paul here says about mediators generally to the particular case of Moses.

329. One may compare various attempts to make it comprehensible in some English versions: "Now an intermediary implies more than one; but God is one" (RSV); "But an intermediary is not needed for one party acting alone, and God is one" (NEB); "Now there can only be an intermediary between two parties, yet God is one" (NJB).

is irrelevant; the issue is the plurality of the *initiating* party.)[330] Paul leaves it to his listeners and readers to draw the implicit conclusion: Since Moses was mediator of the law for the angels (a plurality) mentioned in v. 19d, he could not have been the mediator of the law for God, since God is "one," not a plurality. Paul here appeals to the fundamental conviction of the Israelite faith that God is "one," as attested by the Shema (Deut 6:4).

There are no angels mentioned at the giving of the law in the Hebrew OT, though their presence evidently became an assumption of Jewish tradition and thought in the Hellenistic period, beginning with the LXX of Deut 33:2: "The Lord has come from Sinai; . . . on his right hand his angels with him." The latter phrase is absent from the Hebrew text. The angels add to the majesty and the glory of God; they also add luster to the event described. Stephen's speech in Acts 7 also reflects this tradition of angels, or of one angel (cf. *Jub.* 1.27–2:1), at the giving of the law: Stephen refers to "the angel who spoke to him [Moses] at Mount Sinai," through whom he "received living oracles to give to us" (7:38; cf. 7:53; Heb 2:2). In the first century, the Jewish historian Josephus writes that "we have learned the noblest of our doctrines and the holiest of our laws through angels (*di' angelōn*) instructed by God" (*Ant.* 15.136).[331] Here the angels do not function independently of God, but as mediators on his behalf (without explicit mention of Moses). Paul also uses the construction "through angels" (v. 19d) but pointedly fails to add "instructed by God" or something similar, thereby implying that they acted on their own, as v. 20 further indicates: no life-giving law was given by God. For Paul, at least in his letter to the Galatians, "God was absent at the genesis of the Sinaitic law" (Martyn 366).

Issue 2. The verb "add" (*prostithēmi*) in v. 19b is in this context a near synonym of the verb used in v. 15, "append a codicil to" (*epidiatassō*). The former, just like the latter, was used to mean "add articles to a legal document" (Betz 167 n. 42; cf. LSJ 1527; BDAG 885; Maurer 1972: 167–68). In v. 17 Paul has likened the coming of the law some 430 years after God made the covenant (*diathēkē*) of promise with Abraham to a third party seeking to append further specifications (a codicil) to an already-validated human will (also *diathēkē*). Such tampering has no legal status, since only the testator himself can annul or change his own will. In vv. 15–18, Paul has in effect argued against the new preachers in Galatia that the law is to be understood not as God's own codicil to the Abrahamic promise, but as illegitimate tampering by a third party. Verse 19b, therefore, can only mean that the law "was added" (*prosetethē*) to

---

330. Cf. 1 Tim 2:5 AT: "There is one God and one mediator between God and human beings, the human being Christ Jesus." Here Christ functions as the mediator from a plurality (human beings) to God, who is "one."

331. R. Marcus, the translator of Josephus for LCL, problematically renders the Greek phrase *di' angelōn para tou theou mathontōn* as "from the messengers sent by God," pleading in a footnote that the prophets (or priests) are probably meant.

God's promise by actors other than God himself (against Dunn 189; Matera 128; Longenecker 138), an interpretation further supported by v. 20. In v. 19d, as indicated above, these actors are identified as angels: The law "was added for the sake of the transgressions, . . . having been arranged through angels [*di' angelōn*] by the hand of a mediator." It could be argued that the phrase "through angels" implies that God is the ultimate source of the law (God gave the law "through angels by the hand of a mediator"), but Paul will himself discourage that reading of the phrase in vv. 20–21 (cf. 2:19). The preposition "through" thus implies that the angels were the originating agents rather than the mediating agents in the coming of the law: the law "was arranged through angels," period.[332] God is not expressly mentioned.[333] In this passage, where Paul's primary concern is to place a great distance between God and the law, the angels are, at least by implication, agents acting independently of God. Paul brings his readers "to the edge of an abyss" and compels them to contemplate "the vision of a godless law" (Martyn 358).

The verb *diatassō*, parsed here as the passive aorist participle *diatageis*, has proved difficult to translate. Proposals include "to ordain" (Betz; Longenecker; RSV; cf. LSJ 414; Titus 1:5), "to enact" (Burton), "to institute" (Martyn), "to promulgate" (NJB, NAB; Matera), and "to order" (Lightfoot) in the sense of "to give (detailed) instructions as to what must be done" (BDAG 237–38; cf. 1 Cor 7:17; 9:14; 11:34; 16:1). The expression "to institute a law" (*diatassein nomon*) is found in Hesiod (*Op.* 276) but is not biblical (Martyn 356). A cognate of the verb is used in Acts 7:53, however, where Stephen says, "You [the people of Israel] received the law as enactments [*eis diatagas*] of angels but [despite that fact] did not keep it" (AT).[334] The verb was also used in connection with last wills and testaments, with the meaning "to make testamentary dispositions," "to order by will," or "to bequeath," thus in the passive "to be bequeathed" (LSJ 414, citing for the latter papyrus evidence from the first cent. C.E.; cf. MM 155). The verb is a cognate of the verb used in v. 15, *epidiatassō*, "to add a codicil to." Paul's choice of the verb *diatassō* in v. 19d is probably no accident,

---

332. On this use of the preposition *dia* (instead of *hypo*) with a passive verb, see BDAG 224–25; BDF #223; 1 Cor 1:9 provides an example: "God is faithful, through [*dia*] whom you were called" (AT).

333. Paul's argument here is clearly difficult to square with his unabashed references to "the law of God" in Romans (7:22, 25; 8:7); furthermore, according to Paul in Romans, "the law is spiritual" (7:14) and "holy, and the commandment is holy and just and good" (7:12). But see below on vv. 21–22.

334. The RSV translates Acts 7:53 rather periphrastically: "You who received the law as delivered by angels and did not keep it." According to Fitzmyer (1998: 306), the phrase *eis diatagas* is "strange and difficult to translate." The usual solution (also adopted by Fitzmyer and Martyn 356 n. 205) is to regard the phrase as instrumental, equivalent to *en diatagais* (so BDF #206.1, followed by BDAG 237, 291): "by means of directions/commands of angels." For the common use of the preposition *eis* to mean "for, as," however, see BDAG 290.

therefore, and seeks to carry forward the analogy of a human will (*diathēkē*) in vv. 15–18, whereby God's promissory covenant (*diathēkē*) with Abraham is likened to the last will and testament of a human being (see comment on vv. 15–18, above). The translation "arrange" has been chosen to reflect this testamentary nuance of the verb, as well as the sense of "order" pointed out above. The law is being likened to a bequest, as a set of specifications added to God's promissory *diathēkē* of God with Abraham,[335] "having been arranged through [the intervention of] angels," who used Moses as their mediator to tamper with God's promise, something they had no business doing.[336]

Issue 1. In this passage, then, God seems to have had nothing to do with the coming of the law. "Why then the law?" Why then did the angels add the law to the promise of God, having arranged this step by the hand of Moses? Paul provides his answer: "for the sake of the transgressions," *tōn parabaseōn charin*. The preposition *charin*, derived from the accusative form of the noun for grace (*charis*), follows the noun (here in the gen. pl.) it governs.[337] It can express either cause ("because of the transgressions") or goal ("in order to produce the transgressions"). The phrase can thus in principle mean that the law came on the scene to deal with, identify, or restrain the transgressions that were already taking place (Longenecker 138; Matera 128; Dunn 189; Vouga 82), or to provoke the transgressions that are now taking place, thereby also bringing the reality of Sin (v. 22) into the open (BDAG 1079; Calvin 61; Lightfoot 144; Burton 188; Mussner 245; Betz 165; Martyn 354; cf. Rom 3:20; 5:13, 20; 7:13). There are two reasons why the latter interpretation is to be preferred: (a) The context does not indicate in any way that Paul wants to characterize the addition of the law to the promise through the intervention of angels as a positive, saving step. The angels were tampering with God's *diathēkē* with Abraham, something God did not intend to happen. (b) The noun "transgression," *parabasis*, means the breaking of an existing and recognized law: "Where there is no law there is no transgression" (Rom 4:15 RSV; see comment on Gal 2:17). A transgression thus involves "a transgression *of the law*" (Rom 2:23; cf. 5:14), just as a transgressor is "a transgressor *of the law*" (Rom 2:25, 27; cf. Jas 2:9,

---

335. In vv. 15–18, God's promise to Abraham is the same as his covenant with Abraham (see comment above). It is striking that Paul here reserves the term "covenant" for the promise to Abraham and denies it to the law (cf. 4:24–25, where Paul refers to "two covenants," the one with Abraham and the one with Israel at the giving of the law on Mount Sinai).

336. Paul comes close to regarding the angels he mentions as evil angels, who stand opposed to God, consistent with the traditions of cosmological Jewish apocalyptic eschatology (see Excursus 2). Cf. Schweitzer 69–70.

337. A more-literal translation of the phrase would thus yield "in favor of the transgressions." It seems curious that Paul would here use the preposition *charin*, instead of, say, the preposition *dia*, given its etymological origin. For this nontheological use of the accusative singular of *charis* as a preposition, see Luke 7:47; Eph 3:1, 14; 1 Tim 5:14; Titus 1:5, 11; 1 John 3:12; Jude 16.

The Spirit and the True Heirs of the Promise Made to Abraham 231

11).[338] For these reasons, it can be said that the law was "added" to the promise in order to produce the transgressions of it that are now taking place, whether by Jews or by Gentiles (cf. Rom 2:12–16). It had and has no saving, life-giving function or purpose (Gal 3:21). Paul has already indicated that the law places all human beings under a curse, "the curse of the law" (3:13; see comment on 3:10–13). Some comments that Paul makes in his Letter to the Romans about the function and purpose of the Sinaitic law may be pertinent here, even though they remain unarticulated in Galatians itself: The law brings knowledge of Sin (3:20), enables its presence to be registered (5:14), increases its death-dealing grip on human life (5:20), allows its true nature and power to become discernible (7:13), and effects condemnation (8:1).[339]

What Paul says about the addition of the law to the promise would be bad news for the Galatians and the new preachers visiting Galatia were it not for the fact that he emphasizes that this addition was in force only "until the offspring [Christ, 3:16] should come for whom it [the inheritance, 3:18] had been promised" (cf. Rom 3:23–24; 10:4).[340] Christ, the singular offspring of Abraham, has come (cf. Gal 3:23–26), and with him the Spirit, which is the promised inheritance (cf. 3:14, 18). The law was a mere parenthesis in the history of salvation, not being able to invalidate the promise that God made to Abraham (cf. 3:15–18). The fact that the promise has come to pass demonstrates beyond the shadow of a doubt that the plan of the angels to invalidate God's promise by adding the law had no effect on that promise (cf. 3:1–5). Seen from the perspective of the fulfillment of the promise, the law was not God's life-giving gift to humanity after all. It was really part of the problem, not part of the solution (see below on v. 22).

The second question that Paul asks in this passage, "Is the law then against the promises[341] of God?" (v. 21a), emerges from his answer to the first question, "Why then the law?" (v. 19a). Paul's own answer to this question, "Not at all!" [*mē genoito*, lit., "let it not be so"],[342] would seem to indicate that he wants to prevent his readers from drawing the wrong conclusion from his foregoing argument that the law is somehow "against" (*kata*) the promises of God (cf. Rom 7:7: "What then shall we say? Is the law sin? Not at all!" [AT]). The

---

338. Transgression and sin are not synonymous in Paul; cf. Rom 5:13: "Sin was indeed in the world before the law." See below on v. 22.

339. See de Boer 1988: 165–69.

340. The debate about whether in Judaism the law is eternal (cf., e.g., Sir 24:9) or temporary (cf., e.g., 1QS 9.10–11) seems to be irrelevant here. Paul's notion of the temporality of the law results from his understanding of its function (to produce transgressions), which is in turn an interpretation of the law from the perspective of Christ and his cross.

341. On the peculiar use of the plural, see comment on 3:16 above. The singular is used in v. 22, as in vv. 17 and 18.

342. On this expression, see the comment on 2:17.

point at issue here, however, is probably not the compatibility of the Abrahamic promise and the Mosaic law, as if they somehow need to be reconciled because both are assumed to originate in God (Vos 127–28; Calvin 64; Burton 193–94; Dunn 192; Longenecker 143). Paul's question is not: "Is the law *of God*[343] then against the promises of God?" (cf. Martyn 358 n. 213). Paul's theological and rhetorical purpose in this passage is precisely to dissociate God from the law; he has no interest in bringing God's promises to Abraham and the law into a positive relationship (see comments on vv. 15–18 and 19–20 above), as vv. 21b–22 further attest (see below). Verse 21a cannot be read as Paul's attempt to qualify, or to take back, what he has just said or implied about the law. His answer to the question "Why then the law?" in vv. 19b–20 as well as his argument in vv. 15–18 indicate that the question in v. 21a amounts to asking, "Does the addition of the law through the intervention of angels then constitute an invalidation of God's promises to Abraham?"[344] The answer that Paul himself provides to this question ("Not at all!") now becomes immediately intelligible. It simply reaffirms the argument of v. 17: "The law, having come after four hundred thirty years, does not invalidate a covenant previously validated by God so as to void the promise." Paul's answer therefore does not show that he wants to avoid a separation of the promises and the law (so Betz 173); on the contrary, it shows that he wants emphatically to reaffirm that separation. He wants to prevent the Galatians, under the tutelage of the new preachers, from thinking that the law as appended to God's promises through the intervention of the angels by the hand of Moses represents a divinely approved addition to those promises.

That v. 21a cannot be read as a concession to the new preachers and their positive view of the law becomes clear in vv. 21b–22. As indicated by the conjunction "for" (*gar*), Paul here seeks to clarify his claim that the law is not "against" God's promises:[345]

> ²¹ᵇ For [let me tell you] if a law had been given that is able to make alive [and no such law has in fact been given], justification would indeed be on the basis of the law [*ek nomou*]. ²²But [*alla*] [as it is] the Scripture shut all things [including the law] up under Sin, so that [*hina*] the promise [of

---

343. Given the predilection of commentators to assume that the law here is "the law of God" (Rom 7:22, 25; 8:7), it is surprising that there is no manuscript evidence for this reading as there is for the reading "the promises of God."

344. Cf. Martyn 358–59, who translates v. 21a as follows: "Is the Law, then, effectively opposed to the promises [of God]?" He argues that the law is being conceptualized as "a power opposed to God's promise" (358) and that as such it is not able "to invalidate the promise" (358 n. 214). It seems, however, that the law is here being likened to a legal instrument, a codicil, or a set of specifications added to a will so as to modify its terms (see comments on 3:15, 17, 19).

345. The conjunction *gar* can express cause or reason, or posit an inference (see comment on 1:10), but here it appears to introduce a clarification (cf. BDAG 189–90; BDF #452).

the Spirit] from the faith of Jesus Christ be given to those who believe [in him].

Verse 21b, a present contrary-to-fact conditional sentence, most likely conceals in its form the standpoint of the new preachers in Galatia, who are Christian Jews: "Since a law has been given—the one given by God through angels by the hand of the mediator Moses—which is able make alive [*zōopoiēsai*], justification [*dikaiosynē*] is on the basis of the law." That the law was given by God "for life" (Rom 7:10) is deeply rooted in the OT and in Judaism (cf. Deut 30:15–20; 32:47; Sir 17:11: "the law of life"; Hillel in *m. ʾAbot* 2.7: "The more study of the Torah, the more life"). The verb "to make alive" (*zōopoieō*), however, is elsewhere a soteriological-eschatological term for Paul (Rom 4:17; 8:11; 1 Cor 15:22, 36, 45; 2 Cor 3:6), and it probably has a similar nuance here not only for him but also for the new preachers in Galatia (cf. John 5:21; 6:63; 1 Pet 3:18). For the new preachers, it means "to secure life in the new age beyond the final judgment." According to them, that new life will be granted to those who are justified by God on the basis of their observance of the law (see on 2:16). In this sense, then, the law "is able [*dynamenos*] to make alive," it being (from the new preachers' viewpoint) God's gift for securing salvation ("eternal life"; cf. Dan 12:2 LXX; Gal 6:8 and comment there). The noun *dikaiosynē* for the new preachers in Galatia has the primarily forensic-eschatological meaning (Burton 195; Bultmann 1951: 273) it has also had for them in 2:21: "God's justifying pronouncement" ("justification" by God) or "the status of having been justified by God" (the "righteousness" that comes from God), or both (see on 2:16, 21). Theologically, then, justification is tantamount to eschatological new life, since the former necessarily secures or effects the latter.[346]

Paul does not contest the referential meanings of the terms he uses in v. 21b. He contents himself with disputing the claim of his opponents in Galatia about the law as a life-giving and thus justifying instrument, whether that be in the present or the future. Despite the generalizing formulation, he (like the new preachers) obviously has the Mosaic law in view. It actually makes no difference here for Paul's argument whether the law was given by God (the view of the new preachers) or by angels (evidently Paul's view), since the point is not the origin of the law but its *powerlessness*, no matter what the source, to secure or mediate new life. In his contrary-to-fact formulation, Paul effectively con-

---

346. Sanders (1977: 494) claims that the term "justification" itself *means* "life" in Gal 3:21b, but here Sanders confuses a lexical matter with the theological implication or results of God's justifying action. The *term* here refers to God's eschatological justifying verdict (or the status of eschatological acquittal in God's court). God's actual justifying verdict or action, however, when it occurs, shall mediate, grant, or enable "life." Only for that reason can the event of justification be said to be "mean" life.

cedes that if such a life-giving law had been given, "justification would indeed [*ontōs*] be on the basis of the law," as the new preachers claim. Unfortunately, however, no such life-giving law has been given.

Paul now makes an appeal to "the Scripture" to substantiate the point: "But [*alla*] [as it is] the Scripture shut all things [including the law] up under Sin" (v. 22a). For *this* reason, the law is not able to make alive and deliver justification (v. 21b); it is the captive of Sin, here evidently conceptualized as a power with a domain (see comments on 1:4 and 2:17; cf. Rom 3:9; 5:12–21). Since no specific text is cited or explicitly referred to, "the Scripture" [*hē graphē*] here probably means the Jewish Scriptures in their entirety, as in 3:8 (see comment there), rather than a particular passage, as in 4:30 and elsewhere in Paul's Letters (cf. Rom 4:3; 9:17; 10:11; 11:2). The term is not here synonymous with "the law" (*ho nomos*; Calvin 64; Bruce 180; Hays 268), as if Paul means to say that the law (as legislation to be observed) cannot make alive because the law (as Scripture) shut all things up under Sin. It would then be extremely difficult to explain why Paul uses *graphē* instead of *nomos* to make this point (cf. 4:21).[347] Furthermore, though Paul can use *hē graphē* to introduce a quotation from the Pentateuch (cf., e.g. Rom 4:3, where the citation from Gen 15:6 is so introduced), that does not mean that *hē graphē* is simply interchangeable with *ho nomos*.

"The Scripture" here can perhaps be taken as a synonym for God (cf. Rom 11:32: "God shut all people up in disobedience" [AT], where a *hina* clause also immediately follows), but then we can ask why Paul did not plainly say, "*God* shut all things up under Sin," instead of "the Scripture shut all things up under Sin," even if that is what the thought comes down to. To make God—or "the Scripture" as the expression of God's will (Matera 135)—responsible for the plight of humanity seems far from Paul's mind in this passage, however. As in Gal 3:8, Paul personifies "the Scripture," attributing to it the power to "shut up" or imprison (*synkleiō*). As there, this personification may well be rhetorically motivated and should not therefore be pressed as though Paul were making some grand statement about the authority of Scripture. It is, rather, the new preachers in Galatia who attach great weight to the Scripture; it provides *them* with *the* authority for their gospel of circumcision. It is surely their trump card. Paul now, as in 3:8, solemnly summons "the Scripture" as a witness for his own theology, against the new preachers and their optimistic view of the

---

347. Paul sometimes uses *ho nomos* to designate "the Scripture," referring either to the Pentateuch (Gal 4:21b; 1 Cor 9:9; Rom 3:21b) or to the Jewish Scriptures as a whole (Rom 3:19; 1 Cor 14:21), but that is not his characteristic usage of the term. In Galatians, prior to 4:21b, Paul uses *ho nomos* to refer only to the Sinaitic legislation, never to the Scripture or the Pentateuchal portion thereof; that is also the case in 3:21b. In any case, the issue in v. 22a is not whether *nomos* can mean *graphē*, but rather the reverse.

The Spirit and the True Heirs of the Promise Made to Abraham

law: "The Scripture" that is so important for the new preachers has in fact shut up "all things" (*ta panta*)—and this must then include (the works of) the law—under Sin's power (*hypo hamartian*).[348] What Paul probably means to say is that the powerlessness of the law to make alive by securing the hoped-for justification (cf. 5:5) is attested in the Scripture itself. This reading of v. 22 is in any event consistent with Rom 3:9–10, where Paul, using very similar language, writes that "all people [*pantas*], both Jews and Greeks, are under Sin [*hyph' hamartian*], as it is written: 'No one is righteous, no not one'" (AT). He goes on to cite a catena of passages from the Scripture to buttress the point. In Gal 3:22, however, he does not try to substantiate or to illustrate his claim that "the Scripture shut up all things under Sin" with similar citations from Scripture. He *may* be thinking here especially, if not exclusively, of Ps 143:2 (142:2 LXX), whose language he has used back in 2:16d to assert that "no one shall be justified on the basis of works of the law" (see comment there), since he employs the same language in Romans to encapsulate the preceding argument, including the catena of scriptural passages in 3:9–18: "Therefore, on the basis of works of the law shall no one be justified before him [God], for through the law comes knowledge of Sin" (Rom 3:20 AT; cf. 5:20; 7:13). Others would see in Gal 3:22 an implied reference to the various passages he cites in Rom 3:9–18 (Dunn 194, arguing that Paul may have used this catena in his earlier preaching to the Galatians), or to Deut 27:26, cited in 3:10 (Burton 196–97). Paul does not, however, alert the Galatians to any of these possibilities in v. 22 itself. His point remains simply that, according to the Scripture to which the new preachers appeal, the law like everything else is a captive of Sin. The observance of the law therefore is no solution at all, as his own case as a persecutor of God's church out of loyalty to the law amply illustrates (1:13–14; see comment).

Paul goes on to indicate the God-given alternative to this situation: "so that [*hina*] the promise [of the Spirit] from the faith of Jesus Christ be given to those who believe [in him]." As in v. 18, the word "promise" (*epangelia*) has here a passive sense, "what was promised," namely, the Spirit (cf. 3:14). God did not "give" a life-giving law (v. 21), but God does "give" a life-giving Spirit—"to those who believe" (*tois pisteuousin*). Paul uses the verb *pisteuō* for only the second time since 2:16b (and for the last time in the letter!) to indicate what Christians do: they "believe" or "have faith" (the verb also occurs in 3:6, but

---

348. The neuter plural *ta panta*, "all things," is often taken to mean "all people" (e.g., Longenecker 144), but that begs the question. In the parallel passages of Rom 11:32 (cited just above) and 3:9 (cited just below), Paul uses the masculine plural *pantas* when he means to refer to people. He seems to choose *ta panta* here in order to include the law (also Wilson 2005: 375). To be sure, the captivity of the law "under Sin" also entails the captivity of human beings "under the law," as 3:23 makes plain (see comment there).

there in connection with the believing Abraham, as part of the citation from Gen 15:6). Here it defines their identity as those who believe (have faith). Despite his absolute use of the verb, Paul undoubtedly understands them to believe (have faith) *in Christ* (cf. 2:16b: "We came to believe in Jesus Christ"). Moreover, also for the first time since 2:16 (and again for the last time in the letter!), Paul uses the expression *pistis Iēsou Christou* (governed, as in 2:16c, by the preposition *ek*, "from, on the basis of"). This expression is probably to be rendered "the faith(fulness) *of* Jesus Christ" (referring to his faithful death "for our sins") rather than "(human) faith *in* Jesus Christ" (see Excursuses 9 and 11). The prepositional phrase *ek pisteōs Iēsou Christou* ("from the faith of Jesus Christ") has here been taken to limit the noun *epangelia* ("promise"), signifying that the promised Spirit (3:14) became available as a result of Christ's faithful death on the cross (cf. 3:1–5; Longenecker 145; Matera 135; NRSV). To take the phrase as modifying the verb would not, however, alter the basic sense: "so that the promise might be given on the basis of the faith of Christ to those who believe." The reason is that both the promise and the giving of it are equally dependent on the faithful death of Christ on the cross. So indeed is believing in him (cf. 2:16).

The relationship of the subordinate *hina* clause, just discussed, to the main clause in v. 22a is theologically difficult and challenging. The subordinate conjunction *hina* probably does not point to the Scripture's purpose in confining all things under Sin (though that would be a possible interpretation if the Scripture here stands for God, an interpretation considered above). Rather, it probably expresses *God's* purpose and therefore God's intended result: "so that [as God wills] the promise [of the Spirit] from the faith of Jesus Christ be given [as it now has been] to those who believe [in him]" (see comment on a similar clause in 2:16c). To paraphrase the whole verse: According to the witness of the Scripture itself, all things, including the law, have come into bondage to a power called Sin, making the law ineffectual for securing the justification that is the precondition for life in the new age. As a result, God gives the promised Spirit, which came into the world on the basis of Christ's faithful death, not to those who observe the ineffectual law but to those who believe in Christ.

To sum up: in 3:15–22 Paul has created a huge chasm between God's promise to Abraham, which has found its fulfillment in Christ and his Spirit, and the law of Moses. The latter has absolutely nothing to do with the former. The coming of the law, therefore, cannot invalidate God's promise. The law is part of the problem (a captive of Sin), not part of the solution (the means for justification and life). As shown by the very Scripture to which the new preachers repeatedly appeal to support their views, the law has been shut up under the power of Sin, just like everything else. The result, intended by God, is that the promised Spirit, which came into the world with Christ's faithful death, is given only to those who believe in Christ.

3:23–29 The True Offspring of Abraham

The mention of Christ's faith at the end of the previous passage (3:14–22) causes Paul in the first part of the present passage (3:23–25) to return to the contrast between "faith" and "the law," introduced in 2:15–21 and pursued further in 3:1–5 and 3:6–14. He now characterizes the law as an imprisoning "custodian," from which "we" believers (3:22d) have been released through "faith," meaning "the faith of Jesus Christ" (3:22d). The period of the law came to an end with the coming of Christ and his faith. Paul goes on to clarify what this means for believers in the second part of the passage (3:26–28), citing from a baptismal tradition (marked by the change from "we" to "you"): "You," he reminds the Galatians, are "sons of God through this faith, in Christ Jesus" (3:26), since by being baptized into Christ "you have put on Christ"; "you" were thereby made "one in Christ Jesus" so that the distinction between Jew and Greek (Gentile) no longer defines who "you" are, any more than the distinction between slave and free, or male and female (3:27–28). The passage concludes with the claim that those who belong to Christ are the (true) "offspring of Abraham" (3:29); they are Abraham's "heirs according to a promise." The last verse picks up five terms that were prominent in the preceding passage: not only Christ and Abraham but also promise (*epangelia*), offspring (*sperma*), and inheritance (*klēronomia*). The present passage can thus be as read a continuation and a partial rounding-off of the argument in 3:15–22. (The next paragraph, 4:1–7, will show that Paul is not quite finished.) At the same time, v. 29 echoes the argument begun in 3:6–14 about the identity of the "sons of Abraham." The true "sons," meaning heirs, of Abraham are not those who live from observing the law but those live from the faith of Christ; in him the promise made to Abraham (3:8, 14, 16, 18, 19c, 22) has been fulfilled.

3:23 Before this faith came, we were confined under the law, being shut up until the destined faith should be apocalyptically revealed. **24** As a result the law was our custodian until Christ, so that we might be justified on the basis of faith. **25** Now that this faith has come, we are no longer under a custodian.

26 For all of you are sons of God through this faith, in Christ Jesus.[a]
27 For as many of you as were baptized into Christ have put on Christ.
28 There is neither Jew nor Greek, there is neither slave nor free person, there is no male and female, for all of you are one in Christ Jesus.
29 And if you are Christ's, then you are offspring of Abraham, heirs according to a promise.

a. Instead of *dia tēs pisteōs en Christō Iēsou* ("through this faith, in Christ Jesus"), 𝔓46 has *dia pisteōs Christou Iēsou* ("through [the] faith of Christ Jesus"), omitting not only the article with *pistis* but also the preposition *en* and changing the case of "Christ Jesus"

238   Galatians 3:1–4:7

accordingly from dative to genitive. The text then agrees with that of 2:16a (cf. 3:22d). This reading, though old, is probably secondary since it presents the less-difficult reading.

[23–25] After 3:10 and 3:13–14, and in contrast to 2:16, the first-person plural ("we") in this passage is probably inclusive of Gentiles as well as Jews (Martyn 362; contra, e.g., Burton 199; Longenecker 145). Paul may perhaps have Jews particularly in view, at least in the first instance, but if so he uses their situation "under the law" to be representative of the situation of all humankind (cf. 3:10–14; 4:5).

These three verses further illuminate Paul's understanding of faith and the law in Galatians. He first introduced these terms in 2:16, and what was implicit there and in the intervening verses about both "faith" and the "law" becomes explicit here.

Paul begins v. 23 with a reference to "this faith" (*tēn pistin*, lit., "the faith"). The Greek definite article is being used anaphorically (BDF #252.1), to refer back to a previous instance of the term "faith," hence the translation "this faith." In the previous verse (3:22d) Paul has mentioned "the faith of Jesus Christ" (*pistis Iēsou Christou*). The faith being referred to in v. 23 is, therefore, that of Christ himself (also Hays 270), namely, his faithfulness to (and thus also his trust in and reliance upon) God as disclosed in his self-giving death (see comments on 2:16, 20; 3:22; Excursuses 9 and 11). For this reason, Paul can use the term *pistis* in a personified way, as a virtual synonym for "Christ." To bring out the personification, one could here capitalize the word:

> [23]Before Faith came [*elthein*] [into the world], we [all] were confined under the law, being shut up until the destined Faith should be apocalyptically revealed [*apokalyphthēnai*].[349] [24]As a result the Law was[350] our custodian until Christ [came into the world], so that we might be justified on the basis of Faith. [25]Now that Faith has come [*elthousēs*] [into the world], we are no longer under a custodian.

"Faith" and "Christ" are interchangeable in this passage: Faith "came" onto the world stage at a certain juncture in time (vv. 23a, 25a), just as Christ himself did (3:19). As a result "we are no longer under a custodian" (v. 25b), which means that we are no longer "under the law" (v. 23b), which was "our custodian until Christ [came into the world]" (v. 24a), which means "until Faith should be

---

349. On the translation of this verb, see Excursus 6 and the comments on 1:12 and 1:15. The verb functions here as a synonym of "to come [into the human world from outside]," used in v. 23a.

350. Here NA[27] reads *gegonen*, lit., "has been"; two important witnesses ($\mathfrak{P}^{46}$, B) read *egeneto*, "was." In this context, the distinction between perfect and aorist is meaningless (cf. BDF #343). To interpret the perfect to mean that the law has been and thus continues to be a custodian also for believers (Burton 200) is contextually impossible.

The Spirit and the True Heirs of the Promise Made to Abraham   239

apocalyptically revealed" (v. 23c). With the personification, Paul indicates that the term *pistis* is being used as a metonym for Christ, a particular trait standing for the whole person. Verse 24b, "so that we be justified on the basis of faith," can then only refer to *Christ's* faith, as in 2:16c, "so that we be justified on the basis of the faith of Christ."[351] In Gal 2–3, Paul always seems to use the term "faith" to mean primarily "the faith of Jesus Christ," not "our faith in him" (Excursus 11). *Pistis* refers to Christ's faithful death on the cross, on the basis of which someone is justified (2:16; see comment there).

However, even if *pistis* does here mean, or at least encompass,[352] human faith (believing) in Christ, which is a usage of the term clearly attested elsewhere in Paul's letters (see esp. 1 Thessalonians and Romans), it cannot be construed as an innate or natural human capacity, but only as an apocalyptic-eschatological *novum*[353] that occurs in the life of any particular human being when elicited by the proclamation of the gospel, whose content is the person and work of Christ as God's apocalyptic-eschatological act (cf. Williams 101). Human believing (faith) in Christ thereby corresponds to, participates in, and is defined by Christ's own faith(fulness). Faith is "new creation" (Gal 6:15),[354] an apocalyptic-eschatological reality inseparable from Christ as God's apocalypse (cf. 1:12 and comment there). "Faith" was "apocalyptically revealed" and thereby "came" (3:23, 25) onto the world stage, just as Christ himself did (3:19), as something eschatologically new and thus previously not seen or heard (cf. 1 Cor 2:9). The notion of God's purpose in the coming of faith is indicated by the phrase "the destined faith [*tēn mellousan pistin*]" in v. 23b (BDAG 628; Martyn 361). This passage thus also indicates that for Paul the previous meanings of the term *pistis* (also in the case of Abraham; see comment on 3:6, 9) cannot do justice to what it now has come to mean in Christ. They are at best a rough analogy (cf. Calvin 65).

As in 3:10–12, the positive things that Paul here says about faith function primarily as a foil for the negative things he says about the law. Throughout Section III of the letter, Paul's primary rhetorical concern is to undermine the seemingly convincing way the new preachers in Galatia have caused the

---

351. In contrast to 2:16c, however, the "we" in v. 24b has become inclusive of Gentiles. But even in 2:16c, Paul's point is that "we Jewish Christians" are justified on the same basis as Gentiles: the faith of Christ, not the works of the law. Verse 24b also makes it impossible to construe "faith" in v. 23 (or in v. 25) to mean "the gospel message" (so, e.g., Longenecker 145; cf. BDAG 820), since it must have the same referential meaning as in the parallel clause in 2:16c (see comment on 3:2, 5).

352. Hays (2002) combines the two possibilities by speaking of "the pattern of faithfulness revealed in Jesus." Thus also Martyn 362 ("Christ's faith and . . . the faith kindled by Christ's faith").

353. This means an eschatological (new-age) reality that has invaded the human cosmos from outside. See Martyn (323): "Paul envisions, then, a world that has been changed from without by God's incursion into it, and he perceives that incursion to be the event that has brought faith into existence."

354. Note the parallel between Gal 5:6 (faith working through love) and 6:15 (new creation).

Galatians to contemplate becoming fully law observant, beginning with circumcision (1:6–10; 5:2–3; 6:12–13). In the process, he also makes a number of crucial claims about the theological significance of Christ and faith. It is ultimately from the vantage point of the faith of Christ that Paul carries out his critique of the law.

Paul characterizes the law as "our *paidagōgos*," or "custodian" (cf. Lull; Young; Gordon; Sänger 2006). To have been "under the law" (*hypo nomon*) in v. 23 means to have been "under a custodian" (*hypo paidagōgon*) in v. 25. A *paidagōgos* was "a slave employed in Greek and Roman families to have general charge of a boy in the years from about six to sixteen, watching over his outward behaviour and attending him whenever he went from home, e.g. to school" (Burton 200; cf. BDAG 748; Plutarch, *Mor.* 4A–B; 439F.; Josephus, *Life* 76; Epictetus, *Diatr.* 2.22.26; 3.19.5–6). The *paidagōgos* was a "supervisory guardian" (cf. 1 Cor 4:15), who had "custodial and disciplinary functions" (cf. NRSV, NAB: "disciplinarian," NIV: "supervision"; NJB: "a slave looking after us") "rather than educative or instructional ones" (Longenecker 146).

Those who want to see the *paidagōgos* as a positive figure, either as a disciplinary "schoolmaster" (KJV; Calvin 66) or as a "pedagogue" in the benign English sense of the term, also tend to take the preposition *eis* in v. 24 to express purpose or goal, translating it as "unto": "so that the law was our teacher *unto* Christ." Supporters of this line of interpretation can then also regard Paul's claim in v. 23 that "we were confined under the law" (*ephouroumetha hypo nomon*) in a positive light, to signify a form of protective custody (e.g., Calvin 66; Williams 103; Matera 136; Dunn 197, appealing to this connotation of the verb in 2 Cor 11:32; Phil 4:7; 1 Pet 1:5; Lull). The period of the law was thus for humanity's own good, to protect it from transgressions (3:19) or from Sin (3:22). This line of interpretation, which suits the traditional image of the schoolmaster who both teaches and severely chastises (cf. Luther 1535: 345–46), leads inevitably to speculation about what the law, functioning as a protective if also disciplinary pedagogue, is supposed to have taught his charges during the period of their minority (cf. Luther 1535: 335–51; Calvin 66–67).

This traditional line of interpretation is unconvincing for a number of reasons: (1) A *paidagōgos* was clearly distinguished from a *didaskalos*, or teacher (Plato, *Lysis* 208C; *Leg.* 7.808D–E); he was not then a pedagogue (schoolmaster, teacher). (2) The preposition *eis* also occurs in v. 23 and is there most naturally understood to be temporal: "we were confined under the law, being shut up until [*eis*] this destined faith should be apocalyptically revealed." Verse 25, with its claims that since "this faith has come, we are no longer under a *paidagōgos*," meaning "under the law" (v. 23), only makes sense if the *eis* in v. 24 also has a temporal meaning. (3) In the traditional interpretation, the role of the *paidagōgos* is looked at from a father's viewpoint in putting his child under the care of a *paidagōgos*. By analogy, God is the parent who has put humanity under the protective care, instruction, and discipline of the law. But as in 1 Cor 4:15 (the only other NT instance of the term), Paul looks at the role of the *paidagōgos* from the viewpoint and experience *of the children* involved ("*We* were under a *paidagōgos*"); his assumption is that believers now look back at the period when they were minors as a time when they were unhappily confined "under" (*hypo*) a *paidagōgos* (v. 25). That period was tantamount to being "under a curse"—that of the law (3:10)—and "under Sin" (3:22). To be "under" the *paidagōgos* that is the law is then to be outside the sphere of blessing (see comment on 3:6–9) and under that of the malevolent power against which God's justifying (rectifying) action is directed (see comment on 3:22). (4) The import of the clause "We were confined under the law" in v. 23 is indicated by the qualifying participle "being shut up," being "imprisoned" (*synkleiomenoi*). The same verb has been used in v. 22 in connection with "the Scripture" having "shut all things up under Sin." The custody under the law as a *paidagōgos* cannot then have been protective or pedagogical, but only restrictive and oppressive (Burton 199; Vouga 23; Witherington 268; Sänger 2006: 254–60). The law was a jailer, depriving human beings of their freedom (cf. 2:4; 5:1).[355]

Paul uses the image of the *paidagōgos* primarily to underscore the temporary nature of its control over humanity. Like the regime of the *paidagōgos*, that of the law is not eternal (cf. 3:19): "Now that this faith has come, we are no longer under a custodian" (v. 25). This verse can be said "to encapsulate the message of Galatians" (Martyn 364). The time of faith has arrived, ending the time of the oppressive, confining law that, because it was itself confined under Sin (3:22), was not able to give life (3:21). That new age effectively begins for an individual whenever that person "comes to believe in Christ" (2:16), receives the promised Spirit (3:14, 29), and is baptized into him (3:26–28; see comment below).[356]

The purpose expressed by the subordinate *hina* clause in v. 24b, "so that we might be justified on the basis of faith," pertains to God, not to the law's role as a custodian (see similar instances of such divine purpose clauses in 2:16c and 3:22b). The law was "our custodian until Christ, so that [in accordance with God's purpose] we might [from now on] be justified on the basis of [Christ's] faith [rather than on the basis of the law, which was never God's intention]." The juxtaposition of vv. 24 and 25 indicates that "justification" here entails

---

355. Josephus also writes of being "under the law," but for him this situation implies accountability to the law, not enslavement and oppression, as it does for Paul: "[Moses] our leader made the law the standard and rule, that we might live under it as under [*hypo*] a father [*patēr*] and master [*despotēs*], and be guilty of no sin through willfulness or ignorance" (*C. Ap.* 2.174).

356. The precise relationship between believing, reception of the Spirit, and baptism remains inchoate in Galatians.

liberation from captivity (see comments on 1:4; 2:21; cf. Rom 6:7). Christ has set the captives free (cf. 5:1).

[26–28] Believers know that they are no longer under the custodianship of the law because (*gar*), as Paul now goes on to explain to the Galatians, "all of you are sons [*huioi*] of God through this faith,[357] [that is,] in Christ Jesus." Without punctuation, the latter part of v. 26 reads "through this faith in [*en*] Christ Jesus" (cf. KJV, NIV). This translation gives the misleading impression that Paul is here referring to "human faith [*pistis*] *in* Christ," corresponding to the notion of believing (having faith) *in* Christ back in 2:16b.[358] In the latter, however, Paul has used the preposition *eis*, not *en* (see comment on 2:16b and Excursus 9). For this reason, in v. 26 a comma has been placed in the translation between the two prepositional phrases "through this faith" and "in Christ Jesus."[359] Both are different ways of saying nearly the same thing: "you are all sons of God through this faith, that is, in Christ Jesus."

It is tempting to take the second-person plural here to refer to the Galatian Gentiles (e.g., Burton; Betz; Martyn), but v. 28 ("there is no Jew or Greek") shows that "we Jews by birth" (2:15) are also included, if not rhetorically then substantively. Believers, women as well as men, have come to share in the unique messianic sonship of Christ (cf. 1:15; 4:4–5), because all of them are "heirs according to a promise" (v. 29). That promise, made to Abraham and his offspring (3:16), was fulfilled in the coming of Christ, who was the intended beneficiary of the promise (3:16, 19c). In Rom 8:14–17, Paul can use the phrase "children [*tekna*] of God" as a synonym for "sons of God," there adding that such children are "heirs, heirs of God and fellow heirs with Christ" (RSV; cf. 2 Cor 6:18: "You shall be my sons and daughters"). The designation "sons of God" is occasionally used of the people of Israel (Deut 14:1–2; 3 Macc 6:28; cf. the collective singular in Exod 4:22–23; Hos 11:1; Sir 36:17; *4 Ezra* [2 Esd] 6.58); Paul here applies the designation to define the eschatologically new community of Christ (cf. Hos 2:1 LXX [1:10E]; *Pss. Sol.* 17.27; *Jub.* 1.24–25), consisting not only of Jews but also of Gentiles. Believers have become the eschatological "sons" (heirs) of God "through this faith," that is, through the faithful death of Christ (see on 2:16b; 3:22d; Excursus 9), and thus "in Christ Jesus," in the sphere or territory (the believing community) where the lordship of the one who "died for our sins" (1:4) has already become effective (see comments on 1:22; 2:17; 3:14).

In introducing the theme of believers as "sons of God," Paul appears to be citing and interpreting a baptismal tradition, perhaps already known to the

---

357. Literally, "through *the* faith," *dia tēs pisteōs*. The article is being used anaphorically, as in v. 23, to refer back to a previous use of the term.

358. As noted above, $\mathfrak{P}^{46}$ solves the problem by reading "through (the) faith of Christ Jesus," *dia pisteōs Christou Iēsou*. The text then agrees with that of 2:16a (cf. 3:22d).

359. Here RSV solves the problem by separating the two prepositional phrases in the translation: "for in Christ Jesus you are all sons of God, through faith" (also NRSV).

The Spirit and the True Heirs of the Promise Made to Abraham 243

Galatians (see Excursus 12, below). The tradition, or formula, extends from v. 26 to v. 28. The few words (all in v. 26) that Paul has apparently introduced into this formula to facilitate its aptness for his own argument are italicized:

²⁶*For* all of you are sons of God *through this faith*, in Christ Jesus.
²⁷For as many of you as were baptized into Christ have put on Christ.
²⁸ᵃThere is neither Jew nor Greek,
²⁸ᵇthere is neither slave nor free person,
²⁸ᶜthere is no male and female,
²⁸ᵈfor all of you are one in Christ Jesus.³⁶⁰

In the use of the baptismal formula before (and probably also *by*) Paul, one is to imagine a group of newly baptized believers emerging from the water, putting on articles of clothing, and being addressed by the person who baptized them with the words: "You are all sons of God in Christ Jesus, for as many of you as (= all of you who) were baptized into Christ have put on Christ, and so on." In the formula, both the water into which the believer is immersed (the literal meaning of the verb *baptizō*) and the garment one puts on after emerging from the water symbolize Christ. For this reason the immersion can rightly be called "baptism," a rite of initiation "into Christ." In the formula, as for Paul, being baptized "into Christ" involves "putting him on" as if he were an article of clothing (for similar imagery, see Rom 13:12–14; 1 Thess 5:8; 1 Cor 15:53–54; Eph 4:24; Col 3:10; cf. 2 Chr 6:41; Job 29:14; Ps 132:9; Isa 59:17). The new article of clothing—Christ—bestows a new identity (cf. 2:20). The apostle employs the formula to emphasize the new identity of believers who, by having been immersed into Christ and having put him on, share in his divine sonship (see on 4:5).³⁶¹

In citing the baptismal formula, Paul is interested primarily in the distinction between Jew and Greek (= non-Jew, or Gentile): between people who practice (male) circumcision as the determinative mark of their communal identity and those who do not (cf. 2:7–10; 5:6; 6:15). Elsewhere in Galatians, Paul makes

---

360. Some regard the phrase "in Christ Jesus" in the first and last lines as a Pauline addition as well (e.g., Schüssler Fiorenza 208).
361. Paul interprets this baptismal tradition in different if complementary ways in his other letters. In Rom 6:3 he equates being "baptized into Christ Jesus" with being "baptized into his death," and that could be what he here has in view. In 1 Cor 12:12–13 "Christ" is the "one body" into which "we were all baptized." The Corinthian believers are subsequently and collectively called "the body of Christ and individually members of it" in 12:27; the following verse then refers to "the church," where God has "appointed . . . first apostles, second prophets, third teachers," etc. To be baptized "into Christ" can then mean to be baptized into "the church." The fact, however, that the formula, like Paul in citing it, speaks of being baptized "into Christ" indicates that the focus remains christological rather than ecclesiological. Christ seems here to be a corporate person: those baptized into him participate in his faith and its benefits, one of these being incorporation into a new community.

metaphorical use of the language of slavery and freedom for theological ends (cf. 1:10; 2:5; 4:1–7; 4:21–5:1); yet the *social* distinction between slave and free person in v. 28 plays no further role in Galatians. The sexual (or gender) distinction between male and female also does not appear to be at issue in the remainder of Galatians, despite the frequent references to male circumcision in the letter. The circumcision rite referred to does not distinguish male from female (since not all males are circumcised), nor slave from free person (since men from both groups may or may not be circumcised).[362] It distinguishes Jews (as a community or as an ethnic/religious/cultural entity) from Gentiles.[363] At issue in Galatians is the necessity and priority of the distinction between Jew and Gentile for Christian identity, and that distinction is predicated on the practice of (male) circumcision (2:1–10; 5:2–4, 6; 6:12–13, 15). The point for Paul in making use of the formula, therefore, is that the ethnic/religious/cultural distinction between "Jew" and "Greek," between someone who practices circumcision and someone who does not, no longer matters at all (cf. 5:6; 6:15), any more than does the social distinction between slave and free person, or the sexual distinction between male and female. The underlying message to the Galatians is that it is not necessary for them to undertake the practice of circumcision (and the consequent observance of the remainder of the law), as the new preachers in Galatia are claiming (see Excursus 4 and the comment on 5:2–4).

Believers, whether of Jewish or of Gentile origin, are now "all [*pantes*] . . . one [*heis*] in Christ Jesus." The Greek word for "one" here is grammatically masculine; presumably the Greek word for human being, *anthrōpos*, which is also grammatically masculine, is to be supplied (cf. Col 3:9): They are all "one [human being] in Christ Jesus": where Christ is Lord, the ethnic/religious/cultural distinction between Jew and Gentile (just as the social distinction between slave and free person, and the sexual distinction between male and female) gives way to what amounts to a new humanity, defined by Christ (cf. 1 Cor 15:21–22, 45–49). The "all" (*pantes*) in the original baptismal formula is not emphatic but simply descriptive. For Paul himself, however, and for his Galatian audience, the "all" may carry some emphasis (Betz 185), especially if Paul

---

362. Kahl asks why if sex/gender did not matter to Paul in his argument in Galatians, he did not leave out the line "there is no male and female," as he did in 1 Cor 12:13 and Col 3:11. She points out the following: (1) Circumcision is the major issue in Galatians, and this obviously male matter immediately raises the issue of male and female. (2) The language of "male" (*arsen, arsenikos*) is also used in Gen 17:10–14 (in connection with circumcision). (3) There is also a lot of male body language in Galatians: e.g., foreskin (*akrobystia*), seed (*sperma*). (4) In 2:7, the gospel is defined in male terms, literally as "the gospel of the foreskin" and "the gospel of the circumcision." Still, the primary issue in Galatians is manifestly the relationship between Jews and Gentiles, not between males and females. The practice of circumcision defines Jewish (not male) identity.

363. This means that within the Jewish community, women as well as men practice the circumcision of infant boys on the eighth day; the rite is a community (and a family) matter. See Excursus 4.

is responsible for moving the Greek word *pantes* to the beginning of the formula (so Martyn 374) in vv. 26 and 28d, thus emphasizing it (*pantes gar huioi theou este; . . . pantes gar hymeis heis este*: "for *all* of you are sons of God; . . . for *all* of you are one").[364]

By means of his additions to the formula in v. 26 ("for . . . through this faith . . ."), Paul makes it serve his argument about the termination of the law's custodianship through the faith of Christ (vv. 23–25). Thereby a new identity has been bestowed: *all* those "baptized into Christ" are no longer, at least before God and for each other, Jews or Gentiles (any more than they are any longer, at least before God and for each other, slaves or free persons, or males and females). To the contrary, they are all (metaphorically and eschatologically speaking) "sons—heirs—of God." The citation of the baptismal formula thus serves to *remind* the Galatians of their new identity in Christ (Betz 185), the identity bestowed not through the baptismal rite itself but, according to Paul, "through this faith," the faithful death of Christ.[365] Though Paul does not pause to explore them here, it is clear that this new identity "in Christ" has concrete social and practical implications, as 2:11–14 testifies (see comment there; Horrell 2000; cf. Col 3:5–14).

Excursus 12: The Baptismal Formula in Galatians 3:26–28

Aside from the use of the verb *baptizō* in v. 27, among the reasons for the hypothesis that Paul is citing a pre-Pauline baptismal formula in vv. 26–28 are the following. (1) The sudden change from the first-person plural ("we") in vv. 23–25 to the second-person plural ("you") in vv. 26–28. (2) The identification of believers not as "sons of Abraham," which was the issue posed in 3:7 (cf. 3:29), but as "sons of God."[366] (3) The awkward juxtaposition of the prepositional phrases "through this faith" and "in Christ Jesus" in v. 26, causing a redundancy in the thought. (4) The fact that, of the three pairs in v. 28 (Jew/Greek, slave/free person, male/female), only the first seems to be *directly* relevant to the issue of the practice of circumcision and the observance of the (remainder of the) law by the Gentile believers in Galatia (2:1–10; 5:2–4, 6; 6:12–13, 15). (5) The use of the term "Greek" instead of "Gentile" as the opposite of "Jew" in the first pair (cf. the repeated contrast between "Gentiles" and "Jews" in 2:11–18; 3:8, 14). (6) The near parallels in 1 Cor 12:13 ("For in the one Spirit we were all baptized into one body,

---

364. Cf. 1 Thess 5:5 RSV: "For you are all sons of light [*pantes gar hymeis huioi phōtos este*] and sons of the day."

365. This passage (no more than Rom 6) is not "Paul's teaching on baptism." Paul uses a baptismal tradition and the baptismal language and imagery it contains to make a point about the new identity of believers as "sons of God," an identity surpassing and effectively obliterating their previous identities within the sphere of Christ's lordship.

366. Paul has, however, prepared the way for this step in his analogy of the testament in 3:15–19, whereby God is compared to a testator who makes a promise of inheritance to his designated heirs. See comment on 3:15–19.

whether Jews or Greeks, whether slaves or free" [AT])[367] and Col 3:9–11 ("Put off the old human being . . . and put on the new one, . . . where there is no Greek and Jew, . . . slave, free person" [AT]).

The origin of this baptismal tradition is, however, difficult to trace.[368] A clue is provided by the phrase "there is no male and female," which deviates from the "neither/nor" structure of the two prior pairs. The formulation "male and female" (*arsen kai thēly*) matches the wording found in Gen 1:27 LXX: "And God made the human being, in the image of God he made him, male and female [*arsen kai thēly*] he made them." In making use of this creation language, the formula implies that the new identity of baptized believers, where "there is no [longer] male and female," is tantamount to "new creation": an apocalyptic motif that Paul shares and exploits (cf. 6:15: "for neither circumcision nor uncircumcision is anything, but new creation"; see comment there).

Two sayings attributed to Jesus in the Gospel of Mark (written about twenty years after Galatians) provide further support for this line of interpretation and also indicate that the phrase "male and female" probably concerns marriage (Martyn 381; Schüssler Fiorenza 211). In the first, a teaching rejecting divorce (Mark 10:6–8), Jesus connects God's creation of "male and female" to marriage by juxtaposing a quotation from Gen 1:27 with one from 2:24: "But from the beginning of creation, 'God made them male and female' [Gen 1:27]; 'for this reason a man shall leave his father and mother and be joined to his wife, and the two shall become one flesh' [Gen 2:24]." Marriage brings about a certain kind of unity between a man and a woman in the "old" creation: the two thereby become "one flesh."

In the second saying, a teaching on the resurrection of the dead (Mark 12:25), Jesus points out that in the new age beyond the resurrection of the dead, there is no marriage: "For when they rise from the dead, they neither marry nor are given in marriage, but are like angels in heaven," that is, neither male nor female. If such views provide the background to the claim of the baptismal formula that in Christ "there is no male and female," then the point seems to be that unity between male and female is no longer predicated on marriage ("one flesh") but on baptism into Christ: in him they become "one [human being]."

Such an interpretation of the baptismal tradition seems to lie behind Paul's argument in 1 Cor 7, where he has to point out to certain Corinthian believers that marriage under the present circumstances, while not desirable, is not a sin (1 Cor 7:28, 36). These Corinthians apparently thought that baptism into Christ meant the end of marriage (a stance made credible by Paul's own celibate lifestyle). Paul's nuanced teachings on marriage in 1 Cor 7:1–16 and 7:25–40 sandwich references to the other distinctions found in the baptismal tradition of Gal 3:26–28: the distinction between Jew ("circumcision") and Greek ("uncircumcision") and that between slave and free person (1 Cor 7:17–24). In Galatians, Paul appeals to the end of the distinction between male and female in Christ (as to the end of the distinction between slave and free person in Christ) to undergird the

---

367. Both 1 Cor 7:1–40 and 11:2–16 seem to presuppose knowledge of the formula as cited in Gal 3:26–28, including the part concerning "male and female" (purposely omitted from 1 Cor 12:13?).

368. T. Martin (2003) denies that Paul here cites a formula at all and traces Paul's use of the three pairs back to the influence of Gen 17:9–14.

declaration of the end of the distinction between Jew and Gentile in Christ; thus he also renders observance of the law to be irrelevant and superfluous for determining Christian identity. Unfortunately, it is not possible to ascertain how the Galatians will interpret the "neither slave nor free person" and the "no male and female" parts of the formula or how they will apply it in their own lives as Christians (for possibilities, see Betz 190–93; Meeks; Downing), nor how precisely Paul wants them to do so.[369] Paul remains focused on the end of the distinction between Jew and Gentile as the basis for the Galatians' identity "in Christ." The Galatian believers are no longer to think of themselves as Jews or as Gentiles but as "sons—heirs—of God." Paul drives this point home in Gal 3:29.

[29] Verse 29 has the character of a summary: "And if you are Christ's [as indeed you are], then [*ara*] you are [also] offspring of Abraham, heirs [not on the basis of observance of the law but] according to a promise." Paul here uses the form of a real condition, assuming a fact to be true rather than hypothetical. In the Greek the prepositional phrase "according to a promise" is emphatic, implying a contrast, in this case with the law (Lightfoot 151).The "promise" (*epangelia*) here has a passive sense, "what was promised" (cf. 3:18, 22). What was promised was the Spirit (3:14), and that Spirit has been given (3:1–5)—meaning, in turn, that the promise to Abraham has been fulfilled. Abraham has been mentioned seven times earlier in Gal 3, though for the last time in 3:18 (cf. 3:6, 7, 8, 9, 14, 16). Verse 29 seems to be a recapitulation of the thesis found in 3:7: "Those [who live] from faith," that is, the faith of Christ, are "the sons [heirs] of Abraham." But there also are compatible elements that tie this verse directly to 3:15–22 in particular: Christ (3:16, 22), Abraham (3:16, 18), promise (3:16, 18, 21, 22; cf. 3:14 for the first occurrence), offspring (3:16, 19), and heirs (3:18, "inheritance").

In the immediately prior verses (vv. 26–28), Paul has established that the primary identity of believers in Christ does not actually consist in their being "sons of Abraham" (3:7) but in their being "sons of God." This new identity is not in any way predicated on law observance (vv. 23–25). Indeed, this new identity spells the end of the law's regime over human life, as v. 25 has asserted with utter clarity (see comment). Believers are given their new identity as sons—heirs—of God "in Christ" or, nearly synonymously, "through the faith [of Christ]" (v. 26). Descent from Abraham is thus made subordinate to the descent from God (Martyn 375). Because Jewish and Gentile believers are alike "sons of God" in Christ, they also "are Christ's": they belong to him (v. 29a), having put him on and having become "one [new human being]" in him (v. 28). Those who belong to Christ, for whom Jewish or Gentile identity markers no longer matter, can rightfully claim to be "offspring of Abraham" because they are the heirs of the promise that God made to the patriarch (cf. 3:8, 14, 16, 17,

---

369. Philemon and 1 Cor 7 provide clues, but treatment of these passages falls beyond the scope of this commentary. See further the comment on 4:1–7, below, for the slave/free contrast (cf. 5:1).

18, 19c, 21, 22; 4:23, 28). That promise to Abraham found its fulfillment in the reception of the Spirit (3:2, 5, 14), which is given to those who believe in Christ solely on the basis of his faithful death (3:1–5, 18, 22b). Observance of the law plays no role here whatsoever.

One question remains to be answered: Why does Paul here use the expression "offspring of Abraham [*tou Abraam sperma*]" instead of the expression "sons of Abraham," as in 3:7? After all, the metaphor of "son" is appropriate to the notion of inheritance, with which the verse concludes and which also underlies much of the discussion from 3:15 onward. There are two possible answers to this question:

Answer 1. "Offspring [lit., seed] of Abraham" (*sperma Abraam*) is a slogan of the new preachers in Galatia that Paul hijacks for his own purposes (Burton; Martyn; Vouga). The expression is found already in the Septuagint (Isa 41:8; Ps 104:6 [105:6E]; 2 Chr 20:7), apparently as a synonym for Israel. In Rom 11:1, Paul describes himself as "an Israelite, from the seed of Abraham [*ek spermatos Abraam*]" (KJV; cf. 9:7). Presumably any Jew could do the same. In 2 Corinthians, Paul's opponents use the designation to commend themselves to the Corinthian Christians: "Are they Israelites?" Paul asks. "So am I! Are they offspring of Abraham [*sperma Abraam*]? So am I!" (11:22 AT). In John, certain Jews who have come to believe in Christ (8:31) apparently call themselves "offspring of Abraham [*sperma Abraam*]" (8:33; cf. 8:37), claiming Abraham as their father (8:39). On the basis of this evidence, one could conclude that certain Christian Jews were using the expression "offspring of Abraham" as a self-identification, perhaps originally in opposition to other Jews who were declining to accept the gospel message (cf. Matt 3:9 par. Luke 3:8, where John the Baptist announces to his own generation of Jews: "Do not begin to say to yourselves, 'We have Abraham as our father' [cf. John 8:39]; for I tell you that God is able from these stones to raise up children to Abraham" [alt.]). In this interpretation of the expression, Paul appropriates a Jewish, or a Jewish Christian, identity marker for believers in Christ, whether Jews or Gentiles and apart from any observance of the law. Burton (209) expresses it well: "The prize which the opponents of Paul had held before the eyes of the Galatians, and by which they hoped to persuade them to accept circumcision and become subjects of the law, was the privilege of becoming seed of Abraham, and so heirs of the promise to him and to his seed. This prize, the apostle now assures the Galatians, belongs to them by virtue of the fact that they are Christ's." The identification of the Gentile Galatian believers apart from law observance as "offspring of Abraham" then clearly has a polemical motivation. Paul newly defines the meaning of God's people, the offspring of Abraham, as those who belong to Christ without observing the law (see further on 6:16).

Answer 2. The "offspring of Abraham" is actually Christ, into whom believers are incorporated by the Spirit (Lightfoot; Betz). The basis for this interpretation is Gal 3:16, where "the offspring" of Abraham is explicitly identified as Christ ("the promises were spoken to Abraham and to his [singular] offspring, . . . which is Christ"), as is also the case in 3:19 ("until the offspring for whom it had been promised should come"). Believers have put Christ on, thereby becoming "one [new human being]" in him (v. 28). For this reason, the believers in Galatia (as elsewhere) can be identified as "offspring of Abraham," in effect as the Christ into whom they have been incorporated. In this view, Paul's identification of believers as offspring of Abraham is a result of his corporate Christology.

A decision between the two is difficult. Problems with the first interpretation include the following: (a) Whereas the word "offspring" refers specifically to Christ in 3:16 and 3:19, it is taken in v. 29 to refer to the (plural) descendants of Abraham. This problem is resolved by the second interpretation, where the word "offspring" (*sperma*) has the same referential meaning in all three verses: Christ, regarded as a corporate figure. (b) The standard expression in Greek is *sperma Abraam* (lit., "offspring of Abraham"), not *tou Abraam sperma*, as in v. 29. There Paul uses the article with "Abraham" (probably anaphorically) and the word order is different (lit., "of the Abraham seed"). This double variation could, however, be explained as merely stylistic, to emphasize the point that believers in Christ are "offspring of the aforementioned Abraham." Problems with the second interpretation in turn include the following: (a) The Greek text omits the article with the noun *sperma*. Literally, the text reads: "You are offspring of Abraham." Thus the Galatians are not identified explicitly as *the* offspring of Abraham, namely, as the offspring referred to back in 3:16 and 19, which is Christ, but simply as offspring of Abraham, which could then most naturally be taken to mean "the collective descendants of Abraham" (Burton 209). However, the article may well be presupposed since Greek normally omits the article with a predicate noun after the verb *eimi* ("to be"). (b) The Galatians may not catch the subtlety of this point. Given the presence of the new preachers among them, they will probably understand the expression "offspring of Abraham" as a collective designation for Israel (cf. 6:16), rather than as a reference to Christ. The collective interpretation also makes good sense given the connections with 3:7 and the polemical context. A mediating position would be to say that the Galatians are the collective offspring of Abraham because they have been incorporated into his single offspring, Christ. In either case, the point of v. 29, and indeed of the preceding argument, is that believers in Christ are offspring of Abraham by virtue of their relation to Christ and not by virtue of any relation to the law.

4:1–7 The True Heirs of the Promise

This passage concludes Section III of the letter (3:1–4:7). With its explicit reference to the Spirit, it forms an inclusio with the opening paragraph in 3:1–5. As noted in the introduction to Section III, there is a single, unifying theme:

the Spirit (or more fully, the gift and reception of the promised Spirit). Each of its subsections ends with an explicit or an implicit reference to the Spirit (3:5, 14, 22, 29; 4:6–7). The references to promise (3:14, 16, 18, 19, 22, 29), inheritance (3:18, 29; 4:1, 7), and divine sonship (3:26; 4:5–6) are different ways of articulating this overarching theme.

As the previous subsection has clearly indicated, the gift of the Spirit is closely linked to the identity of the Galatians (cf. 3:7): they are sons of God, offspring of Abraham, heirs according to a promise. The present passage in particular develops the notion of believers in Christ as "heirs" of God's promise of the Spirit to Abraham (3:29), and does so in an individualizing manner ("heir" instead of "heirs"). The passage begins and ends with references to this theme:

4:1: "I say that as long as the *heir* is a child . . ."
4:7: ". . . and if a son [of God], also an *heir* through God."

As 4:7 indicates, the metaphor of the believer as "heir" is closely associated with that of the believer as "son." In 4:6, Paul identifies believers in Christ as God's "sons," an identification anticipated in 3:26 ("All of you are sons of God"). Those identified as "sons of God" have put on Christ and belong to him (3:27–29a), and for that reason are *"heirs* according to a promise," namely, that of the Spirit (3:29; cf. 3:14, 16, 18, 22). Paul thus seems to use the metaphor of sonship to give strength to the metaphor of inheritance. The latter metaphor for salvation was first introduced in 3:18: the inheritance—the Spirit (3:1–5, 14)—is given as the result of a promise, not as the result of law observance (3:18; cf. 3:2, 5, 14, 22).

The notion of the "sonship" of believers seems to belie what Paul has asserted in Gal 3:28, that in Christ "there is no male and female." The latter passage clearly demonstrates, however, that the notion of sonship in 3:26 and in 4:5–7 is to be taken as a metaphor, one whose content and implication are determined by God's action in Christ. As indicated above, the point of the metaphor is that believers become "heirs" of the promise. For a believer in Christ, who has become God's "son" by adoption (4:5), is precisely as such also "an heir" of God's promise (4:1, 7), together with Christ, who is God's unadopted Son (4:4; cf. 3:16; Rom 8:17). As the "sons" of God, believers receive "the Spirit of his Son" (4:6) into their hearts: they receive "the inheritance" (3:18) of "the promised Spirit" (3:14). Equally important for Paul is the event by which the status of sonship is effected: God sent forth his unadopted Son to redeem those enslaved under the law (cf. 3:23–25) precisely so that they might be adopted as God's liberated "sons" (4:4–5; cf. 3:1, 13), thereby becoming "heirs" of the promised Spirit.

The probable views of the new preachers in Galatia can usefully be illustrated with a passage from *Jubilees*, where God says to Moses: "And I shall create for them a holy spirit, and I shall purify them so that they will not turn

The Spirit and the True Heirs of the Promise Made to Abraham 251

away from following me from that day and forever. And their souls will cleave to me and all my commandments. And they will do my commandments. And I shall be a father to them, and they will be sons to me. And they will all be called 'sons of the living God'" (1.23–25). For the new preachers, the coming of Christ and his Spirit represent the fulfillment of such a promise. For the Paul of Galatians, however, the promise to Abraham had nothing to do with observing the law, and neither then does the fulfillment of that promise in the gift of the Spirit. Moreover, according to Paul, the sonship of believers in Christ involves liberation from the law, not its confirmation.

The passage can be divided into three discrete units. In the first (vv. 1–3), Paul uses an analogy to clarify the situation of believers before Christ. That situation was one of enslavement "under the elements of the world." In the second (vv. 4–5), Paul gives a contextually relevant reproclamation of the gospel he first preached to them (1:11; 3:1). Through his Son, God liberated those who were enslaved "under the law" that they might be adopted as God's "sons." In the third section (vv. 6–7), the new identity of believers in Christ as God's adopted "sons" finds confirmation in the cry of the Spirit in the hearts of believers, who recognize God as their own "Father." To be no longer a "slave" is to be a "son," and thus also an "heir."

> 4:1 I say that as long as the heir is a child, he differs in nothing from a slave, even if he is master of everything. 2 However, he is under guardians and household managers until the date set by his father. 3 So also we: when we were children, we were enslaved under the elements of the world.
>
> 4 But when the fullness of time came, God sent forth his Son, having been born of a woman, having existed under the law 5 so that he might redeem those under the law, so that we might receive adoption as sons.
>
> 6 Because you are sons, God sent forth the Spirit of his Son into our hearts, exclaiming, "Abba, Father!" 7 So you are no longer a slave but a son, and if a son, also an heir through God.

[1–3] Paul begins with an analogy in vv. 1–2 in order to illuminate the situation of human beings before Christ as described in v. 3: "We [believers in Christ, both Jewish and Gentile] were [all once] enslaved under the elements of the world." This claim needs to be unpacked first before we can fruitfully turn to the analogy itself. The Greek phrase translated as "the elements of the world," *ta stoicheia tou kosmou*, was a common technical expression, derived primarily from Stoic thought, designating the four elements from which the ancients thought the physical universe was composed: earth, water, air, and fire. In v. 3, Paul uses the expression as a summary designation for a complex of religious beliefs and practices in Galatia, at the center of which were these four elements (*stoicheia*) of the physical universe (for details, see Excursus 13, below). Paul assumes that the Galatians will know what he is referring to. In 4:8–11, Paul will reproach the Galatians for "*returning again* to the ... elements [*ta stoicheia*]," which indicates that the Gentile Galatians were adherents of such religious beliefs and practices before becoming believers in Christ.

Excursus 13: "The Elements of the World" in Galatians

The meaning of this phrase has been debated since antiquity (see Burton 510–18; Lightfoot 166–67).[370] The full expression *ta stoicheia tou kosmou* occurs in Gal 4:3 (as it does in Col 2:8, 20) and is abbreviated to *ta stoicheia* in 4:9. Commentators on the passage routinely cite the four meanings proposed in the English versions of the standard Greek lexicon of Walter Bauer (BAG; BAGD):[371]

1. Elements (of learning), fundamental principles.
2. Elemental substances, the basic elements from which everything in the natural world is made, and of which it is composed: earth, air, fire, and water.
3. Elemental spirits that the syncretistic religious tendencies of later antiquity associated with the physical elements (cf. RSV; NRSV).
4. Heavenly bodies (as in "the twelve *stoicheia* of heaven,"[372] the twelve signs of the zodiac).

One problem has always been to find attestation for the last two meanings, which have had their defenders, in sources earlier than the second or third century C.E.

In the third English edition, prepared by F. W. Danker and published in 2000 (BDAG), these four meanings also recur, but they are evidently grouped according to the principle of "extended definitions" whereby "passages" that "share a given meaning structure" are grouped together under a single heading (BDAG viii):

1. "**Basic components of something, *elements*.**"
   a. "of substances underlying the natural world, the basic ***elements*** fr[om] which everything in the world is made and of which it is composed."
   b. "of basic components of celestial constellations, ***heavenly bodies***."
   c. "of things that constitute the foundation of learning, ***fundamental principles***.
2. "**Transcendent powers that are in control over events in this world, *elements, elemental spirits*.**"[373]

In BDAG, words after an Arabic numeral and in bold type are "extended definitions"; words in bold italic type indicate "formal equivalents" (BDAG viii). The formal

---

370. See de Boer 2007.
371. The same four meanings, given in the same order, recur in the sixth German edition of 1988.
372. *Papyri Osloenses* (1925–36) 4.18 (BAGD 769; BDAG 946).
373. Words in normal type after a letter (a, b, c, etc.) indicate "subsets of a[n extended] meaning or collections of data relating to it" (BDAG viii).

equivalents given agree with the four meanings in the 1979 edition, but meanings nos. 1, 2, and 4 have been placed under one heading in BDAG ("basic components of something"). These definitions are thus regarded as belonging to the same semantic field, for they share, in Danker's words, "a meaning structure" (BDAG viii). The order has also been changed. Of particular interest is that meaning no. 2 in the 1979 edition has been promoted to the first position by Danker (1a).

It is somewhat surprising to observe, however, that BDAG discusses Gal 4:3 (and Col 2:8, 20) only under meanings 1c and 2. In fact, BDAG prefers the meaning 1c for Gal 4:3, favorably quoting the translation "elementary ideas belonging to this world" (found in a footnote of NEB). This interpretation of the phrase *ta stoicheia tou kosmou* follows in the footsteps of the commentators Lightfoot (167: "elementary teaching") and Burton (517: "elementary teaching"; cf. Heb 5:12).[374] Longenecker continues this tradition of interpretation in his commentary (165: "the principles of the world"), as does Matera in his (150: "the rudimentary principles of religious life apart from Christ").

Nevertheless, BDAG's preference for this definition goes against the grain of the research carried out by Blinzler; Schweizer; and Rusam (1992), who have demonstrated beyond any reasonable doubt that meaning 1a ("the basic elements from which the world is made and of which it is composed") must apply to the instances in Galatians (as in Colossians). The research of these three scholars shows that this is by far the most common meaning of the term *stoicheia* and the only meaning attested for the full expression *ta stoicheia tou kosmou* in Paul's time. This referential meaning must then be the starting point for any discussion of the meaning of the phrase *ta stoicheia tou kosmou* in the Galatian (or the Colossian) context (Martyn 394–95; Dunn 1998: 108). With considerable confidence, we can say that, for Paul in the context of his Letter to the Galatians, the phrase *ta stoicheia tou kosmou* is a technical expression referring in the first instance to the four elements of the physical universe: earth, air, fire, water.

The context in which Paul uses this technical term demands, however, that the phrase must indeed be read in some other way, or perhaps better, in some additional way (cf. Martyn 395; Blinzler 441). The phrase does refer specifically to the four building blocks of the universe for the ancients, but Paul's concern can hardly be to expatiate on the natural world as such. Something more is involved, and that is where the other proposed referential meanings of the phrase seem inevitably to come into play as attempts to make sense of Paul's text, even if there is no evidence for the meaning "heavenly bodies" or "elemental spirits" before the second or third century C.E. (Blinzler 439).

While it is difficult to disentangle the meaning that the phrase *ta stoicheia tou kosmou* has for the Galatians in their own historical, cultural context from the argumentative or rhetorical context in which Paul refers to them in the letter, Paul makes two claims about the *stoicheia* in 4:8–11 that arguably provide a window on the views of the Galatians before they will receive Paul's letter and, by extension, of their views before they became believers in Christ.

Claim 1. The *stoicheia* are the *gods the Galatians once venerated.* In 4:8–9, Paul links the putative former gods of the Galatians to the *stoicheia* he has introduced into his argument back in 4:3. The link is provided by the verb *douleuō*, which means "to be a slave" or "to serve or venerate (as a slave)" (BDAG 259):

---

374. Lightfoot gives a useful brief survey of patristic interpretation (166–67).

4:8: You were slaves [*douleuō*] of beings not gods by nature.
4:9: You want to be slaves [*douleuō*] *once more* of *ta stoicheia*.

In 4:9, Paul equates the *stoicheia* with the "beings not gods by nature" in 4:8: both are served as slaves (*douleuō*). He makes this equation without further explanation or justification to his Galatian audience. As Martyn (397) writes, "Paul is able to assume some retrospective comprehension on their part when he links these elements with gods they worshiped before his arrival." The equation thus appears to be a shared assumption.

Claim 2. The veneration of *ta stoicheia* involves *calendrical observances* (4:10). Paul charges the Galatians with wanting to serve (venerate) the *stoicheia* "once again," and he illustrates the charge with the exclamation that they are "observing days and months and seasons and years!" Here, too, there is a shared assumption: veneration of the *stoicheia* involves calendrical observances. (The nature of these calendrical observances will be discussed in the comment on 4:8–11, below.)

These two points, in addition to the primary referential meaning of the full phrase discussed above (a technical expression referring in the first instance to the four elements of the physical universe: earth, air, fire, water), allow us to venture a hypothesis about what these *stoicheia tou kosmou* meant for the Galatians *before* they became believers in Christ: *The Galatians venerated the four elements of the universe as gods; this veneration involved calendrical observances.*

Can this hypothesis find support and even be validated, at least to some extent, from other texts? Two passages, both from the Wisdom of Solomon, appear to be especially pertinent.[375] Terms also found in Galatians appear in italics. The first passage is Wis 7:17–19:

> [17]For it is he [God] who gave me unerring knowledge of what exists, to know the structure of the *world* [*kosmos*] and the activity of the *elements* [*stoicheia*]:[376] [18]the beginning and end and middle of times, the alternations of the solstices and the changes of the *seasons* [*kairoi*], [19]the cycles of the *year* [*eniautos*] and the constellations of the stars. (NRSV).

Likewise, Wis 19:18–20 also mentions *ta stoicheia*, earth, fire, and water being specifically named. The *stoicheia* in Wis 7:17–19 probably refer to the four elements, which are juxtaposed, if not exactly identified, with "times," "solstices," "seasons," "cycles of the year and the constellations of the stars."[377]

---

375. Colossians might also be invoked, but that is a difficult step since this letter was written by either Paul himself or a close disciple. It thus could be dependent on Galatians to some extent.
376. Here NRSV has a semicolon; the Greek text of Rahlfs's standard edition of the LXX (1935) has a comma. The colon suggests that what follows is a specification of "the activity of the elements."
377. Cf. Philo, *Aet.* 107, 109–10:

> There are four elements [*stoicheia*], earth, water, air and fire, of which the world [*kosmos*] is composed; ... all these have transcendent powers. ... For just as the annual seasons circle round and round, each making room for its successor as the years ceaselessly revolve, so, too, the elements of the world [*ta stoicheia tou kosmou*] in their mutual interchanges seem to die, yet, strangest of contradictions, are made immortal as they run their race backwards and forwards and continually pass along the same road up and down. (trans. F. H. Colson, in LCL)

The Spirit and the True Heirs of the Promise Made to Abraham 255

The second passage is Wis 13:1–3, which declares:

¹For all people who were ignorant of God . . . ². . . supposed that either fire or wind or swift air, or the circle of the stars, or turbulent water, or the luminaries of heaven were the *gods* [*theoi*] that rule the world. ³If through delight in the beauty of these things people assumed them to be *gods* [*theoi*], let them know how much better than these is their Lord, for the author of beauty created them. (NRSV)[378]

Here the *stoicheia*, though the word itself is not used, are lined up with the circle of the stars, and the luminaries of heaven, the rulers of the cosmos, as realities that non-Jews supposed to be gods.[379] They are reduced to mere created beings by the author of Wisdom of Solomon.

Wisdom of Solomon is a Jewish text written in Alexandria in the first century B.C.E.[380] It thus tells us of the way Jews in the Diaspora may have looked at pagan religious views and activities in connection with *ta stoicheia tou kosmou*. Paul clearly shares the views about *ta stoicheia* here expressed. Non-Jewish texts do not support the hypothesis as clearly and unequivocally as these texts seem to do, so one could conclude that Paul is imposing a Jewish perspective on *ta stoicheia tou kosmou*, which may bear no relationship to how the Galatians themselves regarded them, or related to them, before becoming believers in Christ. At least two factors suggest otherwise, however:

Factor 1. As the founder of the Galatian churches, Paul must have acquired some knowledge of their pre-Christian religious views. It is therefore unlikely that Paul would refer to *ta stoicheia tou kosmou* unless they in fact were part and parcel of their religious views before they became believers in Christ. He will write in 4:9 of the Galatians "returning again" ("reconverting") to the *stoicheia*. In this connection, it may be relevant to observe, with Martyn, that if "one of Paul's Galatian churches was in Pessinus, . . . Apuleius mentions the temple of Cybele there as the place in which the Phrygians reverence Isis under the name of 'the Pessinuntine Mother of the Gods.' For in the same passage Apuleius identifies Isis as *elementorum omnium domina*, 'mistress of all the elements' (*Metam.* 11.5; cf. 11.25)" (Martyn 396, with further texts in note 34).

---

378. Cf. Philo, *Contempl.* 3–5:

Can we compare those who revere the elements [*ta stoicheia*], earth, water, air, fire, which received different names from different peoples who call fire Hephaestus . . . , air Hera . . . , water Poseidon . . . , and earth Demeter . . . ? Sophists have invented these names for the elements [*ta stoicheia*] but the elements themselves are lifeless matter incapable of movement of itself and laid by the Artificer as a substratum for every kind of shape and quality. (trans. F. H. Colson, in LCL)

379. See Martyn 398, who observes in this connection (398 n. 39): "The claim that no pre-Pauline text includes the stars among the elements can be literally maintained even in the face of Wisdom 13, for the term *stoicheia* does not occur there. It seems clear, however, that in this text the author expands his other references to the elements (7:17; 19:18) to include the stars and, more broadly speaking, the luminaries of heaven." Cf. *Jub.* 2.8–10; *1 En.* 82.7–9.

380. Philo (see notes 377 and 378, above) also lived and worked in Alexandria but in the first century C.E.

Factor 2. Paul equates the *stoicheia* with the gods once worshiped by the Galatians and does so without explanation or justification. As noted above, the equation of the *stoicheia* with their previous gods seems to be a shared assumption.

The hypothesis that the Galatians once venerated the four elements of the universe as gods and that this veneration involved calendrical observances is thus not implausible.

The result of the foregoing analysis is that the phrase *ta stoicheia tou kosmou*, a technical expression referring specifically to the four constituent elements of the physical universe, is being used by Paul in his Letter to the Galatians as *a summary designation* for a complex of religious beliefs and practices centered around the four elements of the physical cosmos, to which the phrase concretely refers. In Paul's usage, the phrase is an instance of *metonymy*, whereby an aspect or attribute stands for a larger whole of which it is a part. In this case *ta stoicheia tou kosmou*—the four elements of physical reality—stand for the religion of the Galatians before they became believers in Christ. Calendrical observances and the physical phenomena associated with such observances—the movements of sun, moon, stars, and planets—were an integral part of these religious beliefs and practices. The gods the Galatians worshiped were so closely linked to the four *stoicheia* that the worship of these gods could be regarded as tantamount to the worship of *ta stoicheia* themselves.[381]

In sum, Paul intends the Galatians to understand the phrase (at least initially), and the Galatians will so understand it—at least on a first reading[382]—as described in the previous paragraph: it is a summary description of their former religious beliefs and practices. These involved venerating the *stoicheia* (the physical elements of the universe) as gods and instituting various calendrical observances in connection with these *stoicheia*. The sense can be captured with the following paraphrase of v. 3: "We were [all once] enslaved under the religious beliefs and practices associated with the four elements of the universe (earth, water, air, and fire)."

Two matters are particularly curious and perplexing in Gal 4:3, however. First, Paul uses the first-person pronoun "we" (*hēmeis*, emphatic in the Greek) in v. 3. This "we" must include Jewish believers such as Paul himself. But Jews,

---

381. Hence, while the *stoicheia tou kosmou* are not the stars as such, Paul's reference to them in v. 3 does imply the worship of stars (or other heavenly bodies) as gods.

382. It is possible that, as Martyn argues, Paul intends the Galatians to hear much more than this on *subsequent* readings of the letter. According to Martyn (405), Paul assumes that "the Galatian congregations will listen to the whole of the epistle several times and with extreme care. He takes for granted, that is, not only great perspicacity but also considerable patience." After such careful rereadings of the letter, and with the presumed perspicacity and patience, the Galatians will come to understand that Paul intends them to *reinterpret* the phrase by taking into account "the baptismal reference to the termination of pairs of opposites" in 3:28 (Jew/Greek, slave/free, male/female) and the "climactic reference to the death of the cosmos made up of the first of those pairs" in 6:14–15 (405). The *kosmos* referred to in the phrase *ta stoicheia tou kosmou* is then the *kosmos* about which Paul speaks in 6:14–15. The Galatians will thus come to understand that "Paul *himself* has in mind not earth, air, fire, and water, but rather the elemental pairs of opposites listed in 3:28, emphatically the first pair, Jew and Gentile, and thus the law and the Not-Law" (404, with added stress). The phrase pertains finally not "to the sensible elements . . . but to the elements of religious distinction" (405–6). For the full argument, see Martyn, 402–6. This commentary focuses on the initial reading of the letter, not on how its subsequent consideration might have conditioned its reception.

The Spirit and the True Heirs of the Promise Made to Abraham 257

for whom God was "one" (Deut 6:4; cf. Gal 3:20), certainly did not as a rule venerate the *stoicheia* as gods, as did (some) non-Jews (cf. Wis 13:1–3; Excursus 13 above). How, then, can Paul claim that Jewish believers and not only Gentile believers were once enslaved under the *stoicheia* when these *stoicheia* evidently concern pagan religious beliefs and practices? Second, in the preceding and following verses, Paul refers to (all) believers having been "under the law [*hypo nomon*]" (3:23–25; 4:4–5; cf. 3:10–14). It would have been consistent with this argumentative context if Paul had written in v. 3, "We were [all once] enslaved *under the law*." Why, then, has Paul introduced a reference to the *stoicheia tou kosmou* into his argument at this point instead?

The answer to the first question probably lies in the fact that Paul has the calendrical observances related to these four elements of the world particularly, even exclusively, in view, as indicated by 4:8–11, where the *stoicheia* are referred to a second time: "You," Paul here reproaches the Galatians, "are returning again to the . . . *stoicheia*, whose slaves you want to be once more: Why, you observe days and months and seasons and years!" Calendrical observances, therefore, were for the Galatians an integral part of the religious beliefs and practices associated with the *stoicheia* prior to their becoming believers in Christ (see Excursus 13, above). Calendrical observances (e.g., Sabbath, Passover) linked to the primal elements and associated phenomena (the movements of sun, moon, planets, stars) were also an integral part of Jewish belief and practice (cf. *Jub.* 2.8–9; *1 En.* 82.7–9; Wis 7:17–19, quoted in Excursus 13 above; see comment on 4:10 below). In this sense both Gentile and Jewish believers in Christ were once "enslaved [together] under *ta stoicheia tou kosmou*."

The reason that Paul has introduced the reference to the *stoicheia tou kosmou* into his argument in v. 3 now also becomes evident: He has done so in order to proclaim to the Galatian believers, tempted to observe the law as the new preachers in Galatia recommend, that their liberation from the *stoicheia* (and the calendrical observance associated with these *stoicheia*) was also, at the same time, their liberation from the law (and the similar calendrical observances associated with that law).[383] If Paul succeeds in convincing the Galatians that they were also freed from the law when they were freed from the

---

383. Martyn (397–400) hypothesizes that Paul introduces a reference to the *stoicheia tou kosmou* because the new preachers in Galatia ("the Teachers," in Martyn's vocabulary) have been speaking about the *stoicheia*. According to Martyn, the new preachers have been instructing the Galatians about how the *stoicheia* are to be properly related to Jewish calendrical observances and the Jewish belief in the one God of Israel. They were thereby seeking to compensate for Paul's failure "to terminate" the Galatians' "ill-informed relation to the elements" (399). This is possible, of course, and Martyn makes a strong case for it. In Gal 4:8–9, however, Paul (1) indicates that the Galatians had indeed fully terminated their relation to the elements at their conversion, (2) assumes that the Galatians will find the prospect of returning to the *stoicheia* distressing, and (3) implicitly asks them to make the connection between Jewish feast days and the calendrical observances related to the *stoicheia* (see comment on 4:8–11).

stoicheia, he will have succeeded in dissuading the Galatians from observing the law as the new preachers in Galatia want them to. He will have made the observance of the law unnecessary in their eyes. Paul's startling equation of the observance of the law with the Galatians' past veneration of the *stoicheia tou kosmou* is part of a rhetorical strategy to keep the Galatians from becoming observers of the law (see Excursus 4).

In vv. 1–2 the *stoicheia tou kosmou* are presented by Paul as analogous to guardians (*epitropoi*) and household managers (*oikonomoi*) who have charge of a child (*nēpios*): "I say that as long as the heir is a child, he differs in nothing from a slave, even if he is master of everything. However, he is under guardians and household managers until the date set by his father." To be "under" *ta stoicheia tou kosmou* before "we" became "[the adopted] sons [of God]" (v. 5b) is thus like being "under" (*hypo*) guardians and household managers when a child, in this case the son and heir, is still a *nēpios*, a minor. The point of comparison between the picture part (left column, below) and the reality part (right column) evidently lies in the notion of slavery (top 3 lines) and its temporary nature (bottom 3 lines):

Picture (analogy)	**Reality**
a child (*nēpios*)	we were children (*nēpioi*)
under *epitropoi* and *oikonomoi*	under *ta stoicheia tou kosmou*
no better than a slave	enslaved / a slave
until the date set by his father	when the fullness of time came
master of everything	adoption as sons
(son and) heir	(adopted) son and thus heir

Making the comparison difficult to assess is the use of personal pronouns, since Paul switches in the reality part from first-person plural ("So also we," v. 3) to third-person plural ("those under the law," v. 5) and then to the second-person, both plural ("You are sons," v. 6) and singular ("You are no longer a slave but a son," 4:7).[384] The use of the first-person plural in v. 3 suggests that Paul has the pre-Christian situation of *both* Jewish and Gentile believers in view (see comment above). The two parallel *hina* clauses in v. 5 (cf. 3:14), along with the causal clause at the beginning of v. 6a, also point to a blurring of the distinction between Jew and Gentile (cf. 3:28):

so that [*hina*] he might redeem *those* under the law,
so that [*hina*] *we* might receive adoption as sons.
Because *you* are sons . . .

---

384. See the similar problem in the immediately preceding passage: "we" in 3:23–25, "you" in 3:26–29, with third person in 3:22. Cf. 3:10–14.

Paul's point, evidently, is that everyone (whether Jew or Gentile) was in the same boat prior to Christ and thus also that everyone (whether of Jewish or Gentile origin) benefits from Christ's redeeming work in the same way, despite initial appearances to the contrary. If Gentile believers were in some sense once "under the law," just as Jewish believers were (see comments on 3:10 and 3:13–14), so too Jewish believers were once in some sense "under the *stoicheia tou kosmou*" just as Gentile believers were! Close analysis of the analogy in its broader argumentative context will show how and why Paul can make such astonishing claims.

Even aside from the problem of the pronouns, the analogy limps a bit (cf. 3:15–18; Rom 7:1–5): The picture part concerns the movement of a child (a son) from the age of minority (childhood) to the age of majority (adulthood), whereas the reality part concerns a movement from a situation of enslavement to that of adopted sonship. In the reality part, the position of the children is, for Paul, actual enslavement to *ta stoicheia tou kosmou*. In the picture part, however, the position of the child is *like* that of a slave, though he is not actually a slave at all; on the contrary, the child is, legally speaking, the master of the whole lot even if he is presently under *epitropoi* and *oikonomoi*. The picture part evidently presupposes that the father is deceased, for an *epitropos* was the "guardian" of a boy whose father had died (cf. 2 Macc 11:1; 13:2; 14:2, where Lysias is the *epitropos* of King Antiochus V Eupator, a minor; Philo, *Somn.* 1.107). This has no correspondence in the reality part: God the Father is alive and well.

Threatening the verisimilitude of the analogy is the claim that a single child, even the heir, would be placed under several guardians. The use of the plural can be explained as an anticipation of the plural *ta stoicheia tou kosmou*, which is a relatively fixed expression. But why, then, the addition of *oikonomoi*, household managers?[385] The combination of the two terms appears to be without linguistic parallel (Martyn 397). According to Betz (204), a household manager could also supervise the slaves of the household. Paul has then added the reference to "household managers" to underscore the slave-like plight of the fatherless son during the period of his minority: "He is no different from a slave [whom the household manager can order about]." In the reality part, Paul's use of "we" indicates that he is looking at the world from the position of the enslaved persons. In the picture part, the situation of the child is described from the viewpoint of an outside observer (Paul), who understands that the position of the child is tantamount to that of a slave even if he is, at least legally speaking, the master of the whole estate.[386] The point is the tremendous contrast between

---

385. Like others, Martyn attributes the plurals of both *epitropoi* and *oikonomoi* to the need to make the picture fit the analogy (1997: 387–88), but Paul could have done so by using *epitropoi* alone.

386. For the legalities in Paul's time, see Betz 202–4. In Paul's analogy, the now-deceased father has evidently set the age of inheritance (which may or may not coincide with the age of adulthood) in his will.

the situation of being a child and that of reaching a certain age when he will take control of what is already rightfully his. That contrast also serves the reality part, where the point is the sharp contrast between the situation of enslavement and that of divine sonship, even if the latter is not a legal right but a gift.

In the analogy, the image of a child "under" guardians and household managers recalls that of *the law* as a "custodian" (*paidagōgos*) back in 3:23–25. Paul here also uses prepositional phrases with "under" (*hypo*): to have been "under the law" (3:23) was to have been "under a custodian" (3:25). Paul thereby implicitly personifies the law by comparing it to a *paidagōgos*; so here he also implicitly personifies *ta stoicheia tou kosmou* by comparing them to guardians and household managers. The "guardians and household managers" of 4:2, whatever their precise functions may have been relative to the son and heir, also are represented by Paul as having had charge of a minor, just like the *paidagōgos* of 3:23–25. Moreover, in Gal 3, Paul adds the image of the custodian to his argument primarily to underscore the temporary nature of its control over humanity, another point of contact with the analogy in 4:1–2. The time of the law was not eternal: "Now that this faith has come, we are no longer under a custodian" (3:25). The time of faith has arrived, ending the time of the law; having been baptized into Christ, believers are now "all sons of God" (3:26). In 4:4–5, the point is similar: "When the fullness of time came, God sent forth his Son, ... being born under the law, to redeem those under the law, that we might receive adoption as sons"; believers in Christ are now "sons" of God (4:6). The import of the phrase "we were confined under the law" in 3:23 is indicated by the qualifying participle "being shut up," "imprisoned" (*synkleiomenoi*). Paul thus interprets the situation "under" the law as restrictive and oppressive (see comment on 3:23–25). The law was a jailer, depriving human beings of their freedom (cf. 2:4; 5:1) and keeping them from righteousness and life (3:21). This interpretation of the law as a confining, oppressive custodian is consistent with the thrust of 4:1–2, where the guardians and household managers are clearly experienced by the child in the same way. The *stoicheia tou kosmou*, just like the law, are realities that enslave human beings.

Paul goes a step further, however, as intimated above, since he appears to maintain that existence under the *stoicheia tou kosmou* was actually tantamount to existence under the law. The conceptual similarity between being "under guardians and household managers" and being "under a custodian [*paidagōgos*]" (in 3:23–25) already points in the direction of this *equation* of the two situations: Both images have to do with the situation of a child, the heir (cf. 3:29), in its minority age. In 3:23–25 the *paidagōgos* functions as a metaphor for the law; the suspicion thus lies to hand that the image of guardians and household managers does likewise, at least implicitly. That suspicion is confirmed by 4:4–5, where Paul uses the phrase "under the law" as an apparent synonym for the phrase "under *ta stoicheia tou kosmou*": "We [both Jewish and Gentile believers] were enslaved under *ta stoicheia tou kosmou*. . . . God

The Spirit and the True Heirs of the Promise Made to Abraham 261

sent forth his Son . . . to redeem those *under the law*, . . . so you [any Gentile believer in Galatia] are no longer a slave [under *ta stoicheia tou kosmou*] but a son." Particularly noteworthy in this connection is the use of the first-person pronoun "we" (*hēmeis*) in v. 3, already noted above, whereby Paul includes Jewish Christians like himself.

To sum up: Picking up from the reference to believers in Christ as "heirs" in 3:29, Paul introduces an analogy for the condition of believers before they were baptized into Christ (3:27–28): they were like an heir who in his minority had been put under guardians and household managers until a time determined by his father in the will (cf. 3:15, 18); in this condition he was no better than a slave even if he was, legally speaking, the master of the estate. In like manner, believers, both Jewish and Gentile, were once enslaved under the *stoicheia tou kosmou*, meaning a body of religious beliefs and practices associated with the four elements of the universe, in particular calendrical observances.

[4–5] Verses 1–3 have prepared the way for what is the central theological announcement of the letter: "When the fullness of time came, *God* . . ."

The image of "the fullness [*plēroma*] of time [*tou chronou*]" (v. 4a)[387] can perhaps be understood in one of two complementary ways.[388]

View 1. The image refers to the moment at which a will or testament finally becomes effective (cf. Lührmann 80). The image of "the fullness of time" corresponds to "the date set by the father" in the analogy in vv. 1–2; that analogy implicitly concerns a will or testament, as the use of the term "heir" indicates (see comment above). In 3:15–18, furthermore, Paul has likened God's promise to Abraham to a last will and testament, which no third party can alter or annul (see comment there). As elsewhere (cf. Rom 7:1–5), the comparison falters (unlike a human testator or father, God does not have to die before his testament, the promise to Abraham, can take effect).

View 2. The image compares the passage of time to a container that runs full (cf. Martyn 389; Dunn 213–14; Ridderbos 154; Schlier 194; Mark 1:15; Eph 1:10). When the point of fullness has been reached, something has to give or more has to happen. It would be wrong, however, to conclude that God's action is somehow dependent on time, on the course of human history. That approach would lead to a futile endeavor to study the history of the Greco-Roman period, or of Israel, around the time of Jesus in order to establish the marks of that fullness.[389]

---

387. See MM 520 for several papyri indicating that the expression *plēroō ton chronon*, "to fulfill the time," is not a Hebraism. Cf. BDAG 830.

388. Martyn (389) mentions a third possibility that seems to me to be less likely: The image refers to the moment that a contract has come to an end.

389. Compare the periodization of history in certain strands of Jewish and Christian apocalyptic eschatology (e.g., Dan 9:24–27; 2 Thess 2:1–12). The essence of apocalyptic eschatology is to be found not in the periodization of history, which is an optional feature, but in the contrast between the two world ages (cf. de Boer 1988; 1998).

For Paul, God's action in Christ in and of itself demonstrates that the fullness (and thus in a sense the "end") of time had—and has—been reached. The event of Christ's being "sent forth" is the proof of the matter. Only in retrospect can a believer recognize "the fullness of time" as "the date set by the Father" (cf. v. 2).

Paul uses the phrase "the fullness of time" for two apparent reasons. (1) He has here particularly in view the concern with calendrical observances (time-keeping schemes) among the Galatians and the new preachers, who are leading them down the path of law observance (see comments on vv. 1–3 above and on 4:8–11 below). (2) In Christ a new time has begun—the time of faith, the time of the Spirit, succeeding the time of the law (cf. "no longer" in 3:25 and 4:7), which is equivalent to "the present evil age," mentioned in 1:4 (see Excursus 2, above). As already indicated in the comment on vv. 1–3 above, the contrast prominent in the analogy of vv. 1–2 (between the age of minority and the age of majority, or between immaturity and maturity) gives way in vv. 4–5 to a contrast between a situation of enslavement "under the law" before Christ and a situation of adopted sonship for believers after "the fulness of time" has come. As its presupposition, adopted sonship has liberation from the law and from the *stoicheia tou kosmou*. The "fullness of time" thus signifies a clean break with the past and may be regarded as an apocalyptic assertion on Paul's part: it announces the end of "the present evil age" (1:4) and the beginning of the "new creation" (6:15).

The remainder of the two verses is artfully and poetically constructed. "Here much is contained in a few words" (Calvin 73):

4bGod sent forth his Son,
4chaving been born [*genomenon*] of a woman,
4dhaving existed [*genomenon*] under the law,
5aso that [*hina*] he [the Son] might redeem those under the law,
5bso that [*hina*] we might receive adoption as sons.

The basic message is easily perceived: God "sent forth [*exapesteilen*] his Son," and he did so for a purpose (*hina*) beneficial to human beings. Because a similar two-step construction occurs elsewhere (Rom 8:3–4: "God, having sent his own Son in the likeness of sinful flesh, . . . so that . . ." [AT]; John 3:17: "God . . . sent his Son into the world . . . so that . . ." [AT]; 1 John 4:9–10: "God sent his only Son into the world so that . . ."), Paul may be using and adapting already-existing formulaic or confessional language (cf. comments on 1:4; 3:13–14; 3:26–28). The cited passages (Rom 8:3–4; John 3:17; 1 John 4:9–10) make clear that the designation of Jesus as God's Son points to his special, unique relationship with God (see comment on 1:16), which is different from that of believers (even apostles), who are "sons" by adoption (v. 5). As God's unique Son, Jesus acts in complete conformity with the will and intention of God the Father, who raised him from the dead (cf. 1:1–4; comment on 1:16a).

The Spirit and the True Heirs of the Promise Made to Abraham 263

The "sending forth" implies the commissioning of the Son for a specific task, found in the first purpose clause in v. 5: "so that he might redeem those under the law." The Son's being "sent forth" could point to his preexistence (cf. Wis 9:9–10, where "wisdom" is "sent forth from the holy heavens"), though the notion of "being sent (forth)" does not in itself make any such claim (cf. e.g., John 1:6; Acts 9:30; Isa 6:8; Jer 7:25; Exod 3:14–15).[390] The wording implies, rather, that the Son's redemptive work constitutes God's apocalyptic invasion of the human world so as to liberate it from enslavement (cf. Gal 3:19, 23, 25).[391] The verb "sent forth" is thus substantially synonymous with "came" in 3:23a, 25 and "be apocalyptically revealed" in 3:23b.

The two participial clauses describing the Son (vv. 4c and d) serve to emphasize that God's Son came to share the human predicament completely: He was "born [*genomenon*] of a woman," meaning that he was a human being (cf. Job 14:1; Matt 11:11).[392] He "existed [*genomenon*] under the law," meaning he shared the human condition of enslavement "under" the law (3:23–25) and, by extension, "under" the elements of the world (v. 3; see comment above).[393] The first clause (his full humanity) thus forms the necessary presupposition of the second (his sharing of the human predicament). Philippians 2:7–8, which also contains two clauses with the past participle *genomenos* ("having become," here nominative), provides the best commentary:

⁷He emptied himself, taking the form of a slave (*doulos*),
having become [*genomenos*] in the likeness of a human being, . . .
⁸he humbled himself,
having become [*genonemos*] obedient unto death,
even death on a cross. (AT)

Before and apart from God's redemptive act, to be a human being is to be a slave under realities that appear to promise freedom, righteousness, and life

---

390. Clearer on this point are 1 Cor 8:6; Phil 2:6–8; Col 1:15–17. See Longenecker 167–70.

391. Martyn 407: "The Son is unlike other human beings in that his becoming a human being was, in a significant sense, God's own advent." Cf. 1:12, 15–16; Excursus 6.

392. Paul's formulation is consistent with the notion of a virgin birth (Matthew, Luke; cf. Luther 1535: 367), but the formulation can also apply to someone with a human father (cf. Burton 217). Verse 4c shows that the preexistence of the Son, if this notion is indeed present in the text, does not call into question the full humanity of Christ in any way. Paul's primary concern in this passage, however, is not Christology (the person of Christ) but soteriology.

393. Jesus' own existence "under the law" undoubtedly includes the fact that he was a Jew (being circumcised), but Paul's concern here is not Jesus' Jewishness or his observance of the law (so Betz 207; Dunn 216; Longenecker 171; Williams 111; Matera 150; Witherington 288). The key point for Paul is that Christ shared the (universal) human predicament of being "under the law." On the universality of existence "under the law" (and its curse), see on 3:10, 13, 23; comment on 4:3, above; and on 4:5, below.

but instead deliver the reverse (cf. 3:21; 4:8). God's Son, Christ (3:23–29), came to share that predicament. He too "existed [*genomenos*] under the law." That means he also shared "the curse of the law" (3:10, 13), "having become [*genomenos*] a curse for us" in his death on the cross (3:13; see comment there).

Paul's theological announcement in 4:4–5 concludes with two *hina* ("so that") clauses (v. 5a and b), the first one emphasizing purpose and the second one result (cf. 3:14). The first *hina* clause indicates that God's act in sending forth his Son had as its goal the redemption of human beings from their enslaved condition "under the law": "God sent forth his Son, . . . so that he [the Son] might redeem [*exagorazō*] those under the law." "Those under the law" are all human beings, Gentiles as well as Jews (cf. on 3:10, 22; Burton 219; Ridderbos 156; Martyn 390; only Jews are in view according to Betz 208; Mussner 270–71; Longenecker 172; Dunn 216; Matera 150). The universal scope of God's redemptive activity in Christ thus corresponds to—and addresses—the universal scope of the human predicament (cf. 1 Cor 15:21–22; Rom 5:18; 11:32). Paul has already used the verb *exagorazō*, "to ransom someone from slavery," in 3:13a: "Christ redeemed [*exēgorasen*] us from the curse of the law, having become a curse for us" (see comment there). As in 3:13, the verb in v. 5a is also a synonym for "to liberate (from)" (BDAG 343; cf. 5:1: "Christ has set us free").[394] Liberation from the law in v. 5a is, therefore, probably tantamount to liberation from the curse of that law (3:13; cf. Hays 2002: 109–10). God's act of liberation from the law has already become effective for "us" (3:13), for those who have come to believe in Christ (2:16b; 3:22b). The fact that the Gentile believers in Galatia too have been redeemed from the law means concretely that they do not have to become observers of that law, as the new preachers in Galatia recommend. The law has absolutely "no jurisdiction" over believers (Luther 1535: 369–70).

The second *hina* clause highlights the consequences of this redemptive act, "so that we [believers in Christ] might receive [as we have] adoption as sons": literally, "so that we might receive the son-adoption [*tēn huiothesia*]." The Greek term used (Latin: *adoptio*) was a technical legal term for adoption (BDAG 1024; cf. Rom 8:15, 23; 9:4; Eph 1:5). The point is that the adopted son obtains the right of inheritance that a natural, legitimate son has (cf. vv. 1–2). Paul uses the language of adoption metaphorically to mean that the (adopted) "sons" of God have become the "heirs" (v. 7; cf. 3:29) of God's promise to Abraham, that promise being the Spirit of Christ (3:14; see below on 4:6–7). For this reason, the metaphor of adopted sonship applies to female as well as to male believers (cf. 3:28). To be God's adopted "son" also means that a believer

---

394. The import of the verb *exagorazō* is thus not to be pressed unduly, as if Christ's redemptive work involved some price he had to pay to someone (e.g., Satan).

The Spirit and the True Heirs of the Promise Made to Abraham

stands in God's favor and has been incorporated into the family of his Son (cf. Martyn 391). It also signifies that a believer, by the power of Christ's Spirit (4:6–7, below; 5:13–6:10), lives in conformity with God's will and intention for human beings, just like "his Son." Paul here once again uses the all-inclusive "we" that he also used in v. 3 (see above): All believers, whether Jewish or Gentile, "receive adoption" to sonship of God (cf. 3:26; 4:6–7).

[6–7] The closing verses of the passage form an inclusio with 3:1–5. The larger unit (3:1–4:7), wherein Paul refutes the false gospel of the new preachers in Galatia and grounds his own gospel, begins and ends with references to the Spirit, that Spirit being the fulfillment of the promise that God made to Abraham (see introduction to 4:1–7 above). In both passages the assumed experience of the Spirit by the Galatians plays a crucial role in the argument.

The initial clause of v. 6 indicates that Paul in this verse tries to further elucidate what adoption to sonship of God for believers (v. 5b) entails: "*Because you are sons [of God], God sent forth the Spirit of his Son into our[395] hearts, exclaiming, 'Abba, Father!'*" Given its relationship to the preceding verse, the initial causal clause is probably not to be interpreted to mean that God's sending forth the Spirit is somehow dependent upon believers' first achieving and recognizing their status as "sons" of God. In 3:1–5, Paul has already said that the Galatians "began" with the Spirit. It is thus more likely that for Paul the sonship of believers becomes evident in the experienced fact that God sent forth the Spirit of his Son into their collective hearts. To paraphrase the point of v. 6: "Because you are God's sons, you also certainly know from your own experience that God sent the Spirit of his Son into all of our hearts, enabling us to acknowledge and address him as Father."

The "heart" (*kardia*) appears here to be regarded especially as the seat of discernment and knowledge (cf. BDAG 508), in this case of the believer's relationship to God (cf. Ezek 36:26: "A new heart I will give you, and a new spirit I will put within you"; Jer 31:33–34: "I will put my law within them, and I will write it on their hearts; and . . . they shall all know me"). This knowledge will first have entered the hearts of believers at their baptism, when they together heard the words: "All of you are sons of God . . . in Christ Jesus, for as many as of you as were baptized into Christ have put on Christ" (3:26–27; see comment there). The words spoken to them would find confirmation in the internal testimony of the Spirit exclaiming, "Abba, Father!" (*abba, ho patēr*), perhaps initially as they rose out of the baptismal water (cf. Martyn 392; Acts 2:38). The verb *krazō* ("exclaim") suggests a fervent shout or cry (BDAG 563–64; cf.

---

395. Other manuscripts read "your" under the influence of the opening clause of v. 6, which uses the second-person plural (Metzger 526). Paul here includes himself and all other believers, whether of Jewish or Gentile origin.

Ps 3:5 LXX [3:4E]) and is here "a sign of certainty and unwavering confidence" in God (Calvin 75).

The term "Abba" has been transliterated from the Aramaic. The addition of the Greek translation (*ho patēr*, lit., "the Father," nominative in form though vocative in function, as in Rom 8:15), is probably traditional, since it is also found in Mark 14:36, where Jesus likewise addresses God as "Abba, Father" (*abba, ho patēr*). The bilingual acclamation probably arose in mission among Greek-speaking people, perhaps initially in Antioch; it is striking that the Aramaic term evidently remained in use in the baptismal rite alongside the Greek, at least for some time in the Pauline mission field (contrast the Lord's Prayer in Luke 11:2; Matt 6:9).

The English translation of v. 6 obscures the fact that in the Greek text it is formally not the "hearts" of believers that exclaim "Abba, Father!" but the very Spirit of God's Son: "God sent forth the Spirit [*pneuma*], . . . exclaiming [*krazon*], 'Abba, Father!'" The participle *krazon*, neuter in the Greek, can only modify the word *pneuma*, which is also grammatically neuter. As the parallel in Rom 8:15–16 shows, however, believers are themselves enabled to make this exclamation as a result of the Spirit within them: "When *we* exclaim [*krazomen*], 'Abba, Father!' it is the Spirit himself bearing witness with our spirit that we are children of God" (alt.). By attributing the exclamation directly to the Spirit in v. 6, Paul also makes it clear that the act of addressing God as "Abba" and/or as "Father" is not an action thought up by human beings themselves, but a human action wrought by God. It is a mark of God's beneficially invasive presence and activity whereby God liberates human beings from slavery, so that they are in a position to recognize God as their caring "Father" (see 1:1–4; 4:4–5).

God's having sent forth (*exapesteilen*) the Spirit parallels his having sent forth (*exapesteilen*) the Son in v. 4b. The sending forth of the Spirit is thereby closely tied to the sending forth of the Son. The link between the two is further underscored by the characterization of the Spirit as "the Spirit *of his Son*" (cf. Phil 1:19; 2 Cor 3:17), in contrast to earlier passages in Galatians where Paul refers simply to "the Spirit" (3:2, 5, 14). In fact, the two sendings are probably to be regarded as coterminous rather than as strictly sequential. The Spirit experienced by believers is another name for the continuing presence and activity of the Son, whom God sent forth. That also means that the Spirit is not a reality immanent to this world; it is not a force inherent in creation. The Spirit is specifically the Spirit of God's Son. The Spirit of God's crucified Son, whom God raised from the dead (1:1) constitutes God's own ongoing invasive—apocalyptic—presence and activity in the world of human beings (see further 5:13–6:10 below). The adoption of the believer as a "son" of God (v. 5b) tangibly occurs whenever God sends the Spirit of his Son into the heart of a human being, enabling that person to exclaim, "Abba, Father!"

"So," Paul writes, drawing a conclusion that pertains to each individual believer in Galatia and summarizes the argument from 3:1 onward, "you are no longer a slave but a son, and if a son, also an heir through God" (v. 7). A believer is no longer a slave of the *stoicheia tou kosmou,* nor then of the law. Liberation from slavery has made the believer a "son" of God. To be a "son" of God (v. 5b, 6; cf. 3:26) means that a believer, male or female (3:28), is "an heir" of God (cf. Rom 8:17), an heir of the promise that God made to Abraham (cf. 3:16, 17, 18, 19, 21, 22, 29; 4:23, 28). As noted earlier, the notion of inheritance was first introduced in 3:15–18, where Paul has likened God's promissory covenant (*diathēkē*) with Abraham (Gen 17:1–8 LXX) to a human testament (also *diathēkē*) that a third party (in this case, the law) cannot tamper with so as to render that promise invalid and void (cf. 3:19–21). The testator of this "testament" is God; the designated heirs of God's "testament" are Christ (3:16, 19) and those who belong to him (3:29). These believers have received his Spirit into their hearts (cf. 3:2, 5; 4:6), this Spirit being "the inheritance" referred to in 3:18 (cf. 3:14). A believer in Christ is not "an heir" of the promise that God made to Abraham "through the law [*dia nomou*]" (2:21), meaning through the observance of the law, as the new preachers in Galatia are claiming; rather, they are heirs "through God [*dia theou*]," that is, through the gracious act of God in Christ (2:21). The phrase "through God" has finally no other theological meaning than the phrase "through [*dia*] a promise" in 3:18 and "through [*dia*] the faith (of Jesus Christ)" in 2:16; 3:14, 26,[396] referring to Christ's faithful death on the cross as God's act of grace on behalf of humanity (see Excursus 9 and comment on 2:16).

Finally, the phrase "no longer" in v. 7 recalls 3:25: "Now that this faith has come, we are *no longer* under a custodian (i.e., under the law)." A regime change has occurred, and above all else Paul wants to make that clear to the Galatians (cf. Martyn 23; Martyn 1997: 121). Paul effectively repeats the point in 4:4–7: "When the fullness of time came, God sent forth his Son . . . [to] redeem those under the law, . . . so you are *no longer* a slave but a son." By wanting to adopt the law with its holy calendar (4:10), the Galatians "are behaving as though Christ had not come, thereby showing that they do not know what time it is" (Martyn 418). Paul announces to the Galatians that God's own (apocalyptic) time as revealed in Christ (4:4–5) has brought to an end the calendrical schemes, which both the law and "the elements of the world" have in common. In sum, Paul seeks to say the following in v. 7: "You are no longer a slave of the elements of the world, or of the law, but a son of God, and if you are a son, as in fact you are, then you are also the rightful heir of God's promise to Abraham, through God's liberating act of grace in Christ."

---

396. Some (lesser) manuscripts indeed read "an heir through (Jesus) Christ," reflected in KJV; Luther 1535: 392–94; Calvin 74. See, further, Metzger 526–27.

Summary of Section III

This section began with Paul's reminding the Galatians in so many words that they had received the Spirit not because they had been observing the law but because they had heard the proclamation of the faithful death of Jesus Christ on the cross. In the following paragraphs, Paul has sought to show again and again that the reception of the Spirit of Christ had and has nothing to do with observing the law. Many things associated with law observance in the views of the new preachers in Galatia—justification, Abraham, blessing, promise, inheritance, divine sonship, yes, even God—are related by Paul to the reception of the Spirit on the basis of Christ's faithful death instead of to the observance of the law. Furthermore, Paul presents the law as a parenthesis in God's dealing with the human world from the time of Abraham. The period of the law was an interval between the promise to Abraham and the fulfillment of that promise at the coming of Christ and his Spirit. Nothing good can be said about that interval: The law extended not a blessing but a curse; its coming represented a dubious attempt to tamper with God's promise to Abraham; it was added to the promise not by God but by angels, who were using Moses as their mediator; it was not able to give life nor the hoped-for justification; it was a jailer closely allied with Sin; it enslaved all human beings, as did the *stoicheia tou kosmou* from which Christ had delivered the Galatians when they came to believe in him. In the process of trashing the law, Paul also reminds the Galatians of what they have already received apart from the law: the Spirit of Christ, representing the rectifying activity of God in the world. The Spirit is what God promised to Abraham; to receive this blessing of Abraham is to become genuine "sons" of Abraham and thus his heirs. Those who have received the Spirit, as the Galatians have, are therefore truly "offspring of Abraham, heirs according to a promise." More important than being "sons" or "offspring" of Abraham, however, is being "sons of God." Through the Spirit of Christ, believers become "sons of God" by adoption and thus heirs, each believer individually, of the promise that God made to Abraham concerning the Spirit. This is all God's doing through the faithful death of Christ.

Section IV: Galatians 4:8–5:12
The Grave Dangers Confronting the Galatians

In the previous section of the epistle (3:1–4:7), Paul has sought to refute the "different gospel" of the new preachers in Galatia and to explicate his own. As if not entirely sure that this argument will have convinced the Galatians, Paul now reviews the dangers that confront the Galatians from the message and the work of the new preachers among them:

4:8–11	The Danger of Returning to Their Previous Religious Servitude
4:12–20	The Danger of Abandoning Paul and His Gospel
4:21–5:1	The Danger of Losing their New Identity through Faulty Exegesis
5:2–6	The Danger of Becoming Separated from Christ and Grace
5:7–12	The Source of the Danger: The Leaven of the New Preachers

The strong Greek adversative conjunction, *alla* ("but"), with which 4:8 begins, signals a sharp break with the preceding passage (and section) and arguably heads the whole section, extending to 5:12. With *alla*, Paul in effect issues a warning at this juncture of the letter: "*But* watch out!" The Galatians, whom he addresses in 4:21 as "you who want to be under the law," are in grave danger of losing everything they have gained if they follow the version of the gospel being proclaimed by the new preachers among them. The new preachers are explicitly mentioned or alluded to in 4:17; 5:7, 10, 12, and they appear to be the unstated target of Paul's formulations throughout (cf. 4:9c–11, 19–20, 21, 29–30; 5:1–4, 8–9, 11).

An urgent tone pervades the whole section. Paul here pulls out all the emotional stops in order to prevent the Galatians from succumbing to the proclamation of the new preachers. He vents feelings of exasperation and incredulity (4:9b, 11; 5:7) as well as those of tenderness and appreciation (4:12, 20). He chides (4:9b), but he also entreats (4:12). He fears for his efforts (4:11), is perplexed about the Galatians (4:20), and concludes with a wincingly crude wish for his opponents in Galatia (5:12).

The thrust of the whole section finds its articulation in 5:1b with its urgent appeal: "Stand fast, therefore, and do not be burdened again with a yoke of slavery!" The "yoke of slavery" refers to is the law-based gospel being propounded by the new preachers in Galatia. The solemn declaration that precedes in 5:1a ("For freedom Christ has set us free!") is arguably an encapsulation of the gospel as Paul has articulated it in Section III (3:1–4:7). It sums up the message of the letter for the Galatians. The urgent appeal in 5:1b is a negative exhortation ("Do *not* . . . again . . ."). The point of the whole section is not to exhort the Galatians to live in a manner that accords with the gospel of Christ, which will be the purpose of Section V (5:13–6:10), but rather to *prevent* them from being burdened by the putative gospel of the new preachers, a step that Paul rather astonishingly equates with the Galatians' going back to their previous situation of religious servitude (4:9c). Section IV, which has been prompted and made necessary by the evidently dire situation of the churches of Galatia, is the rhetorical heart of the letter: it brings Paul's attempt to keep the Galatians from going the route of circumcision and law observance, as the new preachers insist they do, to a sharp focus (see Introduction: Overview). As such, the passage also functions as a transition from what is the theological heart of the epistle in 3:1–4:7 (the indicative) to the paraenesis proper in 5:13–6:10 (the imperative).

4:8–11 The Danger of Returning to Their Previous Religious Servitude

In this short passage, Paul directs the attention of the Galatians to their past (v. 8), equates their desire to become observers of the law with a return to that past (vv. 9–10), and wonders if he has not labored among them in vain (v. 11).

> **4:8** But [*alla*]:[397] Then, when you did not know God, you were slaves of beings not gods by nature. **9** But now, having come to know God, or rather having become known by God, how can you be turning again to the weak and impotent elements of which you are wanting to be slaves[a] once more? **10** You are observing days and months and seasons and years! **11** I fear for you, that I may have labored for you in vain!

a. Mss. ℵ and B read the aorist (*douleusai*) instead of the present (*douleuein*). The aorist could be rendered "become slaves." The present suggests activity that, once begun, continues. Both make good sense.

---

397. As indicated just above, this conjunction (actually, a *dis*junction) appears to provide a heading not just for v. 8 or for vv. 8–11 but for the whole section extending to 5:12.

[8–11] Verses 8–9 exhibit a "on the one hand [*men*] . . . on the other hand [*de*]" construction whereby the past of the Galatians ("then," *tote*) is contrasted with their current situation ("now," *nun*):

⁸ᵃThen [*tote men*], when you did not know God [*ouk eidotes theon*],

⁸ᵇyou were slaves [*edouleusate*] of beings not gods by nature.

⁹ᵃBut now [*nun de*], having come to know God [*gnontes theon*],

⁹ᵇor rather having become known by God,

⁹ᶜhow can you be turning again to the weak and impotent elements of which you are wanting to be slaves [*douleuein*] once more?

In v. 9c, Paul does not write, as one might expect, "You have turned to God from idols to be a slave [*douleuein*] of a living and true God," as he does when writing the Thessalonians (1 Thess 1:9). Instead, he poses an urgent question to the Galatians, making a double equation in the process. (1) To become a slave of "the elements" (*ta stoicheia*) is to become a slave "once more" (*palin anōthen*) of the gods that the Galatians had venerated before becoming believers in Christ (vv. 8b, 9c). (2) To turn to the observance of the law is actually to return to the servitude of "the elements" from which Christ has freed the Galatians (4:3–7; see comment there). Verse 10 ("You are observing days and months and seasons and years!") provides the grounds on which Paul can make this astonishing assertion (see comment, below; and Excursus 13, above). In short, Paul alerts the Galatians to the fact that by turning to the law, as the new preachers recommend, the Galatians are in effect returning to their former religious beliefs and practices! They will then be back to where they started; they will become separated from Christ and will have fallen from grace (5:4). Paul's work among the Galatians will have then been for nought (v. 11). It will be as if he had never been to Galatia to preach the gospel there! Paul here deploys heavy rhetorical artillery in order to keep the Galatians from becoming observers of the law.

In v. 8 Paul reminds the Galatians that when they "did not know God" (as they now do) they "were slaves [*edouleusate*] of beings not gods by nature [*tois physei mē ousin theois*]."[398] Since Paul himself founded the Galatian churches (4:13), he must have been to some extent familiar with their previous beliefs and practices. He had been on-site and had first encountered them before they

---

398. Literally, "the by nature not being gods," or more idiomatically, "the gods who are not such by nature" (Burton 227). The definite article in the Greek (*tois . . . theois*) is probably generic, designating a class (hence the translation given above), though it could also be taken to indicate a reference to the specific gods that the Galatians once worshiped (cf. BDF ##252–54).

had come to believe in Christ. He knows that the Galatians had once been worshipers of "beings not gods by nature." These "gods" (*theoi*) are not here specified; they are simply distinguished from the singular one "God" (*theos*). "By nature" (*physei*) here means simply "in reality" or "in fact": the Galatians had worshiped beings that were not in fact gods at all but part of the "natural" order. Paul would scarcely have used the formulation "beings not gods by nature" if the Galatians had not previously been convinced of the opposite, that the gods they had worshiped were indeed gods in reality. Upon becoming believers in Christ, the Galatians had come to see, following Paul, that the gods they had been worshiping were not really gods at all. He reminds them of this fact, that the gospel had removed the aura of divinity from the beings they had once worshiped, reducing the *stoicheia* to the merely natural phenomena they in fact always were (cf. Wis 13:1–3).

The verb *douleuō*, here translated with "to be a slave," literally means "to serve as a slave" (BDAG 259). Paul uses the term as a virtual synonym for "worship" or "venerate," as in 1 Thess 1:9, where Paul reminds the Gentile believers in Thessalonica how they had "turned to God from idols, to serve [*douleuein*] a living and true God." The latter passage also shows that, for Paul (as for Jews), to "serve" the one God is acceptable, whereas to "serve" other (i.e., false) gods is not (cf. Exod 23:33 LXX; Matt 6:24; Luke 16:13). In v. 8b of the present passage, Paul counts on the Galatians' sharing this negative appraisal of "serving" their former gods. He can count on their doing so for two reasons: (1) Paul works from the (common) pagan assumption that being a slave, even of a god, is a totally undesirable condition. For this reason, Gentiles did not use the verb *douleuō* to characterize their veneration of "the gods." It had no positive religious connotations for them whatsoever (Rengstorf 1964a: 264–65). (2) In the preceding passage (4:1–7), Paul has used other terms for slavery (*doulos*, "slave"; *douloō*, "to enslave") with a thoroughly negative connotation (cf. already 3:28).[399] That negative connotation is carried forward to his use of *douleuō* in v. 8b. In calling the attention of the Galatians to their past in this way, Paul also implicitly reminds them of their new status as liberated "sons of God," the point emphasized in the immediately preceding verses (cf. comment above on 4:6–7).

As just indicated, the contrast between the past and the present of the Galatian believers is highlighted by the parallelism between vv. 8a and 9a: The Galatian Gentiles had not "known" God (v. 8a) but have now "come to know" him (v. 9a). Paul avoids saying what he could have said here, that the Galatian believers had "become slaves" of God, using a form of *douleuō* (cf. again 1 Thess 1:9; Gal 1:10). He avoids this verb probably from rhetorical considerations (its negative connotation for the Galatians). Instead, he uses the language

---

399. Contrast 1:10, where Paul characterizes himself paradoxically as "a slave of Christ."

The Grave Dangers Confronting the Galatians

of coming to know God: the Gentiles in Galatia had moved from ignorance of God to knowledge of God when they heard the gospel that Paul preached (cf. 1:6, 11). The presupposition that the Galatians as Gentiles were ignorant of God appears to be rooted in the OT and Jewish tradition (cf. Jer 10:25; Ps 79:6; 2 Macc 1:27; Acts 17:30; Eph 4:18; 1 Thess 4:5: "the Gentiles . . . do not know God"). Knowledge of God here is not merely intellectual but also, and even primarily, relational. To know God is to be in a proper relationship with God and to live in accordance with God's will.

Most fascinating is that Paul here corrects himself: "But now having come to know God, or rather [what I actually mean to say is:] *having become known by God* . . ." If the language of "coming to know God" is the language of the religious quest for a proper relationship with God, the language Paul chooses is that of God's own initiative, of God's invasive self-disclosure on the earthly stage. A human being becomes known by God: that is, a human being is grasped by God by being "called" into the sphere of "the grace of Christ" (1:6) through the proclamation of the gospel (cf. 1:8–9, 11–12; Excursuses 2 and 6). The gospel is not an instance of the religious quest for God (as common then as it is today), but the expression of God's apocalyptic self-disclosure in Christ (cf. Martyn 37–41).

Given this fact of God's initiative, of having become known by God, Paul now confronts the Galatians with an urgent question, couched in a tone of exasperation and incredulity: "How can you be turning again [*epistrephete palin*] to the weak and impotent elements (*stoicheia*) of which you are wanting to be slaves [*douleuein*] once more [*palin anōthen*]?" (v. 9c). Here Paul for the second time in the letter refers to "the elements" (*ta stoicheia*); these are "the elements of the world" (*ta stoicheia tou kosmou*), introduced in 4:3. "The elements" are here indentified as "the gods" the Galatians once venerated, as the parallelism of vv. 8b and 9c demonstrates (see above). In other words, to be a slave of "the elements" is to be a slave of "the gods" that the Galatians had once venerated. Paul makes this equation without further explanation or justification to his Galatian audience, which suggests that the equation is an assumption shared by Paul and his Galatian audience. The phrase "the elements of the world," *ta stoicheia tou kosmou*, was a technical expression referring to the four constituent elements of the physical universe: earth, water, air, and fire (see Excursus 13, above). That is also manifestly the case for the abbreviated form of the expression "the elements," *ta stoicheia*, in v. 9b (cf. Col 2:8, 20). Paul uses this technical expression in its full or abbreviated form as a summary designation for a complex of religious beliefs and practices centered around the four elements of the physical universe, to which the term concretely refers. As v. 10 shows, calendrical observances—the movements of sun, moon, stars, and planets—were an integral part of these religious beliefs and practices (see comment below). Paul's usage of the full phrase and of its abbreviated form represents an instance of metonymy, whereby an aspect or attribute stands for a larger whole. As the equation evident in vv. 8b and 9c indicates, the gods that the Galatians once worshiped were so closely tied to the four elements that the worship of these gods could be regarded as tantamount to the worship of the elements themselves (see Excursus 13).

The emotionally loaded rhetorical question of v. 9c constitutes part of Paul's attempt to make observance of the law a very unattractive option for the Galatians. The basic problem addressed by the letter, as we have repeatedly noted, is that the Galatians are being encouraged to become observers of the law by new preachers who have come into the Galatian setting (cf. 2:6–9; 3:1–5; 5:2–5; 6:12–13). In 4:1–7 Paul has postulated that existence "under the elements of world [*hypo ta stoicheia tou kosmou*]," which was the situation of the Gentile Galatians before Paul's arrival, was tantamount to existence "under the law [*hypo nomon*]," the situation from which Christ redeems all human beings. The reverse would then also apply: "wanting [*thelontes*] to be under the law," which according to 4:21a is the desire of the Galatians, is tantamount in Paul's eyes to "wanting [*thelete*] to be slaves of the elements" (4:9c) and thus of the gods the Galatians had left behind. Surely, Paul implies, the Galatians do not want to be in *that* position "once more" (*palin anōthen*)![400] As in v. 8b, the argument in v. 9c presupposes that being a slave (*douleuō*) is an entirely undesirable condition no less when it involves being a slave of "the elements" and thus of the gods tied to these elements. By repeating the verb, Paul rhetorically emphasizes the negative implications of returning to the veneration of "the elements" and the gods behind them.[401]

Paul's formulation also indicates that being a slave of a god or gods is a matter of choice. The verb *douleuō* need not necessarily signify enslavement (an imposed condition), as does Paul's use of the cognate verb *douloō* ("enslave") back in 4:3. The *stoicheia* become gods in Paul's view only if and whenever human beings venerate them as such. It is evidently Paul's view that once human beings begin venerating the *stoicheia*, they in effect become enslaved to the gods they have created for themselves. The gospel liberates human beings from such enslaving delusions. For such reasons Paul characterizes the *stoicheia* as "weak and impotent," *asthenē kai ptōcha* (lit., "weak and poor"),[402] which is what they actually are apart from the power that human beings grant to them (cf. Wis 13:18–19). This characterization of the *stoicheia* is part of Paul's rhetorical strategy of dissuading the Galatians from becoming observers

---

400. Cf. 5:1: "Do not be burdened *again* [*palin*] with a yoke of slavery."
401. Attempts to find references to the imperial cult behind these verses (Witulski; Hardin) remain unconvincing.
402. For the translation of *ptōcha* as "impotent," see Martyn 411. Cf. BDAG 896 ("extremely inferior in quality, miserable, shabby").

of the law: The *stoicheia* are just as ineffectual for salvation as the law, which is unable to give life (3:21; Martyn 412). It thus makes no sense to venerate the *stoicheia*, the so-called gods associated with the four elements.

Paul therefore makes clear that for the Galatians to turn to the observance of the law is effectively to *return* (Martyn 401) to the veneration of the *stoicheia* and thus of the gods they had previously worshiped ("you are turning again," *epistrephete palin*). The verb *epistrephō* means "to turn around" and thus by extension "to convert" (cf. BDAG 382; 1 Thess 1:9); the combination *epistrephō palin* evidently means "to *re*convert." In Paul's mind the observance of the law and the veneration of the *stoicheia* are in some sense functionally and thus also conceptually equivalent. Paul has prepared the way for this equation in 4:1–7, as we have seen: Since redemption from the one entailed redemption from the other, to be under the one is tantamount to being under the other. This is clearly Paul's own view of the matter, one he now seeks to impress on the Galatians: He wants the Galatians to see that to turn to the observance of the law is effectively to go *back* to their previous situation, before Christ and apart from Christ. It is this rhetorical agenda that has caused Paul to introduce the references to the *stoicheia* into his argument in 4:3 and 9.[403] Unless there is some similarity, either conceptually or functionally (or both), between the observance of the law and the worship of the *stoicheia*, Paul could not very persuasively make the move of equating the situation under the *stoicheia from* which the Galatians came with the situation under the law *to* which they are now wanting to turn.

In what sense the observance of the law is conceptually and functionally tantamount to the veneration of the *stoicheia* becomes evident in v. 10: "You are observing [*paratēreisthe*] days [*ēmeras*] and months [*mēnas*] and seasons [*kairous*] and years [*eniautous*]!" The verb *paratēreisthe* (present tense) could mean "are [now fully] observing," but the context speaks against this: Paul is doing all he can to prevent the Galatians from taking this contemplated step. The verb is probably to be construed conatively ("You are wanting/intending/beginning to observe"), consistent with the phrase *douleuein thelete* ("You are wanting to be slaves") in v. 9b (cf. 1:7, 10; 6:12) and the conative use of the

---

403. As indicated in the comment on 4:1–7 (see note 383 there), Martyn (397–400) hypothesizes that Paul has introduced the references to the *stoicheia* into his argument because they formed an important part of the message of the new preachers in Galatia ("the Teachers," in Martyn's vocabulary). Martyn argues that the Teachers were trying to wean the Galatians from their problematic relationship to the *stoicheia*, something Paul had failed to do (399–400). In vv. 8–9, however, Paul seems to assume that the Galatians had fully given up venerating the *stoicheia* at the moment they had come to believe in Christ (cf. 1:6–9; 5:7a). He also appears to assume that the Galatians will find the prospect of returning to the *stoicheia* unattractive, and that they had not yet perceived the close connection between Jewish feast days and the calendrical observances related to the *stoicheia* that they had left behind (see comment on v. 10 below).

verb *epistrephete* ("you are turning, intending to turn") in the previous verse.[404] Paul's choice of the verb *paratēreō*, which can mean "to observe scrupulously" (BDAG 771), is undoubtedly for rhetorical effect: it heightens Paul's tone of consternation about what the Galatians are intending to do.

Paul's list of calendrical observances is also interesting. Since the Galatians are ostensibly wanting to turn to the law at the behest of the new preachers present in the Galatian churches (1:6–9; 3:1–5; 5:2–5; 6:12–13), one expects Paul to say to the Galatians in v. 10: "You are observing sabbaths and new moons, and such festivals as the Day of Atonement, Passover, and Firstfruits" (cf. Martyn 416). We may compare Col 2:16, which refers to "a festival or a new moon or a sabbath" (RSV) in connection with another polemic against *ta stoicheia tou kosmou*. Since Paul does not use words such as these, a possible explanation is that he is charging the Galatians with actually wanting to return to the calendrical observances associated with these *stoicheia tou kosmou*, thus to their religious way of life before their coming to faith in Christ (so Martin 1996). Another possible explanation is to argue that, though Paul's list of calendrical observances is not ostensibly Jewish, the terms can cover Jewish holy days: Paul has in view days like the Sabbath and the Day of Atonement, months like the "new moon" (e.g., Num 10:10), seasons like Passover and Pentecost, and years like the Sabbatical Years (Lev 25:5) or the New Year festival (Burton 233–34; Dunn 227–28). Since the Galatians are turning to the law, so the argument runs, the terms must refer specifically to such Jewish calendrically based observances. A better explanation for v. 10 is probably that Paul has here chosen words that could cover both Jewish and pagan calendrical observances (cf. Betz 218; Barclay 1988: 63–64). The Galatians are wanting to turn to the law and the calendrical observances that the law prescribes. For Paul, this turning to the law is tantamount to returning to *ta stoicheia tou kosmou* and the calendrical observances associated with them. With his choice of words, which is neither specifically pagan nor specifically Jewish, but could be either or both (Martin 1996: 112), Paul implies that the Jewish observances that the Galatians are now wanting to observe are no different in kind from the observances linked to *ta stoicheia tou kosmou*. Paul thus intentionally uses terms that cover both Jewish and pagan calendrical observances, for he wants the Galatians to realize that by turning to the law, they are going back to where they came from.[405] The observance of the law is not a step forward,

---

404. Cf. the verb *dikaiousthe* in 5:4 ("You are seeking to be justified in the law"; BDF #319). See Smyth: the conative present "may express an action begun, attempted, or intended" (#1878). The early reading of $\mathfrak{P}^{46}$ (the present participle *paratērountes*) supports this interpretation, for it makes v. 10 part of the question of v. 9, thereby eliminating the seeming contradiction between the two verses (see Betz 217 n. 39).

405. It is possible that, as Martyn (416–17) argues, Paul's language is largely indebted to Gen 1:14 (LXX): "Let there be luminaries in the dome of the sky to separate the day from the night,

but a step backward! In v. 11, Paul draws the inevitable conclusion from his own argument: he fears with respect to the Galatians that he may (*mē pōs*) have labored for them in vain!

4:12–20 The Danger of Abandoning Paul and His Gospel

In the previous passage Paul focused the attention of the Galatian churches on their pagan past as worshipers of false gods, and he warned them of the danger of reverting to that past if they were to become observers of the law, as the new preachers in Galatia insist. They will then have abandoned the God whom they have come to know as believers in Christ and by whom they have come to be known in Christ (4:9ab). In the present passage, Paul focuses the attention of the Galatian churches on a subsequent chapter of their history, the time when he came and preached the gospel to them. He recalls this chapter of their history to warn them of the danger of abandoning *him*, their founding apostle, if they heed the message of the new preachers (cf. 1:6–7 and comment there). He implies that for the Galatians to abandon him is to abandon the gospel that he preached to them at the beginning (cf. 1:11; 3:3), and thus also the God of that gospel. The subject matter of this passage flows directly from 4:11, where Paul has expressed the fear that he may have labored for the Galatians in vain.

The passage can be divided into two units. In the first (vv. 12–14), Paul recalls his initial visit to the Galatians and the generous reception he received from them. In the second (vv. 15–20), he brings up the troubled relationship between him and the Galatians as a result of the missionary work of the new preachers (cf. 4:11).

> **4:12** Become as I am, because I also have become as you are, brethren, I entreat you. You did me no wrong: **13** you know that on account of an infirmity of the flesh I preached the gospel to you the earlier time, **14** and your[a] temptation in my flesh you did not despise or disdain,[b] but you received me as an angel of God, as Christ Jesus.
>
> **15** Where then is your happiness? For I bear you witness that if possible you would have plucked out your eyes and given them to me. **16** So I have become your enemy by being honest with you! **17** They zealously court you but not in a good way; rather, they want to shut you out, so that you might zealously court them. **18** It is good to be courted[c] zealously in a good thing always and not only when I am with you, **19** my children,

---

and let them mark the fixed times of seasons [*kairous*], days [*hēmeras*], and years [*eniautous*]" (as cited by Martyn; cf. Bruce 205). Martyn notes that the list of times found in Gen 1:14 "was sometimes supplemented by the addition of 'months,' and that the times were sometimes put in order of length" (417, referring here to Philo, *Opif.* 55 and 60, and to the work of Lührmann 1980). Cf. *Jub.* 2.8–10; *1 En.* 82.7–9.

with whom I am again in travail until Christ be formed in you. **20** I could wish to be with you now and to change my tone, because I am perplexed about you.

a. Numerous manuscripts, including 𝔓⁴⁶, substitute *mou* ("of me, my") for *hymōn* ("of you, your"). The latter is supported by ℵ, B, D, among others (see Metzger 527).
b. The words "or disdain" (*oude exeptysate*) are omitted by 𝔓⁴⁶.
c. The reading *zēlousthe*, which is either an imperative ("be courted zealously") or an indicative ("you are being courted zealously"), found in ℵ, B, 33, is probably an accidental scribal misspelling of the infinitive *zēlousthai* (*-sthai* and *-sthe* were pronounced alike). The indicative/imperative reading makes no sense.

The tone of this passage on the whole is solicitous. Paul addresses the Galatians fraternally as "brethren" (*adelphoi*) in v. 12 and maternally (rather than paternally!) as "my children" (*tekna mou*) in v. 19. Here Paul's language "overflows with sweet and gentle words" (Luther 1535: 413). Verse 17, however, consists of a warning about the dangerous intentions of the new preachers in Galatia. And that warning points to the underlying issue: the imminent danger of the Galatians' abandoning Paul and "his" gospel.

[12–14] Verse 12a contains the first imperative in the second half of the letter.[406] This imperative, a present tense (*ginesthe*) implying an ongoing state rather than a onetime action, is the only verb in the Greek text of v. 12a. Other verbs have to be supplied: "Become [and remain] as I [am], because I also [have become] as you [are], brethren." As the words in v. 12b indicate ("I entreat you"), the imperative in v. 12a is not a command but an earnest request.[407] The entreaty is patently paradoxical: Paul is asking the Galatians to become like him for the reason that he has already become like them! Since the context clearly indicates that Paul's entreaty functions as part of his campaign to keep the Galatians from becoming observers of the law, the sense appears to be as follows: "Become and remain as I am now, free from the law, because I also have become as you are now, free from the law" (cf. 2:19–21; Lightfoot 174; Burton 237; Longenecker 189; Dunn 232; Betz 222; Matera 159; Martyn 420). The Galatians have not yet succumbed to the message of the new preachers—they are still free from the law—though they are on the verge of doing so. The entreaty has been formulated to underscore the need for reciprocity in action and attitude. The use of the fraternal "brethren" (*adelphoi*), which in

---

406. This fact leads Longenecker (186–87) to surmise that the hortatory section of the letter begins here, not at 5:13. See comment there.
407. The given translation of v. 12a–b follows the Greek word order, but it is still difficult to know what the relationship of v. 12b to v. 12a is, or whether "brethren" (*adelphoi*) goes with v. 12a or v. 12b. One solution is to reverse the word order, as in RSV: "Brethren, I beseech you, become as I am, for I also have become as you are."

Greek includes women as well as men, in turn highlights the equality of the two parties. Paul here addresses the Galatians as intimate friends and equals (Betz 222–23; Martyn 420).

In v. 12c and the following two verses, Paul in one long sentence reminds the Galatians of their relationship when he came to Galatia "the earlier time [*to proteron*]" (v. 13), when he founded the Galatian churches. Classically, *to proteron* refers to the earlier of two occasions, and that could then mean that Paul had been to Galatia a second time before writing the letter (Burton 239; Lightfoot 175). In Hellenistic times, however, *proteron* had come to mean simply "earlier" (BDF #62) and *to proteron* "the first time" or "before" (BDAG 889; cf. John 6:62). Moreover, as Longenecker (190) points out, *to proteron* forms a contrast with the implied *nun* ("now") in v. 16 (cf. NRSV), making a second visit unlikely (see comment below). Along the same lines, Martyn (421) observes that "the picture Paul paints in this paragraph is marked by a simple and striking contrast between the enthusiastic reception the Galatians gave to him and his gospel when he founded their churches and the cool and critical stance the Galatians have adopted due to the influence" of the new preachers. If there had been a second visit, Paul would have reminded the Galatians that even then their relationship had still been good, unlike now. It thus seems that Paul had been to Galatia only once before writing the letter. "The earlier time" refers to the founding visit.

Paul begins his reminder of their common past by recalling that the Galatians "did him no wrong" (v. 12c) when he came to them that first time. What Paul means with this assertion is explicated in vv. 13–14, whereby v. 12c is shown to be an understatement (Tolmie 2005: 158):

> [13]You know that on account of an infirmity of the flesh I preached the gospel [*euēngelisamēn*] to you the earlier time, [14]and your temptation in my flesh you did not despise or disdain, but you received me as an angel of God, as Christ Jesus.

In short, although the Galatians thought Paul had a repulsive bodily condition, they did not turn him away but, amazingly, welcomed him with open arms! This was all to the great credit of the Galatians.

The interpretation of the details of this commendation of the Galatians is difficult, however. Paul was presumably passing through Galatia on his way to another region (cf. Acts 16:6) when he ended up preaching the gospel to the Galatians (cf. 1:8–9, 11). He stopped there only "on account of an infirmity of the flesh [*di' astheneian tēs sarkos*]," because of a bodily ailment. Paul does not divulge what this bodily ailment was, whether a disease or something else. It must have been serious enough to cause him to stop in Galatia. Verse 14, furthermore, indicates that the ailment must have been of such a nature that the

Galatians were tempted to despise and disdain him because of it, though Paul again does not divulge the precise reason for their revulsion. The phrase "your temptation [*peirasmos*] in my flesh" (lit., "the temptation of you") is particularly difficult (the English translation reflects the awkwardness and obscurity of the underlying Greek), in part given its function as direct object of the phrase "you did not despise [*ouk exouthenēsate*] or disdain [*oude exeptysate*]."[408] The noun *peirasmos* can also mean "trial" (cf. RSV) or "test[ing]" (cf. NRSV). The sense of the phrase is apparently passive: "that which tempted/tested you in my flesh," meaning Paul's bodily ailment (Lightfoot 175). With the phrase "in my flesh" (cf. 2 Cor 12:7), Paul is clearly referring back to his "infirmity of the flesh" in v. 13a. Paul's point is probably that there was something in his "physical condition which tempted them [the Galatians] to reject him and his message" (Burton 241; cf. BDAG 352). The verb *ekptyō* ("disdain") literally means "spit out" and seems to have had some connection with the warding off of demons or evil spirits associated with diseases (cf. Betz 225; Dunn 234; Martyn 421). Since the verb was also used metaphorically as a general term for contempt (BDAG 309), no reliable conclusions about either Paul's ailment or the revulsion of the Galatians can be drawn. Paul appears to use the verb simply as a synonym for *exoutheneō*, "despise" (Longenecker 192; cf. *Jos. As.* 2.1).[409] He includes it to emphasize what the Galatians could understandably have done but, surprisingly, did not do.

Instead of despising and disdaining Paul, the Galatians did what can be regarded as the exact opposite: they received (*edexasthe*) him "as an angel of God, as Christ Jesus" (v. 14b). The verb *dechomai* means "to receive" in the sense of "to welcome, to host" (cf. 1 Cor 2:14; 2 Cor 6:1; 7:15; 8:17; 11:4, 16; Phil 4:18; 1 Thess 1:6; 2:13). Despite his problematic illness, the Galatians received Paul into their homes and thus into their midst in the first place as if he were tantamount to "an angel of God," a messenger from God (see comment on 1:8).[410] Paul's choice of words is all the more striking if the Galatians had indeed been tempted to associate Paul's bodily ailment with the presence of a demon (see above on v. 13). In the second place, the Galatians also received him "as Christ Jesus" himself. In receiving Paul, the apostle commissioned by Christ (1:1), the Galatians effectively received the one who had commissioned him (cf. Matt 10:40: "The one who receives you receives me" [RSV, alt.]; Luke 10:16: "The one who rejects you rejects me" [RSV, alt.). But it is remarkable that they did so, given Paul's evidently repulsive physical condition. When Paul was among the Galatians in that condition, he portrayed Christ as crucified before their eyes

---

408. As indicated above, numerous manuscripts, including $\mathfrak{P}^{46}$, seek to resolve the difficulty by substituting *mou* ("of me, my") for *hymōn* ("of you, your"). The latter, however, is the more-difficult reading and is supported by ℵ, B, D, among others (see Metzger 527).

409. That may explain why $\mathfrak{P}^{46}$ has chosen to omit it.

410. Not all "angels" are necessarily "angels *of God*" for Paul (cf. 3:19). In 2 Cor 12:7 he characterizes a bodily ailment (his "thorn in the flesh") as "an angel (messenger) of Satan."

(3:1) so that instead of being offended by "the ugly shape of the cross" (Luther 1535: 420, 421) in Paul's bodily presence (cf. 6:14, 17), they accepted him as the embodiment of Christ's self-giving love (cf. 2:19–20) and thus as "Christ Jesus" himself. In his fleshly infirmity or weakness (*astheneia*), whatever that may have been, Paul evidently became identified in the eyes of the Galatians with Christ, who, as he writes in 2 Cor 13:4, "was crucified in weakness [*astheneia*]" and now "lives by the power [*dynamis*] of God." Though it is not certain whether "the infirmity of the flesh" refers to the same bodily ailment as "the thorn in the flesh" in 2 Cor 12:7 (see n. 410, above), the theological sentiments expressed in the verses that follow may also apply here: Paul three times beseeched Christ to relieve him of that thorn in the flesh, but the answer he received from Christ was: "My grace (*charis*) is sufficient for you, for [my] power [*dynamis*] is made perfect in weakness [*astheneia*]" (2 Cor 12:9a; for "grace," see Gal 1:6, 15; 2:9, 21). Paul then continues: "I will all the more gladly boast of my weaknesses [*astheneiai*], that the power [*dynamis*] of Christ may rest upon me. For the sake of Christ, then, I am content with weaknesses [*astheneiai*], insults, hardships, persecutions, and calamities; for when I am weak [*asthenō*], then I am strong [*dynatos*]" (2 Cor 12:9b–10 RSV; cf. 1 Cor 4:9–13). When Paul is weak in his flesh, suffering bodily ailments and trials, he is "strong," powerful (*dynatos*), in his proclamation of the gospel, as he was among the Galatians (Martyn 421; Vouga 109). Paul's reminder that the Galatians had welcomed him as if he were Christ himself subtly strengthens Paul's authority as Christ's apostle, and thus it also reinforces the entreaty in v. 12 for the Galatians to become as he is.

[15–20] Paul now brings the attention of the Galatians to the present. The relationship between him and the Galatians has soured: "Where then is your happiness [*makarismos*]?" (v. 15a). The noun *makarismos* signifies a blessed (cf. KJV; Dunn; Witherington) or happy frame of mind (BDAG 611), which the renderings of REB, RSV, and NRSV seek to capture: "What has become of the happiness/satisfaction/goodwill you felt?" (cf. Rom 4:6–9). Their happy frame of mind was such that they would have gone to great lengths to be of service to Paul, as he now solemnly attests: "For I bear you witness that if possible you would have plucked out your eyes and given them to me." If Paul had needed them, the Galatians would have given him what for many ancients was the most precious part of the body (LSJ 1278; Vouga 111–12; Betz 227), so great was their affection for him. Paul here resorts to hyperbole; such a gesture, if it had literally been carried out, would not actually have helped him. Given the hyperbolic nature of the imagery, it is difficult to know whether Paul's choice of words *indirectly* discloses that he suffered from a (severe?) eye ailment (is this then "the infirmity of the flesh" referred to in v. 13?). In any case the rhetorical point is clear: the Galatians were extremely well disposed toward Paul—back then.

But not now: "So [*hōste*] I have [now] become your enemy by being honest with you!" (v. 16). This is probably an indignant exclamation (Burton;

Longenecker), rather than a rhetorical question expecting an affirmative answer (RSV, NRSV, NIV; Lightfoot; Betz; Bruce); the conjunction *hōste* at the beginning of an independent clause always introduces an inference elsewhere in Galatians (and the NT), never a question (cf. Gal 2:13; 3:9, 24; 4:7). The phrase "being honest" represents a single Greek word, the participle *alētheuōn*, "to be truthful, to tell the truth" (BDAG 43). Presumably Paul is referring specifically back to 4:8–11, where he has equated the Galatians' desire to become observers of the law with a return to their religious beliefs and practices before they heard the gospel. If they opt for that, it will be as if he had never been to Galatia. That, for Paul, is the honest truth. That argument presupposes "the truth of the gospel" (2:5, 14; cf. 5:7), which means "freedom" from the imposition of the law as a condition for justification (2:4; 5:1, 4, 13). Paul's use of the strong term "enemy" (*echthros*) seems exaggerated in this context, especially since one purpose of the letter is to enable the Galatians to see Paul as Christ's apostle once more (see below on 4:18–20). A possible explanation for the use of the term is that the new preachers, who are clearly alluded to in the next verse, have suggested to the Galatians that Paul with his version of the gospel is actually their enemy, as much as he is theirs (Martyn 420–21). Some law-observant Jewish Christians (the Ebionites) of a later period applied this epithet to Paul (*Ps.-Clem. Ep. Pet.* 2.3; *Ps.-Clem. Recog.* 1.70). It is possible, however, that the word simply expresses Paul's fear that his honesty has caused the originally positive feelings of the Galatians toward him to have taken a 180-degree turn, from friend to enemy.

In the following verse, Paul attempts to indicate that those truly inimical to the best interests of the Galatians are the new preachers, not he: "They zealously court [*zēlousin*] you but not in a good way; rather [*alla*], they want to shut you out, so that you might zealously court [*zēloute*] them." The syntax is garbled. The main thought appears to be: "They zealously court you [and then] not in a good way, . . . [but only so] that you might zealously court them [in turn]." In this reading the purpose clause ("so that you might zealously court them") is dependent on the main clause ("they zealously court you"), not on the subordinate adversative clause ("rather, they want to shut you out"). The main thought thus consists of a play on the verb *zēloō*, literally, "to be zealous [for something or someone]," here translated "to court zealously [i.e., with zeal]" (cf. 1:14). Even without the middle clause, Paul's aim is clearly to cast aspersions on the intentions of the new preachers (Betz 229–30), whom he refers to only indirectly (the Galatians will know whom he is talking about). He claims that the new preachers are zealously courting the Galatians from impure motives, "not in a good way" (*ou kalōs*). Their actual goal is to bind the Galatians to themselves rather than to Christ. They are false friends (Betz 231). It is difficult to know whether Paul is merely vilifying (slandering) his opponents in Galatia or (also) describing what actually is the case: the opponents will undoubtedly protest when the letter is read out to the Galatians.

The manner in which the new preachers try to achieve this goal is to be found in the middle clause: "rather [*alla*], they want [*thelousin*] to shut you out [*ekkleisai hymas*] [from fellowship with Christ]." This clause evidently if awkwardly functions as an explanatory comment for the adverbial phrase "not in a good way" (Vouga 110). In two other places, Paul points to what the new preachers supposedly want: "they want to turn the gospel of Christ into its opposite" by making it conditional upon observing the law (1:7), and "they want to make a good showing in the flesh" by asking the Galatians to practice circumcision (6:12). Here too, then, Paul's image of shutting out or exclusion probably reflects their agenda of wanting to impose the observance of the law on the Galatians, beginning with circumcision (cf. 5:2–4). That is the nub of the matter. The image of exclusion implies that the new preachers are presenting themselves as gatekeepers (Martyn 423), preventing entry into the realm of salvation and the benefits thereof unless their (version of the) gospel is adopted (see Excursus 4). It seems that the new preachers are putting considerable pressure on the Galatians to become observers of the law (cf. 6:12: "they are putting pressure on you to practice circumcision"). On a theological level, this pressure probably takes the form of telling the Galatians that apart from circumcision and further law observance, they remain excluded from membership in God's people, the offspring of Abraham (cf. 3:7, 29; Gen 17:14; Dunn 238). Put otherwise, according to the new preachers, without the law the Galatians fall under the curse of Deut 27:26 (3:10; Martyn 30), whereby they are effectively excluded from "the blessing of Abraham" (cf. 3:14). On a social level the pressure of the new preachers may have taken the form of literally excluding the Galatians from their table fellowship, including the Lord's Supper (cf. Barclay 1988: 59; Martyn 423; Dunn 238). For Paul, this all amounts to exclusion from fellowship with Christ, the one offspring of Abraham (cf. 3:16, 19c, 26–29; 4:19; Lightfoot 177).

In v. 18, again making a play on the verb *zēloo*, Paul contrasts his own zealous courting of the Galatians with that of the new preachers: "It is good [*kalon*] [for you] to be courted zealously [*zēlousthai*] [by me] in a good thing always and not only when I am with you, my children."[411] The true difference between Paul and the new preachers lies not in their zealous courting of the Galatians (cf. 2 Cor 11:2) but in the matter at issue: "a good thing [*kalon*]," with which Paul most probably refers to the gospel he preached (v. 13) or, synonymously, to Christ (vv. 14, 19). In this crucial matter the new preachers fall lamentably and dangerously short. Paul devotes himself to this matter not only when he is

---

411. The verse can also be understood as follows: "It is good [for me] to be courted zealously [by you] in a good thing always and not only [for you to do so] when I am with you, my children" (so, e.g., Ridderbos; Betz). In the interpretation suggested here, v. 18a (Paul's good intentions with respect to the Galatians) is understood to form a contrast with v. 17a (the dubious intentions of the new preachers with respect to the Galatians).

with the Galatians (an allusion to his founding visit) but also now, in his writing of the letter. He is in effect their true friend (Betz 232–33).

Verse 19 is probably to be construed as a continuation of v. 18 (Lightfoot 178; Burton 248).[412] He addresses the Galatians tenderly as his children, while strikingly portraying himself as a pregnant woman and mother-to-be: "my children, with whom I am again in travail [*ōdinō*] . . ." (v. 19a).[413] He is in the process of giving them birth,[414] going through the necessary birth pangs now for the second time. The children who were born when Paul founded the Galatian churches have to be born all over again! Since Paul elsewhere uses the image of birth pains as a metaphor for apocalyptic change (1 Thess 5:3; Rom 8:22–23; cf. Gaventa 1990; 2007: 29–39; Eastman 2007: 89–126; Mark 13:8), he may be doing so here as well, though it not possible to know whether the Galatians will catch the supposed apocalyptic import of the metaphor. In his giving birth to the Galatians now a second time, Paul evidently thinks of himself as standing with them at the juncture of the ages, where new life (the life of the new age) constantly struggles to come into being. The Galatians are addressed and described as those being born again, as people putting their full trust in Christ alone (cf. 2:16b)

The image changes dramatically in the second half of v. 19, however. Paul is once again in travail with the Galatians, he says, "until Christ be formed in you [plural]." Now the Galatian congregations (or the individual members thereof) are likened to a woman in whom Christ is to be conceived (*morphoō*)![415] Paul has earlier noted that those Galatians who were "baptized into Christ have put on Christ" like a set of new clothes (3:27). In v. 19b, then, Paul must mean "until Christ be formed in you *again*." The adverb "again" (*palin*) in the main clause (v. 19a) evidently also covers the subordinate clause (v. 19b). For Christ to be "formed" in them anew probably means that his Spirit must once again invade their collective hearts so that they can say "Abba, Father!" (4:6)—and at the same time say "No!" to the imposition of the law.

In conclusion (v. 20), Paul expresses the wish that he could at the very moment of writing be with the Galatians: "I could wish [*ethelon*] to be with you

---

412. Many other commentators take v. 19 to begin a new (if incomplete) sentence (e.g., Betz; Dunn; Longenecker; Martyn; also Tolmie 2005: 162), as do RSV, NRSV, NIV, because they perceive a sharp change of tone. However, once vv. 18 and 19 are taken to be one sentence, the solicitous tone of v. 19 can also be discerned in v. 18. The solicitous tone is already evident in v. 12 ("brethren").

413. Paul's metaphor may be indebted to Isa 45:10 (Martyn 427–29). In 1 Cor 4:14–15 Paul likens his founding of the church in Corinth to a father who begets children (cf. Phlm 10). That metaphor is also found in Isa 45:10.

414. The verb *ōdinō* when intransitive means "to suffer birth pains," as in the quotation from Isa 54:1 LXX in 4:27. When transitive, as here (*hous . . . ōdinō*, "whom . . . I am bearing in travail"), the verb means "to give birth to a child with birth pains" (cf. Isa 51:2 LXX). See BDAG 1102.

415. For the use of the verb *morphoō* ("to form") in reference to the formation of an embryo in the womb, see BDAG 659, citing Galen (19 [ed. of C. Kühn, 181]) and referring to Philo (*Spec.* 3.117).

The Grave Dangers Confronting the Galatians

now" (cf. v. 18b).[416] The expression "to be with you" (*pareinai pros hymas*) has also been used in v. 18, showing the connection between the two verses, and supporting the view that v. 19 is an appendage to v. 18:

> [18]It is good [for you] to be courted zealously [by me] in a good thing always and not only when I am with you [*pareinai pros hymas*], [19]my children, with whom I am again in travail until Christ be formed in you. [20a]I could wish to be with you [*pareinai pros hymas*] now."

Paul wishes to be with Galatians now "and [also] to change my tone [*phōnē*, voice]" (20b). In other words, if Paul were to be able to talk with the Galatians face-to-face, he would change his tone, presumably from one of consternation and reproach (evident in his written communication) to one of tenderness and concern for the welfare of the Galatians.[417] In effect, he has already made and anticipated that change of tone in this passage, especially in vv. 18–19 ("my children").

The concluding causal clause of v. 20 is probably dependent on the main clause: "I could wish to be with you now . . . because I am perplexed about you."[418] The reason for his perplexity, or bafflement, is clearly given in the opening verse of the next passage: The Galatians "are wanting to be under the law" (4:21a)! Why would they want to do any such thing when they already have the Spirit (cf. 3:1–5)? Paul would dearly like to have a face-to-face encounter with the Galatians in order to determine why they are on the verge of abandoning him and the gospel.[419]

4:21–5:1 The Danger of Losing Their New Identity through Faulty Exegesis

In the two previous passages of Section IV (4:8–5:12), Paul has focused the attention of the Galatians on their past. In 4:8–11 he has recalled for the Galatians their pagan past as worshipers of false gods, and he did so in order to

---

416. The imperfect verb *ēthelon* implies a wish that cannot at the moment be fulfilled (BDF #359.2). The postpositive particle *de* (untranslated) after the verb evidently signals a connection to the prior verse, but also makes it clear that v. 20 cannot be considered one sentence with v. 19.

417. Less likely is another possible meaning: "to exchange my voice [for the letter]" (Betz 236; cf. Longenecker 196). Paul would then be saying that he prefers oral to written communication. But then one would expect him to say, "to exchange my letter [for my voice]."

418. Betz (237) sees a rhetorical ploy here: "Paul acts as if he has run out of arguments." But he clearly has not, as the remainder of the letter indicates.

419. Strikingly, Paul does not indicate that he plans to make his wish to visit the Galatians a reality. He announces no plans to visit the Galatian churches (contrast Rom 15:15, 22–24, 28–29, 32; 2 Cor 12:14, 20–21; 13:1, 10; Phil 2:24; 1 Thess 3:9–13; Phlm 22). We can only speculate about the reasons. Was he too busy with churches founded around the Aegean? Was Galatia too far away? Curiously, he also does not plan to send a trusted coworker (Timothy, Titus) in his place (cf. 1 Cor 4:17; 16:10–11; 2 Cor 12:17–18; Phil 2:19–23, 25–30; 1 Thess 3:2–8).

warn them of the danger of returning to that past if they become observers of the law, as the new preachers in Galatia insist. The Galatians will then have abandoned the God by whom they have come to be known in Christ. In 4:12–20 Paul has directed the attention of the Galatians to the time that he came and preached the gospel to them, and he has done so in order to alert them to the danger of abandoning him, their founding apostle, if they take the route of law observance. They will then have abandoned the gospel that he preached to them initially and thus also the God of that gospel. In the present passage, Paul alerts the Galatians to the danger of losing their new identity through a *wrong exegesis* of Scripture. He has a particular section of the Scripture in view: Gen 16–21, parts of which tell the story of Abraham and his two sons, Ishmael and Isaac; the first is begotten by the slave woman Hagar, and the other is begotten by his wife, Sarah (Gen 16:1–16; 17:15–27; 18:9–15; 21:1–21). Since Paul does not mention Ishmael or Sarah by name in his exposition, while Hagar is not mentioned until v. 24 and Isaac not until v. 28, it appears that the Galatians are assumed to be familiar with at least the basic story found in Gen 16–21.

It is also probable that the new preachers in Galatia are using this very passage in their missionary efforts among the Galatians. This surmise explains not only why the Galatians seem to be familiar with the story but also why Paul feels compelled to call the attention of the Galatians to a passage whose value "from his point of view is anything but obvious" (Barrett 162). The passage cannot, therefore, be convincingly regarded as a "supplementary argument" that the apostle included "apparently as an afterthought" (Burton 251). Paul here tries to disarm the strongest weapon in the arsenal of the new preachers— and therefore, also the greatest danger for his own exposition of the gospel! As Barrett argues, by following the "plain, surface meaning" of the passage, the new preachers in Galatia can claim that "the Jews, who live by the law of Moses, are the heirs of Abraham" through the line established by his son Isaac, who was begotten by Sarah. "It is to Jews that the promise [made to Abraham] applies. . . . Here are the true people of God; and it will follow that Jerusalem is the authoritative centre of the renewed people of God, now called the church. Those who are not prepared to attach themselves to this community by the approved means (circumcision) must be cast out; they cannot hope to inherit promises made to Abraham and his seed" (Barrett 162; cf. 3:15–18; Excursus 4).[420] In this light, it can probably be said that the new preachers regard the Galatians as offspring of Abraham through the line established by Ishmael,

---

420. Cf. *Jub*. 16.17–18, interpreting Gen 21: "And all of the seed of his [Abraham's] sons would become nations. And they would be counted with the nations. But from the sons of Isaac one [Jacob] would become a holy seed and he would not be counted among the nations because he would become a portion of the Most High, . . . a (special) possession from all people, so that he might become a kingdom of priests and a holy people."

begotten by Hagar, Sarah's slave woman (Longenecker 201; Gen 16:10). As those who do not practice circumcision and observe the law, the Galatians, despite being believers in Christ, would not have the status of God's people, but that of Gentile "Ishmaelites" (Gen 37:27).

Paul responds by giving the passage his own "allegorical" interpretation: saying one thing while actually intending something else (see comment on v. 24, below). In doing so, he is *"correcting the exegesis"* of the passage by the new preachers (Barrett 158, stress added; cf. Martyn 450). According to Paul's allegorical reading, the two women of the story represent "two covenants" (v. 24): Hagar stands for the covenant of the law given on Mount Sinai (vv. 24–25), and Sarah stands for the covenant of the promise that God made to Abraham (cf. 3:15–18) and, in fact, to Sarah as well (see comment below). "The slave woman" (Hagar) is thus to be aligned with "the present Jerusalem" (v. 25), standing for the church now sponsoring the new preachers and their law-centered gospel; "the free woman" (Sarah) is to be aligned with "the Jerusalem above" (v. 26), standing for the truly liberated people of God (5:1a; cf. 3:13; 4:4–5). In short, for Paul, believers in Christ who are now free from the law (Paul and his converts in Galatia) are the (spiritual) descendants of Abraham, following the pattern of his son Isaac, who was begotten through God's promise by Sarah, "the free woman" (vv. 22–23, 30–31); those believers in Christ who observe the law beginning with circumcision and now want Gentile believers in Galatia to do the same (the new preachers in Galatia and their sponsors in Jerusalem) are actually the (fleshly) descendants of Abraham via his son *Ishmael*, who was begotten by Hagar, "the slave woman" (vv. 22–23, 30–31)! The "children" of the free woman (the Jerusalem above) are also free, just like their mother; the "children" of the slave woman (the present Jerusalem) are also slaves, just like *their* mother. Paul has thereby managed to "reverse the family relationships of the descendants of Abraham" (Barrett 167)—he has evidently turned the interpretation of the passage by the new preachers in Galatia on its head! As Hays (1989: 112) eloquently puts it: "Like Elijah dousing the sacrifice with water before calling down fire from heaven to consume it [1 Kings 18:20–40], Paul takes on the most difficult case and provocatively raises the stakes. . . . He executes a counterreading that reverses the terms of the discussion, claiming the putatively hostile evidence for his own case." How Paul arrives at his daring interpretation of the Genesis passage is a matter to be addressed in the commentary below.

From this summary of the passage, two consequences follow. (1) The underlying issue here is not "Judaism versus Christianity" (e.g., Burton; Betz), but a mission to Gentiles without the imposition of the law pursued by Paul versus a mission to Gentiles that imposes the law pursued by the new preachers and the church in Jerusalem (so esp. Martyn; see comments on 2:1–14). (2) Because of Paul's peculiar, not to say strained, interpretation of the story in Gen 16–21, it is difficult to maintain, as Tolmie does (2005: 169), that Paul here pursues an argument "based on the authority of scripture." Paul's argument is based rather on a christologically informed authoritative *interpretation* of Scripture. It is doubtful that "Scripture" has any authority for Paul apart from Christ, who enables Paul to read it in a radically new way, from the standpoint of the gospel (see comments on 3:6–14).

Paul turns to the interpretation of the story in Gen 16–21 at this particular point in the letter for two reasons: (1) He perceives that the use the new preachers make of the passage presents a great danger for the steadfastness of the Galatians. (2) He is confident that the Galatians will now accept his daring alternative interpretation of it. The danger that Paul discerns in the reading of the passage by the new preachers is undoubtedly its seemingly self-evident plausibility. He fears that the Galatians will be taken in by this reading of the story and fall victim to the message of the new preachers, thereby losing their new identity. He will now provide the Galatians with an alternative reading of the material for which he has effectively already prepared the way in 3:6–29, with the claim that Christ and those who belong to him by faith are the intended heirs of the promise that God made to Abraham. For Paul, believing in Christ, not observing the law, determines whether or not someone is a descendant of Abraham (see comments on 2:15–3:9). Galatians 4:21–5:1 introduces a new element in that the offspring of Abraham apparently can be divided into "two branches, the slave and the free" (Burton 251). Paul now concedes that the new preachers in Galatia and the church they represent are also Abraham's offspring—but *of the wrong branch*! Paul has also prepared the way for his treatment of Genesis in the immediately preceding two paragraphs (4:8–11, 12–20): the Galatians are now as ready as Paul himself to find a new way of reading the story of Abraham and his sons by Hagar and Sarah, one that will equip them to avoid the dangers to which Paul has called the attention of the Galatians in 4:8–20.

This passage can be divided into three subsections. In the first (vv. 21–23), Paul asks the Galatians, who "want to be under the law," to really listen to "the law," here meaning the Scripture. That Scripture contains the story of Abraham and his two sons by two women, one the slave woman and the other the free woman. Paul summarizes the story in vv. 22–23. In the second subsection (vv. 24–27), Paul gives his allegorical interpretation of the passage, with a significant assist from Isa 54:1, which he quotes in full in v. 27. In the third subsection (4:28–5:1) he applies his interpretation of Gen 16–21 to the Galatians; he tells them that they are "children of promise" and thus "children not of a slave woman but of the free woman." Paul here reaches his penultimate goal: to reaffirm the identity of the believers in Galatia as "children of [God's] promise [to Abraham]" (cf. 3:6–29), a promise that included Sarah. Paul's ultimate goal, however, is to be found in 5:1. This verse begins with a ringing declaration, which sums up what the Galatians already should know by this stage ("For freedom Christ has set us free!"), and concludes with an urgent appeal to the Galatians to stand fast and *not* to allow themselves to "be burdened again with a yoke of slavery," with the Mosaic law that the new preachers seek to impose on them. Now that he has given them the "right" exegesis of Gen 16–21, he can confidently exhort the Galatian believers in Christ to hold their ground and to remain in the freedom for which Christ has set them free.

4:21 Tell me, you who are wanting to be under the law, do you not hear the law? 22 For it stands written that Abraham had two sons, one from the slave woman and one from the free woman. 23 But the one from the slave woman has been born according to the flesh, the one from the free woman through a promise.[a]

24 These things are being said allegorically, for these women are two covenants: on the one hand, one from Mount Sinai, bearing children for slavery, which is Hagar. (25 "Hagar"[b] is Mount Sinai in Arabia.[c]) She belongs with the present Jerusalem, for she is a slave with her children. 26 On the other hand, the Jerusalem above, which is our mother, is free. 27 For it stands written:

"Rejoice, barren one who does not bear,
    break forth and shout, you who are not in labor,
for many [will be] the children of the desolate woman,
    more than of the woman who has a husband."

28 *You*,[d] brethren, like Isaac, are children of promise. (29 But just as at that time the one who was born according to the flesh was persecuting the one according to the Spirit, so also now. 30 But what does the Scripture say? "Throw out the slave woman and her son, for the son of the slave woman shall certainly not inherit with the son of the free woman.") 31 Therefore, brethren, we are children not of a slave woman but of the free woman. 5:1 For freedom Christ has set us free![e] Stand fast, therefore, and do not be burdened again with a yoke of slavery!

    a. The reading "through a promise" occurs in $\mathfrak{P}^{46}$, ℵ, A, et al.; other weighty manuscripts support the reading "through *the* promise" (B, D, et al.).

    b. Here NA^{27} has *to de Hagar* (A, B, D, etc.). Lesser, largely Byzantine manuscripts have *to gar Hagar*, "for Hagar" (Ψ, 062, 33, 1881, etc.).

    c. Some manuscripts ($\mathfrak{P}^{46}$, ℵ, C, F, G, etc.) omit the reference to Hagar, leading to the translation "Mount Sinai is in Arabia." The variation between *de* and *gar* also occurs in these manuscripts; see note b, above. The shorter reading is probably not original: *Hagar* accidentally dropped out from some manuscripts because of the juxtaposition with *gar* (Metzger 527). See footnote 432, below.

d. Some manuscripts have "we," but the best witnesses support "you" (Metzger 528). The latter makes very good sense, given v. 21 ("you"). "We" would also be defensible, however, given v. 31 ("we are") and v. 26 ("our mother").

e. There are a large number of mostly minor textual variants, evidently prompted by two factors: (1) the difficult dative at the beginning of the verse, and (2) the lack of a connecting particle such as *gar* ("for") or *oun* ("then") to mark its relation to the preceding verses. See the extensive discussion in Burton (270–71), who concludes, on the basis of both external evidence and internal considerations, that the reading now found in NA^{27} and relied upon in this commentary is the original one. See also Metzger 528.

Verses 4:21 and 5:1 bracket the passage. The first indicates the basic problem that underlies the whole of section IV (4:8–5:12), indeed the whole letter: the Galatians are "wanting to be under the law." They do so because of the new preachers who have invaded the Galatian churches. The second contains Paul's basic response: Do not yield to the message of the new preachers about the law! Commentators disagree about whether v. 5:1 belongs to this unit (e.g., Bruce; Martyn; Hays; Mussner; Vouga; cf. RSV, NRSV) or the one following (e.g., Burton; Ridderbos; Betz; Longenecker; Dunn; Matera). The verse is probably best understood as belonging to this unit for several reasons. Verses 28 and 31, which apart or together are frequently taken to indicate the goal of the passage, actually repeat in different words, and thus merely reaffirm, the thrust of 3:6–29: those who believe in Christ and have received the promised Spirit (3:14, 18) are on that basis alone the intended and legitimate "sons/offspring of Abraham" (3:8, 29). The new element in the third subsection of the passage is to be found in the admonition to stand fast and refuse to submit to the law in 5:1b. Moreover, 5:1 picks up and concludes the central polarity of the passage, that between freedom and slavery (4:22, 23, 24, 25, 26, 30, 31). That polarity has been anticipated in 2:4 (cf. 3:13, 23–25; 4:1–11), but it here receives its fullest expression.

[21–23] As Paul writes the letter, he knows that the Galatians have come to find themselves caught between him, their founding apostle (4:13), who preached and still preaches a gospel of grace (1:6–9; 2:21), and the new preachers, who have come to Galatia preaching "a different gospel" (1:6), one in which the observance of the law is mandatory. The preaching of the latter has been so effective (cf. 3:1) that the Galatians are seriously contemplating becoming observers of the law. In recognition of this fact and as an expression of his bafflement about the Galatians (4:20; cf. 1:6–7), Paul now addresses the Galatians explicitly as "you who are wanting to be under the law." By this point, however, the Galatians listening to the letter will (Paul hopes) have come to realize that existence "under the law" is not a desirable position to be in, since Paul has emphasized that it involves being imprisoned, confined, and enslaved (2:4; 3:23–4:10). To be "under the law" is effectively to be under its terrible curse (3:10–14). Because the law is Sin's captive and instrument, to be "under the law" is in fact to be "under [the power of] Sin" itself (3:22; see comment).

By this point in Paul's letter and argument, then, the Galatians may no longer be so certain about the desirability of life under the law (*nomos*). For this reason, Paul can now challenge them ("Tell me . . . !") to listen to, and thus to understand, "the law" in a new way ("Do you not *hear* the law?"). For the first time in the letter, Paul does not use the term *nomos* to encapsulate the Sinaitic legislation with its many commandments and prohibitions. He now uses it in a play on words to mean "the Scripture" (v. 30; cf. 1 Cor 14:21; Rom 3:19), in particular the Pentateuch, in which the Sinaitic legislation is recorded (cf. Rom 3:21, which contains a similar wordplay: the righteousness of God has been manifested "apart from the law" even though "the law and the prophets" bear witness to it). In this usage Paul follows existing Jewish (and Jewish Christian) custom and precedent (cf. Prologue to Sirach: "the law and the Prophets and the other books of our ancestors"; Luke 24:44: "the law of Moses, the prophets, and the psalms"; John 1:45: "Moses in the law and also the prophets"). The new preachers, who are Christian Jews (see end of Excursus 4), are therefore probably also using the term in this way. The use of the term *nomos* with this double meaning points to the intimate connection between the written text and the legislation it contains in the thought of the new preachers. Paul will now use this (positive) meaning of "the law" as Scripture to undermine the importance and value of "the law" as legislation to be observed!

The new preachers have apparently been telling the Galatians about a particular story that "stands written" in "the law," namely, that of Abraham and his two sons, found in Gen 16–21 (16:1–16; 17:15–27; 18:9–15; 21:1–21). Paul now asks the Galatians to listen to that passage again: "for [as the new preachers correctly indicate] it stands written that Abraham had two sons, one from the slave woman and one from the free woman" (v. 22). In this case, and unusually, the introductory formula "for it stands written" (cf. 3:10, 13) does not introduce a direct quotation from the OT but a paraphrase of a story found there. The paraphrase is a brief summary, indicating that the Galatians are already familiar with the basic story found in Gen 16–21: Abraham had two sons, one by Hagar (Ishmael) and one by Sarah (Isaac). In his periphrastic summary, however, Paul introduces a word not found in Genesis itself: While Hagar (v. 25) is called "the slave woman" (*paidiskē*)[421] in Gen 16:1–10; 21:10–13 (LXX), Sarah (whose name Paul does not mention) is never there called "the free woman" (*hē eleuthera*). Indeed, the Greek word and its cognates are completely absent from the LXX text of Genesis. Already in his initial summary, then, Paul establishes the contrast between slavery and freedom that determines the dominant polarity of the passage. He thereby associates Sarah explicitly with freedom, the freedom from slavery that Christ has effected for believers in him (cf. 3:13; 4:1–7; 5:1).

---

421. The word is the diminutive of *pais* (girl) and is commonly used in contemporary Greek literature to designate a female slave (BDAG 749–50). See below on vv. 24–25.

Paul clearly assumes that the Galatians will know to whom he is referring with his mention of "the free woman." For this reason, it is possible that this designation for Sarah has been derived from the teaching of the new preachers in Galatia. For them, too, Sarah, Isaac, and freedom undoubtedly belong together (cf. John 8:33, where "the offspring of Abraham" claim to be "free").

In v. 23 Paul expands the summary of the Genesis account by pointing to the different circumstances of the births of the two sons: "But [*alla*] [the decisive point is that] the one from the slave woman has been born according to the flesh, [whereas] the one from the free woman [has been born] through a promise." According to Genesis, Sarah was unable to bear children, leading her to allow Abraham to beget a child by Hagar, her slave woman (16:1–4). The result was that "Hagar bore Abram a son; and Abram named his son, whom Hagar bore, Ishmael" (16:15 LXX). God, however, also promised Abraham that Sarah would bear him a son despite the fact that she was far beyond childbearing age (17:17; 18:11). The promise is repeatedly made (17:21; 18:10, 14; cf. 15:4). Despite the initial skepticism of both Abraham and Sarah (17:17–18; 18:12), Sarah does bear Abraham a son, for "the Lord visited Sarah just as he had said [he would], and the Lord did for Sarah just as he had said, and she conceived and bore to Abraham a son in old age, at the set time just as the Lord had said to him. And Abraham called the name of his son . . . , that Sarah bore to him, Isaac" (21:1–3 LXX). Paul's contrast between the slave woman's son "born according to the flesh" and the free woman's son "[born] through a promise" clearly reflects this account. Presumably, Paul says nothing here with which the new preachers in Galatia will disagree.

Paul does, however, again use terms that are absent from Gen 16–21 LXX itself: "according to the flesh" (*kata sarka*), "through a promise" (*di' epangelias*), and the verb "to bear" (*gennaō*). It is difficult to judge whether Paul is here introducing his own formulations or adopting language already being used by the new preachers. We saw above that the characterization of Sarah as "the free woman," which is also absent from the Genesis account, may have been derived from the teaching of the new preachers. The same is perhaps true of the phrase "according to the flesh"; it does not occur in Paul's earliest letter, 1 Thessalonians. This phrase reflects the fact that Ishmael's birth was the natural result of the sexual (fleshly) union of Abraham and Hagar. The phrase here means "by natural procreative means" (cf. Gen 2:24). It is possible that since the term "flesh" occurs in Gen 16–21 only in connection with circumcision (17:11, 13, 14, 24, 25), Paul here intends an allusion to that practice, thereby subtly connecting the birth of Ishmael to the Jewish practice of circumcision (cf. Gal 3:3).

The term "promise" and its cognates are also absent from the Genesis account, as already noted in the commentary on 3:15–18. The phrase "through a promise" indicates that Isaac's birth was a miracle by any human standard since *both* Abraham and Sarah were very old, too old to be having children

(Gen 17:17; 18:11; cf. Rom 4:19).[422] Both the begetting and the birth, then, are attributed to God's intervention, the result of his promise to both Abraham and Sarah. There is no hint in the Genesis text or in Paul's summary of it that the conception of Isaac did not involve or require the sexual union of Abraham and Sarah. The point is the miraculous nature of Isaac's begetting and birth. "Through a promise" echoes the same phrase in 3:18 and means the same as "through God" in 4:7 (see comment; cf. 3:18, 29).[423]

The verb *gennaō* can mean "to beget" as well as "to bear"; the Greek therefore uses one verb where English needs two, one in connection with women who "bear" children and another in connection with men who "beget" (or "father") them. Since Paul uses the verb *gennaō* in v. 24 with the unequivocal meaning "to bear," it probably has this meaning in v. 23 as well (cf. the birthing imagery in 4:19). In the Genesis account, the verb *tiktō* is used, not the verb *gennaō*, in connection with Hagar and Sarah's bearing their respective sons (see Gen 16:15 and 21:1–3, quoted above). This verb also occurs in Isa 54:1, which Paul quotes in v. 27. It cannot also mean "to beget," unlike *gennaō*. Paul may have chosen the latter verb in v. 23 precisely because of its double meaning (the promise, we saw above, applied to *both* the begetting *and* the birth of Isaac). Both meanings appear to make good sense in v. 23. The meaning "to beget" also allows Paul to allude to the potentially missionary significance of this verb (Martyn 434, 451–52), for he uses it to refer metaphorically to the founding of churches in 1 Cor 4:14–15 ("I begat you in Christ through the gospel" [AT]) and Phlm 10 ("I begat Onesimus" [AT]). If so, Paul already has his eye on the two competing missions to the Gentiles, each with its own "children" (vv. 25, 27, 28, 31), which will be the topic of the allegorical interpretation and application in the verses that follow. This anticipation of the allegorical interpretation of Gen 16–21 and its application to the situation in Galatia is also discernible in Paul's use of the perfect tense "has been begotten/born" (*gegennētai*), instead of the aorist "was begotten/born"(*egennēthē*; cf. aorist passive participle *gennētheis* in v. 29). The perfect tense anticipates Paul's explicitly contemporizing interpretation of the story that begins in v. 24: The begetting and birth of the two sons are not merely historical facts for Paul (or for the new preachers); they have contemporary relevance (see below on vv. 24–27).[424]

---

422. Abraham was 100 at Isaac's birth (Gen 17:17; 21:5), Sarah 90 (17:17). At Ishmael's birth, Abraham was evidently a still-virile 86 (16:16).

423. As indicated above, the reading "through a promise" is supported by $\mathfrak{P}^{46}$, ℵ, A, et al.; other weighty manuscripts support the reading "through *the* promise" (B, D, et al.). In the first reading the emphasis falls on the means by which Isaac was begotten and born (the result of a promise); in the second, on the origin of this event in God's particular promise to Abraham. Yet even in the first reading, God's specific promise to Abraham is in view.

424. See Moule (14–15), who notes other instances of the use of the perfect in seemingly "allegorical" interpretations of OT passages (e.g., Heb 7:6, 9): "It was as though this type of Christian

In sum, in v. 23, Paul sharpens the polarity of slave and free already present in v. 22 with the polarity of flesh and promise. The new polarity is highlighted in the Greek text by the use of a *men* . . . , *de* construction (lit., "on the one hand . . . , on the other hand"), here left untranslated.[425] In vv. 22–23 Paul begins to build a table of opposites that will be further developed ("allegorically interpreted") in the verses that follow:

one son [Ishmael]	the other son (Isaac)
from the slave woman (Hagar)	from the free woman [Sarah]
born according to the flesh	[born] through a promise

With this array of opposites, the new preachers in Galatia will certainly agree. In their view, however, "the law-observant descendants of Abraham through Sarah—the Isaacs—are free people, whereas law-less Gentiles, descendants through Hagar—the Ishmaels—are slaves" (Martyn 434). In the following verses, Paul will pull the rug out from under this understanding of the table of opposites with a radically new interpretation.

[24–27] Paul now proceeds to give an "allegorical" interpretation of the Genesis account: "These things are being said allegorically [in the Genesis narrative], for these women are [i.e., represent] two covenants." Literally, v. 24a reads "*which things [hatina] are being said allegorically [estin allēgoroumena]*"; this relative clause is thus syntactically part of the preceding verse even as it signals a new departure. Paul uses the present tense of *eimi* (*estin*) with a present passive participle (*allēgoroumena*); this combination is the Greek version of the present continuous tense, which is not nearly as common as the English equivalent. It is possible to understand the participle as an indefinite predicate neuter-plural noun, leading to the translation "these things are allegorical matters/utterances" (Martyn; Burton). Others would prefer to translate as "these things are being (or to be) interpreted allegorically" (Betz; Longenecker; Dunn; Hays) largely on the basis of the context, because of what Paul actually does with the Genesis story in the remainder of the verse.

The verb *allēgoreō* ("to say allegorically") comes from the two words *allos* ("other") and *agoreuō* ("say"). Its cognate noun *allēgoria* ("allegory") is defined by Heraclitus (first centuries B.C.E.–C.E.) as "the trope that says one thing but signifies another than what is said" (*All.* 5.2; Di Mattei 107; Lightfoot 180). According to another ancient author from Paul's time, "*Allēgoria* is an enunciation which while signifying one thing literally, brings forth the

---

interpretation viewed the O.T. narratives as 'contemporary,' and could therefore say 'such-and-such an incident *has happened.*' It is, in fact, the logical extension of the Greek perfect used of a past but still relevant event" (with original stress). Cf. BDF 342.5: "The perfect with reference to an OT event can mean that this event still retains its (exemplary) meaning."

425. Some important manuscripts ($\mathfrak{P}^{46}$, B) do not have *men*.

thought of something else" (Tryphon, *De tropis* 1.1; Di Mattei 106). The verb then appears to mean "to say something using the figure of allegory" and thus "to say (or write) allegorically." It remains unclear, however, whether Paul regards the Genesis story he is now interpreting as in fact an allegory (as a literal translation of v. 24a would suggest), whether he effectively makes the story into an allegory through the addition of new elements (as the characterization of Sarah as "the free woman" in v. 23 might suggest), or whether he simply gives it an allegorical interpretation (cf. Verhoef 263–64). The remainder of the verse indicates that he is probably doing the latter, in which case the sense of the opening clause of v. 24 is this: "These things are [now] being said [i.e., interpreted] allegorically [by me], for [in my view] these women are [i.e., represent] *two* covenants [not just one, as the new preachers would have you believe]."

Excursus 14: Allegorical Interpretation

Allegorical interpretation of narratives was not uncommon among the ancient Greeks, who applied the method especially to the stories of the gods found in Homer (Büchsel 260–63). Jews in the Diaspora, especially in Alexandria, evidently adopted the method from the Greeks. Aristobolus of Alexandria interpreted the OT using the allegorical method already in the second century B.C.E. Paul's contemporary, Philo of Alexandria, is probably the best-known practitioner of the method from the ancient world. Even Josephus employs the method occasionally (*Ant.* 3.179–187).

Philo applies the method in numerous places to the figures found in Gen 16–21 (Longenecker 204–5). He understands them to represent abstract virtues or timeless qualities. For example, in *Congr.* 23, Philo writes:

> Sarah, virtue, bears ... the same relation to Hagar, education, as the mistress to the servant-maid, or the lawful wife to the concubine, and so naturally the mind which aspires to study and to gain knowledge, the mind we call Abraham, will have Sarah, virtue, for his wife, and Hagar, the whole range of school culture, for his concubine.

Paul's approach is rather different: he does not use the method "to extract cosmological, psychological or similar lessons from the text. . . . [Rather,] he expounds Scripture as one who lives in the time of its fulfillment (1 C[or] 10:11), . . . so that the true sense of the OT may now be seen. Allegorizing is thus a means to carry through his understanding of Scripture in terms of the centrality of Christ or the cross" (Büchsel 263). In their own way, the new preachers in Galatia may also be reading the Scripture in terms of eschatological fulfillment in Christ, but without the emphasis on the cross that is characteristic of Paul (cf. Gal 3:1; 5:11; 6:12, 14).

Philo does not see his allegorical interpretation as a substitute for a literal understanding of the text, but as a supplement to it: "On the whole, Philo himself intends to maintain the historicity of what is narrated" (Büchsel 262). There is no reason to think that the same observation does not also apply to the use of the Genesis narrative by Paul. He also combines a literal reading of the text with an allegorical application based on the conviction of the eschatological fulfillment of Scripture in Christ (see v. 27 below).

Because Paul's interpretation of the Genesis narrative is not concerned with abstract virtues of timeless qualities but with historical events (in both the past and in the contemporary situation), it is often regarded as actually a form of typology, whereby figures, events, or institutions (e.g., the tabernacle) found in the OT are regarded as "types" foreshadowing or corresponding to later historical figures, events, or institutions, i.e. as relating to Christ and the church. Typological interpretation thus has a historical dimension that allegorical interpretation supposedly lacks. Paul's interpretation of Gen 16–21 has elements that are reminiscent of the typological method since he appears to read the characters and events in the narrative as symbols of realities and developments in his own time and situation, thus as "types." Such typological interpretation can, however, probably also be regarded as an acceptable variant of allegorical interpretation, especially when applied in a sustained way to a longer narrative rather than to isolated figures or events (e.g., Rom 5:14, where Paul refers to Adam as the "type" of Christ). M. H. Abrams (4–5) distinguishes two forms of allegory in modern literature, "the historical and political allegory" and "the allegory of ideas." As an example of the former, Abrams refers to Dryden's *Absalom and Achitophel* (1681), in which "King David represents Charles II, Absalom represents his natural son the Duke of Monmouth, and the biblical plot allegorizes a political crisis in contemporary England." Paul's reading of the Genesis narrative appears to be close to this form of allegory, not to "the allegory of ideas" of which Bunyan's *Pilgrim's Progress* (1678) is the textbook example. Paul's method in any case reflects the definition of "allegory" given by ancient writers. Like Philo, he understands the text to say one thing (at a literal, historical level) but to signify something other than that as well. In contrast to Philo, however, Paul discerns the deeper significance of the text to lie not in abstract ideas or the like but in the historical and eschatological realities of his own time and situation.

The essence of Paul's allegorical reading of the Genesis account is his claim that the two women, Hagar and Sarah, "are [i.e., represent or stand for] two covenants" (v. 24b). It is tempting to see an implicit contrast between "the old covenant" (2 Cor 3:14) of the law and "the new covenant" (1 Cor 11:25; 2 Cor 3:6) of Christ (e.g., Burton; Betz; Longenecker; Becker; Vouga), but it appears that the contrast is rather between the covenant of the law ("Sinai") and the covenant of promise with Abraham (e.g., Lührmann; Matera; Witherington; Hays 1989: 114). The latter covenant (Gal 3:17), for which Paul actually prefers the term "promise" (4:23, 28; cf. 3:14, 16, 18, 19, 21, 22), found its fulfillment in Christ (cf. 3:6–18). The covenant of the law established at Sinai is elaborated in vv. 24c–25, the covenant of promise in vv. 26–27:

> [24c]*On the one hand* [men], one [covenant is] from Mount Sinai,
> bearing children for slavery, which is Hagar. ([25]"Hagar" is

Mount Sinai in Arabia). She belongs with the present Jerusalem, for she is a slave with her children.
²⁶*On the other hand* [*de*], the Jerusalem above, which is our mother, is free. ²⁷For it stands written: "Rejoice, barren one who does not bear, break forth and shout, you who are not in labor, for many [will be] the children of the desolate woman, more than of the woman who has a husband."

Here Paul interprets and expands the table of opposites suggested in vv. 22–23, given above:

Galatians 4:22–23	Galatians 4:22–23
one son [Ishmael]	the other son (Isaac)
from the slave woman (Hagar)	from the free woman [Sarah]
born according to the flesh	[born] through a promise

Galatians 4:24c–25	Galatians 4:26–27
Hagar	[Sarah]
one [covenant]	[the other covenant, of the promise]
from Mount Sinai	[made with Abraham]
the present Jerusalem	the Jerusalem above
a slave	free
her [enslaved] children	[her abundant] free [children]

Paul's argument thus starts off with the two women representing "two covenants" but ends up with them representing two Jerusalems, "the present Jerusalem" and "the Jerusalem above." Paul's construction of the two opposite columns and his movement from two covenants to two Jerusalems are facilitated by the fact that in Greek the words for "covenant" (*diathēkē*) and "Jerusalem" (*Ierousalēm*) are grammatically feminine, as are "Hagar / the slave woman" and "Sarah / the free woman." In the three earlier references to Jerusalem (1:17, 18; 2:1), Paul has used the more Hellenistic neuter plural spelling of the city's name (*Hierosolyma*), perhaps for the sake of his Gentile audience. He here switches to the feminine form (also used in Rom 15:19, 25, 26, 31; 1 Cor 16:3), probably for two reasons: (1) it is the form preferred by the Septuagint, including Second Isaiah, from which he quotes in v. 27 (the neuter-plural spelling occurs only in later deuterocanonical works), and (2) this form facilitates his allegorical-typological interpretation of "Hagar" and "Sarah."

With respect to the initial claim that the two women stand for two covenants, Paul qualifies the understandable claim of the new preachers that Genesis has only one covenant with Abraham and his offspring in view (Gen 15:18; 17:1–14). This one covenant has two important features: (1) it encompasses both the promise of offspring (Gen 15:18; 17:1–8) and the commandment of circumcision (Gen 17:9–14), and (2) it is valid only for the line of descent established through Isaac, not for the line of descent established through Ishmael (Gen 17:19–21). In Paul's view, however, God's one covenant with Abraham (Gal 3:17) evidently did not entail the commandment to practice circumcision (see comment on 3:15–18). In this covenant, the promise of offspring finds its fulfillment not in the people's practicing circumcision, meaning the law-observant people of Israel, but in Christ (3:16) and those who belong to him solely on the basis of faith (2:15–16, 21; 3:6–9; 3:23–29). Paul evidently distinguishes the covenant of promise in Gen 15:18; 17:1–8 from the covenant of circumcision in Gen 17:9–14, regarding them as two separate covenants. In Gal 3:15–18 he has already silently allowed the circumcision commandment to fall under the covenant at Sinai (cf. 5:3: to practice circumcision is to obligate oneself to observe the *whole* law), which by Paul's own reckoning happened some "four hundred and thirty years" (3:17) after the one with Abraham (see comment on 3:17).[426] In 4:24b–25 of the present passage, Paul implicitly provides a rationale for this stunning move: in his view, Hagar stands for the covenant at Sinai, and that means that the commandment to circumcise "the flesh" of the foreskin (Gen 17:11, 13, 14, 24, 25; cf. Gal 3:3; 6:12) has to do, not with Sarah, whose son was born "through a promise" (v. 23b), but with Hagar whose son was "born according to the flesh" (v. 23a; see comment above). The commandment of circumcision is thus valid for the line of Abrahamic descent established through Ishmael, not for the line of Abrahamic descent established through Isaac!

In v. 24b, Paul does not explicitly mention the law, but that is clearly presupposed in the expression "one [covenant] from Sinai" (cf. v. 21). According to Exodus, God made a covenant with the Israelites at this mountain, where he gave them the law by the hand of Moses (Exod 19:5; 23:22, 32; 24:7–8; 34:27–28; cf. 2 Cor 3:12–14; *m.* ʾ*Abot* 1.1: "Moses received the law from Sinai"). The Galatians have evidently been schooled in the matter by the new preachers in Galatia (cf. 3:19–20). In an astonishing and daring exegetical move, Paul reads the covenant at Sinai back into the story found in Gen 16–21, linking it firmly to the slave woman, Hagar, *instead of* to the free woman, Sarah: Of the two covenants, "one [is] from Mount Sinai, bearing children for slavery, which is Hagar" (v. 24b). In contemporary Jewish tradition, the Sinai covenant finds its anticipation in the covenant with Abraham, who was thought to have kept the law fully in advance of its disclosure on Mount Sinai (cf. already Gen 26:5 LXX; see further Sir 44:19–20 LXX; *Jub.* 24.11; comment on Gal 3:6).

---

426. In 3:15–18, Paul does not call the coming of the law "covenant," reserving this term for the promise to Abraham. It is perhaps only the fact that the new preachers focus on the covenant at Sinai in their proclamation that causes Paul to speak initially of "two covenants"; he then drops the term as quickly as he has introduced it.

The Sinai covenant is, then, a reaffirmation of the covenant with Abraham, who after all practiced circumcision (Gen 17:23–27; 21:4). The people of the covenant of the law, in this view, stand in direct genealogical continuity with Abraham through Isaac, the son begotten by his wife, Sarah. By linking Mount Sinai to Hagar the slave woman and her son, Ishmael, instead of to Sarah the free woman and her son, Isaac (as the new preachers are probably doing), Paul polemically plays the covenant at Sinai off against the covenant of promise with Abraham, using polarizing language (slave/free, flesh/promise). When Paul says "two covenants," then, he clearly means "two *different* covenants," or even "two mutually exclusive covenants," since one has to do with slavery, the other with freedom.[427]

How Paul comes to the astonishing identification of Mount Sinai, and thus the covenant of the law, with Hagar is not easily discernible. He apparently works from the assumption that being "under the law" is a form of enslavement, a point he has repeatedly made, especially in 3:23–4:11. For this reason, the covenant from Mount Sinai, now likened to a woman, "is [even now] bearing children for slavery." On the basis of this assumption, Paul makes the connection to Hagar "the slave woman" and by implication to her son, Ishmael, who like his mother was also a slave. What binds the Sinai covenant to Hagar and makes them part of the same oppositional column is the notion of slavery.

Verse 25a appears to be a parenthetical if obtuse attempt to explain the identification of Hagar with Mount Sinai: "[The name] 'Hagar'[428] [in the text of Genesis] is [i.e., stands for] Mount Sinai in Arabia." The verse may not be original to the text (Burton 259). If original, the Galatians will hear it as a simple assertion: "I would have you know that the Hagar mentioned in the Genesis stories is actually a reference to Mount Sinai in Arabia, and thus to the covenant established there with the Israelites by the hand of Moses." As such, v. 25a does not really add anything not already said in v. 24c. The verse does provide an indication of the location of Mount Sinai: It is "in Arabia," which for the Galatians, as for Paul, probably refers to the large undefined dry area to the east and the south of Jerusalem (see comment on 1:17). The reference to Arabia may provide the clue to the verse's significance: Paul may be trying to indicate that Mount Sinai (about which the Galatians have probably been informed) is in "Ishmaelite" territory. According to Josephus (*Ant.* 1.122), the descendants of Ishmael "occupied the whole country extending from the

---

427. For this reason the exposition here is congruent with the one in 3:15–18, where Paul characterizes the coming of the law as an illegitimate attempt to nullify or change the promissory covenant of God with Abraham, which is there likened to a human testament (see comment there).

428. Greek: *to de Hagar* (A, B, D, etc.), where the initial *to* is probably equivalent to quotation marks (Borgen 157). The reading *to gar Hagar*, "for 'Hagar'" (Ψ, 062, 33, 1881, etc.), reinforces the idea that v. 25a functions as an explanation for the daring identification of Hagar with Mount Sinai in v. 24b.

Euphrates to the Red Sea [thus including Mount Sinai],[429] . . . and it is these who conferred their names on the Arabian nation [lit., the nation of the Arabs, *to tōn Arabōn ethnos*]." *Jubilees* 20.13 refers to the descendants of Ishmael as "Arabs or Ishmaelites."[430] "Arabia" is then the land of the descendants of Ishmael, who are called "Hagrites" in Ps 83:6 (cf. Gen 25:13–18). With the geographical note in v. 25a, then, Paul is attempting to point out to the Galatians[431] that the law being promoted by the new preachers originated in Ishmaelite territory (a point they are in no position to dispute or deny), and consequently belongs in the column with Hagar (and Ishmael) rather than in the column with Sarah (and Isaac)![432]

The parenthetical nature of v. 25a is confirmed by the fact that v. 25b is a direct continuation of v. 24c: "one [covenant is] from Mount Sinai, bearing children for slavery, which is Hagar. . . . She [Hagar, now standing for the covenant at Sinai] belongs with the present Jerusalem, for she [Hagar, now standing for the present Jerusalem] is a slave with her children." Noteworthy here is Paul's repeated use of present tenses, whereby he allegorically indicates the relevance of Gen 16–21 for the situation current in Galatia: "Hagar" in Gen 16–21 "is" (stands for) the Sinai covenant, and this covenant "belongs with [*systoichei*] the present Jerusalem [*hē nūn Ierousalēm*]." The verb *systoicheō* has a military origin, referring to troops that stand in line (BDAG 979). The sense here is then that "Hagar," representing the covenant at Sinai, is to be aligned with "the present Jerusalem": they belong to the same oppositional column (Martyn 432, 449; cf. Lightfoot 181: "belongs to the same row or column").[433] If Paul has read the Sinai covenant back into "Hagar" in Gen 16–21, he now brings "Hagar" and the covenant she represents *forward* and aligns her with "the present Jerusalem," here probably signifying, by metonymy, not "Judaism" as such (Betz and others) but *the Jerusalem church* with its own law-based mission to

---

429. No one knew where precisely Mount Sinai was located in this vast region.

430. These Arabs can then stand for Gentiles in general (cf., e.g., Bar 3:23: "the sons of Hagar" [RSV]).

431. Whether they will get the point is a moot question.

432. The formulation "Mount Sinai in Arabia" seems to imply that there may also have been a Mount Sinai in some other region. This wording may explain why some manuscripts ($\mathfrak{P}^{46}$, ℵ, C, F, G, etc.) omit the reference to Hagar, leading to the translation "Mount Sinai is in Arabia." In this reading (adopted as original by Mussner), the Galatians are merely being informed about the geographical location of Mount Sinai (it is "in Arabia"), perhaps as a concession ("To be sure, Mount Sinai is in Arabia, but . . ."). This shorter reading, which is probably not original (Metzger 527), can also be seen, however, as an attempt to make the probable import of the longer reading (the one with "Hagar") explicit ("Mount Sinai is in Arabia, which we all know to be the territory of the descendants of Hagar's son Ishmael").

433. The usual translation of *systoichei* with "corresponds" (RSV, NRSV, NIV, NKJV; cf. BAGD 979; LSJ 1735) could mistakenly be taken to indicate that "Hagar" and "the present Jerusalem" stand in opposite columns, instead of in the same column.

the Gentiles through the work of the new preachers in Galatia (Bruce; Matera; Martyn). Paul has prepared the way for this move in v. 24b with the claim that the covenant (grammatically feminine in Greek) from Mount Sinai is even now "bearing children for slavery" (*eis douleian gennōsa*), for which reason he can then assert that the present Jerusalem (*Ierousalēm*, also feminine in Greek) "is a slave [*douleuei*] with her children." The spiritual children of the present Jerusalem are slaves, even as Ishmael the son of Hagar the slave woman was. Like mother, like children.

Paul began v. 24c with the words "on the one hand [*men*], one [covenant] from Mount Sinai, bearing children for slavery, which is Hagar . . ." The reader therefore expects v. 26 to begin in a corresponding manner: "On the other hand [*de*], the other [covenant] through the promise, bearing children for freedom, which is Sarah . . . ," or words to that effect (cf. 3:6–9, 15–18). His reference to "the present Jerusalem" in v. 25b causes him in v. 26 to leave the notion of a second covenant undeveloped and to introduce "the Jerusalem above," emphasizing her freedom in contrast to the enslaved condition of the present Jerusalem: "On the other hand [*de*], the Jerusalem above, which is our mother, is free [just as Sarah, the mother of Isaac, was]." The Jerusalem "above" clearly does not refer to a heavenly city in a literal sense, but to the church that has been called into being by God (cf. 1:6; 5:8) as the eschatological people of God (see further on 4:28–31). This church, which includes the Galatian believers, has and continues to have its origin in God ("above").[434] Though Paul does not specifically mention Sarah or her son, given vv. 22–23 and 28–31 it is probable that they are both presupposed, and thus that Sarah, "the free woman," stands for the Jerusalem above—corresponding to Hagar, "the slave woman," who stands for the present Jerusalem. The children of the Jerusalem above are then also "free" (cf. 5:1), just as Isaac, the son of Sarah the free woman, was (v. 31). Like mother, like children.

The key opposition in vv. 24–27 ends up being that between "the present Jerusalem" (*hē nun Ierousalēm*) and "the Jerusalem above" (*hē anō Ierousalēm*). Paul here posits what Martyn (440) calls "a distinctly apocalyptic contrast," the present Jerusalem being a reality of the old age (the age of slavery to cosmic powers), and the Jerusalem above a reality of the new age (the age of freedom from inimical cosmic powers). "The Jerusalem above" recalls the new or heavenly Jerusalem found most clearly in somewhat later apocalyptic literature (Rev 3:12; 21:2, 10; *4 Ezra* [2 Esd] 7.26; 8.52; 10.27, 44–46; 13.35–36; *2 Bar.* 4.2–6; cf. Heb 12:22). One would expect the counterpart to the "present" Jerusalem to be the future Jerusalem ("the Jerusalem to come") or, conversely, the counterpart to the Jerusalem "above" to be the Jerusalem on earth below.

---

434. The dangers of ecclesiastical triumphalism signaled by Betz and Mussner do not fall within Paul's purview in this passage. The passage is about the triumph of God's grace.

Paul mixes temporal and spatial categories, a common feature of apocalyptic thinking since the age to come already exists in heaven above, while the present evil age (1:4) describes the current situation on earth. For Paul, furthermore, the Jerusalem above is already making its presence felt on earth over against the present Jerusalem. Not the present Jerusalem, not the church located in that city, is "our mother,"[435] but rather the Jerusalem above is, the church consisting of Jews and Gentiles free from the law. By using the possessive modifier "our," Paul indicates that the Jerusalem above is the mother of all believers, whether they be of Jewish or Gentile origin.

Paul now supports his claims about the Jerusalem above with a quotation from Isaiah (54:1 LXX) in v. 27: "For it stands written:

> Rejoice, barren one who does not bear,
> break forth and shout, you who are not in labor,
> for many [will be] the children of the desolate woman,
> more than of the woman who has a husband.

The verse comes from a part of Isaiah (40–55, known as Second Isaiah) which was probably written to and for Jerusalemites who had become exiles in Babylon (43:14; 48:20) following the destruction of Jerusalem (44:26–28; 49:14–23) early in the sixth century B.C.E. The author, writing around 550 B.C.E., consoles and encourages the exiles with the promise of a new future for Jerusalem and its exiled inhabitants (41:21–23; 42:9; 43:1–7; 44:26–28; 54:1–17). Neither the LXX text nor Paul's citation of it has a verb in the third line (the corresponding text in the MT also has no verb), but the context of the verse within Second Isaiah seems to demand that a future tense of the verb "to be" is presupposed (cf. RSV, NRSV, REB; pres. tense: NJB, KJV, NIV). In Isaiah, these words look to the future and thus promise the restoration of Jerusalem, which is here likened to a barren woman, now desolate because she is without children and thus without a future. However, there will come a time when she will have many more children than the woman who is married. The latter woman is probably not Jerusalem in another phase of her existence (so, e.g., Bruce 222; Willits), but Babylon, which is depicted as a woman in Isa 47:1–4. This interpretation is supported by the Targum to Isaiah (from the rabbinic period but representing earlier traditions), which takes the second woman to represent Rome, the rulers of Judea at that time: "For the children of desolate Jerusalem will be more than the children of inhabited Rome, says the Lord" (trans. Chilton 1987: 105). The link between Babylon and Rome was commonly made

---

435. The new preachers may be claiming that the church in Jerusalem is "our mother" (Martyn 439). On Jerusalem as mother, see comment on v. 27 below.

in Jewish and Christian apocalyptic literature (cf. *4 Ezra* [2 Esd] 3.1–2, 28; *2 Bar.* 11.1–2; 67.6; Rev 14:8; 16:19; 17:5, 18; 18:2). The Targum, in short, has interpreted the implied reference to Babylon ("the woman who has a husband") as a reference to Rome. Like the Targum, Paul evidently reads Isa 54:1 to refer to two distinct cities, those two cities being for him "the Jerusalem above" and "the present Jerusalem." These have been mentioned in vv. 25–26, which means that Paul's interpretation of Isa 54:1 has preceded his citation of it (cf. 3:10 for a similar procedure). The introductory "for" (*gar*) is consequently to be understood as explanatory: Paul explains where his thinking about the two Jerusalems originates: in Isa 54:1.

Excursus 15: Why Isaiah 54:1?

Rabbinic evidence indicates that Isa 54:1 may have served as the so-called haftarah reading to Gen 16 in the liturgy of the synagogue at a later period (Mann lii–liii, 122; Barrett 169 n. 29). Evidence for such haftarah readings—passages from the prophets to complement those taken from the Pentateuch—occurs already in the NT (Acts 13:15; Luke 4:17; John 6:45), though there is no firm indication that the cycle of readings was fixed or uniform in the NT period. The evidence points rather to considerable diversity even in the rabbinic period, with great uncertainty about earlier times (Mann). Furthermore, there is no contemporary evidence to suggest that anyone else had associated Isa 54:1 with the Genesis account prior to Paul. There is also no clear indication that the new preachers are making such a link, and it is difficult to see how the text could support their message. Paul thus appears to be responsible for bringing Isa 54:1 and Gen 16–21 together in the Galatian situation.

The step from Gen 16–21 to Isa 54:1 is not so great in view of the following considerations: (1) Jerusalem in Isa 54:1 is said to be "barren" (LXX: *steira*), as was Sarah, according to Gen 11:30 (LXX: *steira*). In fact, as Barrett (164) observes, "The whole story of Genesis proceeds from the fact that Sarah was barren. . . . This word provides a link with Isa 54:1." Paul's use of Isa 54:1 assumes that the Galatians will also be able to discern the link, if not exactly between Isa 54:1 and Gen 11:30, at least between the barrenness of Jerusalem in the citation and that of Sarah in Gen 16–21 (even if the word itself does not occur in those chapters). Paul has facilitated the discernment of this link in v. 26, where "the Jerusalem above," which is described as "free" and "our mother," has been placed in the same oppositional column as "the free woman" (Sarah) of vv. 22–23. (2) In the whole OT, Sarah is mentioned by name outside Genesis only in Second Isaiah. In the LXX, Isa 51:2 reads: "Look to Abraham your father, and to Sarah, who bears you in travail [*ōdinousan*)]." The verb *ōdinō*, here used transitively to mean "bear children in travail," occurs only once more in Second Isaiah, in Isa 54:1, where it is used intransitively to mean "to be in labor." It is thus possible that Isa 51:2 led Paul to Isa 54:1 (so Verhoef 207; Hays 1989: 120; Brawley 99). (3) Given Isa 51:2, it is possible that the writer of Second Isaiah *intended* the allusion to Sarah and her barrenness in Isa 54:1 (Beuken). If that is the case, it explains why Paul (and Jews of a later period) could discern a link between Isa 54:1 and Gen 16–21.

Paul chose to cite Isa 54:1 instead of Isa 51:2 probably because the passage mentions two women, corresponding to Sarah and Hagar in Paul's interpretation of the oracle, and also alludes to their respective children, corresponding to the apocalyptic contrast between the two Jerusalems. It is true that Sarah in Genesis was not only barren but was also the married one, unlike Hagar the slave woman. Paul's use of Isa 54:1 may thus seem somewhat "arbitrary" (Barrett 167) and inappropriate, at least at first sight. However, the "fit" between Isa 54:1 and Paul's allegorical-typological interpretation of Abraham's two sons and their respective mothers is close enough to suggest that Paul's reflection on Isa 54:1, from the perspective of the gospel and in light of developments in Galatia, has fundamentally shaped his own allegorical-typological interpretation of the Genesis account (de Boer 2004; cf. Martyn 436–37; Brawley 99). The oracle of Isa 54:1, with its picture of two contrasting women, provides Paul with a bridge between the past (cf. v. 22: "Abraham *had* two sons, one from the slave woman and one from the free woman") and the present (cf. vv. 25–26: the one Jerusalem "*is* a slave," the other "*is* free" and is "our mother"). On that basis, Paul can then also correlate the two women of Genesis with "two covenants" (v. 24), the covenant of the law at Sinai, and the covenant of promise with Abraham (and Sarah)—both of which are not only rooted in the past but continue to have contemporary relevance (cf. v. 24) and in fact stand at the center of the theological conflict between Paul and the new preachers.

Paul's quotation of Isa 54:1, originally a consolatory and prophetic word spoken to the barren and desolate Jerusalem, follows immediately upon the interpretation of Sarah as "the Jerusalem above, which is our mother" (v. 26). The "free woman" (Sarah) had also been barren and had borne no children. She too had been in need of consolation, that consolation being God's awesome promise (received by Sarah when she was already far beyond childbearing age) that she would indeed bear a child despite the seeming hopelessness of her situation from a human point of view (Gen 18:9–15). And that promise had come to pass (21:1–2, 6–7). Paul consequently applies the word of consolation and the promise he hears in the words of (Second) Isaiah, not to the earthly Jerusalem (as Second Isaiah does), but to the new or heavenly Jerusalem, represented by Sarah: once barren but now, solely as a result of God's faithfulness to his promise, with many children ("our mother"). The promise that Paul hears in Isa 54:1, therefore, has come to fulfillment in the free children of the heavenly Jerusalem.

As suggested above, the second woman in the oracle, the one with the husband, probably for Paul represents "the present Jerusalem," the Jerusalem that stands in the same column with Hagar and the covenant at Sinai.[436] Since this Jerusalem "is a slave" together "with her children" (v. 25), it has about as much to do with "the Jerusalem above" as Babylon had to do with the earthly Jerusalem of Second Isaiah. They are polar opposites in Paul's thinking. Furthermore, if "the present Jerusalem" refers not to the city as such but to the church located there (see comment on v. 24–25, above), the "husband" mentioned in the fourth line of Isa 54:1 LXX may (in Paul's thinking at any rate) hide an allusion to James, the leader of the Jerusalem church at the writing of the letter (2:12; cf. Acts 21:18), who metaphorically "begets" (*gennaō*; cf. v. 23 and comment

---

436. This despite the fact that in Genesis itself Hagar does not have a husband (see Excursus 14, above).

there) "children" by "the present Jerusalem," doing so "according to the flesh" (v. 23), in other words, through requiring fleshly circumcision of Gentile converts (cf. 3:3; 6:12).

According to Genesis, God promised many descendants to Abraham through *both* Isaac *and* Ishmael (15:1–6; 17:2–6, 16, 20; 22:17–18), and Paul may have this in mind in his christologically shaped apocalyptic interpretation of the prophetic oracle found in Isa 54:1 (see Excursus 2). In Paul's reading of the verse for the situation in Galatia, the children of the free woman (Gentile converts free from the law) will be many, surpassing those of the slave woman (Gentile converts compelled to observe the law). It is possible, then, that Paul (if not Second Isaiah) presupposes a present tense in the third line of Isa 54:1 instead of a future: "for many *are* the children of the desolate one" (cf. NRSV; Burton; Betz; Longenecker; Martyn; otherwise, Vouga). It is difficult to know, however, whether the Gentile Christians converted by Paul in accordance with his law-free gospel already outnumbered (in his perception at any rate) the Gentile Christians converted by Jewish Christian evangelists emanating from Jerusalem. He evidently believes that the promise has been fulfilled or, perhaps better, is now in the process of being fulfilled. Ever since Christ, the one seed of Abraham (3:16, 19), "came" (3:19, 23, 25) into the world to "redeem" those "under the law" (4:4–5), the (eschatological) future belongs, according to Paul's reading of Isa 54:1, to the children given birth by the Jerusalem above.[437]

[4:28–5:1] In Gal 4:28, Paul comes to the penultimate goal of his allegorical reading of the story of Abraham and his two sons by Hagar and Sarah, which is to confirm once again (cf. 3:8–29) the identity of the believers in Galatia as the descendants of the promissory covenant that God made with Abraham and Sarah: "[Despite what the new preachers are saying] You [*hymeis*], brethren [*adelphoi*], like Isaac [*kata Isaak*],[438] are children of promise" (v. 28). Paul once again addresses the Galatians fraternally as *adelphoi* (cf. 1:11; 3:15; 4:12), as sisters and brothers in Christ. The new preachers are probably pointing out to the Galatians that those who observe the law are the direct heirs of Abraham via the line of descent established through Isaac, his son by his wife, Sarah. The observers of the law, meaning the members of the covenant people of Israel, stand in direct historical continuity with Abraham and the covenant that God made with him. That covenant found its continuity in Isaac and the latter's physical descendants. Paul agrees that the birth of Isaac represents the continuity of the covenant with Abraham, but he presents Isaac, whose conception and birth occurred as a result of God's promise, merely as the "type" for believers in Christ in the present, and then particularly and emphatically of the Galatians ("You"). Believers in Christ are offspring of Abraham (cf. 3:29), not by physical descent ("according to the flesh"), but "by a promise" (v. 23), a promise that found its fulfillment in Christ and the Spirit (3:14, 18). The birth of these

---

437. That "those under the law" includes, theologically speaking, Gentiles is evident in 3:13–14; 4:1–7. See comments on these passages (cf. Martyn 334–36).

438. Literally, "in accordance with Isaac," here probably meaning "in the pattern of Isaac" (Martyn).

children is as miraculous as that of Isaac was to the aged Sarah: it was brought about by God. Paul has already established the identity of the Galatians as "sons of Abraham" (3:8) and as "offspring of Abraham" (3:29) on the basis of the faith of Christ rather than works of the law (3:1–29). The idea that the Galatians were thereby children of promise was already implicit in that argument; it is here made explicit.

Verses 29–30 appear to be parenthetical since they interrupt the flow of thought between vv. 28 and 31 (on which see below), but they do anticipate Paul's ultimate goal in 5:1. The continuity with v. 28 lies in Paul's resort to another typological comparison: "But [*alla*] just as at that time the one who was born according to the flesh [Ishmael] was persecuting the one [born] according to the Spirit [Isaac], so also now" (v. 29). The contrast between flesh and promise (vv. 23, 28) now gives way to a contrast between flesh and Spirit (*pneuma*). Ishmael was born (or begotten)[439] "according to the flesh" (*kata sarka*), as v. 23 has already indicated, whereas Isaac was born (or begotten) "according to the Spirit" (*kata pneuma*), which means virtually the same as "through a promise" in v. 23 (cf. "children of promise" in v. 28). The link between the promise and the Spirit has already been made in 3:14, where Paul refers to "the promise of the Spirit" (= the promised Spirit). That link is so close that Paul seems to intimate that the Spirit was present *in spe* (in hope) in the time of Abraham and Sarah, but perhaps the point should not be pressed. Paul's choice of this word here is probably the result of his contemporizing intention ("so also now"): he has his eyes on the presumed persecution of the present children of the Jerusalem above, who are the ones actually born "according to the Spirit" (cf. 3:1–5, 14, 18, 22). He thereby also anticipates the topic of the next chapter, namely, the conflict between the Flesh and the Spirit begun by the coming of Christ (5:13–26; cf. already 3:3).

Just as Ishmael "was persecuting" Isaac, Paul writes, "so also now." There are two issues in this assertion: (1) The Genesis account does not indicate that Ishmael persecuted Isaac. In v. 30, Paul quotes Gen 21:10, and his claim about Ishmael's persecuting Isaac appears to be based on the prior verse, for according to Gen 21:9 "Sarah saw the son of Hagar . . . playing [*paizonta*] with her son Isaac" (LXX). The verb "play" (*paizō*) is evidently understood by Paul to signify something more than innocent playing. Later Jewish treatment of the passage interprets the underlying Hebrew (*měṣaḥēq*, "laugh, play") in a similar way (for texts, cf. Betz 250 n. 116; Bruce 223–24; Longenecker 217). Paul may thus be relying on Jewish tradition here. But whether the Galatians are familiar with Gen 21:9 or with Jewish interpretations of it is not known and perhaps not essential to assume. Paul makes a simple assertion even if there is (as far as

---

439. On the verb *gennaō* as meaning in the passive form both "to be born" and "to be begotten," see comment on v. 23.

The Grave Dangers Confronting the Galatians

we know) little or no basis in the Genesis account for it. (2) It is also unclear in what sense persecution is occurring "now." Other references to persecution in Galatians itself seem to involve the persecution of Christian Jews by other Jews (cf. 1:13, 23; 6:12). In this passage, however, Paul can only be referring to the new preachers (who represent the present Jerusalem in Galatia and are the spiritual descendants of Hagar and her son, Ishmael) and their persecution of the children of promise, which include the Gentile believers in Galatia and their apostle (cf. 5:11: "I am still being persecuted"). It is not clear what this persecution may involve or how strictly Paul intends the verb to be understood in this context. He seems to regard the pressure (6:12) the new preachers in Galatia are exerting on the Galatians to adopt circumcision and the law as tantamount to persecuting the Galatians. Perhaps he also has the threat of exclusion in view (4:17: "they want to shut you out").

Paul's perception and characterization of the situation makes sense of the following verse and its use of Gen 21:10: "But what does the Scripture say? 'Throw out [*ekbale*] the slave woman [Hagar] and her son, for the son of the slave woman shall certainly not [*ou mē*] inherit [what was promised] with the son of the free woman [Sarah] [Gen 21:10 LXX]'" (v. 30). In Genesis, the quoted words are those of Sarah to Abraham: "Throw out this slave woman and her son, for the son of this slave woman shall not inherit with my son Isaac."[440] God approves these words in Gen 21:12, telling Abraham to "Listen to her voice, because in Isaac shall be your offspring" (LXX) The point is the exclusion of Ishmael as Abraham's legitimate heir. Paul makes Sarah's words to Abraham into words of "the Scripture" addressed to the Galatians in the present.[441] He adapts the text accordingly, changing the last phrase "my son Isaac" into "the son of the free woman" (cf. vv. 22–23). The question "What does the Scripture say?" is not to be taken as Paul's acknowledgment of the authority of Scripture and the bringing of that authority to bear in his argument.[442] The point is that the new preachers in Galatia attribute primary authority to Scripture, and Paul now uses this attribution against them. According to the Scripture they hold dear, these preachers are to be actually "thrown out" of the churches of Galatia! Paul here asks his readers in Galatia to make the necessary connections: The

---

440. Cf. *Tg. Ps.-J.* Gen 22:1, which tells of a dispute between Ishmael and Isaac: "Isaac and Ishmael contended. Ishmael said: 'It is right that I should inherit what is the father's, because I am his first-born son.' Isaac said: 'It is right that I should inherit what is my father's, because I am the son of Sarah his wife and you are the son of Hagar the handmaid of my mother'" (Longenecker 200–201).

441. Eastman (2006) contends that since the imperative is singular (*ekbale*), the text cannot be addressed to the (plural) Galatians. The context suggests otherwise, however.

442. This is the third time in the letter that Paul personifies "the Scripture" (3:8, 22). See comment on 3:8 for the possible significance of this. "The Scripture" is here probably another way of saying "the text of Scripture."

"son of the slave woman" stands for the new preachers and their converts. The new preachers are the children of the present Jerusalem, the church under the leadership of James, which is currently sponsoring its own distinctive mission to Gentiles (cf. 2:12 and comment there). These people are to be "thrown out" of the Galatian churches. The verb suggests expulsion or excommunication (cf. John 9:34–35; 3 John 10). The new preachers are to be expelled because they "shall certainly not [*ou mē*, the emphatic double negative] inherit" what was promised: the Spirit (3:14, 18). That inheritance belongs to "the son of the free woman," here standing for the children of the free Jerusalem above, the church called into being by God through Christ. Did Paul mean that the new preachers (and their converts) were literally to be expelled from the Galatian churches? Apparently so, though he leaves it up to the Galatians ("What does the Scripture say?"). Perhaps the point is simply that the Galatians are to reject the message and the missionary efforts of the new preachers active in Galatia.

After the digression in vv. 29–30, the following v. 31 picks up the train of thought found in v. 28, where Paul had reaffirmed the identity of the Galatians as "children of promise," after the pattern of Isaac, who was the son of the free woman (vv. 22–23): "Therefore [*dio*], brethren [*adelphoi*], we are children not of a slave woman but of the free woman." Paul exchanges the "you" of v. 28 for an inclusive "we," for the point actually applies to Jewish believers like Paul as well as to Gentile believers (cf. v. 26b: "our mother"). The new preachers have been telling the Galatians that as Gentiles who do not observe the law, they are "children" (descendants) of a slave woman—of Hagar, the mother of Ishmael. It follows, then, that the Galatian believers in Christ can become children of the free woman, Sarah, only if they become law observant, following the recommendation of the law-observant church in Jerusalem, under whose flag the new preachers are doing their missionary work in Galatia (see Excursus 4 and Introduction: Date). For Paul, however, Hagar the slave woman allegorically represents the covenant at Sinai and stands in the same column with the present Jerusalem, meaning the law-observant church there, whereas Sarah the free woman represents the promissory covenant and stands in the same column with the Jerusalem above, as the law-free church brought into being by the fulfillment of God's promise to Abraham through the coming of Christ and his Spirit (cf. 1:3, 6, 15; 2:21; 3:14, 16, 18, 22; 4:6–7). Believers in Christ ("we") are thus children of "the free woman," allegorically understood as this Jerusalem above (v. 26).

The fact that Paul in both v. 28 and v. 31, whether considered apart or together, substantially repeats a point already made earlier in the letter indicates that neither represents the ultimate goal of his argument in this passage. That is to be found in 5:1, in particular in the exhortation of the second half of that verse: "For freedom Christ has set us free! Stand fast, therefore [*oun*], and do not be burdened again with a yoke of slavery!" Paul thus rounds off the passage

The Grave Dangers Confronting the Galatians

with a ringing declaration (5:1a) followed by an urgent appeal (5:1b). In 5:1a, he makes the christological basis of the freedom of believers explicit: "Christ has set us free!" This declaration is another, christologically focused way of saying that "we" are "children of promise" (4:28), "children of the free woman" (4:31). Christ has set "us" free in order that "we" might have a condition known and experienced as "freedom" (*hē eleutheria*, lit., "the freedom").[443] As the presence of the article in the Greek indicates, Paul has a particular form of freedom in view: what he in 2:4 calls "the freedom [*hē eleutheria*] that we have in Christ Jesus," which is freedom *from the law*. Christ has liberated believers (cf. 1:4; 3:13; 4:4–5) from "under the law" (4:21), the law being conceived of once again as an enslaving power (cf. 3:23–25; 4:1–7). As many a commentator has noted, 5:1a epitomizes the primary message of Galatians, which is a solemn declaration to its readers of what God has done in Christ. It is the positive form of the earlier encapsulation of the letter's message in 3:25 (see comment there). On the basis of Christ's liberating act and its result, Paul now exhorts the Galatians to "stand fast" (hold their ground) and not to "be burdened [*enechesthe*][444] again [*palin*] with a yoke of slavery," which is the law (cf. 5:2–4; Acts 15:10). The two imperatives are conceptually one: Paul is exhorting the Galatians to hold their ground so as not to be burdened with a yoke of slavery. In his choice of the "yoke" metaphor, Paul may be alluding to the paradoxically positive notion of "the yoke of the law," attested in the Mishnah (*m. ʾAbot* 3.5; cf. Matt 11:29–30) and perhaps familiar also to the new preachers in Galatia. In Paul's usage there is no such paradox: the yoke of the law is a yoke of slavery (cf. 1 Tim 6:1), and the Galatians will certainly understand his words in this way. The adverb "again" reflects Paul's view that the Galatians' turn to the law is effectively their return to the condition of enslavement "under the elements of the world" (4:3, 8–11; see comments there). To be under the one is tantamount to being under the other. Both imperatival verbs ("stand fast," "do not be burdened") are present tense in the Greek, probably indicating that ongoing activities are in view: Keep holding your ground and persist in being unburdened by the law. In other words, the Galatians are being exhorted to go on remaining in the freedom for which Christ has set them free.

Paul's exhortation in 5:1b is not based on his allegorical exegesis of the story of Abraham and his two sons by Hagar and Sarah, which is designed to be a correction of the alternative allegorical exegesis of the story by the new preachers in Galatia. The exhortation is based solely on Christ's liberating deed.

---

443. The dative with which the verse begins ("for freedom") evidently expresses purpose or destination (cf. Rom 8:24; Acts 22:25), though it may be instrumental (Lightfoot). It appears to be equivalent in meaning and implication to the prepositional phrase found in 5:13: "You were called into [*epi*] freedom." Cf. Smyth #1531.

444. Cf. BDAG 336: "be loaded down with."

In other words, Paul's concluding exclamatory "imperative" is predicated on the "indicative" of Christ's liberating deed. It is also Christ's liberating work, however, that has provided Paul with the key to his own allegorical exegesis of Gen 16–21, for he reads "the Scripture" through the lens provided by the gospel. Because the Galatians are also beneficiaries of Christ's liberating deed, they can discern with Paul that they are indeed children not of a slave woman, but of the free woman, and thus that Paul's exegesis is actually the "right" one. It is finally only as children of the free woman that the Galatians can be exhorted to stand fast (Martyn 447) so as not to be burdened again with a yoke of slavery.

5:2–6 The Danger of Becoming Separated from Christ and Grace

Beginning at 4:8, Paul has repeatedly called the attention of the Galatians to the dangers of turning to the law: it means a return to previous servitude (4:8–11), an abandonment of Paul and the gospel he preached to them (4:12–20), and the loss of their new identity as the intended heirs of Abraham and Sarah (4:21–5:1). The dangers all come down to the same thing, the loss of Christ, as Paul now makes plain with some vehemence in this passage. The passage has two subunits. In the first (vv. 2–4), Paul emphasizes the dire consequences of beginning with the practice of circumcision. In the second (vv. 5–6), the focus shifts to the positive consequences of "faith," that is, the faith of Christ, mentioned in both verses. Paul here gives another contextualized summary of the gospel.

> 5:2 Look, I, Paul, say to you that if you were to practice circumcision, Christ will avail you nothing. 3 I again testify to everyone practicing circumcision that he [or she] is someone obligated to do the whole law. 4 You have become separated from Christ, you who are seeking to be justified in the law; you have fallen from grace.
>
> 5 For we, through the Spirit from faith, are waiting for the hope of justification, 6 for in Christ Jesus neither circumcision avails anything nor uncircumcision, but faith becoming effective through love.

This passage contains the first explicit mention of circumcision in relation to the Galatians, but it has been implicitly at issue from the beginning (cf. esp. 2:3; 3:3; Excursus 4). The practice of circumcision involves "do[ing] the whole law" and "seeking to be justified in the law." Standing opposed to "the law" (vv. 3–4) is "faith" (vv. 5–6). Paul here then recapitulates the contrast between the law and faith that was first articulated in 2:15–21 and developed further in 3:1–29. In this passage, as in the previous passages, Paul does not urge the Galatians to make *a choice between* Christ and the law. Rather, Paul effectively urges the Galatians *not to choose the law*. They do not need to choose for Christ since they have already been seized by him and his Spirit (3:1–5, 14; 4:6–7).

They have already "become known by God" (4:9); they already stand within the realm of grace (1:6). The problem is that they are contemplating leaving this zone of freedom (5:1) and entering another one, that of enslavement to circumcision and the law (4:21–5:1).

[2–4] In v. 2, Paul calls the Galatians to attention with the full weight of his apostolic authority ("Look, I, Paul, say to you . . ."), making the Galatians take seriously the consequences of the step they are contemplating: "If [*ean*] you [pl.] were to practice circumcision [*peritemnēsthe*], Christ will avail you [pl.] nothing." The verb in the conditional clause is a subjunctive in the Greek, which points to a possibility, not a reality. The form of the conditional clause thus indicates that the Galatians have probably not yet adopted the practice, even if they are seriously contemplating doing so. The present tense implies an activity that will be ongoing if the practice were to be adopted ("if you were to make a practice of circumcising . . .").

The Greek verb *peritemnēsthe* is generally construed to be passive in form and sense (e.g., RSV, NRSV, KJV, NIV, NAB, NJB; Burton; Betz; Longenecker; Martyn; Matera: "If you were to be circumcised," "if you were to receive circumcision," "if you get yourselves circumcised," and the like). This construction of the verb implies that v. 2 is addressed solely, or at least primarily, to the men of the Galatian churches. But this interpretation is not consistent with the use of the present tense, which, as indicated above, implies an ongoing activity or practice. For this reason, the clause cannot pertain to the individual male believer in Galatia contemplating his own punctiliar circumcision, but to the Galatians collectively (3:1), as the use of the plural "you" also suggests. Paul has in view the possible adoption of the *practice* of circumcision in "the churches of Galatia" (1:2). The verb is, therefore, best construed as a middle, indicating a communal practice (see comments below on v. 3 and 6:12–13; cf. 1 Cor 7:18).[445]

The deeper issue in v. 2 is not whether the men in the congregation will allow themselves to be circumcised but whether the churches of Galatia will adopt the practice of circumcision as a distinguishing mark of their religious

---

445. Cf. Smyth #1713: "The middle voice shows that the action is performed with special reference to the subject." In this case, then, the sense is this: "if you Galatians were to practice the rite of circumcision in your churches . . ." Bruce (229) regards the verb as a middle but he translates it as if it were a passive: "if you have yourselves circumcised" (cf. Dunn 266). The middle voice can be used in connection with someone who circumcises himself, as in Jdt 14:10: "When Achior saw all that the God of Israel had done, he believed firmly in God. So he circumcised [*perietemeto*, aor. mid.] the flesh of his foreskin [*tēn sarka tēs akrobystias autou*] and joined the house of Israel until this day" (AT; NRSV translates the relevant phrase concisely as "he was circumcised," as if the verb were a passive). In this case the verb is also accompanied by a direct object. The instances of the verb in Gal 5:2–3 (and 6:12–13) do not have a direct object and do not refer to punctiliar instances of self-circumcision, as in the case of Achior; they refer to the adoption of an ongoing communal practice.

identity. For this reason, the circumcision of males is a community matter, one in which women also have a say as mothers of infant (and older) sons who need to be presented for circumcision. The adoption of male circumcision would signify the adoption of an ongoing communal practice. That practice will also be a family matter. Henceforth parents will together present their infant sons on the eighth day (Gen 17:12) for the rite. Both parents, the mother as well as the father, will thereby acknowledge the importance of the rite for belonging to the Jewish community, with its commitment to observing the remainder of the law (v. 3). In that sense, everyone in the Galatian churches, women as well as men, will be "practicing circumcision."

Paul's primary concern, however, is not to give the Galatians instruction about the rite of circumcision, but to alert them to the fact that the practice of circumcision, once adopted by the Galatian churches, has dire consequences: "Christ will [from then on] avail you [pl.] nothing"! Paul has not only the last judgment in view with his use of a future tense (Betz; Schlier; Witherington) but also the life of the Galatian churches in the present: Christ will be of no further benefit to the Galatians once the practice of circumcision has been adopted. The Galatians will then no longer be "in Christ" (3:28): their identity will no longer be determined by their incorporation into Christ but by their observance of the law. Paul will develop this point especially in v. 4 (see comment below), but it is a point that has lain behind everything he has said from 4:8 onward. This point in turn presupposes the antinomy of Christ and the law first posited in 2:16 (see comment there).

To adopt the practice of circumcision is to adopt the observance of the law, and then not merely some part of it, but the whole law, including all of its many commandments and prohibitions (*b. Mak.* 24a counts 248 commandments and 365 prohibitions, totaling 613). This point is the burden of v. 3, where Paul solemnly formulates a principle for those in Galatia who may be tempted to start practicing circumcision: "I again testify to everyone practicing circumcision that he (or she) is someone obligated to do the whole law." The present tense of the participle ("practicing circumcision," *peritemnomenō*) could be taken to imply that some in Galatia had already begun to practice circumcision (so Martyn 469–70), but that seems unlikely given v. 2 and the thrust of this whole section (4:8–5:12). Paul is desperately trying to keep the Galatians from going that route. This verse is, therefore, best taken as the formulation of a general principle: once begun, the practice of circumcision involves observing "the whole law."

Paul here uses the noun *opheiletēs*, "someone obligated," which is related to the verb *ōpheleō*, "to be of benefit to," in v. 2. The play on words is impossible to reproduce in English, but it indicates that the point of v. 3 (obligation to observe the whole law) complements the point of v. 2 (Christ will be of no benefit). The adverb "again" (*palin*) may indicate that Paul has said this on a previous occasion (Burton), but it more probably emphasizes the point of v. 2 (Martyn; Dunn; Matera), which was to warn the Galatians of the dire consequences of adopting circumcision (cf. 1:9). Paul now individualizes the issue ("everyone," *pas anthrōpos*). As in v. 2, the verb for circumcision is present middle (here in the form of a participle), indicating an ongoing activity or a practice not limited to single male believers contemplating their own circumcision (which is a brief, onetime operation). Paul does not use the word for "man" (*anēr*) here, either (as RSV, NRSV, KJV, NIV, NJB, and NAB assume), but the word for "human being" (*anthrōpos*), and then inclusively: "everyone" (*pas anthrōpos*). The practice of circumcision once adopted involves everyone in the churches of Galatia, whether man or woman (see comment on v. 2 above). Once someone there adopts the practice of male circumcision, that person becomes "someone obligated to do [observe] the whole law."

The assumption behind this claim is that circumcision is not merely an operation or an isolated rite but part of something greater, the Mosaic law. For Gentiles contemplating becoming proselytes to Judaism, it functions as the rite of entry into the Jewish community, the community that lives by the Mosaic law. Once one enters that community by adopting the practice of circumcision, other obligations follow. Paul's phrase "the whole law" (*holos ho nomos*), also found in Matt 22:40, indicates that the law is an undivided whole (cf. 3:10, citing from Deuteronomy: "Accursed is everyone who does not remain in *all* the things written in the book of the law so as to do them"; Jas 2:10: "For whoever keeps the whole law but fails in one point has become guilty of all of it" (RSV); Justin, *Dial.* 8: "If, then, you are willing to listen to me . . . , first be circumcised, then observe what ordinances have been enacted with respect to the Sabbath, and the feasts, and the new moons of God; and, in a word, do *all* the things which have been written in the law"; *Sipra Lev.*, *Kedoshim Pereḳ* 8: "The authorities say, if a proselyte takes upon himself to obey all the words of the Law except one single commandment, he is not to be received"—cited by Moore 1971: 331.

The formulation of v. 3 seems at first sight to indicate that Paul is newly informing the Galatians about the link between the practice of circumcision and the observance of the whole law. Have the new preachers in Galatia failed to tell the Galatians that the adoption of the practice of circumcision involves a commitment to the whole law? Have they perhaps told them about food laws (cf. 2:11–14) and holy times (cf. 4:10) in addition to circumcision, but about no other commandments or obligations (Longenecker; Martyn)? Do they in short have "a policy of gradualism, requiring first some of the major commandments (circumcision, food, days)" while keeping quiet for the time being about the remainder (Sanders 1983: 29)? That seems very unlikely (Dunn; Matera), if only because circumcision would probably be the major stumbling block (Barclay 1988: 46–47). In 6:13, Paul charges that "those who practice circumcision [the new preachers in Galatia] do not themselves keep the law," which seems to imply that the new preachers assume circumcision and law observance to go hand in hand; Paul's reproach is that they do not practice what they preach. In other uses of the term "the law" in Galatians, furthermore, Paul evidently has the whole law in view (e.g., 2:21; 4:21; 6:13), not just some part of it. The phrase "the whole law" in v. 3 probably then means simply "the remainder of the law": if you adopt circumcision, then you are also obligated to keep the remainder of the law, the many other commandments the law contains. The law is a "total way of life" (Dunn 267). By referring explicitly and emphatically to the *whole* law in v. 3, Paul underscores the far-reaching consequences of beginning with circumcision. The new preachers in Galatia undoubtedly believe that the practice of circumcision obligates practitioners to do "the [undivided] law," just as the Christian Jews in Acts 15:5 do, but they do not present this obligation as a terrible burden as Paul now does ("a yoke of slavery," according to 5:1). The underlying implication of v. 3 is that the believer is actually under no obligation whatsoever to observe—to *do* (*poieō*)—the law, whether that be circumcision or any other commandment (see further on 5:13). For Paul, to reject the practice of circumcision as a badge of Christian identity is to reject the observance of the whole law as a badge of Christian identity. The principle of "the whole law" holds as much for him as for the new preachers: the law is a total package, and it is accepted or rejected as such.

In v. 4, Paul is as explicit as he can be about the dire consequences of choosing the law: "You have become separated from Christ, you who are seeking to be justified in the law; you have fallen from grace." Paul addresses the Galatians as those "who [*hoitines*] are seeking to be justified in [the sphere of] the law." The words "You are seeking to be justified" translate the present tense *dikaiousthe* (lit., "you are being justified"), which is here being used to signify an attempt or an intention (BDF #319; Smyth 1956: #1878). Paul clearly does not mean to suggest that the Galatians are in fact being justified in the realm of the law (cf. 3:11: "No one is justified before God in the law"). The sense matches that of 4:21, where Paul addresses the Galatians as "you who are *wanting* [*hoi thelontes*] to be under the law." For Paul, to be "in the law" (3:11) is functionally equivalent to being "under the law" (3:23) and the opposite of being "in Christ" (5:6; cf. 1:22; 2:17; 3:14, 26, 28). "Seeking to be justified in the law" is then equivalent to *not* "seeking [*zētountes*] to be justified in Christ" (2:17, see comment there). Paul's characterization of the Galatians in 5:4 summarizes the basic theological problem he discerns in the Galatian situation as a result of the message of the new preachers: the search for justification "in the law" (in the realm of law observance) rather than "in Christ" (in the realm where Christ's lordship has already become effective, the church).

For Paul, to seek (future) justification in the realm of law observance after having been seized by Christ is to have stepped outside the realm of Christ's grace (cf. 1:6; 2:21). To add weight to the disastrous result of such a step, Paul uses past tenses: "You *have become* separated [*katērgēthēte*] from Christ; ... you *have fallen* from [*exepesate*] [the realm of] grace" (cf. Martyn 471; Bruce 231). In a sense, Paul repeats here the argument found in 4:8–11: if the Galatians choose the route of law observance, they will be back to where they started. It will be as if Christ and his Spirit had never seized them! The rhetorical purpose of this message is crystal clear: Paul wants his Galatian readers to discern once again the realm of freedom (Christ), which has invaded their lives, and thus to stand fast (5:1) against the message of the new preachers, who are insisting that the Galatians must choose the observance of the law if they want to be justified (approved) by God at the last judgment. Verse 6 will show that Paul has no difficulty with the condition of being circumcised or even with the observance of the law as such; the difficulty arises when circumcision and observance of the law are understood to be prerequisites for justification, "for if justification is through the law, Christ died for nothing" (2:21b). To want to predicate justification on circumcision and law observance now that Christ (faith) has come into the world (3:23–25) is to nullify God's grace (2:21a), thus to fall out of the realm of this grace and to become separated from Christ.

[5–6] These two theologically loaded yet compact verses look back to, and summarize, the argument of Section III of the epistle (3:1–4:7). The unifying theme of that section was the Spirit, the gift and the reception of the Spirit on the basis of "faith" (see introduction to Section III). The faithful Christ and his Spirit provide the basis for justification. The second of the two verses, however, also looks forward to Section V (5:13–6:10), where the unifying theme is the love produced by the Spirit. "⁵For we, through the Spirit from faith, are waiting for the hope of justification, ⁶for in Christ Jesus neither circumcision avails anything nor uncircumcision, but faith becoming effective through love." The summarizing quality of these two verses is indicated by the complete absence of definite articles in the Greek text; the nouns are all anarthrous. Paul here uses shorthand formulations as a way to drive the central message of the letter home.

The conjunction "for" (*gar*) in v. 5 is neither inferential nor explanatory but implies a contrast with what has preceded. Paul now states what he believes to be the case: in place of justification in the law (v. 4), there is in fact justification predicated on faith. The initial "we" (*hēmeis*) is emphatic in the Greek. Does Paul mean "we in contrast to [some of?] you Galatians [vv. 2, 4] are waiting for the hope of justification"? Or does he actually mean "you Galatians and I together are waiting for the hope of justification"? The first option would fit with the import of v. 4, where Paul has used the second-person plural with past tenses to characterize the position of the Galatians seeking justification in the realm of the law. It appears to reflect what Paul takes to be the actual situation. The second option is consistent with the aim of the letter as a whole, which is to bring the Galatians to their theological senses (cf. 3:1). Paul is then effectively inviting the Galatians to see the matter as he does, and so to stand fast (5:1).

In any case, "*We . . . are waiting for the hope of justification.*" The verb Paul uses (*apekdechomai*) signifies eager, intense, and confident expectation (cf. Rom 8:19, 25; 1 Cor 1:7; Phil 3:20), though the character of the waiting is not the crucial point of the argument. This is the only instance of the term "hope" (*elpis*) in Galatians (cf. Rom 5:2–5; 8:20–25). "Hope" is not here an attitude or stance (hoping), but an object (that which is hoped for). The content of the hoped-for object is "justification" (*dikaiosynē*), God's vindication of believers in the future (a forensic declaration), but for Paul also (cf. comment on 2:15–21) God's dynamic rectification (setting right) of the world (a liberation of the world from enslaving powers). In both senses, the result will be "righteousness" (*dikaiosynē*), a world rightly related to God because it has been liberated from oppressive powers. Paul does not here contest or qualify the futurity of justification, as he will in Romans (see comment on 2:15–21).[446] The point at issue in Galatians is not the "when" of justification but its basis.

Those who eagerly await the hope of justification do so "*through the Spirit from faith*" (*pneumati ek pisteōs*). The precise import of this phrase has been difficult to determine, as indicated by the variety of proposed translations and punctuations:

> For through the Spirit, by faith, we await the hope of righteousness. (NAB, RSV, NRSV; cf. Betz; Dunn; Martyn)
> For we through the Spirit wait for the hope of righteousness by faith. (KJV; cf. NJB)
> But by faith we eagerly await through the Spirit the righteousness for which we hope. (NIV)

All these translations have two things in common. (1) They translate the two terms involved in the same way: "through the Spirit" (*pneumati*) and "by faith" (*ek pisteōs*). (2) They all separate "through Spirit" from "by faith," either by placing a comma between them or by placing them apart from one another in the sentence. There are good reasons, however, for concluding that the two terms belong together and that the meaning of v. 5 is: "We, through the Spirit

---

446. Some commentators argue that justification (or righteousness) is in this verse a present reality (Matera; Fung), but that argument is consistently substantiated by an appeal to Romans, not by an appeal to other passages in Galatians. This assumption then leads to the forced translation: "We are waiting for the hoped-for reality that present righteousness brings." The line of interpretation can be traced back at least to Luther, who refers to "the righteousness which we already possess by faith" (1535: 25) and interprets "the hope of righteousness" in 5:6 accordingly: "We have indeed begun to be justified by faith. . . . But we are not yet perfectly righteous. Our being justified perfectly still remains to be seen, and this is what we hope for. Thus our righteousness does not yet exist in fact, but it still exists in hope" (1535: 21).

that we received on the basis [*ek*] of Christ's faithful death, are waiting for the hope of justification."

The phrase "by the Spirit from faith" is a concise summary of a key element of Paul's argument in 3:1–4:7 (see esp. 3:1–14, 22–26; 4:4–7). Paul once again employs the prepositional phrase *ek pisteōs*, "from [on the basis of] faith," which he has used six times earlier in Gal 3 (vv. 7, 8, 9, 11, 12, 24). The phrase is there, and for that reason probably here as well, an abbreviation of the longer phrase "from the faith of (Jesus) Christ," *ek pisteōs (Iēsou) Christou*, found in 2:16 and 3:22 (see Excursus 11). The genitive in the latter phrase is probably subjective ("the faith *of* Christ") rather than objective ("faith *in* Christ"). The phrase, therefore, does not have human believing primarily in view but Christ's own faithfulness, particularly as this comes to concrete expression in his faithful death (see Excursus 9; also Choi). In 3:1–5, moreover, Paul has argued that God bestows the Spirit not "on the basis of works of the law" (*ex ergōn nomou*) but "on the basis of what was heard of faith" (*ex akoēs pisteōs*), that is, what the Galatians heard of Christ's faithful death (see comment on 3:1–5, esp. v. 2). Galatians 3:13–14 also links the reception of the Spirit to Christ's faithful death: "Christ redeemed us from the curse of the law," having become a curse "for us" by being hung on a cross, "so that the blessing of Abraham might come to the Gentiles in Christ Jesus, so that we might receive the promise of the Spirit [= the promised Spirit] through [the] faith [of Christ]" (see comment there). Galatians 3:22 in turn refers to "the promise [of the Spirit] from the faith of Jesus Christ" (*hē epangelia [tou pneumatos] ek pisteōs Iēsou Christou*); in this verse, the promised Spirit is given "to those who believe" (*tois pisteuousin*) on the basis of (*ek*) Jesus Christ's faithful death (see comment there; cf. 4:4–7). The expression Paul uses in 5:5, "by the Spirit from faith" (*pneumati ek pisteōs*), is best taken as a restatement in abbreviated form of the clause found in 3:22. It means "by the Spirit that we received on the basis of Christ's faithful death."[447]

Verse 6 now provides a further elaboration in terms of the specific issue of circumcision: "for," as Paul now explains, "in Christ Jesus neither circumcision avails [*ischyei*] anything [for justification] nor uncircumcision [for that matter], but *faith* [*pistis*] [does avail something for justification] becoming effective through love [*agapē*]." "In Christ Jesus," meaning the realm determined by his faithful death (cf. 3:14, cited above), and thus in the church, circumcision does not have the power to bring about justification. "Circumcision" (*peritomē*) can here refer both to the practice of circumcision (cf. Rom 4:11) and to the condition of being circumcised. For good measure, and significantly, Paul also adds

---

447. Burton (278), though he rejects this interpretation, observes that this reading of the relation between *pneuma* and *pistis* in the phrase is "neither grammatically impossible . . . nor un-Pauline in thought."

"uncircumcision" (*akrobystia*, lit., "foreskin"), which appears to refer both to the absence of the practice of circumcision and to the condition of being uncircumcised (cf. 6:15; 1 Cor 7:19).[448] Neither the practice of circumcising nor the lack of this practice, neither the condition of being circumcised nor the absence of that condition, "avails anything" (*ischyei ti*) to secure the sought-for justification.[449] Circumcision and its contrary, uncircumcision, are irrelevant and matters of indifference "in Christ." This religious but also ethnic and cultural distinction is declared to be irrelevant. Paul here restates what he wrote in 3:28: in Christ, there is neither Jew nor Greek. All that matters is "faith," Christ's faith. As God's apocalyptic invasion of the human world (cf. 3:23–25; Excursus 2), this "faith" has the power to secure the sought-for justification. It does so by "becoming effective through love."

This last phrase raises two further questions: (1) Whose love (*agapē*) is Paul here referring to? (2) What is the sense of "becoming effective" (*energoumenē*)? The Greek participle, which is derived from the Greek verb *energeō*, may be either middle or passive. If passive, a reading favored by patristic writers, Paul could mean to say that "[our] faith [is] being made effective through [God's] love." In favor of this reading is the fact that Paul uses the same verb in 2:8 and 3:5 (the only other instances in Galatians), both times in the active voice in connection with God's activity (cf. 1 Cor 12:6, 11; Eph 1:11, 20; 2:2). If middle (with active meaning), Paul means: "faith working [or becoming effective] through love," which is the translation here adopted. In favor of this reading is the frequent use of the middle elsewhere in Paul (Rom 7:5; 2 Cor 1:6; 4:12; 1 Thess 2:13; cf. 2 Thess 2:7; Eph 3:20; Col 1:29). "Faith" is traditionally understood to refer to a human being's faith in Christ even when the verb is construed as a middle, but it probably refers to Christ's own faith, as indicated above. Given 5:13–14, interpreters generally assume that Paul is here referring to the love that believers are to have for one another (cf. also 5:22). In 2:20, however, Paul has defined Christ's faith in terms of his self-sacrificial love. That verse contains the only previous reference to love in the letter and Paul there has presented himself—and by analogy, other believers—as living now "in *faith*, that of the Son of God, the one who *loved* [*agapēsantos*] me and gave himself up for me." Having heard 2:20, the Galatians may, therefore, be inclined to interpret 5:6 to mean "Christ's faith(fulness) becoming effective through his self-giving love for us" (cf. Choi 482–89). Given 2:20, this may also be Paul's intended meaning. If so, Paul is here effectively, just as in

---

448. In 2:7–9 Paul used these same terms metonymically to refer to groups of people practicing (Jews) or not practicing (Gentiles) circumcision (cf. 2:12).

449. According to BDAG 484, the sense of *ischyei* here is "have meaning, be valid, be in force" (cf. Heb 9:17; MM 308), but that seems too weak. In Phil 4:13, Paul uses the verb intransitively to mean "to be strong, to have power" (cf. Jas 5:16; Acts 19:16, 20; Rev 12:8).

2:20, defining Christ's faith in terms of his self-giving death, attributing to that event justifying power (cf. 2:21 and comment there).

Just as Christ's faith has its human correlate (believing in Christ; cf. 2:16; 3:22), so also Christ's love "for us" has its human correlate (loving one another; cf. 5:13–15). Human believing and loving are forms of participation in the antecedent faith and love of Christ. Paul's concise expressions probably encompass both the christological and the anthropological aspects, though the former appear to be primary and in any case the basis for the latter (for the meaning of love, see the comment on 5:13–14, below). Christ, his faith, his love, his Spirit—these, not the law, provide the basis for the hoped-for justification.

5:7–12 The Source of the Danger: The Leaven of the New Preachers

Paul has effectively concluded the section outlining the dangers with which the Galatians are confronted (4:8–5:6) with a concise, contextualized summary of the gospel in 5:5–6. Thus 5:5–6 can be seen as a summary of the letter to this point, and by anticipation, of the remainder of the letter. Ending the passage with a reference to love, Paul now intends to expand on this theme. But before he does so (in 5:13–6:10), he turns his attention briefly, in what amounts to a digression, to the source of the dangers he has outlined: the new preachers active in Galatia (5:7–12).

The passage can be divided into two parts. In vv. 7–10, Paul attacks the teaching of the new preachers while recognizing its persuasive power. Here he makes a play on words having to do with persuasion. In vv. 11–12, he refutes a false charge about him "proclaiming circumcision," closing with the wish that the new preachers will take up the practice of castration.

> 5:7 You were running well. Who hindered you from being obedient to the[a] truth? 8 The persuasion is not from the one who calls you. 9 A little leaven leavens the whole lump. 10 I am confident about you in the Lord[b] that you will think no other way. And the one who is unnerving you will bear the judgment, whoever he may be.
>
> 11 And I, brethren, if I am still[c] proclaiming circumcision, why am I still being persecuted? Then the offense of the cross has been destroyed.
> 12 Would that those who are upsetting you also practice castration!

a. The definite article *hē* ("the") has questionable manuscript support. It is not found in ℵ*, A, B, but its presence is supported by $\mathfrak{P}^{46}$, C, D, F, G, 33, 1739, among other manuscripts.

b. The phrase "in the Lord" is missing from B. The omission is probably accidental.

c. This word (*eti*) is omitted by D and numerous manuscripts of the Byzantine family. Its omission is easier to explain than its inclusion. It is thus probably original.

[7–10] These verses recall the letter's opening, 1:6–10, where Paul has rebuked the Galatians for "so quickly turning from the one who called you ... to a different gospel." In the present passage, Paul uses the image of a footrace in a stadium (cf. 2:2; 1 Cor 9:24–27) to make a similar observation: The Galatians "were running well," but an obstacle successfully impeded their progress (Betz 264: "got in the path"), making it difficult for the Galatians to stay on track, as it were. Or as Paul puts it, someone "hindered" the Galatians "from being obedient [*peithesthai*] to the truth [*alētheia*]" (v. 7). The translation of the verb *peithesthai* (passive in form) with "be obedient" or "obey" (RSV, NRSV, KJV, NIV, NJB; BDAG 792) is not entirely satisfactory. A more literal translation would be "from being persuaded (won over) to the truth." The obedience that Paul has in view involves recognition and acceptance of "the truth," meaning "the truth of the gospel" (2:5, 14; see comment there).[450] In the rhetorical question "Who hindered you?" Paul uses the singular interrogative pronoun "who?" (*tis*), as he has in 3:1 ("Who bewitched you?"). In v. 10b of the present passage, he will refer to "the one who is unnerving you" without specifying who that person is ("whoever he may be"). It is difficult to know whether Paul is speaking generically in these verses or has a particular person (the leader of the group?) in view. Probably the former (see below on v. 10b), since he reverts back to the plural in v. 12 (cf. 1:7; 4:17; 6:12–13). The obstacle in the Galatians' path is the message of the new preachers, specifically their requirement that the Galatians practice circumcision (cf. 5:2–3, 11–12). The subtle allusion to circumcision is evident in the verb "hindered," *enekopsen*, literally, "cut in on" (De Vries; NIV), a cognate of the verb *koptō*, "to cut" (Mark 11:8; Matt 21:8). In v. 12, Paul will use the verb *apokoptō*, "to cut away," in connection with the caricature of circumcision as a form of castration.

"The persuasion [*hē peismonē*]," Paul continues, "is not from the one who calls you" (v. 8). The word *peismonē* is rare, occurring only here in the NT and in no other extant Greek literature prior to Galatians. It can be taken actively (persuading activity) or passively (the condition of being persuaded). Both make good sense and may apply (Burton 283). When looked at as an activity, "the persuasion" is the attractive, convincing message the new preachers present to the Galatians with some rhetorical skill (cf. 3:1, where Paul has asked the Galatians who "bewitched" them; see comment there). The result of the new preachers' persuading activity, however, is also the condition of being persuaded of something other than "the truth" of which v. 7 speaks. This condition, just like the message propounded by the new preachers (the "different gospel" of 1:6), is "not from the one who calls you" (*ek tou kalountos hymas*). The phrase "the one who calls you" is a circumlocution for God, recalling the similar

---

450. That appears to be the case whether or not the article is original with the word "truth" in 5:7 (see textual note above).

The Grave Dangers Confronting the Galatians 321

phrase in 1:6: "the one who called [*kalesantos*] you" (see comment there). The aorist participle used in 1:6 evoked the Galatians' being called by God in the past through the gospel that Paul preached to them (4:9, 13); the present tense used here focuses the attention of the Galatians on the present situation: God (through Paul's letter) is now calling them again (cf. 4:19). Paul does not say where "the persuasion" is from, only where it is not from: it is not from God. It is as if he had written, "God is never inconsistent with himself, and it is he who by my preaching called you to salvation. This new persuasion, then, has come from somewhere else" (Calvin 97).

The metaphorical declaration in v. 9 is a continuation of this line of thought: "A little leaven leavens the whole lump": a small amount of yeast eventually permeates a lump of dough in its entirety. The declaration sounds like a proverb (cf. 1 Cor 5:6, where it recurs), though it is not attested outside of the two instances in Paul's Letters. It certainly points to knowledge or wisdom obtained through experience and observation of natural processes. "Leaven" here has a negative connotation, as in Mark 8:15 ("Beware of the leaven of the Pharisees and the leaven of Herod" [RSV]). Paul does not apply the analogy explicitly to the Galatian situation, but the import is clear enough from the context: The dangerously persuasive message of the new preachers concerning the necessity of circumcision ("a little leaven") is corrupting ("leavens") the Galatian churches ("the whole lump"). The analogy is probably meant as a warning to the Galatian churches not to let matters deteriorate to such an extent since, in the following verse, Paul expresses the confidence that the Galatians will come to share his viewpoint on the matter: "I [*egō*] am confident [*pepoitha*] about you in the Lord that [after hearing this letter] you will think no other way" (v. 10a). The "I" is emphatic in the Greek. Paul's robust confidence over the final outcome finds its ultimate basis "in the Lord," in Christ (cf. 1:3:"the Lord Jesus Christ"), not in the situation in Galatia at the present moment, which is actually a matter of grave concern (cf. 4:11, 20). A more-literal translation of *egō pepoitha* ("I am confident") would be "I am persuaded." The play on words, difficult to capture in English, is evident: Though the Galatians have been hindered from "being persuaded" to the truth of the gospel as preached by Paul (v. 7), Paul is "persuaded in the Lord" (v. 10) that "the persuasion" of the new preachers, which does not come from God (v. 8; cf. 1:1, 6, 10–12), will not finally prevail among the Galatians.

Paul now utters a word of judgment on the new preachers: "The one unnerving [*ho tarassōn*] you will bear the judgment, whoever he may be" (v. 10b). Given the last phrase, Paul appears at first glance to have a specific person of some stature or prominence in view, for example, the leader of the new preachers (Martyn 475; Witherington 372), perhaps even Peter, Barnabas, or James (cf. 1:18–19; 2:7–9, 11–13). His designation of the new preachers back in 1:7 as "those unnerving [*hoi tarassontes*] you," using the plural of the same verb (cf. v. 12), indicates, however, that the singular used in v. 10b is probably to be construed as generic (so most commentators; see comment on v. 7 above). The sense is probably that anyone, whoever that may be, unnerving the Galatians "will [individually] bear the judgment [*to krima*] [of that action]" (RSV; Burton; Betz: "his judgment"; NRSV, NIV: "the penalty"; NAB: "the condemnation"). To "bear" (*bastasei*) the judgment is to "carry" it as one would a burden (cf. Mark 14:13; John 19:17; also Gal 6:2, 5, 17). Here judgment involves condemnation (BDAG 567). In Paul's mind, and given the context, "the judgment" referred to is probably God's (cf. Rom 2:2–3: "the judgment of God," *to krima tou theou*), though it is not certain that the Galatians will realize this on the basis of the word itself. The word for judgment, *krima*, may in some contexts point to the last judgment (Acts 24:25; Heb 6:2; 1 Pet 4:17), but that reference is not inherent in the word itself (cf. BDAG 567; Rom 3:8). The point that Paul wants to put over to the Galatians in v. 10b is that the behavior of the new preachers with respect to the Galatians will surely incur their judgment, their condemnation.

[11–12] Paul could have stopped there, but he concludes this last subsection and thus also the whole of the fourth major section of the letter (4:8–5:12) with an indignant refutation of a potentially very damaging allegation and a wish for his adversaries in Galatia: "And I, brethren, if I am still [in fact] proclaiming circumcision [as the new preachers allege], why am I still being persecuted? [If I am still proclaiming circumcision,] then the offense of the cross has been destroyed. ¹²[Let me tell you and them what I think of circumcision:] Would that those who are upsetting you [go a step further with the circumcising knife and] also practice castration."

The protasis of v. 11, which is a "real" condition in form (*ei peritomēn eti kēryssō*) but an "unreal" (contrary-to-fact) condition in meaning, indicates that the new preachers are claiming that Paul "still proclaims [*kēryssō*] circumcision." Paul signals the absurdity of the allegation at the beginning of v. 11 by using the emphatic first-personal pronoun "I" (*egō*) and by addressing the Galatians as "brethren" (*adelphoi*), meaning sisters and brothers in Christ. Paul underscores the absurdity further in the double apodosis (Lambrecht 1996; otherwise Baarda), one a question ("Why am I still being persecuted?") and the other an assertion ("Then the offense of the cross has been destroyed").

Back in 2:2, Paul has referred to "the gospel [*to euangelion*] that I proclaim [*kēryssō*] among the Gentiles," using the same verb as in v. 11a. Paul's use of this particular verb in this context suggests that he is being charged with "proclaiming" (preaching or advocating) circumcision, as the new preachers are now doing, presumably as part of "the gospel." With his use of the adverb "still" (*eti*), Paul concedes that he had in some unspecified sense once done so. There is no corroborating evidence for this remarkable concession in any of Paul's Letters, and much in Galatians itself speaks against it (cf. 1:1–17; 2:3, 9). Even his claim that circumcision is a matter of indifference just like uncircumcision (5:6; 6:15; cf. 1 Cor 7:19) can hardly be called "proclaiming circumcision"; on the contrary, it relativizes its importance completely. Some interpreters therefore maintain that the charge actually applies to his pre-Christian life (so, e.g., Burton; Longenecker), but it is then difficult to explain how the new preachers could hope to convince the Galatians that Paul was "still" preaching circumcision if in fact he had *never* done so as a preacher of the gospel, after his call and conversion. A possibility is that the charge is based on Paul's acceptance of a mission among Jews (cf. 2:7–9), where circumcision would continue to play an important role (cf. Acts 16:3, which asserts that Paul himself circumcised Timothy, whose mother was Jewish). Paul's acceptance of Christian Jews and their practice of circumcision would then be open to misunderstanding or at least the charge of inconsistency (e.g., Dunn); it could provide the basis for the allegation that in some circumstances he was quite capable of "still proclaiming circumcision," even after his call and conversion. In any case, Paul's concern is not to give information about his past activities but to indicate to the Galatians that he *no longer* "proclaims circumcision" as he once did. Circumcision may once have played a significant role in his life and thought, but it does so no longer, despite what the new preachers are saying. The allegation is absurd.

Paul underscores the absurdity of the allegation in two ways. First, he poses an indignant question, referring to his experience of persecution: "Why am I still being persecuted [*diōkomai*]?" Paul does not say who is persecuting him. He could be referring to non-Christian Jews (cf. 1:13, 23; 6:12) or to the new preachers (cf. 4:29 and comment there). A decision is difficult but could also determine whether the persecution Paul has in view involves actual violence directed to his person (cf. 1:13, 23; 6:12) or simply the ongoing campaign to undermine his gospel and apostolic authority in Galatia (cf. 1:1–2:14). The question in any case implies that Paul is "being persecuted" for rejecting circumcision as obligatory for Gentile believers in Jesus.

Paul underscores the absurdity of the allegation that he still proclaims circumcision, second, by emphasizing the dire theological consequences of such a stance: "Then [*ara*] the offense [*skandalon*] of the cross has been destroyed." This is the first mention of "the cross" (*ho stauros*) as such in Galatians (cf. 6:12, 14). The cross in view is that of the crucified Christ (3:1), as the parallel in 1 Cor 1:23 confirms: "We proclaim [*kēryssomen*] Christ crucified (*estaurōmenon*), an offense [*skandalon*] to Jews" (AT). In Paul's view, the cross, or Christ crucified, is an offense not in some general sense but specifically to Jews, including Christian Jews such as the new preachers in Galatia, because it has (in Paul's understanding of the gospel) effected the destruction of the law as the reliable basis for justification and life (cf. 1:13–16; 2:16, 21; 3:13–14, 21, 23–25; 4:4–5).[451] Earlier in the letter, Paul has formulated its existential application by speaking of himself as having "been crucified with Christ" (2:20; cf. 6:14), meaning that his nomistic self has been killed off. That old self has been replaced by Christ (see comment on 2:19–20). In that event of crucifixion with Christ, the offense also, for Paul, became God's redemptive act of grace (cf. 1:3–5, 6, 15–16; 2:9, 21). Paul may also want the cross to be an offense for the Galatians in the sense that it has brought about the end of a religion based upon "the elements of the world," to which the religion of the law is comparable (4:3, 9; see comments there). Paul's immediate message to the Galatians in v. 11b is that he cannot still be preaching circumcision as the new preachers allege since in that case the offense of the crucified Christ "has been destroyed" (*katērgētai*), i.e., has become void of all significance (cf. 3:17, where the same verb is used; BDAG 525: "the cross has ceased to be an obstacle"). Since it is precisely the crucified Christ whom he proclaims (3:1), Paul cannot be "proclaiming" something (the necessity of circumcision) that is completely inconsistent with this proclamation. The allegation of the new preachers is utterly absurd.

Paul concludes two other major sections of the epistle with a clause beginning with "then [*ara*]" (Section II at 2:21; Section V at 6:10), and the clause in v. 11b can also be taken as the conclusion to Section IV, which begins at 4:8:[452] the dangerous message to which the Galatians have been exposed amounts to the nullification of the cross of Christ, of the gospel of grace (cf. 1:6–7). But Paul does not leave it there. As a token of his indignation with the allegation made by the new preachers (v. 11a), Paul adds a seemingly crude wish: "Would that[453] those who are upsetting you also practice castration!" (v. 12). Paul here characterizes the new preachers as "those who are upsetting you" (*hoi anastatountes hymas*), just as he has earlier called them "those who are unnerving you" (*hoi tarassontes hymas*) in 1:7. The recurrence of the latter term in v. 10b of the present passage (Paul's generic reference to "the one who is unnerving you," *ho tarassōn hymas*) suggests that the choice of another verb with a similar meaning in v. 12 is probably a stylistic variation, though this verb does strengthen Paul's own perception of the new preachers as dangerous troublemakers in the churches of Galatia (cf. BDAG 72; Acts 17:6; 21:38; Betz 270). The new preachers in Galatia are "unnerving" and

---

451. In referring simply to "the cross" Paul is using the figure of metalepsy or double metonymy (Bullinger 608–11): The "cross" stands not only for the very real crucifixion of Christ but also for the soteriological effects of that event. See further comments on 6:12 and 6:14.

452. Cf. 3:29b ("Then [*ara*] you are offspring of Abraham"), which is the conclusion to a significant subsection (3:6–29) within Section III (3:1–4:7) of the epistle.

453. Here $\mathfrak{P}^{46}$ begins the verse with *ara*, probably under the influence of v. 11b, thereby making v. 12 into a third apodosis for the protasis in v. 11a and giving the verse greater significance.

therefore also, in Paul's view, "upsetting" the Galatians by their advocacy of circumcision. In response, Paul expresses the wish that they take the knife for circumcision and use it "also" (*kai*) to "practice castration" (*apokopsontai*), presumably first on themselves (cf. NRSV, NAB: "castrate themselves"; RSV, NJB: "mutilate themselves"; NIV: "emasculate themselves"; Dunn 282: "get themselves castrated").[454] The context indicates that the castration in view is not simply a punctiliar act of self-mutilation (or a series of such acts) but, for Paul and his audience, a recurrent religious rite in some way analogous to circumcision (hence the translation "practice castration").[455] Paul is probably alluding to the ritual castration that occurred in the devotion to the goddess Cybele (Lightfoot 207; S. Elliott; and many others). Pessinus in Galatia was a center of this mystery religion in antiquity. Men so castrated were known as Galli. A second-century tract attributed to Lucian of Samosata provides a description:

> On appointed days, the crowd assembles at the sanctuary while many Galli and holy men . . . perform the rites. . . . On those days, too, men become Galli. For while the rest are playing flutes and performing the rites, frenzy comes upon many, and many who have come simply to watch subsequently perform this act. I will describe what they do. The youth for whom these things lie in store throws off his clothes, rushes to the center with a great shout and takes up a sword, which I believe has stood there for this purpose for many years. He grabs it and immediately castrates himself. . . . This is what they do at the Castration. (*Syr. d.* 50–51)[456]

In rhetorically equating circumcision (*peritemnō*) and castration (*apokoptō*), Paul for polemical purposes adopts the attested Roman perception that circumcision and castration were related forms of male mutilation (Dio Cassius 79.11; Diodorus Siculus 3.31; Lightfoot 207; Vouga 126; S. Elliott 235). In the second century, the emperor Hadrian would ban both (R. Meyer 80). Paul thereby puts circumcision on the same level as the religious practices of the pagan environment that the Galatian believers have left behind (cf. 4:8–11; see comment there). Understood in this way, the verse forms an inclusio with the opening verses of Section IV (4:8–5:12) and brings it to a fitting, if also wincing, climax: Paul expresses the wish that the new preachers practice the

---

454. Paul here uses the construction *ophelon* (a particle meaning "would that" or "I could wish that," which he also uses in 1 Cor 4:8; 2 Cor 11:1) with a future indicative (*apokopsontai*) to express what appears to be an attainable wish (BDF #359.1, #384). (The new preachers will surely not comply).

455. Paul's use of a middle in v. 12 (*apokopsontai*) is analogous to his use of the middle of the verb *peritemnō* (circumcise) in 5:2–3 (see comment above) and 6:12–13 to indicate a recurrent communal practice. The kind of action envisaged by the Greek future (punctiliar, recurrent, continuous) can only be determined from the context.

456. Trans. H. W. Attridge and R. A. Oden, cited from M. Meyer 139.

rite of castration as occurs in the region of Galatia instead of merely the rite of circumcision. The Galatians would then indeed be back to where they started (cf. 4:8–10). By adopting circumcision, "the Galatians were returning in a very marked way to the bondage of their former heathenism" (Lightfoot 207–8; cf. S. Elliott 257). The wish of v. 12 is designed not for the new preachers, who will not pay any attention to it, but for the Galatians, whom Paul wants to alert to the danger involved in adopting the practice of circumcision: it is no better than the practice of castration, a practice that Paul assumes they will find repulsive. As Betz (270) observes, "Paul uses the public disgust with regard to these rituals to discredit his opponents and their ritual of circumcision."

Other interpretations have been proposed:

View 1. The verb Paul uses, *apokoptō*, means simply to "to cut off" (cf. Mark 9:43, 45), and only the context indicates to what this refers. Since Paul does not specify a direct object, the middle form used here (*apokopsontai*) could warrant the translation "Would that those who are upsetting you cut themselves off [from the community]!" (cf. Calvin 99; KJV: "I would they were even cut off which trouble you"). In this case the term would be used metaphorically. Although this interpretation is attractive (it saves Paul from being crude and supposedly loveless with respect to the new preachers), it does not take seriously the immediate context (Paul's references to literal circumcision numerous times in the previous verses) nor the attested middle use of the verb in connection with self-emasculation (Epictetus, *Diatr.* 2.20.19–20; cf. LSJ 203; BDF #317).

View 2. Deuteronomy 23:1 excludes from "the assembly of the LORD" not only a man "whose testicles are crushed" but also a man whose "penis is cut off" (NRSV). The LXX translation of the latter phrase (Deut 23:2) has a form of the verb *apokoptō*, the verb that Paul uses in v. 12. That would seem to suggest that Paul's wish involves "a bungled circumcision" (Williams 142), for he would seem to be hoping that the new preachers take the knife used for circumcision and, through a slip of the knife, also cut off the whole penis in the process. Paul would then be simply venting his frustration with the new preachers, and the verse adds nothing to his argument. Paul's words would amount to a crude joke.[457] Unlike the Hebrew text, however, the LXX of Deut 23:2 does not specify a direct object (it has simply *apokekommenos*, a perfect middle or passive participle). Philo, when he paraphrases this verse and gives it a moralizing interpretation, refers to *apokekommenous ta gennētika tēs psychēs*, "people whose genitals of the soul have been cut away" (passive) or "people who have cut away their genitals of the soul" (middle; *Leg.* 3.8; cf. *Spec.* 1.325). In this

---

457. One might then expect later scribes to soften the impact of this joke or to omit the verse altogether. The fact that no scribe made any such attempt suggests that Paul's words are not to be taken in this way.

light, the corresponding singular in Deut 23:2 LXX need not necessarily have in view someone whose penis has been cut off, but "someone who has been castrated" (passive) or "someone who has castrated himself" (middle).

View 3. Given Deut 23:1, castration was unlike circumcision for Jews in that the former entailed exclusion from the community. Paul can thus be interpreted as expressing the wish that the new preachers exclude themselves from the congregation of the Lord (Burton 289; Dunn 285; Witherington 374). In this interpretation, the knife of circumcision ironically becomes the instrument of exclusion rather than one of inclusion. Verse 12 is actually addressed to the Galatians ("you"), however, even if the wish is meant for the new preachers, and the Galatians will probably not catch the supposed allusion to Deut 23:1 that this interpretation requires. The interpretation of the verse as having in view castration as a religious ritual with which the Galatians were familiar from their cultural environment acknowledges that Paul's primary concern in v. 12 is to make sure that the Galatians reject the version of the gospel being propounded by the new preachers in the churches of Galatia, the version in which the communal rite of circumcision plays a defining role (Tolmie 2005: 187–88). As part of his rhetorical strategy, he puts the ritual circumcision of Gentile Christians by the new preachers on the same level as the ritual castration of the Galli. Paul wants the Galatians to regard circumcision with horror and revulsion (cf. Phil 3:2), just as they do castration. If the new preachers were "practicing castration" instead of circumcision, the Galatians would not now be in danger of "so quickly turning . . . to a different gospel" (1:6), for the new preachers would never have gotten a hearing in Galatia.

Summary of Section IV

In this section, which is the rhetorical heart of the letter, Paul has alerted the Galatians in often-emotional language to the dangers that confront them from the new preachers and their "different gospel" (1:6). By heeding their message, the Galatians are running the risk of returning to their previous condition of religious servitude to "the elements" (4:8–11), of abandoning Paul, their founding apostle, and his gospel, which amounts to abandoning God (4:12–20), of losing their new identity through faulty exegesis of the story of Abraham and his sons by Hagar and Sarah (4:21–5:1), and of becoming separated from Christ and falling from grace (5:2–6). The rhetorical thrust of the whole section, and indeed of the whole letter, is to be found in 5:1 with its urgent appeal: "Stand fast, therefore, and do not be burdened again with a yoke of slavery!" The "yoke of slavery" is the law-based gospel being propounded by the new preachers in Galatia (5:2–4). At the conclusion of his series of warnings, Paul tries to counter the preaching of the new preachers with a (fourth) contextualized summary of the gospel, one that arguably summarizes his theology as formulated in this letter: "For we, through the Spirit from faith, are waiting for the hope of justification, for in Christ Jesus neither circumcision avails anything nor uncircumcision, but faith becoming effective through love" (5:5–6).

Before elaborating on the theme of love, Paul digresses briefly to express his exasperation with the formidable opposition in Galatia. The Galatians "were running well" when he left them. The new preachers, however, are not only "proclaiming circumcision" with persuasive effect; they are also making absurd claims about Paul himself, accusing him of proclaiming circumcision as well. As a result, the new preachers have made a significant impact on the Galatians with their "persuasion," one that has put the Galatians in grave danger. If only the new preachers upsetting the Galatians were practicing castration, Paul wishes at the end. They would then not be getting a hearing as they now are with their gospel of circumcision! Paul thus attempts once again to undermine their efforts to persuade the Galatians to adopt the practice of circumcision. Paul is confident "in the Lord" (if not in himself) that the Galatians will ultimately come to see things as they really are (5:7–12, esp. v. 10) and that anyone unnerving the Galatians will ultimately receive condemnation. And that means that Paul himself will be vindicated.

Section V: Galatians 5:13–6:10
Life at the Juncture of the Ages

In this section of the letter, Paul brings together the central themes of the previous two sections. In Section III (3:1–4:7), the unifying theme was the gift of the Spirit as the basis for participation in God's redemptive action in Christ, whereas in Section IV (4:8–5:12) it was the dangers represented by the message of the new preachers concerning the necessity of observing the Mosaic law, beginning with fleshly circumcision (cf. 3:3; 5:2–4; 6:12–13). Paul now makes explicit what these previous sections already presuppose: the current situation of believers is characterized by ongoing strife (5:17) between the given Spirit (mentioned 10 times in this section) and the Flesh (8 times). The latter has been given a capital F because in this passage the Flesh is depicted as a dangerous, malevolent, suprahuman, and cosmic power (Käsemann 1969: 136; 1971: 25–26; Barclay 1988: 198–209; Martyn 483; 1997: 120; Vouga 132; Becker 88–89; Excursus 16, below), against which only the Spirit (capital S) is of any avail. Believers in Christ now live at "the juncture of the ages" (Martyn 1997: 110), the point at which the Spirit of Christ (4:6) comes into conflict with the world of the Flesh. Paul describes what the daily life in the church looks like under these circumstances (Martyn 481), and he exhorts the Galatians accordingly (cf. the imperatives in 5:13, 15, 16, 25, 26; 6:1, 2, 4, 6, 7, 9, 10). The purpose of Section V is not to keep the Galatians from adopting the views of the new preachers, which was the ostensible purpose of Section IV, but to give them guidance for living at the juncture of the ages, where the new creation (6:15) mediated by Christ and his Spirit invades "the present evil age" (1:4). In this evil age, "the Flesh" holds sway and threatens to destroy the beachhead of the new creation represented by the churches of Galatia. The juncture of the ages signifies the end of the law but also an ongoing conflict of the Spirit with the Flesh.

Paul could have gone directly from 5:12 to 6:11. The preceding passage (5:2–12) and the following one (6:11–18, esp. vv. 12–15) have much in common: (1) the urgent, indignant tone, (2) the repeated references to circumcision and the cross, (3) the mention of persecution, (4) the claim that "neither circumcision nor uncircumcision" matters, and (5) the oblique reference to the new preachers as "those who . . .":

> 5:2Look, I, Paul, say to you that if you were to practice circumcision, Christ will avail you nothing. . . . 6For in Christ Jesus neither circumcision avails anything nor uncircumcision, but faith becoming effective through love. . . . 11If I am still proclaiming circumcision, why am I still being persecuted? Then the offense of the cross has been destroyed. 12Would that those who are upsetting you also practice castration.

One can imagine the apostle snatching the pen out of the hand of his secretary at this point and continuing in his own hand, in order to emphasize the points just made:

> 6:11See with what large letters I am writing to you with my [own] hand! 12*Those who* are wanting to make a good showing in the flesh, these are putting pressure on you to *practice circumcision*, only in order that they may not be *persecuted* for *the cross* of Christ. 13For not even *those who practice circumcision* themselves keep the law, but they are wanting you to *practice circumcision* in order that they may boast in your flesh. 14But let it not be for me to boast except in *the cross* of our Lord Jesus Christ. . . . 15For [as I have just indicated] *neither circumcision is anything nor uncircumcision*, but a new creation.

Paul includes the intervening material in 5:13–6:10 for at least three probable and complementary reasons: (1) The freedom brought by Christ is not (yet) an absolute freedom. Believers in Christ have indeed been liberated from the law and its curse, but the law is still there, as is the world of which it is a part and in which it functions (cf. 2:20: "The life I now live in the flesh . . ."). The situation that has developed after Paul's departure from Galatia has made that painfully clear. The freedom of the Christian is constantly under threat and carries risks. Paul wants to help the Galatians deal with the threat and the risks. (2) The new preachers' exhortation to fleshly circumcision and law observance in Galatia demands a counterexhortation. In their proclamation the new preachers are probably emphasizing the value of the law for daily life, as the divinely authorized remedy for what they are referring to as "the desire [*epithymia*] of the flesh" (see comment on 5:16 and Excursus 16, below). In their view, the freedom from the law as proclaimed by Paul means that the Galatians have been left without a moral compass to guide them on their way and without potent protection from "the desire of the flesh" (Ridderbos 199–200). Paul must indicate why and how the gift of Christ's Spirit rather than the law is the divinely given remedy for this (continuing!) problem. (3) The fleshly circumcision being

Life at the Juncture of the Ages 331

recommended by the new preachers is, for Paul, ironically an indication of a greater problem, that of "the Flesh" (*hē sarx*). Paul widens the scope as it were, moving from the particular instance of the fleshly circumcision being demanded by the new preachers to a consideration of "the Flesh" as a cosmic, apocalyptic power, equivalent to and interchangeable with "Sin" (2:17; 3:22; see comments there). For Paul, "the desire of the flesh" is in fact "the desire of *the Flesh*," and against the Flesh the law is powerless (cf. 3:21). Only the Spirit of Christ is sufficient to counter the Flesh's attacks on human life, especially on relations between human beings. The coming of the Spirit has unmasked this power in all its malignancy and at the same time inaugurated a victorious apocalyptic struggle against it. Such an apocalyptic struggle necessarily has cosmic proportions, encompassing all times and places (see Excursus 2).

In Section V, then, Paul casts the human conflict over fleshly circumcision in Galatia, the explicit topic of both the immediately preceding and following passages, as an instance of the cosmic conflict between the Spirit and the Flesh. This widening of the scope gives Paul's exhortations in Section V a generalizing feel. In what way they also pertain to the actual situation in Galatia must be judged in each instance.

The section has two main subsections: 5:13–24 and 5:25–6:10.[458] In the first the focus falls on the lethal threat presented by the Spirit's opponent, "the Flesh." The passage begins and ends with emphatic references to this malevolent power (5:13, 24), and there are four more references to it in the intervening verses (5:16, 17 [2x], 19). Though the passage focuses on the Flesh and its dangers, it also emphasizes that the Spirit, which is mentioned five times (5:16, 17 [2x], 18, 22), is much more powerful than the Flesh and provides protection against it, primarily by producing a love which is discernibly Christlike. In the second subsection, Paul gives some indications of what life at the juncture of the ages looks like in practice, evidently taking as his point of departure some lingering manifestations of the Flesh's malevolent influence on life within the Galatian churches (5:26). The passage begins and ends with positive exhortations that are predicated on the Spirit's effective presence among the Galatians (5:25; 6:10). The five references to the Spirit (5:25 [2x]; 6:1, 8 [2x]) overshadow the two explicit references to the Flesh (both times in 6:8), though it must be added that there are allusions to the Flesh in the references to unacceptable behavior (cf. 5:25; 6:1, 3, 4).

Though the terms "Flesh" and "Spirit" dominate the section, its central theme appears to be love, since that is the Spirit's major remedy for the danger

---

458. Following Barclay 1988: 149; Schlier; Betz; Martyn; Lührmann; Dunn; Becker; Vouga. Other scholars and commentators end the first subsection with 5:26 and begin the second with 6:1 (Burton; Longenecker; Matera; Mussner; Witherington; Schewe 116). Ridderbos and Mussner end the first subsection with 5:25 and begin the second with 5:26. The transition between the two subsections is fluid.

presented by the Flesh. The exhortation that stands at the head of the passage in 5:13 concerns love: "through love be slaves of another" (5:13c). That exhortation appears to be Paul's interpretation and application of Lev 19:18, which is cited in 5:14: "You will love your neighbor as yourself."[459] In 5:22, love occurs first in the list of "the fruit of the Spirit." Love is the fruit of the Spirit par excellence. Paul does not use the term (either as noun or as verb) in the remainder of Section V, but other exhortations appear to presuppose it and to define its meaning further, especially those in 5:16 ("Walk by the Spirit"); 5:25 ("Let us follow the Spirit"), and 6:2 ("Carry one another's burdens").

One of the most curious features of Section V is the way in which Paul brings love into relationship with the law. In the passages prior to 5:13–6:10, Paul has mentioned the Mosaic law many times, with one notable exception (4:21b), always negatively as an oppressive power, from which Christ liberates human beings. In 5:14, however, Paul supports the exhortation to be slaves of another through love with the astonishing claim that "the entire law has been fulfilled in one word, namely, 'You will love your neighbor as yourself,'" which is the quotation from Lev 19:18 mentioned above. In 6:2 he appears to label this scriptural "word" as "the law of Christ"! It is curious, to say the least, that Paul now uses the term "law" in such a positive way at this point in the letter. Is Paul consistent on this point? We return to this difficult question in the commentary below.

5:13–24 Love and the Spirit's Strife against the Flesh

In this passage, Paul's primary concern is to alert the Galatians to the dangers presented by a malevolent power called "the Flesh" (referred to 6 times). In that sense this passage is an extension of the previous material (4:8–5:12), in which Paul has highlighted the dangers confronting the Galatians from the message of the new preachers in Galatia. He does not now, however, refer to the new preachers, but to "the Flesh," a cosmic force that transcends the specifics of the conflict in Galatia (see Excursus 16, below). Paul gives the Galatians clues to help them recognize its presence in their communal and personal affairs (vv. 19–21). At the same time, he tells them that they do not have to face this malevolent power alone and unaided. Having been freed from the law, they now have the Spirit (vv. 16–18). This claim was already the central point of Section III (3:1–4:7), but the ethical implications now come to the fore. The Spirit manifests its presence in numerous ways (vv. 22–23), but primarily in the Christlike love that believers have for one another (vv. 13–14, 22). That love is the Spirit's primary weapon in its strife against the Flesh.

---

459. For this translation of Lev 19:18 in Gal 5:14, see the comment on 5:14 below and Excursus 17 where I argue that Paul understands Lev 19:18 to be a promise ("You *will* love ...") that has now been fulfilled rather than a command ("You *shall* love ...) that has to be carried out or obeyed.

The passage has four discernible parts. The first (vv. 13-15) warns the Galatians about a malevolent power called the Flesh. The Galatians are free, it is true, but they must not allow this freedom to be exploited and misused by the Flesh. The power of the Flesh is thwarted by mutual love, which represents the fulfillment of "the entire law." The second part of the passage (vv. 16-18) describes the world as it is after the coming of Christ and his Spirit. It is a world in which the Spirit has entered into strife with the Flesh in order to enable human beings to withstand its destructive power. The third part contains an illustrative list of "works of the Flesh" and concludes with the warning that "those who practice such things will not inherit the kingdom of God" (vv. 19-21). The fourth part presents "the fruit of the Spirit" and ends with the striking declaration that "those who belong to Christ Jesus have crucified the Flesh with its passions and desires" (vv. 22-24). The concluding verse forms an inclusio with v. 13 and its initial warning about the danger of the Flesh.

5:13 For you were called into freedom, brethren. Only do not turn this freedom into an opportunity for the Flesh, but through love[a] be slaves of one another. (14 For the entire law has been fulfilled[b] in one word,[c] namely, 'You will love your neighbor as yourself'). 15 But if you bite and tear at each other, see to it that you are not consumed by one another.

16 But I say, walk by the Spirit, and you will *not* carry out the desire of the Flesh. 17 For the Flesh desires against the Spirit, and the Spirit against the Flesh, for these are opposed to one another, so that you do not do these things that you may want. 18 And if you are led by the Spirit, you are not under the law.

19 Now the works of the Flesh are plain, which are sexual immorality, impurity, licentiousness, 20 idolatry, sorcery, hostile actions, strife, jealousy, outbursts of anger, selfish actions, dissensions, factions, 21 acts of envy, bouts of drunkenness, drinking parties,[d] and things like these, about which I say to you in advance, just as I have said before: those who practice such things will not inherit the kingdom of God.

22 But the fruit of the Spirit is love, joy, peace, patience, kindness, goodness, faithfulness, 23 humility, self-control.[e] Against such things there is no law. 24 Those who belong to Christ Jesus[f] have crucified the Flesh with its passions and desires.

a. Some manuscripts read "by the love of the Spirit" (D, F, G, 104, et al.), probably under the influence of 5:22 and Rom 15:30.

b. Some manuscripts read "is fulfilled" (*plēroutai*; D, F, G, Ψ, 0122, 1881, et al.).

c. Marcion's text reads "has been fulfilled *among you*," while Western manuscripts (D*, F, G, ar, b) read "has been fulfilled in one word *among you*." These are attempts to make Paul's line of thought explicit.

d. Some, primarily Western, manuscripts add "adultery" (*moicheia*) at the beginning of the list (in v. 19) and "murders" (*phonoi*) toward the end (cf. v. 21 KJV). These readings were probably added by scribes under the influence of Rom 1:29; Matt 15:19; and Mark 7:21–22. The best manuscripts ($\mathfrak{P}^{46}$, B, 33, 81) do not have them (Metzger 529).

e. Western manuscripts (D*, F, G, it, vg^{cl}) add "purity" (*agneia*).

f. The manuscript evidence for the inclusion or the omission of *Iēsou* ("Jesus") is evenly divided (Metzger 529).

[13–15] In 5:12, Paul has polemically and rhetorically equated the circumcision recommended by the new preachers in Galatia with ritual castration, a religious practice that the Galatians will recognize as part of their religious, cultural environment (see comment on 5:12). Paul has thereby implied that if the Galatians were to adopt the practice of circumcision they would be returning to the world of religious beliefs and practices that they had left behind after becoming believers in Christ (cf. 4:8–10). He has counted on their finding such a prospect unacceptable and repulsive. For that reason, in v. 13a he can remind the Galatians of the "freedom [from the law]" for which "Christ has set us free," about which he has written in 5:1a: Circumcision is no option (the point of 5:12), "for [*gar*; as Paul now reminds them in v. 13a] you were called [by God] into [*epi*] [the realm of] freedom [from the law], brethren." The initial "you" (*hymeis*) is emphatic in Greek, serving to remind the Galatians of their new status: "For *you* were called into freedom, brethren." The preposition *epi* here appears to be equivalent to *eis*, "into" (cf. 1 Thess 4:7; BDF #235.4).[460] If so, freedom is being conceptualized as the realm into which believers "have been called" (*eklēthēte*, aorist of the verb *kaleō*). Paul has used the verb "call" earlier, in phrases that function as circumlocutions for God: "the one who called you" (1:6), "the one who called me" (1:15), and "the one who calls you" (5:8). Paul now uses a passive form with God as the implied subject of the action. As in the previous instances, the verb as used in v. 13a implies more than simply a verbal invitation or summons (see comment on 1:6). Through the liberating work of Christ (cf. 5:1), God's call involves the transfer of the Galatians into the sphere of freedom: they "were called *into* [*epi*] freedom." The freedom in view is specifically "the freedom which we have in Christ Jesus" (2:4), especially freedom from the Mosaic law (cf. 5:2–4).

Verse 13a, writes Burton (291), is "an epitome of the whole preceding argument of the epistle on behalf of the freedom" of the believer, but it also functions "to introduce a wholly new aspect of the matter." That new aspect is signaled by the word "only" (*monon*), with which the following clause begins:

---

460. The translation "with a view to" (Betz) is probably too weak, for it implies choice where there is none. The Galatians do not choose between the Flesh and the Spirit. They already have the Spirit and are told to be on guard against the Flesh.

"Only [do] not [turn] this[461] freedom into [*eis*] an opportunity [*aphormē*] for the Flesh" (v. 13b). As in 2:10, where *monon* is also used to start a clause, Paul omits a verb; it must be mentally supplied. Various possibilities have been proposed (see Burton 292; cf. KJV, NRSV, NIV: "use"). Of these the most likely is the verb *trepō* ("turn"), which can be followed by a prepositional phrase beginning with *eis* (BDAG 1014; *Mart. Pol.* 2.4, where a tyrant seeks through torture to "turn" believers "into [*eis*] denial"). The sense of this negative exhortation is probably that the Galatians must be on their guard for the malevolent and destructive power Paul has dubbed "the Flesh."

The term *aphormē* originally referred to "a base or circumstance from which other action becomes possible, such as the starting point or base of operations for an expedition" (BDAG 158), as in the works of Thucydides and Polybius (Burton 292–93); by extension it came to have a more general meaning of "occasion, opportunity" (BDAG 158), already in the works of Xenophon and others (Burton 292). Paul appears to use the term with this meaning in Rom 7:8; 2 Cor 5:12; 11:12 (cf. 1 Tim 5:14). The military connotations of the term need not, however, be neglected (Martyn 485), especially given Paul's depiction of the warfare between the Spirit and the Flesh in vv. 16–18 (see comment below). Freedom is an "opportunity" for "the Flesh" in the sense that, at the present juncture in the drama of salvation inaugurated by Christ, freedom from the law can be used as a staging area for the Flesh's pernicious assaults on believers.

Paul does not here pause to explain what it is about "the Flesh" that is so dangerous. He will do that in v. 16, where he will write of "the desire [*epithymia*] of the Flesh," which concerns the Evil Inclination or Impulse known from Jewish thought (see Excursus 16, below). The "desire of the Flesh" lies behind the pernicious "works of the Flesh" that Paul will list in vv. 19–21. In this verse, as elsewhere in this passage, "the Flesh" appears to be shorthand for "the [destructive] desire of the Flesh." The problem with "the Flesh" is that it has a "desire" that causes or produces "works" that have a destructive, malignant impact on human affairs (cf. v. 15 below). By introducing "the Flesh" as a specific topic, Paul is here probably responding to the (actual or anticipated) charge that his insistence on freedom from the law has created a moral vacuum in the lives of the new Gentile believers in Galatia, leaving them completely vulnerable to the Evil Inclination (see comments on vv. 14 and 16 below).

Excursus 16: The Flesh as a Cosmic Power

Paul has already used the term *sarx* ("flesh") several times earlier in the letter (1:16; 2:16, 20; 4:13–14) to say something about the universal human condition. As we saw in

---

461. Lit., "the freedom." The definite article is here being used anaphorically, to refer back to the mention of "freedom" in the first half of the verse. Hence, the translation "this freedom."

the comment on 2:20b, "flesh" primarily denotes the substance (containing blood) that covers a human being's bones (BDAG 914) and represents the material substratum of all human existence at the present time (cf. Paul's reference to "my flesh" in 4:14). For this reason, human beings in their totality can be characterized as "flesh and blood" (1:16; cf. 1 Cor 15:50) or as "all flesh" (2:16), whereby they are implicitly distinguished from God. As fleshly creatures, human beings are vulnerable to disease (cf. 4:13: "an infirmity of the flesh"). This is the sphere "in" (*en*) which all human beings live (2:20b), whether they be believers in Christ or not. In none of these passages does "flesh" necessarily have a negative connotation. In 2:20b, however, Paul has indicated that the life that he like everyone else now lives "in the flesh," he like fellow believers in Christ also lives "in faith, [namely,] that of the Son of God." Something has changed: God has invaded the human sphere of the flesh with Christ and his Spirit (cf. 3:1–5; 4:4–7) and somehow qualified it, thereby implicitly casting life "in the flesh" apart from Christ in a new and not necessarily positive light.

In three subsequent passages, moreover, Paul has gone on to *contrast* "the flesh" with "the Spirit" explicitly (cf. Rom 1:3–4; 2:28–29; 1 Cor 5:5; 2 Cor 7:1; Phil 3:3–4; Col 2:5; 1 Tim 3:16), in this way anticipating the antinomy present in the current passage. In 3:3 he has implied that the Spirit and the flesh are mutually exclusive realms, for he has there asked the Galatians, "Having begun with the Spirit, are you now ending up with the flesh?" (cf. Rom 2:28–29; Phil 3:3–4). The question was evidently prompted by the Galatians' desire to become observers of the law, beginning with cutting away the flesh of the foreskin in the rite of circumcision (see comment on 3:3). "Flesh" in 3:3 stands for circumcision and by extension for the remaining "works of the law" (3:2, 5). Paul will use the term "flesh" (*sarx*) explicitly in connection with the rite of circumcision in 6:12–13: "those who are wanting to make a good showing in the flesh . . . are putting pressure on you to practice circumcision. . . . They are wanting you to practice circumcision, in order that they may boast in your [circumcised] flesh." The use of the term in connection with circumcision goes back to Gen 17:10–11, 13 LXX: "Every male of you shall be circumcised. And you shall be circumcised in the *flesh* of your foreskin, and it shall be a sign of a covenant between me and you. . . . And my covenant shall be upon your *flesh* for an everlasting covenant" (cf. LXX: Gen 34:24; Jer 9:26; Sir 44:20; Eph 2:11; Col 2:11, 13). The Galatians will surely have caught the allusion to circumcision upon hearing the reference to "the flesh" in 3:3 (cf. 5:2–3; 6:12–13). The contrast between the flesh and the Spirit took a somewhat different turn in 4:21–5:1, where Paul has contrasted the covenant of Sinai with the covenant of promise (cf. 4:24b–25). He asserted there that Ishmael, the son of Hagar, was begotten "according to the flesh" (4:23, 29), meaning by natural procreative means, whereas Isaac, the son of Sarah, was begotten "according to the Spirit" (4:29), meaning "through [God's] promise" (4:23; cf. 3:14, 18). The meaning of the term "flesh" here is not different from the one found in 2:20, but again by virtue of the contrast with the Spirit and the argumentative context (the polemic against the Sinaitic covenant as a form of slavery), it acquires a negative connotation. That negative connotation has been driven home in 4:29, where Paul has claimed that just as the one begotten "according to the flesh" (Ishmael) "persecuted" the one begotten "according to the Spirit" (Isaac), "so also now"—so also now in Galatia the new preachers with their insistence on the fleshly rite of circumcision and law observance are in some sense persecuting the Gentile believers in Galatia who have received the Spirit (see comment on 4:29). By the time the Galatians will hear 5:13, existence that is oriented to the flesh, which is equivalent to existence that takes its bearings from circumcision and the law, has already been established as a significant problem.

With his personification of the Flesh as a powerful and malevolent actor on the stage of human history in 5:13–6:10, Paul goes a step further. As Martyn (483) writes: "This actor is not a mere component of the human being, a person's flesh as distinguished from his spirit. The Flesh is rather a supra-human power, indeed an inimical, martial power seeking to establish a military base of operations in the Galatian churches, with the intention of destroying them as genuine communities (5:13, 19–21)." Why Paul has taken this remarkable step probably has something to do with the polemical context.

A clue to that context is to be found in 5:16, where Paul refers to "the desire of the Flesh" (*epithymia sarkos*). The simple term "the Flesh" is probably an abbreviation of this expression (Martyn 485). The expression seems to reflect the notion of the Evil Inclination or Impulse (*yetser hara* [= *yēṣer hāraʿ*]) found in Jewish tradition (Martyn 485, 492–93; cf. Marcus 1982; 1986; Urbach 471–83). It has its origins in Gen 6:5 ("every *yēṣer* of the thoughts of his heart was only evil") and 8:21 ("the *yēṣer* of the human heart is evil from youth"; LXX: *dianoia*). The notion of an expressly evil impulse is first clearly attested in Sir 15:14 according to which God "created humankind from the beginning and left them in the power of their own inclination [*yēṣer*; Gk. *diaboulion*]" (AT). This "inclination," which manifestly refers to the human will as capable of making a free choice between good and evil, is, practically speaking, the propensity to make the wrong choice, to sin (cf. Sir 17:31; 25:24; 27:5–6): a propensity that is thwarted by committing oneself to the observance of the law (Sir 21:11: "Whoever keeps the Law controls his thoughts"). Similar views occur in the Dead Sea Scrolls. According to 1QS 5.4–6, "No one should walk in the stubbornness of his heart in order to go astray following his heart and his eyes and the musings of his inclination [*yēṣer*]. Instead he should circumcise in the Community the foreskin of his inclination [*yēṣer*] and of his stiff neck in order to lay a foundation of truth for Israel, for the Community of the eternal covenant." Here the *yēṣer* is metaphorically identified with the foreskin, suggesting that literal circumcision of the fleshy foreskin is a cutting away of the fleshly inclination to do evil (cf. Philo, *Migr*. 92). This is a vivid way of saying that the law (beginning with circumcision) is the remedy for the Evil Inclination, a notion also found in later rabbinic texts, e.g., *Sipre Deut*. #45: "Thus the Holy One, blessed be He, said to Israel: 'My children, I have created for you the Evil Inclination, (but I have at the same time) created for you the Torah as an antidote. As long as you occupy yourselves with the Torah, he shall not have dominion over you" (cited from Urbach 472).

An exact linguistic parallel to the expression Paul uses occurs in 1QH 18.22–23. In this fragmentary and ambiguous passage, the hymnist thanks God with the following words: "Because you have fashioned the sp[irit of your servant and in accordance with] your [wi]ll you have established me. You have not placed my support in robbery, nor in wealth [. . .] my [hea]rt, nor have you placed the inclination of the flesh [*yēṣer bāśār*] as my refuge." The notion of the inclination as "of the flesh" may lie behind the passages cited above in which "flesh" is referred to negatively (1QS 4.19–21; 11.9–10). The reference to "the sin of the flesh" in 1QS 11.12 points in the same direction. It is in this light that the writer of 1QS 11.9–10 can exclaim: "I belong to evil humankind, to *the assembly of unfaithful flesh*; my failings, my iniquities, my sin, . . . with the depravities of my heart belong to the assembly of worms and of those who walk in darkness." What makes human existence problematic is the inclination (*yēṣer*) to evil lodged in "the flesh," a term that in other respects designates "what is merely human" (Barclay 1988: 209; cf. Schewe 94).

That this notion of the Evil Inclination was also known in Jewish Christianity is indicated by the Epistle of James, which uses the term *epithymia*, as Paul does, to designate the Evil Inclination: "Each person is tempted when lured by one's own *epithymia*. Then the *epithymia* when it has conceived gives birth to sin; and sin when it is full-grown brings forth death" (Jas 1:14–15 RSV, alt.). For the Jewish Christian author of James, the solution to this problem is the law: "But the one who looks into the perfect law, the law of freedom, and perseveres, being not a hearer who forgets but a doer who acts, that person will be blessed in their observance [*poiēsis*] [of the law]" (Jas 1:25 AT). On the basis of this and other evidence, Martyn (492) understandably concludes that "Paul is almost certainly following a locution" being used by the new preachers in Galatia "to refer to the Evil Impulse." As Martyn also observes, however, Paul goes further than the new preachers "in that, instead of speaking of an entity that is merely internal to the individual human being, Paul refers to a cosmic power arrayed against God. . . . Seeing the Evil Impulse in its apocalyptic frame, Paul considers it neither a dictator whose power is so great as to relieve the human being of all responsibility nor a mere inclination that can be easily resisted" (Martyn 492–93).

Paul's personification of the Flesh appears to be without parallel, though there is evidence linking the Evil Inclination to the rule of Belial or Satan. In *Testament of Asher* 1.8, when the "soul" gives in to the "inclination" (*diaboulion*) to do evil, it is effectively ruled "by Beliar." Similarly, in 1QH 15.3, "Belial is present [in the activity of the wicked] when their destructive inclination [*yēṣer*] becomes apparent." This correlation of the Evil Inclination with Satan is also found in the rabbinic literature. According to E. Urbach (472), "Rabbinic teaching did to some extent personify 'the Evil Inclination,' to whom were ascribed attributes, aims, and forms of activity that direct man, even before he was explicitly identified, as by the Amora Resh Laqish, with Satan and the Angel of Death."

The personification of the Evil Inclination, and its occasional identification with Satan, reflect the experience of a powerful force in human affairs, one not capable of being brought under control without divine assistance. The explicit rejection or sharp qualification of such personification and identification of the Evil Impulse is a mark of the "forensic" pattern of Jewish apocalyptic eschatology (for the difference between "forensic" and "cosmological" apocalyptic eschatology, see Excursus 2). The emphasis on personal choice and accountability found in this pattern of Jewish apocalyptic eschatology is well articulated by certain passages from Sirach[462]: God "created humankind in the beginning, and he left them in the power of their own inclination. If you choose, you can keep the commandments, and to act faithfully is a matter of your own choice" (Sir

---

462. Sirach is not an apocalyptic work (the dualism of the two ages characteristic of apocalyptic eschatology does not occur), but it articulates certain views that are (1) compatible with the forensic pattern of Jewish apocalyptic eschatology and (2) antagonistic to the cosmological pattern.

Life at the Juncture of the Ages 339

15:14–15, alt.; cf. *Pss. Sol.* 9.4–5). According to Sir 21:27 (LXX), evidently polemicizing against the cosmological pattern of Jewish apocalyptic eschatology, "When an ungodly person curses Satan, he is actually cursing himself"! You cannot claim that Satan made you do it. The new preachers understand the Evil Inclination in a similar way, but then within the framework of forensic Jewish apocalyptic eschatology, with its dualism of the two ages (see Excursus 4). In the apocalypse of *4 Ezra*, which dates from the late first century and is the major representative of this pattern of Jewish apocalyptic eschatology, evil cosmological powers are completely absent. The problem facing humanity is the Evil Inclination, variously referred to as "the evil thought" (7.92), "the evil heart" (3.21, 26; 4.4; 7.48), "the evil root" (3.22), and "the grain of evil seed" (4.30–31). Human existence is a constant struggle with this troublesome reality, one for which devotion to the law provides the God-given solution. *Fourth Ezra* claims that the righteous who have kept the law "perfectly" shall "see with great joy the glory of him who receives them . . . because they have striven with great effort to overcome the evil thought that was formed in them" (7.88–92; cf. 7.127–129). According to *4 Ezra* (2 Esd) 8.53–54, the End will signify not only that "sorrows have passed away" and that "the treasure of immortality is made manifest," but also that "the root of evil is sealed up from you." In the new age, there will be no more strife with the Evil Inclination because it will have been "sealed up."

Paul, however, as we have seen above, understands the notion of the Evil Inclination within a cosmological-apocalyptic framework, causing him to personify it as a dangerous cosmic power akin to Satan. The desire of "the flesh" (Gal 5:16) is for him the desire of "the Flesh." Whenever Paul refers simply to "the Flesh," he has this "desire" in view (see further the comment on 5:16 below). The powerful Spirit of Christ, not the law, is for Paul the God-given solution for this aggressive, malevolent force in human affairs. The fact that Paul refers to the Flesh rather than to Satan in this context is important: It shows that Paul is not interested in cosmological speculation for its own sake and, more important, that cosmological claims about malevolent powers destructive of human life represent attempts to account for anthropological realities and experiences (Käsemann 1971: 27; de Boer 1988: 179) in light of the apocalyptic revelation of Christ (see Excursus 6).

Before turning to instruction about the Flesh (cf. Gal 5:15–21), however, Paul first provides the Galatians with the alternative to letting their freedom turn into an opportunity for the Flesh: "*But [alla]* through love be slaves of one another" (v. 13c). This is the most significant exhortation of Section V. Paul's subsequent exhortations to "walk by the Spirit" in v. 16 and to "follow the Spirit" in v. 25 (and others in 6:1–10) are simply variations of this initial exhortation in v. 13c (see comments below). Here Paul anticipates what in v. 22 he will declare to be the Spirit's first and foremost fruit: love (see comment there).[463] Though free from the law, the believers addressed in this passage are not autonomous human beings but human beings who have received, and are

---

463. Some scribes anticipated v. 22 by changing Paul's text here to read "by the love of the Spirit." See textual note above.

continually given, Christ's Spirit (cf. 3:2, 5, 14, 22; 4:6–7). Paul addresses the Galatians as recipients and beneficiaries of the Spirit (explicitly in v. 16, and then again in v. 25). It is as such that he also exhorts them to mutual love in v. 13c. This mutual love prevents the freedom from the law from turning into an opportunity for the Flesh. The free space created by Christ and his Spirit has to be filled with mutual love if (the desire of) the Flesh is to be kept at bay.

The formulation of the exhortation in v. 13c is noteworthy. Given the quotation from Lev 19:18 in v. 14 ("You will love your neighbor as yourself"), Paul could here simply have written: "but love another [*alla agapate allēlous*]" (cf. 1 Thess 4:9; John 13:34; 15:12), or "but love the brethren" (cf. 1 John 3:10, 14). Instead he writes, interpreting Lev 19:18 for the Galatian situation, "But through love be slaves [*douleuete*] of one another [*allēlois*]" (cf. NRSV: "become slaves to one another"). The common translations "serve one another" (KJV, NIV, NAB) and "be servants of/to one another" (RSV, NJB; Burton), though not wrong, tend to weaken the sense and the offense of Paul's choice of words; they also obscure the paradox of being a slave in freedom. Paul uses not the verb *diakoneō* ("serve," "be a servant") but the verb *douleuō*, which means "to serve *as a slave.*" The present imperative implies an ongoing activity. The sense is probably both that believers are to go on serving one another as slaves and that they are to make a habit of doing so. The phrase "through love" (*dia tēs agapēs*) has already been used in 5:6 (though there without the definite article). As there, the love in view here may in the first instance be that of Christ (cf. 2:20), though the love that believers are to have for another in Christ is also involved (see comment on 5:6), especially given the appeal to Lev 19:18 in v. 14 and the characterization of (human) love as the fruit of the Spirit in v. 22. For Paul, the love that believers have for one another is evidently a form of participation in the antecedent love of Christ. That would then also explain why this love finds its expression and its definition in "being slaves of one another": Love for one another has a christological basis, in Christ himself "having taken the form of slave" (Phil 2:7 AT) or, as Paul puts in Galatians, in the fact that God's Son was "born of a woman" and "existed under the law," thereby sharing the human condition of being "enslaved under the elements of the world" (4:3–5; cf. 3:13). Christ shared the human condition of enslavement to the extreme of a death on a cross (3:13; cf. Phil 2:8), and he did so for the benefit of others, or as Paul has written earlier in this letter, "so that he might redeem those under the law, so that we might receive adoption as sons" (4:5), or back in chapter 3, "so that the blessing of Abraham might come to the Gentiles in Christ Jesus, so that we might receive the promise of the Spirit through faith" (3:14). The "faith" here referred to is that "of the Son of God, the one who loved me [*tou agapēsantos me*] and [*kai*] gave himself up for me [*paradontos heauton hyper emou*]" (2:20). As we indicated in the comment on 2:20, the second participial phrase ("gave himself up for") is probably explanatory of the first ("loved me"). Christ's love is not so much a disposition as a concrete act. That love finds its visible form in his sharing of the human condition as a slave of alien, malevolent forces for the benefit of others. By being slaves of one another (v. 13c), believers become participants in the sacrificial love of Christ for them in that they share or identify with the condition of those whom they love. Love is a form of solidarity with the one loved. In this passage, Paul has specifically in view only the love of believers for one another, not the love of believers for those outside the community of faith (see further on 6:10).[464]

The formulation "Be slaves of one another" will undoubtedly be shocking and paradoxical for the Galatians, especially in light of Paul's use of the same verb and its cognates back in 4:1–11. In 4:7 Paul has declared that the believer in Christ is "no longer a slave [*doulos*], but a son, and . . . an heir" (cf. 3:28). In 4:8–11 he has pointed out to the Galatians that they had once been "slaves [*edouleusate*] of beings not gods by nature." Since coming to know God, or rather to "be known by God" through Christ, they are no longer slaves of such putative gods. In this light they should not, he has argued, want "once more to be slaves [*douleuein*]" of "the elements" (*ta stoicheia*; cf. 4:3), as they evidently want to be by "observing days and months and seasons and years." The assumption shared between Paul and the Galatians behind this argument was that to be a slave of anyone or anything is a completely undesirable condition (see comment on 4:8–11). That is also the shared assumption behind the exhortation in 5:1b to stand fast and not be burdened again with "a yoke of slavery," that yoke being the law (5:2–4). Paul has prepared the way for the new, paradoxical usage in 5:13c with the characterization of himself as "a slave of Christ" back in 1:10. The freedom of the believer paradoxically entails a form of slavery, but the slavery in view is mutual and motivated by love (the well-being of the other). In this mutual slavery of love, it is impossible for one party to lord it over the other in the church or, alternatively, for one party to be the doormat of the other. As in the case of Christ's own love (2:20), the love in view is not so much a disposition or attitude as one or more concrete acts for the benefit, or well-being, of the other.

Paul goes on to buttress his exhortation in v. 13c with an appeal to Lev 19:18 in v. 14: "For the entire Law has been fulfilled in one word, namely, 'You will love your neighbor as yourself.'" As the conjunction "for" (*gar*) indicates, the exhortation of v. 13c probably constitutes Paul's interpretation and application of Lev 19:18 to the Galatian situation before he has cited it in support. That explains why v. 14 appears to interrupt the flow of Paul's argument about the dangers of the Flesh (v. 13b–c), which continues in v. 15: "Only do not turn

---

464. That observation must not lead to the dubious conclusion that, for Paul, love does not need to be extended to those outside the community of faith. Paul's own missionary activity proves the contrary.

this freedom into an opportunity for the Flesh, but through love be slaves of one another.... But if you bite and tear at each other, see to it that you are not consumed by one another."

Verse 14 may thus be considered a parenthesis. This parenthesis has been prompted by the activity of the new preachers active in Galatia and their emphasis on "the law." What makes v. 14 extraordinary is its surprisingly positive appeal to "the law." For this reason, "the law" in v. 14 is probably not the Mosaic legislation (as in every previous use of the term except for 4:21b) but (as in 4:21b) "the Scripture" (3:8, 22; 4:30; see Excursus 17, below, where the interpretation here presented is extensively justified). As in 4:21b, Paul probably has particularly the Pentateuch in view (cf. Rom 3:21: "the law and the prophets"; 1 Cor 9:8–9), though he may also be thinking of the whole of Jewish Scripture (cf. 1 Cor 14:21; Rom 3:19; Matt 5:18; Luke 10:26; 16:17; John 7:49; 10:34; 12:34; 15:25). The scriptural law preserves not only the Mosaic code ("the law" in the legal sense of the term) but also, and what is more important for Paul, contains divine "promises" (3:16, 21) concerning the coming (3:19, 23, 25) of Christ and his Spirit (3:14; 4:6). Specifically in view are the promises God made to Abraham in the Pentateuch (the scriptural law in its narrower and proper sense): the promise of land (Gen 17:8; cf. 12:7; 13:14–17; 15:7, 18–20; 24:7), that of a son and heir (17:15–22; cf. 15:2–4; 18:9–15), and that of many descendants (Gen 17:1–7; cf. 12:2, quoted in Gal 3:8; Gen 15:6, quoted in Gal 3:6; cf. Gen 18:18; 22:17). For Paul, as for the new preachers in Galatia, the Spirit rather than the land constitutes the promised inheritance (3:8, 14; cf. 3:29; 4:1, 7, 30).[465] Furthermore, this one fundamental "promise of the Spirit" (3:14) incorporates the other two, that Abraham would have a son and heir, and that he would through that son and heir become the father of many descendants (Gen 15:4–5; 17:15–22; cf. 28:14; cf. Gal 4:28). For Paul, the latter two promises find their fulfillment not in the historical, law-observant people of Israel (as for the new preachers in Galatia) but (only) in Christ and in those who belong to him on the basis of faith (see on 3:6–9, 29; 4:27; cf. Rom 4:16–18). Since the promises made to Abraham (3:16) actually all concern Christ and his Spirit, they can be spoken of as *one* promise (3:14, 17–18, 19, 22, 29; 4:23, 28). In Paul's view, the love for one another that results among those who have come to believe in Christ (5:13c–14; cf. 5:6) is also evidently another aspect of one and the same eschatological promise, or rather, of its fulfillment: the Spirit is Christ's, and this Spirit brings forth love as its singular fruit (v. 22; see comment there). In short, Paul cites Lev 19:18 not as a commandment of the Mosaic legal code ("You *shall* love your neighbor as yourself") but as a promise of the scriptural law ("You *will* love your neighbor as yourself"), one that has now found its fulfillment in Christ.

---

465. See n. 323 in the comment on 3:18, and on 5:21b below.

Life at the Juncture of the Ages 343

Excursus 17: The Fulfillment of the Law

Paul has used the term "law" (*nomos*) twenty-seven times earlier in Galatians (Gal 2:16 [3x], 19 [2x], 21; 3:2, 5, 10 [2x], 11, 12, 13, 17, 18, 19, 21 [3x], 23, 24; 4:4, 5, 21 [2x]; 5:3, 4). With the exception of 4:21b (where, in a play on words, it refers to the first five books of Jewish Scripture), the term always refers to the Mosaic legislation of commandments and prohibitions as preserved in the Pentateuch.[466] The term also has a persistently negative connotation, particularly noticeable in such phrases as "the curse of the law" (3:13) and "under the law" (3:23; 4:4–5, 21a), a phrase that Paul will use again in 5:18. In v. 23 he will clearly use the term "law" to mean a legal regulation of some sort, again with a negative connotation. Given this pattern of usage, which is understandable in a letter that is seeking to prevent its readers from adopting observance of the Mosaic law, it seems strange that Paul would cite one of the law's seeming commandments positively to support and clarify the admonition that believers in Christ are to be slaves of another through love (cf. John 13:34, where Jesus calls the admonition to love one another "a *new* commandment" rather than an existing one). A partial explanation is that the *content* of Lev 19:18 (loving the neighbor) suits Paul's hortatory agenda very well, but that fact still does not explain why he would present it as the "one word" in which "the entire law has been fulfilled." There are, then, three main issues in the interpretation of v. 14: (1) the precise reference of the phrase "the entire law," (2) the import of the verb "to fulfill," and (3) Paul's use and interpretation of Lev 19:18.

Issue 1: The reference of the phrase "the entire law." A comparison with Gal 5:3 is instructive. In the latter, Paul presents the prospect of being obligated "to do [observe] the whole law" as the thoroughly disastrous consequence of adopting the practice of circumcision. In v. 14, by contrast, he regards loving one another as the very fulfillment of "the entire law." In short:

5:3   Undesirable situation: observance of the whole law
5:14 Desirable situation: fulfillment of the entire law

There is no detectable linguistic difference between "the whole law" (*holos ho nomos*) and "the entire law" (*ho pas nomos*), leading most commentators to conclude that in v. 14, as in v. 3, Paul is referring to the totality of the commandments and prohibitions of the Mosaic legislation (cf. Barclay 1988: 137), with Lev 19:18 giving its "essence" (Tolmie 2005: 195; cf. Betz 276). This line of interpretation finds support in the many previous uses of the term *nomos* in Galatians to refer to the Mosaic law (see above). Further support can then perhaps be found in Rom 8:4 (". . . that the just requirement of the law might be fulfilled in us") and 13:8–10, where Paul quotes Lev 19:18 again and it is understood to be a commandment:

Owe no one anything except to love one another, for the one who loves the other has fulfilled the law. For [the commandments of the Decalogue] "You shall not commit adultery," "You shall not kill," "You shall not steal," "You shall not

---

466. The occurrences in 3:18 and 21b may be references to law in general, though the context demonstrates that the Mosaic code is indirectly in view. In any case the term is used to signify a legal code or regulation in these two verses.

covet," and if there is any other commandment [of the Decalogue and/or the law], are summed up in this word: "You *shall* love your neighbor as yourself." ... Love is therefore the fulfillment [*plērōma*] of the law. (AT)

Following this line of interpretation, Paul presumably wants to say in v. 14: "The just requirement of the entire Mosaic code has been fulfilled among you whenever the commandment found in Lev 19:18 has been put into practice or is observed" (cf. Lightfoot 209; Sanders 1983: 97).

A difficulty with this interpretation, however, is that whereas the construction "the whole law" in 5:3 has a thoroughly negative connotation, the construction "the entire law" in v. 14 has, in its immediate context, a discernibly positive one. If Paul is now suddenly giving "the (Mosaic) law" a positive appraisal, he is also undermining his whole argument to this point. That is not impossible, but it is rather implausible. Another option, and the one here given preference, is to take the formulation "the entire law" to be an indication that Paul is not now referring to the Mosaic legal code at all, as he was in 5:3 with the formulation "the whole law" (cf. Matt 22:40), but to the Scripture (cf. 3:8, 22; 4:30). He has already so used the term "law" in 4:21b (see comment there). The scriptural "law" is something quite positive for Paul, since it not only preserves the Mosaic legislation (a fact of crucial importance for the new preachers in Galatia), but also contains (and this is as important for Paul as for the new preachers) divine promises (3:16, 21), which together can be regarded as *one* promise concerning the coming of Christ and his Spirit (3:14, 17–18, 19, 22, 29; 4:23, 28). That one promise evidently includes the love of one another, apart from which the promise of Christ and his Spirit has no relevance for human life. Paul then means to say in v. 14: "All that God promised in the Scripture has been fulfilled in the fulfillment of the *one* word of Lev 19:18"—and thus, in Paul's view, *apart* from observance of any of the commandments of the Mosaic law (cf. Gal 2:16; 3:1–14). Paul has chosen the word "law" instead of the word "Scripture" here for the same reasons he did in 4:21b: It is a play on words that allows him to refer to the promissory Scripture as "the law" in a situation in which that term, and the scriptural witness to God's promises itself, has become totally identified with the Mosaic code. For the new preachers, the law as Scripture and the law as legal code are one and the same. Paul's repeatedly negative use of the term "law" in the previous argument has run the risk of reinforcing this virtual identification of the scriptural witness to God's promises with the Mosaic code, thereby playing into the hands of his opponents in Galatia. Paul rescues the term from this understandable and traditional identification for his own reading of the scriptural witness, bringing about a distinction, even a bifurcation, between the law as legal code and the law as divine promise.[467] For Paul, these are two

---

[467]. Martyn makes a distinction between "the two voices of the Law," one being "the enslaving voice of the Sinaitic Law" with its many commandments and the other being the promissory voice of "the Abrahamic Law," which "does not consist of commandments at all." He labels the latter "the original, pre-Sinaitic Law that articulates God's own mind" through the medium of Scripture (cf. 558: "the scriptural Law"). Whereas the first voice is "false and cursing," the second is "true and promising" (505–8). The problem with this particular interpretation (one that Martyn [511] seems to sense) is that Lev 19:18 is not pre-Sinaitic; it is difficult to think that Paul is claiming it to be such. It seems, therefore, preferable to speak of one term (*nomos*) being used with two distinct

different laws (corresponding to the two different and opposing covenants of 4:24). In the process of making this distinction, Paul meets the pointed objection from the new preachers that the abandonment of the Mosaic law has effectively left the Galatian churches morally rudderless. For Paul, however, the fulfillment of the law as Scripture containing divine promises has profound moral implications.

This interpretation of the referential meaning of the phrase "the entire law" is perhaps not easily supported by the texts from Romans cited above. Galatians 5:14, however, must be interpreted on its own terms, as part of that letter. In Galatians, in contrast to Rom 13:8–10, Paul avoids the term "commandment" and does not characterize Lev 19:18 as "summing up" the law. Furthermore, when Paul writes Galatians, he has not yet written Romans, which will represent a further development and refinement of his thinking about the law for a very different audience. The churches of Galatia and the new preachers active in them, therefore, do not have access to Romans to assist in the interpretation of Paul's letter to them.[468] Moreover, in Romans no less than in Galatians, the love of neighbor probably comes "in place of the commandments" (Martyn 522) of the Mosaic code, thus neither as a supplement to them nor as an interpretation of their essence. Since, as we shall see below, Paul evidently does not regard the content of Lev 19:18 as part of the Mosaic legal code, as a commandment to be observed, its fulfillment cannot be a fulfillment of "the law" of commandments and prohibitions. It instead fulfills "the law" understood as the scriptural bearer of God's promise(s) about Christ and his Spirit (cf. Vouga 131). "Law" is here then virtually equivalent to "promise."

Issue 2: The import of the verb "to fulfill." Burton (294) acutely observes that the "precise meaning" of v. 14 "turns in no small part on the meaning of *peplērōtai*." The parallel passage in Romans 13:8–10 indicates that the verb has been deliberately chosen. There are four aspects to be noted:

(a) The fact that Paul uses the verb *plēroō* ("fulfill") instead of the verb *poieō* ("do, observe"), which is the verb Paul has used in connection with observing the law in 3:10, 12; 5:3, is significant (Westerholm 1988: 201–5; 2004: 433–39; Barclay 1988: 138–41; Betz 275; Longenecker 242; otherwise Dunn 289–90). For the new preachers, the law was a matter of observance. Throughout the letter to this point, Paul has been seeking to prevent the Galatians from becoming observers of the law, as the new preachers earnestly desire. In v. 14a, however, "the law" is not a matter of observance, but of "fulfillment." With his use of the verb "fulfill," therefore, Paul is probably not suddenly expecting the Galatians to "observe" the law (the Mosaic code), or some crucial part of it (Lev 19:18). In other words, Paul does *not* mean to say to the Galatians: "The entire law has been (fully) observed whenever you take it upon yourselves to observe the commandment to love the neighbor found in Lev 19:18." Another reason for this conclusion is that Lev 19:18 is not presented as a commandment to be observed, but as a promise that has been realized, a point to which we return below.

(b) The verb is passive in form. This passive could be regarded as a circumlocution for God's action ("the entire law has been fulfilled by God") or for Christ's (so Martyn

---

referential meanings as the context and the argument require (Jewish Scripture, particularly the Pentateuch, and the Mosaic legal code).

468. It may also be the case that Rom 13:8–10 has to be read with the assistance of Gal 5:14 rather than the other way around (cf. Martyn 518–23 and note 473 below).

489), but that is unlikely given 6:2, where according to Paul, the Galatians themselves "will fulfill the law of Christ" (cf. Rom 13:8, where "the one who loves the other has fulfilled the law" [AT]). Whenever the Galatians are slaves of one another through love (Gal 5:13c), which is the actualization of the promise heard by Paul in Lev 19:18, the entire law "has been fulfilled"—by them, or rather, in their actual love for one another. Of course, *their* fulfillment of the law can indeed, at a deeper level, be attributed to Christ's redemptive work (Gal 3:13–14; 4:4–5; 5:1), itself an act of love for the other (2:20), and to the work of his Spirit (4:6–7) among them (see 5:22). The point, however, is that the passive form of the verb is probably not to be construed grammatically as a divine passive. Paul regards the Galatians as people who have been liberated from the law and the elements of the world (4:3); for that reason they are fully responsible participants in the drama of salvation inaugurated by Christ.

(c) The verb "fulfill" as used in v. 14a is a perfect indicative (*peplērōtai*). The most common use of the perfect is to express a past action with present effect (BDF #340, #342), and Martyn (489) so understands it. He reads the verse to say in effect: "The [Mosaic] Law has now been fulfilled by Christ in the one word of Lev 19:18." Martyn appeals for this interpretation to 5:1, where "Christ has done something that has affected the Law" (490; cf. 509–10; Longenecker 243; Witherington 382). In short, according to Martyn, Paul refers in v. 14 "to the result of a past action in the Law's history, that past event being an act in which Christ took the [Mosaic] Law in hand" (490; cf. 505; see comment on 6:2). This interpretation depends, however, on taking the passive to be a circumlocution for God's or Christ's action, a possibility rejected as unlikely above. Apart from Martyn, commentators generally regard the perfect as gnomic (e.g., Mussner; Betz), expressing a general truth or a maxim: Whenever the Galatians are slaves of one another in love (v. 13c), the entire law "has been fulfilled" by them.[469] And that seems correct, but has to be properly understood: This fulfilling of the law is always retrospective (Betz 275), never prospective. Paul is "describing, not prescribing" (Westerholm 1988: 201). That is, Paul is not admonishing the Galatians to go and "fulfill the law" (so Sanders 1983: 84) any more than he is admonishing them to "observe" it. The fulfillment of the law is not a goal to be striven for; it is instead presented as the new reality that results whenever believers are in fact loving one another. This situation is one that Paul in v. 22 will call "the fruit," the outcome, of the Spirit's presence. Whenever mutual love happens, those loving (will) "have fulfilled the law."

(d) The basic meaning of the Greek verb *plēroō* from the classical period was "to fill," "to make full" (cf., e.g., Matt 13:48; Luke 2:40; 3:5; John 12:3), but it is here, as elsewhere, used metaphorically to mean "to actualize" or "realize." Contextually such actualization can be understood in one of two ways, either (1) "to obey fully" (Burton 827–29; Westerholm 1988: 204; 2004: 436; cf. 1 Macc 2:55) in the sense of "total realization and accomplishment of the law's demand" (Barclay 1988: 139), or (2) "to complete, bring to completion," as a prophecy or a promise (cf. Martyn 488, 505: "has

---

469. The gnomic understanding of the verb generally leads to the translation "*is* fulfilled" (Betz; cf. KJV, NAB, RSV). This translation would be more appropriate for the (weak) variant found in the majority of manuscripts (D, F, G, etc.), which has a present tense (*plēroutai*). NRSV and NIV both translate "is summed up," which seems to have been influenced by *anakephalaioutai* ("is summed up"), a present passive, in Rom 13:9.

Life at the Juncture of the Ages   347

been brought to completion"; BDAG 828: "complete or finish the law," "bring the law to a designed end"). In the latter sense the verb in effect means "to make a promise (or a prophecy) come true." It is possible that Paul here exploits the ambiguity of the verb (an ambiguity that also extends to the English term "fulfill"), which can cover both possibilities. Westerholm (1988: 205), who adopts the meaning "fully obey," suggests that the verb allows Paul to claim that the conduct of believers "fully satisfies the 'real' purport of the law in its entirety while allowing the ambiguity of the term to blunt the force of the objection that certain individual requirements (with which, Paul would maintain, Christian behavior was never meant to conform) have not been 'done'" (cf. Witherington 382). However, this interpretation, as others,[470] requires that the phrase "the entire law" in v. 14 refer to the Sinaitic legislation, a possibility rejected above as problematic. The second reading of the verb ("complete," "come true") is consistent with the interpretation of the phrase in question as a reference to the law not as legal code but as Scripture.[471]

The passive form of this verb occurs frequently in connection with the fulfillment of Scripture, especially in Matthew (1:22; 2:15, 17, 23; 4:14; 8:17; 12:17; 13:35; 21:4; 26:54, 56; 27:9; cf., e.g., also Mark 14:49; Luke 4:21; 24:44; John 12:38; 13:18; 15:25; 19:24, 36; Acts 1:16; 3:18; 13:27). This fact is all the more interesting in view of Matt 5:17, where Jesus declares that he has not come "to abolish the law and the prophets" but "to fulfill [*plērōsai*] them." This is the only other text in the NT referring to fulfillment of "the law" (cf. Luke 24:44: "it is necessary to fulfill all that was written about me in the law of Moses and the prophets and the psalms" [AT]). Though Jesus in Matthew goes on to speak of "the commandments" (Matt 5:19), the combination "the law and the prophets" suggests that the law as Scripture is here in view, as in Rom 3:21b (cf. John 1:45). As Davies and Allison (486–87) comment, the reference to the prophets indicates that "the verb almost certainly has prophetic content" in Matt 5:17 (cf. 11:13: "the prophets *and the law* prophesied until John"). "So," they conclude, "when Jesus declares, 'I came . . . to fulfill,' he means that his new teaching brings to realization that which the Torah anticipated or prophesied: its 'fulfiller' has come." The parallel to the notion of "fulfilling the law" in Matt 5:17 indicates that Paul is probably not inventing new terms or combinations in Gal 5:14; he is making use of already-existing Jewish Christian tradition.[472] If so, he is probably using terms that the new preachers in Galatia will also understand, because they are *also* using them (see further on 6:2 and "the law of Christ"). The new preachers active in Galatia, just like Paul, use the verb in question "to

---

470. Dunn argues that the verb "fulfill" concerns "a different way of 'doing' the law" (289). Paul "calls here for a life-style which could best be summed up in love of neighbor" as opposed to "a life-style . . . focused in the demand for circumcision," i.e., "a life-style within ethnic or national Judaism" (290), which, he argues, was at issue in 5:3.

471. Whether this interpretation is also valid for Rom 8:4; 13:8–10 is a matter beyond the scope of this commentary. But see Martyn 518–23.

472. The vocabulary of "fulfilling the law" does not occur in the LXX nor in other Greek Jewish literature contemporary with Paul; it also does not have a precise parallel in rabbinic texts. See Barclay 1988: 138, who comes to the conclusion that "Paul is using vocabulary unprecedented in the Jewish tradition." If Matthew, written some decades after Galatians, may count as evidence, such vocabulary was apparently not unprecedented in Jewish-Christian tradition.

describe the total realization of God's will in line with the eschatological fullness of time in the coming of Christ" (Barclay 1988: 140; cf. Gal 4:4). As indicated in the comment on 3:8, the new preachers, just like Paul, believe that the gift of the Spirit to believers in Christ is the fulfillment of a promise that God made to Abraham (the "blessing of Abraham" in 3:14 is for Paul, as for the new preachers, "the promised Spirit"). The promise that God made to Abraham is to be found in "the Scripture" (3:8). The point at which Paul and the new preachers part company concerns the role of observing the Mosaic law in the fulfillment of the promise that God made to Abraham. For Paul, the promise has come true in Christ apart from the observance of the (Mosaic) law.

In short, Paul wants the Galatians and the new preachers among them to understand the verb "has been fulfilled" as follows: "All that God promised in the Scripture concerning Christ and his Spirit has come true in the actualization among you of the one word of Lev 19:18."

Issue 3: Paul's use and interpretation of Lev 19:18 are closely related to the reason for his appeal to this text. There are at least three possible reasons:

(a) As indicated above, the content supports his exhortation in v. 13c. In the latter, Paul admonishes the Galatians to be slaves of one another "through love"; Lev 19:18 concerns "love" of the neighbor. But Paul also presents Lev 19:18 as the "one word" in which "the entire law has been fulfilled." Leviticus 19:18 is thus not cited merely to support his admonition to love in v. 13c.

(b) Paul may be indebted to Jewish tradition. According to the Babylonian Talmud (*Šabb.* 31a), Hillel (a contemporary of Jesus) told a potential proselyte that "the whole law" (*kol-hattôrāh*) is contained in the words "What is hateful to you, do not do to your neighbor," a negative version of Lev 19:18 and of the Golden Rule (cf. Matt 7:12 for the positive version). The rest, according to Hillel, is "commentary." A later tradition attributes to Rabbi Akiba (ca. 50–135 C.E.) the claim that Lev 19:18 is "a great principle in the law" (*Gen. Rab.* 24.7). The Jewish traditions attesting this understanding of Lev 19:18 occur only in texts from the second century C.E. and beyond, and they are not particularly prominent (Wischmeyer). In contrast to these and other rabbinic traditions, moreover, Paul "is not using Lev 19:18 as a summary which includes all the rest of the commands of the law; he does not consider that everything else in the law is commentary on it, to be learned and obeyed" (Barclay 1988: 136).

(c) Paul may be indebted to Jesus and Jewish Christian tradition. In Mark 12:28–34 (par. Matt 22:34–40; Luke 10:25–28), Jesus cites Lev 19:18 as the second most important "commandment," the first being the Shema of Deut 6:4–5 (cf. Jas 2:8; *Did.* 1.2; *T. Iss.* 5.1–2; *T. Dan* 5.3). He then comments: "There is no other commandment [*entolē*] greater than these" (Mark 12:31b). Luke omits this statement, but Matthew reads: "On these two commandments depends the whole law [*holos ho nomos*, as in Gal 5:3] and the prophets" (Matt 22:40 AT). This is not unlike what Jesus says of the Golden Rule in Matt 7:12: "So whatever you wish that people would do to you, do so to them; for this is the law and the prophets" (RSV). As in the Jewish tradition referred to above, love of neighbor is "the principle which sums up and contains" the whole law (Betz 274). As we noted above, a curious feature of Matthew is the extent to which he subsumes the law under the heading of prophecy, for which reason it is also, like the prophets, a matter of fulfillment.

Life at the Juncture of the Ages 349

All things considered, it appears likely that in making an appeal to Lev 19:18, Paul is in dialogue with tradition about Jesus (Betz 276), probably as it is being mediated and applied by the new preachers in Galatia. This tradition will later find a place in the Synoptic Gospels, especially Matthew. In line with this tradition, the new preachers in Galatia probably do not understand Lev 19:18 as making the observance of the other commandments of the Sinaitic legislation superfluous or unnecessary. But, given Paul's argument in Galatians about "works of the law," that is precisely how Paul *does* read Lev 19:18. Paul has thus quoted an ostensibly favorite text of the new preachers against their view that the gift of the Spirit (like that of justification) is dependent on observing the law.

Furthermore, Paul evidently does not regard Lev 19:18 as a commandment of the Mosaic code, nor then as the essence of this code. He refers to Lev 19:18 as a "word" (*logos*), as he will again in Rom 13:9. It is true that *logos* can be used to mean "commandment" (cf. 1 Macc 9:55; Matt 15:3–6; the Ten Commandments are "the Ten Words" in Exod 34:28 MT; Deut 10:4 MT), leading some versions to translate it here with "command" (NIV) or "commandment" (NRSV, NJB), but it is probably no accident that Paul avoids the word "commandment" (*entolē*) in this context (contrast Rom 13:9; cf. Rom 7:9–13). The word *logos* may here mean "sentence" (so Martyn 511; cf. RSV in Rom 13:9). The term is also, however, used in connection with prophecy, for example, in the formulaic expression "the word of the LORD" (e.g., Isa 1:10; 28:14; Hos 1:1; Joel 1:1; Mic 1:1). In 2 Kgdms (2 Sam) 3:13 LXX, David demands that Abner, the commander of Saul's army, make "one promise" (*logon hena*) to him, to return Michal, the daughter of Saul, to him as his lawful wife (cf. 1 Sam 18:19–29). Given his use of the verb "fulfill," Paul evidently understands the "word" of Lev 19:18 to have prophetic or promissory implications (so also, tentatively, Hays 324). The future tense of the verb "love" in the quotation from Lev 19:18 lends further support to this interpretation. In the LXX of Lev 19:18, which Paul cites without alteration, the future clearly has hortatory or imperatival force in its context, thereby accurately reflecting the underlying Hebrew and its context. In classical Greek, this "jussive" use of the future also occurs (Smyth #1917). Nevertheless, the words of Lev 19:18 LXX can also be construed as a promise: "You *will* love [*agapēseis*] your neighbor as yourself." The sense of such a promise would be: "There will come a time when you will indeed love your neighbor as you do yourself." In view of the verb "fulfill," it is likely that Paul intends Lev 19:18 to be so understood here,[473] not as a commandment but as a promise that has been fulfilled.[474] For Paul, then, Lev

---

473. The citation of Lev 19:18 in Rom 13:9 may also perhaps be interpreted in this way, given Rom 13:8b ("the one who [now] loves the other *has fulfilled* the law"; AT) and 13:10b ("Love is the *fulfillment* of the law"; AT). As indicated in note 468 above, however, it falls beyond the scope of this commentary to pursue the matter here.

474. This interpretation is a variant of Martyn's. According to Martyn, "We can be certain that for Paul Lev 19:18 is part of the original [Abrahamic] law that speaks in God's behalf. It is therefore not one of the commandments that make up the plural and cursing law of Sinai (5:3). *We* can see that in form Lev 19:18 is a commandment (belonging literarily to the Sinai legislation), but *Paul* clearly does not consider it to be such, almost certainly avoiding the word 'commandment' when he refers to it as a 'sentence'" (511, with original stress). In form, however, Lev 19:18 is not

19:18 is neither a reduction of the Mosaic law to only one commandment nor an epitome of the Mosaic code, capturing its "essence." It is a singular divine promise that has found its fulfillment in the coming of Christ and his Spirit.

What Paul means to say to the Galatians in 5:14, therefore, is this: "All that God promised in the Scripture concerning Christ and his Spirit has become concrete, visible reality for us in the actualization of the *one* word of promise articulated in Lev 19:18, that in the new creation inaugurated by Christ, you will truly love your neighbor as yourself" (see Excursus 17, above). Whenever believers are slaves of one another in love (v. 13c)—whenever love as the fruit of Christ's Spirit occurs among them (v. 22)—this one promise concerning the coming of Christ and his Spirit *has become* the eschatologically new reality (cf. 5:6; 6:15). This eschatologically new reality constitutes the singular actualization *not* of the Mosaic legal code, which is no longer relevant, and never was,[475] but of the *entire* scriptural "law," containing the promises of God concerning the coming of Christ and his Spirit.

In the text of Lev 19:18 as quoted by Paul, loving oneself does not so much involve liking oneself as looking out for one's own well-being, which is assumed to be a completely natural and universal activity. In the LXX, as in the MT, the "neighbor" is the fellow Israelite (cf. Lev 19:17–18). In this context, it is the fellow believer in Christ, as v. 13c makes clear (also Witherington 384; otherwise, e.g., Lightfoot 209). As indicated, the love that believers now have for one another is the fulfillment of the one word of promise made in Lev 19:18. In the fulfillment of this one promise, the entire law (predominantly the Pentateuch, which contains God's promises to Abraham concerning Christ and his Spirit) has in fact been visibly fulfilled. Christian freedom from the law (as legal code) takes shape as mutual love, an activity that constitutes the fulfillment of the law (as Scripture containing God's promises concerning Christ).

Paul now closes the paragraph with a warning: "But if you bite and tear at each other, see to it that you are not consumed by one another" (v. 15). The imagery is that of wild animals that bite (*daknete*) and tear at (*katesthiete*) each another and end up being consumed (*analōthēte*) by one another. This is a generalization that looks at the animal world as a whole. In particular instances one animal will bite, tear at, and consume another animal; they cannot both be consumed by one another. Paul applies the imagery to the human world,

---

a commandment, and it is questionable whether it is appropriate to refer to it, as Martyn does, as an "imperative" (512). Paul does not present Lev 19:18 as an imperative but as a promise that has been fulfilled in the love that believers have for one another.

475. That, at least, appears to be Paul's view in Galatians (cf. comments on 3:15–18, 19–22, and 23–25). It is arguable that he moderated this extreme position in Romans. In Galatians, however, Paul has no interest whatsoever in referring positively to the Mosaic code. Such a positive reference would undermine his argument to desist from observing the Sinaitic legislation.

Life at the Juncture of the Ages   351

expecting the Galatians to apply it to their own lives. It is not clear, however, whether he has particular circumstances within the Galatian churches in view. The conditional clause with its present indicatives suggests an existing situation but need not do so. The context actually implies that the Galatians are walking by the Spirit and loving one another (see comment on v. 13 above and 16a below). The introduction of the term *sarx* ("flesh") in v. 13b may have prompted the very fleshly imagery here. Paul describes the world outside the church as determined by "the Flesh," a world from which mutual love is absent. It is a world in which biting and tearing at one another inevitably leads to mutual consumption, bringing death and destruction. The world without love, Paul implies, is a dog-eat-dog world. Paul assumes that the Galatians will not want to be part of that world.

[16–18] After raising the specter of mutually assured communal self-destruction in v. 15, Paul calls the Galatians to attention ("But I say . . .") and turns to the God-given solution for the destructive power of the Flesh, which is the Spirit:

> [16]But I say, walk by the [power of the] Spirit, and you will *not* carry out the desire of the Flesh. [17]For the Flesh desires against the Spirit, and the Spirit against the Flesh, for these are opposed to one another, so that you do not do these things that you may want. [18]And if you are led by the [power of the] Spirit, you are not under the law.

Verse 16 largely repeats v. 13, using different words, as the following chiastic arrangement illustrates:

(a) 5:13a: Only let not this freedom turn into an opportunity for the Flesh,
(b) 5:13b: but through love be slaves of one another.
(b´) 5:16a: Walk by the Spirit
(a´) 5:16b: and you [pl.] will *not* carry out the desire of the Flesh.

The verb "walk" (*peripateō*) in v. 16a is here equivalent to the verb "live" (*zaō*) in 2:20 (cf. 3:11–12 and comment there). Both mean "to conduct one's life." This ethical use of the verb "walk" is not attested in classical sources (Bertram 1967; Seesemann) and reflects the frequent ethical use of the Hebrew verb *hālak* in the OT (e.g., Deut 5:33; Prov 8:20) and other Jewish texts (esp. 1QS 3.13–4.26). In the NT the ethical use of the Greek verb is to be found primarily in Paul and John (cf. also Mark 7:5; Acts 21:21; Heb 13:9). It therefore is a safe assumption that the new preachers in Galatia, who are Christian Jews, are also familiar with the ethical associations and uses of this verb. For them, however, to walk by the Spirit is to walk (conduct one's life) by the law in a way that was not possible before the coming of Christ (cf. Matt 5:17–20, esp.

v. 20). For Paul, walking by the Spirit comes in place of walking by the law (cf. below on v. 18: "If you are led by the Spirit, you are *not* under the law"). The "you" in these verses is plural, not singular; Paul is not admonishing not just the individual believer but especially the community of believers in Galatia.

The present imperative (*peripateite*) can mean "keep walking by the Spirit" (if you are already doing so) or "make a habit of walking by the Spirit" (if you are not already doing so). Probably the first is in view, since Paul has assumed from 3:1–5 onward that the Galatians are the recipients of the Spirit. The Galatians are being encouraged to keep going on the road on which they have begun to walk (cf. 3:3). This means that Paul is *not* exhorting his readers "to choose the one or the other" (Ridderbos 203); he is admonishing them to hold fast (cf. 5:1), to live according to the new reality of the Spirit that has overtaken their lives. The admonition to "walk by [or in] the Spirit [*pneumati*]" means essentially the same as the crucial exhortation in v. 13c, "Through love be slaves of one another," where a present imperative is also used ("Keep on being slaves of one another"). To walk by the (power of the) Spirit is to be slaves of one another through love, and vice versa (see comment on v. 13 above).

Unlike the imperative in v. 13c, however, the one in v. 16 has a conditional quality: "*If* you are walking by the Spirit, as you are . . ." This walking by the Spirit becomes the basis for an emphatic promise, as indicated by the use of the double negation (*ou mē*) followed by an aorist subjunctive in the Greek text: ". . . you will *not* carry out [*ou mē telesēte*] the desire of the Flesh" (cf. BDF #365). The verb *teleō* means "to complete, carry out, accomplish" (cf. BDAG 997). To carry out the desire of the Flesh is in fact to give in to it, to let it have its way, and thus to allow one's freedom from the law to become a staging area for the Flesh (v. 13).

Just like the one in v. 13, the admonition in v. 16a does not take place in a vacuum but in recognition of a powerful and lethal threat, that of the Flesh, or as Paul now writes, "the desire [*epithymia*] of the Flesh." The term *epithymia* suggests a strong or inordinate desire. In short, the Flesh is defined by this "desire" (Matera 199: "craving"; KJV: "lust"; NAB: "desire"; RSV, NRSV, NIV: "desires"; NJB: "self-indulgence"). In vv. 19–21, Paul will give some illustrations of how this "desire" concretely and destructively manifests itself in human affairs. The expression "the desire of the Flesh" (*epithymia sarkos*) seems to reflect the notion of the Evil Inclination (*yēṣer hāraʿ*) as found in Jewish and Jewish Christian tradition (see Excursus 16, above). It is probable that the new preachers troubling the Galatians were referring to the Evil Inclination as "the desire of the flesh." For Paul, this "desire of the flesh" is actually the "desire of the Flesh," with a capital *F*. The desire of the Flesh is what Paul has earlier called Sin, with a capital *S* (2:17; 3:22; see comments there). For this reason, the observance of the law is not, in fact cannot be (cf. 3:22), the remedy or

Life at the Juncture of the Ages 353

antidote for the Evil Inclination, as it is in Jewish and Jewish Christian tradition. The powerful Spirit of Christ, manifesting itself in love (5:13–14, 22), is that remedy. If you are walking by the Spirit, Paul promises the Galatians, you will certainly not succumb to the desire of the Flesh. The Spirit "does not make human effort unnecessary, but arouses it and equips it" (Ridderbos 203) to withstand the desire of the Flesh.

Instead of staying on this positive note, Paul in v. 17a returns to the reality of the Flesh's power and its danger for human life in community, giving in the remainder of the verse a description of reality as it has come to be since the advent of Christ: "[17a]For the Flesh desires [*epithymei*] against [*kata*] the Spirit, [17b]and the Spirit [desires] against the Flesh, [17c]for these [two] are opposed to one another, [17d]so that you do not do these things that you may want [to do]." The initial conjunction "for" (*gar*) here signifies a further clarification: "For this is the situation at the present time: . . . ." The verb *epithymeō*, "desire strongly" (BDAG 371–72; KJV: "lusteth"), does not necessarily have a negative connotation (cf. e.g., 1 Tim 3:1) any more than the cognate noun, *epithymia*, used in v. 16, does (cf. e.g., Phil 1:23). For this reason, the verb can also be connected, by implication, with the Spirit's activity. The terms acquire a negative connotation only when brought into connection with the Flesh (cf. esp. v. 19–21, with its list of "works of the Flesh"). Furthermore, the Greek construction *epithymeō kata* ("desire against") is unusual (Martyn 493–94), as is the English translation, and seems to mean "war against."[476] The formulation indicates that the malevolent desire of the Flesh has a particular aim: it is directed "*against* [*kata*] the Spirit." The Spirit, however, gives as good as it gets: It in turn "[desires] *against* [*kata*] the Flesh" (v. 17b). The point is that the "desire" of the Flesh and that of the Spirit are mutually exclusive and hostile toward each other. Or as Paul observes in an explanatory aside: "for these [i.e., the Flesh and the Spirit] are opposed [*antikeitai*] to one another" (v. 17c). The desire against one another points to an adversarial, conflictual relationship (cf. 1 Cor 16:9; Phil 1:28; 2 Thess 2:4; 1 Tim 1:10; 5:14; Luke 13:17; 21:15) between the Flesh and the Spirit. It points to strife or spiritual warfare. The conflict has been inaugurated by the Spirit (see Excursus 16, above) and is apocalyptic in scope and implication (see Excursus 2). As such, the conflict between the Flesh and the Spirit is not solely internal to the individual (Betz 279–80); it also takes place in a visibly communal or social setting, thus on the stage of human history, where people interact and relate to one another (see comment on vv. 19–21).

The notion of warfare between opposing spiritual forces finds a significant parallel in columns 3–4 of the *Community Rule* of Qumran (1QS). According

---

476. Cf. Pol. *Phil.* 5.3: "Every desire [*epithymia*] wars [*strateuetai*] against [*kata*] the Spirit"; Urbach 475–76, for rabbinic texts with a similar notion.

to 1QS 3.17–21, God "created man to rule the world and placed within him two spirits so that he would walk with them until the moment of his visitation: they are the spirits of truth and of deceit." The former is correlated with the rule of "the Prince of Lights" and the latter with "the Angel of Darkness." "God has sorted them into equal parts," according to 1QS 4.16–18, "until the last time, and has put an everlasting loathing between their divisions. Deeds of injustice are an abhorrence to truth and all the paths of truth are an abhorrence to injustice." There is indeed "a violent conflict in respect of all their decrees since they cannot walk together." They are in conflict because they are mutually exclusive. "Until now the spirits of truth and injustice feud in the heart of man: they walk in wisdom or in folly.[477] In agreement with man's inheritance in the truth, he shall be righteous and so abhor injustice; and according to his share in the lot of injustice, he shall act wickedly in it, and so abhor the truth. For God has sorted them into equal parts until the appointed time and the new creation" (1QS 4.23–24). At his final "visitation," God "will refine, with his truth, all man's deeds, and will purify for himself the structure of man, ripping out all spirit of injustice from the innermost part of his flesh, and cleansing him with a spirit of holiness from all wicked deeds" (1QS 4.19–21). While the strife between the Flesh and the Spirit in Galatians is similar to the strife between the two spirits in 1QS 3–4, there are also significant differences (Martyn 530–31; 1997: 120–21). There is first of all Paul's distinctive personification of "the Flesh," implying that the Flesh is a suprahuman, cosmic power (see Excursus 16, above). Furthermore, whereas the conflict between the two spirits in 1QS is inherent to the creation, the conflict between the Flesh and the Spirit (of Christ) is not. The Spirit represents for Paul an eschatological reality that has come into the creation from the outside. It represents and effects the new creation. In 1QS, God's eschatological "visitation" signals the end of the conflict between the warring spirits inherent in the created order (1QS 4.11–14); in Paul, the apocalyptic event of Jesus Christ has actually inaugurated the eschatological conflict between the Flesh and the Spirit. The Spirit's work represents God's apocalyptic "visitation" in the present, as it were, unmasking "the Flesh" for what it is: a cosmic, dangerous power destructive of human life, against which the law is of no avail.

The final clause of v. 17 is ambiguous: "so that [*hina*] you [plur.] do not do these things that you [plur.] may want [to do]." Does this clause indicate purpose (Burton; Mussner; Dunn; Witherington; Vouga) or result (Lightfoot; Betz; Martyn)? Are "these things that you [believers] may want [*ha ean thelēte*] [to do]" good (Lightfoot; Ridderbos; Martyn) or bad (Witherington), or both (Burton; Mussner; Betz; Longenecker; Dunn; Vouga)? The choice made here

---

477. Note how here internal conflict has consequences for how one "walks."

Life at the Juncture of the Ages 355

depends on taking the conjunction to express result and the things believers do not do, which they may want to do, as the works of the Flesh (cf. Barclay 1988: 112). So interpreted, v. 17d modifies v. 17b: "and the Spirit desires against the Flesh, . . . with the result that you [believers] do not do these things [i.e., works of the Flesh] which you may [on account of the Flesh] want [to do]." The intervening clause (v. 17c: "for these are opposed to one another") is taken to be parenthetical, explaining why the Flesh desires against the Spirit, and the Spirit against the Flesh. The message of v. 17d is then consistent with that of v. 16b, with its insistent promise that those who are walking by the Spirit will certainly not carry out the desire of the Flesh.

In v. 18 Paul pointedly reminds the Galatians once again of their new situation of freedom from the law: "But [*de*] if [*ei*] you are [being] led by the [the power of the] Spirit, you are [of course] not under the law." Paul assumes that the Galatians are being led (*agesthe*, present indicative) by the Spirit (see above on v. 16a). The sense is thus that *because* the Galatians are being led by the Spirit, they are not "under the law" (*hypo nomon*), not under its authority (cf. 4:21a, where Paul addresses the Galatians as those "who are wanting to be under the law"). In 3:23 and 4:4–5, Paul emphasized that to be "under the law" is to be confined, imprisoned, and enslaved. Earlier he has claimed that those who live on the basis of the law are in fact "under a curse" (3:10), that "of the law" itself (3:13). According to 3:22 the law is the captive and the instrument of Sin, so that to be "under the law" is in fact to be "under Sin" (3:22; see comment there). In being led by the Spirit, then, the Galatians are not, or no longer, "under the law" (3:25), for the Spirit represents, mediates, and creates the realm of freedom from the law into which the Galatians were called (5:13a) or transferred when they came to believe in Christ (2:16b).

[19–21] Paul now turns to a list of "works of the Flesh" (vv. 19–21):

[19]Now the works of the Flesh are plain, which are sexual immorality, impurity, licentiousness, [20]idolatry, sorcery, hostile actions, strife, jealousy, outbursts of anger, selfish actions, dissensions, factions, [21]acts of envy, bouts of drunkenness, drinking parties, and things like these, about which I say to you in advance, just as I have said before: those who practice such things will not inherit the kingdom of God.

Paul lists fifteen "works [*erga*] of the Flesh." He will follow with a contrasting list headed by love as the singular "fruit of the Spirit" in vv. 22–23 ("love, joy, peace, patience, kindness, goodness, faithfulness, humility, self-control").

Catalogs of vices and virtues (modes of immoral and moral conduct) were common in the Greek philosophical tradition, especially Stoicism, and in Hellenistic Judaism, especially Philo (see Longenecker 250–51; Witherington 404).

It is likely that the Galatians were familiar with some of those traditions.[478] Paul, however, comprehends the listed behaviors within the framework of an apocalyptic conflict between the Flesh and the Spirit (see Excursuses 2 and 16; Martyn 484, 532). Some material in the *Community Rule* of Qumran (1QS) provides the best parallel to Paul's "apocalyptic ethics" (Martyn 534). This material is itself an apocalyptic adaptation of the historic Jewish tradition of the Two Ways, the way of the righteous and the way of the wicked (Ps 1; cf. *T. Ash.* 1–4; *Barn.* 19.1–2; *Did.* 1–2). According to the *Community Rule* (1QS), to "the spirit of deceit," which contends with "the spirit of truth,"

> belong greed, sluggishness in the service of justice, wickedness, falsehood, pride, haughtiness of heart, dishonesty, trickery, cruelty, much insincerity, impatience, much foolishness, impudence for appalling acts performed in lustful passion, filthy paths in the service of impurity, blasphemous tongue, blindness of eyes, hardness of hearing, stiffness of neck, hardness of heart in order to walk in all the paths of darkness and evil cunning. (1QS 4.9–11)

The "spirit of truth," by contrast, is there

> to enlighten the heart of man, straighten out in front of him all the paths of true justice, establish in his heart respect for the precepts of God; it is a spirit of meekness, of patience, generous compassion, eternal goodness, intelligence, understanding, potent wisdom which trusts in all the deeds of God and depends on his abundant mercy; a spirit of knowledge in all the plans of action, of enthusiasm for the decrees of justice, of holy plans with a firm purpose, of generous compassion with all the sons of truth, of magnificent purity which detests all unclean idols, of careful behavior in wisdom concerning everything, of concealment concerning the truth of the mysteries of knowledge. (1QS 4.2–6)

As indicated in the comment on v. 17 above, whereas the conflict between the two spirits in 1QS is inherent to the creation, the conflict between the Flesh and the Spirit (of Christ) is not. The Spirit of Christ is an eschatological reality that has come into the (old) creation from the outside. It represents and effects the new creation.

Paul's list of "the works of the Flesh" is not meant to be exhaustive (cf. "and things like these" in v. 21). Catalogs of vices are also found elsewhere in the Pauline Letters (Rom 1:28–31; 1 Cor 5:9–11; 6:9–10; Eph 4:31; 5:3–4; Col 3:5–8; 1 Tim 1:9–10; 2 Tim 3:2–5; cf. Mark 7:21–22; Matt 15:19; Rev

---

478. Cf. also Harrill, who argues that the *toga virilis* ceremony was "a proclaimed, celebrated, and recognizable Roman institution in the Greek east," including Galatia. The ritual signified the transition from adolescence to manhood. "Inseparable from the *toga virilis* discourse," according to Harrill, "was paraenesis exhorting errant youths to remember the day they 'put on' the toga and to behave accordingly. The *toga virilis* directed vulnerable and morally ambiguous youth toward the responsible use of freedom" (265–66).

Life at the Juncture of the Ages 357

21:8; 22:15; *Did.* 2–5). Two examples from 2 Corinthians and Romans are particularly interesting because they have (italicized) points in common with the present passage from Galatians:

> [20]For I fear that . . . perhaps there may be *strife, jealousy, outbursts of anger, selfish actions*, slanders, gossipings, acts of conceit, and disorders. [21]I fear that when I come . . . I may have to mourn over many of those who sinned before and have not repented of *the impurity, sexual immorality, and licentiousness* which they have practiced. (2 Cor 12:20–21 RSV, alt.)

> [12]Let us cast off the works [*erga*] of Darkness and put on the armor of Light. [13]Let us conduct ourselves becomingly as in the day, not in *drinking parties* and *bouts of drunkenness*, not in debaucheries and *licentious* acts, not in *strife* and *jealousy*. [14]But put on the Lord Jesus Christ [cf. Gal 3:27] and make no provision for the Flesh, for its desires [cf. Gal 5:13, 16, 24]. (Rom 13:12–14 RSV, alt.)

The list in Galatians is thus not particularly unique, even if there are distinctive elements (see below). Moreover, most of the vices listed are also known from the literature of Greek philosophy and Hellenistic Judaism. The Galatians will most probably recognize them as commonly known vices. For this reason, apparently, Paul characterizes the vices listed in vv. 19–21a as "plain" (*phanera*): observable, evident, or known to everyone. Yet Paul notably does not speak of "vices" (*kakiai*) but of "the works of the Flesh" (cf. "the works of Darkness" in Rom 13:12), which means that he regards the behaviors listed not as regrettable character traits nor as poor moral choices ("vices" in common parlance), but instead as the manifestations of a malevolent power that, apart from Christ and his Spirit, determines human life for the worse. Moreover, these "works of the Flesh" have nothing to do with transgressions of the law, intentional or otherwise. Paul here describes the human condition, as it were, apart from the law and its transgression (cf. Rom 5:13).

The expression "the works of the Flesh" (*ta erga tēs sarkos*) is reminiscent of the expression "works of the law" (*erga nomou*), used in 2:16; 3:2, 5, 10. But whereas the works of the law are the deeds required by the Mosaic law (see Excursus 8), the works of the Flesh are the deeds, or activities, caused by the Flesh, here conceived as a malevolent cosmic power that has come to determine the course and the character of human life in a malignant way (see Excursus 16, above). Through his choice of words Paul, here as elsewhere in Galatians, intimates an unholy alliance between the Flesh and the law. The "works of the law," instead of being the solution to "the works of the Flesh," are (inadvertently) part of the problem (see comment on 1:13–14). It is only in Romans, however, that Paul explicitly and emphatically explores the relationship of the law to the Flesh, or Sin (esp. in Rom 7–8). In Galatians, Paul goes no further than to intimate that the law is a tool used by the Flesh, or by Sin (3:22), to increase and solidify its hegemony over human beings (cf. v. 18b above).

Though many today argue for a random collection of "vices" in vv. 19–21a (largely following Betz 283), the significant overlap between the list in vv. 19–21a and those in 2 Cor 12:20–21 and Rom 13:12–14 suggests otherwise—as does v. 21b, where Paul intimates that he has given this list, or something close to it, to the Galatians once before. Furthermore, the works of the Flesh in Paul's list can be classified into four discernible groups (following Lightfoot 210; Burton 304; Vouga 135): the first has to do with sexual misconduct, the second with religious misconduct, the third with sources of communal discord, and the fourth with excessive drinking and its consequences. "In the whole list" Lührmann (111) observes, "Paul is not enumerating attitudes, approaches to life, or ways of thinking, but specific ways of behaving."

Sexual misconduct: "Sexual immorality [*porneia*], impurity [*akatharsia*], licentiousness [*aselgeia*]" (v. 19). Paul refers to the same three forms of misbehavior in 2 Cor 12:21, which indicates that Paul's choice of vices is not entirely random, even if they occur in a slightly different sequence ("impurity, sexual immorality, and licentiousness"). The first two vices are also mentioned together in Col 3:5 and Eph 5:3. The adjective "sexual" can probably cover all three terms in this context. *Porneia* refers to sexual immorality in general (BDAG 854), but in certain instances may have particularly prostitution, adultery, or illicit marriages in view (cf. Mark 7:21; Matt 5:32; 15:19; 19:9; John 8:41; Acts 15:20, 29; 21:25; 1 Thess 4:3; 1 Cor 5:1; 6:13, 18; 7:2). In some cases the term is also used to signify the worship of pagan gods, especially in Revelation (e.g., 19:2), following OT usage (cf. e.g., LXX: Hos 1:2; 2:4, 6 [2:2, 4E]; 4:11–12; 5:4; 6:10; Mic 1:7; Jer 3:9). The most common referential meaning, one that the Galatians would surely know, is prostitution, paying for sexual gratification. *Akatharsia* literally means "uncleanness" (BDAG 34), here used metaphorically to refer to moral impurity. In 1 Thess 4:7 and Rom 6:19 Paul uses "holiness" or "sanctification" (*hagiasmos*) as its opposite. In view is moral depravity, which makes a person unfit for being in God's presence. Given the juxtaposition with *porneia* (as in 2 Cor 12:21; Col 3:5; Eph 5:3), the moral impurity here is probably sexual (cf. Rom 1:24; 1 Thess 2:3; Eph 4:19; Matt 23:27). *Aselgeia* is lack of constraint in behavior (BDAG 141: "self-abandonment"; cf. 1 Pet 4:3; Jude 4). Again, given the context, the lack of constraint or the licentiousness in view is probably sexual, as in 2 Cor 12:21 and Rom 13:13, where the plural is used (cf. Mark 7:22; Eph 4:19; 2 Pet 2:2, 7, 18; Wis 14:26; Philo, *Mos.* 1.305; Josephus, *J.W.* 1.439; 2.121; 4.562).

Religious misconduct: "Idolatry [*eidōlolatria*], sorcery [*pharmakeia*]" (v. 20a). Religious cults in the ancient world often had a sexual component, and that could explain Paul's easy shift from sexual to religious misconduct here (see above, on *porneia*). *Eidōlolatria*, which does not occur in classical writers nor in LXX, refers literally to the worship of idols, and thus from Paul's viewpoint to the worship of false gods (cf. 1 Cor 10:14; Col 3:5, where greed is defined as idolatry; also 1 Pet 4:3; *Did.* 3.4; 5.1; *Barn.* 16.7; 20.1; *T. Jud.* 19.1). This (Gal 5:20) is the oldest attested use of the term. *Pharmakeia* refers to the use of magic or sorcery (Rev 18:23), often involving the use of drugs (cf. LXX: Exod 7:11, 22; 8:3, 14 [8:7, 18E]; Wis 12:4; 18:13; Isa 47:9, 12; Rev 9:21; *Did.* 5.1).

Sources of communal discord: "Hostile actions [*echthrai*], strife [*eris*], jealousy [*zēlos*], outbursts of anger [*thymoi*], selfish actions [*eritheiai*], dissensions [*dichostasiai*], factions [*haireseis*], acts of envy [*phthonoi*]" (v. 20b–21a). This list refers to various sources of conflict between persons; they all have destructive consequences for life in community. All except the second and third are plural[479] (cf. the many plurals in 2 Cor 12:20–21 and Rom 13:12–14, Greek and RSV, above). The singular of *echthrai* is used in classical writers, LXX, and the NT to mean "enmity." The plural *echthrai*, used only here, probably has not merely hostile feelings in view but also, and primarily, hostile actions (BDAG 419). These may be directed to fellow human beings (as in Luke 23:12; Eph 2:14, 16) or to God (as in Rom 8:7; Jas 4:4), in which case this vice may belong with the previous group. The next four terms also occur together in 2 Cor 12:20. *Eris*, an exclusively Pauline term in the NT, denotes strife or discord resulting from rivalry (BDAG 392; cf. Rom 1:29; 13:13; 1 Cor 1:11; 3:3; 2 Cor 12:20; Phil 1:15; 1 Tim 6:4; Titus 3:9). *Zēlos* is frequently paired with *eris* in particular (Rom 13:13; 1 Cor 3:3; 2 Cor 12:20; *1 Clem.* 5.5; 6.4), and can mean zeal or ardor in a positive sense (2 Cor 7:7; 11:2). It here has a negative connotation, as jealousy or envy (BDAG 427). *Thymoi* are outbursts of anger (cf. 2 Cor 12:20; *1 Clem.* 46.5). *Eritheiai* are selfish actions or disputes (BDAG 392). The plural also occurs in 2 Cor 12:20, whereas the singular, which can denote selfish ambition, occurs in Phil 1:17; Rom 2:8; Jas 3:14, 16 (with *zēlos*). *Dichostasiai* are "dissensions" or "sharp disagreements" (cf. BDAG 252; Rom 16:17; *1 Clem.* 46.5; 51.1; 1 Macc 3:29). *Haireseis* are "factions" reflecting differences of opinion (cf. 1 Cor 11:19; Acts 24:14; 2 Pet 2:1) rather than "schools of thought" or "parties" (cf. Acts 5:17; 15:5; 24:5; 26:5; Josephus, *J.W.* 2.137). Only later, in the second century, did the term come to mean "heresies." *Phthonoi* are "acts of envy" or "malice" (cf. v. 26). The plural occurs only here. The singular occurs with *eris* in Rom 1:29; Phil 1:15; and 1 Tim 6:4 (cf. also Titus 3:3; 1 Pet 2:1; Matt 27:18; Mark 15:10; 1 Macc 8:16; 3 Macc 6:7; Wis 2:24; 6:23; in positive sense only in Jas 4:5).

Excessive drinking: "bouts of drunkenness [*methai*], drinking parties [*kōmoi*], and things like these" (v. 21a). *Methai* and *kōmoi* also occur together in Rom 13:13. The only other instance of the plural *methai* in biblical literature is found in Jdt 13:15 (cf. *1 Clem.* 30.1); elsewhere only the singular, meaning

---

479. Some manuscripts also make the second and third sources of conflict into plurals.

"drunkenness," is used (Luke 21:34; LXX: Prov 20:1; 31:6; Isa 28:7; Jer 51:57; Ezek 23:33; 39:19; Joel 1:5; Hag 1:6; Tob 4:15; Sir 31:30; *Pss. Sol.* 8.14). In 1 Cor 5:11 and 6:10, Paul condemns drunkards. The singular of *kōmoi* does not occur in biblical literature. The term was used in connection with a festive procession in honor of Dionysus, the god of wine (BDAG 580). The plural (1 Pet 4:3; Wis 14:23; 2 Macc 6:4) indicates excessive drinking or feasting, perhaps with the implication of sexual misconduct (Ridderbos 206; Longenecker 257: "orgies"). The concluding phrase could refer only to these drinking parties but more probably has the whole list of works of the Flesh in view.

To what extent, Paul's choice of "works of the Flesh" reflects misconduct in Galatia at the moment of writing is not clear. The parallels in 2 Corinthians and Romans quoted above indicate that his selection, while not exactly random, is probably also not wholly determined by his perception or knowledge of the situation of the Galatians at the present time. Moreover, the vices listed seem to articulate the situation of the Galatians before their conversion. This is the world they have presumably left behind (cf. v. 24 below). Unique to this list (when compared with 2 Cor 12:20–21 and Rom 13:12–14) are the following: *eidōlolatria* (idolatry), *pharmakeia* (sorcery), *echthrai* (hostile actions), *dichostasiai* (dissensions), *haireseis* (factions), and *phthonoi* (acts of envy or malice). These then may reflect Paul's particular concerns about the Galatians as he writes the letter. The first two recall Paul's fear in 4:8–11 that the Galatians are in the process of returning to the worship of "the elements" (*ta stoicheia*), which he characterizes as "beings not gods by nature." The remaining works of the Flesh suggest that there are significant threats to communal harmony and unity (cf. v. 15 above), most probably because of the presence of the new preachers among them with their divisive insistence that the Galatians begin practicing circumcision and the remainder of the Mosaic law.

All these are in any event works of the Flesh "about which I say to you in advance [*prolegō*], just as I have said before [*kathōs proeipon*]: those who practice such things will not inherit the kingdom of God" (v. 21b). Thus Paul underscores the seriousness of these works of the Flesh by issuing a warning (cf. 1 Thess 3:4; 2 Cor 13:2). Paul appears to indicate that he has issued the same warning to the Galatians in an earlier visit ("just as I have said before"), though his formulation, which does not indicate explicitly to whom he has said this before, can be taken to mean only that he is here repeating a warning he has made earlier, perhaps in another context and to other churches.

On several grounds it seems that Paul has derived the assertion "those who practice such things will not inherit the kingdom of God" from Jewish Christian tradition. First, the theme of the kingdom of God plays no further role in Paul's Letter to the Galatians. Indeed, in contrast to the Synoptic Gospels, where it forms part of the core teaching of Jesus, Paul's Letters contain very few explicit references to the kingdom of God (Rom 14:17; 1 Cor 4:20; 6:9–10;

15:24, 50; 1 Thess 2:12; cf. Col 4:11; Eph 5:5). Second, Paul has used the language of inheriting earlier in Galatians only in connection with the fulfillment of God's promise to Abraham in the gift of the Spirit (3:18, 29; 4:1, 7, 30). Third, whereas the inheritance of the Spirit is a present reality, the inheritance of the kingdom of God appears to relate to the future, as in 1 Cor 15:50 (NAB: "flesh and blood cannot inherit the kingdom of God, nor does corruption inherit incorruption"). Fourth, the specific formulation that Paul uses in v. 21b, "will not inherit the kingdom of God [*basileian theou ou klēronomēsousin*]," is also found in 1 Cor 6:9–10 in connection with a list of wrongdoers: "Do you not know that the unrighteous will not inherit the kingdom of God [*theou basileian ou klēronomēsousin*]?" (RSV). Paul then gives a list of offenders and declares that none of them "will inherit the kingdom of God [*basileian theou klēronomēsousin*]." The opening rhetorical question in 1 Cor 6:9 ("Do you not know . . . ?") suggests that Paul is relying on traditional material. Fifth, the idea of "inheriting the kingdom of God" also occurs in Matt 25:34 (cf. Jas 2:5: "heirs of the kingdom").

The notion of "inheriting" the kingdom of God as found in Paul and in Matt 25:34 appears to be a variation of the more common notion of "entering into [*eiserchomai eis*] the kingdom of God" (Matt 5:20; 7:21; 18:3; 19:23–24; Mark 9:47; 10:15, 23–25; Luke 18:17, 25; John 3:5). The notion of "entering" or "inheriting" the kingdom of God represents the eschatological adaptation of entering and inheriting the promised land in the OT: "And now, Israel, hear the ordinances and judgments, all that I teach you this day to do: that you may live, and be multiplied, and that you may go in [*eiselthontes*] and inherit [*klēronomēsēte*] the land, which the Lord God of your fathers gives you" (Deut 4:1 LXX).[480] This text also shows that "inheriting" the kingdom of God most probably entails "entering" it. Akin to the promised land, the kingdom of God is conceptualized as a territory or sphere in which God rules as King. In 1 Cor 15:50, Paul regards "the kingdom of God" as the alternative for "corruption" (*phthora*); in Gal 6:8, he so regards "eternal life" (see comment below). The kingdom of God is thus the realm of "eternal life" (cf. "inheriting eternal life" in Matt 19:29; Mark 10:17; Luke 10:25; 18:18). The works of the Flesh have no place there, and those who "practice" them will not inherit it.

The remaining interpretive issue is the precise import of the phrase "those who practice such things [*hoi ta toiauta prassontes*]." As Calvin observes, "This makes it sound as if all are cut off from the hope of salvation; for who is there who does not labour under one or other of these sins?" (104). Calvin's answer is that all who "remain impenitent" (105) will be excluded. The point of the tradition that Paul cites is probably not exclusion from the kingdom of God for occasional or past misconduct, but as the verb suggests, for an

---

480. See the comment on 3:18 with note 323 there.

ongoing, unrepentant lifestyle or practice (Martyn 497; Vouga 138). Paul's primary concern in citing the tradition appears to be to alert the Galatians to the danger of backsliding into their former way of life. The Flesh is a dangerous power; the consequences of carrying out its "desire" (v. 16) are far-reaching and disastrous.

[22–24] Following the warning in v. 21b, Paul goes on to point out that "the fruit of the Spirit is love, joy, peace, patience, kindness, goodness, faithfulness, humility, self-control" (vv. 22–23a; cf. 2 Cor 6:6–10; Eph 4:2–3; Col 3:12–15; 2 Pet 1:5–7). Paul's striking phrase, "the fruit of the Spirit" (*ho karpos tou pneumatos*), raises at least three closely interrelated questions. (1) Why does Paul not refer to the "works" (*erga*) of the Spirit (activities or forms of behavior caused by the Spirit) as he has to the "works" of the Flesh? (2) Why has he chosen the word "fruit" instead? (3) Why does he use the singular "fruit" instead of the plural "fruits"? Burton gives helpful answers to all three questions: Paul probably avoids the term "works" in this connection because of this term's association with the "works of the law" (2:16; 3:2, 5, 10). He has chosen the word "fruit" instead in order to suggest that love, joy, peace, and so forth are "the natural product of a vital relation between the Christian and the Spirit" (Burton 313). And he uses the singular (a) because he always uses the singular "when employing this word in a figurative sense" (cf. Rom 1:13; Phil 1:11; 4:17; etc.)[481] and/or (b) because it "serves to present all the experiences and elements of character in the ensuing list as a unity, together constituting the result of living by the Spirit" (Burton 313).

The singular "fruit" may also indicate that the first item in the list ("love," *agapē*) is the (one) fruit of the Spirit, with the other items to be construed as specifications or aspects of love: "The fruit of the Spirit is love, [which is accompanied or marked by] joy, peace, patience, kindness, goodness, faithfulness, humility, self-control" (cf. Col 3:12–14). Verses 22b–23 can then be understood as a short hymn to love, akin to 1 Cor 13, perhaps as exemplified by Christ himself (Dunn 310). Love "in the context cannot be simply one item beside others, . . . and . . . the following concepts are actually only paraphrases of the love that does not insist on its own way (cf. 1 Cor 13:5)" (Lührmann 111; cf. Matera 210). Paul has already singled out love in vv. 13–14 ("through love be slaves of one another. . . . 'You will love your neighbor as yourself'"; cf. 2:20; 5:6). Love apparently stands in a class by itself, "the source from which all the rest flow" (Burton 314; cf. Longenecker 260). Like the works of the Flesh in vv. 19–21, love as the singular fruit of the Spirit is an activity. Love is loving, as vv. 13–14 show (see also comments on 2:20; 5:6). The remaining items in the list are not activities, however. They describe the circumstances

---

481. The metaphorical use is not limited to Paul (cf., e.g., Jas 3:17–18; Matt 3:8–10; 7:17–18) or the NT (cf. e.g., Isa 5:1–7; Josephus, *Ant.* 20.48; Philo, *Fug.* 176; Epictetus, *Diatr.* 1.4.32).

(joy, peace), dispositions (patience, kindness, goodness), and character traits (faithfulness, humility, self-control) accompanying love, the love that occurs as the singular fruit of the Spirit's presence.

Paul's list does not represent a unique set of "virtues." To a greater or a lesser extent, the nine virtues on his list find their parallels in Greco-Roman philosophy and in contemporary Jewish thought as well as in the OT. In fact, they may represent (a selection of) common aspirations of the time and the culture, perhaps of all times and cultures. There are significant differences, however. For Paul, these aspirations can only become reality "in Christ," meaning in the sphere of Christ's lordship, where his Spirit creates a new world (cf. 6:15). As Betz (286) astutely observes, the "nine concepts" in Paul's list are not "virtues in the Greek sense of the term [*aretai*]. They do not represent qualities of personal behavior" that a person "can elect, cultivate, and appropriate as part" of one's character. "Nor," he continues, "are they 'good deeds' in the sense of Jewish ethics: they do not come from or constitute a code of law which must be obeyed and which can be transgressed." Paul's language here is not prescriptive, but descriptive (Martyn 530, 535). The virtues listed are not matters of decision, nor are they goals to be achieved. They "happen," and when they do, believers in Christ can say: "Ah, the Spirit of Christ, active in our midst!" Martyn emphasizes as well that the virtues in vv. 22b–23a do not primarily concern the individual, as in Greek ethics, but the church: "Paul transforms lists of vices and virtues into something fundamentally different—marks of a community under the sway of the Flesh contrasted with marks of a community under the leading of the Spirit" (Martyn 498).

Many commentators discern no pattern in Paul's list (e.g., Burton 314; Longenecker 260), but some discern three groups of three (as does NA^{27} by means of punctuation). According to Lightfoot (212), the first group (love, joy, peace) "comprises Christian habits of mind in their more general aspect"; the second group (patience, kindness, goodness) "gives special qualities affecting man's intercourse with his neighbor"; and the third group (faithfulness, humility, self-control) "exhibits the principles which guide a Christian's conduct." A similar division is supported by Betz (287–88), according to whom the first three are "different from the rest in that they can be attributed" not only to human beings but also to God and Christ; the second three move "further in the direction of human action"; and the last three are "three famous virtues from Hellenistic ethics." Other commentators also adopt a triadic division but for different reasons (e.g., Ridderbos; Matera; Martyn; Vouga). A triadic division is difficult to prove as Paul's intention, but in any case useful for analysis and comprehension:

Love and its accompanying circumstances: "Love [*agapē*], joy [*chara*], peace [*eirēnē*]." Paul uses the three Greek terms frequently elsewhere, and they seem to be important to him. That is especially true as we have just seen with respect to *agapē* ("love"), which occurs often (Rom 5:5, 8; 8:35, 39; 12:9; 13:10; 14:15; 15:30; 1 Cor 4:21; 8:1; 13:1–4, 8, 13; 14:1; 16:14, 24; 2 Cor 2:4, 8; 5:14; 6:6; 8:7–8, 24; 13:11, 13; Phil 1:9, 16; 2:1–2; 1 Thess 1:3; 3:6, 12; 5:8, 13; Phlm 5, 7, 9; cf. Eph 1:4, 15; 2:4; 3:17, 19; 4:2, 15–16; 5:2; 6:23; Col 1:4, 8, 13; 2:2; 3:14; 2 Thess 1:3; 2:10; 3:5; 1 Tim 1:5, 14; 2:15; 4:12; 6:11; 2 Tim 1:7, 13; 2:22; 3:10; Titus 2:2). Except for the Johannine literature (John 5:42; 13:35; 15:9, 10, 13; 17:26; 1 John 2:5, 15; 3:1, 16–17; 4:7–10, 12, 16–18; 5:3; 2 John 3, 6; 3 John 6), the term is surprisingly rare in the remainder of the NT (Matt 24:12; Luke 11:42; Heb 6:10; 10:24; 1 Pet 4:8; 5:14; 2 Pet 1:7; Jude 2, 12, 21; Rev 2:4, 19). Love plays a special role in the whole list, as we have seen above (cf. 2 Cor 6:6; Eph 4:2; Col 3:14; 2 Pet 1:7). Love, as loving action, is the singular fruit of the Spirit, with the remaining "virtues" describing the socially discernible and relevant circumstances, dispositions, and character traits that accompany love. Love as the fruit of the Spirit seems difficult to square logically with Paul's exhortations in this passage, especially the one in v. 13c: "Through love be slaves of one another" (cf. the imperatives in 5:15, 16, 25, 26; 6:1, 2, 4, 6, 7, 9, 10). Is love something the Galatians must decide to do, or is it the natural outcome of the Spirit's presence? The answer is probably that the Spirit creates the condition (freedom from the law, from Sin, from the elements of the world) in which truly responsible loving action can in fact take place (cf. Martyn; see comment on 6:9–10). Such responsible loving action can thus be understood as the fruit of the Spirit.

The term *chara*, "joy," also occurs frequently in Paul's Letters (Rom 14:17; 15:13, 32; 2 Cor 1:24; 2:3; 7:4, 13; 8:2; Gal 5:22; Phil 1:4, 25; 2:2, 29; 4:1; 1 Thess 1:6; 2:19–20; 3:9; Phlm 7; cf. Col 1:11; 2 Tim 1:4), as does *eirēnē*, "peace" (Rom 1:7; 2:10; 3:17; 5:1; 8:6; 14:17, 19; 15:13, 33; 16:20; 1 Cor 1:3; 7:15; 14:33; 16:11; 2 Cor 1:2; 13:11; Gal 1:3; 5:22; 6:16; Phil 1:2; 4:7, 9; 1 Thess 1:1; 5:3, 23; Phlm 3; cf. Eph 1:2; 2:14–15, 17; 4:3; 6:15, 23; Col 1:2; 3:15; 2 Thess 1:2; 3:16; 1 Tim 1:2; 2 Tim 1:2; 2:22; Titus 1:4). Paul has referred to "peace" earlier in Galatians, in the salutation (1:3). There it is said to come from "God our Father and the Lord Jesus Christ," is closely linked to grace, and points to the eschatological well-being that accompanies the gospel (see comment there). It is the opposite of the situation described in 5:15. Joy and peace are also juxtaposed in Romans, where they together characterize "the kingdom of God" (14:17) and "believing" (15:13). Here joy and peace accompany and characterize the mutual love that is the result of the Spirit's presence and work.

Dispositions that accompany love: "patience [*makrothymia*], kindness [*chrēstotēs*], goodness [*agathōsynē*]." These terms occur rarely outside of the Pauline Letters in the NT and not at all in the Gospels. *Makrothymia* (Rom 2:4; 9:22; 2 Cor 6:6; cf. Eph 4:2; Col 1:11; 3:12; 1 Tim 1:16; 2 Tim 3:10; 4:2; Heb 6:12; Jas 5:10; 1 Pet 3:20; 2 Pet 3:15) implies persistence, steadfastness, and forbearance toward others (Burton 315; Lührmann 111). *Chrēstotēs* (Rom 2:4;

3:12; 11:22; 2 Cor 6:6; cf. Eph 2:7; Col 3:12; Titus 3:4) and *agathōsynē* (Rom 15:14; cf. Eph 5:9; 2 Thess 1:11) serve to underscore patience as a defining disposition of loving action. These terms are all relational.

Character traits that accompany love: "faithfulness [*pistis*], humility [*praütēs*], self-control [*enkrateia*]." Paul probably does not regard these character traits as innate qualities but as marks of the Spirit's presence. While applied to the individual believer, they have social implications since they affect the believer's relationship with other believers. Paul has used the term *pistis* numerous times before in Galatians (2:16; etc.), especially in connection with the faithfulness of Christ (see Excursuses 9 and 11). The term here clearly refers to a believer's faithfulness, probably not in the active sense of trust, reliance, or confidence (in someone or something), but in the passive sense of trustworthiness, honesty, or reliability. *Praütēs* (1 Cor 4:21; 2 Cor 10:1; Eph 4:2; Col 3:12; 2 Tim 2:25; Titus 3:2; Jas 1:21; 3:13; 1 Pet 3:16) can mean "gentleness" (KJV, NRSV, NIV; Hauck and Schulz) but also "meekness" or "humility," "the quality of not being overly impressed by a sense of one's self-importance" (BDAG 861). Its significance for Paul is discernible in 6:1 (see comment there). Humility and faithfulness are two virtues mentioned together in Sirach, who describes "faithfulness and humility" as God's special "delight" (1:27) and claims that God chose Moses "out of all humankind" for "his faithfulness and humility" (45:4 AT). Paul may thus be relying on a traditional juxtaposition in his choice of these two virtues.

Enkrateia has a long history in ancient philosophy, including Plato, Aristotle, and the Stoics (Grundmann 1964a). By Paul's time it had "acquired the meaning 'self-control,' 'mastery of one's own desires and impulses,' but without specific reference to any particular class of such desires" (Burton 318). The noun and the related adjective (*enkratēs*) are absent from the LXX apart from later apocryphal works (e.g., Wis 8:21; Sir 26:15; 4 Macc 5:34). The terms occur frequently in Philo and the Apostolic Fathers. In the NT the adjective occurs only in Titus 1:8, where it is used in connection with the qualifications of a bishop. The noun occurs only twice elsewhere in the NT. Second Peter 1:6 includes it in a catalog of virtues. In Acts 24:25 Paul is depicted as lecturing the Roman prefect of Judea, Felix, and his wife, Drusilla, about "righteousness, self-control and judgment" (NIV). Paul also uses the cognate verb (*enkrateuomai*) in two passages in 1 Corinthians. In 7:9, he recommends marriage as a concession for believers who cannot exercise sexual self-control as he does; in 9:25 he likens himself to an athlete who must exercise self-control in order to win the desired prize. Paul may have chosen to include self-control in his list of Gal 5:23, placing it at the end as a counterpart to the last two vices listed in v. 21a ("bouts of drunkenness, drinking parties"). The basic sense here is thus probably not "sexual asceticism" but "sobriety" or "moderation." The crucial point is not the innate moral goodness of those who exhibit this character trait (and those of faithfulness and humility), but the positive implications for the life of the churches in Galatia as communities of Christ (Martyn; Williams; Witherington; cf. Ukwuegbu). Believers, too, can cultivate these virtues but only within the sphere of the Spirit's strife against the Flesh (cf. 6:2 and comment there). Within that framework, believers cannot entirely escape accountability for the wrong that they do on the one hand, nor can they take full credit for the good that they do on the other.

Paul follows his list of virtues with a seemingly ironic comment: "Against such things [*kata tōn toioutōn*] there is no law" (v. 23b). An alternate translation could be the following: "Against such *people* there is no law." The former is the more likely, given the foregoing list of virtues (cf. "such things," *ta toiauta*, in v. 21b), though there is little or no difference in the sense. Precisely the same phrase is also found in Aristotle (*Pol.* 3.13.1284A), which may or may not be coincidental (cf. Bruce 255–56). Though "law" (*nomos*) here, as in Aristotle, is used in a general sense to mean "legal prescription," Paul probably has particularly the Mosaic law in view. His point is probably not that "these things fully meet the requirements of the [Mosaic] law" (Burton 318; cf. Barclay 1988: 123–24; Schewe 135), but more probably that the virtues just listed fall completely outside its sphere (cf. v. 18: "You are *not* under the law"). They have nothing to do with law or the law. The fruit of the Spirit is not a matter of legal prescription. Paul's peculiar use of the preposition "against" (*kata* + genitive) sharpens the point, especially if Paul intends an allusion back to 3:21, where he has emphatically claimed that the law is *not* "against [*kata* + genitive] the promises of God," meaning that the law cannot invalidate them (see comment on 3:21). Paul's point in 5:23b would then be that the law, coming much later than the promise to Abraham (3:17), cannot invalidate the virtues listed, for they actually represent the fulfillment of God's singular promise as formulated in Lev 19:18 (see comment on 5:14 and Excursus 17, above). This interpretation is consistent with regarding all the virtues listed as aspects or dimensions of love, the singular fruit of the Spirit that stands at the beginning of the list.

Whenever believers in Christ are "walking by the Spirit" (v. 16) or "led by the Spirit" (v. 18), they will manifest the fruit of the Spirit in their daily lives (vv. 22–23a). For this reason Paul can now emphatically say that "those who belong to Christ Jesus have [discernibly] crucified the Flesh with its passions and desires" (v. 24). This verse forms an inclusio with v. 13, the first verse of this subunit, in which Paul raised the specter of a dangerous power loose in the world, something called "the Flesh": "only do not turn this freedom into an opportunity for the Flesh" (v. 13b; see Excursus 16, above). In v. 24, Paul reminds the Galatians of their new situation in Christ with respect to the Flesh: They have crucified it, they have put it to death (cf. Rom 8:13b). The death of the Flesh also means the death of its "passions" (*pathēmata*; cf. Rom 7:5) and "desires" (*epithymiai*). The singular "desire [*epithymia*] of the Flesh," to which

Paul referred in v. 16b (see comment there and Excursus 16), has multifarious manifestations in human life: hence the plural in v. 24. Paul has provided a selection of the many passions and desires of the Flesh for the edification of the Galatians in vv. 19–21 (see comment above).

The use of the verb "crucify" in this connection is surely figurative (cf. 2:19; 6:14; Rom 6:6). It alludes to Christ's death by crucifixion (cf. 3:1; 5:11; 6:12, 14) and implies that this death has also effected the death of the Flesh. This counts for "those who belong to Christ." Nevertheless, Paul's use of this verb in this verse is astonishing for at least two reasons:

Reason 1. He uses a past tense, an aorist (*estaurōsan*). (Since Paul refers to an event in the indefinite past, this aorist is best represented by an English perfect, "have crucified"). In short, Paul declares that the Flesh was put to death sometime in the past, with the undeniable implication that it can no longer pose a threat to the freedom of the Galatians in the present. A primary concern of this passage to this point, however, has been to alert the Galatians to the ongoing danger of the Flesh to this freedom! Paul's exhortation moves between declarations of the new situation effected by Christ and warnings about ongoing danger. His admonitions to "be slaves of one another through love" (v. 13) and to "walk by the Spirit" (v. 16) are addressed to believers in Christ who live at the juncture of the ages and are thus caught between an "already" and a "not yet." The dialectical interplay of the indicative (which assumes an "already") and the imperative (which reckons with a "not yet") evident here has its roots in Paul's apocalyptic construal of Christ's death and resurrection as the event that marks the turn of the ages (see Excursus 2).

Reason 2. Paul makes the Galatian believers the subject of the action. He writes, "*You* have crucified the Flesh," instead of, for example, "since you have been crucified with Christ [cf. 2:19], the Flesh will have no dominion over you" (cf. v. 16). But the latter is in fact what he probably means (also Schewe 137 n. 378). It is not likely that Paul means to say that the Galatians (and other believers after them) have made, or can make, an autonomous decision to put the Flesh to death (Mussner 390; Matera 211). The use of the verb "crucify" is here decisive: It clearly points to Christ's rectifying death on the cross on their behalf. In being crucified with Christ (cf. 2:19; 6:14; see comments there), the Galatian believers can be said to have crucified the Flesh, precisely as faithful participants in Christ's faithful death. That crucifixion of the Flesh occurred when they came to believe and allowed themselves to be baptized into Christ (2:16b; 3:27–28), for at that moment the Spirit was also given to them (3:1–5, 14; 4:6–7). The formulation "You have crucified the Flesh" is thus a *description* of the new, eschatological situation of "those who belong to Christ," which is the result of the gift of the Spirit. Paul's formulation is *not* to be taken as an admonition for believers to go and crucify the Flesh (Dunn 315), for that has already taken place "in Christ." Paul's declaration will enable the Galatians (and subsequent readers of the letter with them) to recognize and to embrace once again the new reality that *has been* established in their lives by the coming of Christ into the world (cf. 4:4–5; 5:1). It is on this basis that Paul can, in the following passage, exhort the Galatians to live accordingly, to "follow the Spirit" (5:25), for it is only by consciously and attentively following the Spirit that they can prevent their freedom from the law from becoming an opportunity for the Flesh to launch attacks on them (5:13).

5:25–6:10 Living by the Spirit and Fulfilling the Law of Christ

Having declared in v. 24 that those who belong to Christ have crucified the Flesh with its diverse passions and desires, Paul can now focus his readers' attention on what life at the juncture of the ages looks like in practice. There are nine imperatives in this passage (5:25, 26; 6:1, 2, 4, 6, 7, 9, 10), more than twice the number found in the previous one (5:13, 15, 16). The Spirit is mentioned five times (5:25 [2x]; 6:1, 8 [2x]) in this subsection; the Flesh appears only twice, both times merely as a foil for the Spirit in 6:8.

It is difficult to discern a structure in the material or its specific relevance for the Galatian situation. Dibelius (3) famously argued that certain of Paul's Letters, this one among them, contain "sayings and groups of sayings very diverse in content, lacking any particular order, and containing no emphasis upon a special thought of pressing importance for a particular situation." According to Dibelius (6), "One saying is attached to another simply because a word or cognate of the same stem appears in both sayings." In support of these claims, he cites Gal 6:2–5, where the verb *bastazō* ("carry") joins seemingly unrelated sayings; 6:7–9, where the verb *therizō* ("reap") does so; and 6:9–10, where the noun *kairos* ("season, opportunity") does the same (1976: 10). For Dibelius, these sayings accordingly do not reflect or address the specific problems or issues in Galatia. Barclay (1988: 154), on the other hand, argues that 5:15 and 5:26 provide "sufficient evidence for communal strife in the Galatian churches, . . . and this may well be the best context in which to understand the various maxims gathered in 5.25–6.10." However, while Dibelius overstates his case, Gal 5:15 and 5:26 do appear to refer to the world of the Flesh in a generalizing way (see comment on 5:15, above; and on 5:26, below). They alert the Galatians to the world outside the sphere of Christ's lordship and to the fact that this world still threatens them on every side (see comment on 5:16–18 above). Christ not only discloses the contours of the "new creation" (6:15); he also discloses the dangerously malignant characteristics of "the present evil age" (1:4). At the present juncture, it is not possible for Paul to mention the first without contrasting it with the second.

The passage appears to have three distinguishable subunits. In the first (5:25–6:1), Paul exhorts the Galatians to "follow" the Spirit, helping them to

Life at the Juncture of the Ages 369

discern what following the Spirit means in practice. In the second (6:2–6), the overarching theme is the carrying of burdens, understood metaphorically. Here occurs the striking notion of "fulfilling the law of Christ." In the third (6:7–10), Paul issues a warning about what is at stake in following, or not following, the Spirit, but he concludes with a promise and words of encouragement. This third subunit functions as a general summary of Section V of the epistle (5:13–6:10). Each subunit begins without a particle or conjunction (such as "and," "but," or "for") connecting it to the preceding subunit. That fact indicates (1) that each subunit is probably an independent literary and semantic whole (see comment below), and (2) that Paul could have varied the sequence of the three subunits without any discernible loss of meaning.

5:25 If we live by the Spirit, let us also follow the Spirit. **26** Let us not become conceited, provoking one another, envying one another. **6:1** Brethren, if someone[a] should indeed be overtaken in any trespass, you who are spiritual restore such a person in a spirit of humility, watching yourself lest you also are tempted.

2 Carry one another's burdens and so you will fulfill[b] the law of Christ. **3** For if someone thinks himself to be something while being nothing, he deceives himself. **4** But let each one scrutinize the work of himself, and then he will have a boast in himself alone and not in the other. **5** For each one will carry his own load. **6** And let the one who is instructed in the word share in all good things with the one who instructs.

7 Do not be deceived, God is not mocked, for whatever someone sows, this also he will reap: **8** Because the one sowing into the Flesh of himself will from the Flesh reap corruption, but the one sowing into the Spirit will from the Spirit reap eternal life. **9** And let us not grow weary of doing what is right, for we shall reap in due season if we do not tire. **10** So then, as we have opportunity, let us accomplish what is good toward all people, and especially toward the members of the household of faith.

a. Some manuscripts add *ex hymōn*, "of you" (Ψ, 0278, 1175, etc.), which is an attempt to clarify Paul's meaning.

b. There is good evidence for the reading *anaplērōsate*, an aorist imperative (ℵ, A, C, D, Ψ, and others). The evidence for the future indicative *anaplērōsete*, however, is also solid ($\mathfrak{P}^{46}$ [*apoplērōsete*], B, F, G, Marcion, and most ancient versions). Given the hortatory context, it is more likely that scribes would here change a future indicative to an aorist imperative than the reverse (Metzger 530).

In Paul's chosen arrangement of the material there is a discernible correspondence between the beginning and the end:

(a) 5:25: Let us follow the Spirit.
(b) 5:26: Let us not become conceited.
(b´) 6:9: Let us not grow weary.
(a´) 6:10: Let us accomplish the good.

The Greek verbs in all four verses are first-person plural subjunctives in the present tense. In 5:25 (a) and 6:10 (a´), the exhortation is positive; in 5:26 (b) and 6:9 (b´) it is negative or prohibitive. The last two verses, therefore, form an inclusio with the first two.

[5:25–6:1] The opening verse is deceptively simple: "If we live by the [power of the] Spirit, let us also follow the Spirit." It is probably the key verse of Section V, encapsulating its message. It deserves careful scrutiny.

Paul begins the verse with the assumption that believers now live by the Spirit: "If [*ei*] we live [*zōmen*] by the Spirit [*pneumati*) [as we do] . . ." (cf. NIV; Longenecker: "Since we live by the Spirit ..."). This is consistent with the preceding verse: On account of the Spirit's presence and work (3:1–5, 14; 5:16–18, 22–23), believers in Christ "*have* crucified the Flesh with its passions and desires" (5:24). For this reason Paul can begin v. 25 with the assumption that believers now live by the Spirit (cf. 5:16, 18). The indicative of this subordinate clause, however, forms the basis for the imperative in the main clause: "[Then] let us also follow the Spirit [*pneumati*]." The conditional clause sums up the import of Paul's argument from 3:1–5 onward (the Galatians have received the Spirit and live by it); the main clause draws the necessary conclusion for life at the present juncture, which remains "in the flesh" (2:20) and under assault by "the Flesh" (5:13–24). The verb "to live" in v. 25a is being used ethically, as a synonym of the verb "to walk" (cf. v. 16), and denotes a manner of conduct or existence (cf. 2:14, 19–20; 3:11–12). Because it concerns life by (and thus also in) the Spirit, that manner of conduct or existence has an eschatological dimension; it entails new life, the life of the age inaugurated by Christ (cf. BDAG 425; comments on 2:19–20; 3:11–12). Its defining characteristic is "being slaves of one another in love" (v. 13; cf. vv. 14, 22).

Paul's use of the verb "to live" (*zaō*) accompanied by a simple dative (here *pneumati*) is a construction that occurs elsewhere in his letters (Rom 6:10–11; 14:7–8; 2 Cor 5:15; Gal 2:19; cf. Luke 20:38; 1 Pet 2:24). In these passages, the dative is always understood by interpreters to be a dative of relation or advantage, leading to the translation "to live [in relation] *to* someone or something" or "*for* [the advantage of] someone or something" (e.g., God, Christ, righteousness). The instance in Gal 2:19 is particularly relevant: "I died to the law, that I might live *to* [or *for*] God [*hina theō zēsō*]." Alone among the commentators, Lightfoot (214) understands the usage in v. 25 in the same way, translating the conditional clause as follows: "If we live *to* the Spirit . . ." He interprets this usage to mean that life in the Spirit is "an ideal" to be attained

Life at the Juncture of the Ages 371

rather than "an actual life." If the dative is one of relation or advantage, however, the more-probable sense would be that "we" believers are *now* living to (or for) the Spirit, just as Paul now lives "to [or for] God," according to 2:19 (cf. 2:20).

Nevertheless, the dative in the conditional clause is probably to be construed as a dative of instrument (Moule 44) or means (Burton 322). That construal of the dative is consistent with the occurrences of *pneumati* (each time without a definite article) in the immediately preceding material:

5:5   For we, through the Spirit [*pneumati*] from faith, are waiting . . .
5:16 But I say, walk by the Spirit [*pneumati*] . . .
5:18 And if you are led by the Spirit [*pneumati*] . . .

Given this usage, the Galatians will probably understand the term in v. 25 in the same way:

5:25 If we live by the Spirit [*pneumati*] . . .

The sense is evidently that the Spirit (of Christ) is the determining factor in the new life of the believers.

This interpretation of the conditional clause provides a warrant for construing the dative *pneumati* in the main clause in the same way, as a dative of instrument or means: "If we live by the Spirit, by the Spirit let us also walk" (so Burton; Ridderbos; RSV). In favor of this reading are (1) the positions of the two instances of *pneumati* in the two clauses (the second instance following directly from the first in the Greek text), (2) the attribution of consistency to Paul in his use of the dative *pneumati* in this context (if he intends a dative of instrument or means in the conditional clause, he probably intends the same in the main clause), and (3) the pleasing chiasm that results:

a   If we live
b   by the Spirit,
b´   by the Spirit
a´   let us also walk.[482]

This way of reading the main clause (b´ + a´) effectively leads to the Galatians' being paradoxically exhorted to do what they are already doing, living or walking by the Spirit.

---

482. An attractive alternative is to construe the dative as locative, as KJV does: "If we live in the Spirit, let us also walk in the Spirit." It can safely be said that life by the Spirit entails life in (the sphere of) the Spirit as well, as the notion of being "in Christ" (3:26–28) demonstrates. On the other hand, if Paul had meant to say "in the Spirit" here, he probably would have used the preposition *en* ("in"), on the model of "in Christ."

The verb translated "walk" in this interpretation is not *peripateō* (cf. 5:16a), however, but *stoicheō* (cf. 6:16; Rom 4:12; Phil 3:16; Acts 21:24).[483] This verb basically means "stand or move in a row or a line" and, like the cognate *systoicheō* in 4:25, has a military origin (LSJ 1647; Barclay 1988: 155; Betz 294; Vouga 144). In its metaphorical use, it means "be in line with a person or thing considered as a standard for one's conduct," in short, "hold to, agree with, follow, conform" (BDAG 946). It takes a dative of association (BDF #193, #198.5), warranting the chosen translation "Let us also follow the Spirit" (so BDAG 946).[484] Acceptable alternatives are "Hold to the Spirit," "Conform to the Spirit," "Walk in line with the Spirit," or "Keep in step with the Spirit" (NIV; Longenecker), where the last two are clearly metaphorical. More periphrastic are such renderings as "Let us also be guided by the Spirit" (NRSV) or "Let us carry out our daily lives under the guidance of the Spirit" (Martyn). There may be an allusion, whether intentional or subconscious, back to the *stoicheia tou kosmou* ("elements of the world"), which the Galatians had once venerated (4:3, 9): Whereas they once "followed" the *stoicheia*, they are now to "follow" (*stoicheō*) the Spirit.

Since the verb in v. 25b is a first-person cohortative subjunctive in the present tense, the sense is "Let us go on following the Spirit" or "Let us make a habit of following the Spirit." The Galatians are being exhorted to go on aligning their lives with the Spirit, by which they now live. This evidently requires some effort and attention. The Spirit enlists believers in its ongoing strife against the Flesh (see 5:17 above). For Paul, only believers in Christ, because they have been liberated from the law and the elements of the world (4:3–5), can be enlisted and thus exhorted in this way. As Martyn writes, "Paul knows . . . that by sending the Spirit into the Galatians' hearts (4:6), God created their churches as addressable communities, communities *able* to hear and heed the divine imperative" (542, with original stress). The gift of the Spirit does not make moral responsibility, discernment, and action superfluous; it makes them possible.

The next two verses provide guidelines for what following the Spirit concretely entails. The first (5:26), however, indicates what following the Spirit does *not* entail: "Let us not become conceited, provoking one another, envying one another" (cf. 5:15). Paul begins the verse with a prohibitive subjunctive (*mē ginōmetha*), the present tense, implying the ongoing or permanent avoidance of an activity. The term *kenodoxoi* ("conceited"), found only here in the

---

483. NRSV perceives the problem presented by RSV but gives a periphrastic rendering of the main clause: "If we live by the Spirit, let us also be guided by the Spirit."

484. Hence, whereas the term *pneumati* in the conditional clause is to be understood to signify instrument or means, the same term in the main clause is to be taken to signify association or accompaniment. Smyth (##503, 1521, 1524) regards the dative of accompaniment as a subcategory of the dative of instrument or means.

NT (cf. *Did.* 3.5; Phil 2:3 uses the cognate noun *kenodoxia*), connotes having an inflated opinion of oneself (BDAG 539). The term frequently occurs in Hellenistic philosophy (Betz 294). This inflated self-perception concretely leads to "provoking [*prokaloumenoi*] one another" and "envying [*phthonountes*] one another." Though common in classical Greek, both terms are absent from the LXX, apart from Tob 4:7, 16 and 2 Macc 8:11 (Lightfoot 214; Burton 324–25; Vouga 145). All three terms occur only occasionally in Hellenistic Jewish texts influenced by popular philosophy (cf. Betz 295). Paul's choice of words thus represents an attempt to make contact with the culture and knowledge of the Greek-speaking Gentile believers in Galatia. Provocation and envy doubtless represent for him two "works of the Flesh" (v. 19–21a). Paul's list of such works includes "acts of envy" (*phthonoi*). To this nonexhaustive list (v. 21a) he could have added "acts of provocation." Such acts belong to the past, which the Galatians have left behind. It is possible that Paul's admonition is designed to meet an existing situation within the Galatian churches (e.g., Burton; Martyn; Barclay 1988: 153), but it is equally possible that he acknowledges a commonplace threat to communal concord (Becker; Vouga). As in 5:13–15, it is as if Paul cannot describe the new world of the Spirit without contrasting it with the old world of the Flesh, a world that the Galatians once knew intimately and that still threatens them on all sides. He assumes, however, if only for the sake of argument, that the Galatians are actually living by the Spirit and want to go on aligning their lives with it (5:25).

In the next verse (6:1), Paul provides a positive indication of what following the Spirit involves: "Brethren, if someone should indeed be overtaken in any trespass, you who are spiritual restore such a person in a spirit of humility, watching yourself lest you also are tempted." The key term in this verse is "humility" (*praütēs*), listed as a fruit of the Spirit in 5:22–23. Humility, as we saw in the comment on the term in 5:23, is "the quality of not being overly impressed by a sense of one's self-importance" (BDAG 861). In other words, to act in "a spirit of humility" is the opposite of being "conceited," of having an exaggerated sense of one's self-importance, in the previous verse.[485] Paul here appears to use the term "spirit" (*pneuma*) in a nontheological sense to refer to an attitude or posture. But there may be a play on words since Paul also regards humility as a fruit of the Spirit. The spirit of humility is, as it were, the humility of the Spirit.

Paul addresses the Galatians directly in 6:1, shifting from the inclusive first-person plural of the previous two verses to the second-person plural in this verse: "Brethren, . . . you who are spiritual restore such a person." The Galatian "brethren" (*adelphoi*, "sisters and brothers") are here characterized as "you who are spiritual," or more literally, "you, the spiritual ones" (*hymeis*

---

485. For this reason, v. 6:1 has been taken to belong with the preceding two verses.

hoi pneumatikoi). This formulation is probably equivalent to "you who have received the Spirit" (cf. 3:2; 4:6). This characterization is sometimes taken to refer to a limited group within the Galatian churches ("the spiritual ones among you"). That then opens the door to various theories about these "spiritual people," whether they were gnostics (Schmithals) or libertines (Lütgert) free from all moral constraint, the opposite of those in Galatia wanting to adopt the law. Another proposal is to equate "you who are spiritual" with those Galatian believers who in fact want to adopt the law: these people are certain that they are the truly spiritual ones (Martyn 546). In these theories, the characterization "you who are spiritual" is to be taken as ironic, even sarcastic, and as disapproving. But the verse does not have a polemical cast; the tone is friendly and fraternal (Calvin; Lightfoot). It seems then that "you who are spiritual" is an inclusive description, coined by Paul himself,[486] of the "brethren" addressed.[487] Elsewhere in Galatians the "brethren" are not some group within the Galatian churches but all the members (1:2, 11; 3:15; 4:12, 28, 31; 5:11, 13). The same is probably true here. There is one exception: the imagined individual overtaken in some trespass, whose nonspiritual activity is regarded as a temporary lapse. The goal, however, is that person's full restoration to the previous condition of being part of the community of spiritual people. The restoration is to be "completely devoid of lasting stigma" (Martyn 547).

In the subordinate clause, Paul posits the possibility of what he hopes is an extremely unlikely, certainly undesirable, circumstance, as indicated by the intensive use of *kai* to mean "indeed" and the use of *ean* ("if") with the subjunctive: "Brethren, if [*ean*] someone should indeed [*kai*] be overtaken [*prolēmphthē*] in any trespass [and of course I hope that does not happen] ..." The "someone" (*anthrōpos*)[488] in view is a member of the Galatian churches (cf. 1 Cor 5:3–5; 2 Cor 2:6–8; Matt 18:15–17; Jas 5:19–20; 1QS 5.24–6.1).[489] The "trespass" (*paraptōma*) remains undefined. Literally, the Greek word implies a misstep leading to a fall (cf. Rom 4:25; 5:15–18, 20; 11:11–12; 2 Cor 5:19; Eph 1:7; 2:1, 5; Col 2:13). A "trespass" so understood is the opposite of following the Spirit (5:25; see comment there). It is probably wrong to translate the term as "transgression" (NRSV, NAB; Betz; Bruce; Longenecker; Witherington; Martyn) since a transgression (*parabasis*) involves the violation of a legal principle or standard (see comment on 2:18; 3:19). A trespass is not the viola-

---

486. He may have coined it for the Galatian situation under the influence of the situation in Corinth. Cf. 1 Cor 2:13–15; 3:1; 12:1; 14:37.

487. For Martyn (546), Paul is being both ironic and inclusive at the same time. Paul takes a term that is being used exclusively by the Galatians who are embracing the law and he uses it inclusively to refer to all the Galatian *adelphoi*.

488. Two manuscripts substitute *tis* for *anthrōpos* (P, sy^p), thereby capturing the sense.

489. Some scribes added "from/of you" (*ex hymōn*) to make this clear (Ψ, 0278, 1175, etc.; also P, sy^p after *tis*).

tion of a law, or of the law, but a falling away or a deviation, in this case, from the guidance of the Spirit. Paul refers to "any" trespass; presumably any one of the works of the Flesh is in view (5:19–21). A trespass thus involves falling back into the old age, where the Flesh still holds sway.

The verb that Paul employs (*prolambanō*) can mean "to detect," "to catch in the act" (NRSV, NAB, NJB, NIV; Betz 295; Dunn 318; Matera 213; Martyn 546) or, more probably in this context, "to overtake by surprise, or unawares," as in Wis 17:16–17 and Josephus, *J.W.* 5.79 (RSV; Burton 327; Longenecker 272; Delling 14; BDAG 872). The imagined misstep is unexpected and unwanted not only by Paul but also by the imagined trespasser. Paul does not have an intentional sin in view, but an unintentional misstep on the part of someone who is living by the Spirit (5:25). A spirit of humility is important in dealing with such a stumbler since anyone helping is in danger of falling as well: "watching yourself lest you [sing.] also are tempted [to deviate from following the Spirit]." In the main clause Paul addresses the Galatians collectively; in this concluding subordinate clause, he individualizes his admonition, thereby making it "more pointed" (Burton 328). As Barclay observes (1988: 149–50), there is a constant interplay between corporate responsibility and individual accountability in this passage. The point of the switch to the singular is not to focus the attention on the subjective feeling of an attraction to evil, but on the danger of finding oneself in the same dire situation as the trespasser whom one is seeking to restore to the community (Burton 329). The verb "tempted" here means "lured to do the same thing," perhaps by the trespasser's behavior itself (Dunn 321). The Galatians, who are spiritual people because they have received the Spirit and live by it, are exhorted to "restore" (*katartizete*) such a trespasser to the community, doing so in a spirit of humility, which involves the constant recognition that the same trespass can overcome everyone unawares. It's a dangerous world out there.

In 5:25–6:1, then, Paul has briefly but concretely indicated what following the Spirit does not entail on the one hand ("becoming conceited") and what it does entail on the other (acting with "a spirit of humility" toward a wayward member of the community).

[2–6] No connective particle joins this passage to the preceding. It stands on its own, though it thematically continues to illustrate what it means to "follow the Spirit" in 5:25b. What sets it apart and unites it is the use of the verb "to carry" (*bastazō*) in vv. 2 and 5 and the use of the synonyms "burden" (*baros*) in v. 2 and "load" (*phortion*) in v. 5:

²Carry [*bastazete*] one another's burdens [*barē*] and so you will fulfill the law of Christ. ³For [*gar*] if someone thinks himself to be something while being nothing, he deceives himself. ⁴But [*de*] let each one scrutinize the work of himself, and then he will have a boast in himself alone and

not in the other. ⁵For [*gar*] each one will carry [*bastasei*] his own load [*phortion*]. ⁶And [*de*] let the one who is instructed in the word share in all good things with the one who instructs.

The verses are joined to each other by conjunctions (*gar* and *de*). Still, the overall impression of this subunit is that of a loose collection of exhortations, each of which could stand on its own. That counts especially for v. 6.

Verse 2 begins literally "Of one another [*allēlōn*] the burdens carry." The placement of *allēlōn* at the beginning of the sentence indicates emphasis and shows that Paul's focus is not so much on the actor as on the beneficiary of the action in view. The verb Paul uses (*bastazete*) is once again a present imperative (cf. 5:13, 16, 25, 26; 6:1), implying that the Galatians are either to "keep on carrying" each other's burdens or to "make a habit of doing so." Both may be in view. To carry one another's burdens is to "follow the Spirit" (5:25b). The Greek verb that Paul uses (*bastazō*) is commonly translated "bear," which has come to have the connotation of "put up with" or "tolerate," perhaps with gritted teeth. That connotation, perhaps present elsewhere (e.g., 5:10; Rom 15:1), is probably not present here (cf. BDAG 171). The point is to do something for someone else that may involve effort, inconvenience, and discomfort (cf. Luke 14:27; Acts 15:10), but then without resentment (cf. 6:17 and comment there). Carrying burdens was predominantly if not exclusively the task of slaves in the ancient world (Barclay 1988: 131). For this reason, Paul's exhortation here is probably synonymous with the exhortation that stands at the head of Section V of the letter in 5:13c: "through love be slaves of one another [*allēlois*]" (see comment there). Paul's language is metaphorical (as, e.g., that of Socrates in Xenophon, *Mem.* 2.7.1, cited by LSJ 307 and Betz 299: "one must share one's burden with one's friends"; cf. Matt 20:12). The "burdens" in v. 2 presumably refer in the first instance to the common cares and concerns that mark life "in the flesh" (2:20): the worry about food, clothing, and shelter; the threats of violence and disease; the debilitating effects of poverty; and the fear of loss, isolation, and death. Some argue that financial burdens may be particularly in view (Strelan; Witherington 423; cf. 1 Thess 2:5–9; 2 Thess 3:8; 2 Cor 12:16; see comment on v. 6 below). Paul may also have in view the burden of becoming, or dealing with, a trespasser (v. 1) who has disrupted community cohesion. Paul's language is as paradoxical as it is metaphorical: Those who are slaves of another through love, through carrying one another's burdens, live in the realm of freedom brought about by Christ and his Spirit (5:1, 13). Making the language doubly paradoxical is the fact that there are no "masters," only "slaves." Christ provides the pattern for this burden bearing (see comment on 5:13c) and his Spirit provides the enabling conditions.

Carry one another's burdens, Paul exhorts, "and so [*houtōs*] you will fulfill [*anaplērōsete*] the law of Christ." Paul has used the simple form of the verb

Life at the Juncture of the Ages 377

"to fulfill" (*pleroō*) in 5:14; he here uses a compound and more intensive form of this verb (*anaplēroō*). The sense may be "completely or thoroughly fulfill." Here Gal 6:2 recalls 5:13c–14:

Galatians 5:13c–14	Galatians 6:2
(a) through love be slaves of one another.	(a) Carry one another's burdens
(b) For the entire law has been fulfilled in one word, namely, "You will love your neighbor as yourself."	(b) and so you will fulfill the law of Christ.

The semantic similarities between 5:13c ("through love be slaves of one another") and 6:2a ("Carry one another's burdens") have been pointed out in the previous paragraph. Both 5:14 and 6:2b speak of "fulfilling the law." As explained in Excursus 17, fulfilling the law is not the same as doing the law. In neither passage, moreover, is fulfillment of "the law" (whatever that may refer to) a commandment or an assignment; in both cases fulfillment is the situation that results from actions of mutual love.[490] If being slaves of another through love (5:13c) constitutes the fulfillment of the promise uttered in Lev 19:18 that "you *will* love your neighbor as yourself" (which is the one "word" of promise whereby "the entire law has been fulfilled"), so also carrying one another's burdens constitutes the fulfillment of the promise that believers "*will* fulfill the law of Christ" (6:2). Furthermore, the sense of the assertion "the entire law has been fulfilled" in 5:14 is clearly "the entire law *will have been* fulfilled [whenever you are being slaves of one another in love]"; so also in v. 2b the sense of the claim "You will fulfill the law of Christ" is "You *will have fulfilled* the law of Christ [whenever you are carrying one another's burdens]." The semantic difference between the perfect in 5:14 and the future in 6:2 is not so great (Horrell 2005: 227) as may appear at first sight.

What however is "the law of Christ"? In 5:14, Paul has apparently used the term "law" to refer not to the Mosaic legal code, as he frequently has in the earlier chapters, but, as in 4:21b, to the Scripture, the Pentateuch in particular, which preserves not only the Mosaic legal code, but also, and this the key for Paul, the promises of God concerning Christ and his Spirit (see comment on 5:14 above along with Excursus 17). For Paul, this scriptural law stands over

---

490. As indicated in the textual note above, some manuscripts have the reading *anaplērōsate*, an aorist imperative (ℵ, A, C, D, Ψ, and others), which is adopted as original by, e.g., Burton 330. The evidence for the future indicative *anaplērōsete*, however, is also strong ($\mathfrak{P}^{46}$ [*apoplērōsete*], B, F, G, Marcion, and most ancient versions) and, since it is more likely that scribes would change a future indicative to an aorist imperative than the reverse, probably original (Metzger 530). Some modern interpreters tend to make the same change: they turn Paul's promise of fulfillment into a command to fulfill (e.g., Sanders 1983: 98: "The law should be fulfilled"; see Excursus 18, below).

against the Sinaitic law; in Paul's radical view, one not shared by the new preachers active in Galatia, the scriptural law is not identical with the Sinaitic law (cf. 4:21–24). Whereas the Sinaitic law is an enslaving and cursing power, the scriptural law contains the promises of the liberating activity of God in Christ. Those promises have now been fulfilled: they have come true. The point of 5:13c–14 was "All that God promised in the Scripture concerning Christ and his Spirit has become concrete, visible reality for us in the realization of the one word of promise articulated in Lev 19:18, namely, that you will in the new creation inaugurated by Christ truly love your neighbor as yourself." Given the points of contact between 5:14 and 6:2b, the reference to "the law of Christ" in v. 2b is probably to be interpreted in a similar way. This law of Christ is the scriptural law that attests to the coming of Christ and his Spirit, the Spirit whose fruit is love. The sense of 6:2b is then probably this: "By carrying one another's burdens, you will indeed fulfill [i.e., you will have fulfilled] the promise contained in the scriptural law concerning the coming of Christ and his Spirit" (see Excursus 18, below). By carrying one another's burdens, the Galatians will each specifically have fulfilled the promise attested by Lev 19:18 that "you [sing.] will love your neighbor as yourself" (see Excursus 17, above). In short, the new creation (6:15) will be a reality—will have become a reality—in their daily lives as a community of those who belong to Christ (cf. 3:29a).

Paul writes that the Galatians themselves "will fulfill the law of Christ." That should not be pressed unduly, as if Paul now regards the Galatians, or believers in Christ generally, as autonomous moral agents (see on 5:24 above). The sense is undoubtedly that believers in Christ will, thanks to Christ and his Spirit, fulfill the law of Christ. Their love for one another, expressed in mutual burden bearing, is after all a fruit of the Spirit (5:22).

Excursus 18: The Law of Christ

Paul's introduction of the expression "the law of Christ" (*ton nomon tou Christou*) in 6:2b is a crux interpretum. There have been four major proposals.

View 1. "The law of Christ" refers to the teachings of Jesus (C. H. Dodd 147–48), which are perhaps to be understood as the messianic law ("the law of the Messiah") suitable for the new age (Davies 143–45). The expression then appears to be a fixed combination, one perhaps derived from the new preachers in Galatia (cf. Betz 300). A difficulty with this proposal is that there is no convincing evidence elsewhere for such a technical use of the expression (Barclay 1988: 127–28). Furthermore, appeals to the (multifarious) teachings of (the pre-Easter) Jesus play no evident role in Paul's argument in Galatians (or for that matter, a significant role elsewhere in his letters). If "the law of Christ" does refer to something that Jesus himself taught, it may be the singular teaching concerning the importance of Lev 19:18 (cf. Mark 12:28–31; Matt 22:34–40;

Luke 10:25-28; see Excursus 17), which Paul quotes in 5:14. That brings us to the second proposal:

View 2. "The law of Christ" is the love commandment, the law of mutual love, as taught and exemplified by Christ (Luther 1535: 113; Bruce 261; Mussner 399; Bultmann 1951: 344; Furnish 1968: 64–65). The proponents of this view appeal to Paul's citation of Lev 19:18 in Gal 5:14. That is the "law of love" both taught and exemplified by Jesus. By carrying one another's burdens (6:2a), or being slaves of another through love (5:13c), believers in Christ will fulfill the commandment to mutual love, as taught by Christ and lived by him. A difficulty with this proposal is that Paul here uses the term "law" (*nomos*) to refer to a single commandment, which is not the way he has used the term earlier in 5:14, where he refers to "the entire law." There Lev 19:18 is referred to as a "word" (*logos*), not as a "law" in the sense of "commandment" (*entolē*). Furthermore, Paul appears to understand Lev 19:18 not as a commandment or a law, but as a promise (see Excursus 17).

View 3. "The law of Christ" is the Mosaic code as redefined, fulfilled, interpreted, lived, or taken in hand by Christ (Barclay 1988:132–34; Matera 220–21; Martyn 548–49; Hays 333; Schewe 156). Here again the expression can be regarded as a fixed combination, presumably derived from the new preachers (Lührmann 116). This interpretation depends upon taking the term "law" in 5:14 as also referring to the Mosaic code and upon emphasizing (Martyn 556–57) the similarity between the expression "the law of Christ" and other such genitive constructions found in Romans, where "the law" is arguably the Mosaic code, such as "the law of faith" in contrast with "the law of works" (3:27) and "the law of the Spirit of life in Christ" in contrast with "the law of Sin and Death" (8:2 AT). In 5:14, however, Paul appears to use the term "law" to refer not to the Mosaic code but to that portion of Scripture (the Pentateuch) commonly known as "the law" and, as Paul has emphasized in Gal 3, containing the promises of God concerning Christ and his Spirit. The same is then probably true for the instance in Gal 6:2b, making the evidence of Romans of dubious value for the interpretation of this verse. In Rom 7–8, furthermore, Paul seeks to exonerate the Mosaic legal code (the problem is not the law itself, but the fact that it has fallen into the hands of Sin); in Galatians, his agenda is the reverse, to point out its complicity with the Flesh (5:13–24) or Sin (3:21–22).

View 4. "The law of Christ" is the "normative pattern" established by Christ through his self-giving death (Hays 1987: 287, followed by Horrell 2005: 228–31; Witherington 423–24; Winger 2000: 538: "the practice which Paul believes should govern the community of believers"; Longenecker 275–75: a collection of "prescriptive principles stemming from the heart of the gospel"). This proposal is attractive because it is consistent with Paul's thought elsewhere in Galatians itself (1:3–4; 2:20; 3:13–14; 4:4–5; see comment on 5:13c). It does, however, attribute a meaning to the term "law" not found earlier in Galatians, not even in 5:14. For Hays, the term must be regarded as "an ironic rhetorical formulation" (1987: 275; cf. Betz 300, who entertains the possibility that Paul's use of the expression is an "ad hoc formulation, a mockery of the Galatians' obsession with the Torah").

Aspects of the last three proposals can be combined. Betz (301), for example, writes that "since the love command is the fulfillment of the whole Torah (Gal 5:14), he who loves fulfills the Torah; and since such love is Christ's love (Gal 2:20), that Torah can be called 'Christ's Torah.'" For Dunn (322–23), "the law of Christ" is a "shorthand" reference to "the Jesus-tradition," indicating "how Jesus interpreted the [Jewish] law in his teaching and actions"; the expression refers to "that law as interpreted by the love command in the light of the Jesus-tradition and the Christ-event" in that it concerns "Jesus' self-giving . . . as a paradigm for Christian relationships." For Matera (221), "the law of Christ" is "the Mosaic law interpreted through the love commandment and exemplified by Jesus' life of self-giving love on behalf of others." According to Horrell (2005: 230), even if the "majority view is correct" that the Mosaic law is in view in 6:2b, also when this Mosaic law is reduced to "the love-command as exemplified (and taught?) by Christ," "it would still be entirely plausible to read Gal 6.2 as indicating the centrality of Christ's self-giving for others as a model for Christian practice."

Crucial for the interpretation adopted in this commentary are two factors. (1) Apart from 5:14 and 6:2, Paul uses the term "law" (*nomos*) with two basic referential meanings in Galatians: It refers either to the Mosaic legal code (2:16 [3x], 19 [2x], 21; 3:2, 5, 10 [2x], 11, 12, 13, 17, 18, 21 [3x], 23, 24; 4:4, 5, 21a; 5:3, 4, 18, 23; 6:13),[491] *or* to "the Scripture," the Pentateuch in particular (4:21b). Obviously, "the law" as Scripture takes its name from the Mosaic legal code that it contains. But the law as Scripture also contains the promises of God concerning Christ and his Spirit, specifically the promise that God made to Abraham concerning offspring in the face of seemingly insuperable natural circumstances (the barrenness of Abraham's wife, Sarah, and the advanced age of both him and his wife). When Paul appealed to "the law" as Scripture in 4:21–5:1, he focused the attention of his readers on this promise at the expense of the Mosaic code (see comment there). (2) The verb "to fulfill," used in 5:14 and 6:2, is appropriate *only* to the second of these meanings, as fully argued in Excursus 17. It would seem then that "the law" in 5:14 and 6:2, as in 4:21b, must refer to "the Scripture." The sense of 6:2 is thus: "Carry one another's burdens, and so you will have brought into reality the scriptural promises concerning Christ." The promise found in Lev 19:18, quoted in 5:14, is probably particularly in view. To carry one another's burdens (v. 6:2a) is synonymous with to be slaves of one another in love (5:13c), which represents the fulfillment of the promise made in Lev 19:18. The fulfillment of this promise is tantamount to the fulfillment of "the entire [scriptural] law [containing the promises of God concerning Christ and his Spirit]" (5:14).

As in 5:14, Paul has in 6:2 chosen the word "law" instead of the word "Scripture" for the same reasons he did so in 4:21b (see Excursus 17): It is a play on words that allows him to refer to the promissory Scripture as "the law" in a situation in which that term, and the scriptural witness to God's promises concerning Christ, have become totally identified with the Mosaic code. Paul's repeatedly negative use of the term "law" in the previous argument has run the risk of reinforcing this virtual identification of the scriptural witness to God's promises with the Mosaic code, thereby playing into the hands of his opponents in Galatia. Paul rescues the term from this understandable and traditional identification for his own reading of the scriptural witness, bringing about a distinction, even a bifurcation, between the law as legal code and the law as divine

---

491. In a few instances Paul appears to speak of "law" (as legal code) in a generalizing way (3:18, 21b; 5:23; 6:13), but even in these verses the Mosaic code is the only law under consideration.

Life at the Juncture of the Ages 381

promise as attested in Scripture. For Paul, these are two different laws. One is "the law of Moses" (1 Cor 9:9), containing legal stipulations (such as the one cited in 1 Cor 9:9 from Deut 25:4: "You shall not muzzle an ox when it is treading out the grain" [RSV]). The other is "the law of Christ," containing divine promises that have been and will be fulfilled (such as the one contained in Lev 19:18: "You will love your neighbor as yourself"). In the process of making this distinction, Paul meets the objection from the new preachers that the abandonment of the Mosaic law has effectively left the Galatian churches morally rudderless, for the fulfillment of the law as Scripture containing divine promises pertaining to Christ has profound moral implications, as this section of the epistle seeks to demonstrate.

Galatians 6:3 is a continuation of the exhortation found in v. 2a: "Carry one another's burdens; . . . for [*gar*] if someone thinks himself to be something while being nothing, he deceives himself." An alternate translation of v. 2b could be, "For if someone thinks herself to be something while being nothing, she deceives herself." "Something" here probably means "something special," while "nothing" means "nothing special" (cf. 2:2, 6, 9; BDF #301.1; Bruce 261). Paul may be relying upon a traditional maxim, derived from popular philosophy (Longenecker 276; Betz 301; cf., e.g., Epictetus, *Diatr.* 4.8.39: "You think you are somebody—fool among fools!"), but in the present context he gives it a christological foundation and a contextually relevant application. Here Paul switches, as he has in 5:25–6:1, above, from a plural collective "we" to an individual "he" or "she" (cf. Lambrecht 1997). This focus on the individual believer continues through v. 6. Paul's concern throughout is "proper individual self-perception as the ground for life in the community" (Kuck 290). Furthermore, as in 5:25–6:1, Paul contrasts daily life in the Spirit with daily life under threat from the Flesh. For someone to "think him or herself to be something [special] while being nothing [special]" is to "become conceited [*kenodoxos*]" (5:26a), which means to indulge in an exaggerated sense of one's own importance. The provocation and envy that result (5:26) are examples of works of the Flesh (see comment on 5:26, above). It is possible that instances of conceit have in fact occurred in the Galatian churches, with its terrible consequences for communal life, but it is equally possible that Paul is merely alerting these churches to potential and all too common dangers (see comment on 5:26, above). Paul's explicit point in any case is that such conceit is self-delusion (cf. 1 Cor 3:18; Jas 1:26). Compared to that "something," a believer in Christ is actually "nothing," being totally dependent on the Spirit for the ability to behave in line with the Spirit (5:25). To be "nothing" in this sense is to be equipped with the ability to bear the burdens of others. Paul's implied point then appears to be that thinking you are something special when you are in fact nothing special gets in the way of mutual burden bearing.

In the following verse, Paul gives an exhortation to combat this manner of thinking: "But [*de*] let each one scrutinize the work of himself [*heauton*], and then he will have a boast in himself [*heauton*] alone and not in the other" (v. 4). An alternate translation could be, "But let each one scrutinize the work of herself, and then she will have a boast in herself alone and not in the other." The Greek conjunction *de* seems here to be adversative, hence the translation "but." The contrast is with v. 3, with thinking oneself to be "something," having an inflated opinion of oneself, when one is actually "nothing," dependent on Christ and his Spirit. The reflexive "himself" (*heauton*) is emphatic in both instances, with the term "alone" (*monon*) strengthening the emphasis in the second instance. Paul's primary concern appears to be that the believer scrutinize one's own work and *not* that of "the other" (*to heteron*), meaning someone else in the church, one's fellow believer. The latter activity leads to an inflated sense of one's own importance.

The term translated as "scrutinize" is the verb *dokimazō*, which here means "to make a critical examination of something" (BDAG 255; cf. NRSV, RSV, NIV: "test"; NJB, NAB: "examine"), thus to examine closely and critically (cf. 1 Cor 11:28; 2 Cor 13:5). The theme of self-examination is common in popular Hellenistic philosophy (Betz 302), but Paul adapts it for his own purposes. The object of such scrutiny is "the work" of oneself. The Greek is *to ergon*, a word Paul has used earlier in the plural with an emphatically negative connotation to designate "works [*erga*] of the law" (2:16; etc.) and "works [*erga*] of the Flesh" (5:19). The term here is used neutrally to mean "what one achieves, the result of one's effort" (Burton 332; cf. 1 Cor 3:13–15). Paul does not have a particular individual action in view, but many actions regarded as a whole. This "work" has to do with living in line with the Spirit (5:25). The believer is to examine closely and critically one's own work for indications of deviation from the Spirit in one's dealings with others in the church (Kuck 293). One is not to carry out such critical scrutiny of "the work" of other believers, which would be a sign of conceit. The result of the critical scrutiny of one's own work is that the believer "will have a boast in oneself alone," rather than "in the other." The preposition "in" (*eis*) here means "with reference to" (cf. 2 Cor 10:13, 15, 16). In this case a "boast" (*kauchēma*) refers to the ground for boasting (cf. RSV, NAB: "reason to boast"; NRSV: "cause for pride"), rather than to the act of boasting (NIV, NJB). The ground for boasting is rigorous scrutiny of the consequences of one's own actions, not those of others. The evident point of the verse can perhaps best be rendered by recasting it in the form of a conditional sentence and by using the second person instead of the third: "If you scrutinize your own work instead of the work of someone else, then you will have a boast with reference to yourself alone and not with reference to someone else."

Paul's positive reference to "a boast with reference to one's self" is difficult. In 6:14 he will indicate that he himself boasts only in the cross of Christ, and that may be what he has in view here: Through self-scrutiny, one discovers anew that the ground of boasting is actually God's grace in Christ (cf. 1:6), in other words, the Spirit, which produces love (5:22) in the form of mutual burden bearing. The "work" to which Paul refers is then the fruit of the Spirit. Furthermore, Paul may be alluding to the new preachers in v. 4, since he does not think they boast in the cross but in their missionary achievements among the Galatians (Martyn 550; Witherington 427): In 6:13 he will accuse them of seeking the circumcision of the Galatians so that they might "boast in their [circumcised] flesh" (see comment there). In short, the new preachers may think that they will have a ground for boasting "in the other," that is, in those Galatians whom they have convinced of the need to practice circumcision. Moreover, the Greek uses the definite article with the noun "boast" [*to kauchēma*, "*the* boast"] in v. 4. Normally this article is understood to be general rather than specific, legitimating the translation "a boast." By including the article, Paul may, however, be referring to "*the* boast" that the new preachers are claiming for themselves on the basis of their missionary successes among the Galatians. For Paul, the ground for boasting (presumably before God) is the scrutiny of one's own work, not the scrutiny of the work of others (e.g., in the matter of circumcision). In the background of the passage, then, stand the missionary efforts of the new preachers as a cautionary tale. If this line of interpretation is near the mark, it is also possible that the "someone" (*tis*) who thinks himself "to be something" in v. 3 is an oblique reference to a leader of the new preachers (cf. comments on 1:9; 3:1; 5:7, 10b). Even so, the admonitions of vv. 3–4 are directed to the Galatians, who are to avoid falling into the errors of the new preachers.

The temporal adverb "then" (*tote* instead of *oun* or *ara*) shows that the future tense of the verb ("will have") is meant temporally, not merely logically. But as a real future, it can still be taken in one of two ways, to refer to the eschatological future or to the imminent (and immanent) future. In the former, the reference is to the final judgment of God (if one scrutinizes now, one will have ground for boasting in oneself at the last judgment); in the latter, it refers to the direct consequences for one's life on earth (whenever one is busy scrutinizing, one will have ground for boasting in oneself). That the eschatological meaning is the probable one is indicated by v. 5, "For [*gar*] each one will carry [*bastasei*] his own load [*to idion phortion*]," even though here too the future has been construed as either eschatological or imminent and immanent (cf. Kuck 289). In v. 2a, Paul has exhorted the Galatian believers in Christ to "carry one another's burdens," using the same verb as in v. 5 (cf. 5:10b). At first glance v. 5 seems to contradict the exhortation in v. 2a (a believer in v. 5 will not carry any else's burden, but only one's own). The contradiction with v. 2a is only apparent, however, since v. 5 is not an exhortation but a prediction, as indicated by the future tense of the verb. Furthermore, Paul here uses another word for "burden" (*phortion*, "load"). To be sure, the word used in v. 5 is a synonym of the one used in v. 2 (*baros*, "burden"), in both its literal and its metaphorical senses (BDAG 1064). Paul's choice of a different term indicates, however, that the (singular) "load" of v. 5 is not simply equivalent to the (many) "burdens" of v. 2a. The metaphorical referent is different; it refers not to the multifarious cares of everyday life (see comment on v. 2a), but to the "work" (*ergon*) of the believer mentioned in v. 4. Self-scrutiny may show that this work was not always in line with the Spirit, for which reason Paul probably likens it to a load one will carry (cf. 5:10b; Schewe 167; Lambrecht 1997: 50). The prediction that "each will carry one's own load" makes good sense if it refers to the last judgment (cf. 2 Cor 5:10; Rom 14:10–12). Each believer will carry the load of one's own "work" before God at the last judgment (cf. *4 Ezra* [2 Esd] 7.104–105: "The day of judgment is decisive; ... no one shall ever pray for another on that day, neither shall anyone lay a burden on another; for then everyone shall bear his [or her] own righteousness or unrighteousness"). A believer is not to examine critically the work of anyone else, for the work of another is not a burden a believer will have to carry before God (cf. 1 Cor 3:13–15; 4:4–5). As Kuck observes, "Each individual is to watch out for himself or herself, examine the self rather than judge others, and look to God's future judgment as the final arbiter of status" (296).[492]

As far as the content is concerned, v. 6 is but loosely connected to the previous verses and appears to be a short appendix to them, as indicated by the conjunction with which it begins: "And [*de*] let the one who is instructed [*ho katēchoumenos*] in the word share in all good things with the one who instructs [*ho katēchōn*]." The fact that each will carry one's own load is now balanced by the exhortation to think of others (Barclay 1988: 163). The imperative of the verb "share" is in the present tense in Greek (*koinōneitō*), which can be taken to mean either "Let the one who is instructed continue sharing," or "Let the one who is instructed make a habit of sharing." The first presupposes an already-existing activity; the second does not, at least not necessarily. The "word" is the message of "the gospel" (1:6, 7, 11; 2:2, 5, 7, 14), whereas the "good things" (*agathois*) are probably material goods such as food, shelter, and money. In short, the one who is taught the word is to support the one who

---

492. An alternative interpretation of v. 4 is to understand the preposition *eis* as indicating direction ("to") rather than reference, the noun *kauchēma* to mean boasting rather than ground for boasting, and the tense of the verb ("will have") as referring to the imminent (and immanent) rather than to the eschatological future. If these assumptions are correct, Paul's point would be that "after testing one's own work one must not flaunt it before others but keep one's boast to oneself" (Barclay 1988: 160–61; also Kuck 294; Martyn 550; cf. Dunn 325; Schewe 164). This reading of v. 4 can be combined with an eschatological interpretation of v. 5 (so Barclay 1988: 162; Kuck 293–94; Martyn 550). This line of interpretation is problematic, however, since one would expect Paul to use either the verb for boasting (cf. 6:13–14) or the noun *kauchēsis*, his normal term for boasting (cf. Rom 3:27; 15:17; 1 Cor 15:31; 2 Cor 1:12; 7:4, 14; 8:24; 11:10, 17; 1 Thess 2:19). Paul occasionally uses *kauchēma* as a synonym for *kauchēsis* (cf. 2 Cor 5:12; 9:3), but that is not his normal usage (cf. Rom 4:2; 1 Cor 5:6; 9:15–16; 2 Cor 1:14; Phil 1:26; 2:16). See BDAG 537; Lightfoot 217; Vouga 148.

Life at the Juncture of the Ages	385

teaches it. The singular is not specific but generic, referring to a class of people: Students are to support their teachers. Paul does not use the common words for teacher or teaching (*didaskalos*, *didaskō*), but the verb *katēcheō*, "to catechize" or "instruct" (cf. Rom 2:18; 1 Cor 14:19; Luke 1:4; Acts 18:25; in Acts 21:21, 24 it means "to inform"), which in Paul's time does not yet have the technical meaning it would later attain, partly on the basis of this passage, to denote instruction of catechumens in the basics of the Christian faith (cf. *2 Clem.* 17.1). Paul uses *katēcheō* elsewhere in connection with theological instruction (Rom 2:18: "instructed in the law"; 1 Cor 14:19: "to instruct others" in the faith), and he does so here as well.

Paul's exhortation presupposes that in the Galatian churches there are people giving instruction in the gospel, and that their function is not unlike that of the congregational "teachers" (*didaskaloi*) mentioned in 1 Cor 12:28 and Eph 4:11, to provide instruction in the gospel as preached or transmitted by the apostle (cf. 1 Cor 15:1–3; Rom 12:7; Acts 13:1). In this passage, however, Paul refers not to "the instructor," which could be taken to indicate a church "office," but to "the one who instructs" (lit., "the one instructing," *ho katēchōn*), which merely indicates an activity that occurs in the churches of Galatians, not a church office. The exhortation of v. 6 does provide a step in the direction of the development of church offices, but that development is beyond Paul's immediate concern or the Galatians' concern. The exhortation of v. 6 is perhaps best understood as a specification of the exhortation to carry one another's burdens (Lightfoot 217; Burton 335; Barclay 1988: 163), which stands at the head of the subunit in v. 2a: Since those giving instruction carry the burden of instructing others in the gospel, the beneficiaries are to carry the burden of supporting those who instruct (cf. 1 Thess 5:12–13; 1 Cor 9:4–14; 2 Cor 11:7–9; Phil 4:10–17).

Why does Paul take the trouble to include this particular admonition in his letter to the Galatians? Paul obviously regards the matter as important enough to make a point of it. The form of Paul's exhortation may presuppose that support for those giving instruction is on the verge of being withheld or has not yet taken root (see above on the verb). What, if anything, lies behind Paul's exhortation? An answer is possible only by reading between the lines. One view is that v. 6 concerns the collection of funds for Jerusalem (see on 2:10; cf. Rom 15:26–27: "For Macedonia and Achaia have been pleased to make some contribution for the poor among the saints at Jerusalem; . . . for if the Gentiles have come to share in their spiritual blessings, they ought also to be of service to them in material blessings" [RSV]). The "one who teaches the word" would then have to represent the Jerusalem church, which is unlikely, given the unflattering connection that Paul posits between the views of that church and those of the new preachers in Galatia (cf. 2:11–14; 4:24–31, with comments). An attractive alternative is that of Martyn (552), who surmises that the instructors in view were those put in place by Paul just before he had left the Galatian churches.

The new preachers have been treating these instructors with hostility and have also tried to replace them with instructors propounding their own understanding of the gospel. This development has reached Paul's ears, and he tries to combat it with the admonition found in v. 6: "Paul would have good reason to reiterate the rule guaranteeing adequate support of the gospel instructor." A difficulty with this proposal is that the form of v. 6 is not discernibly polemical. A third alternative is to argue that v. 6 actually concerns Paul's own relationship with the Galatians (Schewe 169–70; cf. Witherington 430). The "one who instructs in the word" stands for Paul himself, and "the one instructed in the word" for the Galatian churches. The letter itself is the instruction in the word (the gospel) provided by Paul, the teacher, to the Galatians, his students. With his epistolary instruction, Paul is seeking to reestablish the bonds with his churches in Galatia. In v. 6, he tries to encourage the Galatians to take the initiative in reestablishing those bonds by providing him with support. The problem with this proposal is that Paul presents himself earlier in the letter as the preacher of the gospel (cf. 1:11, 16, 23; 3:1–2; 4:13–14), not as its teacher, and that the letter is arguably an attempt to repreach the gospel to the Galatians (on the genre of Galatians, see Excursus 5). A final alternative is to assume that no concrete problem needs to be assumed to explain the inclusion of v. 6: "It is natural that here, as elsewhere in discussing Christian community life, Paul's attention should focus on the teachers" in the Galatian churches (Barclay 1988: 163). All we know is that Paul regards the welfare of those giving instruction in the gospel as important to the daily life of the Galatian churches.

[7–10] Verse 7 contains no transitional particle or conjunction. This passage is therefore probably not to be read as Paul's further commentary on v. 6, with its exhortation to support community instructors materially or financially (e.g., Witherington 431). That these four verses form a unit is indicated by the imagery of sowing and reaping that dominates it in vv. 7–9. Verse 10 contains a concluding exhortation that flows from vv. 7–9.

These four verses have the character of a summary of the whole of Section V of the epistle (5:13–6:10). Paul refers to "the Flesh" for the first time since 5:24, where he has emphatically declared that "those who belong to Christ Jesus have crucified the Flesh with its passions and desires" (see comment there). The passage hence makes explicit that Paul cannot give exhortations about following the Spirit (5:25–6:6) without taking into account the ongoing reality and dangerous threat posed by "the Flesh" (vv. 7–8).

Verses 7–9 may be divided into two parts, the first containing a warning (vv. 7a–8a) and the second a promise (8b–9b):

Warning:
7a Do not be deceived, God is not mocked,
7b for whatever someone sows, this also he will reap:

8a Because the one sowing into the Flesh of himself will from the Flesh reap corruption.

Promise:
8b But the one sowing into the Spirit will from the Spirit reap eternal life.
9a And let us not grow weary of doing what is right,
9b for we shall reap in due season if we do not tire.

The solemn warning in v. 7a is striking in its directness and tone of alarm: "Do not be deceived" (*mē planasthe*)! Do not be misled! This is an idiomatic expression (cf. 1 Cor 6:9; 15:33; Jas 1:16). The sense is probably reflexive (BDAG 822): the Galatians are not to deceive or mislead themselves. The verb is a second-person plural present imperative, which can be taken in one of two ways: "You Galatians are to stop deceiving yourselves as you have been doing," or "You Galatians are never to make a habit of deceiving yourselves." The second option is the more likely, given 5:25, where Paul assumes, if only for rhetorical reasons, that the Galatians he is addressing are indeed living by the Spirit (see comment there). The Galatians are not to make a habit of deceiving themselves with respect to God: "Make no mistake: God is not mocked" (NAB). Paul holds this truth to be self-evident. God does not allow himself to be treated with contempt. The verb Paul uses (*myktērizō*) means literally "to turn up the nose at" (BDAG 660). The sense of v. 7a is this: "Don't kid yourselves about God, because God will not let himself be treated contemptuously." In this way Paul highlights that living according to the Flesh is no laughing matter (vv. 7b–8a).

Verse 7b makes use of an easily understood agricultural metaphor based on observation and experience: there is a direct relationship between a seed put into the ground and the plant that results. Hence, what you sow is what you will also reap (v. 7b). If you plant corn, you will harvest corn, nothing else. Verse 8a shows that Paul's concern is not to impart knowledge of well-known agricultural matters, but to allow the insight gained from nature to illuminate the human situation: "Because [*hoti*] the one sowing into [*eis*] the Flesh of himself will from the Flesh reap corruption" (cf. Job 4:8; Ps 126:5; Prov 22:8 for analogies). An alternate translation could be: "Because the one sowing into the Flesh of herself will from the Flesh reap corruption." Paul here shifts the metaphor from the seed to the soil into which it is sown. In agriculture, what will be harvested is determined not only by the seed, but also by the quality or nature of the soil. In the application of this insight in v. 8b, "the Flesh" is the soil into which is sown (cf. Mark 4:1–20 par.). This soil is a source of "corruption," meaning dissolution, decay, and ultimately death (BDAG 1054–55; cf. 1 Cor 15:42; Rom 8:21). Since this corruption applies not to plants but to people, it is evident that v. 8a is a brief allegory (see Excursus 14): The verb "sow" stands for "indulge," and the verb "reap" stands for "obtain" (or "experience"). If you indulge the Flesh of yourself, you will from the Flesh obtain corruption.

The phrase rather inelegantly rendered "the Flesh of himself" represents the Greek construction *tēn sarka heautou*, which is equally inelegant. This phrase is often translated "his own flesh," but that would normally presuppose a construction with the adjective *idios* (*tēn idian sarka*). The chosen translation, though awkward, makes evident that Paul's concern in both halves of v. 8a is with "the Flesh" (see Excursus 16), a malevolent cosmic power dealt with in 5:13–24 (esp. vv. 13, 17, 19, 24). This power is in conflict with the Spirit (5:16–18, 22). "The Flesh" appears to be Paul's abbreviation for "the desire of the Flesh" (5:16), the Evil Impulse that inhabits and destroys human existence "in the flesh" (2:20; cf. 4:13–14). Paul's peculiar construction "the Flesh of himself" is probably then another way of saying the desire of the Flesh (the Evil Impulse) resident in a flesh-and-blood human being (cf. 1:16). The sense of v. 8b is thus: The one indulging the desire of the Flesh in him- or herself will from the Flesh obtain corruption: death. Paul appears to be referring not to incidental sins or momentary deviations from the life of the Spirit (cf. 6:1, 4), but to a pattern of existence (probably including the practice of fleshly circumcision on the part of the Galatians) whereby someone thumbs one's nose at God (cf. 5:21b and comment there). Paul may have in mind a potential problem to which he will return in Romans: "Are we to continue in sin that grace may abound? By no means!" (Rom 6:1–2 RSV), and "Shall we sin because we are not under law but under grace? By no means!" (Rom 6:15 NIV). Paul may thus be anticipating a possible objection, but it is also conceivable that the new preachers have already indicated to the Galatians that freedom from the law in practice means the free indulgence of fleshly impulses (cf. Rom 3:8). For Paul, circumcision and the law are part of the problem, not part of the solution.

Paul also uses a future tense of the verb "reap" (*therisei*) in v. 8b, thereby qualifying the stern warning of vv. 7–8a with an eschatological promise: "but the one sowing into [*eis*] the Spirit *will* from the Spirit reap eternal life." Continuing with the agricultural metaphor, Paul now likens the Spirit to soil into which seed is sown. The sense here is probably that a person who aligns one's life with the Spirit (5:25) will from the Spirit obtain "eternal life." "Eternal life" (*zoē aiōnios*) is a common expression already known from Dan 12:2 LXX ("Many of them that sleep in the dust of the earth shall awake, some to eternal life, and some to reproach and everlasting shame"). It stands for the life of the new creation (Gal 6:15). Strikingly, there are no imperatives in v. 8. Paul is not asking his readers to choose between Two Ways, as if one's destiny is ultimately in one's own hands (Schlier 277; Mussner 405; see Excursus 16). Believers in Christ have already been grasped by the Spirit: they have no choice to make. Paul is simply describing two modes of being, one before and apart from Christ, the other after his coming into world and in the sphere of his lordship. The person who, in the power of the Flesh, patterns one's life on the Flesh serves as a warning for the person who, grasped by the Spirit, patterns one's life on the Spirit (again cf. 5:21b). For the danger of the Flesh remains (cf. 5:13). In the midst of that stark reality, however, the believer in Christ also receives a divine promise (cf. 5:16): the believer will certainly obtain eternal life by following the Spirit (5:25). "Eternal life" may here presuppose justification: divine vindication and approval (cf. 2:16d; 5:5: "the hope of justification").

What is the significance of the future tense of the verb "reap" (*therisei*) in both clauses of v. 8 (and to anticipate, also in v. 9)? Does it refer to the imminent (and immanent) future (the one sowing into the Flesh and the one sowing into the Spirit will *from now on* reap the appropriate consequences), or to the eschatological future (the one sowing will at the last judgment reap the appropriate consequences)? The opposition between "corruption" and "eternal life" as well as the immediate context (see comment on vv. 4–5 above) seem to plead for the latter. But the issue may not be either-or. As the opposite of "eternal life," "corruption" can stand for that "eternal death" (perdition) that ensues after the last judgment, yet also for the moral death that becomes reality in the present. By the same token, "eternal life" can describe the life of the new age after the last judgment, yet also the quality of life for those who are now "in Christ" (cf. Rom 5:21; 6:23). In the latter case, eternal life remains eschatological since it concerns the life of the new creation brought into the world by Christ (cf. Rom 6:4: "that we . . . might walk in newness of life"). The future has invaded the present. For Paul, patterning one's life on the Flesh (a power that represents the present evil age, mentioned in 1:4) or on the Spirit (the eschatological presence of God's Son sent into "our hearts," according to 4:4–6) has far-reaching consequences, both now and in the future.

The promise with which v. 8 concludes is expanded into an admonition in v. 9a, which is then followed by a repetition of the promise in v. 9b: "Let us not grow weary of doing what is right, for we shall reap [*therisomen*] in due season if we do not tire." The admonition "Let us not grow weary [*mē enkakōmen*] of doing what is right" is probably the counterpart to the admonition found in 5:26, "Let us not become [*mē ginōmetha*] conceited" (see introduction to 5:25–6:10, above). As in 5:26, Paul in 6:9 uses a first-person plural prohibitive subjunctive with the present tense, implying the ongoing or permanent avoidance of an activity. "Doing what is right" also specifies what "sowing into the Spirit" in v. 8b involves. For "what is right," Paul uses the term *to kalon*, literally, "the beautiful thing," which here has a moral meaning, "what is morally right" (cf. 4:18; 1 Thess 5:21). The expression "doing [*poiountes*] what is right" may seem strange in a letter in which "doing the law" (3:10, 12; 5:3) is vehemently rejected. This verse indicates that the problem for Paul is not "doing" as such but the object of that doing: the law *or* "what is morally right," meaning what accords with the Spirit. Doing what is right is the fruit of the Spirit's successful battle with the Flesh (cf. 5:16–23). Paul assumes that the Galatians are in fact doing what is right (cf. 5:25a); he wants them not to grow weary, not to become less enthusiastic about doing that.

There is no reason to grow weary, since (*gar*) "in due season we shall reap," we shall obtain or experience eternal life (v. 8b). The time indicator "in due season" continues the agricultural imagery begun in v. 7b (cf. Matt 13:20; Mark 11:13; Acts 14:17). As a metaphor, it probably refers to a time determined by God (cf. 4:4), though the basic point is that this time will, just like the time for harvesting, certainly come. The "due season" could be the Parousia (cf. 1 Thess 5:1 with 4:13–18; 1 Cor 4:5 and 7:29 with 15:23–28), but not necessarily (BDAG 497–498), since believers may reap (experience) eternal life (the life characteristic of the new creation) at different moments within ongoing human history even before the Parousia (see previous paragraphs). The reaping of eternal life is conditional on perseverance: "If we do not tire [*eklyomenoi*]" (BDAG 306 and Betz 309: "give out"; KJV and Lightfoot 217: "become faint," as in Mark 8:3; Matt 15:32; NAB, NIV, NJB, NRSV: "give up"). The Greek verb used (*elkyomai*, "tire") is a near synonym of the one used at the beginning of the verse (*enkakeō*, "grow weary"). The conditional clause does not signify that Paul now presents salvation as a human achievement. To "tire" is to run the risk of falling away from the realm of the Spirit into that of the Flesh (cf. 5:26). One will then reap not eternal life but corruption (v. 8a). Following the Spirit (5:25) demands effort and attention, for one has to be on guard for the assaults of the Flesh. Believers in Christ must go on doing "what is right" in the face of opposition and assault.

"So then [*ara oun*]," Paul concludes, using a double conjunction to express emphasis, "as we have opportunity [or: while we have time], let us accomplish what is good toward all people, and especially toward the members of the household of faith" (v. 10). Paul's use of a first-person plural form of exhortation (*ergazōmetha*, "let us accomplish," lit., "let us work") entails an inclusio with the similar construction in 5:25, the first verse of this subsection (*stoichōmen*, "let us follow"). In both cases, Paul also uses a present tense, implying continuous or ongoing activity: "Let us go on following the Spirit" and "Let us go on accomplishing the good." The word *kairos*, here translated "opportunity," meanwhile provides a direct verbal link to the preceding verse, where the same term was used to mean "season." Paul's use of the term continues the agricultural metaphor of the preceding verses (Calvin 114). In addition, "accomplishing what is good" (*ergazomai to agathon*) recalls "doing what is right" (*poieō to kalon*) in v. 9. Thus v. 10 functions as a conclusion to this subsection (5:25–6:10), though it also stands in direct continuity with v. 9.

The verb used in v. 10 (*ergazomai*) is a cognate of the noun *ergon*, "work," of which the plural has been used in connection with "works [*erga*] of the law"

Life at the Juncture of the Ages 391

(2:16; etc.) and "works of the Flesh" (5:19). But Paul has used the singular positively in 6:4 to signify what one accomplishes as a believer who lives by the Spirit. The verb, too, has a positive meaning in this context, and its use by Paul in v. 10 shows once again that he sees no problem with doing what is right or with accomplishing (achieving, effecting) what is good (see comments on vv. 4 and 9 above). The concept "what is good" (*to agathon*) signifies "what is beneficial to another" (Burton 346). The exhortation to accomplish what is good is thus another way of underlining the importance of love, the firstfruit of the Spirit (5:22; cf. 5:13–14).

Paul exhorts his readers to accomplish what is good "toward all people, and [*de*] especially toward the members of the household of faith." The latter are undoubtedly other believers in Christ. Paul likens believers to people who share the space under a common roof; they are all "members of the household" (one word in Greek: *oikeious*, lit., "housemates"), members of one and the same "family" (cf. Eph 2:19; 1 Tim 3:15; 5:8). A family in the ancient world could include not only parents and children but also other relatives, as well as slaves, freed persons, and certain business clients. Paul's resort to this description may be indebted to the fact that believers in Christ met in houses and that a household not infrequently formed the nucleus of a so-called house church (cf., e.g., 1 Cor 1:16; 16:15, 19). Various house churches in one city (or region such as Galatia?) might gather in a large house for worship (cf. 1 Cor 14:23: "If the whole church gathers ..."; Rom 16:23: "Gaius ... is host to me and to the whole church"). The image of a household will be especially appropriate when the letter is read aloud to the assembled Galatians. Paul resorts to the image to alert the Galatians to their common bonds, bonds not of kinship, gender, or social status (cf. 3:28) but "of faith," literally, "of *the* faith" (*tēs pisteōs*). The term "the faith" is probably not "the common name for the Christian movement" (Betz 311; cf. Longenecker 283; Vouga 152), but as elsewhere in Galatians, a reference to the "the faith of Christ" (see Excursus 11). Believers in Galatia are being asked to accomplish what is good toward the members of a household who live from the faith of Christ, from his faithful death on the cross (see Excursus 9). The preposition "toward" (*pros* in Greek) is curious; one would expect here a simple dative to express an indirect object, as in Rom 13:10, where the same verb is used: "Love does not work [*ergazetai*] wrong *to* the neighbor" (AT). The preposition "toward" suggests that accomplishing what is good involves being oriented toward someone, in this case, fellow members of the household of faith.

Paul's focus throughout Section V has been on relationships and actions *within* the communities of faith, and that remains the case here as well (Barclay 1988: 166; otherwise Betz 311). Believers in Galatia are being asked to accomplish what is good "especially" (*malista*) toward other believers in Christ. Paul's exhortation to accomplish what is good "toward the members of the household of faith" is thus another way of saying "Be slaves of one another through love" (5:13) or "Carry the burdens of one another" (6:2). But this exhortation is not meant exclusively, as the adverb "especially" indicates. The good that believers are being called upon to accomplish must also be extended "toward all people [*pantas*]." The universal scope of the gospel here comes to expression (cf. 1 Cor 15:23–28; 2 Cor 5:14–15; Rom 5:12–21; 11:32; de Boer 1998: 371–74). Paul's formulation, while calling attention to the priority of the family of faith, effectively prevents intracommunal love from becoming sectarian and exclusively inward-looking.

Summary of Section V

In this section of the letter, Paul has given the Galatians instruction about what life in freedom from the Mosaic law looks like at the present juncture. His instruction involves both description and exhortation. The freedom from the law is not be confused with a moral vacuum, with the absence of morality. That would only give the Flesh an opportunity to launch its pernicious attacks on human beings with disastrous consequences for interpersonal relationships and communal cohesion. No, believers are to be slaves of one another through love, on the pattern of Christ, for such love is in fact the fulfillment of the entire scriptural law containing God's promises concerning Christ and his Spirit. This love is also the singular fruit of the Spirit and has nothing whatsoever to do with observing the Mosaic law or any other legal code.

The present situation, however, is characterized by ongoing strife between the Spirit and the Flesh. Believers must be on their guard for the Flesh. The Spirit is a powerful weapon in this strife, and those who walk by the power of the Spirit will certainly not carry out "the desire of the Flesh." In fact, those who belong to Christ have put the Flesh with its many destructive passions and desires to death. Believers thus live by the power of the Spirit, and on that basis they can be exhorted to go on aligning their lives with the Spirit, while they must always be aware that the Flesh continues to present a very real and mortal threat. Believers are to go on carrying one another's burdens, which is what being slaves of one another through love concretely involves. They must not grow weary in doing so. In this way they will be repeatedly fulfilling "the law of Christ," the scriptural law containing promises pertaining to Christ and his Spirit, in particular the promise contained in Lev 19:18 that "you will love your neighbor as yourself." Such mutual burden bearing, which is love in action and what is right and good, contains the certain promise of "eternal life," the life of the new era inaugurated by the coming of Christ and his Spirit into the world.

Section VI: Galatians 6:11–18
Epistolary Closing

The standard features of Paul's epistolary closings are three: greetings to or from third parties, a "holy kiss" greeting, and a final benediction (White 97). The closing of 1 Corinthians illustrates the point: "All the brethren send greetings. Greet one another with a holy kiss. . . . The grace of the Lord Jesus be with you. . . . Amen" (1 Cor 16:20, 23–24 RSV). Galatians contains only a final benediction (v. 18) and no greetings of any kind. Instead of the joyful exchange of greetings that mark the closing of Paul's other letters, there is a final rebuke of the new preachers who have been "upsetting" the Galatians (5:12) with their insistence on observance of the law, beginning with the rite of circumcision (cf. 5:2–4; Excursus 4). This feature of the closing is consistent with the letter opening (1:1–10). Paul there substituted a rebuke of the Galatians and an imprecation for the new preachers who are "unnerving" them (1:6–9) for the thanksgiving that is a standard component of his other letters.

After the attack on the new preachers in 6:11–13 of the closing, Paul goes on to give a final contextualized summary of the gospel as he has attempted to repreach it through this letter to the Galatians (vv. 14–17). That summary corresponds to the summary given in the prescript to the letter (1:4): the "new creation" of 6:15 is God's apocalyptic alternative for "the present evil age" of 1:4. The distinctive features of the letter closing (as of the letter opening) reflect (1) the circumstances in which the letter is being written, (2) Paul's rhetorical agenda in this epistolary communication, and (3) the message he wants to convey through it. According to Betz (313), the closing "contains the interpretive clues to the understanding of Paul's major concerns in the letter as a whole and should be employed as the hermeneutical key to the intentions of the Apostle." That is probably an overstatement since the closing says nothing about justification (2:15–21; 3:6, 8, 11, 21, 24; 5:5) or the Spirit (3:1–5, 14; 4:6; 5:5; 5:13–6:10). Betz's claim probably counts just as much for the letter opening, though it also makes no mention of justification and the Spirit. The epistolary wrapper (opening and closing) clearly does not tell the whole story, though it does provide relevant clues.

The closing has two subsections. The first (vv. 11–17) constitutes a recapitulation of certain elements of Paul's argument in the foregoing letter; the second, but a single verse (v. 18), contains the final benediction, whereby Paul indicates that the letter is to be read aloud in a worship setting.

6:11–17 Recapitulation

The passage consists of two subunits. The first (vv. 11–13) contains a final rebuke of the new preachers in Galatia, focusing on their central demand for circumcision. The second (vv. 14–17) focuses on the significance of the cross of Christ and provides a final contextualized summary of the gospel as preached by Paul. It also contains a final blessing and a final appeal. The two subunits place over against one another two central topics of the epistle: circumcision and the cross (cf. Weima).

> 6:11 See with what large[a] letters I am writing to you with my hand. 12 Those who are wanting to make a good showing in the flesh, these are putting pressure on you to practice circumcision, only in order that they not be persecuted for the cross of Christ.[b] 13 For not even those who practice circumcision[c] themselves keep the law, but they are wanting you to practice circumcision in order that they may boast in your flesh.
>
> 14 But let it not be for me to boast except in the cross of our Lord Jesus Christ, through which to me the world has been crucified and I to the world. 15 For[d] neither circumcision is anything nor uncircumcision, but a new creation. 16 And all who will follow[e] this standard, peace [be] upon them, and mercy also upon the Israel of God. 17 From now on let no one cause me difficulties, for I carry on my body the scars of Jesus.[f]

a. Instead of *pēlikois*, $\mathfrak{P}^{46}$, B*, and 33 read *ēlikois*, which means the same.

b. After *Christou*, $\mathfrak{P}^{46}$, B, and 1175 add *Iēsou* ("Jesus"). Omitting this word are ℵ, A, C, D, F, G, Ψ, 0278, 33, 1739, et al. The meaning is not affected.

c. The translation "those who practice circumcision" represents a present participial construction construed as a middle, *hoi peritemnomenoi*, which is attested by ℵ, A, C, D, et al. There is also good support for the perfect participle, *hoi peritetmēmenoi*, attested by $\mathfrak{P}^{46}$, B, Ψ, et al. See comment below.

d. The majority of manuscripts (including ℵ, A, C, D) include the phrase "for in Christ Jesus," probably under the influence of 5:6. The shorter reading beginning simply with "for" is supported by $\mathfrak{P}^{46}$, B, Ψ, 33, et al. (Metzger 530). The meaning is not affected.

Epistolary Closing

e. A strongly attested alternate reading is the present tense, *stoichousin* (A, C*, D, F, G, 1739, 1881, *pc* it; Ambst). The future *stoichēsousin* is attested by ℵ, B, Ψ, 33, and others. (𝔓⁴⁶ has an aorist subjunctive, *stoichēsōsin*.) See comment below.

f. There are a host of variants: "Christ," "the Lord Jesus," "the Lord Jesus Christ," and "our Lord Jesus Christ." These are probably liturgically motivated expansions of the simple "Jesus," found in 𝔓⁴⁶, A, B, C, 33, et al.

[11–13] The closing begins with Paul's indicating that he has taken the pen into his own hand in order to write the closing paragraph of the letter himself: "See with what large letters I am writing [*egrapsa*] to you with my [own] hand." In this way Paul indicates to the Galatians that he has been using an amanuensis and, perhaps more important, that he himself is literate (see Keith), no small matter for a letter in which the author's daring interpretation of particular texts from the OT plays a significant role. The reference to "my [own] hand" (as opposed to that of the amanuensis) also has the function that a signature does in a modern letter, to authenticate the letter as coming from the sender named at the beginning (cf. 1:1). This signature can take the form of a greeting. In 1 Corinthians, for example, Paul writes: "The greeting of Paul with my [own] hand" (1 Cor 16:21 AT; cf. Col 4:18; 2 Thess 3:17). Verse 11, however, does not contain a greeting of any sort but is merely a solemn indication that Paul is about to say something important. Paul's Letter to Philemon provides a significant parallel: "If he [Onesimus] has wronged you [Philemon], or owes you something, charge that to my account. I, Paul, write [*egrapsa*] with my [own] hand: I will repay it" (Phlm 18–19 AT). As in Philemon, Paul uses the idiomatic formulation "with my [own] hand" and a conventional epistolary aorist (*egrapsa*, lit., "I wrote"). The latter looks at the letter from the perspective of the recipients rather than that of the writer.

The "large letters" with which Paul writes the closing in his own hand have been explained in various ways: They say something about Paul's penmanship (the result of an injury or hard physical labor?); they indicate that he has difficulty seeing; they provide emphasis and solemnity. The latter is probably the case, given the similarity to the formulation found in Philemon 19 and the rebuke of the new preachers that follows in the next two verses. The large letters are the equivalent of boldface type or italics. Paul calls attention to them so that not only the person reading the letter aloud to the assembled Galatians but also the Galatians themselves will know that he has something important to say in closing (Burton 438).

Verses 12 and 13 are similarly constructed (a main clause followed by a purpose clause beginning with *hina*). Verse 13 thus builds on v. 12. At the same time the two verses together exhibit certain features that suggest a (probably subconscious) chiastic construction for the two verses:

a ¹²ᵃThose who are wanting to make a good showing in the flesh,
  b ¹²ᵇthese are putting pressure on you to practice circumcision,
    c ¹²ᶜonly in order that [*hina*] they not be persecuted for the cross of Christ.
    c´ ¹³ᵃFor not even those who practice circumcision themselves keep the law,
  b´ ¹³ᵇbut they are wanting you to practice circumcision
a´ ¹³ᶜin order that [*hina*] they may boast in your flesh.

The words "boast in your flesh" of the last clause (v. 13c) correspond to the words "make a good showing in the flesh" in the first clause (v. 12a). The middle clauses of both verses (v. 12b and v. 13b) contain references to "practicing circumcision." The last clause of v. 12 and the first of v. 13 in turn both contain a denial concerning the new preachers: they are *not* being persecuted for the cross of Christ, and they are *not* keeping the law. The chiasm is not perfect (e.g., both v. 12a and v. 13b indicate what the new preachers "are wanting") and should not be pressed too far.

The subjects of the six clauses ("those who," "these," "they") all have ostensibly the same referent: the new preachers active in Galatia (cf. 1:6–9; 5:7–12; Excursus 4). The six clauses constitute a catalog of accusations against them. These accusations are a mix of historically plausible facts about the new preachers (vv. 12b, 13b) and unprovable assumptions about their supposed motivations and aims (12a, 12c, 13a, 13c). The two verses together constitute a final rebuke of the new preachers. In the worship setting in which this letter will be read aloud, the new preachers will probably also be present; they will therefore be rebuked not only in the presence of the Galatians but also in the presence of God (see comment on v. 18 and on 1:8–9).

In v. 12, the thread of Paul's thought can probably best be discerned by momentarily reversing the sequence of vv. 12a and 12b:

¹²ᵇThose who are putting pressure on you to practice circumcision,
¹²ᵃthese are wanting to make a good showing in the flesh,
¹²ᶜonly in order that [*hina*] they not be persecuted for the cross of Christ.

The purpose clause of v. 12c is logically dependent on v. 12a, rather than on v. 12b. Paul begins with the reproach of v. 12a rather than with the factual statement of v. 12b because of his anger with the new preachers. Verse 12b indicates the immediate cause of that anger: "*These* [*houtoi*] are [as you Galatians know all too well] putting pressure on [*anankazousin*] you to practice circumcision [*peritemnesthai*]." The first word is emphatic, and it indicates Paul's anger at their motivation, as expressed in v. 12a. Paul has used the verb "put pressure on" (*anankazō*) twice before, first in connection with Titus, "who was not compelled [*ēnankasthē*] to be circumcised" (2:3)[493] on his visit with Paul to Jerusalem; and second in connection with Peter, whom Paul reproached in Antioch for "putting pressure" (*anankazeis*) on Gentile believers to live in a Jewish manner (2:14). Though the nature of the pressure being exerted is not elaborated, v. 12b probably gives an accurate picture of what the new preachers in Galatia are doing there (cf. Excursus 4): neither they nor the Galatians will disagree with what Paul says here.

The verb "practice circumcision" renders the present infinitive of the verb *peritemnō*. The form (*peritemnesthai*), also used in v. 13b, can in principle be construed as a passive ("to be circumcised," "get circumcised," "receive circumcision"; cf. KJV, NIV, RSV, NRSV; commentators), but the present tense makes that unlikely. The present tense indicates ongoing or habitual activity, something that can apply to circumcision only as a recurring communal rite.[494] For this reason, it is better to construe the infinitive as a middle, meaning "to practice circumcision" (cf. 5:2–3, where Paul twice uses a present middle of the same verb). The Galatian churches ("you," plural), consisting of women and men, are all together being asked by the new preachers in Galatia to practice circumcision as a rite of entry into the Jewish community and so become "sons (i.e., heirs) of Abraham" (3:7, 29), whereby they may benefit from the saving work of Christ. The circumcision rite concerns not only men, for the rite is a communal and a family matter (see comment on 5:2; Excursus 4).

In vv. 12a and 12c, Paul attacks what he perceives to be the true motivations of the new preachers: "They are wanting to make a good showing in the flesh," and they do so "only in order that they not be persecuted for [i.e., because of] the cross of Christ." In short, they are motivated by selfish concerns; they do not actually care about the Galatians. These accusations are not subject to proof, either by the Galatians who will receive this letter or by interpreters today. Paul's accusation that the new preachers "are wanting [*thelousin*] to make a good showing [*euprosōpēsai*, lit., "make a good face"] in the flesh" has to do with the pressure they are putting on the Galatians to practice fleshly circumcision (v. 12b). This fact and the parallel with v. 13c—where Paul accuses the new preachers of "wanting you to practice circumcision in order that they may boast in your flesh," meaning in the flesh of the Galatians—show that the phrase "in the flesh" (*en sarki*) in v. 12a has specifically to do with circumcision. Paul virtually accuses the new preachers of counting the number of foreskins

---

493. The aorist indicates pressure successfully applied (hence "compelled"), or with a negative, as here, pressure *un*successfully applied ("not compelled"). That is, the pressure put on Titus to be circumcised did not achieve its goal. See comment on 2:3. The present tense thus signifies an attempt to compel (BDF #319).

494. In connection with a punctiliar act of circumcision, that of Titus, Paul has understandably used the aorist in 2:3, the infinitive *peritmēthēnai*. This infinitive is also passive, to indicate that Titus was to *be* circumcised (by someone else).

severed by the circumcision knife (cf. the reference in v. 15 to "uncircumcision," *akrobystia*, which literally means "foreskin"). They are, he claims, after trophies, presumably (so Paul intimates) in order to impress their fellow Jews, perhaps especially law-observant Christian Jews such as James and the circumcision party in Jerusalem (cf. 2:12). A deeper meaning may be that Paul accuses the new preachers of wanting to make a good showing "in the realm of the Flesh," with a capital F, rather than in that of the Spirit (5:13–6:10; cf. 3:3). Those "wanting to make a good showing in the Flesh" do not know that there has been a change of regimes (3:25); they still orient their lives to the Flesh instead of to the Spirit (cf. 6:8), with all the dangers for communal life that involves (cf. 5:13–24).

Verse 12c recalls 5:11, where Paul has also linked what he there calls "proclaiming circumcision" to the avoidance of persecution for the sake of the cross: "If I am still proclaiming circumcision, why am I still being persecuted? Then the offense (*skandalon*) of the cross has been destroyed." In both passages "circumcision" and "the cross [of Christ]" stand in sharp opposition to one another; to reject the former is to incur persecution for the sake of the latter. "The cross of Christ" is Pauline shorthand for "the crucifixion of Christ" and all that entails with respect to circumcision and the law. Christ's cross is an "offense" to Jews (cf. 1 Cor 1:23 AT: "We preach Christ crucified, an offense to Jews") and Christian Jews such as the new preachers in Galatia because, so Paul claims, it has brought about the end of the law as the reliable basis for righteousness and life (cf. 1:13–16; 2:16, 21; 3:13–14, 21, 23–25; 4:4–5). For Paul, the cross of Christ thus signifies the end of what he has called "Judaism" (*Ioudaïsmos*) in 1:13–14 and "works of the law" (*erga nomou*) in 2:16; 3:2, 5, 10 (see Excursus 8 and comment on 6:14–15 below). Though Paul does not specify in 5:11 or in this verse where the persecution comes from or what form it takes (cf. comment on 4:29), the context and the content of both verses seem to indicate that it comes (or may come) from Jewish opponents of the gospel (cf. 1:13, 23; Jewett 2002; Burton 350; Betz 316; Becker 99). In Paul's view the new preachers are advocating circumcision for the believers in Galatia not from altruistic motives (the presumed salvation of the Galatians through their incorporation into Israel as a first and necessary step), but in order to avoid ongoing persecution (*diōkōntai*, present tense) for the crucified Christ, who put an end to the law as the basis for justification (cf. 2:15–16 and comment there). It is impossible to know whether Paul is right in this charge against the new preachers (the word "only" in any event points to a polemical exaggeration of this charge), or whether he is here merely extrapolating from his own experience, both as a former persecutor of the church and as the persecuted apostle of the crucified Christ. In v. 12c, Paul is effectively accusing the new preachers of being unwilling to discern and to accept the radical implications of the crucifixion for observance of the law (2:16, 21), beginning with the rite of circumcision (2:3; 5:2–4), implications that he himself has painfully experienced in his own body (6:17).

In v. 13a he adds a new accusation: "For not even those who practice circumcision themselves keep the law." The conjunction "for" (*gar*) merely indicates another reason for Paul's ongoing consternation with the new preachers, who are here labeled "those who practice circumcision," *hoi peritemnomenoi* (lit., "the circumcising ones"). As indicated in the textual note above, a strong alternate reading is *hoi peritetmēmenoi*, "those who have practiced circumcision." Both make good sense, even though the present is probably original (it easier to imagine a scribe here changing the present into the perfect than the reverse). The participle, whether present or perfect, is commonly construed as a passive (see above on v. 12b), leading to translations such as "those who are being circumcised," "those who receive circumcision," "those who get themselves circumcised," and "the circumcisers" for the present participle, and for the perfect, "those who have been circumcised" and "the circumcised." What counts for the infinitive of this verb in v. 12c probably also counts for the participle here: it is not a passive but a middle, warranting the translation "those who practice circumcision" (also Schlier 281) for the present form and "those who have practiced circumcision" for the perfect (see on 5:2–3).[495] Either the present or the perfect participle can be taken to refer to the new preachers, who practice and have practiced circumcision.

Some (esp. Burton [352–53] and Munck [87–90]) see a reference here not to the new preachers but to Gentile Christians, whether the (present) participle be construed as a middle or as a passive.[496] This interpretation at first glance makes good sense of v. 13a, which could then be understood to mean the following: "For not even the Gentile Christians who practice circumcision themselves keep the law." For Munck, these Gentile Christians are a group of Paul's own converts in Galatia; for Burton, they are Gentile Christians in general, though there may well be Galatians among them. Such Gentile practitioners of circumcision in Galatia and beyond presumably do not realize that practicing circumcision obligates them "to do the whole law" (5:3); they keep only a part of it (feast days? Cf. 4:10). Munck (89) extrapolates from v. 13a to conclude that all the clauses in vv. 12–13 must refer to such "Judaizing Gentile Christians," a conclusion that he in turn applies to 1:9; 3:1; and 5:7, 10. This interpretation forces the evidence (see Excursus 4) and fails to respect the significant

---

495. To take the middle voice as "causative" (Jewett 2002: 338–39; Lightfoot 222; Bruce 270) in the sense of "those advocating circumcision" seems forced and is most unlikely when one construes the infinitives in vv. 12b and 13b to be middle voice as well; these two infinitives cannot be taken to mean "advocating circumcision" (cf. 5:2–3). It is most natural to interpret the middle in each instance in the same way, to indicate the communal practice of circumcision.

496. Burton and Munck both maintain that the participle is a middle but then translate it as if it were a passive: "they that / those who receive circumcision."

distinction between "they" and "you (Galatians)" in these verses. In v. 13a itself, Burton sees only a reference to Gentile Christians (not necessarily limited to believers in Galatia) who have succumbed to the pressure applied by the new preachers, who are Christian Jews (Burton labels them "judaisers"). This reading of v. 13a is difficult for at least two reasons: (1) The subject in each of the remaining five clauses of vv. 12–13 is always the new preachers ("those who," "these," "they"); it is unlikely that v. 13a constitutes an exception. (2) The most natural reading of the verse is that "those who practice circumcision" in v. 13a are identical with "those who are wanting you [the Galatians] to practice circumcision" in v. 13b.

What, then, does Paul's charge that "not even those who practice circumcision themselves keep the law" signify? To "keep [*phylassō*] the law" (cf. Rom 2:26; Acts 7:53; 21:24) is merely another way of saying to "observe [*poieō*] the law" (5:3). Both expressions are traditional. It can hardly be the case that Paul is reminding the new preachers of something they do not know—that the practice of circumcision, once adopted, obligates one to keep/observe the (whole) law (cf. 5:3). More likely, he here intimates that they do not practice what they themselves preach (cf. 2:14). This accusation is beyond proof, for we do not know what would constitute evidence for such a charge. That is, we do not know on what grounds, if any, the Galatians will be able to say, "That's right—they don't," when they hear the letter. If we may assume that Paul is not merely using invective to vilify his adversaries in Galatia, the charge may be true in one way or another. But we cannot know that it was, and it seems useless to speculate.

Paul concludes with the accusation that the new preachers "are wanting you to practice circumcision [*peritemnesthai*, present middle infinitive as in v. 12b] in order that [*hina*] they may boast in your flesh" (vv. 13bc). That the new preachers want the Galatians to practice circumcision is a shared assumption. There will be no argument on that point in Galatia. The charge in the purpose clause, however, is once again difficult to evaluate or to substantiate. The new preachers, according to Paul, have as their ultimate goal to "boast in the flesh" of the Galatians; they achieve this goal by inducing the Galatian believers in Christ to adopt the practice of fleshly circumcision, whereby they (the Galatians) will be incorporated into the people of Israel (cf. Dunn 339), having thereby become "sons" and thus "heirs" of Abraham (3:7, 29). As suggested above, Paul seems implicitly to suggest that the new preachers are counting how many new converts they have made, presumably to impress their fellow Jews, perhaps especially other Christian Jews, such as "the false brothers" of 2:3–4, who were unable to compel Titus to become circumcised (Martyn 562). It will be difficult for the Galatians to verify this charge of a hidden and selfish motivation when they receive Paul's letter.

[14–17] Paul's charge that the new preachers have as their goal to "boast in the flesh" of the Galatians provides a rhetorical foil for his articulation of what in his view legitimate boasting entails: "But let it not be [*mē genoito*] for me to boast except in the cross of our Lord Jesus Christ" (v. 15a). Paul becomes personal here, as he had in Gal 1–2, for what is at stake here are two forms of evangelism, one carried out by the new preachers (vv. 12–13), the other carried out by Paul (vv. 14–17). Whereas they (according to Paul's perception) aim to boast in the number of converts they have made (cf. 6:4), Paul aims "to boast . . . in the cross of our Lord Jesus Christ." Genuine boasting entails preaching the gospel of the crucified Christ (3:1). The reference to "our Lord Jesus Christ" is highly confessional and solemnly calls attention to the one who is their common Lord. Paul tries to call the new preachers, and the Galatians with them, to their senses, as he had in 3:1–5. He calls their attention to the cross of offense (see comment on v. 12c above). That cross is the end of all boasting, except (paradoxically) the boasting in the cross itself (cf. 1 Cor 1:29, 31; 4:6; 2 Cor 1:12; 11:16–12:10; Rom 5:2–3, 11).

The "cross of our Lord Jesus Christ" is Paul's way of designating the crucifixion of Christ (3:1) and its implications (see above on v. 12c). He here makes these implications explicit; it involves a double crucifixion, of the world and of himself, each in relation to the other: ". . . the cross of our Lord Jesus Christ, through which to me the world has been crucified and I [have been crucified] to the world" (v. 14b). The relative construction "through which [*di' hou*]," which assumes the antecedent to be "the cross," can also be translated "through whom," referring back to "Christ"; both terms are grammatically masculine in Greek. The former is probably the intended reading (cf. Lightfoot 223, who argues that if Paul had wanted to refer back to "Christ," he would have used the construction "in whom" or "with whom"), though there is in fact little or no difference in meaning or implication. Paul announces that with respect to himself ("to me," *emoi*, emphatic by position), "the world [*kosmos*][497] has been crucified," meaning the world that he has earlier characterized as "Judaism" (1:13–14) and as "works of the law" (2:16; 3:2, 5, 10), which includes circumcision (5:2–4; 6:12–13). Paul once regarded this particular "world" of circumcision and the law (Burton 354) as "sacred and dependable" (Martyn 564). He does so no longer. Fleshly circumcision and the law are now regarded as belonging to the realm of "the Flesh with its passions and desires," which the Galatians "crucified" when they became believers in Christ and were given the Spirit (5:24). Paul means that this world has been utterly destroyed—at least with respect to himself ("to me"). He is not here giving his personal, subjective opinion ("As far as I am concerned . . .") but describing what he takes to be an objective situation, the effect of Christ's death on an objective cross and of his own participation in that objective death. For that reason, he can go on to say that with respect to the world of the law, he himself has also been

---

497. On the omission of the article with this word, see BDF #253.4.

crucified ("and I to the world"), a claim that echoes 2:19 ("I have been crucified with Christ"). Here he has in view his nomistic I, the I whose existence is given shape and direction by circumcision and the law (see comment on 2:19). Paul's "previous, cherished and acknowledged identity" (Martyn 564) was put to death and separated from the nomistic world. Both here and in 2:19, Paul employs a perfect tense, indicating a past action with continuing effect on the present. In that verse, as here, Paul refers to himself not in an exclusive sense but as a paradigm for all believers who take their bearings from "the cross of *our* Lord Jesus Christ." Both Paul's nomistic self and the nomistic world that he once inhabited have been painfully put to death by his participation in the crucifixion of Christ. This is Paul's way of emphasizing the complete break with his past as a devotee of the law and the pain this break caused him. For him, a world has been destroyed, and he has suffered the loss of that world.

"For," as he now goes on to explain, "neither circumcision is anything nor uncircumcision but [only] a new creation." On the other side of crucifixion with Christ lie a new world and a new identity. As in 5:6, "circumcision" can here refer both to the practice of circumcision (cf. Rom 4:11) and to the condition of being circumcised. If circumcision means nothing anymore, neither by necessity does uncircumcision (*akrobystia*, lit., "foreskin"). "Uncircumcision" refers both to the absence of the practice of circumcision and to the condition of being uncircumcised (cf. 1 Cor 7:19). Where there is circumcision, there is also uncircumcision. When circumcision (the rite and the condition) becomes irrelevant, so does uncircumcision (the absence of the circumcision rite and the presence of the foreskin). The religious, ethnic, and cultural distinctions caused by a world divided into circumcision and uncircumcision have, in Paul's view, been violently replaced by "a new creation" (*kainē ktisis*). The new creation to which Paul refers evidently replaces "the world of *all* religious differentiation" (Martyn 565, emphasis original; cf. Betz 320; comment on 3:28). The end of the religion of the law ("works of the law") is also the end of the religion of "the elements of the world" (see comments on 4:3, 8–10).

The concept of "a new creation" is at home in Jewish apocalyptic eschatology (cf. Isa 65:17–25; *Jub*. 4.26; *1 En*. 72.1; *4 Ezra* [2 Esd] 7.75; *2 Bar*. 32.6; see Mell and Excursus 2). The new creation to which Paul refers is thus the opposite of "the present evil age" mentioned in 1:4. In Qumran the new creation signifies the end of the struggle between the spirits of truth and falsehood (1QS 4.24–25); according to Paul, the coming of the new creation has inaugurated a struggle between the Spirit and the Flesh (cf. comment on 5:13–24; Excursus 16; Martyn 565 n. 64). It signifies the invasion of "the present evil age" by God's Son, Jesus Christ (1:15–16; 4:5–7), and the creation of a new world for human beings who are "in Christ" (cf. 2 Cor 5:17). The parallel with 5:6 is instructive:

5:6 For in Christ Jesus neither circumcision avails anything nor uncircumcision,
but faith becoming effective through love
6:15 For[498] neither circumcision is anything nor uncircumcision,
but a new creation

This parallel suggests that the new creation of which Paul here speaks is to be equated with (Christ's) faith becoming effective through (Christ's) self-sacrificial love (cf. 2:20) and thus also with the love that believers in Christ even now have for one another as the fruit of the Spirit (5:13–14, 22; see comment on 5:6). The new creation is both God's newly creative act in Christ and the result of this newly creative act, a community of mutual love and service by the Spirit of Christ (cf. 5:13–24), in which the dualities of the present world (Jew/Greek, slave/free, male/female, circumcision/uncircumcison) have been abolished. Verse 15 is Paul's final brief summary of the gospel as he has repreached it to the Galatians through this letter, what he in the next verse calls "this standard."

Paul now moves to the closing of the letter. He begins with a benediction, a wish or prayer for a blessing from God: "And all who [*hosoi*, lit., as many as] will follow[499] this standard, peace [be] upon them . . ." (v. 16a). The main clause lacks a verb, and the reader must supply one: the optative form *eiē* of the verb *eimi* ("to be"), used to express a wish (BDF #128.5). Paul's use of the third person here ("all who . . . upon them") instead of the second person (as in v. 18) suggests that the blessing is not limited to believers in Galatia. Paul evidently has both Jewish and Gentile believers in view (cf. 2:15–16; 3:28); here he generalizes. Nevertheless, the group is restricted since it includes only those who "will follow this standard [*kanōn*]." The word *kanōn*, from which the English word "canon" is derived, literally means "measuring stick" or "ruler"; it is here being used metaphorically to mean "rule" (KJV, NIV, RSV, NRSV), a "norm" or "standard." Paul is referring to the claim made in v. 15 that neither circumcision nor uncircumcision matters but (only) a new creation. The blessing is meant for those who "will [henceforth] follow" (*stoichēsousin*) this standard, as Paul has expounded it throughout the letter. As indicated in the comment on 5:25b, where Paul exhorts the Galatians to "follow the Spirit," the verb *stoicheō* in its metaphorical use means "be in line with a person or thing considered as a standard for one's conduct," in short, "hold to, agree with, follow, conform" (BDAG 946). It takes a dative of association (BDF #193,

---

498. An alternate reading with strong support is "for in Christ Jesus" (ℵ, A, C, D, et al.), probably through the influence of 5:6. See textual note above. The inclusion makes the import explicit.

499. A strongly attested alternate reading is the present tense (A, C*, D, F, G, 1739, 1881, *pc* it; Ambst). The future is attested by ℵ, B, Ψ, 33, and others. See textual note above. If the present tense is original, the sense would be "And all who are now holding to this standard . . ."

#198.5), warranting the translation "follow this standard." Acceptable alternatives would be "hold to, conform to, walk in line with, or keep in step with" this standard. To "follow" this standard is to "follow" the Spirit (5:25b), which involves boasting in Christ's cross (6:14)—nothing else. Peace (*eirēnē*) here is not (simply) the absence of conflict or war, but that condition of eschatological well-being that accompanies the gospel (cf. comment on 1:3; 5:22).

In v. 16b, Paul remarkably includes a second benediction for a second group: ". . . and mercy also upon the Israel of God" (v. 16b). Paul is evidently indebted to, and applying, the language of Jewish liturgical tradition, as in Pss 124:5 LXX (125:5E) and 127:6 LXX (128:5E: "Peace be upon Israel"); *Pss. Sol.* 11.9 ("The mercy of the Lord be upon Israel"); and Benediction 19 of the *Shemonê Esrê* (in the Babylonian Recension; also called Amidah), a synagogue prayer that may go back in some form to Paul's time ("Peace . . . and mercy be upon us and upon all Israel thy people"; Bruce 274–75; Betz 321–22; Dunn 344; Martyn 566; Bachmann 181–84). This fact both clarifies and complicates the interpretation of the verse, since not only "mercy" (v. 16b) but also "peace" (v. 16a) are associated with "Israel" in this tradition. Does Paul intend (and will the Galatians hear?) a combined blessing ("peace and mercy") for a single group of people ("all who will follow this standard" are then identical with "the Israel of God"), a combined blessing for two separate groups ("those who will follow this standard" and "the Israel of God"), *or* separate blessings for two separate groups ("peace" for all who follow the standard and "mercy" for God's Israel)?

In the first option, which lies behind the rendering of the RSV ("Peace and mercy be upon all who walk by this rule, upon the Israel of God"), the Israel of God refers to the church consisting of Jews and Gentiles who adhere to Paul's standard as expressed in v. 15; Paul is then effectively and radically redefining who constitutes "Israel" in v. 16b. In the second option, as in the third, Paul makes a distinction between the church consisting of Jews and Gentiles (v. 16a) and "the Israel of God" (v. 16b). The second option leads to the following literal translation: "And all those who will follow this standard, peace be upon them and mercy, *and* upon the Israel of God." In this case, there is one combined blessing ("peace and mercy"), as in the first option, but for two different groups. The resulting sense is best given by the free translation of NJB: "Peace and mercy to all who follow this rule, *and* to the Israel of God" (cf. KJV, NRSV).[500] With some hesitation and no claim to certainty, the choice has here been made for the third option, separate blessings for two distinct groups (cf. Burton 357; Richardson 84):

---

500. KJV: "And as many as walk according to this rule, peace be on them, and mercy, *and* upon the Israel of God"; NRSV: "As for those who will follow this rule—peace be upon them, and mercy, *and* upon the Israel of God."

¹⁶ᵃAnd [*kai*] all those who will follow this standard, peace
be upon them,
¹⁶ᵇ and [*kai*] mercy also [*kai*] upon the Israel of God.

This translation follows the Greek word order exactly, but also involves decisions with respect to punctuation (the placement of a comma after "upon them" instead of after "mercy") and the translation of the second *kai* in v. 16b as "also" (instead of as "and"). The full argument for this interpretation is to be found in the excursus below. This excursus also addresses the thorny and highly controversial question of the precise referent of the designation "the Israel of God."

Excursus 19: The Israel of God

The crucial issue in the interpretation of v. 16 is the identity of "the Israel of God." The expression is without parallel in contemporary Jewish or Christian sources. Is this expression a designation for (1) the church consisting of Jews and Gentiles (Dahl; Calvin; Lightfoot; Ridderbos; Betz; Longenecker; Matera; Martyn; Hays; Witherington; Becker; Vouga)? Or for (2) the Jewish people, those whom Paul in 1 Cor 10:18 (AT) refers to as "Israel according to the flesh" (Mussner; Bruce; Bachmann 159–89; Eastman 2010)? Or for (3) Jewish Christians who adhere to Paul's standard as given in 6:15 (Schrenk 1949; 1950; Richardson 82–84)? Or for (4) law-observant Jews who believe in Christ, meaning Christian Jews such as the new preachers in Galatia and their sponsors in the church of Jerusalem?[501] The answer to this difficult question is linked to the interpretation of the syntax of the verse and to the significance of the reference to "the Israel of God" in the concluding section of this particular letter. We briefly consider each option in turn.

Option 1. The "Israel of God" refers to *the larger church* made up *of Jews and Gentiles* who adhere to Paul's standard as articulated in v. 15. In this interpretation, Paul is calling a double but unified blessing upon a single group of people: "the Israel of God" of v. 16b is to be equated with "all who will follow this standard" in v. 16a, with all who embrace the gospel as Paul has repreached it in this letter and as he has summarized it in 6:15. This reading in effect places a comma after the word "mercy," presupposes that peace and mercy belong together despite the intervening words (cf. 1:3 for a parallel: "Grace be to you and peace"), and understands the last *kai* of the verse to be explicatory ("i.e.," or "that is to say"): "And all those who follow this standard, peace be upon them and mercy, that is to say, upon the Israel of God." The RSV reflects this interpretation of the verse, providing a smooth translation: "Peace and mercy be upon all who walk by this rule, [i.e.,] upon the Israel of God."

---

501. Burton veers toward this view, since he maintains that the expression refers to "the remnant according to the election of grace, *including even those who had not seen the truth as Paul saw it*, . . . those within Israel who even though as yet unenlightened are the true Israel of God" (358, with added stress).

Contextual factors play a significant role in this interpretation of the verse. Paul has argued in the letter that believers in Christ, including the Gentile believers in Galatia, are "the offspring of Abraham, heirs according to a promise" (3:29) and thus "children of promise, like Isaac" (4:28); they are "children of the free woman [Sarah]" (4:31), who stands for "the Jerusalem above," who is their "mother" (4:26). The identity of God's people is defined by Christ and his Spirit (cf. 4:29), not by incorporation into the empirical people of Israel through circumcision and the observance of the law. The fact that Paul now speaks of the Israel *of God* is important in this argument. As Martyn explains, the new preachers in Galatia

> are identifying Israel on the basis of Law observance, . . . [but] Paul will identify Israel on the basis of God, intending thereby to remind the Galatians that God has identified himself by his promise rather than by the Sinaitic Law. . . . Putting 3:15–29 together with 6:15–16, . . . one can see Paul's intention. He is saying in effect that it is in the promise, rather than in the Law, that God has invested both the power to bring about the *new* creation and the power to provide the identity of his people Israel, the church. The God of Israel is first of all the God of Christ (3:16, 29), and it follows . . . that the Israel of God is the people whom God is calling into existence in Christ (1:6, 13), the community of those who know themselves to be, in Christ, former Jews and former Gentiles. (Martyn 576, emphasis original)

It also follows for Martyn that when Paul "penned Gal 6:16, he was not thinking of the Jewish people" any more than that he was "intending to distinguish a true Israel from a false one, in the sense that the church has now supplanted the synagogue. On the contrary, his attention was focused quite tightly on developments *within* the church" (Martyn 576, emphasis original). It makes no difference to this interpretation that Paul may use the term "Israel" elsewhere in his letters (1 Cor 10:18; 2 Cor 3:7, 13; Rom 9:6, 27, 31; 10:19, 21; 11:2, 7, 25, 26) to designate his "kinsmen according to the flesh" (Rom 9:3 KJV; cf. "Israelite" in Rom 9:4; 11:1; 2 Cor 11:22). The Galatian readers will not have the benefit of these other letters to provide a frame of reference for interpreting the meaning of the designation "the Israel of God"; their only frame of reference will be the letter to the Galatians itself (Martyn 575). In Romans, furthermore, Paul responds to developments that arose *subsequent* to the writing of Galatians (Martyn 577).

There nevertheless remain at least two significant problems with this reading of the verse: (a) The reference to "the Israel of God" is far removed from the one to "all who will follow this standard" (seven words intervene in the Greek text). (b) The syntax much more easily supports the conclusion that two distinct blessings and two distinct entities are in view, and thus that the comma be placed after "upon them." The last *kai* in the verse can then be understood to mean "also": "And all those who will follow this standard, peace be upon them, *and* mercy also upon the Israel of God."

Option 2. The "Israel of God" refers to *the Jewish people*, specifically those *who do not believe in Christ*. In this interpretation, Paul pronounces a blessing of peace on the church consisting of Jews and Gentiles both in Galatia and elsewhere *and* a blessing of mercy on unbelieving Israel. (A possible alternative is that Paul is pronouncing the same double blessing, "peace and mercy," on both the church and Israel.) Paul mentions (unbelieving) Israel here because he realizes that what he has said to this point could be construed as God's rejection of law-observant Israel. But (even unbelieving) Israel remains the Israel *of God*. Paul will work this out further in Rom 9–11 (Mussner 417), where, as in Gal 6:16, there is a notable link between "Israel" and God's "mercy" (*eleos*: Rom 9:23; 11:31; 15:9; *eleeō*: Rom 9:15, 18; 11:30, 31, 32; 12:8). Mercy is God's compassion toward disobedient humanity, in particular, disobedient Israel (Eastman 2010): "Just as you [believers in Rome] were once disobedient to God but now have received mercy because of their [Israel's] disobedience, so they have now been disobedient in order that by the mercy of God shown to you they also may receive mercy. For God has consigned all to disobedience, that he may have mercy upon all" (Rom 11:30–32 RSV). In Gal 6:16, then, Paul has in view God's ultimate mercy for disobedient Israel.

The problem with this interpretation is twofold: (a) It assumes that the referential meaning for "Israel" in Gal 6:16 must be consistent with that found in Rom 9–11 (see the critique of this assumption in the discussion of the first option above). (b) It leaves unexplained why Paul would include a blessing of mercy over non-Christian Jews but not one over Christian Jews, such as the new preachers in Galatia, who do not share Paul's understanding of the gospel and who have been the target of his argument throughout the letter.

Option 3. The "Israel of God" refers to *Jewish Christians who follow Paul's standard.* This proposal in effect reads the verse as follows: "And all Gentile believers in Christ who will henceforth follow this standard, peace be upon them, and mercy also upon God's Israel, Jewish believers in Christ who will henceforth follow this standard." The advantage of this reading is that justice is done to the genitive "of God," as in the first interpretation. The Israel *of God* is the remnant of Israel (cf. Rom 9:27; 11:5) that believes in Christ (cf. Rom 9:6–8 RSV: "Not all who are descended from Israel belong to Israel. . . . It is not the children of the flesh who are the children of God, but the children of the promise"). The problem with this solution, however, is that Paul uses a third-person construction in v. 16a. One expects him to write: "And *you* Gentile believers in Galatia, who will follow this standard, peace be upon *you*, and mercy also upon God's Israel, Jewish believers in Christ elsewhere who will follow this standard." Furthermore, Jewish believers in Christ who are loyal to Paul's gospel are probably already included in the reference to "all who follow this standard" in v. 16a.

Option 4. The "Israel of God" refers to *Jewish believers in Christ who remain law observant.* It is sometimes suggested that the new preachers in Galatia are using the term "Israel" (Martyn 574), or even the full expression "the Israel of God" (Betz 323; Longenecker 298), to designate law-observant believers in Christ such as themselves. It is not possible to prove that they used the expression, but it is certainly not implausible that they did so. The hypothesis helps to explain why Paul resorts to the expression seemingly "out of the blue." The designation as used by the new preachers would encompass not only themselves and any Gentile converts in Galatia and elsewhere, but also the mother church in Jerusalem, to which Paul seems to have referred in 1:13 as "the church *of God*" (see comment there). This church is currently sponsoring the mission to the Gentiles being carried out by the new preachers in Galatia (see Excursus 4 and comment on 4:25–26). Paul has adopted their self-designation ("Israel" or "Israel of God") in order to invoke God's compassionate mercy upon the wayward Jerusalem church and its missionaries, including those in Galatians. This interpretation does justice to 6:16, which invokes separate blessings on two distinct groups: And all those who will follow this standard, meaning churches of the Pauline mission, consisting of Jews and Gentiles who do not practice circumcision and do not observe the law, peace be upon them—and mercy also upon the Israel of God, meaning the churches of the Petrine mission, consisting of Jews who continue to practice circumcision and to observe the law, especially the mother church in Jerusalem now under the leadership of James (cf. 2:7–9).

As argued in the preceding excursus, the designation "the Israel of God" probably refers to Jewish believers in Christ who remain fully law observant. Paul calls these believers in Christ "the Israel of God" and invokes a blessing of mercy upon them because he realizes that what he has written in v. 15, which is a summary of his argument from 2:15 onward, could be construed as *God's* rejection of the law-abiding church of Jerusalem and of its proper mission (to Jews not to Gentiles). Paul believes this mission, which was being led by Peter, to have been authorized by God (cf. 2:7–9).[502] The church in Jerusalem, together with "the churches of Judea that are in Christ" (1:22), remains the Israel *of God*, that is, God's possession. By authorizing a mission of circumcision to Gentiles (in Galatia) and thereby betraying the agreement reached in Jerusalem (2:6–10; cf. 2:11–14), this church has, to be sure, fallen into grievous error (cf. 2:4: "false brethren"). For this church and all those who identify themselves with its present posture, Paul nevertheless invokes a blessing of mercy (*eleos*), which is God's compassion toward his disobedient people (cf. Exod 34:6–7; Isa 49:13), in this specific case, the church in Jerusalem and its missionaries in Galatia, upon whom Paul has invoked God's anathema in 1:6–9. Mercy looks to their eventual conversion to Paul's understanding of the gospel and indicates that the anathema of 1:6–9 is not eternal. In Rom 9–11, Paul will apply the same line of thought to Israel, understood as those Jews who are currently "enemies" of the gospel (Rom 11:28). In Galatians, however, mercy is invoked for the law-observant Jerusalem church and its allies, who are odiously pursuing a mission requiring that Gentile believers in Christ adopt the practice of circumcision and become fully law observant.

This interpretation of v. 16 helps to make sense of v. 17, which begins with Paul uttering neither "a gruff remark" (so Lührmann 122) nor one of "an impatient grumpiness" (so Dunn 346), but an earnest if indirect plea to the new preachers in Galatia (and their allies elsewhere?): "From now on, let no one cause me difficulties" (v. 17a). He wants to be left alone "from now on" (*tou loipou*), meaning "in the future" (BDAG 602), which indicates that matters

---

502. This interpretation is an answer to the objection that Paul would scarcely want to bless the new preachers and the church supporting their missionary activities at the end of a letter in which he has vigorously opposed them (Betz 322; Dahl 168; Weima 105; Tolmie 2005: 225–26).

Epistolary Closing 409

have been different up to this point. Paul seems to imply that he hopes the letter will bring a permanent end to the (unspecified) "difficulties" he has received from that quarter. The expression "cause difficulties" (*parechō kopous*) is an idiom (cf. Matt 26:10; Mark 14:6; Luke 11:7; 18:5), which is commonly translated with the corresponding English idiom "make trouble" (BDAG 558; NRSV) or a near equivalent (cf. KJV, NIV, RSV). The verb in the Greek is a third-person imperative in the present tense (*parechetō*), the sense of which can be captured by the following paraphrase: "Let no one repeatedly cause me difficulties in the future." The indefinite singular pronoun "no one" (*mēdeis*) is here construed as generic. It is possible, however, that Paul (also) has a leader of the new preachers particularly in view, as in 1:9; 3:1; 5:7, 10b, where he also uses a singular in connection with the new preachers (see comments on these verses and Excursus 4). If so, the sense of v. 17a may be captured by the following rendering: "Let someone [and you Galatians know who I mean] henceforth stop causing me difficulties."

Paul's indirect appeal to the new preachers to stop causing him difficulties is predicated on his suffering for Christ: "for [*gar*]," as Paul now explains, "I carry on my body the scars of Jesus" (v. 17b). The "I" is here emphatic (*egō*) and may imply a contrast: Paul in effect claims that *he*, unlike the new preachers active in Galatia, carries "the scars [*stigmata*] of Jesus" on his body. When Paul refers to "the scars of [the crucified] Jesus on my body," he probably does not mean that the specific wounds the crucified Christ suffered to his body (hands, feet, side) are literally present (and thus observable!) as scars on his (Paul's) body. The expression "the scars of Jesus" is probably rather an oblique reference to the scars Paul has acquired from "countless beatings" (2 Cor 11:23), including the five times he was whipped, the three times he was beaten with rods, and a stoning (2 Cor 4:8–10; 6:4–5; 11:23–25), all for preaching the gospel of the crucified Christ. By calling these marks on his body "the scars of Jesus," he also indicates that they have some deeper theological significance. The word *stigmata*, which may originally have been used in connection with religious tattooing (Betz 324), could also be used to refer to brands placed on slaves to indicate ownership (cf. BDAG 945; MM 590; Betz 1964), sometimes by a god (cf. Herodotus, *Hist.* 2.113; 3 Macc 2:29). Paul regards himself as "a slave of Christ" (1:10), and the scars of his suffering are marks indicating that he belongs to Christ (cf. NRSV, NJB: "the marks of Jesus branded on my body"). In this case, like Christ the Lord, like his slave. His bodily condition thus itself becomes a manner of testimony, of preaching the gospel of Christ crucified (cf. 3:1; 4:13–14; and comments there; Martyn 568–69).

In sum, after vilifying his opponents, the advocates of circumcision for Gentile believers in Galatia, Paul provides a last brief summary of the gospel. Neither circumcision nor uncircumcision means anything anymore. That world of religious, cultural, and ethnic differentiation came to an end in the cross, the crucifixion of Christ. What matters now is the new creation, which has replaced the world divided by circumcision and uncircumcision. May peace come to those who will follow this standard. And may mercy come upon the Israel of God, the law-observant church in Jerusalem and its missionaries in Galatia: may they yet come to see the truth of the gospel, which is the truth of Christ crucified, as Paul himself can personally testify with the scars on his body.

6:18 The Final Benediction

Paul brings his letter to a close with a parting benediction addressed to the Galatians directly:

6:18 The grace of our Lord Jesus Christ [be] with your spirit, brethren. Amen.

The Greek omits the verb; as in v. 16, the verb to be supplied is probably the optative *eiē* (of the verb *eimi*, "to be"), which expresses a wish. Paul closes his other letters with a "grace" benediction (Rom 16:20; 1 Cor 16:23; 2 Cor 13:13 (14 RSV, NIV); Phil 4:23; 1 Thess 5:28; Phlm 25), but the inclusion of the address "brethren" (*adelphoi*) is peculiar to Galatians. The form is masculine, but the term is inclusive of both women and men. Paul has used it several times earlier in the letter (1:2, 11; 3:15; 4:12, 28, 31; 5:11, 13; 6:1) as a way of emphasizing the fraternal bond that he feels with the Galatians, despite his consternation at their current situation (1:6–9; 5:2–4). By including the term in his final benediction, he indicates how important these fraternal bonds are to him. "Grace" is a standard item in Paul's benedictions, but it plays a central role in Paul's theological reflection in this letter, beginning with the opening salutation (1:3, 6; 2:9, 21; 5:4; see comments there). For Paul, it functions as a one-word summary of the gospel itself, for it is "the grace of our Lord Jesus Christ" (cf. 1:6). Paul asks that this grace be "with your spirit." He uses the same formulation in Phil 4:23 and Phlm 25 (cf. 2 Tim 4:22), which indicates that it is a Pauline convention. Paul means the "spirit" of the Galatians as invaded and captured, thereby liberated, by "the Spirit" of Christ (cf. 4:6; 5:1; 5:13–6:10; further Rom 8:16).

The final "Amen" (cf. Rom 15:33; 16:27; 1 Cor 16:24) indicates that Paul expects his letter to the Galatians to be read aloud in the context of a gathering for worship, thus "in the acknowledged presence of God" (Martyn 21). With the concluding "Amen," Paul invites the Galatians who will be listening to his letter to join him in a solemn affirmation of God's grace, explicitly mentioned in v. 18 and expounded in the remainder of the letter. Paul has written a letter that is the substitute for a sermon: in fact, an intensely apocalyptic sermon (see end of Excursus 5). In this apocalyptic sermon from his hand, Paul has been

Epistolary Closing

trying to repreach the gospel of the crucified Christ whereby (so he believes) God will once again secure the liberation of the Galatians from malevolent forces seeking to hold them in captivity, in particular Sin and the law (1:4; 3:13, 22–23; 4:4–5).

Did Paul's apocalyptic sermon accomplish what Paul hoped, even expected, it would in the churches of Galatia? We shall never know for sure. We have no direct information about the outcome. In his later letter to the Romans, Paul's failure to mention the churches of Galatia in connection with the collection for the poor in Jerusalem (Rom 15:25–27; contrast 1 Cor 16:1–3) seems to indicate that the letter did not do what Paul had hoped. The preservation of the letter, however, is itself an indication that it had an impact, not only in Galatia but beyond. In none of Paul's remaining letters—which apart from 1 Thessalonians were written after Galatians—nor in fact in the other books of the NT is the circumcision of Gentile believers in Christ any longer the make-or-break issue it was when Paul wrote Galatians in 51 C.E. (see Introduction: Date). Paul may have lost the battle over this issue in Antioch (see comment on 2:11–14), but through this letter he seems nevertheless to have won the war. Apart from pockets of churches consisting of law-observant Christian Jews in Palestine, Christian identity was no longer determined by the practice of circumcision and the observance of the law, that is, by incorporation into the Jewish people. Christian identity would henceforth be determined solely by one's relationship to Christ. For Paul and his followers, that relationship to Christ meant, and would always mean, participation in his crucifixion, his faithful death on the cross.

INDEX OF ANCIENT SOURCES

OLD TESTAMENT

Genesis
Ref	Pages
1:14	276–77n405
1:27	246
2:24	246, 292
6:1–6	31
6:5	337
6:15	246
8:21	337
11:30	303
12:2	190
12:1–3	196
12:2	224, 342
12:2–3	194, 216
12:3	58n83, 189, 193–94, 195, 195n282, 215
12:7	196, 224, 342
13:14–17	224, 342
13:14–18	196
13:15	222n319
13:16	194
15:1–6	221, 305
15:2–4	224, 342
15:2–5	189, 194, 196, 216
15:3–4	224
15:4	292
15:4–5	224
15:5	224
15:6	142, 149, 187–91, 190n270, 193–94, 196–97, 234, 236, 342, 287
15:7	224
15:7–8	224
15:13	221n318
15:18	196, 218, 220n317, 221, 222n319, 297–98
15:18–20	224, 342
16	303
16–21	286–289, 291–93, 295–96, 298, 300, 303, 310
16:1–4	292
16:1–10	291, 291n421
16:1–16	286, 291
16:10	287
16:15	292–93
16:16	293n422
17	177
17:1	179
17:1–7	224, 342
17:1–8	216, 218, 220–22, 267
17:1–14	297–98
17:2	222n319
17:2–6	305
17:4	222n319
17:4–7	224
17:4–8	196
17:5	196
17:7	222n319
17:8	219, 222n319, 222–24, 342
17:9–14	54, 57, 58, 58n83, 185, 187, 218, 220–21, 246n368
17:10–11	177, 336
17:10–14	244n362
17:11	292, 298
17:12	55n77, 312
17:13	177, 336
17:13–14	292, 298
17:14	283
17:15–22	224, 342
17:15–27	286, 291
17:16	305
17:16–21	196
17:17	292–93, 293n422
17:17–18	292
17:19–21	298
17:20	305
17:21	292
17:23–27	299
17:24–25	292, 298
18:9–15	224, 286, 291, 304, 342
18:10–12	292–93
18:14	292
18:18	58n83, 189, 195n282, 195–96, 216, 224, 342
20:9	146
21	286n420
21:1 2	304
21:1–3	292–23
21:1–4	221
22:1–19	188, 196
21:1–21	286, 291
21:4	299
21:5	293n422
21:6–7	304
21:9	306–7
21:9–10	306
21:10	224, 307
21:10–13	291, 291n421
21:12	307
21:27	219n315
21:32	219n315
22:16–17	222–23
22:17	224, 342
22:17–18	196, 305
22:28	195
24:7	222n319, 223–24, 342
25:13–18	300
26:4	195
26:5	187, 298
26:28	219n315
28:3–4	214
28:4	224
28:14	196, 224, 342
31:14	224n322
31:44	219n315
34:24	336
37:27	287
44:15	146

414 *Index of Ancient Sources*

Exodus		13:16	45	2 Chronicles	
3:14–15	263	13:17	45	6:41	243
4:22–23	242	14:1–2	242	20:7	248
4:25	55n77	14:3–21	134	12	63
7:11	359	16:19	118		
7:22	359	20:17	45	Ezra	
8:7	359	21:22–23	212	4:17	27n37
8:18	359	21:23	209, 211n305,	5:7	27n37
12:40	221n318		211, 212–13nn309–10;		
18:20	146		213–14	Nehemiah	
19:5	298	23:1	327	10:29	226n326
23:12	146	23:1–2	326	13:1	88
23:22–32	298	23:1–4	88	Esther	
23:33	272	25:1	153	8:17	138
24:7–8	298	25:4	381		
31:18	226n326	27:26	56, 146, 185,	Job	
34:27–28	298		198–201,	4:8	387
34:6–7	408		199–200nn288–90;	14:1	263
34:28	349		203–4, 206–7,	29:14	243
			212–13, 234,	Psalms	
Leviticus			283, 313	1	356
11:1–23	134	28:54	170	2:7	94
12:3	221	28:58	199	2:7–9	25
17:8–9	134	29:19	199	3:4	266
17:10–15	134	30:10	199	18:50	24
18:5	146, 198, 202–3,	30:15–20	233	65:2	152
	205–8, 208n300	30:16	207	79:6	273
19:15	118	32:2	327	83:6	300
19:16	379	33:2	228	89:26–27	94
19:17–18	350	27–30	184, 198	89:26–29	25
19:18	147, 147n214, 332,	32:47	233	105:6	248
	332n459, 340–43,			106:31–32	188
	344n467, 345–46,	Joshua		110:1	25
	348–50, 350n474,	6:17–18	45	119:1–8	153
	366, 377–81, 344–45,	7:11–13	45	125:5	404
	349nn473–74	7:12	45	126:5	387
25:5	276	9:15–20	219n315	128:5	404
25:6–15	188			132:9	243
26:46	227n327	1 Samuel		136:25	152
27:28	45	2:10	24	143:2	145n211, 152n224,
		2:35	24		152–54, 153n225,
Numbers		12:3	24		235
3:8	190n271	12:5	24	145:21	152
10:10	276	18:19–29	349		
22–24	63	20:30	79	Proverbs	
23:13	63			8:20	351
25:6–15	87	2 Samuel		20:1	360
26:46	226n326	3:13	349	22:8	387
		4:10	41	31:6	360
Deuteronomy		7:12–14	94, 223		
1:17	118	7:12–17	25	Isaiah	
4:1	361			1:10	349
5:33	351	1 Kings		5:1–7	362n481
6:4	228, 257	14:6	21	6:8	263
6:4–5	348	18:20–40	287	14:5	135
7:26	45			28:7	360
10:4	349	1 Chronicles		28:14	349
10:17	118	28:8	88	40–55	302

Index of Ancient Sources 415

40:9	41
41:8	248
41:8–9	90
41:21–23	302
42:1	90
42:4	90
42:6–7	90
42:9	302
43:1–7	302
43:9	153
43:14	302
43:25–26	154n228
43:26	153
44:3	215
44:26–28	302
45:10	284n413
47:1–4	302
47:9	359
47:12	359
48:20	302
49:1	79
49:1–6	90–91
49:5–6	90
49:6	79
49:13	408
49:14–23	302
50:8	153
51:2	303–4
52:7	41
52:10	79
53:1	79, 175, 190n270
53:11	153
54:1	79, 288, 293, 302–5
54:1–2	284n414
54:1–17	302
59:17	243
60:6	41
65:1	156
65:17–25	402

Jeremiah

1:5	90
1:10	90
1:15–16	90
3:9	358
7:25	263
9:26	336
10:25	273
24:9	211
26:6	211
31:33–34	265
44:8	211
51:57	360

Lamentations

4:20	24
23:33	360
39:19	360

Ezekiel

11:19–20	181
36:26	265

Daniel

1–12	78
1:8	134
4:1	27n37
9:24–27	261n389
11:31	222n320
12:2	31, 233, 388

Hosea

1:1	349
1:2	358
1:10	242
2:2	358
2:4	358
4:11–12	358
5:4	358
6:10	358
11:1	242

Joel

1:1	349
1:5	360
2:31	43
3:5	41

Amos

9:11	223

Micah

1:1	349
1:7	358
7:8	154n228
7:9	153, 163

Habakkuk

2:4	192n276, 198, 202–8, 203n295
3:13	24

Haggai

1:6	360

Zechariah

14:11	45

NEW TESTAMENT

Matthew

1	263n392
1–28	40
1:1	222
1:22	347
2:3	42
2:15	347
2:17	347
2:23	347
3:5	103n157
3:8–10	362n481
3:9	248
4:14	347
5:3	127
5:5	224n323
5:17	347
5:17–20	153, 181, 351
5:18	342
5:19	347
5:20	352, 361
5:32	358
6:9	266
6:24	272
6:33	156
7:38	228
7:12	348
7:17–18	362n481
7:21	361
7:53	228–29
8:17	347
10:3	99
10:40	280
11:11	263
11:13	347
11:29–30	309
12:17	347
12:32	30
12:36–37	153
13:20	390
13:35	347
13:48	346
14:2	182
14:26	42
14:62	25
15:3–6	349
15:19	334, 356, 358
15:32	390
16:17	92, 95
16:18	98, 121
16:19	25
18:3	361
18:15–17	374
19:9	358
19:23–24	361
19:29	224n323, 361
20:12	376
21:4	347
21:8	320
22:34–40	348, 378
22:40	313, 344, 348
22:44	25
23:27	358
24:12	364
25:34	224n323, 361
26:10	409
26:28	30
26:54	347

Index of Ancient Sources

Matthew (*continued*)
26:56   347
26:64   25
27:9   347
27:18   359

Mark
1–16   40
1:1   93
1:14   261
2:1   8n17, 107n158
3:18   99
4:1–20   387
6:3   99
6:50   42
7:1–5   87n136
7:3–5   85n133
7:5   351
7:21   358
7:21–22   334, 356
7:22   358
8:3   390
8:15   321
8:31   7
9:43   326
9:45   326
9:47   361
10:6–8   246
10:15   361
10:17   224n323, 361
10:23–25   361
10:30   30
11:13   390
11:22   149–50n219
12:25   246
12:26   25
12:28–31   378
12:28–34   348
12:31   348
13   78
13:8   284
14:6   409
14:13   322
14:36   25, 94, 266
14:49   347
14:61   93
14:71   45
15:5   98
15:10   359
15:50   95, 361
16:1   127

Luke
1   263n392
1–24   40
1:4   385
1:12   42
2:13   108
3:8   248
3:23   108
4:17   303
4:21   347
6:13   22
6:15   99
7:6   108
7:13–14   108
7:47   230n337
8:6   108
8:16   108
9:10   22
10:16   280
10:25   224n323, 361
10:25–28   348, 379
10:26   342
11:2   266
11:7   409
11:21   108
11:42   364
12:18   108
13:17   353
14:27   376
16:13   272
16:17   342
17:5   22
18:5   409
18:17   361
18:18   224n323, 361
18:25   361
18:30   30
20:21   118
20:34–35   30
20:38   370
20:42–43   25
21:5   45
21:15   353
22:69   25
23:12   359
24:25   170n252
24:36–49   22
24:38   42
24:44   291, 347
24:49   209, 215–16

John
1:6   263
1:17   226n326
1:41   24
1:42   97, 120
1:45   291, 347
2:6   108
3:2   342
3:5   361
3:14   342
3:16   342
3:17   262
3:19   342
3:21   342
3:23   342
4:6   342
4:25   24
5:7   42
5:21   233
5:29   174
5:42   364
6:45   303
6:62   10, 279
6:63   233
7:49   342
8:31   248
8:33   248, 292
8:37   248
8:39   248
8:41   358
9:34–35   308
10:34   342
11:33   42
12:3   346
12:27   42
12:34   342
12:38   347
13:16   21
13:18   347
13:21   42
13:34   340, 343
13:35   364
14:1   42
14:27   42
15:9   364
15:10   364
15:12   340
15:13   364
15:25   342, 347
17:26   364
19:17   322
19:24   347
19:36   347
20:22   173, 209, 215
20:31   93
21:34   360

Acts
1–5   121
1–28   30n43, 20–21, 40, 59n86, 88n139, 125
1:4–5   209, 215–16

Index of Ancient Sources

1:8	91	9:26–31	100	14:4	22–23, 95, 115n169
1:9–11	22	9:27	107		
1:10	261	9:27–28	100	14:8–10	182
1:13	87n137, 99–100	9:30	7, 100, 101n152, 263	14:14	5, 22–23, 95, 115n169
1:15	100	9:31	101, 102n153	14:17	390
1:15–16	108n161	9:32–11:18	102, 102n153	14:21–24	10n20
1:15–26	22	10:1–48	133	14:21–27	4
1:16	347	10:1–11:18	59, 120	14:24–28	22, 115n169
1:17–19	23	10:9–11:18	132	15	10n20, 43, 107n159, 127n184
1:22	22	10:28	135, 135nn193–94	15:1	43, 58, 107n159, 133, 136
1:26	22, 95, 100	10:34–11:18	84		
2:14	100	10:39	22, 212	15:1–2	107, 112
2:20	43	10:41	22	15:1–29	8n18, 107n159
2:22	182	10:44–45	59	15:1–35	130
2:33	209, 215–16	10:45	73, 113, 115n169, 133	15:2	107
2:33–35	25	11:2	73, 113, 115n169	15:4–5	110, 113, 115
2:37	22	11:2–3	133, 135	15:4–29	115
2:37–38	100	11:4–18	133	15:5	55n78, 59, 107n159, 113, 133, 136, 314, 359
2:38	209, 173, 215	11:17–18	59		
2:42	124	11:18	133	15:6	107, 110
3:1	84, 123	11:19–26	59	15:6–22	58
3:1–12:19	98	11:19–30	130	15:7	98
3:3–4	123	11:19–15:35	23	15:7–10	131
3:11	123	11:22	107	15:7–11	120
3:18	347	11:25–26	7, 100, 107	15:10	309, 376
4:13	123	11:25–15:35	7, 100	15:12	182
4:19	123	11:26	26n32, 112	15:13	99–100, 123
5:6–22	43	11:27–30	127, 127n184, 128, 128n185	15:13–29	133–34n191
5:17	359			15:20	134, 358
5:29	22	11:28–30	108n161	15:21	110
5:30	212	11:30	8n18, 10n20, 107, 107n159	15:22–35	73
6–8	88n138			15:23	7, 19n26, 27, 100
6:12	95	12:1–2	123	15:24	43, 59, 132n189
7:6	221n318	12:2	99	15:28	107n159
7:38	27	12:11	35	15:29	125n182, 134, 358
7:47	230n337	12:17	99–100, 123	15:35	107
7:53	229n334, 400	12:25	8n18, 107, 107n159	15:36	110
8:1–3	6, 85n129, 87			15:37–39	108, 110
8:1–40	59, 102n153	13–14	4–5, 107	15:41	7, 27, 100, 110
8:14	123	13–15	121	16:1–3	111, 111nn164–65
9:1	87	13:1	107, 385	16:1–5	4n7
9:2	85n128	13:1–3	22–23, 108n161, 115n169	16:3	323
9:3	96			16:6	4, 4n11, 9–10, 279
9:3–9	6, 78, 90	13:1–14:20	10n20	16:9–10	108n161
9:4–5	85n128	13:1–14:28	130	16:10–17	6n12
9:10–19	95	13:13–14:23	4	16:16–18	182
9:11	7, 100	13:15	303	17:1–2	126
9:13	87	13:27	347	17:6	324
9:15	23, 84, 91	13:33	25, 94	17:27	156
9:19	88	13:43	5	17:30	273
9:20	93	13:47	91	18	182
9:21	6, 85n131, 87	14:1	5	18:1	6, 11
9:22–23	111n165				
9:23	7, 97				
9:23–25	7, 100				

Index of Ancient Sources

Acts (*continued*)
18:2–3	171
18:3	98
18:5	11
18:11	11
18:12	9
18:23	4, 10
18:23–24	11n22
18:25	385
19:11–12	182
19:16	318n449
19:20	318n449
19:32	27
19:39	27
19:40–41	27
20:5–15	6n12
20:7–12	182
20:28	88
20:32	224n323
21:1–18	6n12
21:17–26	133, 133–34n191
21:18	99–100, 123, 304
21:20–22	59
21:21	351, 385
21:24	372, 385, 400
21:25	134, 358
21:38	324
21:39	7, 100
22:3	7, 85n133, 100
22:4	6, 85n128, 87
22:6	96
22:6–11	6, 78, 90
22:7–8	6, 85n128
22:10	23
22:12–16	95
23:12	45
23:14	45
22:14–15	23
22:21	84, 91
22:25	309n443
23:6	85n127
23:21	45
23:26	19n26, 27
23:34	7, 100
24:5	359
24:14	359
24:17	8n17, 107n158, 133–34n191
24:25	322, 365
25:14	110
26:5	85n127, 359
26:10	87
26:11	6, 85n128
26:12	96
26:12–18	6, 78, 90
26:14–15	6, 85n128
26:17	84
26:17–18	91
26:17–19	23
26:20	96
27:1–28:16	6n12
28:1–9	182

Romans
1–16	2, 20–21, 147n213, 156n133, 165n251, 192n275, 239, 406
1:1	65, 90, 93
1:1–4	81, 94
1:3	93
1:3–4	336, 177
1:4	25
1:5	122, 125, 150, 192
1:7	27, 364
1:8	39
1:9	93
1:13	37, 362
1:14	170
1:16	28n38, 44n57
1:16–18	81
1:17	92, 150, 188, 192n276, 192, 204, 205n299
1:18–32	81
1:24	358
1:28–31	356
1:29	334, 359
2:2–3	322
2:4	364
2:5	80–81
2:5–8	153
2:7	31, 156
2:8	359
2:10	364
2:12–15	201
2:12–16	231
2:13	153
2:18	385
2:23	230
2:25	158, 230
2:26	119, 400
2:27	158, 230
2:28–29	177, 336
3:3	149n219, 204n297
3:8	42, 322, 349, 388
3:8–19	235
3:9	157, 234, 235n348
3:9–18	235
3:12	364
3:17	364
3:19	234n347, 291, 342
3:20	145–46, 148, 152, 231, 235
3:21	234n347, 291, 342, 347
3:21–26	150, 154
3:22	148, 193, 209
3:23	157, 264
3:23–24	231
3:25	30, 30n42, 145n211, 154–55, 193, 210, 215
3:25–26	155n230
3:26	148, 192
3:27	379, 384n492
3:27–28	146
3:28	145, 152
3:30	119, 192
3:30–31	193
4:1–8	154
4:2	146, 189, 384n492
4:3	190n270, 234
4:4	146
4:5	155
4:6	146
4:6–8	30n42, 154–55
4:6–9	281
4:9	119
4:10–12	146, 221
4:11	317, 402
4:12	133, 149, 372
4:13–14	224n323
4:15	158n236, 158, 230
4:16	149, 192
4:16–18	224, 342
4:17	40, 190n270, 196, 220, 233
4:19	293
4:21	190
4:24	145n211
4:25	30, 150, 155n230, 211, 374
5:1	28, 192, 364
5:1–10	154
5:2	40n53
5:2–3	401
5:2–5	316
5:5	181, 364
5:6	155
5:8	155, 172, 364
5:8–9	30, 154
5:9	81
5:10	28n38, 44n57, 94
5:11	401

Index of Ancient Sources   419

5:12	33, 113	8:18–19	80	11:23		144
5:12–21	33, 157,	8:19	316	11:25–26		406
	234, 392	8:20–25	316	11:28		408
5:12–6:23	155	8:21	387	11:30–32		407
5:13	230, 231n238	8:22–23	284	11:31		407
5:14	230–31, 296	8:23	94	11:32		234, 235n348,
5:15–18	374	8:24	309n443			264, 392
5:18	264	8:25	316	12:2		30
5:19	150	8:30	40, 154	12:3		198
5:20	230–31,	8:32	94	12:7		385
	235, 374	8:34	25	12:8		407
5:20–21	113	8:35	364	12:9		364
5:21	31, 33, 389	8:38	33	13:8		346
6	245n365	8:39	364	13:9		346n469, 349
6:1–10	161n241	9–11	407–8	13:8–10		147, 343–45,
6:2	159, 207	9:1	99			345n468,
6:6	161, 367	9:3	45, 406			347n471
6:7	242	9:4	264, 406	13:9–10		349n473
6:9	212	9:6	406	13:10		364, 391
6:10–11	159, 370	9:6–8	407	13:12		357
6:14–15	210n302	9:7	248	13:12–14		243, 357–60
6:15	388	9:12	40	13:13		358, 359
6:19	358	9:15	407	13:14		178
6:22	31	9:17	234	14:7–8		370
6:23	31, 389	9:18	407	14:10–12		384
7	160n240	9:22	364	14:15		364
7–8	357, 379	9:23	407	14:17		31, 360, 364
7:1–5	259, 261	9:27	406–7	14:19		364
7:4	160	9:30	192	14:23		192
7:5	120n178, 318, 366	9:31	406	15:1		376
7:6	159	9:32	192	15:3		29
7:7	231	10:3	156	15:4		171
7:8	335	10:4	231	15:4–5		342
7:9–13	349	10:5	206	15:9		407
7:10	233	10:6	192	15:13		183n268, 364
7:12	147, 229n333	10:8	109n162	15:14		365
7:13	230–31, 235	10:9	28	15:15		285n419
7:14	229n333	10:10	28n38, 44n57	15:16		125, 130
7:22	229n333, 232n343	10:11	234	15:17		384n492
7:25	229n333, 232n343	10:14	142	15:18		125
8:1	231	10:15	41, 144	15:19		182, 183n268, 297
8:2	379	10:16	79, 190n270	15:22–24		285n419
8:3	94	10:16–17	175	15:23		100
8:3–4	262	10:19	406	15:25–26		297
8:4	343, 347n471	10:20	156	15:25–27		22, 127,
8:6	364	10:21	406			133–34n191
8:7	229n333,	11:1	248, 406	15:25–28		118
	232n343, 359	11:2	234, 406	15:26		3n5, 124, 127
8:11	233	11:5	407	15:26–27		385, 411
8:13	366	11:6	224	15:28–29		285n419
8:14–17	242	11:7	406	15:30		333, 364
8:15	25, 94, 264, 266	11:11	28n38, 44n57	15:31		297
8:15–16	266	11:11–12	374	15:32		285n419, 364
8:16	410	11:13	125	15:33		364, 410
8:17	224n323, 250, 267	11:22	364	15:50		336

Index of Ancient Sources

Romans (*continued*)
16:5	3n5
16:15	130
16:17	359
16:20	33, 364, 410
16:23	391
16:27	410

1 Corinthians
1–16	20–21
1:1	22, 25
1:2	88
1:3	27, 364
1:4–9	39
1:7	79–80, 316
1:8	79
1:9	40, 94, 124, 229n332
1:11	37, 359
1:12	118n173, 120
1:16	391
1:17	64n96
1:18	84, 172
1:18–19	172
1:20	30
1:22	156
1:23	84, 109n162, 172, 323, 398
1:24	172
1:29	401
1:31	188, 401
2:1–2	64n96, 172
2:1–5	183
2:2	84
2:6	30
2:6–8	33
2:8	30
2:10	80, 92
2:1–5	183
2:2–5	183
2:9	239
3:13	80
2:13–15	374n486
2:14	280
3:1	374n486
3:3	359
3:10–17	124n180
3:13–15	382, 384
3:18	30, 381
3:19	30
3:22	118n173, 120
4:1–5	65
4:4–5	384
4:5	390
4:6	401
4:8	325n454
4:9–13	281
4:14–15	284n413, 293
4:15	240–41
4:17	285n419
4:18	42
4:20	31, 360
4:21	364–65
4:25	162
5:1	358
5:3–5	374
5:5	33, 177, 336
5:6	321, 384n492
5:9–11	356
5:10	30
5:11	360
5:12	335
5:28	94
6:9	31, 361
6:9–10	224n323, 356, 360–61
6:10	31, 360
6:11	145n211, 154, 155n230
6:13	358
6:15	141, 156n133
6:18	358
7	247n369
7:1	42
7:1–16	246
7:1–40	246n367
7:2	358
7:5	33
7:9	365
7:15	40n53, 364
7:17	229
7:17–24	246
7:18	311
7:19	318, 323, 402
7:25–40	246
7:28	246
7:29	390
7:31	30
7:36	246
8:1	364
8:1–6	134
8:5–6	28
8:6	263n390
8:8	144
9:1	22, 78, 91, 95
9:1–5	117
9:1–6	118
9:2	122
9:4–14	385
9:5	99, 118n173, 120
9:5–6	95
9:6	95, 107, 118n173
9:8–9	342
9:9	234n347, 381
9:14	229
9:15–16	384n492
9:16	65, 144
9:20	126n183, 126
9:24–26	110
9:24–27	320
9:25	365
10:11	31, 295
10:14	359
10:16	124
10:16–17	134n192
10:18	405–6
10:23–30	134
10:30	30
10:32	88
11:2–16	246n367
11:8	320
11:12	335
11:16	88
11:17–34	132n188
11:19	359
11:22	88
11:23	77n119, 82
11:25	296
11:28	382
11:32–33	6–7
11:34	229
12	183
12:1	374n486
12:3	28, 37, 45
12:4–11	182
12:6	120n178, 318
12:9–10	41
12:10	183
12:11	318
12:12	183
12:12–13	243n361
12:13	244n362, 245, 246n367, 245–46
12:17	175n259
12:26	180
12:27	243n361
12:28	385
12:28–29	182–83
13	362
13:1	144
13:1–4	364
13:5	362
13:8	364
13:13	364

14	81	15:45–49	33, 244	4:13–14	183
14:1	364	15:50	31, 224n323, 361	5:5	224n323
14:6	80	15:53–54	243	5:10	384
14:6–7	144	15:54–56	162n245	5:12	384n492
14:9	144	15:56	33	5:14	364
14:11	144	16:1	3, 26–27, 128, 229	5:15	370
14:19	385	16:1–3	127, 411	5:17	31, 402
14:21	234n347, 291, 342	16:1–4	127, 133–34n191	5:19	30, 30n42, 374
14:23	391	16:3	297	6:1	280
14:26	80	16:5	3n5	6:2	28n38, 44n57
14:28	144	16:9	353	6:6	364
14:29–31	80	16:10–11	285n419	6:6–10	362
14:30	80, 92	16:11	364	6:14	124
14:33	364	16:14	364	6:15	33
14:37	374n486	16:15	3n5, 391	6:18	242
15:1	37, 46, 75–76	16:17	42	7:1	177, 336
15:1–3	82, 385	16:19	3, 3n5, 101, 391	7:4	364, 384n492
15:1–5	77n119, 83n125, 83–84	16:22	45	7:5	3n5
		16:20	393	7:7	359
15:1–9	118	16:21	395	7:8	114n168
15:1–11	22n28, 83	16:23	410	7:13	364
15:3	46, 150, 153, 172, 209, 211	16:23–24	393	7:14	384n492
		16:24	364, 410	7:15	280
15:3–4	171			8–9	127, 133–34n191
15:3–5	83–84, 210	**2 Corinthians**		8:1	3, 3n5, 37, 75–76, 101
15:3–8	117	1–13	20–21, 59		
15:4–5	25	1:1	3n5, 22, 25, 280	8:2	364
15:5	98, 118n173, 120, 123	1:2	27, 364	8:4	124
		1:3	39	8:6	57n81, 177, 180
15:5–8	95	1:6	120n178, 180, 318	8:7–8	364
15:5–9	92	1:8	3n5, 37, 280	8:17	280
15:7	99	1:12	384n492, 401	8:23	22, 95, 108
15:7–9	22	1:14	384n492	8:24	364, 384n492
15:8	78	1:19	93–94	9:2	3n5
15:8–9	95	1:24	364	9:3	384n492
15:9	86–87	2:3	364	9:13	124
15:10	90	2:4	364	10:1	365
15:11	109n162	2:6–8	374	10:2	42
15:12	42	2:8	364	10:13	382
15:12–18	84	2:11	33	10:15–16	382
15:17	211	2:13	3n5, 108	10:16	125
15:20–28	34	2:40	346	11:1	325n454
15:21	212	3:1	42	11:2	283, 359
15:21–22	33, 244, 264	3:5	346	11:3	33
15:22	233	3:6	233, 296	11:4	41, 60n87, 280
15:23–28	79, 390, 392	3:7	406	11:7–9	385
15:24	30–31, 33, 361	3:12–14	298	11:9	3n5
15:25	25	3:14	296	11:10	3nn5–6; 100, 384n492
15:26	33, 162n245	3:17	266		
15:27	202	4:2	64n96	11:14	33
15:31	384n492	4:4	30, 33	11:16	280
15:33	387	4:5	28	11:16–12:10	401
15:36	144, 233	4:6	92	11:17	384n492
15:42	387	4:8–10	409	11:22	248, 406
15:45	233	4:12	120n178, 318	11:22–23	60n87

2 Corinthians (*continued*)		1:3–4	379	1:10–12	37n51, 71
11:23	409	1:3–5	44n57, 71	1:11	2n4, 16, 25, 37, 39–41, 46, 50, 61, 68, 76nn115–16; 103, 109n162, 125, 168–69, 218, 251, 273, 277, 279, 305, 384, 386, 410
11:23–25	409	1:3–6	324		
11:24	126n183, 126	1:4	15, 17, 28n38, 29n40, 30n43, 35n48, 40, 44, 63, 71–72, 78, 80, 83, 83n125, 113–14, 139, 150, 154–55, 161, 162–65, 172, 192, 198, 209–11, 210n303, 214, 234, 242, 262, 302, 309, 329, 368, 389, 393, 402, 411		
11:26	114				
11:31	99				
11:32	240				
11:32–33	96, 100				
12:1	81			1:11–12	15–16, 48, 63, 71–72, 98, 104, 119, 150, 273
12:1–4	80–81				
12:5–7	81				
12:7	33, 80, 280–81, 280n410			1:11–17	8, 14, 24, 73, 75–96, 104, 128
12:9	281			1:11–24	16, 23, 72–73, 105, 110
12:9–10	281				
12:12	182	1:5	36n50	1:11–2:14	45n58, 51, 60, 70
12:14	285n419	1:6	11n21, 28, 40n52, 91, 111, 113, 115, 119, 122, 130, 136, 153, 163–65, 225, 273, 281, 290, 301, 308, 311, 315, 320–21, 327, 334, 382, 406, 410		
12:16	376			1:11–2:21	12, 14–15, 37, 72–165, 104, 128
12:17–18	285n419				
12:20	359			1:11–6:10	12, 14
12:20–21	285n419			1:12	6, 6n14, 22, 24–25, 31n44, 53, 77n118, 77–78n120, 78n122, 83n124, 89n141, 109, 144, 155, 238n349, 239, 263n391
12:21	358				
12:20–21	357–60				
13:1	285n419	1:6–7	15–16, 24, 76, 114, 169, 171, 277, 290, 324, 384		
13:2	360				
13:4	281				
13:5	382	1:6–9	5, 10, 12, 17, 33n45, 34, 36, 60n87, 84, 119, 145, 180, 209, 225, 275n403, 276, 290, 393, 396, 408, 410	1:12–2:14	68
13:10	285n419			1:12–16	159–60
13:11	364			1:13	6, 27n34, 73, 102, 102n153, 103, 123–24n180, 307, 323, 398, 406–7
13:13	124, 364				
13:13–14	410				
		1:6–10	12, 14–15, 19, 23, 37–71, 64n96, 72, 240, 320		
Galatians					
1–2	11, 127n184, 401			1:13–14	64, 72, 86n135, 103, 133, 161, 235, 357, 398, 401
1–6	411, 192n275				
1:1	9, 28n39, 40, 61, 63, 72, 74, 77, 84, 86, 89, 94–95, 100, 104, 110, 117, 122n179, 144, 150, 160, 211, 214, 266, 321, 395	1:6–11	68		
		1:6–6:10	67	1:13–16	324, 398
		1:6–6:17	12	1:13–24	104
		1:7	12, 15, 74, 77, 164, 194, 200n290, 275, 283, 320–21, 324	1:13–2:14	5, 72–73
				1:13–2:21	162n242
				1:14	85n132, 89n140, 282
1:1–4	94, 262, 266	1:8	81, 144	1:15	38, 40, 51, 73, 90n144, 113, 119, 130, 136, 163, 225, 238n349, 242, 281, 308, 334
1:1–5	11–12, 14, 19–36, 67	1:8–9	15, 72, 109n162, 131, 200n290, 273, 279, 396		
1:1–6	10				
1:1–10	14, 37, 19–37, 66, 19–71, 393	1:9	47n62, 82, 170, 313, 383, 399, 409	1:15–16	5–8, 15, 22, 24–25, 28, 48, 71, 78n120, 104, 107n158, 109, 122, 89nn142–43; 155, 263n391, 324, 402
1:1–17	323	1:9–11	76		
1:1–2:14	323	1:9–12	63–64		
1:2	3, 5, 47n62, 50, 53, 101, 311, 374, 410	1:10	29, 74–75, 86, 90, 232n345, 244, 272, 272n399, 340, 409		
1:3	15, 28n39, 38, 40, 65, 91, 113, 157, 163, 225, 308, 321, 364, 404–5, 410			1:15–17	6–7, 73, 97
				1:16	25, 31n44, 40, 72, 103, 109n162, 116n170,
		1:10–11	45		

Index of Ancient Sources

	125, 145n211,	2:4	10, 59, 63, 102,		147, 194, 195n282,
	161–62, 195n282,		111n165, 113n166,		304, 308,
	262, 335–36,		164, 241, 260, 282,		318n448, 398
	386, 388		290, 309, 334, 408	2:12–13	137n197, 158
1:16–17	94n147, 101	2:4–5	111n164, 136, 210	2:13	5, 22, 73, 107–8,
1:17	3n6, 6–7, 21, 99,	2:5	8, 16, 65, 72–73,		108n160, 110,
	117, 144, 299		159, 168, 244, 282,		115n169, 282
1:17–18	98, 297		320, 384, 401	2:14	16, 54n74, 65,
1:17–19	123	2:6	3, 117n172,		72–73, 104,
1:17–23	125		116nn170–71; 381		120–21, 137n198,
1:17–24	104	2:6–9	274		144, 153, 205, 207,
1:18	6–8, 72–73, 76,	2:6–10	8–10, 120, 408		136nn195–96; 282,
	97n149, 106,	2:7	16, 72, 99,		320, 370, 384,
	107, 107n158, 110,		118n175, 142n205,		397, 400
	114, 119–21,		144, 149n218,	2:14–16	139, 195n282
	127n1841:18–19,		244n362, 384	2:15	12n23, 44,
	95, 123, 321	2:7–8	41n54, 74, 91,		135–36, 137n197,
1:18–20	73, 111		102, 119–21,		141n203, 226,
1:18–24	8, 14, 73,		120n177		242, 408
	96–104, 128	2:7–9	48, 72, 97,	2:15–16	16, 16n25,
1:19	9n19, 28, 72,		102n154, 129, 132,		33n45, 57,
	95, 117, 122–23		135, 147, 318n448,		103, 115n169,
1:20	99n150		321, 323, 408		119, 129, 132,
1:21	3n6, 6–8, 73, 115	2:7–10	98–99, 243		137, 193n278,
1:21–24	73	2:8	91n145, 95,		200, 209, 298,
1:22	3, 27n34, 103n157,		122n179, 318		398, 403
	242, 314, 408	2:8–9	23, 95, 195n282	2:15–21	14, 34, 44, 46,
1:22–23	88	2:9	5, 9, 9n19, 22, 28,		61n91, 68, 72–74,
1:23	72, 82, 84n126, 93,		40, 72, 74, 91, 95,		78n120, 84, 104,
	102n153, 103n157,		99, 116n171,		175–76, 186, 139–65,
	109n162, 149, 193,		118nn174–75;		237, 310, 316, 393
	193n280, 307, 323,		123–24nn180–81;	2:15–3:9	288
	386, 398		130, 132, 133–34n191,	2:15–4:7	199
2–3	239		136, 139, 163, 225, 281,	2:16	26n32, 30, 44, 56,
2:1	5–6, 8, 22, 73,		323–24, 381, 410		61, 61n92, 84, 102,
	76, 95, 100,	2:10	127n184, 335,		103n156, 130, 136,
	101n151, 108n160,		385, 401		139nn200–202;
	127n184, 130–32, 297	2:10–14	49		142n204, 143n206,
2:1–3	8	2:11	6–7, 9, 72–73,		144n210, 148nn216–17;
2:1–10	8, 8n18, 10n20,		100, 120–21,		149n218, 152nn222;
	14, 73, 84, 101,		173, 374		224; 165n250, 166,
	104–28, 131,	2:11–12	112		168, 172–73, 177,
	107n159, 126n183,	2:11–13	107, 140, 321		181, 183–85, 188,
	127n184, 130, 133,	2:11–14	5, 10, 14, 23,		190–95, 194n281,
	244–45		73–74, 102, 108,		198, 201, 203–4,
2:1–14	287		110, 117, 147,		210, 214–15,
2:1–21	16, 72–73, 105		128–38, 245,		215n312, 226, 233,
2:2	15–16, 72, 80, 82,		313, 385,		235–36, 238–239,
	91n145, 114n167,		408, 411		239n351, 241–42,
	195n282, 320,	2:11–18	245		242n358, 264, 267,
	322, 381, 384	2:11–21	104		284, 312, 317, 319,
2:3	138, 144, 147, 173,	2:12	5, 9n19, 23, 72–73,		324, 335–36, 343–44,
	310, 323, 399,		99, 112–13, 118n173,		355, 357, 362, 365,
	397nn493–94		123, 131n187,		367, 380, 389, 391,
2:3–4	400		132n190, 135,		398, 401

Galatians (*continued*)

2:16–17	194		167, 185, 193, 195, 202, 209, 215, 225–26, 231, 236–37, 247–50, 168–84, 265, 274, 276, 285, 306, 310, 317, 336, 352, 367, 370, 393, 401		236, 245, 247–50, 267, 283, 397, 400
2:17	35, 102, 137n197, 156n234, 230, 231n342, 234, 242, 314, 331, 352			3:7–9	168, 317
				3:8	34, 44n57, 61, 72, 144, 151, 154n227, 165–67, 169, 195n282, 216, 221, 224–25, 227, 234, 245, 247, 290, 306, 307n442, 342, 344, 348, 393
2:18	164n247, 374	3:1–6	190		
2:19	154n226, 159n238, 161n241, 206, 343, 367, 370, 380, 402	3:1–14	317, 344		
		3:1–29	306, 310		
		3:1–4:6	12		
2:19–20	78n120, 80, 89, 93, 172, 281, 324, 370–71	3:1–4:7	13–14, 165–268, 216, 249, 265, 269–70, 315, 317, 329, 332	3:8–29	305
				3:9	282
				3:9–12	239
2:19–21	91, 94, 113, 171–72, 176, 205, 272, 278	3:1–4:31	68	3:10	35, 44, 56, 58, 145, 153, 165n250, 168, 199n288, 201n291, 202n293, 216, 235, 238, 241, 259, 263n393, 264, 283, 291, 303, 313, 345, 355, 357, 362, 380, 389, 398
		3:2	13, 44, 58–59, 81, 145, 159, 161, 193n277, 198, 174nn257–58; 176nn260–61; 248, 266–67, 336, 340, 343, 357, 362, 374, 380, 398, 401		
2:20	25, 29, 91, 94, 103, 103n156, 158n237, 162n243, 175, 193, 198n285, 205, 207, 209, 211, 214, 229, 238, 243, 318, 324, 330, 335–36, 340, 346, 351, 362, 370, 376, 379, 388, 403				
				3:10–12	146
				3:10–13	231, 343
		3:2–3	56–57nn80–81	3:10–14	203n296, 238, 257, 258n384, 290
		3:2–5	239n351		
		3:2–26	192	3:10–15	167
2:20–21	192, 319	3:3	56, 138, 152n223, 177n263, 191, 277, 292, 298, 305–6, 310, 329, 336, 352, 398	3:10–21	146
2:21	28, 38, 40, 44, 48, 51, 61, 115, 119, 122, 130, 136, 164nn246, 249; 166, 184–85, 188, 191–92, 194, 200–201, 206, 208, 215n312, 224–25, 233, 242, 267, 281, 290, 298, 308, 314–15, 324, 343, 380, 398, 410			3:11	12, 34, 144, 148, 154n227, 157, 165–66, 169, 192n276, 205n298, 218, 226, 202nn292–93; 314, 393
		3:5	13, 44, 56, 58–59, 120n178, 145, 161, 181n267, 198, 226n325, 248, 250, 266–67, 318, 336, 340, 343, 357, 362, 380, 398	3:11–12	168, 198n285, 203n294, 317, 351, 370
				3:11–13	380
				3:12	144, 153, 208n300, 345, 389
		3:5–6	267	3:13	5, 29, 34–35, 63, 113–14, 160n240, 165, 167, 169, 172, 191, 210n303, 211n304, 212nn306, 308; 216, 231, 250, 263n393, 264, 287, 290–91, 309, 343, 355, 406, 411
3	139, 260, 379	3:6	34, 61, 142, 149n218, 165–66, 169, 224, 227, 235, 239, 298, 342, 393		
3–4	11, 152				
3:1	4–5, 12n23, 13, 26, 46, 50n65, 52–53, 53n70, 61, 84, 94, 161, 170n252, 171nn255–56; 192, 200n290, 250–51, 267, 280–81, 290, 295, 311, 316, 320, 323–24, 367, 383, 399, 401, 409				
		3:6–7	149, 226		
		3:6–8	224n321		
		3:6–9	60n87, 224, 241, 247, 298, 301, 342		
		3:6–14	14, 167–68, 217, 184–216, 237, 288	3:13–14	238, 259, 262, 305n437, 317, 324, 346, 379, 398
		3:6–18	296		
3:1–2	11, 56, 177n262, 386	3:6–22	61n91	3:14	13, 44n57, 56, 82, 102, 143n207, 161, 167–68, 173, 195n282, 216–17, 223, 225–26, 231,
		3:6–29	57, 324n452, 288, 290		
3:1–3	41	3:7	56, 150n220, 191n273, 216, 222,		
3:1–5	14, 44, 46, 50, 57, 60n87, 80, 168–84,				

Index of Ancient Sources

	235–36, 241–42, 245, 247–48, 250, 258, 264, 266–67, 283, 290, 296, 305–6, 308, 310, 314, 317, 336, 340, 342, 344, 348, 367, 370, 393	3:21	3, 34, 141, 156n133, 165–66, 169, 187, 216n313, 232n344, 233n346, 241, 260, 264, 275, 314, 324, 343, 343n466, 344, 366, 380, 380n491, 393, 398	3:26	13, 28, 143n207, 102, 167, 193, 210, 242nn357–59; 250, 260, 265, 267, 314
				3:26–27	265
				3:26–28	241n356, 243n360, 245, 246n367, 262, 245–47, 371n482
3:14–18	197n283, 298, 298n426, 299n427	3:21–22	164, 168, 229n333, 234n347, 248, 267, 296, 379	3:26–29	258n384, 283
3:14–22	197, 237			3:27	284, 357
3:15	163, 219n315, 220n316, 232n344, 248, 261, 305, 374, 410	3:22	13, 26n32, 35, 142, 144, 148, 150, 150n220, 157, 162, 165n250, 167, 177, 191–93, 204, 215n311, 231nn338, 341; 238, 240–41, 242, 242n358, 247–48, 250, 258n384, 264, 290, 306, 307n442, 308, 317, 319, 340, 342, 344, 352, 355, 358	3:27–28	367
				3:27–29	250, 261
				3:28	102–3, 113, 184, 184n269, 209, 250, 256n382, 258, 264, 267, 272, 312, 314, 318, 340, 344, 391, 402–3
3:15–18	164n248, 225n324, 230n335, 259, 261, 267, 286–87, 292, 301, 350				
				3:28–29	224
3:15–19	245n366			3:29	13, 26n32, 56, 60n87, 167, 185, 195, 216, 222–24, 226, 250, 260, 264, 267, 283, 290, 293, 305–6, 324n452, 342, 344, 361, 378, 397, 400, 406
3:15–22	14, 167–68, 172, 216–36, 237, 247				
3:15–29	406	3:22–23	35, 411		
3:16	82, 144, 167, 187, 216n313, 231n341, 242, 247–50, 267, 283, 296, 305, 308, 342, 344, 366, 406	3:22–25	149		
		3:22–26	317		
		3:22–29	223		
		3:23	35, 81–82, 198, 201, 235n348, 242n357, 260, 263, 263n393, 305, 343, 355		
3:16–19	168, 247–48, 267			4:1	13, 167–68, 342, 361
3:17	54, 159, 220n316, 232n344, 296, 298, 324			4:1–2	184n269
		3:23–24	16, 343, 380	4:1–3	210
		3:23–25	34n46, 71, 167, 175, 193, 202–3, 239n351, 241n355, 250, 257, 258n384, 260, 263, 290, 239nn352–53, 309, 315, 318, 324, 350, 398	4:1–5	164
3:17–18	231n341, 380			4:1–6	34, 36
3:17–19	342–44			4:1–7	14, 16, 165, 167, 184n269, 237, 244, 247n369, 274–75, 275n403, 291, 305n437, 309, 249–68
3:18	44, 247–48, 250, 261, 267, 293, 305–6, 308, 336, 342n465, 343n466, 361, 361n72, 380n491				
				4:1–8	272
		3:23–26	103, 168, 198, 210, 231	4:1–10	78n120
3:18–19	13, 167, 250, 296			4:1–11	290, 340
3:19	48, 54, 82, 149, 193, 230n336, 232n344, 238–42, 249–50, 263, 267, 280n410, 283, 305, 374	3:23–29	14, 167–68, 264, 237–49, 298	4:2	35, 144, 259nn385–86; 298, 303
		3:23–4:10	290		
		3:23–4:11	299	4:3	26, 35, 78n120, 82, 167, 256n381, 263n393, 273–75, 309, 324, 340, 346, 372, 402
		3:24	34, 144, 154n227, 165–66, 169, 193, 204, 218, 238n350, 282, 317, 393		
3:19–20	167, 298				
3:19–21	267				
3:19–22	164, 200, 206, 225n324, 350	3:24–25	82	4:3–4	34
		3:24–26	184	4:3–5	35, 340, 343, 372
3:19–23	160n240, 161	3:25	16–17, 35, 82, 167, 172, 262–63, 267, 305, 309, 355, 398	4:3–7	271
3:19–25	210			4:4	25, 212n307, 261nn387–88; 263n392, 348, 390
3:20	227nn328–29; 257				
		3:25–29	225n324		

Galatians (*continued*)
4:4–5   16–17, 35, 94,
         113–14, 161, 167,
         172, 198, 210, 212–13,
         242, 287, 305, 309,
         324, 346, 355, 379–80,
         386, 398, 411
4:4–6   389
4:4–7   202, 317, 336
4:5   35, 63, 148, 165,
         169, 172, 238, 243,
         263n393, 340
4:5–6   265n395
4:5–7   13, 167, 402
4:6   25, 80, 92, 94, 161,
         162n242, 173, 183,
         195, 284, 329, 372,
         374, 393, 410
4:6–7   13, 28, 94, 308,
         310, 340, 346, 367
4:7   13, 167–68, 282,
         293, 340, 342, 361
4:7–8   144
4:7–5:12 12–14, 70n111,
         269–328, 270n297,
         285, 290, 312
4:8   35, 82, 271n398,
         312, 324
4:8–9   5, 142, 257n383,
         275n403
4:8–10   125, 201n291,
         326, 334, 402
4:8–11   13–14, 26, 172,
         252–54, 257,
         257n383, 262, 269,
         274n401, 282,
         309–10, 315, 325,
         327, 340, 270–77, 360
4:8–20   288
4:8–5:6 319
4:8–5:12 322, 325,
         329, 332
4:9   35, 40, 77n122, 252,
         255, 269, 274n402,
         311, 321, 324, 372
4:9–10   276n404
4:9–11   269
4:10   61, 147, 257, 267,
         275n403, 313, 399
4:11   68, 269, 277, 321
4:11–12 270
4:12   13, 269, 278n407,
         284n412, 305,
         374, 410
4:12–15 5
4:12–20 14, 171, 269,
         286, 310, 327,
         277–85
4:13   9–10, 11n22, 26,
         44, 47n62, 50, 72,
         75, 109n162, 171,
         271, 290, 321,
         334, 336
4:13–14 9, 26, 46,
         162n244, 335, 386,
         388, 409
4:14   47–48, 144,
         280nn408–10; 336
4:17   42–44, 53, 54n75,
         56, 138, 144,
         269, 307, 320
4:17–18 283n411
4:18   389
4:18–19 284n412
4:19   284n415, 293, 321
4:19–20 385n416
4:19–21 269
4:20   39, 67, 269–70,
         290, 321,
         385nn417–18
4:21   11, 13, 35, 41,
         55, 61, 159,
         198–99, 201n291,
         210, 234, 234n347,
         269, 274, 314, 332,
         342–44, 355, 377, 380
4:21–24 378
4:21–30 177
4:21–31 114
4:21–5:1 14, 60, 164n248,
         184n269, 191, 197,
         216, 244, 269,
         285–311, 327,
         336, 380
4:23   144, 216, 248, 267,
         293n423, 294n425,
         306n439, 336, 342, 344
4:24   345
4:24–25 230n335,
         291n421,
         299n428, 336
4:24–31 385
4:25   3n6, 54, 159,
         217, 372
4:25–26 300nn429–33;
         407
4:25–27 74, 118n173,
         123, 133–34n191
4:26   74, 406
4:26–27 133
4:27   79, 224, 284n414,
         302n435, 342
4:27–28 223
4:28   184n269, 190, 248,
         267, 305n438, 342,
         374, 406, 410
4:29   13, 180, 216, 323,
         336–37, 398, 406
4:29–30 269
4:29–31 144
4:30   13, 49, 234, 291,
         307n441, 342,
         344, 361
4:31   374, 406, 410
5–6   11
5:1   11, 13, 17, 34–36,
         55n78, 63, 82,
         113–14, 165, 201n291,
         241–42, 247n369, 260,
         264, 264n394, 270,
         274n400, 282, 287–89,
         308–9, 309n444, 311,
         314–15, 316, 327, 334,
         340, 346, 352, 368,
         376, 410
5:1–4   269
5:1–6   269
5:1–6:10 68
5:2   13n24, 330
5:2–3   53n72, 60n88,
         137n199, 147, 153,
         173, 240, 311n445,
         320, 325n455, 336,
         397, 399, 399n496
5:2–4   10–11, 17, 46, 55,
         86, 106, 111n164, 138,
         151, 185, 244–45, 283,
         309, 327, 329, 334,
         340, 393, 399, 401, 410
5:2–5   274, 276
5:2–6   14, 310–19, 327
5:2–7   171
5:2–12   329
5:3   49, 55, 55n78, 59,
         136, 138, 153, 298,
         343, 344–45, 347n470,
         348, 349n474, 389, 400
5:3–4   41, 343, 380
5:4   28, 39–41, 44, 56,
         61, 113, 122, 143–44,
         144n208, 147–48,
         153, 154n227, 157,
         157n235, 201n291, 203,
         208, 218, 271, 276,
         276n404, 282, 410

Index of Ancient Sources

5:4–5	34, 139, 163, 165		329–92, 330, 337,	6:9	390
5:5	13, 34, 36, 153–54,		369, 393, 398, 410	6:9–10	329
	159, 184, 192, 194,	5:14	147, 147n214, 172,	6:10	324, 340
	204, 215n312, 235,		332n459, 345n468,	6:11	17, 54
	317n447, 371, 389, 393		377, 378–80	6:11–13	393
5:5–6	17, 193n280,	5:14–15	392	6:11–15	330
	328	5:15	368, 372	6:11–17	12, 14, 68,
5:6	60n88, 64, 71, 102,	5:15–16	329, 368		394–410
	111n164, 144, 147,	5:16	165, 173, 178,	6:11–18	12, 14, 67,
	239n354, 243–45,		183, 198n285, 205,		329, 393–410
	316n446, 323, 330,		207, 330, 370–71,	6:12	5, 46, 65, 111,
	340, 342, 350, 362,		376, 389		111n164, 115, 137,
	402–3, 403n498	5:16–18	368, 370, 388		137n199, 153, 180,
5:6–7	68n106	5:16–19	331		185, 275, 283,
5:7	10, 42, 46, 50n65,	5:16–23	390		295, 298, 305,
	53, 55, 110, 169–70,	5:16–24	35		307, 323,
	269, 275n403, 282,	5:17	329, 372		324n451, 367
	320n450, 383,	5:18	35, 370–71, 380	6:12–13	10, 17, 41, 44,
	399, 409	5:19	382, 391		53n72, 54, 54n76,
5:7–12	14, 17, 269,	5:19–21	162, 373, 375		55–56, 60n88, 106,
	319–28, 396	5:21	31, 49, 224n323,		138, 147, 151,
5:8	40, 301, 334		342n465, 389		152n223, 173, 177,
5:8–9	269	5:22	17, 28, 172,		240, 244–45, 274,
5:8–12	144		192, 192n274,		276, 311, 311n445,
5:10	28, 42, 46, 50n65,		193nn279–80; 318,		320, 325n455, 329,
	53, 59, 61, 170,		331, 339n463, 342,		336, 399n495
	200n290, 269, 376,		370, 378, 383, 388,	6:12–15	329
	383–84, 399, 409		391, 403–4	6:13	54n73, 55n78,
5:10–11	55	5:22–23	373		59, 144, 200,
5:11	64–65, 109n162,	5:23	380, 380n491		313–14, 380,
	147, 172, 269, 295,	5:24	26n32, 160–61,		380n491, 383
	307, 367, 374,		172, 378, 386, 401	6:13–14	384n492
	398, 410	5:25	17, 198n285, 205,	6:14	28–29, 160, 165,
5:11–12	324n453, 330		331–32, 339, 340,		172, 281, 295,
5:12	13, 26, 53, 53n71,		368, 372nn483–84;		323–24, 324n451,
	54, 61, 269–70,		387, 403–4		367, 382
	325n455, 334, 393	5:25–26	329, 331n458,	6:14–15	18, 172,
5:12–13	278n406		364		256n382
5:12–6:11	12, 329	5:25–6:10	14, 331, 368–92	6:14–17	393
5:13	11, 13, 63n95, 114,	5:26	331, 389	6:15	17, 31, 60n88,
	144, 282, 309n443,	6:1	331, 373n485,		64, 71, 91,
	314, 339, 334n460,		376, 378, 410		111n164, 144, 147,
	368, 374, 376,	6:1–2	329, 364		172, 194n281, 239,
	379–80, 389,	6:1–10	339		239n354, 243–45,
	392, 410	6:2	147, 172, 322, 332,		262, 318, 323, 329,
5:13–14	17, 318, 370,		346–47, 366, 377–79		350, 363, 368,
	377–79, 391, 403	6:3–4	331		388, 393
5:13–15	319, 373	6:4	243n361, 329,	6:16	18, 28, 248–49,
5:13–24	14, 162n245,		364, 401		364, 372,
	331–68, 370, 379,	6:4–5	384n492		405n501, 410
	388, 398, 402–3	6:5	322	6:17	18, 65, 332, 376
5:13–26	56n80, 306	6:6–7	329, 364	6:18	12, 14, 18, 28,
5:13–6:10	13–14, 51, 68,	6:9–10	364		38, 40, 71, 393,
	177–78, 265–66,	6:8	31, 233, 331,		396, 403,
	270, 315, 319		361, 398		410–11

Ephesians		1:2	27, 364	Colossians	
1–6	20–21	1:3	38–39	1–4	20–21
1:1	22	1:4	364	1:1	22
1:2	364	1:5	124	1:2	364
1:4	364	1:6	57n81, 177, 180	1:4	364
1:5	264	1:9	364	1:8	364
1:7	30, 374	1:11	362	1:11	364
1:11	318	1:12	37	1:13	364
1:13	209	1:15	359	1:15–17	263n390
1:14	224n323	1:16	364	1:29	318
1:15	364	1:17	359	2:2	364
1:17	80	1:19	28n38, 44n57, 266	2:5	149, 177, 366
1:18	224n323	1:23	353	2:8	252, 253,
1:20	25, 318	1:25	364		254n375, 273
1:21	30	1:26	384n492	2:11	336
2:1	374	1:28	353	2:13	336, 374
2:2	30, 318	1:29	142, 180	2:16	149, 276
2:4	364	2:1	124	2:20	252–53,
2:5	374	2:1–2	364		254n375, 273
2:7	30, 364	2:2	364	3:1	25, 156
2:11	336	2:3	373	3:5	358
2:14	158, 359	2:6–8	263n390	3:5–8	356
2:14–15	364	2:7	340	3:5–14	245
2:16	359	2:7–8	212n307, 263	3:9	244
2:17	364	2:8	340	3:9–11	246
2:19	391	2:9–11	22n28	3:10	243
2:21	124n180	2:11	28	3:11	244n362
3:1	230n337	2:13	120n178	3:12	364–65
3:3	84, 171	2:16	110, 384	3:12–14	362
3:6	84	2:19–23	285n419	3:12–15	362
3:14	230n337	2:24	285n419	3:14	364
3:17	364	2:25	22, 95	3:15	364
3:19	364	2:25–30	285n419	3:24	224n323
3:20	318	2:29	364	4:11	31, 132–33, 361
4:2	364–65	3:2	60n87, 327	4:16	66
4:2–3	362	3:3–4	177, 336	4:18	395
4:3	364	3:4–9	86		
4:5–16	364	3:5	64, 85	**1 Thessalonians**	
4:11	385	3:5–6	87	1–5	11, 20, 165, 194n281,
4:18	273	3:6	92		239, 292, 411
4:19	358	3:9	143n207, 148	1:1	25, 27, 27n35, 364
4:22	85	3:10	124	1:2–3	38
4:24	243	3:15	80, 92	1:3	127, 364
4:31	356	3:16	372	1:5	37
5:2	29, 163, 364	3:20	316	1:6	280, 364
5:3	358	4:1	364	1:7–8	3n5
5:3–4	356	4:3	25	1:9	272, 275
5:5	31, 224n323, 361	4:7	240, 364	1:10	81, 94
5:9	365	4:9	82, 364	2:3	358
5:25	29, 163	4:10–17	385	2:4–5	62–63
6:15	364	4:13	318n449	2:4–6	64n96
6:23	364	4:15	3n5	2:5–9	376
		4:17	362	2:9	171
Philippians		4:18	280	2:12	31, 40, 361
1–4	59	4:20	36n49	2:13	82, 120n178, 175,
1:1	25	4:23	410		280, 318

Index of Ancient Sources 429

2:14	3, 88, 102, 180	1:9–10	356	5	364		
2:16	126n183	1:10	353	6	124, 247n369		
2:17	114n168	1:14	364	7	364		
2:18	33	1:16	31, 364	9	364		
2:19	384n492	1:17	36n49	10	293		
2:19–20	364	2:5	228n330	15	114n168		
3:1–2	11	2:6	29	18–19	395		
3:2–8	285n419	2:13–14	33	22	285n419		
3:4	360	2:15	364	25	410		
3:5	33	3:1	353				
3:6	11, 364	3:5	88	**Hebrews**			
3:9	364	3:15	88, 391	1:3	25		
3:9–13	285n419	3:16	177, 336	1:5	94		
3:12	364	4:2	85	1:13	25		
4:1	82	4:12	364	1:14	224n323		
4:3	358	5:8	391	2:17	150		
4:5	273	5:14	230n337, 335, 353	2:2	228		
4:7	40n53, 334, 358	6:1	309	3:2	150		
4:9	83n124, 340	6:4	359	5:5	94		
4:10	3n5	6:11	364	5:12	253		
4:13–18	34, 79, 390	6:12	31	6:2	322		
5:1	390			6:5	30		
5:3	284, 364	**2 Timothy**		6:10	364		
5:5	245n364	1–4	20–21	6:12	364		
5:8	243, 364	1:1	22	7:6	293–94n424		
5:10	20	1:2	364	7:9	293–94n424		
5:12–13	385	1:4	364	8:1	25		
5:13	364	1:7	364	9:15	209		
5:21	389	1:13	364	9:17	318n449		
5:23	364	2:3–5	356	10:12–13	25		
5:24	40	2:22	364	10:24	364		
5:27	66	2:25	365	10:38	203		
5:28	410	3:10	364	11:17	223		
		4:2	364	12:2	25		
2 Thessalonians		4:10	108	12:22	301		
1:2	364	4:18	36n49	13:7	85, 127		
1:3	364	4:22	410	13:9	351		
1:5	31			13:16	124		
1:7	79	**Titus**		13:21	36n49		
1:11	365	1–3	20–21				
2:1–12	261n389	1:2	31	**James**			
2:3	79	1:4	108	1:1	19n26, 27		
2:4	353	1:5	229, 230n337	1:14–15	338		
2:6	79	1:8	365	1:16	387		
2:7	318	1:11	230n337	1:21	365		
2:8	79	2:2	364	1:25	338		
2:10	364	2:14	29	1:26	381		
3:5	364	3:2	365	2:5	224n323, 361		
3:8	376	3:3	359	2:7–9	408		
3:16	364	3:4	365	2:8	348		
3:17	395	3:7	31, 224n323	2:9	158, 230		
		3:9	359	2:10	58n84, 313		
1 Timothy				2:11	158, 231		
1–6	20–21	**Philemon**		2:21–23	179		
1:1	22	1–25	11, 20	2:23–24	188		
1:2	364	3	27, 364	3:13	85, 365		
1:5	364	4	39	3:14	359		

James (continued)

3:16	359
3:17–18	362n481
4:4	359
4:5	359
5:10	364
5:16	318n449
5:19–20	374

1 Peter

1–5	120
1:1	22
1:4	224n323
1:5	240
1:15	85
1:18	85
2:1	359
2:12	85
2:24	212, 370
3:1–2	85
3:9	224n323
3:16	85
3:18	233
3:20	364
3:22	25
4:3	358–60
4:8	364
4:11	36n49
4:12–14	180
4:17	322
5:9	180
5:14	364

2 Peter

1:1	22
1:5–7	362
1:6	365
1:7	364
2:1	359
2:2	358
2:4	31
2:7	85, 358
2:18	358
3:11	85
3:15	364
3:16	66

1 John

1:3	124
1:6–7	124
2:5	364
2:15	364
2:16	178
3:1	364
3:10	340
3:12	230n337
3:14	340
3:16–17	364
3:20–21	131
4:7–10	364
4:9–10	262
4:12	364
4:16–18	364
5:3	364

2 John

3	364
6	364

3 John

6	364
10	308

Jude

2	364
4	358
6	31
12	364
16	230n337
21	364

Revelation

1–22	36n49, 78
1:1	31, 31n44, 78, 78n121
1:4	27, 364
1:5	150
2:19	364
3:12	124n180, 301
3:14	150
3:22	25
9:21	359
12:8	318n449
14:8	303
16:19	303
17:5	303
17:18	303
18:2	303
18:23	359
19:2	358
19:11	150
21:2	301
21:7	224n323
21:8	357
21:10	301
21:14	23, 95
22:15	357

APOCRYPHA

Additions to Esther

14:17	134

Baruch

3:23	300n430

2 Esdras (see *4 Ezra* below)

Judith

12:1–4	134
13:15	359
14:10	311n445
16:19	45

1 Maccabees

1:34	135
1:47	134
1:62–63	134
2:23–28	87, 188
2:48	135
2:50–51	188
2:52	188, 196
2:55	346
3:29	359
6:58	124
8:16	359
9:55	349
12:11	127

2 Maccabees

1:1	27n37
1:27	273
2:13	45
2:21	86
3:9	110
6:4	360
6:7	134
6:18–21	134
6:23	85
7:1	134
7:24	39
7:32–38	30n41
8:1	86
8:3	30n41
8:11	373
9:16	45
11:1	259
11:24	39
13:2	259
14:2	259
14:38	86

3 Maccabees

2:29	409
6:28	242
6:7	359

4 Maccabees

4:26	86

Index of Ancient Sources

5:20–21	58n84	18:13	359	86.1–6	31
5:34	365	19:18	255n379	98.4–5	32
6:27–29	30n41	19:18–20	254	106.13–17	31
17:21–22	30n41				
18:1	222n320	**PSEUDEPIGRAPHA**		*4 Ezra* (**2 Esdras**)	
18:12	87			1–16	33, 33n45, 78
18:24	36nn49–50	*Assumption of Moses*		3.1–2	303
		1.14	227n327	3.5–7	32
Sirach		10	32	3.20–21	32
1–51	338n462	10.1	31	3.21	339
1:27	365			3.22	339
11:27	79	*2 Baruch*		3.26	339
11:31	43	1–87	33, 33n45	3.28	303
14:14–15	339	4.2–6	301	4.4	339
14:18	95	11.1–2	303	4.30–31	32, 339
15:14	337	14.12	153	6.9	30
17:11	233	14.13	30	6.58	242
17:31	95, 337	15.5	201	7	153
21:11	337	15.8	30	7.12–13	30
21:27	339	17.2–3	32	7.26	301
22:22	79	17.4	32	7.28–29	94n146
25:24	32, 337	23.4	32	7.37	201
26:15	365	32.6	31, 402	7.48	339
27:5–6	337	38.1–2	32, 153	7.50	30
31:30	360	44.8–15	30	7.75	31, 402
36:17	242	44.14	163	7.88–92	339
44:19–20	187, 298	46.6	153	7.89	154n229
44:19–21	196	48.22	32, 153	7.92	339
44:20	188, 336	48.40	201	7.104–5	384
45:4	365	48.42–43	32	7.113	30
45:23–24	87	51.3	153	7.118–119	32
		51.16	32	7.127–129	339
Tobit		52.7	153	8.1	30
1:10–11	134	54.5	32, 153	8.52	301
4:7	373	54.14	32	8.53–54	339
4:15	360	54.15	32	10.27	301
4:16	373	54.19	32	10.44–46	301
14:15	36n49	56.6	32	13.32	94n146
		56.12–15	31	13.35–36	301
Wisdom of Solomon		57.2	153	13.37	94n146
2:23–24	31	67.6	303	13.52	94n146
2:24	359	78.2–3	27n37	14.9	94n146
6:23	359	83.4–9	30		
7:17	255n379	85.7	32	*Joseph and Aseneth*	
7:17–19	254, 257			2.1	280
8:21	365	*1 Enoch*			
9:9–10	263	1–108	33	*Jubilees*	
10:1	32	1–36	32	1.23–24	181
12:4	359	6–19	31	1.23–25	242, 250–51
13	255n379	64.1–2	31	1.27–2.1	228
13:1–3	255, 257, 272	69.4–5	31	2.8–9	257
13:18–19	274	69.6	32	2.8–10	255n379, 276–77n405
14:23	360	71.15	30		
14:26	358	72.1	31, 402	3.17–25	32
17:16–17	375	82.7–9	255n379, 257, 276–77n405	4.15	31
				4.22	31

Jubilees (continued)

4.26	402
4.29–30	32
5.1–8	31
10.4–5	31
15.3	179
16.17–18	286n420
17.15–16	188, 196
20.13	300
22.16	135
23.10	179, 187
24.1	298
24.11	187, 196

Liber antiquitatum biblicarum

13.8–9	32
34.1–5	31

Odes of Solomon

13.32	79

Psalms of Solomon

1–18	33n45
1.1–8	135
2.34–35	153
3.3–12	155n229
5.9–10	224n323
8.14	360
9.4–5	32, 339
9.7	155n229
11.9	404
13.7	155n229
13.10–11	155n229
13.11–12	153
14.1–3	153, 207
14.2	155n229, 157, 164
14.5	224n323
14.9–10	153
15.10–11	224n323
15.12–13	153, 155n229
17.23	224n323
17.27	242
17.32	24

Testament of Asher

1–4	356
1.8	338

Testament of Dan

5.3	348

Testament of Issachar

5.1–2	348

Testament of Judah

19.1	359

Testament of Naphtali

3.5	31

Testament of Reuben

5.6–7	31

RABBINIC LITERATURE

BABYLONIAN TALMUD

Berakot

9.5	30

Makkot

24a	312

Šabbat

31a	348

MISHNAH

	179n266

ʾAbot

1.1	77n119, 298
2.1	58n84
2.7	233
3.5	309
4.1	30
4.2	58n84

Nedarim

3.11	179

Sanhedrin

10.1	30

OTHER RABBINIC WORKS

Genesis Rabbah

24.7	348
Rabbi Akiba	348
Rabbinic traditions	124n180

Sipra Leviticus, Kedoshim Pereḳ

8	313

Sipre Deuteronomy

45	337

QUMRAN

CD	33
CD 2.14–16	179
CD 2.17–3.1	31
CD 16.1–3	33
1QH 15.3	338
1QH 18.22–23	337
1QM	33
1QM 4.10	88
1QM 14.7	127
1QMelch 2.15–24	41
1QpHab 8.1–3	204
1QS 1–4	33
1QS 1.8	179
1QS 1.13–18	58n84
1QS 2.2	179
1QS 3–4	33, 353–54
1QS 3.1–11	154n229
1QS 3.3–4	179
1QS 3.9	178n264, 179
1QS 3.13–4.26	351
1QS 3.17–21	354
1QS 4.2–6	356
1QS 4.9–11	356
1QS 4.11–14	354
1QS 4.16–18	354
1QS 4.19–21	178n264, 337, 354
1QS 4.22	154n229
1QS 4.23–24	354
1QS 4.24–25	402
1QS 4.25	146
1QS 5.4–5	178
1QS 5.4–6	337
1QS 5.20–21	146
1QS 5.23–24	146
1QS 5.24	179
1QS 5.24–6.1	374
1QS 6.17	146
1QS 6.18	146
1QS 8.1	154n229
1QS 9.2	179
1QS 9.5–6	179
1QS 9.8–9	179
1QS 9.10–11	231n340
1QS 9.19	179
1QS 11.9	178n264
1QS 11.9–10	337, 338
1QS 11.11–15	154n228
1QS 11.12	337
1QS 11.17	179
1QSa 2.11–12	94n146
4Q174	94n146
4Q174 1.10–13	94
4Q246	94n146
4Q398 2.7	146
4Q398 frg. 14–17 2.2–4	145
4QFlor (4Q174) 1.10–11	223
4QMMT (4Q398)	145, 188
4QpNah	212
11QTemple 64.6–13	212

Index of Ancient Sources

OTHER JEWISH WORKS

Aristobolus of Alexandria
295

Josephus 45, 86

Antiquities
1.122	299
1.192	54
2.204	221n318
3.179–87	295
3.259–60	134
3.268	108
4.123	63
4.137	134
8.255	63
10.135	87
12.271	87
13.297	85n133
15.136	228, 228n331
17.226	218n314
17.300	21
18.112	96
18.328–29	124
20.44–45	58
20.48	362n481
20.50–51	127n184
20.139	171n254

Jewish War
1.439	358
1.635	131
2.121	358
2.137	359
2.420	41
2.454	138, 171n254
2.463	138
4.168	41
4.405	87
4.534	87
4.562	358
4.656	41
5.79	375
5.159	96
5.382	221n318
6.81	98
7.154	131

Life
14	134
76	240
191	85n133

Liturgy
Shemonê Esrê 19   404

Philo 21, 45, 86, 295, 365

Allegorical Interpretation
3.8   326

Contemplative Life
3–5   255n378

Creation of the World
55	276–77n405
60	276–77n405

De congressu eruditionis gratia
23   295

Dreams
1.107	259
1.143	227n327
2.181	170n252

Eternity of the World
107	254n377
109–10	254n377

Flight and Finding
176   362n481

Life of Abraham
60–88   187

Life of Moses
1.305	358
2.166	227n327

Migration of Abraham
92   337

Special Laws
1.56	87
1.325	326
2.253	85n133
3.117	284n415

Targums

Targum Onqelos
Lev 18:5   208n300

Targum Pseudo-Jonathan
Lev 18:5	208n300
Gen 22:1	307n440

Targum to Isaiah
Isa 47:1–4   302–3

EARLY CHRISTIAN WRITINGS

APOSTOLIC FATHERS   365

Barnabas
16.7	359
19.1–2	356
20.1	359

1 Clement
1–65	20
5.2	120
5.5	359
6.4	359
30.1	359
46.5	359
47.1	120
51.1	359

2 Clement
17.1   385

Didache
1–2	356
1.2	348
2–5	357
3.4	359
3.5	373
5.1	359
6.2	179
12.2	98

Eusebius
Historica ecclesiastica
2.23.4–18   123, 133–34n191

Hegesippus
Commentaries
5   123, 133–34n191

Ignatius
To the Ephesians
6.1   202
To the Magnesians
10.3   86, 138
To the Philadelphians
6.1   86

Justin Martyr
Dialogue with Trypho
8   58, 313

Marcion
Marcionite Prologue   60n90

Polycarp
To the Philippians
5.3   353

Polycarp's Friends
Martyrdom of Polycarp
2.4   335

Index of Ancient Sources

Pseudo-Clement

Epistle of Peter
2.3   282

Homilies
17.19   131

Recognitions
1.70   282

Ascents of James
                                 59n85

Preaching of Peter
                                 59n85

GRECO-ROMAN LITERATURE

Rhetoric to Alexander
1436B–1437A   64n96

[Anon.]

Rhetoric to Herennius
                                 67n104

Apuleius

Metamorphoses
11.5   255
11.25   255

Aristotle

Politics
3.13.1284A   366

Rhetoric
                                 67n104
1.2.1355B   67
1.2.1356A   64, 70

Cicero   66

Letters to Atticus
8.14.1   70n112
9.10.1   70n112
12.53   70n112

Letters to Friends
2.4.1   70n112
9.21.1   69
12.30.1   70n112
16.16.2   70n112

Rhetorical Invention
                                 67n104

Demetrius

Elocution (Style)
227   70n112

233   70n112

Dio Cassius

Roman History
79.11   325

Diodorus Siculus

Historical Library
3.31   325
15.7.1   210
19.94.1   96
36.2.2   210

Epictetus

Discources
1.4.32   362n481
2.20.19–20   326
2.22.26   240
3.19.5–6   240
4.8.39   381

Galen

Opera omnia (Kühn, 1821–33)
Vol. 19:181   284n415

Heraclitus

Allegoriae (Quaestiones homericae)
5.2   294

Herodotus

Histories
2.113   409

Hesiod

Works and Days
276   229

Hesychius of Alexandria

Alphabetical Collection of All Words
                                 113

Homer   295

Julius Victor

Rhetorical Art
69, 70n112

Lucian of Samosata

Goddess of Syria
50–51   325

Philostratus   70n112

Plato

Apology of Socrates
21B   107
41E   107

Gorgias
452E   62, 66–67
472A   107

Laws
7.808D–E   240

Lysis (Friendship)
208C   240

Protagoras
352E   62

Pliny the Younger   66

Plutarch

Cicero
7.6   138

Moralia
439F   240
4A–B   240

Pelopidas
29   45

Polybius

Universal History
                                 335
21.46.11   110

Pseudo-Demetrius

Typoi epistolikoi
68n105, 69n108

Pseudo-Libanius

Epistolimaioi characteres
2.58   68n105, 69,
                                 69n108,
                                 70n112

Quintilian

Institutes of Oratory
67n104, 71
2.13.7   69n110
2.15.38   67n102
3.4.3   69

Seneca

Moral Epistles   66
40.1   70n112
75.1   70n112

Index of Ancient Sources

Sophocles
Antigone
286   45

Tacitus
Histories
5.5.2   54, 134

Thucydides
Peloponnesian War
     335

Tryphon
De tropis
1.1   295

Xenophon
Memorabilia
     335
2.7.1   376

INSCRIPTIONS AND PAPYRI

Megara Inscription 46n59
Papyri 19n26, 27n37, 39, 229
Papyri Osloenses
4.18   252n372

INDEX OF SUBJECTS AND AUTHORS

Abba, 25, 94, 167, 251, 265–66, 284
Abner, 349
Abraham
  age of, at Isaac's birth, 293n422
  and birth of Isaac, 221, 292–93, 305–6, 392n422
  blessing of, 44n57, 167, 184–91, 193–98, 195n282, 200–202, 209–10, 214–16, 268, 348
  Christ as offspring of, 221–25, 231, 248–49, 283, 305
  circumcision and, 177, 179, 186–87, 221
  covenant between God and, 57, 177, 185, 186–87, 217–22, 220n317, 226–32, 230n335, 267, 296–99, 299n427, 344n467
  on eating with Gentiles, 135
  faith of, 149, 190n271, 193–94, 196
  God's promise of son to, 221, 292, 293n423, 304, 342, 380
  God's promise to, and law of Moses, 216–36, 267, 342, 350
  Isaac as offspring and heir of, 184n269, 189–90, 196, 223, 224, 286–310, 307n440, 406
  justification and, 188–90, 193–94
  near sacrifice of Isaac by, 179, 188, 196
  new preachers in Galatia on, 186–87, 196–97
  obedience of, to God, 187–88, 196
  as patriarch, 124n180, 187
  perfection and, 179
  physical descendants of, 197, 197n283
  righteousness of, 187, 189–90
  sons of, by Hagar and Sarah, 184n269, 286–310, 327, 336
  true offspring of, 16, 56–58, 166, 167, 184–86, 188, 189, 191, 195–97, 221–25, 237–49, 268, 290, 305–6, 406
Abrams, M. H., 296
Achior, 311n445

Acts of the Apostles
  on Antioch church, 112, 127n184, 128n185, 130, 133n191
  on apostles, 22–23, 100
  on Apostolic Council in Jerusalem, 43, 59, 107, 115
  on circumcision, 43, 58–59, 112, 113–14, 133, 323
  on collection for poor in Jerusalem, 127n184, 128n185, 133n191
  date of, 6n12, 20
  depiction of Paul in, versus Paul's own letters, 6n12, 21, 59, 59n86, 126n183
  epistolary conventions in, 19n26
  on James's meeting with Paul in Jerusalem, 133–34n191
  on law, 229n334
  on miracles of Paul, 182
  on mission to Gentiles, 125n182
  on observation of the whole law by Christian Jews, 314
  on Paul as Pharisee and persecutor of Christians, 85n133, 86–88
  on Paul's conversion, 93
  on Paul's missionary career and apostolic vocation, 20–21, 59, 90–91
  on Paul's visit to Jerusalem, 100
  on Peter in Caesarea, 133, 135–36
  on Peter's rescue, 35
  on promise of the Spirit, 209
  on prophecy of Joel, 43
  and salutations of letters, 27
  on Stephen, 229
  temporal notation in, 8n17
  on virtues, 365
Adam, 32, 33, 296
adelphoi (brethren), 3, 25, 39, 76, 169, 218, 278–79, 278n407, 305, 308, 322, 373–74, 410
adultery, 358
agapē (love), 317, 318–19, 340, 362–64. *See also* love

agathois, agathon (good things), 384–85, 390–91
agathōsynē (goodness), 364, 365
agorazō (redeem), 212
agricultural imagery, 369, 386–92
akatharsia (uncleanness), 358
Akiba, Rabbi, 233, 348
akrobystia (uncircumcision, foreskin), 119, 244, 318, 398, 402
allēgoria (allegory), 294–95
allegorical interpretation, 293–94n424, 294–304
amanuensis, 395
Amos, Book of, 223
anankazō (to put pressure on), 54, 111, 111n164, 115, 137–38, 396–97
anaplēroō (fulfill), 376–77, 377n490
anastrophē (manner of life, conduct, behavior), 84–85, 92
anathema, 45–47, 46n59, 50, 62, 63, 64–65, 76
Anderson, Roger Dean, Jr., 37, 41n55, 66n99, 66n100–101, 67–70, 200
anethemēn (share with, communicate to), 110
angels
 apocalyptic eschatology and, 31, 33
 evil angels, 230n336, 280n410
 fall of, 31
 God's glory and, 228
 hypothetical situation of angel preaching "different gospel," 47–49, 66
 law and, 221, 227–30, 229n334, 232, 233, 268
 as mediators, 228
 Moses and, 221, 227–28
 revelation and, 48, 79, 81
animal imagery, 350–51
anoētoi (unthinking), 169–70
anthrōpos (human being), 244, 313, 374
Antioch
 Barnabas in, 5, 9, 10, 23, 74, 107, 108, 115, 121, 124, 130
 charges against Paul in, 156–58
 and circumcision of Gentiles, 5, 9, 43, 59, 73, 107, 112–13, 115, 117, 128–38, 142, 411
 and collection for poor in Jerusalem, 127–28, 133n191
 conflict in, over circumcision, 9, 49, 73, 104, 117, 128–38
 false brethren in, 112–14
 importance of, in Roman Empire, 100
 Jerusalem church and, 23, 43, 59, 126–28
 location of, 130
 Lord's Supper in, 132n188, 134n192
 Paul in, 7, 9, 10, 22, 23, 24, 49, 100, 110, 121, 124, 130
 Paul's break with church in, and break with Barnabas, 5, 9, 49, 73, 74, 104, 107, 108, 110, 128
 population of, 130
Antiochus Epiphanes, 87
Antiochus IV Epiphanes, 86
Antiochus V Eupator, 259
aphesis (forgiveness), 30n42. *See also* forgiveness
aphormē (occasion, opportunity, base from which other action becomes possible), 335
Apocalypse of John. *See* Revelation, Book of
apocalyptic eschatology
 angels and, 31, 33, 230n336
 blessing of Abraham and, 216
 cosmological pattern of, 31–34, 338, 339
 evil age and, 29–36, 30n43, 72, 81, 161, 165, 172, 198, 210, 262, 302, 368, 389
 forensic pattern of, 31, 32–34, 33n45, 163–64, 194, 338, 338n462
 Judaism and, 30–36, 33n45, 36n50, 153, 230n336
 justification and, 153–54
 law and, 32–33
 and link between Babylon and Rome, 302–3
 new preachers in Galatia and, 33n45, 34
 opening verse of Revelation and, 31n44
 periodization of history and, 261n389
 and present Jerusalem versus Jerusalem above, 301–5, 308
 redemptive death of Jesus Christ and, 161, 165, 184
 Spirit and, 183
 Spirit versus Flesh and, 354
 two world ages and, 30–34, 93, 161, 172, 198, 210, 261n389, 262, 301–2, 389
 See also apocalyptic revelation; last judgment
apocalyptic revelation
 childbirth metaphor and, 284
 criterion for true gospel and, 84
 crucifixion of Christ and, 81, 83, 84, 172
 different uses of term *apokalypsis*, 79–81
 and disclosure of divine mysteries through the Spirit, 80
 faith and, 81–82, 84, 239
 and God's cataclysmic invasion of the world in Christ, 81
 language of, 77, 78n122, 79–96
 Parousia and, 79–80, 81, 205, 390
 and Paul's conversion and call to apostleship, 89–96, 89n143, 159, 161–62

Index of Subjects and Authors 439

Paul's trips to Jerusalem and, 108–9, 108n161
and reception of gospel by Paul, 83
truth of gospel and, 109–10
See also apocalyptic eschatology
apokalypsis, apokalypsai, apokalyptō (revelation, unveiling, apocalypse, apocalyptically reveal), 78–82, 89, 91, 93, 109
apokoptō (to cut away), 320, 326
apokoptō, apokopsontai (practice castration), 325–26, 325nn454–455. *See also* castration
apostasy, 39
apostles
  Acts on, 22–23, 100
  appearance of risen Christ to, 95, 98, 117
  as commissioned by human beings, 21, 22, 24
  as commissioned by Jesus Christ and God, 21–25, 22n27, 28n39
  as companions of Jesus Christ, 22–23
  in Jerusalem, 23, 48, 72, 89, 94–96, 100
  origin and meaning of term, 21
  status of pillar apostles, 117–18
  types of, 22–24
  use of term in Galatians, 21–31
  See also specific apostles
Apostolic Council (Jerusalem), 8, 9, 10, 10n20, 43, 58–59, 104–19, 121, 123, 138, 408
Apuleius, 255
Aquila, 211n305, 213n310
Arabia, 94–96, 300, 300n432
areskō (please), 62–63
aretai (virtues), 363. *See also* virtues
Aretas IV, King, 7, 96
Aristobolus of Alexandria, 295
Aristotle, 62, 64, 67, 67n104, 70, 365, 366
arsen, arsenikos (male), 244n362, 246
ascension of Jesus Christ, 23n28
aselgeia (licentiousness), 358
Assumption of Moses, 23
astheneia (weakness), 281
athlete imagery, 320, 365
Attridge, H. W., 325n456
Aune, David E., 12, 39
Aus, Roger D., 124n180

Baarda, Tjitze, 322
Babylon, 302–3
Babylonian Talmud, 348
Bachmann, Michael, 49, 146, 404, 405
Balaam, 63
Balak, 63
baptism and baptismal formula, 237, 241, 241n356, 242–49, 243n361, 260, 265

Barclay, John M. G., 50n64, 51n67, 56, 58, 60n89, 61nn93–94, 90, 91, 161, 173, 276, 283, 313, 329, 338, 343, 345, 346, 347n472, 348, 355, 366, 368, 372, 373, 376, 378, 379, 384, 384n492, 385, 386
Barnabas
  Antioch church and, 5, 9, 10, 23, 104, 107, 108, 115, 120, 121, 124, 130
  as apostle, 22, 23, 95
  and Apostolic Council in Jerusalem, 59
  break between Paul and, at Antioch church, 5, 9, 49, 73, 74, 104, 107, 108, 110, 128
  and circumcision of Gentiles, 5, 9, 10, 107, 111–13, 115, 131, 132, 136, 138, 142
  Galatian churches and, 4–5
  in Jerusalem, 8, 100, 105–12, 107n159, 114, 115, 117, 118, 120–24
  Jerusalem apostles and, 74, 105–6
  missionary activities of, to Gentiles, 117, 118, 120–25
  and new preachers in Galatia, 321
  Paul and, 4–5, 9, 49, 73, 100, 105–7, 108n160, 109–10, 114, 117, 118, 118n173, 120–25
  and Paul's travel to Antioch, 7, 100
  references to, in Galatians, 5
Barnikol, Ernst, 120
baros (burden), 375–76, 383–84
Barrett, C. K., 286, 287, 303, 304
Bauckham, Richard J., 5
Bauer, W., 252
Becker, Jürgen, 13, 121, 296, 329, 398, 405
Behm, Johannes, 45
Beker, J. Christiaan, 31
Belial, 33, 338
benediction, 18, 403–5, 410–11
Bertram, Georg, 43, 351
Betz, Hans Dieter, 13, 21, 37, 37n51, 39, 40, 42, 43, 47–49, 51n67, 56n81, 59n85, 62, 67–68, 70, 76n116, 85n132, 98, 102n155, 109n163, 118, 119, 120n178, 121, 138, 148n217, 161–62nn241–242, 170, 170n252, 171, 173, 177n263, 179, 189, 191n272, 202, 209, 210n303, 212n306, 223, 226n325, 228–30, 232, 242, 244, 245, 247, 248, 259, 259n386, 263n393, 264, 276, 276n404, 278–82, 283–84n411–412, 285nn417–418, 287, 290, 294, 296, 300, 301n434, 305, 306, 311, 312, 316, 322, 324, 326, 334, 343, 345, 346, 346n469, 348, 349, 353, 354, 358, 363, 372–76, 378–82, 390, 391, 393, 398, 402, 404, 405, 407, 408n502, 409

Beuken, W. A. M., 303
birthing and pregnancy imagery, 284, 284nn414–415, 293, 302, 303
Blinzler, Josef, 253
boast, boasting, 382–83, 384n492, 394, 396, 397, 400–401
Brawley, Robert L., 303, 304
Breytenbach, Cilliers, 4*n*10, 5, 29
Brondos, David, 210n303
Bruce, F. F., 12n23, 13, 50n64, 60n89, 62, 99–101, 121, 131, 173, 218n314, 227n328, 234, 277n405, 282, 290, 301, 302, 306, 311n445, 366, 374, 379, 381, 399n495, 404, 405
Büchsel, Frederich, 295
Bullinger, E. W., 324n451
Bultmann, Rudolf, 62, 155n230, 233, 379
Bunyan, John, 296
Burton, Ernest De Witt, 8, 13, 22, 24, 41, 47, 62, 64, 74, 76n116, 85n132, 92, 94n147, 98, 99, 103, 109n163, 111, 113–15, 119, 122n179, 124, 126, 131, 132n190, 144, 144n210, 148n217, 157, 162, 163, 170, 171, 173, 174n257, 194–96, 200, 202, 203n295, 209, 211, 212n308, 213, 215n312, 219, 219n315, 226n325, 229, 230, 232, 233, 235, 238, 238n350, 240–42, 248, 249, 252, 263n392, 264, 271n398, 278–81, 284, 286, 287, 290, 294, 296, 299, 305, 311, 313, 317n447, 320, 322, 327, 334, 335, 340, 345, 346, 354, 358, 362, 363, 365, 366, 371, 373, 375, 377n490, 382, 385, 391, 395, 398–401, 399n496, 404, 405n501

Caesarea, 133, 135–36
Calvin, John, 35n47, 47, 48, 87n136, 88, 200, 213, 230, 232, 234, 239, 240, 262, 267n396, 361, 374, 405
Campbell, Douglas, 192n276
carrying one another's burdens, 369, 375–78, 380, 381, 383, 385, 392
carrying one's own burden, 383–84
castration, 54, 319, 322, 325–27, 325nn454–455, 334
Cephas. *See* Peter (Cephas)
chairein (greetings), 27
Chalcedonian Creed, 24
character traits, 365–66
chara (joy), 363, 364
charis (grace), 27–28, 36–37, 224–25, 230, 230n337. *See also* grace
charismata (gifts), 182
Chester, Stephen, 155n232
Chibici-Revneanu, Nicole, 207

childbirth imagery. *See* birthing and pregnancy imagery
children
  Galatians addressed as, by Paul, 284–85, 288–89
  slave-like plight of, 258–61
children of God, 242–43. *See also* sons of God
children of promise, 216, 288–89, 306–9, 406
Chilton, Bruce, 302
Choi, Hung-Sik, 317, 318
chrēstotēs (kindness), 364–65
Christ. *See* Jesus Christ
church
  ekklēsia as term for, 26–27, 27n34, 86–88
  Israel of God as, 405–6, 408
  as Jerusalem above, 301–5
Cicero, 66, 67n104, 69
Cilicia, 7–9, 73, 97, 100, 101, 107, 111
circumcision
  of Achior, 311n445
  Antioch church and, 5, 8, 8n18, 9, 10, 43, 58–59, 73, 128–38, 411
  castration equated with, 54, 319, 322, 325–27, 334
  and Christian Jews versus Jewish Christians, 60n88
  as community and family matter, 312, 313, 397
  conflict between Paul and Peter over, in Antioch, 9, 49, 73, 104, 117, 128–38
  and covenant between God and Abraham, 177, 178, 186–87, 221
  danger of, as separation from Christ and grace, 310–15
  decision by Apostolic Council (Jerusalem) on Paul's circumcision-free mission to Gentiles, 8, 9, 10, 10n20, 43, 58–59, 104–19, 121, 123, 138, 408
  "false brethren" supporting, 112–19, 115n169, 136, 138, 408
  false charges against Paul regarding, 319, 322–24
  as fleshly act, 152n223, 177–79, 298, 330–31, 336, 388, 397–98
  Genesis on, 57, 177, 179, 221, 244n362, 292, 336
  irrelevance of, for justification, 317–18, 328, 330, 394, 402, 403, 409–10
  Izates and, 58
  James and, 9, 10, 128–30, 132, 132n189, 133, 133n191, 135–37, 140, 304–5
  Jerusalem's circumcision party, 113–19, 115n169, 123, 135–36, 140, 142, 398, 408

Index of Subjects and Authors

of Jesus Christ, 263n393
Justin Martyr and, 58
of Moses, 55n77, 58
new preachers in Galatia on, 5, 10, 17, 41, 43, 44, 53–58, 54–58nn73–83, 60–61, 137–38, 164, 177–79, 200–201, 239–40, 283, 298, 307, 313–14, 330–31, 383, 393–400
and obligation to observe the whole law, 312–14, 343, 344, 399, 400
and Paul's pre-Christian life, 64
perfection and, 179–80
Philippians on, 60
as rite of entry to Judaism, 313
Titus and, 105, 106, 108, 111–12, 111n164, 115, 138, 396–97, 397nn493–494, 400
Claudius, Emperor, 127n184
Clement, First Letter to, 20, 120
closing of Letter to the Galatians
  benedictions in, 18, 403–5, 410–11
  on circumcision, 54
  features of summarized, 393–94
  functions of, 17–18
  on Israel of God, 394, 404–10
  recapitulation in, 17–18, 393–405
  in structure of letter, 12, 14
Collins, John J., 33
Colossians, Letter to
  authorship of, 20, 254n375
  on elements of the world, 252
  prescript in, 21
  on sexual misconduct, 358
commandments. *See* Ten Commandments
communal discord, 359
conceit, conceited (*kenodoxoi*), 372–73, 375, 381, 389
conversion
  of Corinthians, 183
  definition of, 77–78n120
  of Paul, 6, 23, 73, 75–79, 88–96, 89n141, 89n143, 100, 122, 159, 161–62
Corinth
  Christian Jewish missionaries in, 60
  conversion of Corinthians, 183
  Paul in, 11, 172, 284n413
  See also Corinthians, First Letter to; Corinthians, Second Letter to
Corinthians, First Letter to
  on Adam, 33
  on *akoē* (message as heard), 175
  on anathema, 45
  on *apokalypsis*, 79, 80
  "apostle" as term in, 21, 22, 95
  on appearances of risen Christ, 92
  authorship of, 20

441

on baptismal formula, 243n361
on begetting (founding) of churches, 284n413, 293
on Cephas/Peter, 120
closing of, 393
on congregational teachers, 385
on crucifixion, 398
on death and resurrection of Christ, 83–84, 150, 172, 211
dēlon hoti as phrase in, 202
on divine origin of gospel, 77n119
on drunkenness, 360
epistolary conventions in, 37
geographical terms in, 3, 3n5
on gifts of the Spirit, 182
on glossolalia, 81
on God as the one who called you, 40
on God's deeds of power, 183
on grace, 40n53
greeting in, 395
on Israel according to the flesh, 405
on kingdom of God, 361
on love, 362
on marriage, 246
on Mosaic law, 381
on old and new covenants, 296
opening of, 25, 26
on *paidagōgos* (custodian), 241
on preaching to Jews by Paul, 126, 126n183
on reception of gospel by Paul, 83
salutation in, 27
on Satan, 33
thanksgiving section of, 39
Corinthians, Second Letter to
  "apostle" as term in, 21, 22
  authorship of, 20
  on Christian-Jewish missionaries' resistance to Paul, 59–60, 60n87
  on crucifixion, 281
  epistolary conventions in, 37
  geographical terms in, 3, 3n5
  on Jesus Christ as Son of God, 93
  and miracles of Paul, 182–83
  on offspring of Abraham, 248
  on old and new covenants, 296
  opening of, 25, 26
  on Paul's bodily ailment, 281
  salutation in, 27
  on Satan, 33
  on sins, 357, 358, 359, 360
  on synagogue punishment for Paul, 126, 126n183
  thanksgiving section of, 39
  Titus in, 108
  on visions and revelations, 80–81

Cornelius, 133
Cosgrove, Charles H., 221
cosmic powers
  of the Flesh, 33–34, 56n80, 71, 162, 178, 301, 329, 331–43, 354, 362, 388, 389, 392
  of law, 198, 210
cosmological apocalyptic eschatology, 31–34, 338, 339. *See also* apocalyptic eschatology
covenant
  between Abraham and God, 57, 177, 185, 186–87, 217–22, 220n317, 226–32, 230n335, 267, 296–99, 299n427, 344n467
  between God and Israel, 151, 230n335
  human will or testament as analogy of, 218–20, 224, 230, 245n366
  new preachers on, 297–98
  Sinai covenant/Sinaitic law, 296–301, 298n426, 299n428, 304, 308, 344n467, 378
  two covenants represented by Hagar and Sarah, 287, 289, 294–303, 298n426, 344–45
covenantal nomism, 151–52, 220
creation of human beings, 246, 338
cross, 323–24, 324n451, 330, 340, 394, 398, 401–2, 404, 409, 411. *See also* crucifixion
crucifixion
  as apocalyptic event, 81, 83, 84, 172
  and Christ as accursed by law, 210–14, 210n303, 212n308
  cross and, 323–24, 324n451, 330, 340, 394, 398, 401–2, 404, 409, 411
  date of, 5
  Deuteronomy on, 209, 211–14
  end of world of law due to, 172
  First Corinthians on, 83–84, 150
  of the Flesh, 333, 366–68, 370, 386
  justification by faith and, 16, 84, 89, 93, 140, 150, 152, 163, 164, 166, 190–93, 197, 202, 203
  new preachers in Galatia and, 398–99
  Paul's being "crucified with Christ," 24, 160–62, 164, 394, 401–2
  Paul's preaching on, in Galatia, 171–73
  redemption and freedom through, 29, 113, 114, 160, 162–66, 172, 185, 190, 262–68, 340
  risen Christ and, 94
  See also faith of Jesus Christ
curse of the law, 167, 184–86, 191, 197–216, 203n296, 231, 263–64, 268, 343, 355

custodianship of the law, 237–42, 260, 267
Cybele, 325

Dahl, Nils A., 405, 408n502
Damascus, 6, 7, 96, 97, 100
Daniel, Book of, 78, 388
Danker, F. W., 252–53
Das, A. Andrew, 144
David, 223, 349
Davies, W. D., 178, 378
Dead Sea Scrolls, 32–33, 94n146, 145–46, 154n229, 212, 337
death
  animal imagery on, 350–51
  corruption and desires of the Flesh causing, 351, 387, 388, 389
  eternal death after last judgment, 32, 389
  fear of, 376
  of Flesh, 366–67, 392, 401
  and mortality of the flesh, 162
  sin and, 32–34, 113, 231, 338, 379
  See also crucifixion; flesh/The Flesh; sins
De Boer, Martinus C., 31, 33, 50n64, 79, 92, 152n224, 155, 155n230, 162n245, 231n339, 252n370, 304, 339, 392
Deissmann, Adolf, 66
Delling, Gerhard, 375
desire of the Flesh, 330, 335, 337–39, 352–53, 362, 366–67, 388. *See also* flesh/The Flesh
Deuteronomy, Book of
  on angels, 228
  on assembly of Yahweh, 88
  on castration, 326–27
  on circumcision, 200
  on crucifixion, 209, 211–14
  on curse versus blessing, 56, 184–85, 198–201, 200n290, 207, 209, 211–14, 211n305, 283, 313
  on God as one, 228, 256
  on law, 200–201, 200n290, 203, 204, 206–7, 313, 381
  Shema in, 228, 348
  on sons of God, 242
De Vries, Carl E., 320
diatassō (to ordain, enact, institute, order), 229–30
diathēkē (will or testament, covenant), 219, 220, 220n316, 221, 225, 226, 228, 230, 267, 297
Dibelius, 368
dichostasiai (dissensions), 359, 360
didaskalos, didaskō (teacher, teaching), 240, 385
dikaioi, dikaiosynē, dikaiousthai (justifies, justification), 34, 139, 140, 143–44, 151–53,

Index of Subjects and Authors 443

152n222, 153n225, 156, 157n235, 164, 165, 186, 187, 190, 193, 194, 207–8, 233, 276, 314, 316. *See also* justification
ho dikaios (the just one), 205–6, 205n298
Di Mattei, Steven, 294, 295
Dio Cassius, 325
Diodorus Siculus, 210, 325
Dionysus, 360
Dodd, C. H., 98, 378
dokimazō (scrutinize), 382
Donaldson, Terence L., 87n137
doulos, douleuō (slave, to be a slave), 253–54, 272–75, 301, 340, 341. *See also* slavery
Downing, F. Gerald, 247
drunkenness, 359–60, 365
Drusilla, 365
Dryden, John, 296
Dunn, James D. G., 8, 13, 28, 37, 41–43, 47, 49, 51n67, 62, 92, 95, 98, 100, 110, 114n167, 115, 117, 135, 143, 144, 147, 147n215, 148nn216–217, 173, 176, 189, 200, 202, 212n306, 213, 219, 229, 230, 232, 235, 240, 253, 261, 263n393, 264, 278, 280, 281, 283, 284n412, 290, 294, 313, 314, 316, 323, 325, 327, 345, 347n470, 354, 362, 367, 375, 380, 384n492, 400, 404, 408
Du Toit, André, 43
dynamis, dynameis (power), 182–84, 281

Eastman, Susan, 170n253, 284, 307n441, 405, 407
Ebionites, 282
echthrai (hostile actions), 359, 360
echthros (enemy), 282
Edgar, C. C., 19n26, 39
edouleusate (slaves), 35, 271, 341. *See also* slavery
eidōlolatria (idolatry), 358–59, 360
eirēnē (peace), 27–28, 27n37, 36–37, 363, 364, 404
ekklēsia (assembly, gathering, church), 26–27, 27n34, 86–88
ek pisteōs, ek pisteōs (Iēsou) Christou (from the faith of Jesus Christ), 72, 139, 149, 167, 191–93, 204–6, 236, 316–17. *See also pistis Iēsou Christou* (faith of Christ)
ek tou kalountos hymas (from the one who calls you), 320–21
Eleazar, 58
elements of the world, 13, 251–61, 254–55n377–379, 256n381, 267, 270–76, 327, 341, 360, 372, 402
eleos (mercy), 407, 408

eleutheria, eleutheroō (freedom, set free), 35, 113, 309. *See also* freedom
Elijah, 287
Elliott, J. Keith, 41
Elliott, John H., 170n253
Elliott, Susan M., 61n93, 325, 326
elpis (hope), 316. *See also* hope
enekopsen (cut in on), 320
en emoi (in me, through me, within me, in my former manner of life), 89, 92–93, 103, 159, 161
enkrateia (self-control), 365
entire law, 343–45, 379. *See also* law; whole law
entolē (commandment), 348–49, 379
envy, 359, 360, 373, 381
epangelia (promise), 215, 216, 222, 235, 236, 237, 292. *See also* promise
Epaphroditus, 22
Ephesians, Letter to, 20, 29, 358, 385
Ephesus, 11n22
Epictetus, 240, 326, 381
epikataratos (accursed), 211–13
epistles versus letters, 66. *See also* letters
epistolary closing. *See* closing of Letter to the Galatians
epistolary writing style of Paul, 12, 15, 19–20, 27–28, 36–39, 66–71, 76, 393, 410
epiteleisthe (ending up with/perfecting or completing of what was already there), 56–57n81
epithymia (desire), 335, 337, 338, 352–53, 366–67
erga nomou (works of the law), 143–46, 148, 382, 390, 398. *See also* works of the law
ergon (work), 382, 384, 390–91
eris (strife), 359
eritheiai (selfish actions), 359
eschatological mysticism, 161n241
eschatology. *See* apocalyptic eschatology
Esler, Philip F., 26, 64n96, 66n99, 67, 69, 134, 134n192, 138
estaurōsan (they crucified), 367–68
Esther, Book of, 138
eternal death, 32, 389
eternal life, 31, 388–90, 392
ethnē (Gentiles, nations), 195, 195n282, 196
ēthos (character argument), 64, 70
euangelion (gospel), 38, 40–41, 46, 50, 76, 322. *See also* gospel
euangelizetai (preach-good-news), 46, 47, 76, 90, 92
euangelizomai (preach-good-news), 109n162
eulogian (blessing), 186, 196
eutheōs (immediately), 94n147

evangelists, 51n66
evil
  angels as, 230n336, 280n410
  apocalyptic eschatology and evil age, 29–36, 30n43, 72, 81, 161, 165, 172, 198, 210, 262, 302, 368, 389
  Calvin on, 35n47
  desire of the Flesh and, 335, 337–39, 352–53, 388
  flesh associated with, 178, 335, 337–39, 352–53, 388, 389
  free choice between good and, 337, 338
  human susceptibility to, 162n245
  of new preachers in Galatia, 170–71
  personification of Evil Inclination/Impulse, 337–39, 352–53, 388
  rescue from, 35–36
  slavery of, 33–35, 210
  See also flesh/The Flesh; sins
exagorazō (redeem), 35
exaireō (rescue), 35–36
ex akoēs pisteōs (from what is heard of faith), 173–84, 193, 317. *See also* faith
Exodus, Book of, 146, 179, 221n318, 226n326, 298
Ezekiel, Book of, 265
Ezra, Fourth Book of, 339

Fairchild, Mark R., 87n137
faith
  of Abraham, 149, 190n271, 193–94, 196
  apocalyptic revelation and, 81–82, 84, 239
  of believers in Jesus Christ, 148–49, 149n218, 154
  and blessing of Abraham versus curse of the law, 167, 184–216, 268
  household of, 391–92
  interpretations of *ex akoēs pisteōs*, 173–84, 193
  justification by, 16, 17, 34, 56–57, 72, 82, 84, 139–44, 148–66, 152n222, 173–74, 181, 193, 202, 203, 213, 226, 239n351, 317
  law versus, 16–17, 56–57, 82, 84, 104–5, 207–16, 310–11, 314
  living in Christ and, 161–62
  love and, 317, 318–19
  meaning of *pistis*, 174
  as metonym for Christ, 103, 193
  as obedience, 150
  as personification of Christ, 238–39
  preaching the faith, 103–4
  promise to Abraham and law of Moses, 216–36
  and sharing in God's eschatological revelation, 81

Spirit and, 13, 14, 16–17, 181
  as synonym for the gospel, 103–4
  works versus, 16, 104–5
  See also faith of Jesus Christ
faith of Jesus Christ
  crucifixion and, 139nn201–202, 145n211, 148–66, 154, 165n250, 175–76, 192, 193, 202, 203, 236, 238, 267
  as faith of believers, 148–49
  as faith of Christ, 149–50, 191–92
  interpretation of, 139nn201–202, 148–50
  justification by, 145n211, 148–66, 165n250, 190–93, 197, 202, 203, 226, 241–42, 315, 318
  law of Christ and, 391
  love and, 317, 318–19
  Martyn on, 145n211, 239, 239n352
  new creation and, 403
  new identity for humans through, 245
  pistis as personification of Christ, 238–39
  positive consequences of, 310, 315–19
  promise of the Spirit and, 236, 247, 317, 340
  reception of the Spirit and, 166–68, 217, 315
  sons of God and, 242–43, 247–48, 262–67, 340
  See also justification
false brethren, 112–19, 115n169, 136, 138, 408
Fee, Gordon D., 80, 182, 183, 183n268
Felix, 365
female/male distinction. *See* male/female distinction
fides (faith), 103
Fitzmyer, Joseph A., 6n12, 205, 205n299, 212, 229n334
flesh/The Flesh
  animal imagery and, 350–51
  circumcision and, 152n223, 177–79, 292, 298, 330–31, 336, 388, 397–98
  cosmic power of, 33–34, 56n80, 71, 162, 178, 301, 329, 331–43, 354, 362, 388, 389, 392
  crucifixion of, 333, 366–68, 370, 386
  death of, 366–67, 392, 401
  desire of, 330, 335, 337–39, 352–53, 362, 366–67, 388
  Evil Inclination/Impulse and, 337–39, 352–53, 388
  freedom as opportunity for, 335, 341–42, 351, 352, 366, 392
  Hagar and Ishmael associated with, 292, 294, 298, 336
  human beings as flesh and blood, 75, 89, 94–95, 162, 336, 361, 388

Index of Subjects and Authors 445

list of works of, 333, 353, 355–62, 373
love and Spirit's strife against, 331–68, 392
new preachers in Galatia and realm of, 398
perseverance against falling into realm of, 390
sins and evil associated with, 33–35, 56n80, 162, 178, 207, 333, 335, 337–39, 352–53, 388, 389
sowing and reaping imagery on dangers of, 386–89
Spirit versus, 35, 56, 56n80, 162–63, 169, 177–79, 306, 331–42, 351, 351–68, 388, 402
works of the law and, 198n285, 357–58
See also death
food laws of Judaism, 134–36, 134n192, 138, 147, 313
footrace imagery, 320
forensic apocalyptic eschatology, 31, 32–34, 33n45, 163–64, 194, 338, 338n462. *See also* apocalyptic eschatology
forgiveness, 30, 30n42, 154–55, 155nn229–230
freedom
of choice between good and evil, 337, 338
christological basis of, 113, 114, 270, 289, 308–10, 315, 330, 334
exhortation on, 308–10, 315
of gospel, 115, 282
from observance of the law, 257–58, 262, 264, 270, 282, 309, 330, 334, 350, 355, 392
as opportunity for the Flesh, 335, 341–42, 351, 352, 366
Sarah associated with, 291–92, 294, 295, 297, 301, 304–5
from *stoicheia*, 257–58, 262
threats to, 330
fulfillment of law of Christ, 332, 333, 341–92, 347n472
fullness of time, 261–62, 267
Fung, Ronald Y. K., 13, 144n210, 215n312, 316n446
Furnish, Victor Paul, 182–83, 379

Galatia
audience for Paul's preaching in, 171–72
danger of abandoning Paul and his gospel in, 277–86, 327
danger of becoming separated from Christ and grace in, 310–19
danger of returning to previous religious servitude in, 269–77, 334
dangers confronting Galatians, 13, 14, 17, 55, 269–328
ethnic Galatians, 4, 4nn9–10, 5, 169

founding of churches in and Paul's visits to, 5, 7–11, 11n22, 26, 49, 108, 114–15, 277, 279–81, 284
as geographic region and location of churches in, 3–5, 4n11, 26
gospel brought by Paul to, 46, 48, 50, 53, 56, 60n90, 72, 171–72
Jews not living in northern Galatia, 5
mystery religion of Cybele in, 325
new preachers as source of danger in, 319–28
"North Galatia" hypothesis, 5, 11n22, 26
Paul's bodily ailment and Galatians, 279–81
Paul's desire for face-to-face encounter with Galatians, 284–85
persecution of Gentile Christians in, 180
reception of the Spirit in, 167–84
"South Galatia" hypothesis, 5, 10n20, 26
spiritual people in, 374–75
See also circumcision; Galatians, Letter to; new preachers in Galatia
Galatians, Letter to
addressees of, 3–5, 3n6, 26, 169–70
apocalyptic eschatology and, 31–36, 31n44
on apocalyptic revelation of gospel, 77, 79–96
"apostle" as term in, 21–31
autobiographical narrative in, 72–79, 96–119, 128–38
on baptismal formula, 237, 242–49
on blessing of Abraham and curse of the law, 167, 184–216, 268
chronology leading up to writing of, 5–11
on circumcision controversy and conflict with Cephas/Peter in Antioch, 128–38
closing of, 12, 14, 17–18, 54, 393–411
cosenders of, 20, 25
on danger of abandoning Paul and his gospel, 277–86, 327
on danger of becoming separated from Christ and grace, 310–19
on danger of losing new identity through false exegesis of Ishmael and Isaac story, 285–310, 327
on danger of returning to previous religious servitude, 269–77, 334
on dangers confronting the Galatians, 13, 14, 17, 55, 269–328
date of, 5–11, 10n20
on divine origin of gospel, 14, 15–16, 72, 75–104
on elements of the world, 251–61, 270–76, 327
on eternal life, 31, 388–90, 392

Galatians, Letter to (*continued*)
  exhortations, or paraenesis in, 17, 308–10, 315, 331, 332, 340, 381–82, 384–85, 390–92
  on faith, 16–17, 139–44, 148–65, 166–68, 192–216
  on Flesh as cosmic power, 329, 331–43, 388
  on fulfillment of law of Christ, 332, 341–92
  genre of, and Paul's use of rhetorical forms and conventions in, 66–71
  geographical terms in, 3–4, 3n6
  on Greek phrase *ex akoēs pisteōs,* 173–84
  historical-critical approach to, 1–2, 2n4
  on Israel of God, 394, 404–10
  on living at juncture of ages, 329–32, 368–92
  on living by the Spirit and fulfilling the law of Christ, 368–92
  on love, 14, 17, 329–92
  Marcionite Prologue to, 60n90
  oath in, 99
  opening of, 12, 14, 15, 19–71
  outcome of, 411
  overview of commentary on, 15–18
  on Paul's conversion and call to apostleship, 75–79, 88–96
  and Paul's credibility, 16, 45, 61–65, 74, 99
  on Paul's visit with Peter/Cephas in Jerusalem, 96–104
  prescript of, 15, 19–37
  problem of verses 2:7b–8 in, 119–28
  on promise of the Spirit, 13, 14, 16–17, 166–68, 249–68
  on promise to Abraham and law of Moses, 216–36
  reading aloud of, 27, 36, 66–67, 71nn113–114, 99, 256n382, 410
  recapitulation of themes of, 17–18, 393–405
  on reception of the Spirit, 167–84
  salutation in, 15, 27–29, 27n37, 28n39
  on Spirit's strife against the Flesh and love, 332–68
  structure of, 11–15, 67–68
  summaries of gospel in and theme of, 15, 16, 17, 18, 29, 72, 401–3, 409–10
  translation of, 2–3
  on true heirs of promise of the Spirit, 167, 168, 184, 215–16, 249–67
  on true offspring of Abraham, 16, 56–58, 166, 167, 184–86, 188, 191, 195–97, 221–25, 237–49, 268, 290, 305–6
  on truth of gospel, 14, 15–16, 47–49, 66, 72, 73, 104–65
  on works of the law, 16, 84, 104–5, 139–48, 151, 152

  See also circumcision; law; love; new preachers in Galatia
Galen, 284n415
Galli, 325, 327
Gaventa, Beverly Roberts, 75, 77–78n120, 86, 284
Genesis, Book of
  on Abraham's faith in God's promise, 149, 187–91, 193–97
  on Abraham's sons by Hagar and Sarah, 184n269, 286–310, 327, 336
  allegorical interpretation of, 294–304
  on blessing of Abraham, 187–91, 193–97, 195n282, 214–16
  on circumcision, 57, 177, 179, 221, 244n362, 292, 336
  on covenant between God and Abraham, 57, 177, 187, 219–22, 220n317, 298
  on creation of human beings, 246
  on evil, 337
  haftarah readings of, 303
  on marriage, 246
  on offspring of Abraham, 221–24, 222n319, 224n322
  pisteuō (believe) in, 142
  on seasons, days, months, and years, 276–77n405
  gennaō (to beget, to bear, to be born), 292, 293, 304–5, 306n439
Gentile/Jew distinction. *See* Jew/Gentile distinction
Georgi, Dieter, 124n181, 127, 127n184, 128, 181n267
gnostics, 60n89
God
  as Abba, Father, 25, 94, 167, 251, 265–66, 284
  apostles commissioned by, 21–23, 22n27
  believers as sons of, 94, 242–47, 245n365, 250–51, 258, 260–67, 272, 340
  cataclysmic invasion of world in Christ by, 81
  coming to know God, 272–73
  fatherhood of, and believers, 25n31, 28, 94, 166, 240–47, 245n365, 250–51, 260–67, 272, 340
  fatherhood of, and Jesus Christ, 24–25, 24n30, 28, 94, 167, 251, 265–66, 284
  forgiveness by, 154, 155n229
  glory of, 228
  glory to, 36
  grace of, 150, 224–25, 410
  grace of, for Paul, 75, 89–91, 106, 109, 110, 122
  humans created in image of, 246
  impartiality of, 118

Index of Subjects and Authors

Israel of God, 394, 404–10
Jesus Christ as Son of, 25, 93–94, 162–63, 262–67
  as Judge, 32, 33, 34, 153, 315, 322, 383
  law of, 32–33
  love of, as grace, 91
  Luther on, 24
  mercy of, 407–8
  as "the one who called/calls you," 40, 320–21, 334
  power and righteousness of, 81, 92, 182–84
  redemption and, 24, 28, 29–30, 34, 35, 262–67
  resurrection of Jesus Christ by, 24–25, 28n39, 36, 72, 81, 94, 190n271, 213–14, 262
  revelation from, 48
  Scripture as synonym for, 234
  sovereignty of, in age to come, 34
  Spirit and, 182
  wrath of, 81
  See also covenant
Golden Rule, 348
goodness, 284–85, 364, 365, 390–92
Gordon, David T., 240
gospel
  apocalyptic revelation of, 77, 79–96
  authority of, 194, 194n281
  as brought by Paul to Galatia, 46, 48, 50, 53, 56, 60n90, 72
  criterion of true gospel, 84
  "different gospel" of new preachers in Galatia, 12, 37–66, 84, 86
  divine origin of, 14, 15–16, 72, 75–104
  faith as synonym for, 103–4
  freedom of, 115, 282
  Galatians in danger of abandoning, 277–86, 327
  grace and, 40, 51, 72, 115, 119, 122
  instructors of, 384–86
  Jerusalem pillar apostles and truth of, 117
  meaning of term for Christians, 40–41, 56
  one gospel for all believers, 119
  Paul's loyalty to true gospel, 65–66
  reception of, by Paul, 82–83
  summaries of, 15, 16, 17, 18, 29, 401–3, 409–10
  as theme of Galatians, 72
  truth of, 14, 15–16, 47–49, 66, 72, 73, 104–65, 117, 320
  universal scope of, 392
  See also specific gospels, such as John, Gospel of
grace
  in benediction, 410
  of Christ, 38–40, 40nn52–53, 44, 51, 65, 72

Galatians in danger of becoming separated from, 310–19
  for Gentiles, 84
  of God, 150, 224–25, 410
  gospel and, 40, 51, 72, 115, 119, 122
  as love of God, 91
  Paul's calling by grace of God, 75, 89–91, 106, 109, 110, 122
  as redemptive power and manner of living, 113
  in salutation of letter, 27–28
  thanksgiving for, in First Corinthians, 39
graphē (Scripture), 234, 234n347
Greek/Jew distinction. *See* Jew/Gentile distinction
Grundmann, Walter, 48, 365

Habakkuk, Book of, 192n276, 202–8, 203n295
Hadrian, 325
Häfner, Gerd, 49
haftarah readings, 303
Hagar, 184n269, 286–310, 299n428, 300nn432–433, 327, 336
haireseis (factions), 359, 360
Hall, Robert G., 68, 71
hamartia (sin), 157. *See also* sins
Hanse, Hermann, 202
Hansen, G. Walter, 31, 39, 68, 86
happiness, 277, 281. *See also* joy
Hardin, Justin K., 274n401
Harrill, J. Albert, 356n478
Hauck, Frederich, 365
Hays, Richard B., 13n24, 92, 147, 148n217, 150, 173–75, 190n271, 193, 200, 202, 205n298, 209, 234, 238, 239n352, 264, 287, 290, 294, 296, 303, 349, 379, 405
heart, 265–67
Hebrews, Letter to, 30, 150
Hegesippus, 123, 134n191
heirs. *See* inheritance
heirs of promise of the Spirit, 167, 168, 184, 249–67, 340, 361
Hengel, Martin, 87
heresies, 359
Herod Agrippa, King, 35, 123
Herodotus, 409
Hesiod, 229
Hesychius, 113
Hillel, 233, 348
historēsai (visit), 98, 110
Holmberg, Bengt, 136, 137, 138
holos ho nomos (the whole law), 312–14, 343
Homer, 295
Hooker, Morna D., 214
hope, 316, 328, 389

horaō (see), 91
Horrell, David G., 377, 379, 380
house churches, 391
household of faith, 391–92
Hultgren, Arland J., 101, 214
humility, 365, 369, 373, 375
Hunt, Arthur Surridge, 19n26, 39
hypocrisy, 132

idolatry, 31, 134, 187, 271–72, 333, 358–59, 360. *See also* elements of the world
Ignatius, 86
inheritance
  and Abraham's true offspring, 16, 56–58, 166, 167, 184–86, 188, 189, 191, 195–97, 237–49, 268, 290, 305–6, 406
  in ancient patriarchal society, 184n269
  children of God, 242–43
  heirs of promise of the Spirit, 167, 168, 184, 215–16, 249–67, 361
  of Isaac from Abraham, 184n269, 189–90
  of sons of God, 242–47, 245n365, 250–51, 258, 260–68, 272, 340
  wills and testaments for, 218–20, 224, 229–30, 245n366, 261
ioudaïzein (to practice Judaism), 137–38
Isaac
  Abraham's age at birth of, 293n422
  as begotten by the Spirit, 336
  birth of, 221, 292–93, 305–6, 392n422
  inheritance of, from Abraham, 184n269, 189–90
  Ishmael as brother of, 286–310
  Ishmael's relationship with, 306–7, 307n440
  near sacrifice of, by Abraham, 179, 188, 196
  as offspring of Abraham, 184n269, 189–90, 196, 223, 224, 286–310, 307n440, 406
  as patriarch, 124n180
  as "type," 305
Isaiah, Book of, 79, 90–91, 156, 215, 284nn413–414, 288, 293, 302–5
Ishmael, 286–310, 300n432, 307n440, 336
Ishmaelites, 287, 299–300
Isis, 255
Israel of God, 394, 404–10
Izates, King of Adiabene, 58

Jacob, 90, 91, 124n180, 135, 196
James
  appearance of risen Christ to, 95, 117
  as brother of Jesus, 99, 100, 117, 123
  and circumcision, 9, 10, 128–30, 132, 132n189, 133, 133n191, 135–37, 140, 304–5

  Jerusalem church and, 48, 72, 73, 97, 98, 99, 102, 104–7, 110, 123, 133–34n191, 308, 408
  leadership of, 117–18, 120, 123–24, 308
  mission of, to Jews, 120
  and new preachers in Galatia, 48, 74, 321, 398
  and Paul's missionary activities, 105–6, 110, 116–19
  Paul's relationship with, 118n173, 133–34n191
  Paul's visits with, in Jerusalem, 97, 98, 99, 102, 104, 105–6
  truth of gospel and, 104, 105
James, Letter of, 188, 313, 338
James (son of Alphaeus), 99
James (son of Zebedee), 99, 123
Jeremiah, 90, 265
Jerusalem
  Antioch church and, 23, 59
  apocalyptic contrast between present Jerusalem and Jerusalem above, 301–5, 308
  Apostolic Council in, 8, 9, 10, 10n20, 43, 58–59, 104–19, 121, 123, 138, 408
  Barnabas in, 8, 100, 105–12, 107n159, 114, 115, 117, 118, 120–24, 127n184
  church in, 87–88, 97, 98, 103–7, 408
  circumcision party in, 113–19, 115n169, 123, 135–36, 140, 142, 398, 408
  collection of funds for poor in, 126–28, 127n184, 128n185, 133n191, 385, 411
  devastation of, 63, 87, 302
  Israel of God and church in, 408
  James and church in, 48, 72, 73, 97, 98, 99, 102, 104–7, 110, 123, 133–34n191, 308, 408
  new preachers in Galatia and Jerusalem church, 48, 74, 98, 107, 123–25, 300–301, 308, 321–22, 385
  partnership between Antioch church and, 126–28
  Paul's visits to, 6–10, 8n18, 10n20, 73, 74, 84, 96–119, 107n159, 121–22, 127n184, 133–34n191
  pillar apostles in, 23, 48, 72, 89, 94–96, 100, 105–7, 117–28, 123–24n180
  status of pillar apostles in, 117–18
  support by Jerusalem church for Paul's circumcision-free mission to Gentiles, 104–19
  support for Paul's missionary activities by apostles in, 102n154, 105–6, 110–11, 116–19
Jesus Christ
  apokalypsis of, 79–80
  apostles and, 21–25, 22n27

Index of Subjects and Authors

ascension of, 23n28
baptism of, 22
circumcision of, 263n393
divine origin of the gospel and, 77
divinity of, 24–25, 93–94
fulfillment of law of, 332, 341–92
Galatians in danger of becoming separated from, 310–19
God's fatherhood of, 24–25, 24n30, 28, 94, 167, 251, 265–66, 284
grace of, 40, 40nn52–53, 44, 51, 72
human condition of, 24n29, 263n392, 340–41
law and, 61, 61n91, 263–64, 263n393, 312, 340
law of Christ and, 378–80
as Lord, 28–29, 113, 215, 363, 389
love of, 163, 172, 211, 318–19, 340–41, 346, 379–80
meaning of "Christ," 24
as mediator, 228n330
as Messiah, 61n91, 88, 94, 139, 214, 223
as offspring of Abraham, 221–25, 231, 248–49, 283, 305
Parousia and, 31, 34, 36, 79–81, 166, 205, 390
resurrection of, 23–25, 23n28, 28n39, 36, 72, 81, 83–84, 94, 190n271, 211, 213–14, 262
as Son of God, 25, 93–94, 162–63, 262–67
virgin birth of, 263n392
See also crucifixion; faith of Jesus Christ; gospel; redemption; Spirit
Jewett, Robert, 7, 54n76, 56n81, 133, 398, 399n495
Jew/Gentile distinction, negation of, 237, 243–47, 256n382, 258–59, 318
Joel, Book of, 43
John
  as apostle, 95, 117
  appearance of risen Christ to, 117
  in Jerusalem, 72, 105–7, 117–18, 123
  leadership of, 117–18, 120, 123–24
  mission of, to Jews, 120, 123, 125
  and new preachers in Galatia, 48
  Paul's missionary activities and, 105–6, 116–19
  Peter and, 123, 125
  truth of gospel and, 104, 105
John, Gospel of
  on law, 226n326
  Letter to the Galatians informed by, 24
  on love, 343
  meaning of *proteron* in, 10
  on Mosaic law, 291

on offspring of Abraham, 248, 292
on "resurrection of life," 174n258
John the Baptist, 182, 248
Josephus, 21, 41, 45, 54, 58, 63, 85n133, 86, 87, 96, 98, 108, 124, 127n184, 131, 134, 138, 218n314, 221n318, 228, 228n331, 240, 241n355, 295, 299–300, 358, 359, 362n481, 375
Joshua, 77n119
joy, 363, 364. *See also* happiness
Jubilees, 33, 135, 179, 181, 187, 188, 250–51, 300
Judaism
  allegorical interpretation of Scripture and, 295–96
  apocalyptic eschatology and, 30–36, 33n45, 36n50, 153, 230n336
  calendrical observances of, 257, 267, 276
  Christian Jews in Jerusalem, 133–34n191
  Christian Jews versus Jewish Christians, 60n88
  circumcision as rite of entry to, 313
  food laws and, 134–36, 134n192, 138, 147, 313
  in Galatia, 5
  Israel of God as Jewish people, 406–7
  on love of neighbor, 348
  negation of Jew/Gentile distinction, 237, 243–47, 256n382, 258–59, 318
  new creation and, 402
  Paul as Pharisaic Jew before his conversion, 64, 72–73, 77, 84–89, 84–89nn126–140, 92–93, 96, 159, 161–62
  Paul's use of term, 86, 86n135, 398
  rabbinic Judaism, 86n135
  Sabbath and, 147
  and verb *ioudaïzein* (to practice Judaism), 137–38
  See also circumcision; law; Pentateuch; Scripture; Torah; *and specific books of Old Testament*
Judaizers and Judaizing, 54n74, 86n135, 400
Judas, 22
Judea, 59, 97, 100–104, 101n152, 102n153
Judith, Book of, 311n445, 359
Julius Victor, 69
justification
  Abraham and, 188–90, 193–94
  apocalyptic eschatology and, 153–54
  charges against Paul in Antioch regarding, 156–58
  cosmological-eschatological meanings of, 34–35
  by faith, 16, 17, 34, 56–57, 72, 82, 84, 139–44, 148–66, 173–74, 181, 193, 197, 202, 203, 213, 226, 239n351, 317

justification *(continued)*
  by faith of Jesus Christ, 145n211, 148–66, 165n250, 190–93, 197, 202, 203, 226, 241–42, 315, 318
  forensic-eschatological meanings of, 34, 194
  forgiveness and, 154–55, 155n230
  by God, 190–91, 190n271
  hope of, 316, 328, 389
  irrelevance of circumcision or uncircumcision for, 317–18, 328, 330, 394, 402, 403, 409–10
  language of, in Paul's letters generally, 11
  at last judgment, 315
  Letter of James on, 188
  as liberation from captivity, 241–42
  new life and, 233, 233n346
  new preachers in Galatia on, 34, 44, 55–57, 61, 72, 151, 153–54, 154n226, 163–65, 167–68, 195–97, 208n300, 233–34
  and phrase "seeking to be justified," 156–58, 156n234, 157n235
  in present versus future, 155, 156, 164, 194, 316, 316n446
  rectification and, 161, 166, 184, 205, 316
  righteousness and, 316, 316n446
  seeking to be justified in the law, 314–15
  Spirit and, 215n312, 315–17
  works of the law as irrelevant for, 2, 16, 56, 57, 72, 84, 104–5, 132, 139–48, 144n210, 151–56, 158–67, 173, 181, 197, 202–8, 213, 226, 247, 315, 398
Justin Martyr, 58, 313

Kahl, Brigitte, 244n362
kainē ktisis (new creation), 402
kaleō (call), 40, 334
kalon (what is right), 389–90
kanōn (norm, standard), 403
kardia (heart), 265
Käsemann, Ernst, 151, 155, 329, 339
katara (curse), 211
katara theou (curse of God), 211n305
kataskopēsai (to spy out), 113
katēcheō (to catechize, to instruct), 385
kauchēma, kauchēsis (boasting, ground for boasting), 382–83, 384n492
Keck, Leander E., 31
Keith, Chris, 395
Kennedy, George A., 67, 67n102, 68, 69, 70
kenodoxoi (conceited), 372–73, 375, 381
Kern, Philip H., 68, 69
kēryssō (proclaim), 109n162, 322–23
Kim, Seyoon, 200, 202
kindness, 364–65

kingdom of God, 31, 34, 333, 360–62, 364
klēronomeō, klēronomeō (inheritance, to inherit), 224, 224n322, 237
Knox, John, 8, 59n86, 100
Koch, Dietrich-Alex, 4n11, 5, 191n272
Koet, Bart J., 86, 90
koinōnia (fellowship), 124
koinōneitō (share), 384–85
kōmoi (drinking parties), 359–60
koptō (to cut), 320
kosmos (world), 254, 254n377, 256n382, 401
Kremendahl, Dieter, 68n106
krima (judgment), 322
Kuck, David W., 381–84, 384n492
kyrios (Lord), 28–29

Lambrecht, Jan, 322, 381, 384
last judgment, 32, 33, 34, 153, 315, 322, 383–84, 389
Lategan, Bernard C., 74
law
  Abrahamic promise versus Mosaic law, 216–36
  angels and, 221, 227–30, 229n334, 232, 233, 268
  being "under the law," 16, 35, 81, 148, 149, 158, 159, 171n254, 193, 201n291, 209–13, 210n302, 235n348, 237–41, 241n355, 250–51, 257–64, 263n393, 267, 269, 274–75, 285, 288–91, 299, 305, 309, 314, 333, 343, 351, 352, 355, 366, 388
  as captive of sin, 234, 235n348, 236, 355, 357–58
  of Christ, 377–92
  Christian Jews as zealots for, 133, 134n191
  circumcision and obligation to observe the whole law, 312–14, 343, 344, 399, 400
  cosmic power of, 198, 210
  curse of, 167, 184–86, 191, 197–216, 203n296, 231, 263–64, 268, 343, 355
  custodianship of, 237–42, 260
  "dying to the law" and justification by faith, 158–65
  elements of the world (*stoicheia*) and, 270–77
  end of, due to Christ's crucifixion, 172
  entire law, 343–45, 379
  faith versus, 16–17, 56–57, 82, 84, 104–5, 207–16, 310–11, 314
  food laws, 134–36, 134n192, 138, 147, 313
  forensic apocalyptic eschatology and, 32–33, 163–64, 194
  freedom from observance of, 257–58, 262, 264, 270, 282, 309, 330, 334, 350, 355, 392

Index of Subjects and Authors

fulfillment of, 332, 333, 341–92, 347n472
function and purpose of, 217–18, 226–31, 337, 338
God as Judge and, 32, 33, 34, 153
Jesus Christ and, 61, 61n91, 263–64, 263n393, 312, 340
last judgment and, 153, 315
life-giving law, 233–35
new preachers in Galatia on Mosaic law, 10, 54–61, 55n78, 140, 142, 233, 313–14
number of commandments and prohibitions under Mosaic law, 312
origin of, in Moses, 77n119
Paul and Mosaic law, 86–89, 133–34n191, 401–2
Paul's rejection of legalism, 147
Paul's rejection of select laws, 147–48
in Pentateuch, 54, 146, 159, 173, 199, 291, 342, 343, 345n467, 350, 377–80
promises of God and, 231–36, 232n344, 342
as remedy for evil inclinations, 337, 338
ritual law versus moral law, 148
Romans on, 113, 146, 147, 152, 158, 160, 210n302, 229n333, 231, 231n338, 343, 345, 347, 350n475, 379
Scripture as, 234, 234n347, 291, 342, 344, 347, 380–81
seeking to be justified in the law, 314–15
Sinai covenant/Sinaitic law, 296–301, 298n426, 299n428, 304, 308, 344n467, 378
sinners versus transgressors of, 158n236
slavery of, 16–17, 35, 55n78, 114, 164, 167, 201n291, 260–61, 263, 267, 268, 270, 309–11, 314
temporality of, 231n340
transgressions of, 158n236, 230–31, 374
virtues and, 366
yoke metaphor for, 309–10, 314, 327, 341
See also circumcision; new preachers in Galatia; Ten Commandments; works of the law
law of Christ
and carrying one's own burdens, 383–84
and conceit as self-delusion, 381, 389
and doing what is right, 389–92
eternal life and, 388–90, 392
exhortations on, 381–82, 384–85, 390–92
as love commandment, 378–81
meanings of, 378–81
mutual burden bearing and, 381, 383, 385, 392
perseverance in following the Spirit, 390
and self-perception and self-examination, 381–84

sowing and reaping imagery and, 369, 386–92
and support for community instructors in the gospel, 384–86
See also love
leaven metaphor, 321
letters
definition of, 66, 70n112
epistles versus, 66
length of Paul's letters compared with other letter writers, 66
Paul's epistolary writing style, 12, 15, 19–20, 27–28, 36–39, 66–71, 76, 393, 410
for reading out loud, 27, 36, 66–67, 71nn113–114, 99, 410–11
in Roman society, 66n101
See also specific letters by Paul, such as Galatians, Letter to
Leviticus, Book of
Abrahamic law and, 349–50n474
on law, 203, 205–7
on love, 147, 332, 332n459, 340, 341, 343–46, 344n467, 348–51, 378, 379, 381, 392
on Moses, 226n326, 227n327
and new preachers in Galatia, 349
targums and, 208n300
Libanius (or Proclus), 68n105, 69n108
liberation. *See* freedom
Lightfoot, J. B., 13, 39, 47, 87n137, 92, 94n147, 99, 107n159, 115, 131, 144n210, 176n261, 178n265, 182, 189, 213n310, 222n320, 226n325, 229, 230, 247, 248, 252, 253, 253n374, 278–80, 282, 283, 284, 294, 300, 309n443, 325, 326, 344, 350, 354, 358, 363, 370–71, 373, 374, 384n492, 385, 390, 399n495, 401, 405
logos (logical argument), 70
logos (word), 349, 379
Longenecker, Bruce W., 170n253
Longenecker, Richard N., 8, 13, 39, 40n53, 43, 62, 66n99, 68, 71, 76n116, 94n147, 98, 99, 101, 106, 109n163, 114, 119, 121, 127, 131, 132n190, 133, 138, 144n210, 148n217, 158n236, 161n241, 170, 173, 175, 188, 191n273, 194, 200, 202, 208n300, 212n306, 213, 219, 219n315, 221n318, 229, 230, 232, 235n348, 236, 238, 239n351, 253, 263n390, 263n393, 264, 278, 278n406, 279, 282, 284n412, 285n417, 287, 290, 294–96, 305, 306, 307n440, 311, 313, 345, 346, 354, 355, 360, 362, 363, 370, 372, 374, 375, 379, 381, 391, 405

lordship of Jesus Christ, 28–29, 113, 215, 363, 389
Lord's Prayer, 266
Lord's Supper, 56, 132n188, 134n192, 283
love
  being slaves of one another through, 63n95, 332, 333, 339–43, 346, 348–52, 362, 364, 367, 370, 376–78, 380, 392
  and carrying one another's burdens, 369, 375–78, 380, 381, 383, 385, 392
  exhortations on, 63n95, 332, 340, 381–82, 391–92
  faith and, 317, 318–19
  as fruit of the Spirit, 332, 333, 339–40, 342, 355, 362–64, 392
  as fulfillment of the law, 332, 333, 343–68
  God's grace as, 91
  Golden Rule and, 348
  of human beings for each other generally, 319
  of Jesus Christ, 163, 172, 211, 318–19, 340–41, 346, 379–80
  Jewish tradition on, 348
  as law of Christ, 378–80
  Leviticus on, 147, 332, 332n459, 340, 341, 343–46, 344n467, 348–51, 378, 379, 381, 392
  of neighbor as self, 147, 332, 333, 340–45, 347n470, 348–50, 362, 377–78, 381, 392
  as new commandment, 343
  new creation and, 350, 378, 403
  Romans on, 147, 333, 345, 349n473, 391
  Spirit and, 14, 17, 332, 333, 339–40, 342, 355
  and Spirit's strife against the Flesh, 331–68, 392
  See also law of Christ
Lucian of Samosata, 325
Lüdemann, Gerd, 8, 100
Lührmann, Dieter, 79, 99, 121, 201, 207, 221n318, 261, 277n405, 296, 362, 379, 408
Luke, Gospel of, 23n28, 40, 291
Lull, David J., 240
Lütgert, Wilhelm, 60n89, 374
Luther, Martin, 24, 45, 49n63, 62, 96, 155nn231–232, 240, 263n392, 264, 267n396, 278, 281, 316n446, 379
Lyons, George, 62, 86
Lysias, 259

Maccabees, First Book of, 86, 134, 188, 196
Maccabees, Second Book of, 86, 373
Maccabees, Fourth Book of, 86
makarismos (happiness), 281

makrothymia (patience), 364
male/female distinction, negation of, 184, 184n269, 237, 243–47, 244n362, 250, 256n382, 264, 267, 402
Malherbe, Abraham J., 68n105, 69, 69n108, 70n112
Mann, Jacob, 303
Marcionites, 120
Marcus, Joel, 201, 337
Marcus, R., 228n331
Mark, Gospel of
  on God addressed as "Abba, Father," 266
  "gospel" as term in, 40
  on leaven of Pharisees and Herod, 321
  on love, 348
  on marriage, 246
  Synoptic apocalypse in, 78
  temporal notation in, 7, 8n17
marriage, 246, 365
Martin, Dale, 65n97
Martin, Troy W., 62, 276
Martyn, J. Louis, 5, 13, 24, 27, 31, 33, 35, 37n51, 41–44, 47, 48, 50, 50n64, 51n67, 59, 59n85, 61–63, 61n91, 70–71, 71n114, 74, 75, 79, 87n136, 91, 92, 98, 100, 101, 102n154, 106, 108, 109, 109n163, 114n167, 117, 119, 121, 123, 126n183, 128, 131, 135, 143, 145n211, 148n217, 155n230, 163, 164, 170n252, 171, 173, 174n258, 176, 178, 180, 181n267, 189, 191, 191n273, 200–202, 205, 208n301, 213, 220, 223, 228–30, 232, 232n344, 239, 239nn352–353, 241, 242, 246–48, 253–55, 255n379, 256–57nn382–383, 259, 259n385, 261, 261n389, 263n391, 264, 265, 267, 273, 274n402, 275, 275n403, 276–77n405, 278–83, 284nn412–413, 287, 290, 293, 294, 300, 301, 304, 305, 305nn437–438, 310–13, 316, 321, 329, 335, 337, 338, 344n467, 345–46, 345n468, 347n471, 349, 349–50n474, 353, 354, 356, 362, 363, 366, 372–75, 374n487, 379, 384n492, 400–402, 404–7, 409, 410
Mason, Steve, 86n135
Matera, Frank J., 13, 23, 37, 62, 68, 89, 126, 148n217, 191, 215, 219, 229, 230, 234, 236, 240, 253, 263n393, 264, 278, 290, 296, 301, 311, 313, 316n446, 352, 362, 363, 367, 375, 379, 380, 405
Matlock, Barry, 148n217
Mattathias, 87
Matthew, Gospel of
  on apostles, 280
  on fulfillment of Scripture, 347

Index of Subjects and Authors   453

on Golden Rule, 348
"gospel" as term in, 40
on greatest commandments, 348
on John the Baptist, 182
on kingdom of God, 361
on the whole law, 313
Maurer, Christian, 39, 228
Meeks, Wayne A., 247
Meiser, Martin, 1
Mell, Ulrich, 402
mercy, 394, 404–8, 404n500, 410
Merk, Otto, 13
Messiah, 24, 25, 34, 61n91, 88, 94, 94n146, 139, 214, 223
metastrephōn (turning), 43
metastrepsai (pervert, distort), 43, 44
metatithesthe (turn), 39
methai (drunkenness), 359–60
Metillus, 138
metonymy, 256, 273–74, 300, 318n448
Metzger, Bruce Manning, 20, 38, 76, 106, 169, 265n395, 267n396, 280n408, 289–90, 334, 369, 377n490, 394
Meyer, Marvin W., 325n456
Meyer, Paul W., 149n218, 151
Meyer, Rudolf, 325
Michael (angel), 33
Michal, 349
miracles, 182–83
mishnah, 179, 179n266, 309
Mitchell, Stephen, 5
Moore, George, 313
Morland, Kjell, 46
Mosaic law. *See* circumcision; law; Moses; works of the law
Moses
circumcision of, 55n77, 58
commandments and, 181, 226n326, 298
faithfulness and humility of, 365
God's fatherhood and, 250–51
Josephus on, 241n355
law received by, 54, 77n119, 159, 241n355, 298
as mediator of the law, 217, 221, 227–28, 227nn327–328, 230, 232, 233, 268
teaching of law by, 146
See also law
Moule, C. F. D., 174n257, 293–94n424, 371
Mount Sinai, 54, 187, 217, 226–27n326–327, 228, 230n335, 287, 289, 296–301, 300n429, 300n432
Mullins, Terence Y., 39
Munck, Johannes, 60n88, 399, 399n496
Murphy-O'Connor, Jerome, 7, 26, 66n99, 68, 69, 69n110, 96

Mussner, Franz, 13, 47, 64, 200, 211, 230, 264, 290, 300n432, 301n434, 346, 354, 367, 379, 388, 405, 407
mysticism, 161n241

Nanos, Mark D., 39, 50, 60n89, 69, 69n107, 138, 170n253
Nehemiah, Book of, 88, 226n326
new creation
as apocalyptic alternative for present evil age, 17, 31, 71, 246, 262, 329, 393, 394, 402–3
baptismal formula and, 246
blessings of salvation and, 44n57
Christ's redemptive death and, 172
description of, 402–3
eternal life and, 388–90, 392
faith as, 239, 239n354
faith of Jesus Christ and, 403
following the Spirit and, 17
fullness of time for, 262
God's grace and, 91
and God's refinement of human deeds, 354
irrelevance of circumcision/uncircumcision for, 246, 330, 402, 403, 409–10
Israel of God and, 406, 410
love and, 172, 350, 378, 403
present evil age versus, 368
Spirit and, 356, 403
vision of, 71
new preachers in Galatia
on Abraham, 186–87, 196–97
and Abraham's two sons Ishmael and Isaac, 286–309
aims and motivations of, 51, 51n67, 61, 397–401
anathema against, 45–47, 46n59, 50, 62, 63, 64–65, 76, 408
arrival of, after Paul's founding of Galatian churches, 50
Barnabas and, 108n160, 321
bewitching of Galatians by, 52, 169–70, 172, 200, 320
boasting by, 383, 394, 396, 397, 400–401
charges by, against Paul as people pleaser and freebooter, 64–65, 73–74, 99
on circumcision and Mosaic law, 10–11, 17, 41, 43, 44, 53–58, 54–58nn73–83, 60–61, 137–38, 140, 142, 164, 177–79, 186–87, 200–201, 239–40, 283, 298, 307, 313–14, 330–31, 383, 393–400, 406
conclusions about and information on, 50–61
content of "different gospel" of, 56, 60–61

new preachers in Galatia (*continued*)
  on covenant between Abraham and God, 220, 297–98
  crucifixion and, 398–99
  different interpretations of Paul's perception of, 52
  different terms for, 51nn66–67
  effectiveness of and persuasive power of, 52–53, 61, 170–71, 290, 319–21, 328
  expulsion of, from Galatian churches, 307–8
  and false charges against Paul regarding circumcision, 319, 322–24
  forensic apocalyptic eschatology and, 33n45, 34, 194
  identity of, 60, 139
  on Israel of God, 407–8
  Jerusalem church and, 48, 74, 98, 107, 111, 123–25, 300–301, 308, 321–22, 385, 398
  on justification by works of the law, 34, 44, 55–57, 61, 72, 151, 153–54, 154n226, 163–65, 167–68, 195–97, 208n300, 233–34
  Leviticus and, 349
  negative impact of, 42–45, 47, 50, 51, 61, 65–66, 170–71, 269–328
  on new life, 233
  on offspring of Abraham, 248, 249
  in opening of Letter to the Galatians, 15, 17, 23–24, 37–66
  as outsiders and interlopers, 50, 52–53, 60
  Paul's appeal to, to stop causing him difficulties, 408–9
  Paul's authority and credibility versus, 45, 61–65, 74, 99
  and Paul's community instructors on gospel, 385–86
  Paul's disproving of "new gospel" of, 172–73
  Paul's rebuke of, 12, 17–18, 64, 65, 321–22, 393–401
  Paul's rebuke of Galatians for following "different gospel" of, 12, 37–66, 84, 86, 320
  persecution of children of promise by, 307, 322, 323, 336–37
  questioning of Paul's apostolic mission by, 23–24
  on reception of the Spirit, 181
  Scripture as authority for, 194, 199–201, 214, 234–35, 307
  as serious about Galatians and their salvation, 53
  as source of danger to Galatians, 319–28
  on *stoicheia* and Jewish calendrical observances, 257n383, 267, 275n403
  turning gospel into its opposite by, 43–45, 47, 50, 51
  undermining authority of, by Paul, 45–49
  as "unnerving" the Galatians, 42–43, 47, 50, 51, 51n67, 53, 55, 56, 61, 319–22, 324–25, 328, 393
  on works of the law, 44, 151, 152n224, 167–68, 173, 179–81, 195–96
  worship services by, in Galatian churches, 181n267
  zeal of, in courting Galatians, 53, 277–78, 282, 283
Neyrey, Jerome H., 170n253
Nicene Creed, 24
Noah, 31
ton nomon tou Christou (the law of Christ), 378–81
nomos (law), 159, 159n238, 199, 234, 234n347, 290, 343, 344–45n467, 366, 379, 380. *See also holos ho nomos* (the whole law); *ho pas nomos* (the entire law); law; *ton nomon tou Christou* (the law of Christ)
ho nomos (the Scripture), 234n347
Numbers, Book of, 87

obedience
  of Abraham, 187–88, 196
  faith as, 150
  to truth of gospel, 320
Oden, R. A., 325n456
Oepke, Albrecht, 79
oikeious (household), 391
Old Testament. *See* Pentateuch; Scripture; Torah; *and specific books and persons of the Old Testament*
opening of Letter to the Galatians
  apocalyptic eschatology and, 31–36
  "apostle" as term in, 21–31
  cosenders mentioned in, 20, 25
  modifications of conventional epistolary style in, 19–20, 27–28, 36–39
  on negative impact of new preachers, 42–45, 47, 50, 51, 61, 65–66
  on new preachers in Galatia, 15, 23–24, 37–66
  on new preachers turning gospel into its opposite, 43–45, 47, 50, 51
  on Paul's authority and credibility versus new preachers, 45, 61–65
  prescript of, 15, 19–37
  rebuke and imprecation in, 15, 37–71
  rhetorical forms and conventions in, 36–37, 66–71
  salutation in, 15, 27–29, 27n37, 28n39

Index of Subjects and Authors 455

in structure of letter, 12, 14
summary of gospel in, 15, 29
themes of letter in, 15
undermining authority of new preachers in, 45–49

paidagōgos (custodian), 240–41, 260, 267
paidiskē (slave woman), 291, 291n421
pantas (people), 235, 235n348, 392
pantes (all), 244–45
parabasis (transgression), 230
paralambanō (receive), 82–83
paraptōma (trespass), 374–75
paratēreō (to observe), 275–76, 276n404
parechō kopous (cause difficulties), 409
pareisaktous (secretly-brought-in), 112–15, 115n169, 136, 138. *See also* false brethren
Parousia, 31, 34, 36, 79–81, 166, 205, 390
to pas nomos (the entire law), 343–45
Pastoral Epistles, 20, 21
pathēmata (passions), 366
pathos (emotion argument), 70
patience, 364
Paul
  amanuensis used by, 395
  in Antioch, 7, 9, 10, 22, 23, 100, 110, 121, 124, 130
  as apostle, 21–31, 28n39, 86
  in Arabia, 94–96
  Barnabas and, 4–5, 9, 49, 73, 100, 105–7, 108n160, 114, 117, 118, 120–25
  beatings of, and scars from beatings, 409
  birthplace of, 7, 100
  break between Barnabas/Antioch church and, 5, 9, 49, 73, 74, 104, 107, 108, 110, 128
  chronology leading up to writing of, 5–11
  conversion and call to apostleship of, 6, 23, 73, 75–79, 88–96, 89n141, 89n143, 100, 122, 159, 161–62
  in Corinth, 11, 172, 284n413
  in Damascus, 7, 96, 97, 100
  depiction of, in Acts versus his own letters, 6n12, 21, 59, 59n86, 126n183
  in Ephesus, 11n22
  epistolary writing style of, 12, 15, 19–20, 27–28, 36–39, 66–71, 76, 393, 410
  escape from Damascus by, 7
  and fear of rejection by Jerusalem apostles, 110–11
  founding of Galatian churches and travels to Galatia by, 5, 7–11, 11n22, 26, 49, 108, 114–15, 277, 279–81, 284
  Galatians in danger of abandoning, 277–86, 327

  illness and physical ailments of, 26, 279–81, 280n410, 409
  Jerusalem visits by, 6–10, 8n18, 8n20, 73, 74, 84, 96–119, 107n159, 121–22, 127n184, 133–34n191
  literacy of, 395
  method of using Old Testament by generally, 191n272
  miracles of, 182–83
  missionary career of, to Gentiles, 4–11, 6n12, 8n18, 10n20, 20–23, 59, 73, 94–96, 100–104, 110–11, 116–28, 341n464
  Mosaic law and, 86–89, 133–34n191, 401–2
  opponents and critics of, 59, 59n85, 133–34n191, 156–58
  parallel missions of Peter and, to Gentiles and Jews, 102, 102n154, 119–28
  persecution against, by non-Christian Jews or new preachers in Galatia, 307, 322, 323, 330, 398
  persecution of Christians by, 6, 73, 84n126, 85–89, 85nn128–131, 92–96, 102, 103, 159, 161–62, 398
  Peter's conflict with, in Antioch concerning circumcision, 9, 49, 73, 104, 117, 128–38
  Peter's visit with, in Jerusalem, 6, 7, 96–104
  as Pharisaic Jew before his conversion, 64, 72–73, 77, 84–89, 84–89nn126–140, 92–93, 96, 159, 161–62
  preaching by, to Jews and Gentiles, 5, 126, 126n183
  synagogue punishment of, 126, 126n183
  in Syria and Cilicia, 7–9, 73, 97, 100, 101, 107, 110
  Titus and, 108–9, 111–12, 111n164
  as unknown in Judea, 100–104, 101n152, 102n153
  See also specific letters by Paul
peace, 27–28, 27n37, 36–37, 363, 364, 394, 403–5, 404n500, 410
peismonē (persuasion), 320–21
peithesthai (obey), 320
peithō (persuade), 62–63
Pentateuch, 54, 138, 146, 159, 173, 199, 234, 234n347, 291, 303, 342, 343, 345n467, 350, 377–80, 379. *See also* law
peplērōtai (fulfill), 345–48
perfection, 178–80
peripateō (walk), 351–52, 372
peritomē, peritemnēsthe (circumcision, practice circumcision), 119, 311, 317–18, 396–97, 397n494, 399, 400. *See also* circumcision

persecution of Christians
  in Galatia, 180, 307
  by new preachers in Galatia, 307, 322, 323, 336–37
  against Paul by non-Christian Jews or new preachers in Galatia, 307, 322, 323, 330, 398
  by Saul/Paul, 6, 73, 84n126, 85–89, 85nn128–131, 92–96, 102, 103, 159, 161–62, 398
Peter, Second Letter of, 365
Peter (Cephas)
  in Antioch, 9, 49, 73, 104
  as apostle, 95, 117
  appearance of risen Christ to, 95, 117
  in Caesarea, 133, 135–36
  and circumcision of Gentiles, 9, 10, 128–38, 142
  grace given to, 122
  in Jerusalem, 6, 7, 72, 96–106, 110, 121
  as Jew, 136–37, 143
  leadership of, 98, 100, 105–7, 117–18, 120, 122–23
  and new preachers in Galatia, 48, 74, 321
  origin of name of, 97–98
  parallel missions of Paul and, to Gentiles and Jews, 102, 102n154, 119–28, 408
  Paul's conflict with, in Antioch concerning circumcision, 9, 49, 73, 104, 117, 128–38, 397
  Paul's later relationship with, 118n173
  and Paul's missionary activities, 102n154, 105–6, 110–11, 116–20
  Paul's visits with, in Jerusalem, 6, 7, 96–106
  references to both Cephas and Peter in Galatians, 119–21, 120n177
  rescue of, from Herod, 35
  truth of gospel and, 104, 105
Pharisees. *See* Judaism
pharmakeia (sorcery), 358, 359, 360
Philemon, Letter to
  authorship of, 20
  on begetting, 293
  benediction in, 410
  opening of, 26
  Paul's writing of, with his own hand, 395
  salutation in, 27
  thanksgiving section of, 38–39
Philippi, 60. *See also* Philippians, Letter to
Philippians, Letter to
  authorship of, 20
  benediction in, 410
  on Christian-Jewish missionaries' resistance to Paul, 59–60
  on circumcision, 60
  on crucifixion, 212n307, 263
  on Epaphroditus as apostle, 22
  epistolary conventions in, 37
  on faith of Christ, 148
  geographical terms in, 3n5
  ischyei (to have meaning, to be strong) in, 318n449
  kenodoxia (conceitedness) in, 373
  opening of, 25, 26
  on Paul as Pharisee before his conversion, 85
  salutation in, 27
  on sins, 359
  thanksgiving section of, 38–39
Philo of Alexandria, 21, 45, 86, 187, 227n327, 254n377, 255n378, 255n380, 259, 277n405, 284n415, 295–96, 326, 355, 358, 362n481, 365
Phinehas, 188
phortion (burden), 383–84
phthonoi (acts of envy), 359, 360, 373, 381
pisteuō, pisteuein (believe, believing), 142, 190, 191, 235–36
pistis (faith, faithfulness), 81, 103n156, 139, 149, 149n219, 150, 162, 174–76, 183, 192–217, 192n274, 238–39, 242, 317, 365. *See also* ek pisteōs, ek pisteōs (Iēsou) Christou (from the faith of Jesus Christ); *ex akoēs pisteōs*; faith; *pistis Iēsou Christou* (faith of Christ)
pistis Iēsou Christou (faith of Christ), 139, 139nn201–202, 143–45, 148–50, 149n218, 154, 175–76, 191–93. *See also* faith of Jesus Christ
Plato, 62, 66, 107, 170, 240, 365
plēroō, plērōma (to fulfill, fulfillment), 344–47, 346–47nn469–470, 376–77
Pliny the Younger, 66
Plutarch, 45, 138, 240
pneuma, pneumati (Spirit), 266, 306, 352, 370–71, 372n484, 373. *See also* Spirit
pneumati ek pisteōs (through the Spirit from faith), 316–17, 317n447
Polybius, 110, 335
poor, 126–28, 133n191, 385, 411
porneia (sexual immorality), 358
portheō (destroy), 87
praütēs (humility), 365
preachers in Galatia. *See* new preachers in Galatia
pregnancy. *See* birthing and pregnancy imagery
Proclus (or Libanius), 68n105, 69n108
prolambanō (to detect, to catch in the act), 375

Index of Subjects and Authors

promise
 children of promise, 216, 288–89, 306–9, 406
 God's promise of son to Abraham and Sarah, 221, 292–93, 293n423, 304, 342, 380
 God's promise to Abraham, 216–36, 342, 350, 406
 heirs of promise of the Spirit, 167, 168, 184, 249–67, 340, 361
 redemption and promise of the Spirit, 317
 relationship of law to promises of God, 231–36, 232n344
 of the Spirit, 13, 14, 16–17, 166–68, 215–16, 247, 249–68, 306, 317, 342
 See also covenant
prophets, 77n119
prostitution, 358
Psalms, 145n211, 152, 152n224, 153, 153n225, 154, 188, 300, 404
Psalms of Solomon, 207–8, 404
Pseudo-Demetrius, 68n105, 69n108

Quintilian, 67n102, 67n104, 69–70, 69n110, 71
Qumran, 178, 179, 188, 337–38, 353–54, 356, 402

Räisänen, Heikki, 144n210
rectification, 161, 166, 184, 205, 316. *See also* justification
redemption
 apocalyptic eschatology and, 161, 165
 and believers as sons of God, 264–65
 and Christ as accursed by law, 210–14, 210n303, 212n308
 through crucifixion, 29, 113, 114, 160, 162–65, 166, 172, 185, 190, 262–68
 from "curse of the law," 185–86, 208–16
 freedom through, 270, 289
 in fullness of time, 261–62, 267
 God and, 24, 28, 29–30, 34, 35
 by Jesus Christ, 15, 16, 24, 28–30, 34–36, 72, 113, 114, 160, 162–65, 185–86, 190, 208–16, 262–68
 language of, in epistles, 28n38, 44n57
 liberation from the law and, 264
 in Old Testament, 30n41
 promise of Spirit and, 317, 340
 of slave, 210
Rehoboam, 63
religious misconduct, 358–59
Rengstorf, Karl Heinrich, 21
resurrection of Jesus Christ, 23–25, 23n28, 28n39, 36, 72, 81, 83–84, 94, 190n271, 211, 213–14, 262

Revelation, Book of
 as Apocalypse of John, 78
 on death of Jesus Christ, 150
 genre and contents of, 78
 on idolatry, 358
 opening verse of, 31n44, 78, 78n12
rhetoric
 in ancient Greco-Roman world, 67, 67n104, 68n105, 69, 69n108
 categories of, 67
 definition of, 62, 66, 67n102
 deliberative rhetoric, 67, 68–69, 70n111
 of diatribe preachers, 170n252
 epideictic rhetoric, 67, 69
 forensic rhetoric, 67–68, 68n106, 69
 of Galatians, 66–71
 negative evaluation of sophistry, 62, 67n103
 of new preachers in Galatia, 170–71
 and Paul's letters being read out loud, 27, 36, 66–67, 71nn113–114, 99, 410–11
 Quintilian on, 69–70, 69n110, 71
 of religion, 70–71
 standard strategem of, 64, 64n96
 and three modes of artistic proof, 70
 See also epistolary writing style of Paul
Richardson, Peter, 404, 405
Riches, John, 1
Ridderbos, Herman N., 63, 219, 261, 264, 283n411, 290, 330, 352–54, 360, 363, 405
Rohde, Joachim, 37, 39, 213
Romans, Letter to
 on Adam, 33, 296
 akoē (message as heard) in, 175
 on anathema, 45
 "apostle" as term in, 21
 authorship of, 20
 on baptismal formula, 243n361
 on children of God, 242
 on collection for poor in Jerusalem, 411
 compared with Galatians, 2, 160n240, 161n241, 165n251
 on dying to the law, 160
 epistolary conventions in, 37
 on faith, 81, 150, 239
 on faith of Abraham, 149
 on faith of God, 149n219
 on faith of Jesus Christ, 148, 154
 on forgiveness, 154
 geographical terms in, 3n5
 on grace, 224
 on Israel and God's mercy, 407
 on Jesus Christ as Son of God, 93
 on justification, 154, 156, 211, 316

Romans, Letter to (*continued*)
  on law, 113, 147, 158, 210n302, 229n333, 231, 231n338, 343, 345, 347, 350n475, 379
  on *logos* (word), 349
  on love, 147, 333, 345, 345n468, 349n473, 391
  on new life, 389
  on offspring of Abraham, 248
  Old Testament quotations in, 189, 190n270, 192n276, 204
  opening of, 26
  on Paul as apostle to Gentiles, 125
  on poor in Jerusalem, 127
  on power and righteousness of God, 81, 92
  salutation in, 27
  on Satan, 33
  on sins, 157, 158, 235, 357, 358, 359, 360, 388
  thanksgiving section of, 38–39
  on works of the law, 146, 152
Ropes, James Hardy, 60n89
Rusam, Dietrich, 148n217, 253
Russell, David Syme, 32

Sabbath, 147, 257, 276
Salu, 87, 188
salvation. *See* justification; redemption
Samuel, Second Book of, 223
Sanders, E. P., 33, 50n64, 56, 134, 135, 151, 155n230, 233n346, 313, 344, 377n490
Sänger, Dieter, 66n99, 70, 214, 240, 241
Sarah, 184n269, 286–310, 293n422, 327, 336, 380, 406
sarx (flesh), 331, 335–36, 351
Satan, 33, 34, 210, 264n394, 280n410, 338–39. *See also* evil; sins
Schewe, Susanne, 338, 379, 384, 384n492, 386
Schlier, Heinrich, 13, 261, 312, 388, 399
Schmidt, Andreas, 121
Schmithals, Walter, 52, 60n89, 374
Schrenk, Gottlob, 405
Schulz, Siegfried, 365
Schüssler Fiorenza, Elisabeth, 243n360, 246
Schweitzer, Albert, 33, 161n241, 230n336
Schweizer, Eduard, 253
Scripture
  on Abraham's sons by Hagar and Sarah, 184n269, 286–310, 327, 336
  allegorical interpretation of, 293–94n424, 294–304
  christologically informed authoritative interpretation of, 288
  false exegesis of, 285–310

  fulfillment of, 347
  law (*nomos*) as, 234, 234n347, 291, 342, 344, 347, 380–81
  new preachers in Galatia and, 194, 199–201, 214, 234–35, 307
  personification of, as shutting up all things under sin, 232, 234–36, 241
  Septuagint of, 21, 45–46, 248, 297
  as synonym for God, 234
  typological interpretation of, 296, 305
  See also Pentateuch; Torah; *and specific books of the Old Testament*
Seesemann, Heinrich, 351
self-control, 365–66
self-examination, 382–84
Seneca, 66
Septuagint, 21, 45–46, 248, 297
Servant Song, 90–91
sexual distinctions. *See* male/female distinction
sexual misconduct, 358
Shema, 228, 348
Shishak, King of Egypt, 63
Silas/Silvanus, 4, 25
Silva, Moisés, 107n159
Sinai covenant/Sinaitic law, 296–301, 298n426, 299n428, 304, 308, 344n467, 378. *See also* covenant; law
sins
  of Adam, 32
  being "under the law" and, 355
  death and, 32–34, 113, 231, 338, 379
  flesh associated with, 35, 56n80, 162, 178, 207, 333, 335, 337–38
  forgiveness of, 30, 30n41, 154–55, 155nn229–230
  free will and, 32, 33
  Jesus Christ's death for, 29, 29n40, 113, 114, 160, 162–65, 166, 172
  law as bringing knowledge of, 230–31, 235
  law as captive of, 234, 235n348, 236, 355, 357–58
  list of works of the Flesh, 333, 353, 355–62, 373
  origin of, before the law, 231n338
  Paul and Peter charged as sinners in Antioch, 156–58
  punishment for, 32
  Romans on, 157, 158, 235, 357, 358, 359, 360, 388
  Scripture as shutting up all things under, 232, 234–36, 241
  sinners versus transgressors of the law, 35, 158n236
  See also death; evil; flesh/The Flesh

rach, Book of, 43, 187, 188, 196, 291, 338–39, 338n462
very
being slaves of one another through love, 63n95, 332, 333, 339–43, 346, 348–52, 362, 364, 367, 370, 376–78, 380, 392
brands put on slaves, 409
carrying burdens as task of slaves, 376
children compared with slaves, 258–61
Christ taking form of slave, 340–41
under elements of the world, 251–67, 270–76, 327, 341
of evil, 33–35, 210
of Hagar, 184n269, 286–310, 327, 336
household managers of slaves, 258–60
of human beings, 210
of law, 16–17, 35, 55n78, 114, 164, 167, 201n291, 257, 260–61, 263, 267, 270, 309–11, 314
negation of free person/slave distinction, 237, 243–45, 403
paidagōgos (custodian) as slave, 240
Paul as slave of Christ, 62, 63, 63n95, 64, 65, 86, 90, 341, 409
redemption of slave, 210
of sin, 164
yoke of, 309–10, 314, 327, 341
it, Joop, 68–69
yth, Herbert Weir, 109n162, 162n243, 276n404, 309n443, 311n445, 314, 349, 372n484
ards, M. L., 156n234
crates, 376
lomon, 223
ns of God, 242–47, 245n365, 250–51, 258, 260–68, 272, 340
phocles, 45
cery, 358, 359, 360
wing and reaping imagery, 369, 386–92
erma (offspring, seed), 222–23, 225, 237, 244n362, 248–49
irit
Abraham's true offspring and, 166, 167, 184–86, 188, 191, 195, 221–25, 237–49, 268, 290, 305–6
apokalypsis as disclosure of divine mysteries through, 80
blessing of Abraham and, 44n57, 167, 184–91, 193–98, 195n282, 200–202, 209–10, 214–16, 268, 348
Christ's death and Galatians' reception of, 175–77
eternal life and, 388–90, 392
exhortations predicated on effectiveness of, 331, 332

faith and, 13, 14, 16–17, 181
faith of Jesus Christ and promise of, 149, 236, 247, 317
Flesh versus, 35, 56, 56n80, 162–63, 169, 177–79, 306, 331–42, 351, 351–68, 388, 402
following the Spirit, 17, 368–78, 390–91
fruits of, 332, 333, 339–40, 342, 355, 362–66, 392
gifts of, 182–83
God's supplying of, 182
justification and, 215n312, 315–17
life-giving Spirit, 235
and living at juncture of ages, 329–32, 368–92
living by the Spirit and fulfilling the law of Christ, 17, 332, 368–92
love and Spirit's strife against the Flesh, 331–68, 392
and love generally, 14, 17
new creation and, 356, 403
perseverance in following, 390
pneumati ek pisteōs (through the Spirit from faith), 316–17
promise of, 13, 14, 16–17, 166–68, 215–16, 247, 249–68, 306, 317, 342
questions on reception of, 169, 173, 177–81, 177n262
reception of, in Galatia, 166–84, 247–48, 265, 315
redemption and, 317
sowing and reaping imagery on, 387, 388–91
true heirs of promise of, 167, 168, 184, 215–16, 249–67, 340, 361
walking by the Spirit, 351–52, 366, 367, 371–72, 371n482
Stanley, Christopher D., 194n281, 200, 208, 213
stauros (cross), 323–24. *See also* cross; crucifixion
Stephen, 85n129, 228, 229
stigmata, 409
stoicheia (elements), 13, 252–62, 255nn378–379, 256n381, 257n383, 270–77, 275n403, 341, 360, 372
stoicheō (walk, follow), 372, 403–4
Stoicism, 251, 355, 365
Strelan, John G., 376
Syria, 7–9, 73, 97, 100, 101, 107, 110
systoichei (belongs with), 300, 300n433, 372

Tacitus, 54, 134
ta panta (all things), 235, 235n348

tarassō (disturb, confuse, unnerve), 42, 53, 59, 321–22, 324
targums, 208n300, 302–3
Tarsus, as Paul's birthplace, 7, 100
ta stoicheia tou kosmou (elements of the world), 252–62, 255nn378–379, 256n382, 257n383, 270–77, 275n403, 341, 360, 372
teleios (perfect), 179
temporal measurement. *See* time measurement
Ten Commandments, 147, 181, 226n326, 298, 343–44, 349. *See also* law
Testament of Asher, 338
thanksgiving section of Paul's letters, 38–39
thaumazō (astonish), 39
Theodotion, 27n37, 211n305, 213n310
theoi (gods), 271–72
theos (God), 272
Thessalonians, First Letter to
  akoē (message as heard) in, 175
  authorship of, 20
  epistolary conventions in, 37
  on faith, 239
  on Gentiles not knowing God, 273
  geographical terms in, 3, 3n5
  justification language absent from, 165
  on moral impurity versus holiness, 358
  Old Testament not quoted in, 194n281
  opening of, 25, 26
  Paul in Corinth during writing of, 11
  peri versus *hyper* in, 20
  on pleasing God versus pleasing humans, 63
  salutation in, 27, 27n35
  on sons of light, 245n364
  thanksgiving section of, 38–39
  on turning to God from idols, 272
Thessalonians, Second Letter to, 20, 79
Thucydides, 335
Thurén, Lauri, 39, 53
thymoi (anger), 359
time measurement, 7–11, 7n15, 8n17, 11n21, 97, 101n151, 107, 107n158
Timothy, 4, 25, 285n419, 323
Timothy, First Letter to, 20, 29, 228n330
Timothy, Second Letter to, 20
Titus, 8, 105–9, 111–12, 111n164, 115, 138, 285n419, 396–97, 397nn493–494, 400
Titus, Letter to, 20, 29, 365
Tobias, Book of, 373
toga virilis ceremony, 356n478
Tolmie, D. François, 70, 194n281, 200, 213, 279, 284n412, 288, 327, 343, 408n502
ton nomon tou Christou (the law of Christ). *See* law of Christ

topos (standard topic), 64
Torah, 145–46, 188, 226n325, 233, 337, 347, 379–80
transgressions, 35, 158n236, 230–31, 374
trechō (run), 109n163
trespass, 374–75
truth
  freedom and truth of gospel, 115
  of gospel, 14, 15–16, 47–49, 66, 72, 73, 104–65, 117, 320
  Jerusalem pillar apostles and truth of the gospel, 117
  Qumran on "spirit of truth," 356
Trypho, 58
Tryphon, 295
two world ages, 30–34, 93, 161, 172, 198, 210, 261n389, 262, 301–2, 389. *See also* apocalyptic eschatology
typological interpretation of Scripture, 296, 3[?]

Ukwuegbu, Bernard O., 366
uncircumcision, 119, 244, 318, 398, 402, 40[?], 409–10
"under the law," 16, 35, 81, 148, 149, 158, 159, 171n254, 193, 201n291, 209–13, 210n302, 235n348, 237–41, 241n355, 250–51, 257–64, 263n393, 267, 269, 274–75, 285, 288–91, 299, 305, 309, 3[?] 333, 343, 351, 352, 355, 366, 388. *See also* law
Urbach, Ephraim E., 337, 338, 353n476

Van Manen, Willem Christiaan, 120
Verhoef, Eduard, 203, 295, 303
vices. *See* evil; sins
virtues, 332, 333, 339–40, 342, 355–56, 362–66
Vos, Johan S., 13, 23, 64, 67n103, 232
Vouga, François, 13, 61, 63, 68, 101, 121, 170, 189, 202, 211, 219, 221n318, 230, 241, 248, 281, 283, 290, 296, 305, 325, 329, 345, 354, 358, 362, 363, 372, 373, 384n492, 391, 405

Walker, William O., 60n89, 120, 144n210
Wedderburn, Alexander J. M., 128
Weima, Jeffrey A. D., 408n502
Westerholm, Stephen, 147, 148, 159, 345–4[?]
White, John L., 12, 20, 27, 37, 71n113, 393
whole law, 312–14, 343, 344, 399, 400. *See also* entire law; law
Wilckens, Ulrich, 124n180
Williams, Sam K., 13, 148n217, 161, 174n257, 200, 202, 202n293, 211, 215n312, 240, 263n393, 326, 366

Willits, Joel, 302
wills and testaments, 218–20, 224, 229–30, 245n366, 261
Wilson, Todd A., 210, 235n348
wisdom of Solomon, 254–55
Witherington, Ben, III, 43, 47, 68, 103, 114n167, 119, 170n252, 176n261, 200, 202, 209, 215n312, 241, 263n393, 281, 296, 312, 321, 327, 346, 347, 350, 354, 355, 366, 374, 376, 379, 386, 405
Witulski, Thomas, 274n401
women
  creation of, 246
  marriage of, 246, 365
  negation of male/female distinction, 184, 184n269, 237, 243–47, 244n362, 250, 256n382, 264, 267, 402
  practice of circumcision and, 244n363, 312, 313, 397
works of the flesh, 333, 353, 355–62, 373, 391
works of the law
  Abraham and, 179
  curse of law versus blessing of Abraham, 167, 184–86, 191, 197–216, 203n296
  definition of, 173
  Dunn on, 147–48nn215–216

as irrelevant for justification, 2, 16, 56, 57, 72, 84, 104–5, 132, 139–48, 144n210, 151–56, 158–67, 173, 181, 197, 202–8, 213, 226, 247, 315, 398
last occurrence of, in Galatians, 165n250
new creation versus, 402
new preachers in Galatia on, 44, 151, 152n224, 167–68, 173, 179–81, 195–96
perfection and, 179–80
questions for Galatians on, 169, 173, 177–81, 177n262
works of the flesh and, 357–58
See also justification; law
Wright, N. T., 151, 154n226, 200, 202

Xenophon, 335, 376

yoke of slavery, 309–10, 314, 327, 341
Young, Norman H., 240

zaō, zēsontai (live), 206–8, 370–71
zealots, 87n137
zēloō, zēlōsai, zēlousin (be zealous, court zealously), 87, 278, 282, 283
Ziesler, John, 160, 164
Zimri, 87, 188
Zipporah, 55n77
zoē aiōnios (eternal life), 388–89

www.ingramcontent.com/pod-product-compliance
Lightning Source LLC
Chambersburg PA
CBHW032021290426
44110CB00012B/625